T0215027

Lecture Notes in Computer Science 9888

Commenced Publication in 1973
Founding and Former Series Editors:
Gerhard Goos, Juris Hartmanis, and Jan van Leeuwen

Advanced Research in Computing and Software Science
Subline of Lecture Notes in Computer Science

More information about this series at http://www.springer.com/series/7407

Cyril Gavoille · David Ilcinkas (Eds.)

Distributed Computing

30th International Symposium, DISC 2016
Paris, France, September 27–29, 2016
Proceedings

 Springer

Editors
Cyril Gavoille
University of Bordeaux
Talence Cedex
France

David Ilcinkas
CNRS & University of Bordeaux
Talence Cedex
France

ISSN 0302-9743   ISSN 1611-3349   (electronic)
Lecture Notes in Computer Science
ISBN 978-3-662-53425-0   ISBN 978-3-662-53426-7   (eBook)
DOI 10.1007/978-3-662-53426-7

Library of Congress Control Number: 2016950389

LNCS Sublibrary: SL1 – Theoretical Computer Science and General Issues

Printed on acid-free paper

This Springer imprint is published by Springer Nature
The registered company is Springer-Verlag GmbH Berlin Heidelberg

Preface

DISC, the International Symposium on Distributed Computing, is an international forum on the theory, design, analysis, implementation, and application of distributed systems and networks. DISC is organized in cooperation with the European Association for Theoretical Computer Science (EATCS).

This volume contains the papers presented at DISC 2016, the 30th International Symposium on Distributed Computing, held during September 27–29, 2016, in Paris, France. The volume includes the citation for the 2016 Edsger W. Dijkstra Prize in Distributed Computing, jointly sponsored by DISC and PODC (the ACM Symposium on Principles of Distributed Computing), which was presented at PODC 2016 in Chicago and split between Noga Alon, Laszlo Babai, and Alon Itai; and Michael Luby for their two seminal papers both published in 1986: "A Fast and Simple Randomized Parallel Algorithm for the Maximal Independent Set Problem" and "A Simple Parallel Algorithm for the Maximal Independent Set Problem". The volume also includes the citation for the 2016 Doctoral Dissertation Award, also jointly sponsored by DISC and PODC, which was presented at DISC 2016 in Paris. This year the award was split between Hsin-Hao Su, who completed his dissertation "Algorithms for Fundamental Problems in Computer Networks" in July 2015, under the supervision of Seth Pettie at the University of Michigan, and Shahar Timnat, who completed his dissertation "Practical Parallel Data Structures" in July 2015, under the supervision of Erez Petrank at Technion.

In total, 132 regular papers and 13 brief announcements were submitted and peer reviewed. The Program Committee selected 32 contributions out of the 132 submissions for regular presentations at the symposium. Each presentation was accompanied by a paper of up to 14 pages in this volume. Every submission was read and evaluated by at least three members of the Program Committee (PC). The PC was assisted by 148 external reviewers. Following a 10-day discussion period, the PC held a physical meeting in Paris, France, on July 4, 2016, with some of the PC members participating by conference call. Revised and expanded versions of several selected papers will be considered for publication in a special issue of the journal Distributed Computing. Four of the regular submissions that were rejected, but generated substantial interest among the members of the PC, were invited to be published as brief announcements. In total, 10 brief announcements were accepted for a short presentation and accompanied by a 3-page publication presented in the back-matter pages of this volume. Each brief announcement summarizes ongoing work or recent results, and it can be expected that these results will appear as full papers in later conferences or journals.

The Best Paper Award for DISC 2016 was presented to Dan Hefetz, Fabian Khun, Yannic Maus, and Angelika Steger for their paper "A Polynomial Lower Bound for Distributed Graph Coloring in a Weak LOCAL Model". This year three papers have been nominated for the Best Student Paper Award. It will be awarded after a vote on the student talk at the conference during a special session. The nominated students are

Amir Abboud and Seri Khoury for their paper "Near-Linear Lower Bounds for Distributed Distance Computations, Even in Sparse Networks" (co-authored by Keren Censor-Hillel), Ohad Ben-Baruch for his paper "Lower Bound on the Step Complexity of Anonymous Binary Consensus" (co-authored by Hagit Attiya and Danny Hendler), and Lili Su for the paper "Non-Bayesian Learning in the Presence of Byzantine Agents" (co-authored by Nitin H. Vaidya).

The program featured three invited lectures, presented by Javier Esparza (Technische Universität München), Serge Abiteboul (Inria & ENS Cachan), and Graham Cormode (University of Warwick). An abstract of each invited lecture is included in the front-matter pages of the proceedings. Three workshops were co-located with the DISC symposium this year. The 5th Workshop on Advances on Distributed Graph Algorithms (ADGA) chaired by Danupon Nanongkai, the 6th Research Meeting on Distributed Computing by Mobile Robots (MAC) co-chaired by Paola Flocchini and Maria Potop-Butucaru, and the 1st Workshop on Dynamic Graph in Distributed Computing (DGDC) co-chaired by Arnaud Casteight and Swan Dubois. The workshops AGDA and MAC were held on September 26, and DGDC on September 30.

We wish to thank the many contributors to DISC 2016: the authors of the submitted papers, the PC members, who performed a huge and difficult job, the three invited speakers, the conference general chair and local organizers led by Maria Potop-Butucaru for the great effort they put in, the logistics chair Lélia Blin, the sponsoring chair Petr Kuznetsov, the publicity chair Swan Dubois, the web chair Stéphane Rovedakis, the workshop organizers led by the workshop chair Colette Johnen, the Steering Committee for its guidance led by Shlomi Dolev.

DISC 2016 acknowledges the use of the EasyChair system for handling submissions, managing the review process, and producing the proceedings.

July 2016   Cyril Gavoille
                                                             David Ilcinkas

Organization

Program Committee

Silvia Bonomi	Sapienza Università di Roma, Italy
Carole Delporte-Gallet	University Paris Diderot, France
Swan Dubois	UPMC Sorbonne Universités & Inria, France
Michael Elkin	Ben-Gurion University of the Negev, Israel
Panagiota Fatourou	FORTH ICS & University of Crete, Greece
Pascal Felber	University of Neuchâtel, Switzerland
Paola Flocchini	University of Ottawa, Canada
Cyril Gavoille	University of Bordeaux, France
Chryssis Georgiou	University of Cyprus, Cyprus
Seth Gilbert	National University of Singapore, Singapore
Emmanuel Godard	Université Aix-Marseille, France
Vincent Gramoli	The University of Sydney, Australia
Rachid Guerraoui	EPFL, Switzerland
Magnús M. Halldórsson	Reykjavik University, Iceland
David Ilcinkas	CNRS & University of Bordeaux, France
Matthew P. Johnson	City University of New York, USA
Christoph Lenzen	MPI for Informatics, Germany
Toshimitsu Masuzawa	Osaka University, Japan
Mikhail Nesterenko	Kent State University, USA
Paolo Penna	ETH Zürich, Switzerland
Luís Rodrigues	University of Lisbon, Portugal
Elad Michael Schiller	Chalmers University of Technology, Sweden
Johannes Schneider	ABB Corp. Research, Switzerland
Christian Sommer	Apple Inc., USA
Jennifer L. Welch	Texas A&M University, USA
Philipp Woelfel	University of Calgary, Canada

Additional Reviewers

Adamek, Jordan
Agathangelou,
  Chrysovalandis
Ahmadi, Mohamad
Akhoondian Amiri, Saeed
Anceaume, Emmanuelle
Bampas, Evangelos
Barenboim, Leonid
Baruch, Mor
Beauquier, Joffroy
Bhattacharya, Sayan
Blin, Lelia
Bramas, Quentin
Brown, Trevor
Burman, Janna
Busnel, Yann
Casteigts, Arnaud
Castéran, Pierre
Censor-Hillel, Keren
Chalopin, Jérémie
Christoforou, Evgenia
Clementi, Andrea
Crain, Tyler
Crescenzi, Pierluigi
Das, Shantanu
Denysyuk, Oksana
Dereniowski, Dariusz
Devismes, Stéphane
Di Luna, Giuseppe
Eisenstat, David
Fauconnier, Hugues
Filmus, Yuval
Foreback, Dianne
Fuegger, Matthias
Függer, Matthias
Gafni, Eli
Garnica, Ramsey
Gelashvili, Rati
Giakkoupis, George
Glacet, Christian
Golab, Wojciech
Hamza, Jad

Holzer, Stephan
Hood, Kendric
Huang, Jeff
Izumi, Taisuke
Jurdzinski, Tomasz
Kakugawa, Hirotsugu
Kanellou, Eleni
Kerber, Michael
Konrad, Christian
Korhonen, Janne H.
Kranakis, Evangelos
Krinninger, Sebastian
Kropf, Peter
Kuns, Kassidy
Kutten, Shay
Kuznetsov, Petr
Labourel, Arnaud
Lamani, Anissa
Levi, Reut
Liaskos, Christos
Luccio, Fabrizio
Luchangco, Victor
Marcoullis, Ioannis
Markou, Euripides
Maurer, Alexandre
Mavronicolas, Marios
Maymounkov, Petar
Medina, Moti
Mendes, Hammurabi
Mercier, Hugues
Mery, Dominique
Millet, Laure
Monnet, Sébastien
Morrison, Adam
Mostéfaoui, Achour
Natale, Emanuele
Navarra, Alfredo
Neiman, Ofer
Nicolaou, Nicolas
Nikoletseas, Sotiris
Nisse, Nicolas
Ooshita, Fukuhito

Pandurangan, Gopal
Pasin, Marcelo
Pasquale, Francesco
Patt-Shamir, Boaz
Paz, Ami
Perdereau, Eloi
Perrot, Kévin
Persiano, Giuseppe
Petrank, Erez
Pettie, Seth
Pratikakis, Polyvios
Querzoni, Leonardo
Rabie, Mikaël
Radeva, Tsvetomira
Rajsbaum, Sergio
Robinson, James
Robinson, Peter
Rodeh, Yoav
Romano, Paolo
Ropars, Thomas
Ruppert, Eric
Santoro, Nicola
Schmid, Stefan
Shapiro, Marc
Sharma, Gokarna
Shibata, Masahiro
Stachowiak, Grzegorz
Su, Hsin-Hao
Sudo, Yuichi
Suomela, Jukka
Sutra, Pierre
Talmage, Edward
Tonoyan, Tigran
Travers, Corentin
Turau, Volker
Vasudev, Yadu
Viglietta, Giovanni
Vilaça, Xavier
Wada, Koichi
Yamauchi, Yukiko
Zemmari, Akka

Sponsoring Organization

DISC 2016 is sponsored by

DISC 2016 is hosted by

The 2016 Edsger W. Dijkstra Prize in Distributed Computing

The Dijkstra Prize Committee has decided to grant the 2016 Edsger W. Dijkstra Prize in Distributed Computing jointly to Noga Alon, László Babai, Alon Itai, and Michael Luby, for the following two papers:

- "A Fast and Simple Randomized Parallel Algorithm for the Maximal Independent Set Problem" by Noga Alon, László Babai, and Alon Itai, published in *Journal of Algorithms*, 7(4):567–583, 1986
- "A Simple Parallel Algorithm for the Maximal Independent Set Problem" by Michael Luby, published in the *Proceedings of the 17th Annual ACM Symposium on Theory of Computing (STOC)*, pp. 1–10, May 1985, and in *SIAM Journal on Computing*, 15(4):1036–1053, 1986

The Prize is awarded for outstanding papers on the principles of distributed computing, whose significance and impact on the theory and/or practice of distributed computing have been evident for at least a decade.

In these seminal works, the authors present, simultaneously and independently, an $O(\log n)$ time randomized distributed/parallel algorithm for the Maximal Independent Set (MIS) problem. MIS is regarded as a crown jewel of distributed symmetry breaking problems, and a central problem in the area of locality in distributed computing. The nominated papers provide a fascinatingly simple, elegant, and efficient randomized solution for this problem. While many variations exist, at their core, the algorithms are as simple as this:

> *Repeat until done: each node picks an $O(\log n)$-bit random number; strict local minima join the MIS, and get removed from the graph along with their neighbors.*

The algorithm has played a significant role in popularizing Distributed Computing to the broader Computer Science community. It is one of the most well-known distributed algorithms, and perhaps the one covered most frequently in general algorithms courses and textbooks, especially those on randomized algorithms.

The algorithm leads to $O(\log n)$ time randomized distributed/parallel algorithms for many other basic symmetry breaking problems such as $(\Delta + 1)$-coloring, Maximal Matching, and Ruling Sets. The awarded papers were among the pioneers in demonstrating the striking power of randomization in Distributed Computing, and have received more than 1,000 citations. Interestingly, they were also among the first in observing the simple yet powerful fact that one can derandomize parallel/centralized algorithms that use only d-wise independent randomness for constant d. This fact is used in the papers to derive deterministic parallel MIS algorithms, and it is now viewed as one of the basic derandomization techniques.

Thanks to its simplicity, the algorithm and its variations have been in widespread use, in various settings, from wireless networks to biological systems where symmetry breaking is required. This algorithmic result has also given rise to a host of fundamental and rich theoretical questions. Although to this day many of the questions remain open and continue intriguing the researchers, the follow up work on these questions have advanced our understanding of locality considerably.

The E.W. Prize is sponsored jointly by the ACM Symposium on Principles of Distributed Computing (PODC) and the EATCS Symposium on Distributed Computing (DISC). The prize is presented annually, with the presentation taking place alternately at PODC and DISC. This year it will be presented at PODC to be held at Chicago, IL, USA, July 25–29, 2016.

The 2016 Dijkstra Prize Committee:

Shlomi Dolev   Ben-Gurion University of the Negev
Pierre Fraigniaud   CNRS and University Paris Diderot
Cyril Gavoille   University of Bordeaux (Chair)
Dahlia Malkhi   VMware Research
Andrzej Pelc   Université du Québec en Outaouais
David Peleg   Weizmann Institute

The 2016 Doctoral Dissertation Award
in Distributed Computing

The Doctoral Dissertation Award Committee has awarded the 2016 Principles of Distributed Computing Doctoral Dissertation Award to Dr. Hsin-Hao Su and to Dr. Shahar Timnat:

- "Algorithms for Fundamental Problems in Computer Networks" by Dr. Hsin-Hao Su supervised by Professor Seth Pettie at University of Michigan, Ann Arbor.

    Dr. Hsin-Hao Su completed his dissertation "Algorithms for Fundamental Problems in Computer Networks" in July 2015, under the supervision of Professor Seth Pettie, at the University of Michigan, Ann Arbor.

    Hsin-Hao's thesis provides efficient algorithms for fundamental graph problems that arise in networks, in both sequential and distributed settings. Among the latter, the most prominent are his results concerning graph coloring. He showed that numerous existential results in graph theory can be viewed as distributed algorithms with a tiny probability of success (guaranteed by the Lovasz Local Lemma) and that a fast distributed algorithm for the constructive LLL could be used to amplify the success probability to nearly 1. Hsin-Hao presented a $O(\log n)$-time randomized algorithm for the LLL, and illustrated how it could be applied to graph coloring problems where the existence of the coloring is not obvious. Moser and Tardos observed that any LLL algorithm in their "resampling" framework requires $\Omega(\log n)$ time, so this result is optimal within a natural design space. Hsin-Hao used his LLL algorithm to establish an $O(\log n)$-time algorithm for $(4 + o(1))\Delta/\ln\Delta$-coloring triangle-free graphs. This result more than any other exhibits the technical virtuosity of Hsin-Hao: he discovered not only a great algorithm, but a new bound on the chromatic number of triangle-free graphs.

    Before Hsin-Hao's work many symmetry-breaking problems appeared to have similar complexity: $(\Delta + 1)$-coloring seemed similar to the Maximal Independent Set (MIS) problem and $(2\Delta - 1)$-edge coloring seemed similar to Maximal Matching. Hsin-Hao developed new tools for analyzing randomized coloring algorithms in locally sparse graphs, one consequence of which is that $(2\Delta - 1)$-edge coloring is provably easier than maximal matching.

- "Practical Parallel Data Structures" by Dr. Shahar Timnat supervised by Professor Erez Petrank at Technion.

    Dr. Shahar Timnat completed his dissertation "Practical Parallel Data Structures" in July 2015 under the supervision of Professor Erez Petrank at Technion.

    Shahar's dissertation provides an outstanding advance in our understanding of concurrent algorithms, including novel efficient practical algorithms and a theoretical study of their fundamental properties. The literature on highly-concurrent data structures focuses on lock-freedom, which guarantees that some thread will eventually make progress, and wait-freedom, which guarantees that all threads will eventually make progress in spite of failures and delays of other threads. It was believed that the overhead and complexity required to achieve wait-freedom is too high for practical systems. Shahar's thesis changes this traditional belief by showing that lock-free algorithms can be made wait-free automatically and with a small performance penalty. His construction is realistic and practical.

Shahar provides a practical wait-free iterator, an original construct that no one knew how to do before. Another contribution is a novel and helpful analysis of the common "helping" pattern that is typically used for constructing wait-free algorithms. This analysis shows that there exist circumstances where some form of helping is required. Like many lower bounds, this has practical impact because it spares data structure designers from wasting their time trying on other approaches. Finally, the thesis proposes a simple transactional interface that is well-adapted both to architectures that provide hardware support for transactions, and to those that do not, yielding a way to design data structures that easily can be ported from one platform to another.

The 2016 Doctoral Dissertation Award Committee:

Yoram Moses	Technion
Andrzej Pelc	Université du Québec en Outaouais (Chair)
Paul Spirakis	University of Liverpool

Invited Lectures

Verification of Population Protocols

Javier Esparza

Technische Universität München

Abstract. Population protocols (Angluin et al., PODC 2004) are a formal model of sensor networks consisting of identical mobile devices. When two devices come into the range of each other, they interact and change their states. Computations are infinite sequences of pairwise interactions where the interacting processes are picked by a fair scheduler. A population protocol is well specified if for every initial configuration C of devices and for every fair computation starting at C, all devices eventually agree on a consensus value that only depends on C. If a protocol is well-specified, then it is said to compute the predicate that assigns to each initial configuration its consensus value. The main two verification problems for population protocols are: Is a given protocol well-specified? Does a given protocol compute a given predicate?

While the class of predicates computable by population protocols was already established in 2007 (Angluin et al., Distributed Computing), the decidability of the verification problems remained open until 2015, when my colleagues and I finally managed to prove it (Esparza et al., CONCUR 2015, improved version to appear in Acta Informatica). In the talk I report on our results and discuss some new developments.

Personal Information Management Systems and Knowledge Integration

David Montoya[1], Thomas Pellissier Tanon[2], and Serge Abiteboul[3]

[1] Engie Ineo & ENS Cachan & Inria
[2] ENS Lyon
[3] INRIA & ENS Cachan

Abstract. Personal data is constantly collected, either voluntarily by users in emails, social media interactions, multimedia objects, calendar items, contacts, etc., or passively by various applications such as GPS of mobile devices, transactions, quantified self sensors, etc. The processing of personal data is complicated by the fact that such data is typically stored in silos with different terminologies/ontologies, formats and access protocoles. Users are more and more loosing control over their data; they are sometimes not even aware of the data collected about them and how it is used.

We discuss the new concept of Personal Information Management Systems (PIMS for short) that allows each user to be in a position to manage his/her personal information. Some applications are run directly by the PIMS, so are under direct control of the user. Others are in separate systems, that are willing to share with the PIMS the data they collect about that particular user. In that later case, the PIMS is a system for distributed data management. We argue that the time has come for PIMS even though the approach requires a sharp turn from previous models based on the monetisation of personal data. We consider research issues raised by PIMS, either new or that acquire a new avor in a PIMS context.

We also present works on the integration of users data from different sources (such as email messages, calendar, contacts, and location history) into a PIMS. The PIMS we consider is a Knowledge Base System based on Semantic Web standards, notably RDF and schema.org. Some of the knowledge is episodical (typically related to spatio-temporal events) and some is semantic (knowledge that holds irrelative to any such event). Of particular interest is the cross enrichment of these two kinds of knowledge based on the alignment of concepts, e.g., enrichment between a calendar and a geographical map using the location history. The goal is to enable users via the PIMS to query and perform analytics over their personal information within and across different dimensions.

Matching and Covering in Streaming Graphs

Graham Cormode

Department of Computer Science, University of Warwick, UK

Abstract. Problems related to (maximum) matchings and vertex covering in graph have a long history in Combinatorics and Computer Science. They arise in many contexts, from choosing which advertisements to display to online users, to characterizing properties of chemical compounds. Stable matchings have a suite of applications, from assigning students to universities, to arranging organ donations. These have been addressed in a variety of different computation models, from the traditional RAM model, to more recent sublinear (property testing) and external memory (MapReduce) models. Matching has also been studied for a number of classes of input graph: including general graphs, bipartite graphs, weighted graphs, and those with some sparsity structure.

We focus on the streaming case, where each edge is seen once only, and we are restricted to space sublinear in the size of the graph (ie., no. of its vertices). In this case, the objective is to find (approximately) the size of the matching. Even here, results for general graphs are either weak or make assumptions about the input or the stream order. In this talk, we describe work which seeks to improve the guarantees in various ways. First, we consider the case when we are given a promise on the size of the solution: the matching is of size at most k, say. This puts us in the realm of parameterized algorithms and kernelization, but with a streaming twist. We show that algorithms to find a maximal matching can have space which grows quadratically with k. Second, we consider restricting to graphs that have some measure of sparsity – bounded arboricity, or bounded degree. This aligns with reality, where most massive graphs have asymptotically fewer than $O(n^2)$ edges. In this case, we show algorithms whose space cost is polylogarithmic in the size of the input, multiplied by a constant that depends on the level of sparsity, in order to estimate the size of the maximum matching. The techniques used rely on ideas of sampling and sketching, developed to handle data which arrives as a stream of observations, coupled with analysis of the resulting randomized algorithms.

G. Cormode—Supported in part by European Research Council grant ERC-2014-CoG 647557 the Yahoo Faculty Research and Engagement Program and a Royal Society Wolfson Research Merit Award.

Contents

Brief Announcements

Fast Two-Robot Disk Evacuation
with Wireless Communication

Ioannis Lamprou[✉], Russell Martin, and Sven Schewe

Department of Computer Science, University of Liverpool, Liverpool, UK
{Ioannis.Lamprou,Russell.Martin,Sven.Schewe}@liverpool.ac.uk

Abstract. In the fast evacuation problem, we study the path planning problem for two robots who want to minimize the worst-case evacuation time on the unit disk. The robots are initially placed at the center of the disk. In order to evacuate, they need to reach an unknown point, the exit, on the boundary of the disk. Once one of the robots finds the exit, it will instantaneously (using wireless communication) notify the other agent, who will make a beeline to it.

The problem has been studied for robots with the same speed [8]. We study a more general case where one robot has speed 1 and the other has speed $s \geq 1$. We provide optimal evacuation strategies in the case that $s \geq c_{2.75} \approx 2.75$ by showing matching upper and lower bounds on the worst-case evacuation time. For $1 \leq s < c_{2.75}$, we show (non-matching) upper and lower bounds on the evacuation time with a ratio less than 1.22. Moreover, we demonstrate that a different-speeds generalization of the two-robot search strategy from [8] is outperformed by our proposed strategies for any $s \geq c_{1.71} \approx 1.71$.

Keywords: Evacuation · Different speeds · Disk · Wireless · Fast robots

1 Introduction

Consider a pair of mobile robots in an environment represented by a circular disk of unit radius. The goal of the robots is to find an *exit*, i.e. a point at an unknown location on the boundary of the disk, and both move to this exit. The exit is only recognized when a robot visits it. The robots' aim is to accomplish this task as quickly as possible. This problem is referred to as the *evacuation problem*. The robots start at the center of the disk and can move with a speed not exceeding their maximum velocity (which may be different from one another). They can coordinate their actions in any manner they like, and can communicate wirelessly (instantaneously).

1.1 Related Work

Evacuation belongs to the realm of distributed search problems, which have a long history in mathematics, computer science, and operations research, see, e.g. [3].

© Springer-Verlag Berlin Heidelberg 2016
C. Gavoille and D. Ilcinkas (Eds.): DISC 2016, LNCS 9888, pp. 1–15, 2016.
DOI: 10.1007/978-3-662-53426-7_1

Salient features in search problems include the *environment* (e.g. a geometric one or graph-based), *mobility* of the robots (how they are allowed to move), *perception* of and *interaction* with the environment, and their *computational* and *communication abilities*. Typical tasks include exploring and mapping an unknown environment, finding a (mobile or immobile) target (e.g. cops and robbers games [4] and pursuit-evasion games [17]; the "lost at sea" problem [12]; the cow-path problem and plane-searching problem [2,5,14,15]), rendezvous or gathering of mobile agents [16], and evacuation [7,8,10]. (Note that we distinguish between the distributed version of evacuation problems involving a search for an unknown exit, and centralized versions, typically modeled as (dynamic) capacitated flow problems on graphs, where the exit is known.) A general survey of search and rendezvous problems can be found in [1]. Also related is the task of patrolling or monitoring, i.e. the periodic (re)visitation of (part of) the environment [6,9,18].

In most of these settings, the typical cost is the time required to finish the task (in a synchronous environment), or the total distance moved by the robots to finish it (in an asynchronous setting). (Patrolling has a different "cost", the time between consecutive visits to any point in the region, the so-called "idle time".)

A little explored feature of the robots is their *speed*. Most past work has focused on the case where all robots share the same (maximal) speed. Notable exceptions of which the authors are aware include [7], which considers the evacuation problem on the infinite line with robots with distinct maximal speeds, [9], which introduces a non-intuitive ring patrolling strategy using three robots with distinct maximal speeds, and [11,13], where the rendezvous problem with different speeds in a cycle is studied. It is this feature, robots with different maximal speeds, that we explore in this paper.

The most relevant previous work is [8,10], which explores the evacuation problem in the unit disk with two robots with identical speeds ($s = 1$).

1.2 Our Results

We consider the evacuation problem in the unit disk using two robots with distinct maximal speeds (one with speed 1, the second with speed $s \geq 1$). The robots share a common clock and can communicate instantaneously when they have found the exit (wireless communication) and so can synchronize their behavior in the evacuation procedure. We assume that the robots can measure distances to an arbitrary precision (equivalently, they can measure time to an arbitrary precision), and can vary their speeds as they desire, up to their maximum speed.

We show that, even in the case of two robots, the analysis involved in finding (time) optimal evacuation strategies can become intricate, with strategies that depend on the ratio of the fast robot's to the slow robot's maximal speed.

For large s, we introduce an efficient and non-obvious search strategy, called the Half-Chord Strategy (Fig. 1). We generalize a strategy from [8] for small s, the "Both-to-the-Same-Point Strategy" (BSP), where the two robots move to the same point on the boundary and then separately explore the boundary in clockwise and counterclockwise directions to find the exit. For values of $s \geq c_{1.86}$ (with $c_{1.86} \approx 1.856$), we show that BSP is not optimal by demonstrating that the Half-Chord Strategy is superior to it. Moreover, we improve on this with the Fast-Chord Strategy (Fig. 4), which outperforms Half-Chord for $1.71 \approx c_{1.71} < s < c_{2.07} \approx 2.07$. We obtain optimality for all $s \geq c_{2.75} \approx 2.75$, in the wireless setting, as we demonstrate matching upper and lower bounds on the evacuation time. For $s \in (1, c_{2.75})$, we provide lower bounds on the evacuation time that do not match the bounds provided by the respective search strategies (BSP for $s < c_{1.71}$, Fast-Chord for $s \in [c_{1.71}, c_{2.07})$, and Half-Chord for $s \geq c_{2.07}$). The worst ratio between our upper and lower bound, 1.22, is realized for $s = c_{1.71}$.

Section 2 contains a more formal definition of the problem we consider. Section 3 contains our upper bounds on the evacuation time, while Sect. 4 has our lower bounds. In the interests of space, parts of the proofs are omitted from this version, and we trust the reader to rely upon the supplied diagrams for the intuition of our results.

2 Problem Definition and Strategy Space

In this section, we formally define the problem in question. Furthermore, we provide a partition of the strategy space and some observations, which will be useful in the bounds to follow.

Definition 1 (The Fast Evacuation Problem). *Given a unit disk and two robots starting at its center (the former with maximum speed $s \geq 1$ and the latter with maximum speed 1), provide an algorithm such that both robots reach an unknown exit lying on a boundary point of the disk. The two robots, called Fast and Slow, are allowed to move within the entire unit disk, can only identify the exit when they stand on it, and can communicate wirelessly at any time.*

Definition 2. *An "evacuation strategy" is an algorithm on how each robot moves such that both robots have evacuated the disk at the end of its execution.*

The following remark is a direct consequence of the geometric environment in which this fast evacuation scenario takes place.

Remark 1. In any evacuation strategy, when either robot discovers the exit, the optimal strategy of the other one immediately reduces to following a beeline to the exit.

We now proceed with identifying key aspects of potential strategies.

Definition 3. *A "both-explore" strategy is a strategy for both robots to evacuate the disk, where (in the worst-case) both of them explore at least two distinct points on the boundary. We define the set of all both-explore strategies as BES.*

Definition 4. *A "fast-explores" strategy is a strategy where only Fast explores the boundary searching for the exit. Slow, eventually, only reaches the exit point and at any time it reaches no other point on the boundary of the disk. We define the set of all fast-explores strategies as FES.*

Definition 5. *A "slow-explores" strategy is a strategy where only Slow explores the boundary searching for the exit. Fast, eventually, only reaches the exit point and at any time it reaches no other point on the boundary of the disk. We define the set of all slow-explores strategies as SES.*

Notice that, for $s = 1$, if only one robot explores the boundary, we randomly assign such a strategy to FES or SES. Below, let ALL stand for the set of all evacuating strategies.

Proposition 1.   *(BES, FES, SES) forms a partition of ALL.*

We remark that, when considering SES and FES strategies, it can become a burden to forcefully keep the non-exploring robot away from the boundary. E.g., if we only want Slow to explore in an SES strategy, the optimal behavior of Fast would be to mimic the behavior of Slow. For FES strategies with $s \leq 2$, it also proves to be most natural to allow Slow to move on the boundary, but to ignore it when Slow finds the exit first. For this reason we use FES and SES strategies in this sense. Alternatively, one could also let the non-exploring robot to move ε-close to the boundary.

We do not consider SES strategies in our analysis. An optimal SES strategy is obviously to go to the boundary and explore the boundary (counter)clockwise. The worst case time is $1 + 2\pi$.

3   Upper Bounds

3.1   The Half-Chord Strategy

The idea for this strategy stems from the proof of the FES lower bound to follow. The worst-case analysis is performed for $s \in [2, \infty)$. For the strategy details below, please refer to Fig. 1. The center of the disk is denoted by O. Fast's trajectory is given with *double arrows*, while Slow's is given with *single arrows*. All angles and arcs are considered in counterclockwise order.

The Strategy. Initially, both robots move in beelines with an angle of $\pi + 1/2$ between them until *Fast* reaches the boundary (i.e. for $\frac{1}{s}$ time). Let B be the first boundary point reached by *Fast*. From now on, *Fast's* strategy reduces to exploring the boundary. On the other hand, *Slow* continues on its beeline for another $\frac{1}{s}$ time until it reaches point C (where $|OC| = \frac{2}{s}$). Then, it takes an arc from C to M on the disk with radius $\frac{2}{s}$ centered at O (where M is the middle point of chord BA, where A is the point with arc distance $2\arccos\left(-\frac{2}{s}\right)$ from B). Finally, *Slow* traverses MB. Below, we provide a more structured and formal strategy definition.

Fast moves as follows until the exit is found:

- for $t \in \left[0, \frac{1}{s}\right]$: moves toward B and
- for $t \in \left(\frac{1}{s}, \frac{1+2\pi}{s}\right]$: traverses the boundary counterclockwise.

Slow moves as follows until the exit is found:

- <u>Phase I</u>: for $t \in \left[0, \frac{2}{s}\right]$ moves toward C,
- <u>Phase II</u>: for $t \in \left[\frac{2}{s}, \frac{1+2\arccos(-2/s)}{s}\right]$ moves toward M via CM on disk $\left(O, \frac{2}{s}\right)$,
- <u>Phase III</u>: for $t \in \left[\frac{1+2\arccos(-2/s)}{s}, \frac{1+2\pi}{s}\right]$ moves toward B via the MB segment.

In Table 1, we shortly outline some core measurements on the emerging shape, e.g. angles and lengths, which will be useful in the proofs that follow. We now continue with some useful propositions.

Table 1. Measurements for Half-Chord Strategy

$\|OC\| = \frac{2}{s}$	by choice
$BA = 2\arccos\left(-\frac{2}{s}\right)$	by choice
$\phi = \angle BOC = \pi + 1/2$	by choice
$\|CM\| = \frac{1}{s}(2\arccos\left(-\frac{2}{s}\right) - 1)$	slow on M exactly when fast on A
$\theta = \angle COM = \frac{s}{2}\|CM\| = \arccos\left(-\frac{2}{s}\right) - 1/2$	arc-to-angle
$\psi = \angle MOB = 2\pi - \phi - \theta = \pi - \arccos\left(-\frac{2}{s}\right)$	sum of angles around O
$\|AB\| = 2\sin\left(2\arccos\left(-\frac{2}{s}\right)/2\right) = 2\sqrt{1 - \frac{4}{s^2}}$	arc-to-chord computation
$\|AM\| = \|MB\| = \|AB\|/2 = \sqrt{1 - \frac{4}{s^2}}$	since M is the middle of the chord
$\angle OMB = \pi/2$	perpendicular bisector through center

Proposition 2. *Fast reaches A exactly when Slow reaches M.*

Proposition 3. *Fast explores the whole boundary before Slow reaches B.*

The aforementioned proposition, together with the fact that it takes $\frac{1+2\pi}{s}$ time for Fast to explore the whole boundary, provides us with the endtime for Phase III and the strategy in general.

The main result of this section follows from the combination of the upper bounds proved for Phases I, II, and III.

Theorem 1. *For any $s \geq 2$, the worst-case evacuation time of the Half-Chord strategy is at most* $\frac{1+2\arccos\left(-\frac{2}{s}\right)}{s} + \sqrt{1 - \frac{4}{s^2}}.$

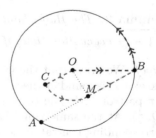

Fig. 1. The Half-Chord Strategy (case $s = 4$)

Phase I

Lemma 1. *The Half-Chord evacuation strategy takes at most*

$$\frac{(1 + 2\arccos(-2/s))}{s} + \sqrt{1 - \frac{4}{s^2}}$$

evacuation time, if the exit is found during Phase I.

Proof. We need only care about the time $t \in [1/s, 2/s]$, since for less time Slow has not yet reached the boundary. Imagine that the exit is discovered after $(1+a)/s$ time (for $a \in [0,1]$). For a visualization, the reader can refer to Fig. 2a. Slow has covered $(1+a)/s$ distance on the OC segment, while Fast has explored an a part of BA. Slow now takes a segment from its current position (namely D) to the exit E. To compute $|DE|$ we use the law of cosines in $\triangle DOE$. Let $\omega = \angle DOE$. In case $a \leq \frac{1}{2}$, $\omega \leq \pi$, and more accurately $\omega = a + \psi + \theta = \pi + a - \frac{1}{2}$. In case $a > \frac{1}{2}$, $\omega > \pi$, and more accurately $\omega = 2\pi - a - \psi - \theta$. Since $\cos(2\pi - x) = \cos(x)$, we can consider the two cases together. We compute,

$$|DE| = \sqrt{|OE|^2 + |OD|^2 - 2|OE||OD|\cos(\omega)} = sqrt1 + \frac{(1+a)^2}{s^2} + 2\frac{1+a}{s}\cos(1/2 - a)$$

Overall, the worst-case evacuation time is given by

$$\max_{a \in [0,1]} \left\{ \frac{1+a}{s} + \sqrt{1 + \frac{(1+a)^2}{s^2} + 2\frac{1+a}{s}\cos(1/2 - a)} \right\}.$$

To conclude the proof, it suffices to observe that $\frac{2}{s} + \sqrt{1 + \frac{2^2}{s^2} + 2\frac{2}{s}}$ is an upper bound to the above quantity, since $a \leq 1$ and $\cos(\cdot) \leq 1$. Finally, $\frac{2}{s} + \sqrt{1 + \frac{2^2}{s^2} + 2\frac{2}{s}} \leq \frac{1 + 2\arccos\left(-\frac{2}{s}\right)}{s} + \sqrt{1 - \frac{4}{s^2}}$ for any $s \geq 2$. □

Phase II

Lemma 2. *The Half-Chord evacuation strategy takes at most* $\frac{1 + 2\arccos\left(-\frac{2}{s}\right)}{s} +$ $\sqrt{1 - \frac{4}{s^2}}$ *evacuation time, if the exit is found during Phase II.*

Proof. We prove that the worst-case placement for the exit is point A. Suppose the exit E is found at the time when Slow lies on point S and has not yet covered a τ part of CM. The corresponding central angle is $\frac{s\tau}{2}$, since CM is an arc on $(O, \frac{2}{s})$. At the same time, Fast has not yet explored an $s\tau$ part of BA with a corresponding central angle of size $s\tau$. Then, Slow can move backwards on the boundary of $(O, \frac{2}{s})$ for another τ distance to point D. Now, the central angle from D to M is $\frac{s\tau}{2} + \frac{s\tau}{2} = s\tau$ and matches the central angle between E and A. Thence, due to shifting by the same central angle, we get $\angle EOD = \angle EOA + \angle AOD = \angle DOM + \angle AOD = \angle AOM$. Moreover, since $|OD| = |OM| = \frac{2}{s}$ and $|OE| = |OA| = 1$, triangles $\triangle EOD$ and $\triangle AOM$ are congruent meaning that

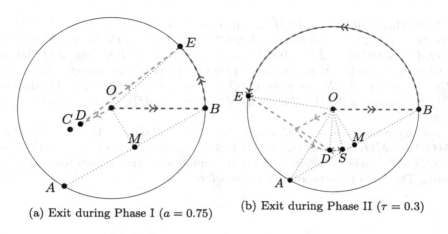

(a) Exit during Phase I ($a = 0.75$)   (b) Exit during Phase II ($\tau = 0.3$)

Fig. 2. Exit during Phases I &II (Examples for $s = 4$)

$|ED| = |AB|$. To sum up, if the exit is discovered τ time before Slow reaches M, it takes at most another $\tau + \sqrt{1 - \frac{4}{s^2}}$ time for it to reach it. At the same time, it would take $\tau + \sqrt{1 - \frac{4}{s^2}}$ for it to reach A. Hence, exiting through A is the worst-case scenario and yields a total time of $\frac{1 + 2\arccos\left(-\frac{2}{s}\right)}{s} + \sqrt{1 - \frac{4}{s^2}}$.   □

Phase III

Lemma 3. *The Half-Chord evacuation strategy takes at most $\frac{1 + 2\arccos\left(-\frac{2}{s}\right)}{s} + \sqrt{1 - \frac{4}{s^2}}$ evacuation time, if the exit is found during Phase III.*

Proof. Since $\frac{1 + 2\arccos\left(-\frac{2}{s}\right)}{s}$ time has already passed at the beginning of Phase III, it suffices to show that at most $\sqrt{1 - \frac{4}{s^2}}$ time goes by when the exit is discovered within AB.

Suppose that the exit is discovered τ time units after the beginning of Phase III. Then, Slow lies at C (Fig. 3), τ distance away from M on the MB segment. On the other hand, Fast lies on E, an $s\tau$ distance away from A on AB.

Consider a disk with center C and radius $r = \sqrt{1 - \frac{4}{s^2}} - \tau$. One can notice that (C, r) intersects $(O, 1)$ at two points: one of them is B and the other one is D, where D is included in AB, since $|AC| \geq r$ for any choice of $\tau \geq 0$. Moreover, we draw the chord DB and its middle point, say M'. Now, notice that OM' is perpendicular to DB, since DB is a chord of $(O, 1)$ and also that OM' passes through C, since DB is also a chord of (C, r). To conclude, we exhibit that E is included in DB. Equivalently, that $|AE| \geq |AD|$. We look into two cases.

First, that $\angle AOD \leq \angle AOM$. In this case, we compute $\angle AOD = \angle AOM - \angle DOM = \angle MOB - \angle DOM = \angle MOM' + \angle M'OB - \angle DOM = \angle MOM' + \angle DOM' - \angle DOM = 2 \cdot \angle MOM'$, since $\angle AOM = \angle MOB$ and $\angle M'OB = \angle DOM'$ from the fact that OM (OM') bisects AB (DB). Moreover, $\angle DOM' - \angle DOM = \angle MOM'$. We compute $\angle MOM' = \arctan(s\tau/2)$ by the right triangle $\triangle MOC$. Finally, $\angle AOD = 2\arctan(s\tau/2) \leq s\tau = \angle AOE$, since $\arctan(x) \leq x$ for $x \geq 0$.

For the second case, $\angle AOD > \angle AOM$. Then, $\angle AOD = \angle AOM + \angle MOD = \angle MOB + \angle MOD = \angle MOM' + \angle M'OB + \angle MOD = \angle MOM' + \angle DOM' + \angle MOD = 2 \cdot \angle MOM'$, again by using the equalities deriving from bisecting the chords. The rest of the proof follows as before. □

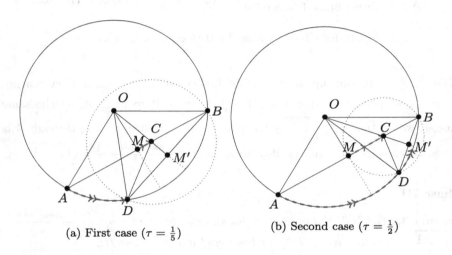

(a) First case ($\tau = \frac{1}{5}$)　　　　(b) Second case ($\tau = \frac{1}{2}$)

Fig. 3. Exit during Phase III (when $s = 4$; exit E lies at the end of Fast's arrow)

3.2 The Half-Chord Strategy for $1 \leq S \leq 2$

We first observe that, for $s = 2$, the name "Half-Chord" is slightly misleading, as the points A, B, and M coincide. The time needed for $s = 2$ is, as shown in Theorem 1, $\frac{1+2\pi}{s}$. Note also that the Half-Chord strategy is a BES strategy for $s = 2$.

For $s < 2$, Slow can simply move even slower, namely with speed $\frac{s}{2}$. Using the same paths as for $s = 2$, this provides the same upper bound of $\frac{1+2\pi}{s}$.

Theorem 2. *For $1 \leq s \leq 2$, the (generalized) Half-Chord strategy leads to a $\frac{1+2\pi}{s}$ evacuation time.*

3.3 The Both-to-the-Same-Point Strategy

This *BES* strategy follows the same key idea presented in [8] where it is proven to be optimal for $s = 1$.

The Strategy. In the *Both-to-the-Same-Point Strategy* (shortly *BSP* strategy), initially both robots set out toward the same boundary point moving in a beeline. Once they arrive there, they move to opposite directions along the boundary. This goes on, until the exit has been found by either robot or the robots meet each other on the boundary. We restrict the analysis of BSP for $s \in [1, 2]$, since for $s > c_{1.71}$ this strategy becomes non-dominant.

Theorem 3. *The BSP strategy requires evacuation time at most*

$$1 + 2\sqrt{1 - \frac{1}{(s+1)^2}} + \frac{2\arccos(-\frac{1}{s+1}) - s + 1}{s+1}$$

when $s \in [1, 2]$.

3.4 The Fast-Chord Strategy

In the Half-Chord strategy for $s = 2$, we observe that the final point reached after Phase I, i.e. point C, lies on the disk boundary. Thence, after that, Slow explores CB, but so does Fast (since by its strategy it explores the whole boundary). This seems like an unnecessary double-exploring of this part of the boundary. Thus, we propose a new strategy, where Fast reaches C as usual, but then traverses the CB chord, instead of CB. Furthermore, we could vary the position of C, in order for Fast to reach B (for the second time) exactly when Slow reaches D (a point before B) and so get Fast to explore some part of the boundary in clockwise fashion as well. In this case, Slow does not traverse the whole CB. Let us now describe more formally this *Fast-Chord* family of strategies. All arcs are considered in *counterclockwise* fashion unless otherwise stated. Below, let $|BA| = s - 1$, $x_1 = |AC|$, $x_2 = |CB|$, $x_3 = |DB|$ and $y = |CB|$; see Fig. 4.

The Strategy. *Fast* moves as follows until the exit is found:

- for $t \in \left[0, \frac{1}{s}\right]$ moves toward B,
- <u>Phase I</u>: for $t \in \left(\frac{1}{s}, 1\right]$ traverses BA,
- <u>Phase IIa</u>: for $t \in \left(1, 1 + \frac{x_1}{s}\right]$ traverses AC,
- <u>Phase IIb</u>: for $t \in \left(1 + \frac{x_1}{s}, 1 + \frac{x_1+x_2}{s}\right]$ traverses CB and
- <u>Phase IIc</u>: for $t \in \left(1 + \frac{x_1+x_2}{s}, 1 + \frac{x_1+x_2}{s} + \frac{x_3}{s+1}\right]$
  moves toward D (clockwise) till it meets Slow.

Slow moves as follows until the exit is found:

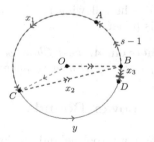

Fig. 4. The Fast-Chord Family of Strategies

- for $t \in [0, 1]$ moves toward C,
- for $t \in (1, 1 + y]$ traverses CD,
- for $t \in \left(1 + y, 1 + y + \frac{x_3}{s+1}\right]$ traverses DB till it meets Fast.

The following system of equations describes the relationship between the variable distances:

$$\begin{cases} x_1 + y + x_3 + s - 1 = 2\pi & \text{(I)} \\ x_2 \qquad\qquad\quad = 2\sin\left(\frac{x_3+y}{2}\right) & \text{(II)} \\ x_1 + x_2 \qquad\quad = s \cdot y & \text{(III)} \end{cases}$$

Equation (I) suggests how the disk boundary is partitioned. Equation (II) suggests that x_2 is the chord of an arc with length $x_3 + y$. Equation (III) suggests that Fast traverses x_1 and x_2 at the same time as slow traverses y. That is, since Fast lies on A exactly when Slow lies on C, then Fast arrives at B (for the second time) exactly when Slow arrives at D. The latter happens at time $1 + y = 1 + \frac{x_1 + x_2}{s}$. The remaining x_3 part of the boundary can be explored in time $\frac{x_3}{s+1}$, since both robots explore it concurrently until they meet. Hence, within $\frac{x_3}{s+1}$ time, they can explore a distance equal to $s \cdot \frac{x_3}{s+1} + \frac{x_3}{s+1} = (s+1) \cdot \frac{x_3}{s+1} = x_3$. All variables are non-negative representing distance.

The idea behind this paradigm is to try different values for x_3 and then solve the above system to extract x_1, x_2 and y. Nonetheless, due to the $\sin(\cdot)$ function in equation (II), it is not possible to obtain a symbolic solution. Thence, we hereby provide bounds computed *numerically*. For any value of s, we iterate over all possible x_3 values and then solve the above system numerically. For each x_3 value and for each exploration phase, we use a small time step and compute the worst-case evacuation time. Then, we can select the x_3 value which minimizes this worst-case time. All this numerical work is implemented in Matlab. We iterate over x_3 in the interval $[0, 2\pi - s + 1]$. The upper bound for x_3 stems from the case $x_1 = y = 0$. Indeed, notice that, for $s = 1$, Fast-Chord is exactly BSP when we set $x_1 = y = 0$. For the time parameter, namely t, we iterate in the interval $\left[0, 1 + \frac{x_1 + x_2}{s} + \frac{x_3}{s+1}\right]$. Finally, we use a parametric representation of the disk (where the center O lies on coordinates $(0, 0)$) to calculate the distance between the two robots.

By studying the numerical bounds we obtain via the Fast-Chord method, we state the following result, in comparison to the other two strategies studied in this paper.

Theorem 4. *Fast-Chord performs better than (Generalized) Half-Chord for $s \in (c_{1.71}, c_{2.07})$. It also performs better than Both-to-the-Same-Point for $s \geq c_{1.71}$.*

4   Lower Bounds

The main tool behind our lower bounds is the following lemma from [8].

Lemma 4 (Lemma 5 [8]**).** *Consider a boundary of a disk whose subset of total length $u + \epsilon > 0$ has not been explored for some $\epsilon > 0$ and $\pi \geq u > 0$. Then there exist two unexplored boundary points between which the distance along the boundary is at least u.*

4.1 Fast Explores

Lemma 5. *Any FES-strategy takes at least*

- $\frac{1+2\pi}{s}$ *time for any $s \in [1, 2]$ and*
- $\frac{1+2\arccos\left(-\frac{2}{s}\right)}{s} + \sqrt{1 - \frac{4}{s^2}}$ *time for any $s \geq 2$.*

Proof. For any s, Fast needs at least $\frac{1+2\pi}{s}$ time to explore the whole boundary. We now show a better bound for $s \geq 2$. At time $\frac{1+a}{s}$ (where $a \geq 0$), Fast has explored at most an a part of the boundary. Then, if we consider the time $\frac{1+a-\epsilon}{s}$ (where $\epsilon > 0$), a $2\pi - (a - \epsilon) = 2\pi - a + \epsilon$ subset of the boundary has not yet been explored. We bound $a \in [\pi, 2\pi)$ such that $0 < 2\pi - a \leq \pi$ holds. We now apply Lemma 4 with $u = 2\pi - a$ and ϵ. Thence, there exist two unexplored boundary points between which the distance along the boundary is at least u. Let us now consider the perpendicular bisector of the chord connecting these two points. Depending on which side of the bisector Slow lies, an adversary may place the exit on the boundary point lying at the opposite side. The best case for Slow is to lie exactly on the point of the bisection. That is, Slow will have to cover a distance of at least $\frac{2\sin\left(\frac{u}{2}\right)}{2} = \sin\left(\frac{a}{2}\right)$, where $2\sin\left(\frac{u}{2}\right)$ is the chord length. In this case, the overall evacuation time is equal to $\frac{1+a}{s} + \sin\left(\frac{a}{2}\right)$ and for the best lower bound we compute $\max_{\pi \leq a < 2\pi} \left\{\frac{1+a}{s} + \sin\left(\frac{a}{2}\right)\right\}$. □

4.2 Both Explore

The following lower bound is a result of applying Lemma 4 to obtain a generalization of the lower bound proved in [8]. The proof considers a timestep when both robots have explored some part of the boundary and lie on the opposite ends of a long chord. Then, an adversary acts according to his best interests. He either places the exit on the end opposite Fast or in the end being farthest to Slow; the latter leading to a chord bisection argument similar to the one used in Lemma 5.

Lemma 6. *Any BES-strategy takes at least*

- $1 + \frac{2}{s}\sqrt{1 - \frac{s^2}{(s+1)^2}} + \frac{-s+2\arccos\left(-\frac{s}{s+1}\right)+1}{s+1}$ *time for $s \in [1, 2)$,*

- $1 + \sqrt{1 - \frac{4}{(s+1)^2}} + \frac{-s+2\arccos\left(-\frac{2}{s+1}\right)+1}{s+1}$ *for $s \in [2, c_{4.84}]$ (where $c_{4.84} \approx 4.8406$)*
  and

- $1 + \sin\left(\frac{s-1}{2}\right)$ *time for $s \in (c_{4.84}, 2\pi + 1)$.*

The above lower bound loses its value as s grows. Hence, there is a need to capture a lower bound for the case where Slow has not explored any part of the boundary yet. This is possible, since we can apply an *FES* lower bound idea when s is big enough.

Lemma 7. *Any BES-strategy takes at least*

- $1 + \sin\left(\frac{s-1}{2}\right)$ *time for $s \in (\pi + 1, c_{4.97})$, where $c_{4.97} \approx 4.9699$, and*
- $\frac{1 + 2\arccos\left(-\frac{2}{s}\right)}{s} + \sqrt{1 - \frac{4}{s^2}}$ *time for $s \geq c_{4.97}$.*

4.3   An Improvement for Both Explore

We now obtain numerical values for a stronger *BES* lower bound by performing a more complex analysis on the *Original BES* lower bound proof given in Lemma 6. The main idea behind the improvement is to provide a better bound for the subcase when the adversary places the exit on the farthest endpoint from Slow's current position. Apparently, the best play for Slow is to lie exactly on the midpoint of the chord with the unexplored endpoints. Nevertheless, in order for Slow to be there, it needs to spend some of its time, originally destined for exploration, within the disk interior. We hereby examine the best possible scenario for

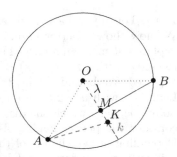

Fig. 5. An Improved *BES* Lower Bound

Slow in terms of its distance from the midpoint following the above reasoning. Let us refer to this lower bound as *Improved BES*.

Lemma 8. *Improved BES is greater or equal to Original BES for any $s \geq 1$.*

Proof. At time $1 + y$, where $y \geq 0$ is a variable, Fast has explored at most an $s - 1 + sy$ part of the boundary and Slow has explored at most a y part of the boundary. Now suppose that Slow has spent k time, where $k \in [0, y]$, *not exploring* the boundary, i.e. moving within the disk interior.

Notice that it takes $1 + \frac{2\pi - s + 1}{s+1}$ time for the whole perimeter to be explored, when both robots are only exploring after timestep 1. Thence, we upper-bound $y \leq \frac{2\pi - s + 1}{s+1}$. To lower-bound y, we restrict the unexplored part $u = 2\pi - s + 1 - (s+1)y + k \leq \pi$. That is, we get $y \geq \max\{\frac{\pi - s + 1 + k}{s+1}, 0\}$. Moreover, $u > 0$ is already covered by the aforementioned upper bound.

Now, we are ready to apply Lemma 4: There exist two unexplored points (say A, B) with arc distance $\geq 2\pi - s + 1 - (s+1)y + k$, which implies that the chord between them has length at least $2\sin\left(\frac{2\pi - s + 1 - (s+1)y + k}{2}\right) = 2\sin\left(\frac{s - 1 + (s+1)y - k}{2}\right)$. An adversary could place the exit on any of the two endpoints. If Slow reaches an endpoint first (case I), then the exit is placed on the other side, such that Slow has to traverse the chord. If Fast reaches an endpoint first, then the exit is placed either on the other side (case II), meaning that Fast has to traverse the chord, or on the endpoint that lies the farthest from Slow's current position (case III), meaning that Slow has to traverse at least half the chord. We assume that both the robots and the adversary behave optimally. Hence, the robots will always avoid case I.

Let us now examine more carefully what happens in case III. For a depiction of the proof, see Fig. 5. The ideal location for Slow is to lie exactly on the chord midpoint, say M. Nevertheless, this may not be possible due to it only spending k time within the disk interior. Let us consider the minimum distance from the chord midpoint to the boundary. This is exactly $1-\lambda$, where $\lambda = |OM|$ is the distance from the midpoint to the center of the disk. Notice that OM intesects AB *perpendicularly*, since M is the midpoint of chord AB. Using the Pythagorean theorem in $\triangle AMO$, we get $\lambda = \sqrt{1 - \sin^2\left(\frac{s-1+(s+1)y-k}{2}\right)}$. If we consider the case when $1-\lambda > k$, then the ideal position for Slow is to lie k distance away from the boundary and on the extension of OM (i.e. on point K). From there, Slow can take a beeline to the exit, yielding a $\sqrt{\sin^2\left(\frac{s-1+(s+1)y-k}{2}\right) + (1-\lambda-k)^2}$ distance again by the Pythagorean theorem, now in $\triangle AMK$.

To conclude, Slow will try to minimize this beeline distance over k, while the adversary will select a case between II and III that maximizes the total distance. Overall, the optimization problem reduces to computing:

$$
\max_{y\in[y_{min},y_{max})} \left\{ 1+y+\max\left\{ \begin{array}{l} \min_{k\in[0,y]} \frac{2}{s}\sin\left(\frac{s-1+(s+1)y-k}{2}\right), \\ \min_{k\in[0,y]} \sqrt{\sin^2\left(\frac{s-1+(s+1)y-k}{2}\right) + \max\{1-\lambda-k,0\}^2} \end{array} \right\} \right\} \quad (1)
$$

Note that the above bound matches the original one for $1 - \lambda < k$.

Last but not least, we need also consider the case where the adversary chooses to place the exit on the last boundary point to be explored. In the current setting, it takes at least $\frac{u}{s+1} = \frac{2\pi-s+1-(s+1)y+k}{s+1}$ extra time for both robots to explore the rest of the boundary, since Fast explores $s\frac{u}{s+1}$ while Slow explores $\frac{u}{s+1}$ for a total distance of u. Overall, we are looking to compute $\max_{y\in[y_{min},y_{max})} \left\{ 1+y+\frac{2\pi-s+1-(s+1)y}{s+1} \right\}$, since Slow wishes to minimize k. Due to the inherent complexity of the optimization problem (1), we compute *numerical* bounds. The computational work is done in Matlab, where we iterate over feasible values of y and k. The resulting bounds show that, for all $s \in [1, 2\pi + 1)$, this lower bound is greater or equal to the lower bound given in Lemma 6 with $k = 0$ *always* selected as the minimizer. $\qquad\square$

5   Comparison and Future Work

Regarding the lower bounds, for each value of s we select the minimum (weakest) lower bound between the (maximum) *BES* and *FES* ones as our overall lower bound. We see that Improved *BES* is strictly stronger than Original *BES* for any $s \geq c_{1.71} \approx 1.71$. Moreover, Improved BES is stronger than the FES lower bound for $s \geq c_{2.75} \approx 2.75$.

As far as the upper bounds are concerned, we notice that Half-Chord outperforms BSP for any $s \geq c_{1.86} \approx 1.856$. Besides, Fast-Chord outperforms BSP for any $s \geq c_{1.71} \approx 1.71$. Finally, Fast-Chord outperforms Half-Chord for any $s \leq c_{2.07} \approx 2.072$. That is, the introduction of Fast-Chord yields a better upper bound for any $s \in [c_{1.71}, c_{2.07}]$.

By comparing upper and lower bounds, we see that Half-Chord is optimal for $s \geq c_{2.75}$, since the matching FES lower bound is the weakest in this interval. On the other hand, for $s < c_{2.75}$ the ratio between the bounds is at most 1.22 (maximized when $s = c_{1.71}$), where the strategy changes from BSP to Fast-Chord. The best strategy to use is BSP when $s < c_{1.71}$, Fast-Chord when $c_{1.71} < s < c_{2.07}$ and Half-Chord for $s \geq c_{2.07}$.

Optimality for the case $1 < s < c_{2.75}$ remains open. Regarding further work, one could consider a more-than-two-robots evacuation scenario. Moreover, the non-wireless case for two-robots fast evacuation seems to be quite challenging given that exact optimality is complex to obtain even for $s = 1$ [10].

References

1. Alpern, S., Gal, S.: The Theory of Search Games and Rendezvous. International Series in Operations Research and Management Science, vol. 55. Kluwer Academic Publishers, Dordrecht (2002)
2. Baeza-Yates, R.A., Culberson, J.C., Rawlins, G.J.E.: Searching in the plane. Inform. Comput. **106**, 234–252 (1993)
3. Beck, A.: On the linear search problem. Naval Res. Logist. **2**, 221–228 (1964)
4. Bonato, A., Nowakowski, R.J.: The Game of Cops and Robbers on Graphs. American Mathematical Society, Golovach (2011)
5. Bose, P., De Carufel, J.-L., Durocher, S.: Revisiting the problem of searching on a line. In: Bodlaender, H.L., Italiano, G.F. (eds.) ESA 2013. LNCS, vol. 8125, pp. 205–216. Springer, Heidelberg (2013)
6. Chevaleyre, Y.: Theoretical analysis of the multi-agent patrolling problem. In: IAT 2004, pp. 302–308 (2004)
7. Chrobak, M., Gąsieniec, L., Gorry, T., Martin, R.: Group search on the line. In: Italiano, G.F., Margaria-Steffen, T., Pokorný, J., Quisquater, J.-J., Wattenhofer, R. (eds.) SOFSEM 2015-Testing. LNCS, vol. 8939, pp. 164–176. Springer, Heidelberg (2015)
8. Czyzowicz, J., Gąsieniec, L., Gorry, T., Kranakis, E., Martin, R., Pajak, D.: Evacuating robots via unknown exit in a disk. In: Kuhn, F. (ed.) DISC 2014. LNCS, vol. 8784, pp. 122–136. Springer, Heidelberg (2014)
9. Czyzowicz, J., Gąsieniec, L., Kosowski, A., Kranakis, E.: Boundary patrolling by mobile agents with distinct maximal speeds. In: Demetrescu, C., Halldórsson, M.M. (eds.) ESA 2011. LNCS, vol. 6942, pp. 701–712. Springer, Heidelberg (2011)
10. Czyzowicz, J., Georgiou, K., Kranakis, E., Narayanan, L., Opatrny, J., Vogtenhuber, B.: Evacuating robots from a disk using face-to-face communication (Extended Abstract). In: Paschos, V.T., Widmayer, P. (eds.) CIAC 2015. LNCS, vol. 9079, pp. 140–152. Springer, Heidelberg (2015)

11. Feinerman, O., Korman, A., Kutten, S., Rodeh, Y.: Fast rendezvous on a cycle by agents with different speeds. In: Chatterjee, M., Cao, J., Kothapalli, K., Rajsbaum, S. (eds.) ICDCN 2014. LNCS, vol. 8314, pp. 1–13. Springer, Heidelberg (2014)
12. Gluss, B.: An alternative solution to the "lost at sea" problem. Naval Res. Logistics Q. **8**, 117–122 (1961)
13. Huus, E., Kranakis, E.: Rendezvous of many agents with different speeds in a cycle. In: Papavassiliou, S., Ruehrup, S. (eds.) Ad-hoc, Mobile, and Wireless Networks. LNCS, vol. 9143, pp. 195–209. Springer, Heidelberg (2015)
14. Jeż, A., Łopuzański, J.: On the two-dimensional cow search problem. Inf. Process. Lett. **131**, 543–547 (2009)
15. Kao, M.-Y., Reif, J.H., Tate, S.R.: Searching in an unknown environment: An optimal randomized algorithm for the cow-path problem. Inform. Comput. **131**, 63–80 (1996)
16. An, H.-C., Krizanc, D., Rajsbaum, S.: Mobile agent rendezvous: a survey. In: Flocchini, P., Gąsieniec, L. (eds.) SIROCCO 2006. LNCS, vol. 4056, pp. 1–9. Springer, Heidelberg (2006)
17. Parsons, T.D.: Pursuit-evasion in a graph, in theory and applications of graphs. In: Proceedings of the Michigan May 11–15, pp. 426–441 (1976)
18. Yanovski, V., Wagner, I.A., Bruckstein, A.M.: A distributed ant algorithm for efficiently patrolling a network. Algorithmica **37**, 165–186 (2003)

Deterministic Leader Election in $O(D + \log n)$ Time with Messages of Size $O(1)$

Arnaud Casteigts$^{(\boxtimes)}$, Yves Métivier, John Michael Robson, and Akka Zemmari

Université de Bordeaux - Bordeaux INP LaBRI, UMR CNRS 5800,
351 cours de la Libération, 33405 Talence, France
{acasteig,metivier,robson,zemmari}@labri.fr

Abstract. This paper presents a distributed algorithm, called $\mathcal{STT}$, for electing deterministically a leader in an arbitrary network, assuming processors have unique identifiers of size $O(\log n)$, where n is the number of processors. It elects a leader in $O(D + \log n)$ rounds, where D is the diameter of the network, with messages of size $O(1)$. Thus it has a bit round complexity of $O(D + \log n)$. This substantially improves upon the best known algorithm whose bit round complexity is $O(D \log n)$. In fact, using the lower bound by Kutten et al. [13] and a result of Dinitz and Solomon [8], we show that the bit round complexity of $\mathcal{STT}$ is optimal (up to a constant factor), which is a step forward in understanding the interplay between time and message optimality for the election problem. Our algorithm requires no knowledge on the graph such as n or D.

1 Introduction

The election problem in a network consists of distinguishing a unique node, the leader, which can subsequently act as coordinator, initiator, and more generally performs some special role in the network (see [22] p. 262). Once a leader is established, many problems become simpler. For this reason, election algorithms are often considered as building blocks for other distributed algorithms and election, together with consensus, is probably the most studied task in distributed computing literature [7], starting with the works of Le Lann [14] and Gallager [10] in the late 70's.

A distributed algorithm solves the election problem if it always terminates and in the final configuration exactly one process (or node) is in the *elected* state and all others are in the *non-elected* state. It is also required that once a process becomes elected or non-elected, it remains so for the rest of the execution. The vast body of literature on election (see [2,15,19,23] and references therein) actually covers a number of different topics. They include the feasibility of deterministic election in anonymous networks, starting with the seminal paper of Angluin [1] and the key role of coverings; the complexity of *deterministic* election in networks *with identifiers*; and the complexity of probabilistic election in anonymous (or sometimes identified) networks.

A full version of this paper can be found on arXiv (http://arxiv.org/abs/1605.01903).

© Springer-Verlag Berlin Heidelberg 2016
C. Gavoille and D. Ilcinkas (Eds.): DISC 2016, LNCS 9888, pp. 16–28, 2016.
DOI: 10.1007/978-3-662-53426-7_2

The present work is in the second category. We assume that each node has a unique identifier which is a positive integer of size $O(\log n)$, and the nodes exchange messages with their neighbours in synchronous rounds. The exact complexity of deterministic leader election in this setting has proven elusive for decades and even some simple questions remain open [13]. Assuming the size of messages is logarithmic (i.e. messages of size $O(\log n)$), we know since Peleg [16] that $O(D)$ rounds are sufficient to elect a leader in arbitrary networks. This was recently proven optimal by Kutten et al. [13] using a very general $\Omega(D)$ lower bound (that applies even in the probabilistic setting). Independently, Fusco and Pelc [9] showed that the time complexity of leader election is $\Omega(D + \lambda)$ where λ is the smallest depth at which some node has a unique view, called the *level of symmetry* of the network. (The view at depth t from a node is the tree of all paths of length t originating at this node.) If nodes have unique identifiers, then $\lambda = 0$, which implies the same $\Omega(D)$ bound as in [13].

Regarding message complexity, Gallager [10] presents the first election algorithm for general graphs with $O(m + n \log n)$ messages, where m is the number of edges, and a running time of $O(n \log n)$. Santoro [18] proves a matching $\Omega(m + n \log n)$ lower bound for the number of messages. A few years later, Awerbuch [3] presents an algorithm whose message complexity is again $O(m + n \log n)$, but time complexity is taken down to $O(n)$.

A number of questions remain open for election. Peleg asks in [16] whether an algorithm could be both optimal in time and in number of messages. The answer depends on the setting, but remains essentially open [13]. In the conclusion of their paper, Fusco and Pelc [9] also observe that it would be interesting to investigate other complexity measures for the leader election problem, such as *bit complexity*. This measure can be viewed as a natural extension of communication complexity (introduced by Yao [24]) to the analysis of tasks in a distributed setting.

Following [11], the bit round complexity of an algorithm $\mathcal{A}$ is the total number of *bit rounds* it takes for $\mathcal{A}$ to terminate, where a bit round is a round with single bit messages. This measure has become popular recently, as it captures into *a single quantity* aspects that relate both to time and to the amount of information exchanged. In this framework, the time-optimal algorithm of Peleg [16] results in a bit round complexity of $O(D \log n)$ (i.e. $O(D)$ rounds with $O(\log n)$ message size), and the message-optimal algorithm of [3] results in a $O(n \log n)$ bit round complexity (i.e. $O(n)$ time with $O(\log n)$ message size).

In this paper, we present a bit round complexity *optimal* leader election algorithm for arbitrary synchronous networks. Our algorithm requires $O(D + \log n)$ bit rounds, and we show this is optimal by combining a lower bound from [13] and a recent communication complexity result by Dinitz and Solomon [8]. This work is thus a step forward in understanding election, and a partial answer to whether optimality can be achived both in time and in the *amount* of information exchanged. (As opposed to measuring time on the one hand, and the number of messages *of a given size* on the other hand.) In this respect, our result illustrates the benefits of studying optimality under the unified lenses of bit complexity.

1.1   Contributions

We present an election algorithm $\mathcal{STT}$, having time complexity of $O(D + \log n)$ with messages of size $O(1)$, where D is the diameter of the network. Algorithm $\mathcal{STT}$ solves the *explicit* (i.e. strong) variant of the problem defined in [13], namely, the identifier of the elected node is eventually known to all the nodes. It also fulfills requirements from [8], such as ensuring that every non-leader node knows which local link is in direction of the leader, and these nodes learn the maximal id network-wide (*MaxF*), as a by-product of electing this specific node in the *explicit* variant.

The architecture of our algorithm follows the same principle as many election algorithms, such as those of Gallager [10] or Peleg [16]. It relies on a competition of spanning tree constructions that works by extinction of those trees originating at nodes with lower identifiers (see Algorithm 4 in [2] and discussion therein). Eventually, a single spanning tree survives, whose root is the node with highest identifier. This node becomes elected when it detects termination (recursively from the leaves up the root). Difficulty arises from designing such algorithms with the extra constraint that only constant size messages must be used. Of course, one might simulate $O(\log n)$-size messages in the obvious way paying $O(\log n)$ bit rounds for each message. But then, the bit round complexity would remain $O(D \log n)$. Our algorithm takes it down to $O(D + \log n)$.

For ease of exposition, we split the $\mathcal{STT}$ algorithm into three components described below, whose execution is joint in a specific way.

1. A spreading algorithm $\mathcal{S}$ which pipelines the maximal identifier bitwise to each node, in a mix of battles (comparisons), conquests (progress of locally higher prefixes), and correction waves of bounded amplitude;
2. A spanning tree algorithm that executes in parallel of $\mathcal{S}$ and whose union with $\mathcal{S}$ is denoted $\mathcal{ST}$. It consists in updating the tree relations based on what neighbour brought the highest prefix so far;
3. A termination detection algorithm that executes in parallel of $\mathcal{ST}$ and whose union with $\mathcal{ST}$ is denoted $\mathcal{STT}$. This component enables the node with highest identifier (and only this one) to detect termination of the spanning tree construction rooted whose root it is.

An extra component can be added to broadcast a (constant size) termination signal from the root down the tree, once election is complete. This component is trivial and therefore not described here.

Lower Bound: Dinitz and Solomon [8] prove a lower bound (Theorem 1 below) on the leader election problem among two nodes.

Theorem 1 (*[8]*). *Let M be an integer such that $M \geq 2$. Let G be the graph with two nodes linked by an edge each node has a unique identifier taken from the set $Z_M = \{0, \cdots, M\}$. The bit round complexity of the Leader task and of the MaxF version is exactly $2\lceil \log_2((M + 2)/3.5) \rceil$.*

Table 1. Best known solutions in terms of time and number of messages, compared to our algorithm.

	Time	Number of messages	Message size	Bit round complexity
Awerbuch [3]	$O(n)$	$\Theta(m + n\log n)$	$O(\log n)$	$O(n\log n)$
Peleg [16]	$\Theta(D)$	$O(Dm)$	$O(\log n)$	$O(D\log n)$
This paper	$O(D + \log n)$	$O((D + \log n)m)$	$O(1)$	$\Theta(D + \log n)$

This theorem implies that the time complexity of an election algorithm with messages of size $O(1)$ is $\Omega(\log n)$, and thus the bit round complexity of Algorithm $\mathcal{STT}$ is $\Omega(\log n)$.

On the other hand, the lower bound by Kutten et al. in [13], establishing that $\Omega(D)$ time is required with logarithmic size messages, obviously extends to constant size messages. Put together, these results imply that the bit complexity of leader election with messages of size $O(1)$ and identifiers of size $O(\log n)$ is $\Omega(D + \log n)$, which makes our algorithm bit-optimal (up to a constant factor).

In fact, the lower bound holds for arbitrary sizes $|id|$ of identifiers (necessarily larger than $\log n$, though, since they are unique). Likewise, the complexity of our algorithm is expressed relative to identifiers of arbitrary sizes (see Theorem 25). Hence, the bit round complexity of the election problem is in fact $\Theta(D + |id|)$. Table 1 summarises these elements.

Outline: After general definitions in Sect. 2, we present the three components of the algorithm: the spreading algorithm $\mathcal{S}$ (Sect. 3), its joint use with the spanning tree algorithm ($\mathcal{ST}$, Sect. 4), and the adjunction of termination detection ($\mathcal{STT}$, Sect. 5). We conclude in Sect. 6 with some remarks.

2   Model and Definitions

2.1   The Network

We consider a failure-free message passing model for distributed computing. The communication model consists of a point-to-point communication network described by a connected graph $G = (V, E)$ where the nodes V represent network processes (or nodes) and the edges E represent bidirectional communication channels. Processes communicate by message passing: a process sends a message to another by depositing the message in the corresponding channel.

Let n be the size of V. We assume that each node u is identified by a unique positive integer of $O(\log n)$ bits, called identifier and denoted Id_u (in fact, Id_u denotes both the identifier and its *binary representation*). We do not assume any global knowledge on the network, not even the size or an upper bound on the size, neither do the nodes require position or distance information. Every node is equipped with a port numbering function (i.e. a bijection between the set of incident edges I_u and the integers in $[1, |I_u|]$), which allows it to identify which channel a message was received from, or must be sent to. Two nodes u and v are said to be neighbours if they can communicate through a port.

Finally, we assume the system is fully synchronous, namely, all processes start at the same time and time proceeds in synchronised rounds composed of the following three steps:

1. Send messages to (some of) the neighbours,
2. Receive messages from (some of) the neighbours,
3. Perform local computation.

The time complexity of an algorithm is the number of such rounds needed to complete the execution in the worst case.

2.2   Further Definitions

The paper uses a number of definitions from graph theory and formal language theory. Although most readers may be familiar with them, we remind the most important ones. Next we define the bit round complexity.

Definitions on graphs: These definitions are selected from [17] (Chapter 8). A tree is a connected acyclic graph. A rooted tree is a tree with one distinguished node, called the root, in which all edges are implicitly directed away from the root. A spanning tree of a connected graph $G = (V, E)$ is a tree $T = (V, E')$ such that $E' \subseteq E$. A forest is an acyclic graph. A spanning forest of a graph $G = (V, E)$ is a forest whose node set is V and edge set is a subset of E. A rooted forest is a forest such that each tree of the forest is rooted. A child of a node u in a rooted tree is an immediate successor of u on a path from the root. A descendant of a node u in a rooted tree is u itself or any node that is a successor of u on a path from the root. The parent of a node u in a rooted tree is a node that is the immediate predecessor of u on a path to u from the root.

Definitions on languages: These definitions are selected from [17] (Chapter 16). Let A be an alphabet, A^* is the set of all words over A, the empty word is denoted by ϵ. If x is a non empty word over the alphabet A of length p then x can be written as the concatenation of p letters, i.e., $x = x[1]x[2] \cdots x[p]$ with each $x[i]$ in A. If $a \in A$ and i is a positive integer then a^i is the concatenation i times of the letter a. Let x and y be two words over alphabet A, x is said to be a prefix (*resp.* proper prefix) of y if there exists a word (*resp.* non-empty word) z such that $y = xz$.

Bit round complexity: The bit complexity in general may be viewed as a natural extension of communication complexity (introduced by Yao [24]) to the analysis of tasks in a distributed setting. An introduction to the area can be found in Kushilevitz and Nisan [12]. In this paper, we follow the definition from [11], that is, the bit round complexity of an algorithm $\mathcal{A}$ is the total number of *bit rounds* it takes for $\mathcal{A}$ to terminate, where a bit round is a synchronous round with single bit messages. This measure captures into a single quantity aspects that relate both to time and to the amount of information exchanged. Other definitions are considered in the literature, in [4–7] the bit complexity is the total number of bits sent until global termination. In [20], it is the maximum number of bits sent through a same channel. In both variants, silences may convey much information, which is why we consider the definition from [11] in terms of *round* complexity as more comprehensive.

3   A Spreading Algorithm

This section presents a distributed spreading algorithm using only messages of size $O(1)$ which allows each node to know the highest identifier among the set of all identifiers with a time complexity of $O(D + \log n)$, where D is the diameter of G.

3.1   Preamble

Given a node u and the binary representation Id_u of its identifier. We define $\alpha(Id_u)$ as the word

$$\alpha(Id_u) = 1^{|Id_u|}0Id_u.$$

For instance, if u has identifier 23, then $Id_u = 10111$ and $\alpha(Id_u) = 11111010111$. This encoding has the nice property that it extends the natural order $<$ of integers into a lexicographic order $\prec$ on their α-encoding.

Remark 2. Let u and v be two nodes with identifiers Id_u and Id_v. Then:

$$Id_u < Id_v \Leftrightarrow \alpha(Id_u) \prec \alpha(Id_v).$$

As a result, the order between two identifiers Id_u and Id_v is the order induced by the first letter which differs in $\alpha(Id_u)$ and $\alpha(Id_v)$. This property is key to our algorithm, in which the spreading of identifiers progresses bitwise and comparisons occur consistently.

3.2   The Algorithm $\mathcal{S}$

Variables: Each node can be *active* or *follower*, depending on whether it is still a candidate for becoming the leader (i.e. no higher identifier was detected so far). Each node u also has variables Y_u, Z_u and Z_u^v (one for each neighbour v of u) which are words over the alphabet $\{0, 1\}$. Y_u is a shorthand for $\alpha(Id_u)$, it is set initially and never changes afterwards. Z_u is a prefix of Y_w, for some node w (possibly u itself). It indicates the highest prefix known so far by u. On each node, this variable will eventually converge to the α-encoding of the highest identifier. Finally, for each neighbour v of u, Z_u^v is the lastest value of Z_v known to u.

Initialisation: Initially every node u is *active*, all the Z_u's are set to the empty word ϵ, and the Z_u^v's are accordingly set to the empty word (wlog, we assume that a preliminary round made it possible for all nodes to know what neighbours they have).

Main Loop: In each round, the algorithm executes the following actions.

1. update Z_u,
2. send to all neighbours a signal indicating how Z_u was updated,
3. receive such signals from neighbours,
4. update all the Z_u^v accordingly.

The main action is the update of Z_u (step 1). It depends on the values of Z_u^v for all neighbours v and Z_u itself at the end of the previous round. This update is done according to a number of rules. For instance, as long as u remains *active* and Z_u is a proper prefix of Y_u, the update consists in appending the next bit of Y_u to Z_u. Most updates are more complex and detailed further below. The three other actions (step 2, 3, and 4 above) only serve the purpose of informing the neighbours as to how Z_u was updated, so that all Z_u^v are correctly updated. In fact, Z_u can only be updated in *seven* possible ways, each causing the sending of a particular signal among $\{append0, append1, delete1, delete2, delete3, change, null\}$, with following meaning:

- *append0* or *append1*: Z_u was updated by appending a single 0 or a single 1;
- *delete1*, *delete2*, or *delete3*: Z_u was updated by deleting one, two or three letters from the end;
- *change*: Z_u was updated by changing the last letter from 0 to 1;
- *null*: Z_u was not modified.

Each node updates its variables Z_u^v based on these signals (step 4).

Remark 3. By the end of each round, it holds that $Z_u^v = Z_v$ for any neighbour v of u. Thus from now on, Z_u^v is simply written Z_v.

We now describe the way Z_u is updated by each node u. One property that the update guarantees is that by the end of each round, if u and v are two neighbours, then Z_u and Z_v must have a common prefix followed, in each case, by at most six letters. This fact is later used for analysis.

Update of Z_u in each round: Let us denote the state of some variable X *at the end* of round t by X^t. For instance, we write $Z_u^0 = \epsilon$, where round 0 corresponds to initialisation. The computation of Z_u at round t results from u being active or follower, and the values of Z_u^{t-1} and Z_v^{t-1} for all neighbours v of u. It is done according to the following rules given in order of priority, i.e., $R_{1.1}$ has a higher priority than $R_{1.2}$, having itself a higher priority than R_2, *etc.* Whenever a rule is applied, the subsequent rules are ignored.

-R_1 (delete). The relationship between Z_u^{t-1} and Z_v^{t-1} for any neighbour v of u may mean that a delete operation is possible. If any delete is possible, one will be carried out; if more than one is possible, the greatest will be carried out.

   -$R_{1.1}$ If some Z_v^{t-1} is a proper prefix of Z_u^{t-1} and v's last action was a *delete*, delete $min\{|Z_u^{t-1}| - |Z_v^{t-1}|, 3\}$ letters from the end of Z_u^{t-1};

   -$R_{1.2}$ If $Z_u^{t-1} = z0x$ with $x \neq \epsilon$ and some $Z_v^{t-1} = z1y$, delete $|x|$ letters from the end of Z_u^{t-1};

-R_2 (change). if $Z_u^{t-1} = z0$ and some $Z_v^{t-1} = z1y$ then change Z_u^{t-1} to $z1$ and change u's state to *follower* if it is *active*;

-R_3 (append). if for some v, $Z_v^{t-1} = Z_u^{t-1}1x$, then Z_u^t is obtained by appending 1 to Z_u^{t-1};

-R_4 (append). if for some v, $Z_v^{t-1} = Z_u^{t-1}0x$, then Z_u^t is obtained by appending 0 to Z_u^{t-1};

-R_5 (append). if u's state is *active* and $t < |Y_u|$, append $Y_u[t]$ to Z_u^{t-1};

If none of these actions apply, then Z_u remains unchanged and a *null* signal is sent. Otherwise, a signal corresponding to the resulting action is sent. We now prove some properties on Algorithm $\mathcal{S}$.

Lemma 4. *Whenever a node u carries out a delete operation at round t, u's operation at round $t + 1$ must be another delete operation or a change operation.*

Proof. The proof proceeds by induction on t (details in the long version).

Lemma 4 induces immediately:

Corollary 5. *A sequence of delete operations on a node u ends with a change operation on u.*

Remark 6. If a node u applies $R_{1.1}$, $R_{1.2}$, R_2, R_3, or R_4 then there exists a node v such that $Y_u \prec Y_v$.

Remark 7. Let u be a node. If there exists a neighbour v of u and a round t such that $|Z_u^t| < |Z_v^t|$ then u becomes *follower*.

Lemma 8. *Let u and v be two neighbours. Let t be a round number. The words Z_u^t and Z_v^t will always take one of the following forms (up to renaming of u and v) where p and w are words and a is 1 or 0:*

1. $Z_u^t = p$ and $Z_v^t = p$,
2. $Z_u^t = p$ and $Z_v^t = pw$ with $1 \le |w| \le 2$,
3. $Z_u^t = p0$ and $Z_v^t = p1a$,
4. $Z_u^t = p1$ and $Z_v^t = p0w$ and $|w| \le 3$,
5. $Z_u^t = p$ and $Z_v^t = pw$ and $3 \le |w| \le 6$ and u has performed a delete.

Proof. The proof proceeds by examination of all possible cases (detailed proof in the long version).

The application of rule $R_{1.2}$ corresponds to item 4, thus:

Corollary 9. *If $R_{1.2}$ is applied then $0 < |x| \le 3$ and $y = \epsilon$.*

Lemma 8 implies:

Theorem 10. *Let G be a graph of size n and diameter D such that each node u is endowed with a unique identifier Id_u which is a non negative integer. Let X be the highest identifier. After at most $|\alpha(X)| + 6D$ rounds, algorithm $\mathcal{S}$ terminates and for each node u, $Z_u = \alpha(X)$.*

Proof. The proof proceeds by induction on the distance of a node from the highest node (detailed proof the long version).

4   A Spanning Tree Algorithm

This section explains how the computation of a spanning tree may be associated to the spreading algorithm $\mathcal{S}$ by selecting for each node u the edge through which Z_u was modified.

Let u be a node, we add for each neighbour v, a variable $status_u^v$ whose possible values are in $\{child, parent, other\}$: it indicates the status of v for u; initially $status_u^v = other$. The computation of the spanning tree occurs concurrently with the spreading algorithm $\mathcal{S}$ as follows. If R_2, R_3, or R_4 is applied at round t relative to neighbor v, then u choses v as parent (if not already the case). Then, in addition to the signals of the spreading algorithm (indicating how Z_u was updated), u sends a signal *parent* to v and a signal *other* to its previous parent (if different from v).

After receiving signals from neighbours, in addition to the computation of the new value of Z_v for each neighbour v by Algorithm $\mathcal{S}$, u updates $status_u^v$. Algorithm $\mathcal{ST}$ denotes the algorithm obtained with Rules of the spreading algorithm $\mathcal{S}$ and actions described just above.

Remark 11. A node has no parent if and only if it is active.

Remark 12. A node has at most one parent.

The next definition introduces for each node u a word T_u that is used to prove that the graph induced by all the *parent* relations has no cycle.

Definition 13. *Let u be a node, let t be a round number of the spreading algorithm $\mathcal{S}$; T_u^t is equal to:*

- Z_u^t *if $t = 0$ or if Z_u^t has been obtained from Z_u^{t-1} thanks to R_2 or R_3 or R_4 or R_5;*
- $Z_u^{t'}$ *if Z_u^t has been obtained from Z_u^{t-1} thanks to $R_{1.1}$ or $R_{1.2}$ and $t' < t$ is the last round where $Z_u^{t'}$ has not been obtained by a delete operation.*

The following lemma is a direct consequence of the definition of T_u^t, and of R_2, R_3 and R_4:

Lemma 14. *Let t be a round number of the spreading algorithm $\mathcal{S}$. If v is parent of u then $T_u^t \preceq T_v^t$; furthermore if v becomes parent of u at round t then $T_u^t \prec T_v^t$ or $T_u^t = T_v^t$ and $T_u^{t-1} \prec T_v^{t-1}$.*

Corollary 15. *Let t be a round number. Let u_1 be a node. Let $(u_i)_{1 \le i \le p}$ be nodes of G such that, at round t, for $2 \le i \le p$ u_i is parent of u_{i-1}. Then $u_1 \ne u_p$.*

Proof. Let t be a round, and let u_1 be a node. Let $(u_i)_{1 \le i \le p}$ be nodes of G such that, at round t, for $2 \le i \le p$ u_i is parent of u_{i-1}. The previous lemma implies that $(T_{u_i}^t)_{1 \le i \le p}$ is increasing. Considering a couple (u_j, u_{j+1}) where R_2, or R_3, or R_4 has been applied for the last time before t, we obtain the result. $\square$

Corollary 16. *Let t be a round number. Let u_1 be a node. Then either u_1 is active or there exist $(u_i)_{1 \le i \le p}$ nodes of G such that: for $2 \le i \le p$ u_i is parent of u_{i-1} and u_p is active.*

Definition 17. *We denote by $ST(G)$ the subgraph of $G = (V, E)$ having V as node set and there is an edge between the node u and the node v if u is the parent of v or v is the parent of u when algorithm ST terminates.*

When Algorithm ST terminates there is exactly one *active* node: the node with highest identifier. Now, from Remark 12 and Corollary 16:

Proposition 18. *Let G be a connected graph such that each node has a unique identifier. Let u be the node with the highest identifier. When algorithm ST terminates, the graph $ST(G)$ is a spanning tree of G.*

5   Termination Detection of Algorithm ST

This section presents some actions which, added to algorithm ST, enable the node with the highest identifier to detect termination of algorithm ST; furthermore, as it is the only one, when it detects the termination it becomes elected. Our solution is a bitwise adaptation of the propagation process with feedback introduced in [21] and further formalised and studied in Chapter 6 and 7 of [23].

Definition 19. *Let v be a node. Let t be a round number of the spreading algorithm. The variable Z_v^t is said to be well-formed if there exists an identifier Id such that $Z_v^t = \alpha(Id)$.*

Each node v is equipped with a boolean variable $Term_v$ which is *true* iff v and all of its subtree have terminated. Whenever a rule of the spreading algorithm is applied to node v, the variable $Term_v$ is set to *false*, and a signal is sent to its neighbours to indicate that $Term_v = false$. Indeed, this variable can be updated several times for a same node before stabilizing to *true*.

We describe an extra rule to be added to the ST algorithm in order to allow the node with highest identifier to learn that it is so by detecting termination of the spanning tree algorithm. This rule is considered *after* those of algorithm ST in each round. Let us denote by N_v the set of neighbours of v, and by $Ch_v \subseteq N_v$ those which are v's children. Also recall that we omit the round number in the expression on variables when it is non ambiguous.

The rule: Given a node v, if (v is follower) and ($Term_v = false$) and (Z_v is well-formed) and ($\forall w \in N_v$ $Z_w = Z_v$) and ($\forall w \in Ch_v$ $Term_w = true$) then $Term_v := true$. Furthermore v sends to his parent a signal indicating that $Term_v = true$.

We denote by $\mathcal{STT}$ the algorithm obtained by putting together the rules of Algorithm $\mathcal{ST}$ and this extra rule for termination detection.

Remark 20. Let v be a node, if $Term_v = true$ then Z_v has the same value it had when $Term_v$ became $true$ the last time.

Remark 21. If $Ch_v = \emptyset$, i.e., v is a leaf, and Z_v is well-formed and for each neighbour w of v $Z_w = Z_v$ then v sets $Term_v$ to $true$ right away (and v sends to his parent a signal indicating that $Term_v = true$).

Remark 22. Let u be the node with highest identifier. Let v be a node. If $Z_v = \alpha(Id_u)$ then Z_v will never change.

Theorem 10 and Proposition 18 imply:

Proposition 23. *Let G be a graph such that each node has a unique (integer) identifier. Algorithm $\mathcal{STT}$ terminates. Furthermore, if the node u has the highest identifier then, after a run of algorithm $\mathcal{STT}$, for each neighbour v of u $Z_v = \alpha(Id_u)$ and $Term_v = true$ and the node u receives from each node v in Ch_u the signal indicating that $Term_v = true$.*

The next proposition established that only the node with highest identifier can receive a termination signal from all neighbors.

Proposition 24. *Let G be a graph such that each node has a unique identifier. Let v be a node which has not the highest identifier and such that $Z_v = \alpha(Id_v)$ and for each neighbour w of v $Z_w = Z_v$. Then there exists a neighbour v' of v such that $Term_{v'} = false$.*

Proof. The proof relies on transitive relations between $Term_v$ values within the tree (detailed proof in the long version).

If the node u with highest identifier, becomes *elected* as soon as, for each neighbour v of u, $Z_v = \alpha(Id_u)$ and $Term_v = true$ and it receives from each child v the signal indicating that $Term_v = true$ we deduce:

Theorem 25. *Let G be a graph such that each node has a unique identifier which is an integer. Let u be the node with the highest identifier. There exists an election algorithm for G with messages of size $O(1)$ which terminates after at most $|\alpha(Id_u)| + 6D$ rounds.*

6   Conclusion

Concerning deterministic election algorithms with identifiers, we may consider three complexity measures: time complexity, message complexity, and bit (round) complexity. Santoro [18] proved that $\Omega(|E| + n \log n)$ is a lower bound for the number of messages and Awerbuch [3] presented an algorithm that matches this bound. Kutten et al. [13] shows that concerning the time complexity $\Omega(D)$ is a lower bound and [16] implies that $O(D)$ is a tight upper bound. For bit (round) complexity, we deduced from [13] and [8] that $\Omega(D + \log n)$ is a lower bound and we presented an algorithm that matches this bound with a running time of $O(D + \log n)$ bit rounds. Our algorithm requires no knowledge on the graph such as the size or the diameter.

References

1. Angluin, D.: Local and global properties in networks of processors. In: Proceedings of the 12th Symposium on Theory of Computing, pp. 82–93 (1980)
2. Attiya, H., Welch, J.: Distributed Computing: Fundamentals, Simulations, and Advanced Topics. Wiley, Hoboken (2004)
3. Awerbuch, B.: Optimal distributed algorithms for minimum weight spanning tree, counting, leader election and related problems (detailed summary). In: Proceedings of 19th Symposium on Theory of Computing, New York, USA, pp. 230–240 (1987)
4. Bar-Noy, A., Naor, J., Naor, M.: One-bit algorithms. Distrib. Comput. **4**, 3–8 (1990)
5. Bodlaender, H.L., Moran, S., Warmuth, M.K.: The distributed bit complexity of the ring: from the anonymous case to the non-anonymous case. Inf. Comput. **114**(2), 34–50 (1994)
6. Bodlaender, H.L., Tel, G.: Bit-optimal election in synchronous rings. Inf. Process. Lett. **36**(1), 53–56 (1990)
7. Dinitz, Y., Moran, S., Rajsbaum, S.: Bit complexity of breaking and achieving symmetry in chains and rings. J. ACM **55**(1), 167–183 (2008)
8. Dinitz, Y., Solomon, N.: Two absolute bounds for distributed bit complexity. Theor. Comput. Sci. **384**(2–3), 168–183 (2007)
9. Fusco, E.G., Pelc, A.: Knowledge, level of symmetry, and time of leader election. Distrib. Comput. **28**(4), 221–232 (2015)
10. Gallager, R.G.: Finding a leader in a network with $o(e + n \log n)$ messages. Technical Report Internal Memo., M.I.T., Cambridge, MA (1979)
11. Kothapalli, K., Onus, M., Scheideler, C., Schindelhauer, C.: Distributed coloring in $O(\sqrt{\log n})$ bit rounds. In: 20th International Parallel and Distributed Processing Symposium (IPDPS), Rhodes Island, Greece. IEEE (2006)
12. Kushilevitz, E., Nisan, N.: Communication complexity. Cambridge University Press, New York (1999)
13. Kutten, S., Pandurangan, G., Peleg, D., Robinson, P., Trehan, A.: On the complexity of universal leader election. J. ACM **7**, 7: 1–7: 27 (2015)
14. LeLann, G.: Distributed systems: Towards a formal approach. In: Gilchrist, B. (ed.), Information processing 1977, pp. 155–160. North-Holland (1977)
15. Lynch, N.A.: Distributed algorithms. Morgan Kaufman, San Francisco (1996)
16. Peleg, D.: Time-optimal leader election in general networks. J. Parallel Distrib. Comput. **8**(1), 96–99 (1990)
17. Rosen, K.H. (ed.): Handbook of Discrete and Combinatorial Mathematics. CRC Press, Boca Raton (2000)
18. Santoro, N.: On the message complexity of distributed problems. Int. J. Parallel Program. **13**(3), 131–147 (1984)
19. Santoro, N.: Design and analysis of distributed algorithm. Wiley, New York (2007)

20. Schneider, J., Wattenhofer, R.: Trading bit, message, and time complexity of distributed algorithms. In: Peleg, D. (ed.) Distributed Computing. LNCS, vol. 6950, pp. 51–65. Springer, Heidelberg (2011)
21. Segall, A.: Distributed network protocols. IEEE Trans. Inf. Theor. **29**(1), 23–24 (1983)
22. Tanenbaum, A., van Steen, M.: Distributed Systems - Principles and Paradigms. Prentice Hall, Upper Saddle River (2002)
23. Tel, G.: Introduction to distributed algorithms. Cambridge University Press, Cambridge (2000)
24. Yao, A.C.: Some complexity questions related to distributed computing. In: Proceedings of 11th Symposium on Theory of Computing (STOC), pp. 209–213. ACM Press (1979)

Near-Linear Lower Bounds for Distributed Distance Computations, Even in Sparse Networks

Amir Abboud[1](✉), Keren Censor-Hillel[2](✉), and Seri Khoury[2](✉)

[1] Stanford University, Department of Computer Science, Stanford, USA
abboud@cs.stanford.edu
[2] Department of Computer Science, Technion, Haifa, Israel
{ckeren,serikhoury}@cs.technion.ac.il

Abstract. We develop a new technique for constructing sparse graphs that allow us to prove near-linear lower bounds on the round complexity of computing distances in the CONGEST model. Specifically, we show an $\widetilde{\Omega}(n)$ lower bound for computing the diameter in sparse networks, which was previously known only for dense networks. In fact, we can even modify our construction to obtain graphs with constant degree, using a simple but powerful degree-reduction technique which we define.

Moreover, our technique allows us to show $\widetilde{\Omega}(n)$ lower bounds for computing $(\frac{3}{2} - \varepsilon)$-approximations of the diameter or the radius, and for computing a $(\frac{5}{3} - \varepsilon)$-approximation of all eccentricities. For radius, we are unaware of any previous lower bounds. For diameter, these greatly improve upon previous lower bounds and are tight up to polylogarithmic factors, and for eccentricities the improvement is both in the lower bound and in the approximation factor.

Interestingly, our technique also allows showing an almost-linear lower bound for the verification of (α, β)-spanners, for $\alpha < \beta + 1$.

Keywords: Distributed computing · Approximations · Lower bounds · Diameter · Radius · Eccentricity · Spanners

1 Introduction

The diameter and radius are two basic graph parameters whose values play a vital role in many applications. In distributed computing, these parameters are even more fundamental, since they capture the minimal number of rounds needed in order to send a piece of information to all the nodes in a network. Hence, understanding the complexity of computing these parameters is central to distributed computing, and has been the focus of many studies in the CONGEST

A. Abboud—Supported by Virginia Vassilevska Williams's NSF Grants CCF-1417238 and CCF-1514339, and BSF Grant BSF:2012338.
K. Censor-Hillel and S.Khoury—Supported by ISF Individual Research Grant 1696/14.

© Springer-Verlag Berlin Heidelberg 2016
C. Gavoille and D. Ilcinkas (Eds.): DISC 2016, LNCS 9888, pp. 29–42, 2016.
DOI: 10.1007/978-3-662-53426-7_3

model of computation, where in every round each of n nodes may send messages of up to $O(\log n)$ bits to each of its neighbors. Frischknecht et al. [21] showed that the diameter is surprisingly hard to compute: $\widetilde{\Omega}(n)$ rounds are needed even in networks with constant diameter[1]. This lower bound is nearly tight, due to an $O(n)$ upper bound presented simultaneously and independently by [26,34] to compute all pairs shortest paths in a network. Naturally, approximate solutions are a desired relaxation, and were indeed addressed in several cornerstone studies [21,24,26,28,34], bringing us even closer to a satisfactory understanding of the time complexity of computing distances in distributed networks. However, several central questions remained elusive.

Sparse Graphs. The graphs constructed in [21] have $\Theta(n^2)$ edges and constant diameter, and require any distributed protocol for computing their diameter to spend $\widetilde{\Omega}(n)$ rounds. Such a high lower bound makes one wonder if the diameter can be computed faster in networks that we expect to encounter in realistic applications. Almost all large networks of practical interest are very sparse [29], e.g. the Internet in 2012 had $\approx$ 4 billion nodes and $\approx$ 128 billion edges [30].

The only known lower bound for computing the diameter of a sparse network is obtained by a simple modification to the construction of [21] which yields a much weaker bound of $\widetilde{\Omega}(\sqrt{n})$. This leaves hope that the $\widetilde{\Omega}(n)$ bound can be beaten significantly in sparse networks. Our first result rules out this possibility.

Theorem 1. *The number of rounds needed for any protocol to compute the diameter of a network on n nodes and $O(n \log n)$ edges of constant diameter in the CONGEST model is $\Omega(\frac{n}{\log^2 n})$.*

We remark that, as in [21], our lower bound holds even for networks with constant diameter. Throughout the paper we say that a graph on n nodes is sparse if it has $O(n \log n)$ edges. Due to simple transformations, e.g. by adding dummy nodes, all of our lower bounds will also hold for the more strict definition of sparse graphs as having $O(n)$ edges, up to a loss of a log factor.

As explained next, the sparsity in our new lower bound construction allows us to extend the result in some interesting ways.

Approximation Algorithms. Another important question is whether we can bypass this near-linear barrier if we settle for knowing only an approximation to the diameter. An α-approximation algorithm to the diameter returns a value $\hat{D}$ such that $D \leq \hat{D} \leq \alpha \cdot D$, where D is the diameter of the network. From [21] we know that $\widetilde{\Omega}(\sqrt{n} + D)$ rounds are needed, even for computing a $(\frac{3}{2} - \varepsilon)$-approximation to the diameter, for any constant $\varepsilon > 0$.

Following this lower bound, almost-complementary upper bounds were under extensive research. It is known that a $\frac{3}{2}$-approximation can be computed in a sublinear number of rounds: Holzer and Wattenhofer [26] showed a $O(n^{3/4} + D)$-round algorithm and (independently) Peleg et al. [34] obtained a $O(D\sqrt{n} \log n)$ bound, later these bounds were improved to $O(\sqrt{n} \log n + D)$ by Lenzen and

---

[1] The notations $\widetilde{\Omega}$ and $\widetilde{O}$ hide factors that are polylogarithmic in n

Peleg [28], and finally Holzer et al. [24] reduce the bound to $O(\sqrt{n \log n} + D)$. When D is small, these upper bounds are near-optimal in terms of the round complexity – but do they have the best possible approximation ratio that can be achieved within a sublinear number of rounds? That is, can we also obtain a $(\frac{3}{2} - \varepsilon)$-approximation in $\widetilde{O}(\sqrt{n} + D)$ rounds, to match the lower bound of [21]?

Progress towards answering this question was made by Holzer and Wattenhofer [26] who showed that any algorithm that needs to decide whether the diameter is 2 or 3 has to spend $\widetilde{\Omega}(n)$ rounds. However, as the authors point out, their lower bound is not robust and does not rule out the possibility of a $(\frac{3}{2} - \varepsilon)$-approximation when the diameter is larger than 2, or an algorithm that is allowed an additive $+1$ error besides a multiplicative $(\frac{3}{2} - \varepsilon)$ error. Furthermore, when the diameter is 2 or 3 as in the construction of [26], any $(\frac{3}{2} - \varepsilon)$-approximation must return the exact diameter. Thus, to explain why we cannot save time by settling for a $(\frac{3}{2} - \varepsilon)$-approximation, we need a more general construction.

The Main Challenge. Perhaps the main difficulty in extending the lower bound constructions of [21, 26] to resolve these gaps was that their original graphs are dense. Our new sparse construction technique allows us to tighten the bounds and negatively resolve the above question. In other words, we show a $\widetilde{\Omega}(n)$ lower bound for computing a $(\frac{3}{2} - \varepsilon)$-approximation to the diameter.

At a high level, the reason that the density matters is as follows. The lower bound technique reduces the 2-party communication complexity problem of Set-Disjointness to a distributed algorithm for approximating the diameter. This is done by constructing a graph in which the existence of some of the edges depends on the inputs of the players, and partitioning the graph between the two players, inducing a cut in it. The dependence is such that having a good approximation to the diameter induces an answer to the Set-Disjointness problem. The players then simulate the distributed algorithm, and pay in communicating the bits that are sent on edges that cross the cut between their two partitions. Therefore, a known lower bound on the 2-party communication complexity of Set-Disjointness implies a lower bound on the number of rounds required for a distributed approximation algorithm for the diameter. The larger the cut, the smaller the lower bound for the distributed problem.

Having *a sparse graph with a small cut*, is what allows us to make this leap in the lower bound. The key idea of achieving a sparse graph with a small cut, is to connect the nodes to a set of nodes that represent their binary value, and the only nodes on the cut are the nodes of the binary representation. We call this graph structure a *bit-gadget*, and it plays a central role in all of our graph constructions. This is inspired by graph constructions for different settings (e.g. [3], see discussion in Sect. 1.1). Our main result follows.

Theorem 2. *For all constant $0 < \varepsilon < 1/2$, the number of rounds needed for any protocol to compute a $(3/2 - \varepsilon)$-approximation to the diameter of a sparse network in the CONGEST model is $\Omega(\frac{n}{\log^3 n})$.*

Radius. In many scenarios we want one special node to be able to efficiently send information to all other nodes. In this case, we would like this node to be the one that is closest to every other node, i.e. the *center* of the graph. The *radius* of the graph is the largest distance from the center, and it captures the number of rounds needed for the center node to transfer a message to another node in the network. While radius and diameter are closely related, the previous lower bounds for diameter do not transfer to radius and it was conceivable that the radius of the graph could be computed much faster. Obtaining a non-trivial lower bound for radius has been stated as an open problem in [26]. A third advantage of our technique is that it extends to computing the radius, for which we show that the same strong near-linear barriers above hold.

Theorem 3. *For all constant $0 < \varepsilon < 1/2$, the number of rounds needed for any protocol to compute a $(3/2 - \varepsilon)$-approximation to the radius of a sparse network in the CONGEST model is $\Omega(\frac{n}{\log^3 n})$.*

Eccentricity. The eccentricity of a node is the largest distance from it. Observe that the diameter is the largest eccentricity in the graph while the radius is the smallest. As pointed in [26], given a $(\frac{3}{2} - \varepsilon)$-approximation algorithm to all the eccentricities, we can achieve $(\frac{3}{2} - \varepsilon)$-approximation algorithm to the diameter by a simple flooding. This implies an $\widetilde{\Omega}(\sqrt{n} + D)$ lower bound for any $(\frac{3}{2} - \varepsilon)$-approximation algorithm for computing all the eccentricities. Our construction allows us to improve this result by showing that any algorithm for computing even a $(\frac{5}{3} - \varepsilon)$-approximation to all the eccentricities must spend $\Omega(\frac{n}{\log^3(n)})$ rounds. This improves both in terms of the number of rounds, and in terms of the approximation factor, which we allow to be even larger. Interestingly, it implies that approximating all eccentricities is even harder than approximating just the largest or the smallest one.

Theorem 4. *For all constant $0 < \varepsilon < 2/3$, the number of rounds needed for any protocol to compute a $(5/3 - \varepsilon)$ approximation of all eccentricities of a sparse network in the CONGEST model is $\Omega(\frac{n}{\log^3 n})$.*

Verification of Spanners. Finally, our technique allows us to obtain a lower bound for the verification of (α, β)-spanners. An (α, β)-spanner of a graph G, is a subgraph H in which for any two nodes u, v it holds that $d_H(u, v) \leq \alpha \cdot d_G(u, v) + \beta$. When spanners are sparse, i.e., when H does not have too many edges, they play a vital role in many application, such as routing, approximating distances, synchronization, and more. Hence, the construction of sparse spanners has been a central topic of many studies, both in centralized and sequential computing.

Here we address the problem of verifying that a given subgraph H is indeed an (α, β)-spanner of G. At the end of the computation, each node outputs a bit indicating whether H is a spanner, with the requirement that if H is indeed a spanner with the required parameters then all nodes indicate this, and otherwise at least one node indicates that it is not. We obtain the following lower bound.

Theorem 5. *Given an unweighted graph $G = V, E$, a subgraph $H \subset E$ of G, the number of rounds needed for any protocol to decide whether H is an (α, β)-spanner of G in the CONGEST model is $\Omega(\frac{n}{(\alpha+\beta)\log^3 n})$, for any $\alpha < \beta + 1$.*

Notice that for any reasonable value of $\alpha, \beta = O(poly \log n)$, the lower bound is near-linear. This is another evidence for a task for which verification is harder than computation in the CONGEST model, as initially brought into light in [18]. This is, for example, because $(+2)$-purely additive spanners with $O(n^{3/2} \log n)$ edges can be constructed in $O(\sqrt{n} \log n + D)$ rounds (this appears in [28], and can also be deduced from [26]), and additional various additive spanners can be constructed fast in CONGEST [14].

Roadmap. Section 2 contains our lower bound for computing the exact or approximate diameter. Due to space limitations we give our lower bounds for computing the exact or approximate radius, computing eccentricities and verifying spanners in the full version [2]. The degree-reduction technique appears in the full version as well.

1.1   Additional Related Work

Communication Complexity and Distributed Computing. A well-known technique to prove lower bounds in the $CONGEST$ model is to use a reduction from communication complexity to distributed computing. Peleg and Rubinovich [35] apply a lower bound from communication complexity to show that the number of rounds needed for any distributed algorithm to construct a minimum spanning tree (MST) is $\widetilde{\Omega}(\sqrt{n} + D)$. Many recent papers were inspired by this technique. In [20] Elkin extended the result of [35] to show that any distributed algorithm for constructing an α-approximation to the MST must spend $\widetilde{\Omega}(\sqrt{\frac{n}{\alpha}})$ rounds. Das Sarma et al. [18] show that any distributed verification algorithm for many problems, such as connectivity, $s - t$ cut and approximating MST requires $\widetilde{\Omega}(\sqrt{n} + D)$ rounds. Nanongkai et al. [32] showed an $\Omega(\sqrt{\ell \cdot D} + D)$ lower bound for computing a random walk of length ℓ. Similar reductions from communication complexity were adapted also in the $CONGEST$ $Clique$ $Broadcast$ model [19,25], where in each round each node can broadcast the same $O(\log n)$-bit message to all the nodes in the network.

Similar to the technique used in [18,19,21,25,26], our lower bounds are obtained by reductions from the Set-Disjointness problem in the two-party number-in-hand model of communication complexity [39]. Here, each of the players Alice and Bob receives a k-bit string, S_a and S_b respectively, and needs to decide whether the two strings are disjoint or not, i.e., whether there is some bit $0 \le i \le k - 1$ such that $S_a[i] = 1$ and $S_b[i] = 1$. It is shown in [27] that in order to solve the Set-Disjointness problem, Alice and Bob must exchange $\Omega(k)$ bits. The high level idea for applying this lower bound in the $CONGEST$ model, is to define a graph $G = (V, E)$ based on the input strings of Alice and Bob, such that G has some property p (e.g., diameter at most 4) if and only if the two strings of Alice and Bob are not disjoint. Given an algorithm for deciding whether a graph has property p, Alice and Bob can simulate this algorithm on G in order to solve the Set-Disjointness problem.

More on Distributed Distance Computation. Distance computation problems have also been recently studied in weighted distributed networks. Nanongkai [31] presented an $\widetilde{O}(n^{\frac{1}{2}} \cdot D^{\frac{1}{4}})$ upper bound for the $(1 + o(1))$-approximation to the single source shortest paths problem. More recently, this result was improved by Henzinger et al. [23] as they presented an $\widetilde{O}(n^{\frac{1}{2}+o(1)} + D^{1+o(1)})$ algorithm for the same approximation factor and showed that this also implies a $(2 + o(1))$-approximation algorithm to the diameter. Moreover, such problems have also been considered in the *congested clique* model [13,23,31], where $(1 + o(1))$-approximate all pairs shortest paths can be computed in $O(n^{0.158})$ rounds [13].

Intuitively, the technical difficulty in extending the proof for diameter to work for radius as well is the difference in types between the two problems: the diameter asks for a pair of nodes that are far ($\exists x \exists y$) while radius asks for a node that is close to everyone ($\exists x \forall y$). Recent developments in the theory of (sequential) algorithms suggest that this type-mismatch could lead to fundamental differences between the two problems. Recall that classical *sequential* algorithms solve APSP in $O(nm)$ time [17] and therefore both diameter and radius can be solved in quadratic $O(n^2)$ time in sparse graphs.

Due to the lack of techniques for proving *unconditional* super-linear $\omega(n)$ lower bounds on the runtime of sequential algorithms for any natural problem, a recent line of work seeks hardness results conditioned on certain plausible conjectures (a.k.a. "Hardness in P"). An interesting example of such result concerns the diameter: Roditty and Vassilevska W. [36] proved that if the diameter of sparse graphs can be computed in truly-subquadratic $O(n^{2-\varepsilon})$ time, for any $\varepsilon > 0$, then the Strong Exponential Time Hypothesis (SETH) is false[2], by reducing SAT to diameter. Since then, many other problems were shown to be "SETH-hard" (e.g. [1,4,6,7,9] to name a few) but whether a similar lower bound holds for radius is an open question [3,5,10,11,16,36]. In fact, Carmosino et al. [12] show that there is a formal barrier for reducing SAT to radius[3], and Abboud, Vassilevska W. and Wang [5] introduce a new conjecture to prove an $n^{2-o(1)}$ lower bound for radius[4] (which has a similar $\exists \forall$ type). Diameter and radius seem to behave differently also in the regime of dense and weighted graphs where the best known algorithms take roughly cubic $O(n^3/2^{\sqrt{\log n}})$ time [15,37] and it is known that radius can be solved in truly-subcubic $O(n^{3-\varepsilon})$ time if and only if APSP can [3], but showing such a subcubic-equivalence between APSP and diameter is a big open question [3,8,38].

---

[2] SETH is a pessimistic version of the $\mathsf{P} \neq \mathsf{NP}$ conjecture, which essentially says that CNF-SAT cannot be solved in $(2-\varepsilon)^n$ time. More formally, SETH is the assumption that there is no $\varepsilon > 0$ such that for all $k \geq 1$ we can solve k-SAT on n variables and m clauses in $(2 - \varepsilon)^n \cdot poly(m)$ time.

[3] It would imply a new co-nondeterministic algorithm for SAT and refute the Nondeterministic-SETH, which is a strong version of $\mathsf{NP} \neq \mathsf{CONP}$.

[4] A truly-subquadratic algorithm for computing the radius of a sparse graph refutes the Hitting Set Conjecture: there is no $\varepsilon > 0$ such that given two lists A, B of n subsets of a universe U of size $poly \log n$ we can decide whether there is a set $a \in A$ that intersects all sets $b \in B$ in $O(n^{2-\varepsilon})$ time.

The framework and set-up in our *unconditional* lower bound proofs for distributed algorithms are very different from the ones in the works on *conditional* lower bounds for sequential algorithms discussed above. Still, some of our graph gadgets are inspired by the constructions in those proofs, e.g. [3,5,11,16,36]. Thus, it is quite surprising that our hardness proof for diameter transfers without much difficulty to a hardness proof for radius.

1.2   Model and Basic Definitions

We consider a synchronized network of n nodes represented by an undirected graph $G = (V, E)$. In each round, each node can send a different message of b bits to each of its neighbors. This model is known as the $CONGEST(b)$ model, and as the $CONGEST$ model when $b = O(\log(n))$ [33]. The graph parameters we consider are formally defined as follows.

Definition 1 *(Eccentricity, Diameter and Radius). Let $d(u,v)$ denote the length of the shortest path between the nodes u and v. The eccentricity $e(u)$ of some node u is $max_{v \in V} d(u, v)$. The Diameter (denoted by D) is the maximum distance between any two nodes in the graph: $D = max_{u \in V} e(u)$. The Radius (denoted by r) is the maximum distance from some node to the "center" of the graph: $r = min_{u \in V} e(u)$.*

Finally, we define what we mean when we say that a graph is sparse.

Definition 2 *(sparse network). A sparse network $G = (V, E)$ is a network with n nodes and at most $O(n \log(n))$ edges.*

Recall, however, that all our results can be obtained for graphs that have a strictly linear number of $\Theta(n)$ edges, at the cost of at most an additional $O(\log n)$ factor in the lower bound.

2   Computing the Diameter

In this section we present lower bounds on the number of rounds needed to compute the diameter *exactly* and *approximately* in sparse networks. First, in Sect. 2.1 we present a higher lower bound on the number of rounds needed for any algorithm to compute the exact diameter of a sparse network, and next, in Sect. 2.2 we show how to modify our sparse construction to achieve a higher lower bound on the number of rounds needed for any algorithm to compute a $(\frac{3}{2} - \varepsilon)$-approximation to the diameter.

2.1   Exact Diameter

To prove Theorem 1 we describe a graph construction $G = (V, E)$ and a partition of G into (G_a, G_b), such that one part is simulated by Alice (denoted by G_a), and the second is simulated by Bob (denoted by G_b). Each player receives an input string defining some additional edges that will affect the diameter of G. The proof is organized as follows: in Sect. 2.1 we describe the graph construction, and next, in Sect. 2.1, we describe the reduction from the Set-Disjointness problem and deduce Theorem 1.

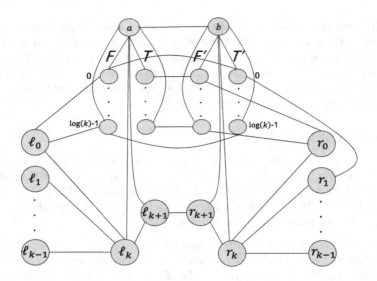

Fig. 1. Graph Construction (diameter). Some edges are omitted, for clarity.

Graph Construction. Let i^j denote the value of the bit j in the binary representation of i. The set of nodes V is defined as follows (see also Fig. 1):[5] First, it contains two sets of nodes $L = \{\ell_i \mid 0 \le i \le k-1\}$ and $R = \{r_i \mid 0 \le i \le k-1\}$, each of size k. All the nodes in L are connected to an additional node ℓ_k, which is connected to an additional node ℓ_{k+1}. Similarly, all the nodes in R are connected to an additional node r_k, which is connected to an additional node r_{k+1}. The nodes ℓ_{k+1} and r_{k+1} are also connected by an edge.

Furthermore, we add four sets of nodes, which are our bit-gadget: $F = \{f_j \mid 0 \le j \le \log(k) - 1\}$, $T = \{t_j \mid 0 \le j \le \log(k) - 1\}$, $F' = \{f'_j \mid 0 \le j \le \log(k) - 1\}$, $T' = \{t'_j \mid 0 \le j \le \log(k) - 1\}$, each of size $\log(k)$. We connect the sets F, T with F', T' by adding edges between f_i and t'_i, and between t_i and f'_i, for each $0 \le i \le \log(k) - 1$. To define the connections between the sets L, R and the sets F, T, F', T', we add the following edges: For each $\ell_i \in L$, if $i^j = 0$, we connect ℓ_i to f_j, otherwise, we connect ℓ_i to t_j. Similarly, for each $r_i \in R$, if $i^j = 0$ we connect r_i to f'_j, otherwise, we connect r_i to t'_j.

To complete the construction we add two additional nodes $\{a, b\}$. We connect a to all the nodes in $F \cup T \cup \{\ell_k, \ell_{k+1}\}$, and similarly, we connect b to all the nodes in $F' \cup T' \cup \{r_k, r_{k+1}\}$. We also add an edge between the nodes a and b. The proofs of the following two claims appears in the full version [2].

Claim 2.1. *For every $i, j \in [k-1]$ it holds that $d(\ell_i, r_j) = 3$ if $i \ne j$, and $d(\ell_i, r_j) = 5$ otherwise.*

Claim 2.2. *For every $u, v \in V \backslash (L \cup R)$ it holds that $d(u, v) \le 3$.*

---

[5] Note that for the sake of simplicity, some of the edges are omitted from Fig. 1.

Corollary 1. *For every u, v such that $u \in (V_a \backslash L)$ or $v \in (V_b \backslash R)$, it holds that $d(u, v) \leq 4$.*

Reduction from Set-Disjointness. To prove Theorem 1, we show a reduction from the Set-Disjointness problem. Following the construction defined in the previous section, we define a partition ($G_a = (V_a, E_a)$, $G_b = (V_b, E_b)$):

$$V_a = L \cup F \cup T \cup \{\ell_k, \ell_{k+1}, a\}, \ E_a = \{(u, v) | u, v \in V_a \wedge (u, v) \in E\}$$
$$V_b = R \cup F' \cup T' \cup \{r_k, r_{k+1}, b\}, \ E_b = \{(u, v) | u, v \in V_b \wedge (u, v) \in E\}$$

The graph G_a is simulated by Alice and the graph G_b is simulated by Bob, i.e., in each round, all the messages that nodes in G_a send to nodes in G_b are sent by Alice to Bob. Bob forwards these messages to the corresponding nodes in G_b. All the messages from nodes in G_b to nodes in G_a are sent in the same manner. Each player receives an input string (S_a and S_b) of k bits. If the bit $S_a[i] = 0$, Alice adds an edge between the nodes ℓ_i and ℓ_{k+1}. Similarly, if $S_b[i] = 0$, Bob adds an edge between the nodes r_i and r_{k+1}.

Observation 6. *For every $u, v \in V_a$, it holds that $d(u, v) \leq 4$. Similarly, $d(u, v) \leq 4$ For every $u, v \in V_b$.*

This is because $d(u_a, \ell_{k+1}) \leq 2$ for any $u_a \in V_a$, and $d(u_b, r_{k+1}) \leq 2$ for any node $u_b \in V_b$.

Lemma 1. *The diameter of G is at least 5 if and only if the sets of Alice and Bob are not disjoint.*

The proof appears in the full version [2].

Proof of Theorem 1. From Lemma 1, we get that any algorithm for computing the exact diameter of the graph G can be used to solve the Set-Disjointness problem. Note that since there are $O(\log(k))$ edges in the cut (G_a, G_b), in each round Alice and Bob exchange $O(\log(k) \cdot \log(n))$ bits. Since $k = \Omega(n)$ we deduce that any algorithm for computing the diameter of a network must spend $\Omega(\frac{n}{\log^2(n)})$ rounds, and since $|E| = O(n \log(n))$ this lower bound holds even for sparse networks.

2.2 $(\frac{3}{2} - \varepsilon)$-approximation to the Diameter

In this Section we show how to modify our sparse construction to achieve a stronger lower bound for $(\frac{3}{2} - \varepsilon)$-approximation algorithms.

Graph Construction. The main idea to achieve this lower bound is to stretch our sparse construction by replacing some edges by paths of length P, an integer which will be chosen later. Actually, we only apply the following changes to the construction described in Sect. 2.1 (see also Fig. 2 where $P = 3$):

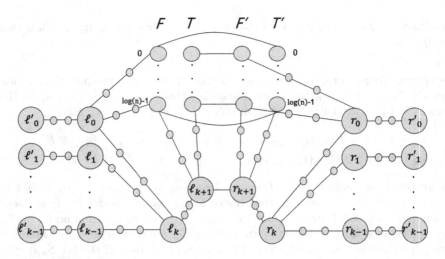

Fig. 2. Graph construction, $P = 3$ (diameter approximation). Some edges are omitted.

1. Remove the nodes a, b and their incident edges.
2. Replace all the edges incident to the nodes ℓ_k, r_k by paths of length P.
3. Replace all the edges (u, v) such that $u \in L$ and $v \in (F \cup T)$ by paths of length P. Similarly, Replace all the edges (u, v) such that $u \in R$ and $v \in (F' \cup T')$ by paths of length P.
4. Add two additional sets $L' = \{\ell'_i \mid 0 \le i \le k - 1\}$, $R' = \{r'_i \mid 0 \le i \le k - 1\}$ each of size k. Connect each ℓ'_i to ℓ_i by a path of length P. Similarly, connect each r'_i to r_i by a path of length P.

Furthermore, to simplify our proof, we connect each $u \in (F \cup T)$ to ℓ_{k+1} by a path of length P. Similarly, connect each $u \in (F' \cup T')$ to r_{k+1} by a path of length P.

Definition 3. $(Y(u,v))$ *For each $u, v \in V$ such that u and v are connected by a path of length P, denote by $Y(u, v)$ the set of all nodes on the P path between u and v (without u and v).*

The proofs of the following two claims appears in the the full version [2].

Claim 2.3. *For every $u, v \in V \backslash (L' \cup R' \bigcup_{i \in [k-1]} Y(\ell'_i, \ell_i) \bigcup_{i \in [k-1]} Y(r'_i, r_i))$ it holds that $d(u, v)$ is at most $4P + 1$.*

Claim 2.4. *For every $i, j \in [k - 1]$ it holds that $d(\ell'_i, r'_j) = 4P + 1$ if $i \ne j$, and $d(\ell'_i, r'_j) = 6P + 1$ otherwise.*

Reduction from Set-Disjointness. Following the construction described in the previous section, we define a partition $(G_a = (V_a, E_a), G_b = (V_b, E_b))$:

$$V_a = \bigcup_{\substack{i\in[k-1]\\ j\in[\log(k)-1]\\ i^j=0}} Y(\ell_i, f_j) \quad \bigcup_{\substack{i\in[k-1]\\ j\in[\log(k)-1]\\ i^j=1}} Y(\ell_i, t_j) \quad \bigcup_{i\in[k-1]} Y(\ell_i', \ell_i)$$

$$\bigcup_{i\in[k-1]} Y(\ell_i, \ell_k) \cup Y(\ell_k, \ell_{k+1}) \cup L' \cup L \cup F \cup T \cup \{\ell_k, \ell_{k+1}\}$$

$$E_a = \{(u,v) \mid u,v \in V_a \wedge (u,v) \in E\}$$

$$V_b = \bigcup_{\substack{i\in[k-1]\\ j\in[\log(k)-1]\\ i^j=0}} Y(r_i, f_j') \quad \bigcup_{\substack{i\in[k]\\ j\in[\log(k)-1]\\ i^j=1}} Y(r_i, t_j') \quad \bigcup_{i\in[k-1]} Y(r_i', r_i)$$

$$\bigcup_{i\in[k-1]} Y(r_i, r_k) \cup Y(r_k, r_{k+1}) \cup R' \cup R \cup F' \cup T' \cup \{r_k, r_{k+1}\}$$

$$E_b = \{(u,v) \mid u,v \in V_b \wedge (u,v) \in E\}$$

Each player receives an input string (S_a and S_b) of k bits. If $S_a[i] = 0$, Alice adds an edge between the nodes ℓ_i and ℓ_{k+1}. Similarly, if $S_b[i] = 0$, Bob adds an edge between the nodes r_i and r_{k+1}.

Claim 2.5. *Let $0 \le i \le k - 1$ be such that $S_a[i] = 0$ or $S_b[i] = 0$. Then the distance from the node $\ell_i \in L$ to any node $u \in (R \cup \{r_{k+1}\})$ is at most $2P + 2$.*

The proof appears in the full version [2]. Note that any node in V_b is connected by a path of length at most P to some node in $R \cup \{r_{k+1}\}$, and any node in L' is connected by a path of length P to some node in L. Thus, combining this with Claim 2.5 we conclude the following.

Corollary 2. *Let $0 \le i \le k - 1$ be such that $S_a[i] = 0$ or $S_b[i] = 0$. Then $d(u, v_b) \le 4P + 2$ for any $u \in \{\ell_i'\} \cup Y(\ell_i', \ell_i)$ and any $v_b \in V_b$. Symmetrically, $d(u, v_a) \le 4P + 2$ for any $u \in \{r_i'\} \cup Y(r_i', r_i)$ and any $v_a \in V_a$.*

Lemma 2. *The Diameter of G is $6P+1$ if the two sets of Alice and Bob are not disjoint, and $4P+2$ otherwise.*

The proof appears in the full version [2].

Proof of Theorem 2. To complete the proof we need to choose P such that $(\frac{3}{2} - \varepsilon) \cdot (4P+2) < (6P+1)$, this holds for any $P > \frac{1}{2\varepsilon} - \frac{1}{2}$. Note that $k = \Omega(\frac{n}{\log(n)})$ for a constant ε. Thus, we deduce that any algorithm for computing $(\frac{3}{2} - \varepsilon)$-approximation to the diameter requires at least $\Omega(\frac{n}{\log^3(n)})$ rounds. Furthermore, the number of nodes and the number of edges are both equal to $\Theta(k \log(k) \cdot P)$. Thus, this lower bound holds even for graphs with linear number of edges.

3   Discussion

We introduce a new technique for reducing the Set-Disjointness communication problem to distributed computation problems, in a highly efficient way. Our reductions encode an instance of Disjointness on k bits into a graph on only $\widetilde{O}(k)$ nodes and edges with a small "communication-cut" of size $O(\log k)$. All previous lower bound constructions had a cut of $poly(k)$ size (e.g., [18, 21, 25, 26]). This efficiency allows us to answer several central open questions regarding the round complexity of distance computation problems in the $CONGEST$ model.

There are several interesting directions for future work. First, there is still a $\log n$ factor gap between the upper and lower bounds on the round complexity of computing the diameter in the $CONGEST$ model. Due to the fundamentality of the diameter, we believe that it will be interesting to close this small gap.

Second, while our ideas greatly improve the state of the art lower bounds for shortest paths problems on *unweighted* graphs, their potential in the regime of *weighted* graphs is yet to be explored.

Finally, following our strong barriers for sparse graphs, it is important to seek further natural restrictions on the networks that would allow for much faster distance computation. Planar graphs are an intriguing setting in this context. s A promising recent work of Ghaffari and Haeupler [22] showed that computing a minimum spanning tree can be done in $\widetilde{O}(D)$ rounds in planar graphs, despite the $\widetilde{\Omega}(\sqrt{n})$ lower bound for general graphs [18]. Can the diameter of a planar network be computed in $\widetilde{O}(D)$ rounds? While the graphs in our lower bounds are highly non-planar, it is interesting to note that they have a relatively small treewidth of $O(\log n)$.

Acknowledgement. We thank Ami Paz for many discussions and helpful suggestions.

References

1. Abboud, A., Backurs, A., Hansen, T.D., Williams, V.V., Zamir, O.: Subtree isomorphism revisited. In: Proceedings of the Twenty-Seventh Annual ACM-SIAM Symposium on Discrete Algorithms, SODA (2016)
2. Abboud, A., Censor-Hillel, K., Khoury, S.: Near-linear lower bounds for distributed distance computations, even in sparse networks. CoRR, abs/1605.05109 (2016)
3. Abboud, A., Grandoni, F., Williams, V.V.: Subcubic equivalences between graph centrality problems, APSP and diameter. In: Proceedings of the Twenty-Sixth Annual ACM-SIAM Symposium on Discrete Algorithms, SODA (2015)
4. Abboud, A., Williams, V.V.: Popular conjectures imply strong lower bounds for dynamic problems. In: 55th IEEE Annual Symposium on Foundations of Computer Science, FOCS (2014)
5. Abboud, A., Williams, V.V., Wang, J.R.: Approximation and fixed parameter subquadratic algorithms for radius and diameter in sparse graphs. In: Proceedings of the Twenty-Seventh Annual ACM-SIAM Symposium on Discrete Algorithms, SODA (2016)

6. Abboud, A., Williams, V.V., Weimann, O.: Consequences of faster alignment of sequences. In: Esparza, J., Fraigniaud, P., Husfeldt, T., Koutsoupias, E. (eds.) ICALP 2014. LNCS, vol. 8572, pp. 39–51. Springer, Heidelberg (2014)
7. Abboud, A., Williams, V.V., Yu, H.: Matching triangles and basing hardness on an extremely popular conjecture. In: Proceedings of the Forty-Seventh Annual ACM on Symposium on Theory of Computing, STOC (2015)
8. Aingworth, D., Chekuri, C., Indyk, P., Motwani, R.: Fast estimation of diameter and shortest paths (without matrix multiplication). SIAM J. Comput. **28**(4) (1999)
9. Backurs, A., Indyk, P.: Edit distance cannot be computed in strongly subquadratic time (unless SETH is false). In: Proceedings of the Forty-Seventh Annual ACM on Symposium on Theory of Computing, STOC (2015)
10. Borassi, M., Crescenzi, P., Habib, M.: Into the square - on the complexity of quadratic-time solvable problems. CoRR, abs/1407.4972 (2014)
11. Cairo, M., Grossi, R., Rizzi, R.: New bounds for approximating extremal distances in undirected graphs. In: Proceedings of the Twenty-Seventh Annual ACM-SIAM Symposium on Discrete Algorithms, SODA (2016)
12. Carmosino, M.L., Gao, J., Impagliazzo, R., Mihajlin, I., Paturi, R., Schneider, S.: Nondeterministic extensions of the strong exponential time hypothesis and consequences for non-reducibility. In: Proceedings of the 2016 ACM Conference on Innovations in Theoretical Computer Science (2016)
13. Censor-Hillel, K., Kaski, P., Korhonen, J.H., Lenzen, C., Paz, A., Suomela, J.: Algebraic methods in the congested clique. In: Proceedings of the 2015 ACM Symposium on Principles of Distributed Computing, PODC (2015)
14. Censor-Hillel, K., Kavitha, T., Paz, A., Yehudayoff, A.: Distributed construction of purely additive spanners. Manuscript (2016)
15. Chan, T.M., Williams, R.: Deterministic APSP, orthogonal vectors, and more: quickly derandomizing Razborov-Smolensky. In: Proceedings of the Twenty-Seventh Annual ACM-SIAM Symposium on Discrete Algorithms, SODA (2016)
16. Chechik, S., Larkin, D.H., Roditty, L., Schoenebeck, G., Tarjan, R.E., Williams, V.V.: Better approximation algorithms for the graph diameter. In: Proceedings of the Twenty-Fifth Annual ACM-SIAM Symposium on Discrete Algorithms, SODA (2014)
17. Cormen, T.H., Leiserson, C.E., Rivest, R.L., Stein, C.: Introduction to Algorithms, 3rd edn. The MIT Press, Cambridge (2009)
18. Das Sarma, A., Holzer, S., Kor, L., Korman, A., Nanongkai, D., Pandurangan, G., Peleg, D., Wattenhofer, R.: Distributed verification and hardness of distributed approximation. SIAM J. Comput. **41**(5) (2012)
19. Drucker, A., Kuhn, F., Oshman, R.: On the power of the congested clique model. In: ACM Symposium on Principles of Distributed Computing, PODC (2014)
20. Elkin, M.: Unconditional lower bounds on the time-approximation tradeoffs for the distributed minimum spanning tree problem. In: Proceedings of the 36th Annual ACM Symposium on Theory of Computing (2004)
21. Frischknecht, S., Holzer, S., Wattenhofer, R.: Networks cannot compute their diameter in sublinear time. In: Proceedings of the Twenty-Third Annual ACM-SIAM Symposium on Discrete Algorithms, SODA (2012)
22. Ghaffari, M., Haeupler, B.: Distributed algorithms for planar networks II: low-congestion shortcuts, mst, and min-cut. In: Proceedings of the Twenty-Seventh Annual ACM-SIAM Symposium on Discrete Algorithms, SODA (2016)
23. Henzinger, M., Krinninger, S., Nanongkai, D.: An almost-tight distributed algorithm for computing single-source shortest paths. CoRR, abs/1504.07056 (2015)

24. Holzer, S., Peleg, D., Roditty, L., Wattenhofer, R.: Distributed 3/2-approximation of the diameter. In: Distributed Computing - 28th International Symposium, Proceedings, DISC (2014)
25. Holzer, S., Pinsker, N.: Approximation of distances and shortest paths in the broadcast congest clique. CoRR, abs/1412.3445 (2014)
26. Holzer, S., Wattenhofer, R.: Optimal distributed all pairs shortest paths and applications. In: ACM Symposium on Principles of Distributed Computing, PODC (2012)
27. Kushilevitz, E., Nisan, N.: Communication Complexity. Cambridge University Press, New York (1997)
28. Lenzen, C., Peleg, D.: Efficient distributed source detection with limited bandwidth. In: ACM Symposium on Principles of Distributed Computing, PODC (2013)
29. Leskovec, J., Krevl, A.: SNAP Datasets: stanford large network dataset collection (2014)
30. Meusel, R., Vigna, S., Lehmberg, O., Bizer, C.: The graph structure in the web - analyzed on different aggregation levels. J. Web Sci. 1(1) (2015)
31. Nanongkai, D.: Distributed approximation algorithms for weighted shortest paths. In: Symposium on Theory of Computing, STOC (2014)
32. Nanongkai, D., Sarma, A.D., Pandurangan, G.: A tight unconditional lower bound on distributed randomwalk computation. In: Proceedings of the 30th Annual ACM Symposium on Principles of Distributed Computing, PODC (2011)
33. Peleg, D.: Distributed computing: a locality-sensitive approach. In: Society for Industrial Mathematics (2000)
34. Peleg, D., Roditty, L., Tal, E.: Distributed algorithms for network diameter and girth. In: Czumaj, A., Mehlhorn, K., Pitts, A., Wattenhofer, R. (eds.) ICALP 2012, Part II. LNCS, vol. 7392, pp. 660–672. Springer, Heidelberg (2012)
35. Peleg, D., Rubinovich, V.: A near-tight lower bound on the time complexity of distributed MST construction. In: 40th Annual Symposium on Foundations of Computer Science, FOCS (1999)
36. Roditty, L., Williams, V.V.: Fast approximation algorithms for the diameter and radius of sparse graphs. In: Symposium on Theory of Computing Conference, STOC (2013)
37. Williams, R.: Faster all-pairs shortest paths via circuit complexity. In: Symposium on Theory of Computing, STOC (2014)
38. Williams, V.V., Williams, R.: Subcubic equivalences between path, matrix and triangle problems. In: 51th Annual IEEE Symposium on Foundations of Computer Science, FOCS (2010)
39. Yao, A.C.: Some complexity questions related to distributive computing (preliminary report). In: Proceedings of the 11th Annual ACM Symposium on Theory of Computing, April 1979

Fast Distributed Algorithms for Testing Graph Properties

Keren Censor-Hillel, Eldar Fischer, Gregory Schwartzman$^{(\boxtimes)}$,
and Yadu Vasudev

Department of Computer Science, Technion – Israel Institute of Technology,
Haifa, Israel
{ckeren,eldar,gregory}@cs.technion.ac.il, yaduvasudev@gmail.com

Abstract. We provide a thorough study of *distributed property testing* – producing algorithms for the approximation problems of property testing in the CONGEST model. In particular, for the so-called *dense* graph testing model we emulate sequential tests for nearly all graph properties having 1-sided tests, while in the *general* and *sparse* models we obtain faster tests for triangle-freeness, cycle-freeness and bipartiteness, respectively. In addition, we show a logarithmic lower bound for testing bipartiteness and cycle-freeness, which holds even in the LOCAL model.

In most cases, aided by parallelism, the distributed algorithms have a much shorter running time as compared to their counterparts from the sequential querying model of traditional property testing. The simplest property testing algorithms allow a relatively smooth transitioning to the distributed model. For the more complex tasks we develop new machinery that may be of independent interest.

1 Introduction

The performance of many distributed algorithms naturally depends on properties of the underlying network graph. Therefore, an inherent goal is to check whether the graph, or some given subgraph, has certain properties. However, in some cases this is known to be hard, such as in the CONGEST model [29]. In this model, computation proceeds in synchronous rounds, in each of which every vertex can send an $O(\log n)$-bit message to each of its neighbors. Lower bounds for the number of rounds of type $\tilde{\Omega}(\sqrt{n} + D)$ are known for *verifying* many global graph properties, where n is the number of vertices in the network, D is its diameter and $\tilde{\Omega}$ hides polylogarithmic factors (see, e.g. Das-Sarma et al. [34]).

To overcome such difficulties, we adopt the relaxation used in graph property testing, as first defined in [17,19], to the distributed setting. That is, rather than aiming for an exact answer to the question of whether the graph G satisfies a certain property P, we settle for distinguishing the case of satisfying P from the case of being ϵ-*far* from it, for an appropriate measure of being far.

Apart from its theoretical interest, this relaxation is motivated by the common scenario of having distributed algorithms for some tasks that perform better

Supported in part by the Israel Science Foundation (grant 1696/14).

C. Gavoille and D. Ilcinkas (Eds.): DISC 2016, LNCS 9888, pp. 43–56, 2016.
DOI: 10.1007/978-3-662-53426-7_4

given a certain property of the network topology, or given that the graph *almost* satisfies that property. For example, Hirvonen et al. [23] show an algorithm for finding a large cut in triangle-free graphs (with additional constraints), and for finding an $(1 - \epsilon)$-approximation if at most an ϵ fraction of all edges are part of a triangle. Similarly, Pettie and Su [30] provide fast algorithms for coloring triangle-free graphs.

We construct fast distributed algorithms for testing various graph properties. An important byproduct of this study is a toolbox that we believe will be useful in other settings as well.

1.1   Our Contributions

We provide a rigorous study of property testing methods in the realm of distributed computing under the CONGEST model. We construct *1-sided error distributed ϵ-tests*, in which if the graph satisfies the property then all vertices output `accept`, and if it is ϵ-far from satisfying the property then at least one vertex outputs `reject` with probability at least 2/3. Using the standard amplification method of invoking such a test $O(\log n)$ times and having a vertex output `reject` if there is at least one invocation in which it should output `reject`, gives rejection with higher probability at the price of a multiplicative $O(\log n)$ factor for the number of rounds.

The definition of a graph being ϵ-far from satisfying a property is roughly one of the following (see the preliminaries section in the full version, [8], for precise definitions): (1) Changing any ϵn^2 entries in the adjacency matrix does not give a graph that satisfies the property (dense model), or (2) changing any $\epsilon \cdot \max\{n, m\}$ entries in the adjacency matrix does not give a graph that satisfies the property, where m is the number of edges (general model). A particular case here is when the degrees are bounded by some constant d, and any resulting graph must comply with this restriction as well (sparse model).

In a *sequential ϵ-test*, access to the input is provided by queries, whose type depends on the model. In the dense model these are asking whether two vertices v, u are neighbors, and in the general and sparse models these can be either asking what the degree of a vertex v is, or asking what the i-th neighbor of v is (the ordering of neighbors is arbitrary). While a sequential ϵ-test can touch only a small handful of vertices with its queries, in a distributed test the lack of ability to communicate over large distances is offset by having all n vertices operating in parallel.

Our first contribution is a general scheme for a near-complete emulation in the distributed context of ϵ-tests originating from the dense graph model (Sect. 2). This makes use of the fact that in the dense model all (sequential) testing algorithms can be made *non-adaptive*, which roughly means that queries do not depend on responses to previous queries (see the preliminaries section in the full version for definition). In fact, such tests can be made to have a very simple structure, allowing the vertices in the distributed model to "band together" for an emulation of the test. There is only one additional technical condition (which we define in Sect. 2), since in the distributed model we cannot handle properties whose counter-examples can be "split" to disjoint graphs. For example, the distributed model cannot hope to handle the property of the graph having no disjoint union of two triangles, a property for which there exists a test in the dense model.

Theorem 1. *Any ϵ-test in the dense graph model for a non-disjointed property that makes q queries can be converted to an $O(q^2)$-round distributed ϵ-test.*

We next move away from the dense graph model to the sparse and general models, that are sometimes considered to be more realistic. In the general model, there exists no test for the property of containing no triangle that makes a number of queries independent of the number of graph vertices [2]. Here the distributed model can do better, because the reason for this deficiency is addressed by having all vertices operate concurrently. In Sect. 3 we adapt the interim lemmas used in the best testing algorithm constructed in [2], and construct a distributed algorithm whose number of rounds is independent of n.

Theorem 2. *There is a distributed ϵ-test in the general graph model for triangle-freeness, that requires $O(\epsilon^{-2})$ rounds.*

The sparse and general models inherently require *adaptive* property testing algorithms, since there is no other way to trace a path from a given vertex forward, or follow its neighborhood. Testing triangle-freeness sequentially uses adaptivity only to a small degree. However, other problems in the sparse and general models, such as the one we explore next, have a high degree of adaptivity built into their sequential algorithms, and we need to take special care for emulating it in the distributed setting.

In the sparse model (degrees bounded by a constant d), we adapt ideas from the bipartiteness testing algorithm of [18], in which we search for odd-length cycles. Here again the performance of a distributed algorithm surpasses that of the test (a number of rounds polylogarithmic in n vs. a number of queries which is $\Omega(\sqrt{n})$ – a lower bound that is given in [19]). The following is proved in Sect. 4.

Theorem 3. *There is a distributed ϵ-test in the bounded degree graph model for the property of being bipartite, that requires $O(poly(\epsilon^{-1}\log(n\epsilon^{-1})))$ rounds.*

In the course of proving Theorem 3 we develop a method that we consider to be of independent interest[1]. The algorithm performs $2n$ random walks concurrently (two starting from each vertex). The parallel execution of random walks despite the congestion restriction is achieved by making sure that the walks have a uniform stationary distribution, and then showing that congestion is "close to average", which for the uniform stationary distribution is constant.

In Sect. 5 we show a fast test for cycle-freeness. This makes use of a combinatorial lemma that we prove, about cycles that remain in the graph after removing edges independently with probability $\epsilon/2$. The following summarizes our result for testing cycle-freeness.

---

[1] This was recently independently and concurrently devised in [16] for a different use.

Theorem 4. *There is a distributed ϵ-test in the general graph model for cycle-freeness, that requires $O(\log n/\epsilon)$ rounds.*

We also prove lower bounds for testing bipartiteness and cycle-freeness that match the upper bound for the latter property. Roughly speaking, these are obtained by using the probabilistic method with alterations to construct graphs which are far from being bipartite or cycle-free, but all of their cycles are of length that is at least logarithmic. This technique bears some similarity to the classic result by Erdös [12], which showed the existence of graphs with large girth and large chromatic number. The following are given in Sect. 6.

Theorem 5. *Any distributed 1/100-test in the bounded degree or general graph model for the property of being bipartite requires $\Omega(\log n)$ rounds of communication.*

Theorem 6. *Any distributed 1/100-test in the bounded degree graph or general model for cycle-freeness requires $\Omega(\log n)$ rounds of communication.*

Roadmap: The paper is organized as follows. The remainder of this section consists of related work and historical background on property testing. The emulation of sequential tests for the dense model is given in Sect. 2. In Sect. 3 we give our distributed test for triangle-freeness. In Sect. 4 we provide a distributed test for bipartiteness, along with our new method of executing many random walks, and in Sect. 5 we give our test for cycle-freeness. Section 6 gives our logarithmic lower bounds for testing bipartiteness and cycle-freeness. We conclude with a short discussion in Sect. 7.

1.2   Related Work

The only previous work that directly relates to our distributed setting is due to Brakerski and Patt-Shamir [7]. They show a *tolerant* property testing algorithm for finding large (linear in size) *near-cliques* in the graph. An ϵ-near clique is a set of vertices for which all but an ϵ-fraction of the pairs of vertices have an edge between them. The algorithm is tolerant, in the sense that it finds a linear near-clique if there exists a linear ϵ^3-near clique. That is, the testing algorithm considers two thresholds of being close to having the property (in this case – containing a linear size clique). We are unaware of any other work on property testing in this distributed setting.

Testing in a different distributed setting was considered in Arfaoui et al. [4]. They study testing for cycle-freeness, in a setting where each vertex may collect information of its entire neighborhood up to some distance, and send a short string of bits to a central authority who decides whether the graph is cycle-free.

Related to having information being sent to, or received by, a central authority, is the concept of proof-labelling schemes, introduced by Korman et al. [26] (for extensions see, e.g., Baruch et al. [5]). In this setting, each vertex is given some external label, and by exchanging labels the vertices need to decide whether a given property of the graph holds. This is different from our setting in which no information other than vertex IDs is available. Another setting that is related to proof-labelling schemes, but differs from our model, is the prover-verifier model of Foerster et al. [14].

Sequential property testing has the goal of computing without processing the entire input. The wider family of *local computation algorithms* (LCA) is known to have connections with distributed computing, as shown by Parnas and Ron [28] and later used by others. A recent study by Göös et al. [22] proves that under some conditions, the fact that a centralized algorithm can query distant vertices does not help with speeding up computation. However, they consider the LOCAL model, and their results apply to certain properties that are not influenced by distances.

Finding induced subgraphs is a crucial task and has been studied in several different distributed models (see, e.g., [9–11,25]). Notice that for *finding* subgraphs, having *many* instances of the desired subgraph can help speedup the computation, as in [10]. This is in contrast to algorithms that perform faster if there are *no* or only *few* instances, as explained above, which is why we test for, e.g., the property of being *triangle-free*, rather for the property of *containing* triangles. (Notice that these are not the same, and in fact every graph with $3/\epsilon$ or more vertices is ϵ-close to having a triangle.)

Parallelizing many random walks was addressed in [1], where the question of graph covering via random walks is discussed. It is shown there that for certain families of graphs there is a substantial speedup in the time it takes for k walks starting from the same vertex to cover the graph, as compared to a single walk. No edge congestion constraints are taken into account. In [35], it is shown how to perform, under congestion, a single random walk of length L in $\tilde{O}(\sqrt{LD})$ rounds, and k random walks in $\tilde{O}(\sqrt{kLD} + k)$ rounds, where D is the diameter of the graph. Our method has no dependence on the diameter, allowing us to perform a multitude of *short walks* much faster.

1.3 Historical Overview

The first papers to consider the question of property testing were [6] and [33]. The original motivations for defining property testing were its connection to some Computerized Learning models, and the ability to leverage some properties to construct Probabilistically Checkable Proofs (PCPs – this is related to property testing through the areas of Locally Testable Codes and Locally Decodable Codes, LTCs and LDCs). Other motivations since then have entered the fray, and foremost among them are sublinear-time algorithms, and other big-data considerations. Since virtually no property can be decidable without reading the entire input, property testing introduces a notion of the allowable approximation to the original problem. In general, the algorithm has to distinguish inputs satisfying the property, from inputs that are ϵ-*far* from it. For more information on the general scheme of "classical" property testing, consult the surveys [13,20,31].

The older of the graph testing models discussed here is the dense model, as defined in the seminal work of Goldreich, Goldwasser and Ron [17]. The dense graph model has historically kick-started combinatorial property testing in earnest, but it has some shortcomings. Its main one is the distance function, which makes sense only if we consider graphs having many edges (hence the name "dense model") – any graph with $o(n^2)$ edges is indistinguishable in this model from an empty graph.

The stricter and at times more plausible distance function is one which is relative to the actual number of edges, rather than the maximum $\binom{n}{2}$. The general model was defined in [2], while the sparse model was defined already in [19]. The main difference between the sparse and the general graph models is that in the former there is also a guaranteed upper bound d on the degrees of the vertices, which is given to the algorithm in advance (the query complexity may then depend on d, either explicitly, or more commonly implicitly by considering d to be a constant).

2 Distributed Emulation of Sequential Tests in the Dense Model

We begin by showing that under a certain assumption of being *non-disjointed*, which we define below, a property P that has a sequential test in the dense model that requires q queries can be tested in the distributed setting within $O(q^2)$ rounds. We prove this by constructing an emulation that translates sequential tests to distributed ones. We first introduce a definition of a *witness* graph and then adapt [21, Theorem 2.2], restricted to 1-sided error tests, to our terminology.

Definition 1. *Let P be a property of graphs with n vertices. Let G' be a graph with $k < n$ vertices. We say that G' is a* witness against P, *if it is not an induced subgraph of any graph that satisfies P.*

Notice that if G' has an induced subgraph H that is a witness against P, then by the above definition G' is also a witness against P. The work of [21] transforms tests of graphs in the dense model to a canonical form where the query scheme is based on vertex selection. This is useful in particular for the distributed model, where the computational work is essentially based in the vertices. We require the following special case for 1-sided error tests.

Lemma 1 ([21, Theorem 2.2]). *Let P be a property of graphs with n vertices. If there exists a 1-sided error ϵ-test for P with query complexity $q(n, \epsilon)$, then there exists a 1-sided error ϵ-test for P that uniformly selects a set of $q' = 2q(n, \epsilon)$ vertices, and accepts iff the induced subgraph is not a witness against P.*

Our emulation leverages Lemma 1 under an assumption on the property P.

Definition 2. *We say that P is a* non-disjointed *property if for every graph G that does not satisfy P and an induced subgraph G' of G such that G' is a witness against P, G' has some connected component which is also a witness against P. We call such components* witness components.

We are now ready to formally state our main theorem for this section.

Theorem 1. *Any ϵ-test in the dense graph model for a non-disjointed property that makes q queries can be converted to an $O(q^2)$-round distributed ϵ-test.*

We claim that not satisfying a non-disjointed property cannot rely on subgraphs that are not connected, which is exactly what we need to forbid in a distributed setting. Formally, the property P is a non-disjointed property if and only if all minimal witnesses that are induced subgraphs of G are connected. Here *minimal* refers to the standard terminology, which means that no proper induced subgraph is a witness against P.

Next, we give the distributed test (its pseudo-code form appears in the full version). The test has an outer loop in which each vertex picks itself with probability $5q/n$, collects its neighborhood of a certain size of edges between *picked* vertices in an inner loop, and rejects if it identifies a witness against P. The outer loop repeats two times because not only does the sequential test have an error probability, but also with some small probability we may randomly pick too many or not enough vertices in order to emulate it. Repeating the main loop twice reduces the error probability back to below $1/3$. In the inner loop, each vertex collects its neighborhood of picked vertices and checks if its connected component is a witness against P. To limit communications this is done only for components of picked vertices that are sufficiently small: if a vertex detects that it is part of a component with too many edges then it accepts and does not participate until the next iteration of the outer loop.

To analyze the algorithm, we begin by proving (see full version) that there is a constant probability of at least $2/3$ for the number of picked vertices to be sufficient and not too large, namely, between q and $10q$. Now, we can use the guarantees of the sequential test to obtain the guarantees of our algorithm.

Lemma 2. *Let P be a non-disjointed graph property. If G satisfies P then all vertices output* accept *in the emulation algorithm. If G is ϵ-far from satisfying P, then with probability at least $2/3$ there exists a vertex that outputs* reject.

We now address the round complexity. Each vertex only sends and receives information from its q-neighborhood about edges between the chosen vertices. If too many vertices are chosen we detect this and accept. Otherwise we only communicate the chosen vertices and their edges, which requires $O(q^2)$ rounds using standard *pipelining*[2]. Together with Lemma 2, this proves Theorem 1.

Applications: k-colorability and perfect graphs. We provide some examples of usage of Theorem 1. A result by Alon and Shapira [3] states that all graph properties closed under induced subgraphs are testable in a number of queries that depends only on ϵ^{-1}. We note that, except for certain specific properties for which there are ad-hoc proofs (such as k-colorability), the dependence is usually a tower function in ϵ^{-1} or worse (asymptotically larger).

---

[2] Pipelining means that each vertex has a buffer for each edge, which holds the information (edges between chosen vertices, in our case) it needs to send over that edge. The vertex sends the pieces of information one after the other.

From this, together with Lemma 1 and Theorem 1, we deduce that if P is a non-disjointed property closed under induced subgraphs, then it is testable, for every fixed ϵ, in a constant number of rounds. Our emulation implies a distributed 1-sided error ϵ-test for *k-colorability* that requires $O(\text{poly}(k\epsilon^{-1}))$ rounds, and a distributed 1-sided error ϵ-test for being a *perfect graph*[3] whose running time depends only on ϵ (see full version for complete details).

3   Distributed Test for Triangle-Freeness

In this section we show a distributed ϵ-test for triangle-freeness. Notice that since triangle-freeness is a non-disjointed property, Theorem 1 gives a distributed ϵ-test for triangle-freeness under the dense model with a number of rounds that is $O(q^2)$, where q is the number of queries required for a sequential ϵ-test for triangle-freeness. However, for triangle-freeness, the known number of queries is a tower function in $\log(1/\epsilon)$ [15].

Here we leverage the inherent parallelism that we can obtain when checking the neighbors of a vertex, and show a test for triangle-freeness that requires only $O(\epsilon^{-2})$ rounds. Importantly, our algorithm works not only for the dense graph model, but for the general graph model (where distances are relative to the actual number of edges), which subsumes it. In the sequential setting, a test for triangle-freeness in the general model requires a number of queries that is some constant power of n by [2]. Our proof, which appears in the full version, actually follows the groundwork laid in [2] for the general graph model – their algorithm picks a vertex and checks two of its neighbors for being connected, while we perform the check for all vertices in parallel.

Theorem 2. *There is a distributed ϵ-test in the general graph model for triangle-freeness, that requires $O(\epsilon^{-2})$ rounds.*

4   Distributed Bipartiteness Test for Bounded Degree Graphs

In this section we show a distributed ϵ-test for being bipartite for graphs with degrees bounded by d. Our test builds upon the sequential test of [18] and, as in the case of triangle freeness, takes advantage of the ability to parallelize queries. While the number of queries of the sequential test is $\Omega(\sqrt{n})$ [19], the number of rounds in the distributed test is only *polylogarithmic* in n and polynomial in ϵ^{-1}. As in [18], we assume that d is a constant, and omit it from our expressions (it is implicit in the O notation for L below).

Let us first outline the algorithm of [18], since our distributed test borrows from its framework and our analysis is in part derived from it. The sequential test basically tries to detect odd cycles. It consists of T iterations, in each of

---

[3] A graph G is said to be *perfect* if for every induced subgraph G' of G, the chromatic number of G' equals the size of the largest clique in G'.

which a vertex s is selected uniformly at random and K random walks of length L are performed starting from the source s. If, in any iteration with a chosen source s, there is a vertex v which is reached by an even prefix of a random walk and an odd prefix of a random walk (possibly the same walk), then the algorithm rejects, as this indicates the existence of an odd cycle. Otherwise, the algorithm accepts. To obtain an ϵ-test the parameters are chosen to be $T = O(\epsilon^{-1})$, $K = O(\epsilon^{-4}\sqrt{n}\log^{1/2}(n\epsilon^{-1}))$, and $L = O(\epsilon^{-8}\log^6 n)$.

The main approach of our distributed test is similar, except that a key ingredient is that we can afford to perform much fewer random walks from every vertex, namely $O(\text{poly}(\epsilon^{-1}\log n\epsilon^{-1}))$. This is because we can run random walks in parallel originating from all vertices at once. However, a crucial challenge that we need to address is that several random walks may collide on an edge, violating its congestion bound. To address this issue, our central observation is that *lazy* random walks (chosen to have a uniform stationary distribution) provide for a very low probability of having too many of these collisions at once. The main part of the analysis is in showing that with high probability there will never be too many walks concurrently in the same vertex, so we can comply with the congestion bound. We begin by formally defining the lazy random walks we use.

Definition 3. *A* lazy *random walk over a graph G with degree bound d is a random walk, that is, a (memory-less) sequence of random variables $Y_1, Y_2, \ldots$ taking values from the vertex set V, where the transition probability $Pr[Y_k = v | Y_{k-1} = u]$ is $\frac{1}{2d}$ if uv is an edge of G, $\frac{1-deg(u)}{2d}$ if $u = v$, and 0 otherwise.*

The stationary distribution for the lazy random walk of Definition 3 is uniform [32, Section 8]. Next, we describe a procedure to handle one iteration of moving the random walks (Algorithm 1). Our distributed test for bipartiteness (its pseudo-code form is in the full version) initiates only 2 lazy random walks from every vertex concurrently, and searches for odd cycles that can be detected if an even prefix and an odd prefix of 2 such random walks collide at some vertex.

It is quite immediate that Algorithm 1 takes $O(\xi)$ rounds (the value of ξ is given below). Our main result here is that using L iterations of Algorithm 1 indeed provides a distributed ϵ-test for bipartiteness.

Theorem 3. *There is a distributed ϵ-test in the bounded degree graph model for the property of being bipartite, that requires $O(\text{poly}(\epsilon^{-1}\log(n\epsilon^{-1})))$ rounds.*

The number of rounds is immediate from the algorithm – it is dominated by the L calls to Algorithm 1, making a total of $O(\xi L)$ rounds, which is indeed $O(\text{poly}(\epsilon^{-1}\log(n\epsilon^{-1})))$. To prove the rest of Theorem 3 we need some notation, and a lemma from [18] that bounds from below the probabilities for detecting odd cycles if G is ϵ-far from being bipartite.

Given a source s, if there is a vertex v which is reached by an even prefix of a random walk w_i from s and an odd prefix of a random walk w_j from s, we say that walks w_i and w_j *detect a violation*. Let $p_s(k, \ell)$ be the probability that, out of k random walks of length ℓ starting from s, there are two that detect a violation. Using this notation, $p_s(K, L)$ is the probability that the sequential

---

Algorithm 1. Move random walks once with input ξ

Variables: W_v walks residing in v (multiset), H_v history of walks through v
Input: ξ, the maximum congestion per vertex allowed
`# each walk is characterized by` (i, u) `where` i `is the number of actual`
`    moves and` u `is the origin vertex`
1 for each *vertex* v **simultaneously**
2   if $|W_v| \leq \xi$ then `# give up if exceeded the maximum allowed`
3   for *every* (i, u) *in* W_v do
4   draw next destination w (according to the lazy walk scheme)
5   if $w \neq v$ then `# walk exits` v
6   send $(i+1, u)$ to w
7   remove (i, u) from W_v

8   *wait* until the maximum time for all other vertices to process up to ξ walks
9   add the walks received by v to W_v and H_v `# walks entering` v

---

algorithm outlined in the beginning rejects in an iteration in which s is chosen. Since we are only interested in walks of length L, we denote $p_s(k) = p_s(k, L)$. A good vertex is a vertex for which this probability is bounded as follows.

We say a vertex s is called *good* if $p_s(K) \geq 1/10$. In [18] it was proved that if G is ϵ-far from being bipartite then at least an $\epsilon/16$-fraction of the vertices are good. In contrast to [18], we do not perform K random walks from every vertex in each iteration, but rather only 2. Hence, what we need for our analysis is a bound on $p_s(2)$. To this end, we use K as a parameter, and express $p_s(2)$ in terms of K and $p_s(K)$, by showing that for every vertex s, $p_s(2) \geq 2p_s(K)/K(K-1)$.

Using this relationship between $p_s(2)$, K and $p_s(K)$, we prove that our algorithm is an ϵ-test. First we prove this for the random walks themselves, ignoring the possibility that Algorithm 1 will skip moving random walks due to its condition in Line 2.

Lemma 3. *If G is ϵ-far from being bipartite, and we perform η iterations of starting 2 random walks of length L from every vertex, the probability that no violation is detected is bounded by $1/4$.*

As explained earlier, the main hurdle on the road to prove Theorem 3 is in proving that the allowed congestion will not be exceeded. We prove the following general claim about the probability for k lazy random walks of length ℓ from each vertex to exceed a maximum *congestion factor* of ξ walks allowed in each vertex at the beginning of each iteration. Here, an iteration is a sequence of rounds in which all walks are advanced by one step (whether or not they actually switch vertices).

Lemma 4. *With probability at least $1 - 1/n$, running k lazy random walks of length ℓ originating from every vertex will not exceed the maximum congestion factor of $\xi = \gamma + k = 3(2 \ln n + \ln \ell) + k$ walks allowed in each vertex at the beginning of each iteration, if $\gamma > k$.*

If G is bipartite then all vertices output **accept** in our bipartiteness test, because there are no odd cycles and thus no violation detecting walks. If G is ϵ-far from bipartite, we use Lemma 3, in conjunction with Lemma 4 with parameters $k = 2$, $\ell = L$ and $\gamma = 3(2 \ln n + \ln L)$ as used by our bipartiteness test. By a union bound the probability to accept G will be bounded by $1/4 + 1/n < 1/3$ (assuming $n > 12$), providing for the required bound on the rejection probability. This, with the communication complexity analysis of our distributed bipartiteness test, gives Theorem 3.

5   Distributed Test for Cycle-Freeness

In this section, we give a distributed algorithm to test if a graph G with m edges is cycle-free or if at least ϵm edges have to be removed to make it so. Intuitively, in order to search for cycles, one can run a breadth-first search (BFS) and have a vertex output **reject** if two different paths reach it. The downside of this exact solution is that its running time depends on the diameter of the graph. To overcome this, a basic approach would be to run a BFS from each vertex of the graph, but for shorter distances. However, running multiple BFSs simultaneously is expensive, due to the congestion on the edges. Instead, we use a simple prioritization rule that drops BFS constructions with lower priority, which makes sure that one BFS remains alive.[4]

Our technique consists of three parts. First, we make the graph G sparser, by removing each of its edges independently with probability $\epsilon/2$. We denote the sampled graph by G' and prove that if G is far from being cycle-free then so is G', and in particular, G' contains a cycle.

Then, we run a partial BFS over G' from each vertex, while prioritizing by ids: each vertex keeps only the BFS that originates in the vertex with the largest id and drops the rest of the BFSs. The length of this procedure is according to a threshold $T = 20 \log n/\epsilon$. This gives detection of a cycle that is contained in a component of G' with a low diameter of up to T, if such a cycle exists, since a surviving BFS covers the component. Such a cycle is also a cycle in G. If no such cycle exists in G', then G' has some component with diameter larger than T. For large components, we take each surviving BFS that reached some vertex v at a certain distance ℓ, and from v we run a new partial BFS in the *original* graph G. These BFSs are again prioritized, this time according to the distance ℓ. Our main tool is proving that with high probability, if there is a shortest path in G' of length $T/2$ between two vertices, then there is a cycle in G between them of length at most T. This allows our BFSs on G to find such a cycle. We start with the following combinatorial lemma that shows the above claim.

---

[4] A more involved analysis of multiple prioritized BFS executions was used in [24], allowing all BFS executions to fully finish in a short time without too much delay due to congestion. Since we require a much weaker guarantee, we can avoid the strong full-fledged prioritization algorithm of [24] and settle for a simple rule that keeps one BFS tree alive. Also, the multiple BFS construction of [27] does not fit our demands as it may not reach all desired vertices within the required distance, in case there are many vertices that are closer.

Lemma 5. *Given a graph G, let G' be obtained by independently deleting each edge in G with probability $\frac{\epsilon}{2}$. Then, with probability at least $1 - \frac{1}{n^3}$, every vertex $v \in G'$ that has a vertex $w \in G'$ at a distance $\frac{10 \log n}{\epsilon}$, has a closed path passing through it in G, that contains a simple cycle, of length at most $\frac{20 \log n}{\epsilon}$.*

Next, we prove that indeed there is a high probability, of at least $1 - e^{-\epsilon^2 m/32}$, that G' contains a cycle if G is ϵ-far from being cycle-free.

In the full version we provide pseudocode for both our prioritized multiple BFS and an ϵ-test for cycle freeness.

Theorem 4. *Our algorithm is a distributed ϵ-test in the general graph model for the property of being cycle-free, that requires $O(\log n/\epsilon)$ rounds.*

6 Lower Bounds

In this section, we prove that any distributed algorithm for ϵ-testing bipartiteness or cycle-freeness in bounded-degree graphs requires $\Omega(\log n)$ rounds of communication. This applies even to the less restricted LOCAL model, which does not limit the size of the messages. We construct bounded-degree graphs that are ϵ-far from being bipartite, such that all cycles are of length $\Omega(\log n)$. We argue that any distributed algorithm that runs in $O(\log n)$ rounds does not detect a witness for non-bipartiteness. We also show that the same construction proves that every distributed algorithm for ϵ-testing cycle-freeness requires $\Omega(\log n)$ rounds of communication. Formally, we prove the following theorem.

Theorem 5. *Any distributed $1/100$-test in the bounded degree or general graph model for the property of being bipartite requires $\Omega(\log n)$ rounds of communication.*

To prove Theorem 5, we show the existence of a graph G' that is far from being bipartite, but all of its cycles are at least of logarithmic length. Since in T rounds of a distributed algorithm, the output of every vertex cannot depend on vertices that are at distance greater than T from it, no vertex can detect a cycle in G' in less than $O(\log n)$ rounds, which proves Theorem 5. To prove the existence of G' we use the probabilistic method with alterations, and prove the following.

Lemma 6. *Let G be a random graph on n vertices where each edge is present with probability $1000/n$. Let G' be obtained by removing all edges incident with vertices of degree greater than 2000, and one edge from each cycle of length at most $\log n/\log 1000$. Then with probability at least $1/2 - e^{-100} - e^{-n}$, G' is $1/100$-far from being bipartite.*

Since a graph that is ϵ-far from being bipartite is also ϵ-far from being cycle-free, we immediately obtain the same lower bound for testing cycle-freeness:

Theorem 6. *Any distributed $1/100$-test in the bounded degree graph or general model for cycle-freeness requires $\Omega(\log n)$ rounds of communication.*

7   Discussion

This paper provides a thorough study of distributed property testing. It provides an emulation technique for the dense graph model and constructs fast distributed algorithms for testing triangle-freeness, cycle-freeness and bipartiteness. We also present lower bounds for both bipartiteness and cycle-freeness.

This work raises many important open questions, the immediate of which is to devise fast distributed testing algorithms for additional problems. One example is testing freeness of other small subgraphs. More ambitious goals are to handle dynamic graphs, and to find more general connections between testability in the sequential model and the distributed model. Finally, there is fertile ground for obtaining additional lower bounds in this setting, in order to fully understand the complexity of distributed property testing.

References

1. Alon, N., Avin, C., Koucký, M., Kozma, G., Lotker, Z., Tuttle, M.R.: Many random walks are faster than one. Comb. Probab. Comput. **20**(4), 481–502 (2011)
2. Alon, N., Kaufman, T., Krivelevich, M., Ron, D.: Testing triangle-freeness in general graphs. SIAM J. Discrete Math. **22**(2), 786–819 (2008)
3. Alon, N., Shapira, A.: A characterization of the (natural) graph properties testable with one-sided error. SIAM J. Comput. **37**(6), 1703–1727 (2008)
4. Arfaoui, H., Fraigniaud, P., Ilcinkas, D., Mathieu, F.: Distributedly testing cycle-freeness. In: Kratsch, D., Todinca, I. (eds.) WG 2014. LNCS, vol. 8747, pp. 15–28. Springer, Heidelberg (2014)
5. Baruch, M., Fraigniaud, P., Patt-Shamir, B.: Randomized proof-labeling schemes. In: Proceedings of the ACM Symposium on Principles of Distributed Computing, (PODC), pp. 315–324 (2015)
6. Blum, M., Luby, M., Rubinfeld, R.: Self-testing/correcting with applications to numerical problems. J. Comput. Syst. Sci. **47**(3), 549–595 (1993)
7. Brakerski, Z., Patt-Shamir, B.: Distributed discovery of large near-cliques. Distrib. Comput. **24**(2), 79–89 (2011)
8. Censor-Hillel, K., Fischer, E., Schwartzman, G., Vasudev, Y.: Fast distributed algorithms for testing graph properties. CoRR abs/1602.03718 (2016)
9. Censor-Hillel, K., Kaski, P., Korhonen, J.H., Lenzen, C., Paz, A., Suomela, J.: Algebraic methods in the congested clique. In: Proceedings of the ACM Symposium on Principles of Distributed Computing, (PODC), pp. 143–152 (2015)
10. Dolev, D., Lenzen, C., Peled, S.: "Tri, tri again": finding triangles and small subgraphs in a distributed setting. In: Aguilera, M.K. (ed.) DISC 2012. LNCS, vol. 7611, pp. 195–209. Springer, Heidelberg (2012)
11. Drucker, A., Kuhn, F., Oshman, R.: The communication complexity of distributed task allocation. In: Proceedings of the ACM Symposium on Principles of Distributed Computing (PODC), pp. 67–76 (2012)
12. Erdös, P.: Graph theory and probability. J. Math. **11**, 34G38 (1959)
13. Fischer, E.: The art of uninformed decisions: a primer to property testing. Current Trends Theor. Comput. Sci. Challenge New Century I **2**, 229–264 (2004)
14. Foerster, K.T., Luedi, T., Seidel, J., Wattenhofer, R.: Local checkability, no strings attached. In: Proceedings of the 17th International Conference on Distributed Computing and Networking (ICDCN), pp. 21: 1–21: 10 (2016)

15. Fox, J.: A new proof of the graph removal lemma. CoRR abs/1006.1300 (2010)
16. Ghaffari, M., Kuhn, F., Su, H.H.: Manuscript (2016)
17. Goldreich, O., Goldwasser, S., Ron, D.: Property testing and its connection to learning and approximation. J. ACM **45**(4), 653–750 (1998)
18. Goldreich, O., Ron, D.: A sublinear bipartiteness tester for bounded degree graphs. Combinatorica **19**(3), 335–373 (1999)
19. Goldreich, O., Ron, D.: Property testing in bounded degree graphs. Algorithmica **32**(2), 302–343 (2002)
20. Goldreich, O., Ron, D.: Algorithmic aspects of property testing in the dense graphs model. In: Goldreich, O. (ed.) Property Testing. LNCS, vol. 6390, pp. 295–305. Springer, Heidelberg (2010)
21. Goldreich, O., Trevisan, L.: Three theorems regarding testing graph properties. Random Struct. Algorithms **23**(1), 23–57 (2003)
22. Göös, M., Hirvonen, J., Levi, R., Medina, M., Suomela, J.: Non-local probes do not help with graph problems. CoRR abs/1512.05411 (2015)
23. Hirvonen, J., Rybicki, J., Schmid, S., Suomela, J.: Large cuts with local algorithms on triangle-free graphs. CoRR abs/1402.2543 (2014)
24. Holzer, S., Wattenhofer, R.: Optimal distributed all pairs shortest paths and applications. In: Proceedings of the 2012 ACM Symposium on Principles of Distributed Computing, pp. 355–364. ACM (2012)
25. Kari, J., Matamala, M., Rapaport, I., Salo, V.: Solving the induced subgraphproblem in the randomized multiparty simultaneous messages model. In: Proceedings of the 22nd International Colloquium on Structural Informationand Communication Complexity (SIROCCO), pp. 370–384 (2015)
26. Korman, A., Kutten, S., Peleg, D.: Proof labeling schemes. Distrib. Comput. **22**(4), 215–233 (2010)
27. Lenzen, C., Peleg, D.: Efficient distributed source detection with limited bandwidth. In: Proceedings of the ACM Symposium on Principles of Distributed Computing (PODC), pp. 375–382 (2013)
28. Parnas, M., Ron, D.: Approximating the minimum vertex cover in sublinear time and a connection to distributed algorithms. Theor. Comput. Sci. **381**(1–3), 183–196 (2007)
29. Peleg, D.: Distributed computing: a locality-sensitive approach. Soc. Ind. Appl. Math. **157**, 2153–2169 (2000)
30. Pettie, S., Su, H.: Distributed coloring algorithms for triangle-free graphs. Inf. Comput. **243**, 263–280 (2015)
31. Ron, D.: Property testing: a learning theory perspective. Found. Trends Mach. Learn. **1**(3), 307–402 (2008)
32. Ron, D.: Algorithmic and analysis techniques in property testing. Found. Trends Theor. Comput. Sci. **5**(2), 73–205 (2009)
33. Rubinfeld, R., Sudan, M.: Robust characterizations of polynomials with applications to program testing. SIAM J. Comput. **25**(2), 252–271 (1996)
34. Sarma, A.D., Holzer, S., Kor, L., Korman, A., Nanongkai, D., Pandurangan, G., Peleg, D., Wattenhofer, R.: Distributed verification and hardness of distributed approximation. SIAM J. Comput. **41**(5), 1235–1265 (2012)
35. Sarma, A.D., Nanongkai, D., Pandurangan, G., Tetali, P.: Distributed random walks. J. ACM **60**(1), 2 (2013)

Further Algebraic Algorithms in the Congested Clique Model and Applications to Graph-Theoretic Problems

François Le Gall[(✉)]

Graduate School of Informatics, Kyoto University, Kyoto, Japan
legall@i.u-kyoto.ac.jp

Abstract. Censor-Hillel et al. [PODC'15] recently showed how to efficiently implement centralized algebraic algorithms for matrix multiplication in the congested clique model, a model of distributed computing that has received increasing attention in the past few years. This paper develops further algebraic techniques for designing algorithms in this model. We present deterministic and randomized algorithms, in the congested clique model, for efficiently computing multiple independent instances of matrix products, computing the determinant, the rank and the inverse of a matrix, and solving systems of linear equations. As applications of these techniques, we obtain more efficient algorithms for the computation, again in the congested clique model, of the all-pairs shortest paths and the diameter in directed and undirected graphs with small weights, improving over Censor-Hillel et al.'s work. We also obtain algorithms for several other graph-theoretic problems such as computing the number of edges in a maximum matching and the Gallai-Edmonds decomposition of a simple graph, and computing a minimum vertex cover of a bipartite graph.

1 Introduction

Background. The congested clique model is a model in distributed computing that has recently received increasing attention [2, 6–11, 17–19, 22, 23]. In this model n nodes communicate with each other over a fully-connected network (i.e., a clique) by exchanging messages of size $O(\log n)$ in synchronous rounds. Compared with the more traditional congested model [24], the congested clique model removes the effect of distances in the computation and thus focuses solely on understanding the role of congestion in distributed computing.

Typical computational tasks studied in the congested clique model are graph-theoretic problems [2, 6–8, 11, 22], where a graph G on n vertices is initially distributed among the n nodes of the network (the ℓ-th node of the network knows the set of vertices adjacent to the ℓ-th vertex of the graph, and the weights of the corresponding edges if the graph is weighted) and the nodes want to compute properties of G. Besides their theoretical interest and potential applications, such problems have the following natural interpretation in the congested clique

© Springer-Verlag Berlin Heidelberg 2016
C. Gavoille and D. Ilcinkas (Eds.): DISC 2016, LNCS 9888, pp. 57–70, 2016.
DOI: 10.1007/978-3-662-53426-7_5

model: the graph G represents the actual topology of the network, each node knows only its neighbors but can communicate to all the nodes of the network, and the nodes want to learn information about the topology of the network.

Censor-Hillel et al. [2] recently developed algorithms for several graph-theoretic problems in the congested clique model by showing how to implement centralized algebraic algorithms for matrix multiplication in this model. More precisely, they constructed a $O(n^{1-2/\omega})$-round algorithm for matrix multiplication, where ω denotes the exponent of matrix multiplication (the best known upper bound on ω is $\omega < 2.3729$, obtained in [16,29], which gives exponent $1 - 2/\omega < 0.1572$ in the congested clique model), improving over the $O(n^{2-\omega})$ algorithm mentioned in [7], in the following setting: given two $n \times n$ matrices A and B over a field, the ℓ-th node of the network initially owns the ℓ-th row of A and the ℓ-column of B, and needs to output the ℓ-th row and the ℓ-column of the product AB. Censor-Hillel et al. consequently obtained $O(n^{1-2/\omega})$-round algorithms for several graph-theoretic tasks that reduce to computing the powers of (some variant of) the adjacency matrix of the graph, such as counting the number of triangles in a graph (which lead to an improvement over the prior best algorithms for this task [6,7]), detecting the existence of a constant-length cycle and approximating the all-pairs shortest paths in the input graph (improving the round complexity obtained in [22]). One of the main advantages of such an algebraic approach in the congested clique model is its versatility: it makes possible to construct fast algorithms for graph-theoretic problems, and especially for problems for which the best non-algebraic centralized algorithm is highly sequential and does not seem to be implementable efficiently in the congested clique model, simply by showing a reduction to matrix multiplication (and naturally also showing that this reduction can be implemented efficiently in the congested clique model).

Our results. In this paper we develop additional algebraic tools for the congested clique model.

We first consider the task of computing in the congested clique model not only one matrix product, but multiple independent matrix products. More precisely, given k matrices $A_1, \ldots, A_k$ each of size $n \times m$ and k matrices $B_1, \ldots, B_k$ each of size $m \times m$, initially evenly distributed among the n nodes of the network, the nodes want to compute the k matrix products $A_1 B_1, \ldots, A_k B_k$. Prior works [2,7] considered only the case $k = 1$ and $m = n$, i.e., one product of two square matrices. Our contribution is thus twofold: we consider the rectangular case, and the case of several matrix products as well. Let us first discuss our results for square matrices ($m = n$). By using sequentially k times the matrix multiplication algorithm from [2], k matrix products can naturally be computed in $O(kn^{1-2/\omega})$ rounds. In this work we show that we can actually do better.

Theorem 1 (Simplified version). *In the congested clique model k independent products of pairs of $n \times n$ matrices can be computed with round complexity*

$$\begin{cases} O(k^{2/\omega} n^{1-2/\omega}) \ if \ 1 \le k < n, \\ O(k) \qquad\qquad if \ k \ge n. \end{cases}$$

This generalization of the results from [2] follows from a simple strategy: divide the n nodes of the network into k blocks (when $k \leq n$), each containing roughly n/k nodes, compute one of the k matrix products per block by using an approach similar to [2] (i.e., a distributed version of the best centralized algorithm computing one instance of square matrix multiplication), and finally distribute the relevant part of the k output matrices to all the nodes of the network. Analyzing the resulting protocol shows that the dependence in k in the overall round complexity is reduced to $k^{2/\omega}$. This sublinear dependence in k has a significant number of implications (see below).

The complete version of Theorem 1, given in Sect. 3, also considers the general case where the matrices may not be square (i.e., the case $m \neq n$), which will be crucial for some of our applications to the All-Pairs Shortest Path problem. The proof becomes more technical than for the square case, but is conceptually very similar: the main modification is simply to now implement a distributed version of the best centralized algorithm for rectangular matrix multiplication. The upper bounds obtained on the round complexity depend on the complexity of the best centralized algorithms for rectangular matrix multiplication (in particular the upper bounds given in [15]). While the major open problem is still whether the product of two square matrices can be computed in a constant (or nearly constant) number of rounds, our results show that for $m = O(n^{0.651\cdots})$, the product of an $n \times m$ matrix by an $m \times n$ matrix can indeed be computed in $O(n^\epsilon)$ rounds for any $\epsilon > 0$. We also show lower bounds on the round complexity of the general case (Proposition 1 in Sect. 3), which are tight for most values of k and m, based on simple arguments from communication complexity.

We then study the following basic problems in linear algebra: computing the determinant, the rank or the inverse of an $n \times n$ matrix over a finite field $\mathbb{F}$ of order upper bounded by a polynomial of n, and solving a system of n linear equations and n variables. We call these problems $\mathsf{DET}(n, \mathbb{F})$, $\mathsf{Rank}(n, \mathbb{F})$, $\mathsf{INV}(n, \mathbb{F})$ and $\mathsf{SYS}(n, \mathbb{F})$, respectively (the formal definitions are given in Sect. 2). While it is known that in the centralized setting these problems can be solved with essentially the same time complexity as matrix multiplication [1], these reductions are typically sequential and do not work in a parallel setting. In this paper we design fast deterministic and randomized algorithm for these four basis tasks, and obtain the following results.

Theorem 2. *Assume that $\mathbb{F}$ has characteristic greater than n. In the congested clique model, the deterministic round complexity of $\mathsf{DET}(n, \mathbb{F})$ and $\mathsf{INV}(n, \mathbb{F})$ is $O(n^{1-1/\omega})$.*

Theorem 3. *Assume that $\mathbb{F}$ has order $|\mathbb{F}| = \Omega(n^2 \log n)$. In the congested clique model, the randomized round complexity of $\mathsf{DET}(n, \mathbb{F})$, $\mathsf{SYS}(n, \mathbb{F})$ and $\mathsf{Rank}(n, \mathbb{F})$ is $O(n^{1-2/\omega} \log n)$.*

The upper bounds of Theorems 2 and 3 are $O(n^{0.5786})$ and $O(n^{0.1572})$, respectively, by basing our implementation on the asymptotically fastest (but impractical) centralized algorithm for matrix multiplication corresponding to the upper bound $\omega < 2.3729$. These bounds are $O(n^{2/3})$ and $O(n^{1/3} \log n)$, respectively, by basing our implementation on the trivial (but practical) centralized algorithm for matrix multiplication (corresponding to the bound $\omega \leq 3$). These algorithms are obtained by carefully adapting to the congested clique model the relevant known parallel algorithms [5,12–14,25] for linear algebra, and using our efficient algorithm for computing multiple matrix products (Theorem 1) as a subroutine. An interesting open question is whether $\mathsf{INV}(n, \mathbb{F})$ can be solved with the same (randomized) round complexity as the other tasks. This problem may very well be more difficult; in the parallel setting in particular, to the best of our knowledge, whether matrix inversion can be done with the same complexity as these other tasks is also an open problem.

Applications of our results. The above results give new algorithms for many graph-theoretic problems in the congested clique model, as described below and summarized in Table 1.

Table 1. Summary of the applications of our algebraic techniques to graph-theoretic problems in the congested clique model. Here n both represents the number of vertices in the input graph and the number of nodes in the network.

Problem	Round complexity	Previously
APSP (undirected, weights in $\{0, 1, \ldots, M\}$)	$\tilde{O}\left(M^{\frac{2}{\omega}} n^{1-\frac{2}{\omega}}\right)$	$\tilde{O}\left(Mn^{1-\frac{2}{\omega}}\right)$
APSP (directed, constant weights)	$O(n^{0.2096})$	$\tilde{O}(n^{1/3})$
Diameter (undirected, weights in $\{0, 1, \ldots, M\}$)	$\tilde{O}\left(M^{\frac{2}{\omega}} n^{1-\frac{2}{\omega}}\right)$	$\tilde{O}\left(Mn^{1-\frac{2}{\omega}}\right)$
Computing the size of a maximum matching	$O(n^{1-\frac{2}{\omega}} \log n)$	—
Computing allowed edges in a perfect matching	$O(n^{1-1/\omega})$	—
Gallai-Edmonds decomposition	$O(n^{1-1/\omega})$	—
Minimum vertex cover in bipartite graphs	$O(n^{1-1/\omega})$	—

Our main key tool to derive these applications is Theorem 7 in Sect. 3, which gives an algorithm computing efficiently the distance product (defined in Sect. 2) of two matrices with small integer entries based on our algorithm for multiple matrix multiplication of Theorem 1. Computing the distance product is a fundamental graph-theoretic task deeply related to the All-Pairs Shortest Path (APSP) problem [27,28,30]. Combining this result with techniques from [28], and observing that these techniques can be implemented efficiently in the congested clique model, we then almost immediately obtain the following result.

Theorem 4. *In the congested clique model, the deterministic round complexity of the all-pairs shortest paths problem in an undirected graph of n vertices with integer weights in $\{0, \ldots, M\}$, where M is an integer such that $M \leq n$, is $\tilde{O}(M^{2/\omega} n^{1-2/\omega})$.*

Since computing the diameter of a graph reduces to solving the all-pairs shortest paths, we obtain the same round complexity for diameter computation in the same class of graphs. This improves over the $\tilde{O}(Mn^{1-2/\omega})$-round algorithm for these tasks (implicitly) given in [2]. The main application of our results nevertheless concerns the all-pair shortest paths problem over directed graphs (for which the approach based on [28] does not work) with constant weights. We obtain the following result by combining our algorithm for distance product computation with Zwick's approach [30].

Theorem 5. *In the congested clique model, the randomized round complexity of the all-pairs shortest paths problem in a directed graph of n vertices with integer weights in $\{-M, \ldots, 0, \ldots, M\}$, where $M = O(1)$, is $O(n^{0.2096})$.*

Prior to this work, the upper bound for the round complexity of this problem was $\tilde{O}(n^{1/3})$, obtained by directly computing the distance product (as done in [2]) in the congested clique model. Again, Theorem 5 follows easily from Theorem 7 and the observation that the reduction to distance product computation given in [30] can be implemented efficiently in the congested clique model. The exponent 0.2096 in the statement of Theorem 5 is derived from the current best upper bounds on the complexity of rectangular matrix multiplication in the centralized setting [15].

Theorems 2 and 3 also enable us to solve a multitude of graph-theoretic problems in the congested clique model with a sublinear number of rounds. Examples described in this paper are computing the number of edges in a maximum matching of a simple graph with $O(n^{1-2/\omega} \log n)$ rounds, computing the set of allowed edges in a perfect matching, the Gallai-Edmonds decomposition of a simple graph, and a minimum vertex cover in a bipartite graph with $O(n^{1-1/\omega})$ rounds. These results are obtained almost immediately from the appropriate reductions to matrix inversion and similar problems known the centralized setting [3,20,26] — indeed it is not hard to adapt all these reductions so that they can be implemented efficiently in the congested clique model. Note that while non-algebraic centralized algorithms solving these problems also exist (see, e.g., [21]), they are typically sequential and do not appear to be efficiently implementable in the congested clique model. The algebraic approach developed in this paper, made possible by our algorithms for the computation of the determinant, the rank and the inverse of matrix, appears to be currently the only way of obtaining fast algorithms for these problems in the congested clique model.

Remarks on the organization of the paper. Due to space constraints, most of the technical proofs are not included, but can be found in the full version of the present paper. The discussion of randomized algorithms for the determinant (Theorem 3) is also omitted from this version. The whole discussion detailing the applications of our algebraic methods is omitted as well, with the exception of the statement of Theorem 7 given in Sect. 3.

2 Preliminaries

Notations. Through this paper we will use n to denote the number of nodes in the network. The n nodes will be denoted $1, 2, \ldots, n$. The symbol $\mathbb{F}$ will always denote a finite field of order upper bounded by a polynomial in n (which means that each field element can be encoded with $O(\log n)$ bits and thus sent using one message in the congested clique model). Given any positive integer p, we use the notation $[p]$ to represent the set $\{1, 2, \ldots, p\}$. Given any $p \times p'$ matrix A, we will write its entries as $A[i, j]$ for $(i, j) \in [p] \times [p']$, and use the notation $A[i, *]$ to represent its i-th row and $A[*, j]$ to represent its j-th column.

Graph-theoretic problems in the congested clique model. As mentioned in the introduction, typically the main tasks that we want to solve in the congested clique model are graph-theoretical problems. In all the applications given in this paper the number of vertices of the graph will be n, the same as the number of nodes of the network. The input will be given as follows: initially each node $\ell \in [n]$ has the ℓ-th row and the ℓ-th column of the adjacency matrix of the graph. Note that this distribution of the input, while being the most natural, is not essential; the only important assumption is that the entries are evenly distributed among the n nodes since they can then be redistributed in a constant number of rounds as shown in the following Lemma by Dolev et al. [6], which we will use many times in this paper.

Lemma 1. *[6] In the congested clique model a set of messages in which no node is the source of more than n messages and no node is the destination of more than n messages can be delivered within two rounds if the source and destination of each message is known in advance to all nodes.*

Algebraic problems in the congested clique model. The five main algebraic problems that we consider in this paper are defined as follows.

$\mathsf{MM}(n, m, k, \mathbb{F})$ — Multiple Rectangular Matrix Multiplications
> Input: matrices $A_1, \ldots, A_k \in \mathbb{F}^{n \times m}$ and $B_1, \ldots, B_k \in \mathbb{F}^{m \times n}$ distributed among the n nodes
>> (Node $\ell \in [n]$ has $A_1[\ell, *], \ldots, A_k[\ell, *]$ and $B_1[*, \ell], \ldots, B_k[*, \ell]$)
>
> Output: the matrices $A_1 B_1, \ldots, A_k B_k$ distributed among the n nodes
>> (Node $\ell \in [n]$ has $A_1 B_1[\ell, *], \ldots, A_k B_k[\ell, *]$ and
>> $A_1 B_1[*, \ell], \ldots, A_k B_k[*, \ell]$)

$\mathsf{DET}(n, \mathbb{F})$ — Determinant
> Input: matrix $A \in \mathbb{F}^{n \times n}$ distributed among the n nodes
>> (Node $\ell \in [n]$ has $A[\ell, *]$ and $A[*, \ell]$)
>
> Output: $\det(A)$ (Each node of the network has $\det(A)$)

$\mathsf{Rank}(n, \mathbb{F})$ — Rank
> Input: matrix $A \in \mathbb{F}^{n \times n}$ distributed among the n nodes
>> (Node $\ell \in [n]$ has $A[\ell, *]$ and $A[*, \ell]$)

Output: rank(A)   (Each node of the network has rank(A))

INV($n, \mathbb{F}$) — Inversion

Input: invertible matrix $A \in \mathbb{F}^{n \times n}$ distributed among the n nodes
(Node $\ell \in [n]$ has $A[\ell, *]$ and $A[*, \ell]$)

Output: matrix A^{-1} distributed among the n nodes
(Node $\ell \in [n]$ has $A^{-1}[\ell, *]$ and $A^{-1}[*, \ell]$)

SYS($n, \mathbb{F}$) — Solution of a linear system

Input: invertible matrix $A \in \mathbb{F}^{n \times n}$ and vector $b \in \mathbb{F}^{n \times 1}$, distributed among
the n nodes (Node $\ell \in [n]$ has $A[\ell, *]$, $A[*, \ell]$ and b)

Output: the vector $x \in \mathbb{F}^{n \times 1}$ such that $Ax = b$ (Node $\ell \in [n]$ has $x[\ell]$)

Note that the distribution of the inputs and the outputs assumed in the above five problems is mostly chosen for convenience. For instance, if needed the whole vector x in the output of SYS($n, \mathbb{F}$) can be sent to all the nodes of the network in two rounds using Lemma 1. The only important assumption is that when dealing with matrices, the entries of the matrices must be evenly distributed among the n nodes.

We will also in this paper consider the distance product of two matrices, defined as follows.

Definition 1. *Let m and n be two positive integers. Let A be an $n \times m$ matrix and B be an $m \times n$ matrix, both with entries in $\mathbb{R} \cup \{\infty\}$. The distance product of A and B, denoted $A * B$, is the $n \times n$ matrix C such that $C[i,j] = \min_{s \in [m]} \{A[i,s] + B[s,j]\}$ for all $(i,j) \in [n] \times [n]$.*

We will be mainly interested in the case when the matrices have integer entries. More precisely, we will consider the following problem.

DIST(n, m, M) — Computation of the distance product

Input: an $n \times m$ matrix A and an $m \times n$ matrix B, with entries in
$\{-M, \ldots, -1, 0, 1, \ldots, M\} \cup \{\infty\}$
(Node $\ell \in [n]$ has $A[\ell, *]$ and $B[*, \ell]$)

Output: the matrix $C = A * B$ distributed among the n nodes
(Node $\ell \in [n]$ has $C[\ell, *]$ and $C[*, \ell]$)

Centralized algebraic algorithms for matrix multiplication. We now briefly describe algebraic algorithms for matrix multiplication and known results about the complexity of rectangular matrix multiplication. We refer to [1] for a detailed exposition of these concepts.

Let $\mathbb{F}$ be a field and m, n be two positive integer. Consider the problem of computing the product of an $n \times m$ matrix by an $m \times n$ matrix over $\mathbb{F}$. An algebraic algorithm for this problem is described by three sets $\{\alpha_{ij\mu}\}$, $\{\beta_{ij\mu}\}$ and $\{\lambda_{ij\mu}\}$ of coefficients from $\mathbb{F}$ such that, for any $n \times m$ matrix A and any $m \times n$ matrix B, the equality

$$C[i,j] = \sum_{\mu=1}^{t} \lambda_{ij\mu} S^{(\mu)} T^{(\mu)}$$

holds for all $(i,j) \in [n] \times [n]$, where $C = AB$ and

$$S^{(\mu)} = \sum_{i=1}^{n} \sum_{j=1}^{m} \alpha_{ij\mu} A[i,j], \qquad T^{(\mu)} = \sum_{i=1}^{n} \sum_{j=1}^{m} \beta_{ij\mu} B[j,i],$$

for each $s \in [t]$. Note that each $S^{(\mu)}$ and each $T^{(\mu)}$ is an element of $\mathbb{F}$. The integer t is called the rank of the algorithm, and corresponds to the complexity of the algorithm.

For instance, consider the trivial algorithm computing this matrix product using the formula

$$C[i,j] = \sum_{s=1}^{m} A[i,s] B[s,j].$$

This algorithm can be described in the above formalism by taking $t = n^2 m$, writing each $\mu \in [n^2 m]$ as a triple $\mu = (i', j', s') \in [n] \times [n] \times [m]$, and choosing

$$\lambda_{ij(i',j',s')} = \begin{cases} 1 & \text{if } i = i' \text{ and } j = j', \\ 0 & \text{otherwise,} \end{cases}$$

$$\alpha_{ij(i',j',s')} = \begin{cases} 1 & \text{if } i = i' \text{ and } j = s', \\ 0 & \text{otherwise,} \end{cases} \qquad \beta_{ij(i',j',s')} = \begin{cases} 1 & \text{if } i = j' \text{ and } j = s', \\ 0 & \text{otherwise.} \end{cases}$$

Note that this trivial algorithm, and the description we just gave, also works over any semiring.

The exponent of matrix multiplication. For any non-negative real number γ, let $\omega(\gamma)$ denote the minimal value τ such that the product of an $n \times \lceil n^\gamma \rceil$ matrix over $\mathbb{F}$ by an $\lceil n^\gamma \rceil \times n$ matrix over $\mathbb{F}$ can be computed by an algebraic algorithm of rank $n^{\tau+o(1)}$ (i.e., can be computed with complexity $O(n^{\tau+\epsilon})$ for any $\epsilon > 0$). As usual in the literature, we typically abuse notation and simply write that such a product can be done with complexity $O(n^{\omega(\gamma)})$, i.e., ignoring the $o(1)$ in the exponent. The value $\omega(1)$ is denoted by ω, and often called the exponent of square matrix multiplication. Another important quantity is the value $\alpha = \sup\{\gamma \mid \omega(\gamma) = 2\}$.

The trivial algorithm for matrix multiplication gives the upper bound $\omega(\gamma) \leq 2 + \gamma$, and thus $\omega \leq 3$ and $\alpha \geq 0$. The current best upper bound on ω is $\omega < 2.3729$, see [16,29]. The current best bound on α is $\alpha > 0.3029$, see [15]. The best bounds on $\omega(\gamma)$ for $\gamma > \alpha$ can also be found in [15].

3   Matrix Multiplication in the Congested Clique Model

In this section we discuss the round complexity of Problems $\mathsf{MM}(n, m, k, \mathbb{F})$ and $\mathsf{DIST}(n, m, M)$.

Our first result is the following theorem.

Theorem 6 (Complete version). *For any positive integer $k \leq n$, the deterministic round complexity of $\mathsf{MM}(n, m, k, \mathbb{F})$ is*

$$\begin{cases} O(k) & \text{if } 0 \leq m \leq \sqrt{kn}, \\ O(k^{2/\omega(\gamma)} n^{1-2/\omega(\gamma)}) & \text{if } \sqrt{kn} \leq m < n^2/k, \\ O(km/n) & \text{if } m \geq n^2/k, \end{cases}$$

where γ is the solution of the equation

$$\left(1 - \frac{\log k}{\log n}\right)\gamma = 1 - \frac{\log k}{\log n} + \left(\frac{\log m}{\log n} - 1\right)\omega(\gamma). \tag{1}$$

For any $k \geq n$, the deterministic round complexity of $\mathsf{MM}(n, m, k, \mathbb{F})$ is

$$\begin{cases} O(k) & \text{if } 1 \leq m \leq n, \\ O(km/n) & \text{if } m \geq n. \end{cases}$$

The proof of Theorem 1, which will also show that Eq. (1) always has a solution when $k \leq n$ and $\sqrt{kn} \leq m < n^2/k$, can be found in the full version of the paper (a short discussion of the proof ideas was presented in the introduction). As briefly mentioned in the introduction, the round complexity is constant for any $k \leq \sqrt{n}$, and we further have round complexity $O(n^\epsilon)$, for any $\epsilon > 0$, for all values $k \leq n^{(1+\alpha)/2}$ (the bound $\alpha > 0.3029$ implies $(1+\alpha)/2 > 0.6514$). For the case $m = n$ the solution of Eq. (1) is $\gamma = 1$, which gives the bounds of the simplified version of Theorem 1 presented in the introduction.

We now give lower bounds on the round complexity of $\mathsf{MM}(n, m, k, \mathbb{F})$ that show that the upper bounds of Theorem 1 are tight, except possibly in the case $\sqrt{kn} \leq m < n^2/k$ when $k \leq n$.

Proposition 1. *The randomized round complexity of $\mathsf{MM}(n, m, k, \mathbb{F})$ is*

$$\begin{cases} \Omega(k) & \text{if } 1 \leq m \leq n, \\ \Omega(km/n) & \text{if } m \geq n. \end{cases}$$

Proof. We first prove the lower bound $\Omega(km/n)$ for any $m \geq n$. Let us consider instances of $\mathsf{MM}(n, m, k, \mathbb{F})$ of the following form: for each $s \in [k]$ all the rows of A_s are zero except the first row; for each $s \in [k]$ all the columns of B_s are zero except the second column. Let us write $C_s = A_s B_s$ for each $s \in [k]$. We prove the lower bound by partitioning the n nodes of the network into the two sets $\{1\}$ and $\{2, \ldots, n\}$, and considering the following two-party communication problem. Alice (corresponding to the set $\{1\}$) has for input $A_s[1, j]$ for all $j \in [m]$ and all $s \in [k]$. Bob (corresponding to the set $\{2, \ldots, n\}$) has for input $B_s[i, 2]$ for all $i \in [m]$ and all $s \in [k]$. The goal is for Alice to output $C_s[1, 2]$ for all $s \in [k]$. Note that $C_s[1, 2]$ is the inner product (over $\mathbb{F}$) of the first row of A_s and the second column of B_s. Thus $\sum_{s=1}^{k} C_s[1, 2]$ is the inner product of two vectors of size km. Alice and Bob must exchange $\Omega(km \log |\mathbb{F}|)$ bits to compute this value [4], which requires $\Omega(km/n)$ rounds in the original congested clique model.

We now prove the lower bound $\Omega(k)$ for any $m \geq 1$. Let us consider instances of $\mathsf{MM}(n, m, k, \mathbb{F})$ of the following form: for each $s \in [k]$, all entries of A_s are zero except the entry $A_s[1, 1]$ which is one; for each $s \in [k]$, $B_s[i, j] = 0$ for all $(i, j) \notin \{(1, j) \mid j \in \{2, \ldots, n\}\}$ (the other $n - 1$ entries are arbitrary). Again, let us write $C_s = A_s B_s$ for each $s \in [k]$. We prove the lower bound by again partitioning the n nodes of the network into the two sets $\{1\}$ and $\{2, \ldots, n\}$, and considering the following two-party communication problem. Alice has no input. Bob has for input $B_s[1, j]$ for all $j \in \{2, \ldots, n\}$ and all $s \in [k]$. The goal is for Alice to output $C_s[1, j]$ for all $j \in \{2, \ldots, n\}$ and all $s \in [k]$. Since the output reveals Bob's whole input to Alice, Alice must receive $\Omega(k(n - 1) \log |\mathbb{F}|)$ bits, which gives round complexity $\Omega(k)$ in the original congested clique model. $\square$

One of the main applications of Theorem 1 is the following result, which will imply all our results on the all-pairs shortest paths and diameter computation, including Theorems 4 and 5.

Theorem 7. *For any $M \leq n$ and $m \leq n$, the deterministic round complexity of* $\mathsf{DIST}(n, m, M)$ *is*

$$
\begin{cases}
O(M \log m) & \text{if } 0 \leq m \leq \sqrt{Mn \log m}, \\
O\left((M \log m)^{2/\omega(\gamma)} n^{1-2/\omega(\gamma)}\right) & \text{if } \sqrt{Mn \log m} \leq m \leq n^2/(M \log m), \\
O\left(mM \log m / n\right) & \text{if } n^2/(M \log m) \leq m \leq n,
\end{cases}
$$

where γ is the solution of the equation $\left(1 - \dfrac{\log M}{\log n}\right) \gamma = 1 - \dfrac{\log M}{\log n} + \left(\dfrac{\log m}{\log n} - 1\right) \omega(\gamma)$.

The proof of Theorem 7 is omitted, but can be found in the full version of the paper. The idea is to show that $\mathsf{DIST}(n, m, M)$ reduces to $\mathsf{MM}(n, m, k, \mathbb{F})$ for $k \approx M \log m$ and a well-chosen finite field $\mathbb{F}$, and then use Theorem 1 to get a factor $(M \log m)^{2/\omega(\gamma)}$, instead of the factor M obtained in a straightforward implementation of the distance product, in the complexity. This reduction is done by first applying a standard encoding of the distance product into a usual matrix product of matrices with integer entries of absolute value $\exp(M)$, and then using Fourier transforms to split this latter matrix product into roughly $M \log m$ independent matrix products over a small field.

4   Deterministic Computation of Determinant and Inverse Matrix

In this section we present deterministic algorithms for computing the determinant of a matrix and the inverse of a matrix in the congested clique model, and prove Theorem 2. Our algorithms can be seen as efficient implementations of the parallel algorithm by Preparata and Sarwate [25] based on the Faddeev-Leverrier method.

Let A be an $n \times n$ matrix over a field $\mathbb{F}$. Let $\det(\lambda I - A) = \lambda^n + c_1 \lambda^{n-1} + \cdots + c_{n-1} \lambda + c_n$ be its characteristic polynomial. The determinant of A is $(-1)^n c_n$ and, if $c_n \neq 0$, its inverse is

$$A^{-1} = -\frac{A^{n-1} + c_1 A^{n-2} + \cdots + c_{n-2}A + c_{n-1}I}{c_n}.$$

Define the vector $c = (c_1, \ldots, c_n)^T \in \mathbb{F}^{n \times 1}$. For any $k \in [n]$ let s_k denote the trace of the matrix A^k, and define the vector $s = (s_1, \ldots, s_n)^T \in \mathbb{F}^{n \times 1}$. Define the $n \times n$ matrix

$$S = \begin{pmatrix} 1 & & & & \\ s_1 & 2 & & & \\ s_2 & s_1 & 3 & & \\ \vdots & \vdots & \vdots & \ddots & \\ s_{n-1} & s_{n-2} & s_{n-3} & \cdots & s_1 & n \end{pmatrix}.$$

It can be easily shown (see, e.g., [5,25]) that $Sc = -s$, which enables us to recover c from s if S is invertible. The matrix S is invertible whenever $n! \neq 0$, which is true in any field of characteristic zero or in any finite field of characteristic strictly larger than n. The following proposition shows that the inverse of an invertible triangular matrix can be computed efficiently in the congested clique model.

Proposition 2. *Let $\mathbb{F}$ be any field. There is a deterministic algorithm with round complexity $O(n^{1-2/\omega})$ that solves $\mathsf{INV}(n, \mathbb{F})$ when the input A is an invertible lower triangular matrix.*

We are now ready to give the proof of Theorem 2.

Proof (of Theorem 2). For convenience we assume that n is a square, and write $p = \sqrt{n}$. If n is not a square we can easily adapt the proof by taking $p = \lceil \sqrt{n} \rceil$. Observe that any integer $a \in \{0, 1, \ldots, n - 1\}$ can be written in a unique way as $a = (a_1 - 1)p + (a_2 - 1)$ with $a_1, a_2 \in [p]$. Below when we write $a = (a_1, a_2) \in [n]$, we mean that a_1 and a_2 are the two elements in $[p]$ such that $a = (a_1-1)p+(a_2-1)$.

For any $\ell \in [n]$, let R_ℓ be the $p \times n$ matrix such that the i-th row of R_ℓ is the ℓ-th row of $A^{(i-1)p}$, for each $i \in [p]$. Similarly, for any $\ell \in [n]$, let C_ℓ be the $n \times p$ matrix such that the j-th column of C_ℓ is the ℓ-th column of A^{j-1}, for each $j \in [p]$. For each $\ell \in [n]$ define $U_\ell = R_\ell C_\ell$, which is a $p \times p$ matrix. Observe that, for any $k = (k_1, k_2) \in [n]$, the identity

$$s_k = \sum_{\ell=1}^{n} U_\ell[k_1, k_2] \tag{2}$$

holds. We will use this expression, together with the equation $c = -S^{-1}s$ to compute the determinant in the congested clique model.

In order to compute the inverse of A we then use the following approach. For any $(a_1, a_2) \in [p] \times [p]$, define the coefficient $c_{a_1, a_2} \in \mathbb{F}$ as follows:

$$c_{a_1, a_2} = \begin{cases} c_{n-1-(a_1-1)p-(a_2-1)} & \text{if } (a_1, a_2) \neq (p, p), \\ 1 & \text{if } (a_1, a_2) = (p, p). \end{cases}$$

For any $a_2 \in [p]$, define the $n \times n$ matrix E_{a_2} as follows:

$$E_{a_2} = \sum_{a_1=1}^{p} c_{a_1,a_2} A^{(a_1-1)p}.$$

Note that the following holds whenever $c_n \neq 0$:

$$A^{-1} = -\frac{\sum_{a=0}^{n-1} c_{n-1-a} A^a}{c_n} = -\frac{\sum_{a_1=1}^{p} \sum_{a_2=1}^{p} c_{a_2,a_1} A^{(a_1-1)p+(a_2-1)}}{c_n},$$

which gives

$$A^{-1} = -\frac{\sum_{a_2=1}^{p} E_{a_2} A^{a_2-1}}{c_n}. \tag{3}$$

The algorithm for $\mathsf{DET}(n,\mathbb{F})$ and $\mathsf{INV}(n,\mathbb{F})$ is described in Fig. 1. Steps 1 and 7.2 can be implemented in $O(p^{2/\omega} n^{1-2/\omega})$ rounds from Theorem 1 (or its simplified version in the introduction). Step 5 can be implemented in $O(n^{1-2/\omega})$ rounds, again from Theorem 1. At Steps 2, 3 and 6 each node receives n elements from the field $\mathbb{F}$, so each of these three steps can be implemented in

---

1. The matrices $A^{(a_1-1)p}$ and A^{a_2-1} are computed for all $a_1, a_2 \in [p]$ using the distributed algorithm of Theorem 1. At the end of this step node $\ell \in [n]$ has the whole $p \times n$ matrix R_ℓ and the whole $n \times p$ matrix C_ℓ.
2. Node $\ell \in [n]$ locally computes U_ℓ, and sends $U_\ell[k_1, k_2]$ to each node $k = (k_1, k_2) \in [n]$.
3. Node $k = (k_1, k_2) \in [n]$, who received $U_\ell[k_1, k_2]$ for all $\ell \in [n]$ at the previous step, locally computes s_k using Equation (2). Node k then sends s_k to all the nodes.
4. Node $\ell \in [n]$, who received $\boldsymbol{s}$ at Step 3, locally constructs $S[\ell, *]$ and $S[*, \ell]$.
5. The matrix S^{-1} is computed using the algorithm of Proposition 2. At the end of this step, node $\ell \in [n]$ has $S^{-1}[\ell, *]$ and $S^{-1}[*, \ell]$.
6. Node $\ell \in [n]$ locally computes c_ℓ from $S^{-1}[\ell, *]$ and $\boldsymbol{s}$, and sends c_ℓ to all nodes.
7. The determinant of A is $(-1)^n c_n$. If $c_n = 0$ the matrix A is not invertible. Otherwise the nodes compute A^{-1} as follows:
    7.1 Node $\ell \in [n]$ computes $E_{a_2}[\ell, *]$ for each $a_2 \in [p]$ (this can be done locally since $\boldsymbol{c}$ and each row $A^{(a_1-1)p}[\ell, *]$ are known from Steps 6 and 1, respectively).
    7.2 The matrices $E_{a_2} A^{a_2-1}$ are computed for all $a_2 \in [p]$ using the distributed algorithm of Theorem 1 (since, besides $E_{a_2}[\ell, *]$ obtained at the previous step, each node $\ell \in [n]$ knows $A^{a_2-1}[*, \ell]$ from the result of the computation of Step 1). At the end of this step, node $\ell \in [n]$ has the ℓ-th row and the ℓ-th column of the matrix $E_{a_2} A^{a_2-1}$ for all $a_2 \in [p]$.
    7.3 Node $\ell \in [n]$ computes locally $A^{-1}[\ell, *]$ and $A^{-1}[*, \ell]$ using Equation (3).

Fig. 1. Distributed algorithm for computing the determinant of an $n \times n$ matrix A and computing A^{-1} if $\det(A) \neq 0$. Initially each node $\ell \in [n]$ has as input $A[\ell, *]$ and $A[*, \ell]$.

two rounds from Lemma 1. The other steps (Steps 4, 7.1 and 7.3) do not require any communication. The total round complexity of the algorithm is thus $O\left(p^{2/\omega}n^{1-2/\omega}\right) = O\left(n^{1-1/\omega}\right)$, as claimed. $\qquad\square$

Acknowledgments. The author is grateful to Arne Storjohann for precious help concerning the computation of the determinant and to anonymous reviewers for their comments. This work is supported by the Grant-in-Aid for Young Scientists (A) No. 16H05853, the Grant-in-Aid for Scientific Research (A) No. 16H01705, and the Grant-in-Aid for Scientific Research on Innovative Areas No. 24106009 of the Japan Society for the Promotion of Science and the Ministry of Education, Culture, Sports, Science and Technology in Japan.

References

1. Bürgisser, P., Clausen, M., Shokrollahi, M.A.: Algebraic Complexity Theory. Springer, Heidelberg (1997)
2. Censor-Hillel, K., Kaski, P., Korhonen, J.H., Lenzen, C., Paz, A., Suomela, J.: Algebraic methods in the congested clique. In: Proceedings of the 34th Symposium on Principles of Distributed Computing, pp. 143–152 (2015)
3. Cheriyan, J.: Randomized $\tilde{O}(M(|V|))$ algorithms for problems in matching theory. SIAM J. Comput. **26**(6), 1635–1669 (1997)
4. Chu, J.I., Schnitger, G.: Communication complexity of matrix computation over finite fields. Math. Syst. Theor. **28**(3), 215–228 (1995)
5. Csanky, L.: Fast parallel matrix inversion algorithms. In: Proceedings of the 16th Annual Symposium on Foundations of Computer Science, pp. 11–12 (1975)
6. Dolev, D., Lenzen, C., Peled, S.: "Tri, tri again": finding triangles and small subgraphs in a distributed setting. In: Aguilera, M.K. (ed.) DISC 2012. LNCS, vol. 7611, pp. 195–209. Springer, Heidelberg (2012)
7. Drucker, A., Kuhn, F., Oshman, R.: On the power of the congested clique model. In: Proceedings of the ACM Symposium on Principles of Distributed Computing, pp. 367–376 (2014)
8. Hegeman, J.W., Pandurangan, G., Pemmaraju, S.V., Sardeshmukh, V.B., Scquizzato, M.: Toward optimal bounds in the congested clique: Graph connectivity and MST. In: Proceedings of the ACM Symposium on Principles of Distributed Computing, pp. 91–100 (2015)
9. Hegeman, J.W., Pemmaraju, S.V.: Lessons from the congested clique applied to mapreduce. In: Halldórsson, M.M. (ed.) SIROCCO 2014. LNCS, vol. 8576, pp. 149–164. Springer, Heidelberg (2014)
10. Hegeman, J.W., Pemmaraju, S.V., Sardeshmukh, V.B.: Near-constant-time distributed algorithms on a congested clique. In: Kuhn, F. (ed.) DISC 2014. LNCS, vol. 8784, pp. 514–530. Springer, Heidelberg (2014)
11. Henzinger, M., Krinninger, S., Nanongkai, D.: A deterministic almost-tight distributed algorithm for approximating single-source shortest paths. In: Proceedings of the 48th Annual ACM Symposium on Theory of Computing, pp. 489–498 (2016)
12. Kaltofen, E., Pan, V.Y.: Processor efficient parallel solution of linear systems over an abstract field. In: Proceedings of the 3rd Annual ACM Symposium on Parallel Algorithms and Architectures, pp. 180–191 (1991)

13. Kaltofen, E., Pan, V.Y.: Processor-efficient parallel solution of linear systems II: the positive characteristic and singular cases (extended abstract). In: Proceedings of the 33rd Annual Symposium on Foundations of Computer Science, pp. 714–723 (1992)

14. Kaltofen, E., Saunders, B.D.: On Wiedemann's method of solving sparse linear systems. In: Proceedings of the 9th International Symposium on Applied Algebra, Algebraic Algorithms and Error-Correcting Codes, pp. 29–38 (1991)

15. Le Gall, F.: Faster algorithms for rectangular matrix multiplication. In: Proceedings of the 53rd Annual IEEE Symposium on Foundations of Computer Science, pp. 514–523 (2012)

16. Le Gall, F.: Powers of tensors and fast matrix multiplication. In: Proceedings of the 39th International Symposium on Symbolic and Algebraic Computation, pp. 296–303 (2014)

17. Lenzen, C.: Optimal deterministic routing and sorting on the congested clique. In: Proceedings of the ACM Symposium on Principles of Distributed Computing, pp. 42–50 (2013)

18. Lenzen, C., Wattenhofer, R.: Tight bounds for parallel randomized load balancing: extended abstract. In: Proceedings of the 43rd ACM Symposium on Theory of Computing, pp. 11–20 (2011)

19. Lotker, Z., Pavlov, E., Patt-Shamir, B., Peleg, D.: MST construction in $o(\log \log n)$ communication rounds. In: Proceedings of the Fifteenth Annual ACM Symposium on Parallelism in Algorithms and Architectures, pp. 94–100 (2003)

20. Lovász, L.: On determinants, matchings, and random algorithms. In: Fundamentals of Computation Theory, pp. 565–574 (1979)

21. Lovász, L., Plummer, M.D.: Matching Theory. American Mathematical Society (2009)

22. Nanongkai, D.: Distributed approximation algorithms for weighted shortest paths. In: Proceedings of the 46th Symposium on Theory of Computing, pp. 565–573 (2014)

23. Patt-Shamir, B., Teplitsky, M.: The round complexity of distributed sorting: extended abstract. In: Proceedings of the 30th Annual ACM Symposium on Principles of Distributed Computing, pp. 249–256 (2011)

24. Peleg, D.: Distributed computing: a locality-sensitive approach. Society for Industrial and Applied Mathematics (2000)

25. Preparata, F.P., Sarwate, D.V.: An improved parallel processor bound in fast matrix inversion. Inf. Process. Lett. **7**(3), 148–150 (1978)

26. Rabin, M.O., Vazirani, V.V.: Maximum matchings in general graphs through randomization. J. Algorithms **10**(4), 557–567 (1989)

27. Seidel, R.: On the all-pairs-shortest-path problem in unweighted undirected graphs. J. Comput. Syst. Sci. **51**(3), 400–403 (1995)

28. Shoshan, A., Zwick, U.: All pairs shortest paths in undirected graphs with integer weights. In: Proceedings of the 40th Annual Symposium on Foundations of Computer Science, pp. 605–615 (1999)

29. Vassilevska Williams, V.: Multiplying matrices faster than coppersmith-winograd. In: Proceedings of the 44th Symposium on Theory of Computing, pp. 887–898 (2012)

30. Zwick, U.: All pairs shortest paths using bridging sets and rectangular matrix multiplication. J. ACM **49**(3), 289–317 (2002)

Towards a Universal Approach for Monotonic Searchability in Self-stabilizing Overlay Networks

Christian Scheideler, Alexander Setzer, and Thim Strothmann[✉]

Paderborn University, Paderborn, Germany
{scheidel,asetzer,thim}@mail.uni-paderborn.de

Abstract. For overlay networks, the ability to recover from a variety of problems like membership changes or faults is a key element to preserve their functionality. In recent years, various self-stabilizing overlay networks have been proposed that have the advantage of being able to recover from *any* illegal state. However, the vast majority of these networks cannot give any guarantees on its functionality while the recovery process is going on. We are especially interested in *searchability*, i.e., the functionality that search messages for a specific identifier are answered successfully if a node with that identifier exists in the network. We investigate overlay networks that are not only self-stabilizing but that also ensure that *monotonic* searchability is maintained while the recovery process is going on, as long as there are no corrupted messages in the system. More precisely, once a search message from node u to another node v is successfully delivered, all future search messages from u to v succeed as well. Monotonic searchability was recently introduced in OPODIS 2015, in which the authors provide a solution for a simple line topology. We present the first *universal* approach to maintain monotonic searchability that is applicable to a wide range of topologies. As the base for our approach, we introduce a set of primitives for manipulating overlay networks that allows us to maintain searchability and show how existing protocols can be transformed to use theses primitives. We complement this result with a generic search protocol that together with the use of our primitives guarantees monotonic searchability. As an additional feature, searching existing nodes with the generic search protocol is as fast as searching a node with any other fixed routing protocol once the topology has stabilized.

1 Introduction

In this paper, we continue our research started in [16] and investigate protocols for self-stabilizing overlay networks that guarantee the *monotonic* preservation of a characteristic that we call *searchability*, i.e., once a search message from node u to another node v is successfully delivered, all future search messages from u to

This work was partially supported by the German Research Foundation (DFG) within the Collaborative Research Center "On-The-Fly Computing" (SFB 901).

C. Gavoille and D. Ilcinkas (Eds.): DISC 2016, LNCS 9888, pp. 71–84, 2016.
DOI: 10.1007/978-3-662-53426-7_6

v succeed as well. Instead of focusing on a specific topology, as done in [16], we present an approach that is aimed at universality. As a base, we present a set of primitives for overlay network maintainance for which we prove that they enable monotonic searchability. On top of that, we give a generic search protocol that, together with a protocol that solely uses these primitives, guarantees monotonic searchability. Additionally, we show that existing self-stabilizing overlay network protocols can be transformed to use our primitives.

To the best of our knowledge, we are the first to investigate monotonic searchability as an attempt to explore maintaining properties beyond the traditional "time and space" metrics during stabilization. We believe that the question of how to maintain monotonic searchability and similar properties during topological stabilization has a lot of potential for future research.

1.1 Model

We consider a distributed system consisting of a fixed set of nodes in which each node has a unique reference and a unique immutable numerical identifier (or short id). The system is controlled by a protocol that specifies the variables and actions that are available in each node. In addition to the protocol-based variables there is a system-based variable for each node called *channel* whose values are sets of messages. We denote the channel of a node u as $u.Ch$ and it contains all incoming messages to u. Its message capacity is unbounded and messages never get lost. A node can add a message to $u.Ch$ if it has a reference of u. Besides these channels there are no further communication means, so only point-to-point communication is possible.

There are two types of *actions* that a protocol can execute. The first type has the form of a standard procedure $\langle label \rangle(\langle parameters \rangle) : \langle command \rangle$, where *label* is the unique name of that action, *parameters* specifies the parameter list of the action, and *command* specifies the statements to be executed when calling that action. Such actions can be called locally (which causes their immediate execution) and remotely. In fact, we assume that every message must be of the form $\langle label \rangle(\langle parameters \rangle)$, where *label* specifies the action to be called in the receiving node and *parameters* contains the parameters to be passed to that action call. All other messages are ignored by nodes. The second type has the form $\langle label \rangle : \langle guard \rangle \longrightarrow \langle command \rangle$, where *label* and *command* are defined as above and *guard* is a predicate over local variables. We call an action whose guard is simply **true** a *timeout* action.

The *system state* is an assignment of values to every variable of each node and messages to each channel. An action in some node u is *enabled* in some system state if its guard evaluates to **true**, or if there is a message in $u.Ch$ requesting to call it. In the latter case, when the corresponding action is executed, the message is processed (and it is removed from $u.Ch$). An action is *disabled* otherwise. Receiving and processing a message is considered as an atomic step.

A *computation* is an infinite fair sequence of system states such that for each state S_i, the next state S_{i+1} is obtained by executing an action that is enabled in S_i. This disallows the overlap of action execution, i.e., action execution is *atomic*.

We assume *weakly fair action execution* and *fair message receipt*. Weakly fair action execution means that if an action is enabled in all but finitely many states of a computation, then this action is executed infinitely often. Note that a time-out action of a node is executed infinitely often. Fair message receipt means that if a computation contains a state in which there is a message in a channel of a node that enables an action in that node, then that action is eventually executed with the parameters of that message, i.e., the message is eventually processed. Besides these fairness assumptions, we place no bounds on message propagation delay or relative nodes execution speeds, i.e., we allow fully asynchronous computations and non-FIFO message delivery. A *computation suffix* is a sequence of computation states past a particular state of this computation. In other words, the suffix of the computation is obtained by removing the initial state and finitely many subsequent states. Note that a computation suffix is also a computation. We say a state S' is reachable from a state S if starting in S there is a sequence of action executions such that we end up in state S'. We use the notion $S < S'$ as a shorthand to indicate that the state S happened chronologically before S'.

We consider protocols that do not manipulate the internals of node references. Specifically, a protocol is *compare-store-send* if the only operations that it executes on node references is comparing them, storing them in local memory and sending them in a message. In a compare-store-send protocol, a node may learn a new reference of a node only by receiving it in a message. A compare-store-send protocol cannot create new references. It can only operate on the references given to it.

The overlay network of a set of nodes is determined by their knowledge of each other. We say that there is a (directed) *edge* from a to b, denoted by (a, b), if node a stores a reference of b in its local memory or has a message in $a.Ch$ carrying the reference of b. In the former case, the edge is called *explicit*, and in the latter case, the edge is called *implicit*. Messages can only be sent via explicit edges. Note that message receipt converts an implicit edge to an explicit edge since the message is in the local memory of a node while it is processed. With NG we denote the directed *network (multi-)graph* given by the explicit and implicit edges. ENG is the subgraph of NG induced by only the explicit edges. A *weakly connected component* of a directed graph G is a subgraph of G of maximum size so that for any two nodes u and v in that subgraph there is a (not necessarily directed) path from u to v. Two nodes that are not in the same weakly connected component are *disconnected*. We assume that the positions of the processes in the topology are encapsulated in their identifier and that there is a distance measure which is based on the identifiers of the processes and which can be checked locally. That is, for a given identifier ID, each node u can decide for each neighbor v whether v is closer to the node w with $id(w) = ID$ if such a node exists (we also say that $id(v)$ is closer to ID than $id(u)$ or $ds(id(v), ID) < ds(id(u), ID)$). For a node u, we define $R(u, ID)$ as the set containing u and all processes v for which there is a path Q from u to v via explicit edges such that for each edge (a, b) that is traversed in Q it holds that $ds(id(b), ID) < ds(id(a), ID)$. Furthermore, for a set U, we define $R(U, ID) := \bigcup_{u \in U} R(u, ID)$.

We are particularly concerned with search requests, i.e., SEARCH($v, destID$) messages that are routed along ENG according to a given search protocol, where v is the sender of the message and $destID$ is the identifier of a node we are looking for. We assume that SEARCH() requests are initiated locally by an (possibly user controlled) application operating on top of the network. Note that $destID$ does not need to be an id of an existing node w, since it is also possible that we are searching for a node that is not in the system. If a SEARCH($v, destID$) message reaches a node w with $id(w) = destID$, the search request *succeeds*; if the message reaches some node u with $id(u) \neq destID$ and cannot be forwarded anymore according to the given search protocol, the search request *fails*.

1.2　Problem Statement

A protocol is *self-stabilizing* if it satisfies the following two properties as long as no transient faults occur: (i) **Convergence:** starting from an arbitrary system state, the protocol is guaranteed to arrive at a legitimate state and (ii) **Closure:** starting from a legitimate state the protocol remains in legitimate states thereafter.

A self-stabilizing protocol is thus able to recover from transient faults regardless of their nature. Moreover, a self-stabilizing protocol does not have to be initialized as it eventually starts to behave correctly regardless of its initial state. In *topological self-stabilization* we allow self-stabilizing protocols to perform changes to the overlay network NG. A legitimate state may then include a particular graph topology or a family of graph topologies. We are interested in self-stabilizing protocols that stabilize to *static topologies*, i.e., in every computation of the protocol that starts from a legitimate state, ENG stays the same, as long as the node set stays the same.

In this paper we are not focusing on building a self-stabilizing protocol for a particular topology. Instead we are interested in providing a reliable protocol for searching in a wide range of topologies that fulfill certain requirements. Traditionally, search protocols for a given topology were only required to deliver the search messages reliably once a legitimate state has been reached. However, it is not possible to determine when a legitimate state has been reached. Furthermore, searching reliably during the stabilization phase is much more involved. We say a self-stabilizing protocol satisfies *monotonic searchability* according to some search protocol R if it holds for any pair of nodes v, w that once a SEARCH($v, id(w)$) request (that is routed according to R) initiated at time t succeeds, any SEARCH($v, id(w)$) request initiated at a time $t' > t$ will succeed. We do not mention R if it is clear from the context. A protocol is said to satisfy *non-trivial* monotonic searchability if (i) it satisfies monotonic searchability and (ii) every computation of the protocol contains a suffix such that for each pair of nodes v, w, SEARCH($v, id(w)$) requests will succeed if there is a path from v to w in the target topology. Throughout the paper we will only investigate non-trivial monotonic searchability. Consequently, whenever we use the term monotonic searchability in the following, we implicitly refer to non-trivial monotonic searchability.

A *message invariant* is a predicate of the following form: If there is a message m in the incoming channel of a node, then a logical predicate P must hold. A protocol may specify one or more message invariants. An arbitrary message m in a system is called *corrupted* if the existence of m violates one or multiple message invariants. A state S is called *admissible* if there are no corrupted messages in S. We say a (self-stabilizing) protocol *admissibly satisfies* a predicate P if the following two conditions hold: (i) the predicate is satisfied in all computation suffixes of the protocol that start from admissible states, and (ii) every computation of the protocol contains at least one admissible state. A protocol *unconditionally satisfies* a predicate if it satisfies this predicate starting from any state.

The following was proven in [16]:

Lemma 1. *No self-stabilizing compare-store-send protocol can unconditionally satisfy monotonic searchability.*

Consequently, to prove monotonic searchability for a protocol (according to a given search protocol R) it is sufficient to show that: (i) in every computation of the protocol that starts from an admissible state, every state is admissible, (ii) in every computation of the protocol there is an admissible state, and (iii) the protocol satisfies monotonic searchability according to R in every computation that starts from an admissible state. Note that we have not defined any invariants yet and it is possible to pick invariants such that the set of admissible states equals the set of legitimate states, in which the problem becomes trivial. However, for the invariants we provide, any initial topology can be an admissible state. In particular, as long as no corrupt messages are initially in the system, our protocols satisfy monotonic searchability throughout the computation.

We will show that a broad class of existing self-stabilizing protocols can be transformed to satisfy monotonic searchability. More specifically, we will consider protocols that fulfill the MDL *property*, i.e., for any action a of the protocol it holds that (i) a node u executing action a will always keep a reference of another node v in its local memory if an edge (u, v) is part of the final topology, and (ii) if a node u executing action a in state S decides not to keep a reference of another node v in its local memory, every other action of the protocol executed by u in a subsequent state will decide to not keep the reference of v, and (iii) a node u executing action a decides *deterministically* and solely based on its *local* memory whether to send and where to send the reference of v, and (iv) in every legitimate state, for every reference of a node v contained in a message m in the channel of a node u (i.e., for any implicit edge (u, v)), there are fixed cycle-free paths $(u = u_1, u_2, \ldots, u_k)$ such that u_i sends the reference of v to u_{i+1}, and u_k has an explicit edge (u_k, v) (note that there is only one path if the reference is never duplicated), i.e., the reference of v is forwarded along fixed paths until it finally fuses with an existing reference. Informally speaking, the first two properties imply that the protocol *monotonically* converges to its desired topology, since edges of the topology are always kept and edges that are not part of the topology are obviated over time. The last property implies that in legitimate states, all implicit edges will eventually merge with explicit edges. Note that the MDL property is generally not a severe restriction. Most existing protocols that stabilize to static topologies naturally fulfill this property.

In addition to the MDL property and the assumption that the final topology is static, we have one more condition on the topologies and their distance measures. The generic search protocol we will use to achieve monotonic searchability assumes that in the target topology for every pair of nodes u, v within the same connected component, there is a path of explicit edges from u to v with the property that each edge on the path strictly decreases the distance to v (i.e., for each edge (a, b) that is traversed in the path, $ds(id(b), id(v)) < ds(id(a), id(v))$). Note that many topologies naturally fulfill this property (in particular, whenever the distance is defined as the number of nodes on a shortest path).

1.3 Our Contribution

To the best of our knowledge, we are the first to solve the problem of searching reliably during the stabilization phase in self-stabilizing topologies. Although routing with a low dilation is a major motivation behind the use of overlay topologies, prior to this work, one could not rely on the routing paths in such topologies[1]: In previous approaches, it can happen that a node u is able to send a message to a node v, while it is unable to do so in a later state, only because the system has not stabilized yet (which is not locally detectable by the nodes). In our solution, once a search message from a node u has successfully arrived at a node v, every further search message from u to v will also arrive at its destination, regardless of whether the system has fully stabilized or not.

We present a universal set of primitives for manipulating edges that protocols should use and a simple generic search protocol, which together satisfy monotonic searchability. Moreover, we provide a general description of how a broad class of self-stabilizing protocols for overlay networks can be transformed such that they use these primitives, thus satisfying monotonic searchability afterwards.

Our results of Sect. 3 may be of independent interest, where we reinvestigate the fundamental primitives for manipulating edges introduced in [13] and strengthen the results concerning the universality of these primitives.

2 Related Work

The idea of self-stabilization in distributed computing was introduced by E.W. Dijkstra in 1974 [4], in which he investigated the problem of self-stabilization in a token ring. In order to recover certain network topologies from any weakly connected state, researchers started with simple line and ring networks (e.g., [7,18]). Over the years more and more topologies were considered, ranging from skip lists

---

[1] Note that [16] did solve the problem of monotonic searchability for the list, but the list has a worst-case routing time of $\Omega(n)$, thus not offering a low dilation.

and skip graphs [8,14], to expanders [6], and small-world graphs [12]. Also a universal algorithm for topological self-stabilization is known [1].

In the last 20 years many approaches have been investigated that focus on maintaining safety properties during convergence phase of self-stabilization, e.g. snap-stabilization [2,3], super-stabilization [5], safe convergence [11] and self-stabilization with service guarantee [10]. Closest to our work is the notion of *monotonic convergence* by Yamauchi and Tixeuil [19]. A self-stabilizing protocol is monotonically converging if every change done by a node p makes the system approach a legitimate state and if every node changes its output only once. The authors investigate monotonically converging protocols for different classical distributed problems (e.g., leader election and vertex coloring) and focus on the amount of non-local information that is needed for them.

Research on monotonic searchability was initiated in [16], in which the authors proved that it is impossible to satisfy monotonic searchability if corrupted messages are present. In addition, they presented a self-stabilizing protocol for the line topology that is able to satisfy monotonic searchability.

3 Primitives for Topology Maintenance

An important property for every overlay management protocol is that weak connectivity is never lost by its own actions. Therefore, it is highly desirable that every node only executes actions that preserve weak connectivity. Koutsopoulos et al. [13] introduced the following four primitives for manipulating edges in an overlay network.

Introduction. If a node u has a reference of two nodes v and w with $v \neq w$, u *introduces* w to v if u sends a message to v containing a reference of w while keeping the reference.

Delegation. If a node u has a reference of two nodes v and w s.t. u, v, w are all different, then u *delegates* w's reference of v if u sends a message to v containing a reference of w and deletes the reference of w.

Fusion. If a node u has two references v and w with $v = w$, then u *fuses* the two references if it only keeps one of these references.

Reversal. If a node u has a reference of some other node v, then u *reverses* the connection if it sends a reference of itself to v and deletes its reference of v.

Note that the four primitives can be executed locally by every node in a wait-free fashion. Furthermore, for the Introduction primitive, it is possible that $w = u$, i.e., u introduces itself to v. The authors show that these four primitives are safe in a sense that they preserve weak connectivity (as long as there is no fault). This implies that *any* distributed protocol whose actions can be decomposed into these four primitives is guaranteed to preserve weak connectivity.

We define $\mathcal{IDF}$ as the set containing the first three primitives: Introduction, Delegation and Fusion. Let $\mathcal{P}_{\mathcal{IDF}}$ denote the set of all distributed protocols where all interactions between processes can be decomposed into the primitives of $\mathcal{IDF}$. According to [13] these protocols even preserve strong connectivity in a sense that for any pair of nodes u, v with a directed path in NG there will always be a directed path from u to v in NG. To the best of our knowledge, all self-stabilizing topology maintenance protocols proposed so far (such as the list [7, 15, 18], the Delaunay graph [9], etc.) satisfy this property. Moreover, in [13], the four primitives were shown to be *universal*, i.e. the primitives allow one to get from any weakly connected graph $G = (V, E)$ to any other weakly connected graph $G' = (V, E')$ for NG. In fact, only the first three primitives (i.e., $\mathcal{IDF}$) are necessary to get from any weakly connected graph to any *strongly* connected graph, which is sufficient in our case ([13] denote this by *weak universality*). Note that the notion of universality for a set of primitives is not constructive, i.e., only *in principle* the primitives allow one to get from any weakly connected graph to any other weakly connected graph. We strengthen the results concerning universality of the primitives with the following theorem (the proof can be found in the full version [17]).

Theorem 1. *Any compare-store-send protocol that self-stabilizes to a static strongly-connected topology and preserves weak connectivity can be transformed such that the interactions between nodes can be decomposed into the primitives of $\mathcal{IDF}$.*

4   Primitives for Monotonic Searchability

Although the primitives of [13] are general enough to construct any conceivable overlay, they do not inherently satisfy monotonic searchability. This is due to the fact that the Delegation primitive replaces an explicit edge (u, v) by a path (u, w, v) consisting of an explicit edge (u, w) and an implicit edge (w, v) and thus a search message from u to v issued after the delegation may be processed by w before there is a path from w to v via explicit edges, causing the search message to fail (even though an earlier message sent while (u, v) was still an explicit edge was delivered successfully). Consequently, we are going to introduce a new set of primitives that enables monotonic searchability. We say a set of primitives is *search-universal* according to a set of Invariants $\mathcal{I}$ if the following holds:

1. the set of primitives is weakly universal,
2. starting from every state in which the invariants in $\mathcal{I}$ hold, for every pair of nodes u and v as soon as there is a path via explicit edges from u to v, there will be a path via explicit edges from u to v in every subsequent step.

We are now going to introduce a modified set of primitives that are search-universal. Moreover, we will show that these new primitives are also general enough to cover all self-stabilizing protocols that can be built by the original primitives. Consequently, we ultimately aim at a result similar to Theorem 1 for the new primitives.

Remember that we assume the MDL property. Therefore, in every fixed state S in every execution of a self-stabilizing protocol, each node u can divide its explicit edges into two subsets: the *stable edges* and the *temporary edges* (not to be confused with implicit edges). The first set contains those explicit edges that

u wants to keep, given its current neighborhood in S; the second set holds the explicit edges that are not needed from the perspective of u in S. Note that the set of temporary edges can also be the empty set.

For the new primitives, a node does not only store references of its neighbors, but additionally stores sequence numbers for every reference in its local memory, i.e., every node u stores for each neighbor v an entry $u.eseq[id(v)]$ (or $u.eseq[v]$, in short). We keep the Introduction primitive as in Sect. 3 and change Delegation and Fusion in the following way:

Safe-Delegation. Consider a node u that has references of two different nodes v and w. In order to perform *Safe-Delegation*, u has to distinguish between (u, w) being implicit or temporary.

If (u, w) is an implicit edge, it is delegated as in the original delegation primitive (we will later refer to this case as an *implicit delegation* or IMPLDELEGATE(t) o avoid confusion with the original primitives). If (u, w) is a temporary edge, it can only be delegated to a node v if (u, v) is a stable edge. Whenever an explicit edge (u, w) is to be delegated to another node v, u sends a DELEGATEREQ($u, w, eseq$) message to v, where $eseq = u.eseq[w]$. Additionally, it sets $u.eseq[v]$ to $max\{u.eseq[v], u.eseq[w] + 1\}$. Any node v that receives a DELEGATEREQ($u, w, eseq$) message, adds (v, w) to its set of explicit edges (if it does not already exist), sets $v.eseq[w]$ to $max\{v.eseq[w], eseq + 1\}$ and sends a DELEGATEACK($w, eseq$) message back to u. Upon receipt of this message, u checks whether $eseq = u.eseq[w]$ and whether (u, w) is actually a temporary edge (note that the last check is necessary to handle corrupt initial states). If both conditions hold, u removes the temporary explicit edge to w and sends an IMPLDELEGATE(w) message to one of its neighbors. Otherwise, u simply acts as it would upon receipt of an IMPLDELEGATE(w) message.

Fusion. If a node u has two references v and w with $v = w$, then u *fuses* the two references if it only keeps one of these references. Note that when a node u receives a DELEGATEREQ(v,w,eseq) message and already stores a reference of w, it also behaves as described in the Safe-Delegation primitive.

We define $\mathcal{ISF}$ as the set containing the three primitives Introduction, Safe-Delegation and Fusion. Throughout the paper we assume that DELEGATEREQ() and DELEGATEACK() messages are only sent in the Safe-Delegation primitive. Analogous to $\mathcal{P}_{\mathcal{IDF}}$, let $\mathcal{P}_{\mathcal{ISF}}$ denote the set of all distributed protocols where all interactions between processes can be decomposed into the primitives of $\mathcal{ISF}$. Likewise to the MDL property, we say that a protocol fulfills the *stable* MDL property, if the protocol fulfills the MDL property with respect to stable explicit edges. More specifically, for any action a of the protocol it holds that a node u executing action a will always keep a reference of another node v in its local memory (i.e., the stable edge (u, v)) if an edge (u, v) is part of the final topology, and if a node u executing action a in some state S decides to not keep a reference of another node v in its local memory (i.e., the temporary or implicit edge (u, v)), every other action of the protocol executed by u in any state $S' > S$ will decide to not keep the reference of v.

4.1 Universality of the New Primitives

To show that our primitives are search-universal we first show that they are weakly universal. The corresponding proof can be found in the full version.

Lemma 2. $\mathcal{ISF}$ *is weakly universal.*

In order to enable monotonic searchability, we define the following two **message invariants**:

1. If there is a DELEGATEREQ(u,w,eseq) message in $v.Ch$, then there exists a path $P = (u = x_1, x_2, \ldots, x_k = v)$ that does not contain (u, w) and for every $1 \leq i < k$, $x_i.eseq[x_{i+1}] > u.eseq[w]$, or $u.eseq[w] > eseq$.
2. If there is a DELEGATEACK(w,eseq) message in $u.Ch$, then there exists a path $P = (u = x_1, x_2, \ldots, x_k = w)$ that does not contain (u, w) and for every $1 \leq i < k$, $x_i.eseq[x_{i+1}] > u.eseq[w]$, or $u.eseq[w] > eseq$.

Intuitively, Invariant 1 says that whenever node v has a DELEGATEREQ(u,w,eseq) message in $v.Ch$ (i.e., node u asked v to establish the edge (v, w) such that it may remove its own (u, w) edge), then there is a path from u to v that does not use the edge (u, w). Invariant 2 states that whenever a node u has a DELEGATEACK(w,seq) message in $u.Ch$ (i.e., some other node v which u asked to establish the edge (v, w) has already done so), then there is a path from u to w that does not use the edge (u, w). However, both statements only need to hold if the value of ESEQ indicates that the messages belong to a current safe-delegation, i.e., if $u.seq[w] > eseq$, the DELEGATEREQ() or DELEGATEACK() message can be ignored.

We define the predicate $E(u, v)$ to be true if and only if there exists a directed path from u to v via explicit edges. In order to show search-universality, we prove the following lemma.

Lemma 3. *Consider a computation of a protocol* $P \in \mathcal{P}_{\mathcal{ISF}}$ *that fulfills the stable* MDL *property. If there is a state* S *such that Invariants 1 and 2 hold, then they will hold in every subsequent state. Additionally, for every state* $S' \geq S$ *it holds that if* $E(u, v) \equiv TRUE$ *in* S', *then* $E(u, v) \equiv TRUE$ *in every state* $S'' \geq S'$.

Lemmas 2 and 3 imply the following corollary:

Corollary 1. $\mathcal{ISF}$ *is search-universal according to Invariants 1 and 2.*

We conclude this section by showing that a protocol $A \in \mathcal{P}_{\mathcal{IDF}}$ that fulfills the MDL property and self-stabilizes to some topology can be transformed into a protocol $B \in \mathcal{P}_{\mathcal{ISF}}$ that fulfills the stable MDL property and for which it holds that in every computation of B there is a state in which Invariant 1–2 hold. The corresponding proof can be found in the full version [17].

Theorem 2. *Consider a protocol $A \in \mathcal{P}_{\mathcal{IDF}}$ that self-stabilizes to a strongly-connected topology T and that fulfills the* MDL *property. Then A can be transformed into another protocol $B \in \mathcal{P}_{\mathcal{ISF}}$ such that B fulfills the stable* MDL *property, B self-stabilizes to the same topology, and in every computation of B there exists a computation suffix in which Invariants 1 and 2 hold.*

5   The Generic Search Protocol

In this section we describe a generic search protocol such that every protocol in $\mathcal{P}_{\mathcal{ISF}}$ fulfilling the stable MDL property satisfies monotonic searchability according to that search protocol. We assume that when a node u wants to search for a node with identifier ID, it performs an INITIATENEWSEARCH(ID) action in which a SEARCH(u, ID) message is created. The search request is regarded as answered as soon as the SEARCH(u, ID) message is either dropped, i.e., it *fails*, or is received by the node w with $id(w) = ID$, i.e. it *succeeds*.

The principle idea of the *generic search protocol* is the following: A node u with a SEARCH(u, ID) message does not directly forward this message through the network but buffers it. Instead, u initiates a probing algorithm whose goal is to either receive the reference of the node w with $id(w) = ID$, or to get a negative response in case this node does not exist or cannot be reached yet. In the former case, u directly sends SEARCH(u, ID) to w. In the latter case, u drops SEARCH(u, ID). Whenever an additional SEARCH(u, ID) message for the same identifier ID is initiated at u while a probing for ID is still in progress, this message is combined with previous SEARCH(u, ID) messages waiting at u.

For the probing, a node u with a buffered SEARCH(u, ID) message periodically initiates a new PROBE() message in its TIMEOUT action. This PROBE() message contains four arguments: First, a reference *source* of the source of the PROBE() message., i.e., a reference of u. Second, the identifier *destID* of the node that is searched, i.e., ID. Third, a set *Next* that holds references of all neighbors of u with a closer distance to *destID* than $id(u)$. Last, a sequence number *seq* that is used to distinguish probe messages that belong to different probing processes from the same node and for the same target, i.e., $seq = u.seq[ID]$, where $u.seq[ID]$ is a value stored at u. This is necessary because in each execution of the TIMEOUT action, a new probe message is sent, although upon receival of the first response to such a message, the set of buffered search messages is sent out to the target or dropped completely. Thus, future replies may arrive afterwards and u has to know that these are outdated. All in all, u initiates a PROBE(*source, destID, Next, seq*) message and sends this message to the node in *Next* whose identifier has the maximum distance to ID (i.e., it is the closest to u).

Any intermediate node v that receives a PROBE(*source, destID, Next, seq*) message first checks whether $id(v) = destID$. If so, v sends a reference of itself to *source* via a PROBESUCCESS(*destID, dest*) message with $dest = v$. Otherwise, v removes itself from *Next* and adds all its neighbors to *Next* that have a closer distance to *destID* than itself. If *Next* is empty after this step, v responds to *source* via a PROBEFAIL(*destID, seq*) message. Otherwise,

v forwards the PROBE($source, destID, Next, seq$) message (with the already described changes performed to $Next$) to the node in $Next$ whose identifier has the maximum distance to ID. If the initiator u of a probe receives a PROBE-SUCCESS($destID, dest$) or a PROBEFAIL($destID, seq$) message, it first checks whether $seq \geq u.seq[destID]$, i.e., it checks whether the received message is a response to the current batch of search requests. If it is from an earlier probe, u simply drops the received message. Otherwise, u acts depending on the message it received: In case of a PROBESUCCESS($destID, dest$) message, u sends out all (possibly combined) SEARCH($u, destID$) messages waiting at u to $dest$ (thus stopping the probing). In case of a PROBEFAIL($destID, seq$) message, u drops all SEARCH($u, destID$) messages waiting at u to $dest$ (thus also stopping the probing). In both cases, u additionally increases $u.seq[destID]$ such that probe messages that are still in the system at this point in time cannot have any effects on future requests. The pseudocode of the generic search protocol and supplementary details can be found in the full version [17].

Using the protocol as specified above could cause a high dilation because each probe message in each step is always sent to the node with the highest distance to the target in $Next$, even if a shorter path is possible. Luckily, if there exists a fast routing protocol for the stabilized target topology (i.e., $o(n)$ hops in the worst case), it is possible to speed up search messages in legitimate states (and possibly even earlier). Details can be found in the full version [17].

As the generic search protocol cannot guarantee to function properly under the presence of corrupt messages, we define the following additional invariants that are maintained during the execution of the generic search protocol (that did not start with corrupt messages):

3. If there is a PROBE($source, destID, Next, seq$) message in $u.Ch$, then
   (a) $u \in Next$ and $\forall w \in Next \setminus \{u\} : ds(id(w), destID) \leq ds(id(u), destID)$,
   (b) $R(Next, ID) \subseteq R(source, ID)$, and
   (c) if v exists with $id(v) = destID$ and $v \notin R(Next, destID)$, then for every admissible state with $source.seq[destID] < seq$, $v \notin R(source, destID)$.
   If there is a FASTPROBE($source, destID$) message in $u.Ch$, then
   (d) $u \in R(source, destID)$.
4. If there is a PROBESUCCESS($destID, dest$) message in $u.Ch$, then $id(dest) = destID$ and $dest \in R(u, destID)$.
5. If there is a PROBEFAIL($destID, seq$) message in $u.Ch$, then if v exists such that $id(v) = destID$, then for every admissible state with $u.seq[destID] < seq$, $v \notin R(u, destID)$.
6. If there is a SEARCH($v, destID$) message in $u.Ch$, then $id(u) = destID$ and $u \in R(v, destID)$.

We say a protocol for the self-stabilization of a topology is *monotonic-searchability-sufficient* (*ms-sufficient*) if (i) all interactions between processes can be decomposed into the primitives in $\mathcal{ISF}$, (ii) it fulfills the stable MDL property, (iii) it uses the generic search protocol for searching, (iv) no PROBE(),

PROBESUCCESS(), PROBEFAIL(), or SEARCH() message is sent at any other occasion than the ones specified in the generic search protocol, and (v) in every computation of the protocol there is a state in which the first two invariants hold. Note that Theorem 2 implies the following:

Corollary 2. *Any conventional protocol $A \in \mathcal{P}_{\mathcal{IDF}}$ that self-stabilizes to a strongly-connected topology T and that fulfills the* MDL *property can be transformed into an ms-sufficient protocol that stabilizes the same topology.*

For an *ms*-sufficient protocol, we define a state as admissible if all six invariants hold. The proof of the following theorem can be found in the full version [17].

Theorem 3. *Every ms-sufficient protocol satisfies monotonic searchability according to Invariant 1–6.*

The following result follows from the description of the generic search protocol:

Corollary 3. *Every ms-sufficient protocol P that stabilizes to a topology T and in which the generic search protocol uses a routing strategy with a worst-case routing time of $O(T(n))$ for the fast search as described in the protocol, then P answers successful search requests in legitimate states in time $O(T(n))$.*

6   Conclusion and Outlook

In this work we further strengthened the notion of monotonic searchability introduced in [16] by presenting a universal approach for adapting conventional protocols for topological self-stabilization such that they satisfy monotonic searchability. Even more, we carved out some design principles that protocols should adhere to in order to enable reliable searches even during the stabilization phase.

Although our results solve the problem of monotonic searchability for a wide range of topologies, there are certain aspects that have not been studied yet. For example, we did not consider the additional cost of convergence (i.e., the amount of additional messages to be sent), nor the impact of our methods on the convergence time of the topology. Additionally, while our generic search protocol enables us to search existing nodes in legitimate states with a low dilation, searching for a non-existing node can still cause a message to travel $\Omega(n)$ hops, even in a legitimate state. Whether this is provably necessary or could be improved is still an open question.

References

1. Berns, A., Ghosh, S., Pemmaraju, S.V.: Building self-stabilizing overlay networks with the transitive closure framework. Theor. Comput. Sci. **512**, 2–14 (2013)
2. Bui, A., Datta, A.K., Petit, F., Villain, V.: Snap-stabilization and PIF in tree networks. Distrib. Comput. **20**(1), 3–19 (2007)
3. Delaët, S., Devismes, S., Nesterenko, M., Tixeuil, S.: Snap-stabilization in message-passing systems. J. Parallel Distrib. Comput. **70**(12), 1220–1230 (2010)

4. Dijkstra, E.W.: Self-stabilizing systems in spite of distributed control. Commun. ACM **17**(11), 643–644 (1974)
5. Dolev, S., Herman, T.: Superstabilizing protocols for dynamic distributed systems. Chicago J. Theor. Comput. Sci. **1997** (1997)
6. Dolev, S., Tzachar, N.: Spanders: distributed spanning expanders. Sci. Comput. Program. **78**(5), 544–555 (2013)
7. Gall, D., Jacob, R., Richa, A.W., Scheideler, C., Schmid, S., Täubig, H.: A note on the parallel runtime of self-stabilizing graph linearization. Theory Comput. Syst. **55**(1), 110–135 (2014)
8. Jacob, R., Richa, A.W., Scheideler, C., Schmid, S., Täubig, H.: Skip$^+$: a self-stabilizing skip graph. J. ACM **61**(6), 36:1–36:26 (2014)
9. Jacob, R., Ritscher, S., Scheideler, C., Schmid, S.: Towards higher-dimensional topological self-stabilization: a distributed algorithm for delaunay graphs. Theor. Comput. Sci. **457**, 137–148 (2012)
10. Johnen, C., Mekhaldi, F.: Robust self-stabilizing construction of bounded size weight-based clusters. In: D'Ambra, P., Guarracino, M., Talia, D. (eds.) Euro-Par 2010, Part I. LNCS, vol. 6271, pp. 535–546. Springer, Heidelberg (2010)
11. Kakugawa, H., Masuzawa, T.: A self-stabilizing minimal dominating set algorithm with safe convergence. In: 20th International Parallel and Distributed Processing Symposium (IPDPS 2006), Proceedings, 25–29 April 2006. Rhodes, Island, Greece (2006)
12. Kniesburges, S., Koutsopoulos, A., Scheideler, C.: A self-stabilization process for small-world networks. In: 26th IEEE International Parallel and Distributed Processing Symposium, IPDPS 2012, Shanghai, China, 21–25 May 2012, pp. 1261–1271 (2012)
13. Koutsopoulos, A., Scheideler, C., Strothmann, T.: Towards a universal approach for the finite departure problem in overlay networks. In: Pelc, A., Schwarzmann, A.A. (eds.) SSS 2015. LNCS, vol. 9212, pp. 201–216. Springer, Heidelberg (2015)
14. Nor, R.M., Nesterenko, M., Scheideler, C.: Corona: a stabilizing deterministic message-passing skip list. Theor. Comput. Sci. **512**, 119–129 (2013)
15. Onus, M., Richa, A.W., Scheideler, C.: Linearization: locally self-stabilizing sorting in graphs. In: Proceedings of the Nine Workshop on Algorithm Engineering and Experiments, ALENEX 2007, New Orleans, Louisiana, USA, 6 January 2007
16. Scheideler, C., Setzer, A., Strothmann, T.: Towards establishing monotonic searchability in self-stabilizing data structures. In: Principles of Distributed Systems - 19th International Conference, OPODIS 2015, Proceedings (2015)
17. Scheideler, C., Setzer, A., Strothmann, T.: Towards a universal approach for monotonic searchability in self-stabilizing overlay networks (full version). ArXiv e-prints, July 2016
18. Shaker, A., Reeves, D.S.: Self-stabilizing structured ring topology P2P systems. In: Fifth IEEE International Conference on Peer-to-Peer Computing (P2P 2005), 31 August–2 September 2005, Konstanz, Germany, pp. 39–46 (2005)
19. Yamauchi, Y., Tixeuil, S.: Monotonic stabilization. In: Lu, C., Masuzawa, T., Mosbah, M. (eds.) OPODIS 2010. LNCS, vol. 6490, pp. 475–490. Springer, Heidelberg (2010)

Asynchronous Embedded Pattern Formation Without Orientation

Serafino Cicerone[1], Gabriele Di Stefano[1], and Alfredo Navarra[2](✉)

[1] Dipartimento di Ingegneria e Scienze dell'Informazione e Matematica,
Università degli Studi dell'Aquila, Via Vetoio, Coppito, 67100 L'aquila, Italy
{serafino.cicerone,gabriele.distefano}@univaq.it
[2] Dipartimento di Matematica e Informatica, Università degli Studi di Perugia,
Via Vanvitelli 1, 06123 Perugia, Italy
alfredo.navarra@unipg.it

Abstract. We consider the Embedded Pattern Formation (EPF) problem introduced in [Fujinaga et al., *SIAM J. on Comput., 44(3), 2015*]. Given a set F of distinct points in the Euclidean plane (called here *fixed-points*) and a set R of robots such that $|R| = |F|$, the problem asks for a distributed algorithm that moves robots so as to occupy all points in F. Initially, each robot occupies a distinct position.

Robots operate in standard Look-Compute-Move cycles. In one cycle, a robot perceives the current configuration in terms of the robots' positions and the fixed-points (Look) according to its own coordinate system, decides whether to move (Compute), and in the positive case it moves (Move). Cycles are performed asynchronously for each robot. Robots are oblivious, anonymous and execute the same algorithm.

In the mentioned paper, the problem has been investigated by assuming chirality, that is robots share a common left-right orientation. The obtained solution has been used as a sub-procedure to solve the Pattern Formation problem, without fixed-points but still with chirality.

Here we investigate the other branch, that is, we are interested in solving EPF without chirality. We fully characterize when the EPF problem can be accomplished and we design a deterministic distributed algorithm that solves the problem for all configurations but those identified as unsolvable. Our approach is also characterized by the use of logical predicates in order to formally describe our algorithm as well as its correctness.

1 Introduction

The pattern formation problem has been largely investigated in the last years under different assumptions [7,9,13,15]. One of the latest results, see [12], solves

The work has been partially supported by the European project "Geospatial based Environment for Optimisation Systems Addressing Fire Emergencies" (GEO-SAFE), contract no. H2020-691161 and by the Italian projects: PRIN 2012C4E3KT "AMANDA – Algorithmics for MAssive and Networked DAta"; "RISE: un nuovo framework distribuito per data collection, monitoraggio e comunicazioni in contesti di emergency response", Fondazione Cassa Risparmio Perugia, code 2016.0104.021.

© Springer-Verlag Berlin Heidelberg 2016
C. Gavoille and D. Ilcinkas (Eds.): DISC 2016, LNCS 9888, pp. 85–98, 2016.
DOI: 10.1007/978-3-662-53426-7_7

the problem for robots empowered with few capabilities. Initially, no robots occupy the same location, and they are assumed to be: *Dimensionless*: modeled as geometric points in the plane; *Anonymous*: no unique identifiers; *Autonomous*: no centralized control; *Oblivious*: no memory; *Homogeneous*: they all execute the same deterministic algorithm; *Asynchronous*: there is no global clock that synchronizes their actions; *Silent*: no means of communication; *Chiral*: they share a common left-right orientation.

Robots operate in standard *Look-Compute-Move* cycles. In one cycle a robot takes a snapshot of the current global configuration (Look) in terms of robots' positions according to its own coordinate system. Successively, in the Compute phase it decides whether to move along a specific trajectory toward a target position or not, and in the positive case it moves (Move).

Cycles are performed asynchronously, i.e., the time between Look, Compute, and Move phases is finite but unbounded, and it is decided by an adversary for each robot. Moreover, during the Look phase, a robot does not perceive whether other robots are moving or not. Hence, robots may move based on outdated perceptions. In fact, due to asynchrony, by the time a robot takes a snapshot of the configuration, this might have drastically changed when it starts moving. The scheduler determining the Look-Compute-Move cycles timing is assumed to be fair: each robot performs its cycle within finite time and infinitely often.

The distance traveled within a move is neither infinite nor infinitesimally small. More precisely, the adversary has also the power to stop a moving robot before it reaches its destination, but there exists an unknown constant $\delta > 0$ such that if the destination point is closer than δ, the robot will reach it, otherwise the robot will be closer to it of at least δ. Note that, without this assumption, an adversary would make it impossible for any robot to ever reach its destination.

In order to solve the problem within the described model, the authors of [10–12] first introduced the so-called *Embedded Pattern Formation* (EPF) problem. In this variant, during the Look phase robots can also detect $|R|$ distinct points from now on called *fixed-points*, and the problem asks to move the robots to occupy all such points. In practice, the pattern to be formed is provided as a set of points in the plane.

In this paper, we are interested in the EPF problem, but we want to get rid of the assumed chirality. This represents a step forward for the main open question left in [12] concerning the resolution of the more general Pattern Formation problem in the described setting but without fixed points and without chirality.

So far, the only sub-problems solved within the weakest setting are the circle-formation problem [8], where robots must form a regular n-gon, the gathering problem [4], where robots must move toward a common point, and the case of asymmetric configurations [2]. Further research directions concern randomized approaches like in [1,16]. Instead of exploring yet another specific case, we investigate on a different branch, that is the EPF problem without chirality.

Intuitively, having fixed-points instead of chirality or randomness increases difficulties in designing distributed algorithms. In fact, usually main troubles come from symmetries. To this respect, chirality or randomness are powerful means to break possible symmetries. Having fixed points, instead, might be helpful in some cases where the matching between robots and fixed-points is trivial, but in general this is not the case, and the provided strategies must cope with unbreakable symmetries. It comes out that some configurations for EPF are unsolvable, that is, they do not admit any deterministic algorithm. This unsolvability result holds even though synchronous robots are considered. Any algorithm designed for solving EPF must take care of this result, since unsolvable configurations must be avoided by robots during their movements.

In this paper, we fully characterize the configurations for EPF that can be solved, and we provide a resolution algorithm. The formalization of the algorithm and the proof of correctness are provided by making use of basic predicates, that composed in a Boolean logic way provide all the invariants needed to be checked during the execution of the algorithm. This methodology reveals to be rather effective, and it could be very useful for formal verifications like in [5, 6, 14].

2   Definitions and Impossibility Results

In this section, we formally define the EPF problem, and then we recall from [3] the *view of a configuration* and some relations between *configuration symmetries* and the view. We conclude by providing a characterization result about configurations where the EPF problem cannot be solved.

Problem definition. The system is composed of $n \geq 1$ mobile *robots*. At any time, the multiset $R = \{r_1, r_2, \ldots, r_n\}$, with $r_i \in \mathbb{R}^2$, contains the *positions* of all the robots. $F = \{f_1, f_2, \ldots, f_n\}$ is a set of n distinct *fixed-points* in the plane. The pair $C = (R, F)$ represents a system *configuration*. If more than one robot occupies the same position, a *multiplicity* occurs. Robot are not endowed with any multiplicity detection, that is they do not realize from their view whether a point is occupied by more than one robot. A robot is said to be *stationary* in a configuration C if it is not moving and either the last snapshot acquired is C or it will perform the Look phase as next operation. A configuration C is said to be *stationary* if all robots are stationary in C. A configuration C is *initial* if it is stationary and all robots have distinct positions. Unlike the initial configuration, in general, not all robots are stationary in a non-initial configuration C', but at least one robot that takes the snapshot C' is stationary by definition. A configuration C is *final* if it is stationary and $R \equiv F$.

The EMBEDDED PATTERN FORMATION problem (shortly, EPF), asks to transform an initial configuration into a final one. An *algorithm* for EPF is a deterministic distributed algorithm able to bring the robots to a final configuration in a finite number of cycles from any given initial configuration I, regardless of the activation scheduling and delays (which are decided by the adversary). We say that an initial configuration I is *unsolvable* if there are no algorithms for EPF with respect to I.

Configuration view and symmetries. Given a configuration $C = (R, F)$, $cg(F)$ is the *center of gravity* of points in F, that is the point whose coordinates are the mean values of the coordinates of the points of the set. In [3], it has been defined a data structure called *view* and computable by each robot r for any point $p \in R \cup F$. Essentially, a robot r that needs to compute the view of a configuration C from a point p, first computes $cg(F)$ and then, starting from the half-line from p to $cg(F)$ and looking around from p (in clockwise and counter-clockwise manner), it determines the order in which all robots and fixed-points appear. For instance, in Fig. 1, the counter-clockwise sequence of points perceived by r from itself is $(r, f_1, r_1, r_2, f_2, r_3, f_3)$. Each point in such a sequence is then replaced by information referred to angles, distances, and type of points (i.e., robots, fixed-points). The result of this process computed by r is a pair of strings $\mathcal{V}_r^+(p)$ and $\mathcal{V}_r^-(p)$ representing the clockwise and counter-clockwise view of C from the point p. For instance, in Fig. 1, robot r gets $\mathcal{V}_r^-(r) = (0°, d(r, cg(F)), \mathbf{r}, \alpha_1, d(r, f_1),$ $\mathbf{f}, \alpha_2, d(r, r_1), \mathbf{r}, \alpha_2, d(r, r_2), \mathbf{r}, \alpha_3, d(r, f_2), \mathbf{f}, \alpha_4, (r, r_3), \mathbf{r}, \alpha_5, d(r, f_3), \mathbf{f})$. It is possible to define a lexicographic order that leads to define the view from p as $\mathcal{V}_r(p) = \min\{\mathcal{V}_r^+(p), \mathcal{V}_r^-(p)\}$, and then $\mathcal{V}_r(C) = \bigcup_{p \in R \cup F}\{\mathcal{V}_r(p)\}$. Notice that clockwise and counter-clockwise directions always refer to the local coordinate system of each robot. Moreover, even though robots do not share a common left-right orientation (chirality), by computing $\mathcal{V}_r(C)$, every robot r acquires the same information.

Every robot r can use $\mathcal{V}_r(C)$ not only to share a common view about C but also to determine whether a configuration is "symmetric" or not. A map $\varphi : \mathbb{R}^2 \to \mathbb{R}^2$ is called an *isometry* or distance preserving if for any $a, b \in \mathbb{R}^2$ one has $d(\varphi(a), \varphi(b)) = d(a, b)$. Examples of isometries in the plane are *rotations* and *reflections*. An *isometry of a configuration* $C = (R, F)$ is an isometry in the plane that maps robots to robots (i.e., points of R into R) and fixed-points to fixed-points (i.e., points of F into F). If C admits only

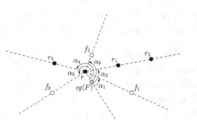

Fig. 1. A sequence of points and angles in C perceived by robot r.

the identity isometry, then C is said *asymmetric*, otherwise it is said *symmetric* (i.e., C admits rotations or reflections). If C is symmetric due to an isometry φ, a robot cannot distinguish its position at $r \in R$ from $r' = \varphi(r)$. In such a case we say that r and r' are *equivalent*. As a consequence, two equivalent robots can decide to move simultaneously, as any algorithm is unable to distinguish between them. In such a case, there might be a so called *pending move*, that is, without loss of generality r performs its entire Look-Compute-Move cycle while r' does not terminate the Move phase, i.e. its move is pending. Clearly, all the other robots performing their cycles are not aware whether there is a pending move, that is they cannot deduce the global status from their view. This fact greatly increases the difficulty to devise a distributed algorithm for symmetric configurations.

The following result from [3] states that each robot r can use the view $\mathcal{V}_r(C)$ to determine whether C is symmetric or not.

Lemma 1. *[3] Let $C = (R, F)$, $|F| > 1$, be a configuration without multiplicities and let $r \in R$ be a robot that has taken a snapshot of C during its last Look phase. Then, (1) C admits a reflection iff there exist two points $p, q \in R \cup F$, not necessarily distinct, such that $\mathcal{V}_r^+(p) = \mathcal{V}_r^-(q)$, and (2) C admits a rotation iff there exist two distinct points $p, q \in R \cup F$, such that $\mathcal{V}_r^+(p) = \mathcal{V}_r^+(q)$.*

From this result we get that, for an asymmetric configuration C, it is unique the point (robot or fixed-point) having the minimum view.

Unsolvable configurations. The following lemmata provide a characterization about configurations that cannot be solved in the EPF problem, even in the synchronous setting.

Lemma 2. *If $C = (R, F)$ is a configuration containing a multiplicity, then the EPF problem is unsolvable even though robots are synchronized and endowed with the multiplicity detection.*

In the following, we denote by $\mathcal{I}$ the set of all the initial configurations. Then a configuration $C = (R, F) \in \mathcal{I}$ implies that R is a set with distinct elements. We provide a sufficient condition for a configuration in $\mathcal{I}$ to be unsolvable: if this applies, then the EPF problem cannot be solved.

Lemma 3. *Let $C = (R, F) \in \mathcal{I}$. If C admits an axis of reflection ℓ such that $\ell \cap F \neq \emptyset$ and $\ell \cap R = \emptyset$, then C (and hence the EPF problem) is unsolvable even though robots are synchronized.*

Figure 2.*i* shows an unsolvable configuration. By Lemma 3, if the EPF problem can be solved in a configuration that admits an axis of reflection ℓ with fixed-points, then there must be robots on ℓ, see Fig. 2.*ii*.

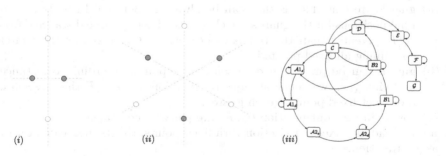

(i)   (ii)   (iii)

Fig. 2. (i): an unsolvable configuration for the EPF problem (cf. Lemma 3). White and black circles represent fixed-points and robots, respectively; dashed lines are axes of reflection. (ii): a solvable configuration where it is necessary to move robots out of the axes, otherwise, given the symmetry, a multiplicity might be created in $cg(F)$ (cf. Lemma 2). (iii) Transitions among phases (cf. Theorem 1).

3   The Algorithm for EPF

The general idea of our algorithm is based on the following observation. If the initial configuration $C = (R, F)$ is asymmetric, then we can solve EPF by proceeding in two phases.

In the first phase a unique robot is chosen and moved far from $cg(F)$ in such a way it always guarantees the configuration remains asymmetric, regardless of the movements of other robots. Once such a "guard" is positioned, the second phase can start. In the second phase still one unique robot per time is chosen. This is the one not on a point in F, closest to a non-occupied fixed-point, and of minimum view in case of ties. By Lemma 1, we are ensured that always one single robot will be selected since the configuration is asymmetric. The selected robot is then moved toward one of the closest fixed-point until it reaches such a point. In the following, we will refer to this approach as *distmin-approach*. This is iterated until only the guard has to move toward the unique empty fixed-point remained. By Lemma 2, all moves must be performed so as to avoid the occurrence of multiplicities. It follows that sometimes movements are not straightforward toward the target point but robots may deviate their trajectories.

Such an approach can be generalized in order to deal also with symmetric configurations. In particular, the strategy selects a set of (possibly) equivalent robots $G \subseteq R$ called *guards* and move them in specific positions so that (G, F) has no axis with fixed-points only. In this situation the EPF problem can be solved in the sub-configuration formed by the remaining robots, by means of the *distmin-approach*. In particular, to solve the EPF problem our algorithm performs five main steps:

1. select a set $G \subseteq R$ of pairwise equivalent robots in C among the furthest robots from $cg(F)$;
2. if required, move the selected robots, denoted as *guards*, such that:
   (a) guards are placed so as they can be always recognized. In particular, as final positions for the guards, we chose a sufficiently large distance d from $cg(F)$, greater than the radius of O_F, where O_F is the smallest circle containing all fixed-points in F;
   (b) guards can be pre-assigned to some fixed-points according to distances and view (i.e., we define an injective function $\mu : G \to F$ that associates a distinct fixed-point to each guard);
   (c) robots in the configuration (G, F) are pairwise equivalent.
3. if (G, F) admits axes of reflection with fixed-points, robots in G cannot serve as guards. Hence:
   (a) select a new set G' of guards among the robots belonging to the axes of reflection,[1] and pull them along the axes until reaching a certain distance $d' > d$ from $cg(F)$;

---

[1] The existence of such robots is guaranteed by the fact that the initial configuration was solvable, and hence by Lemma 3 there were no axes with only fixed-points. Moreover, the moves performed from the initial configuration until the current step guarantee to not create such kind of axes.

(b) break the reflection symmetry by rotating the robots in G' along the circle of radius d';
(c) define $G = G'$ and go back to Step 3.
4. partially solve the EPF problem by using (a variant of) the *distmin-approach*, but limited to the robots in $R \setminus G$ and the fixed-points in $F \setminus \mu(G)$.
5. finalize the pattern by moving each guard $r \in G$ toward its pre-assigned fixed-point $\mu(r)$.

One difficulty arising from the above strategy is that symmetric and asymmetric configurations cannot be managed really separately as it is likely to happen that a symmetric configuration becomes asymmetric after some moves. Moreover, from a symmetric configuration where some robots are equivalent, it is not always possible to break the symmetry due to the impossibility to select one single robot to move. To handle such situations we sometimes apply a sort of "simulation", to check whether the current configuration could have been obtained from a symmetric one. If yes, then moves to (re-)establish the symmetry are performed, otherwise the strategy for asymmetric configurations is applied. It follows that sometimes configurations that start as asymmetric are transformed into symmetric ones by our strategy. Also, it might happen that the set of guards selected in step 1 is bigger than the current set of robots furthest from $cg(F)$.

By Lemma 3, there are configurations in $\mathcal{I}$ (from now on denoted by $\mathcal{U}$) that are unsolvable. Hence, our algorithm solves the EPF problem when the input configuration belongs to $\mathcal{I} \setminus \mathcal{U}$. We construct our algorithm in such a way that the execution consists of a sequence of *phases* denoted by $\mathcal{A}1$, $\mathcal{A}2$, $\mathcal{B}1$, $\mathcal{B}2$, $\mathcal{C}$, $\mathcal{D}$, $\mathcal{E}$, and $\mathcal{F}$, see Table 3. To each phase, we assign an invariant such that every configuration satisfies exactly one of the invariants so that robots can correctly recognize the phase they have to perform. Moreover, each time robots switch to a different phase, the current configuration is stationary, that is each phase is initiated from a stationary configuration. This property is crucial to prove the correctness of our algorithm, as it implies specific configurations (a sort of check-points) that robots eventually reach without leaving pending moves. The possible transitions among phases are shown in Fig. 2.*iii*. Since we will show that each configuration satisfies exactly one of the invariants, then each phase has a natural association with a subset of $\mathcal{I} \setminus \mathcal{U}$. It follows that, if $\mathcal{G}$ denotes the set of all the final configurations for the EPF problem where no moves have to be performed, then $\{\mathcal{A}1, \mathcal{A}2, \mathcal{B}1, \mathcal{B}2, \mathcal{C}, \mathcal{D}, \mathcal{E}, \mathcal{F}, \mathcal{G}\}$ is a partition of $\mathcal{I} \setminus \mathcal{U}$.

Concerning the informal description of the algorithm provided above, the phases/subsets play the following roles: $\mathcal{C}$ performs Steps 1 and 2, $\mathcal{A}1$ and $\mathcal{A}2$ perform Step 3.(a), $\mathcal{B}1$ and $\mathcal{B}2$ perform Step 3.(b), $\mathcal{D}$ performs Step 4, and $\mathcal{E}$ and $\mathcal{F}$ perform Step 5.

3.1 Formal Details

To formally define our algorithm, let $C = (R, F)$ be a configuration, then:

- $Axes(C)$ is a set containing all the axes of reflection of C; for sake of simplicity, we write $Axes(F)$ instead of $Axes((\emptyset, F))$;
- $Axes^f(C) \subseteq Axes(C)$ contains only the axes with fixed-points, i.e. each $\ell \in Axes(C)$ such that $\ell \cap F \neq \emptyset$. Symmetrically, $Axes^{\neg f}(C) = Axes(C) \setminus Axes^f(C)$.
- $SemiAxes(C)$ contains the *semi-axes* of C, that is all the half-lines starting from $cg(F)$ and lying on an axis of $Axes(C)$;
- $SemiAxes^f(C) \subseteq SemiAxes(C)$ contains only the semi-axes lying on some element of $Axes^f(C)$; Symmetrically, $SemiAxes^{\neg f}(C) = SemiAxes(C) \setminus SemiAxes^f(C)$.
- $Rays(F)$ contains the half-lines starting from $cg(F)$ and passing through elements in $F \setminus cg(F)$;
- O_F is the smallest circle centered in $cg(F)$ enclosing all points of F (cf. Fig. 3.i);
- An *orbit* is a circle O_k centered at $cg(F)$ and with radius $k \cdot \rho_F / n$, $k \geq 1$ integer, where ρ_F is the radius of O_F (cf. Fig. 3.i). The radius of O_k is denoted by ρ_k.
- O_t is the smallest orbit enclosing all robots in R (cf. Fig. 3.ii);
- A_t is the annulus of $\mathcal{C}$, that is the area comprised between O_t and O_{t-1}, including O_{t-1} but excluding O_t;
- let $\alpha = \frac{2\pi}{2n^2}$ (cf. Fig. 3.iv) and $\ell \in SemiAxes(F)$: p_0^ℓ is the point at $\ell \cap O_t$, $P_{1/2}^\ell$ is the set containing the points p such that $\sphericalangle(p_0^\ell, cg(F), p) = \alpha/2$ (where $\sphericalangle(a, b, c)$ is the angle centered at point b and with sides $[a, b]$ and $[b, c]$), and P_1^ℓ is the set containing the points p such that $\sphericalangle(p_0^\ell, cg(F), p) = \alpha$;
- $Rob(\cdot)$ is a function that takes a region of the plane (e.g., annulus, orbit, axis, ray, ...) as input and returns the set of robots lying in the given region;
- R_t denotes the set containing all robots on O_t, i.e. $R_t = Rob(O_t)$ (e.g., in Fig. 3.ii there are four robots in R_t);
- R_t^f denotes the set containing all robots both on O_t and on some element of $Axes^f(F)$, i.e. $R_t^f = Rob(O_t \cap Axes^f(F))$;
- $R_t^{\neg f}$ denotes the set containing all robots on O_t but those in R_t^f, i.e. $R_t^{\neg f} = R_t \setminus R_t^f$ (e.g., in Fig. 3.iii there are two robots in R_t^f and four in $R_t^{\neg f}$);
- $\mu : R_t \to F$, defined when each robot in R_t is not on an axis of $Axes^{\neg f}(F)$. Function $\mu(r)$ returns the fixed-point furthest from $cg(F)$ on the half-line in $Rays(F)$ closest to r. In case of ties, that is there are two candidate fixed-points f_1 and f_2, if (R_t, F) is asymmetric, then $\mu(r)$ selects among f_1 and f_2 the point with minimum view in (R_t, F); if (R_t, F) is symmetric then, as it will better specified later, necessarily (R_t, F) admits a rotation and hence $\mu(r)$ selects the first point among f_1 and f_2 met in the direction induced by the minimum view in (R_t, F) (cf. Lemma 1).

The phases required by our algorithm are defined in Table 3 according to the invariants specified in Tables 1 and 2. In particular, Table 3 shows that the algorithm essentially consists of a single move associated to each phase (i.e., robots that detect the membership of the current configuration to a phase, simply perform the move associated to the detected phase). Details about moves are

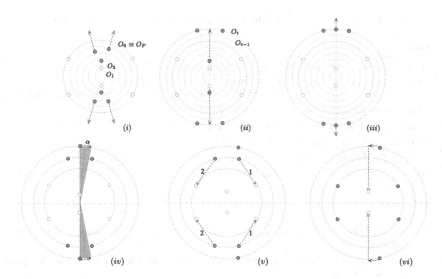

Fig. 3. Configurations in phase $\mathcal{C}$ (i), $\mathcal{A}1_s$ and $\mathcal{A}1_d$ (ii), $\mathcal{A}2_s$ and $\mathcal{A}2_d$ (iii), $\mathcal{B}1$ and $\mathcal{B}2$ (iv), $\mathcal{D}$ (v), $\mathcal{E}$ and $\mathcal{F}$ (vi). In (v), the numbers close to movement directions represent the order in which the moves are performed.

given in Table 4. It is worth to remark that each phase is started from a stationary configuration. All the moves described in Table 4 are simple, except for m_3 and m_6 that require the sub-procedures SIMULATE and DISTMIN, respectively. Here we just provide an intuition of their roles, while the pseudo-codes and the correctness proofs are omitted.

When the algorithm deals with symmetric configurations, move m_3 could be performed at the same time by a set of equivalent robots. In particular, move m_3 is responsible of setting the guards at a sufficiently large distance from $cg(F)$, Steps 1 and 2 of the above informal description. Since the adversary may stop some of the guards at different distances from the target, then Procedure SIMULATE is used to identify all the robots that have to complete their movements. This is the case where asymmetric configurations may become symmetric as the simulation performed by SIMULATE outputs a set of equivalent robots.

Once guards have been suitably positioned, that is, the movements of the other robots cannot generate unsolvable configurations, DISTMIN is invoked. This procedure moves all robots but the guards toward suitable fixed-points, Step 4 of the above informal description. Once all robots but the guards have reached their final destinations, guards are all equivalent, and they are all matched with different fixed-points not yet occupied by robots.

The possible transitions among phases are shown in Fig. 2.*iii*.

Theorem 1. *If the algorithm described in Table 3 processes an initial configuration $C \in \mathcal{I} \setminus \mathcal{U}$, then it leads to a final configuration in $\mathcal{G}$, eventually.*

Table 1. Basic Boolean variables used to define the phases' invariants.

Var	Definition
a_0	(1) $\rho_{t-1} > \rho_F$ and SIMULATE$(C) = \emptyset$ and (2) $Rob(A_t) = \emptyset$
a_1	let $C' = (R_t^{-f}, F)$; (1) $\rho_{t-1} > \rho_F \wedge$ SIMULATE$(C) = \emptyset$, and (2) $Rob(A_t \setminus Axes^f(C')) = \emptyset \wedge \forall \ell \in SemiAxes^f(C') : |Rob(\ell) \cap Rob(A_t \cup O_t)| \le 1$
b	all robots in R_t are on some element of $Axes(F)$
c_0	$C' = (R_t^{-f}, F)$ has axes with fixed-points, i.e. $\exists\, \ell \in Axes(C')$ s. t. $\ell \cap F \ne \emptyset$
c_1	let $C' = (R_t^{-f}, F)$; $\forall\, \ell \in Axes(C')$ s. t. $\ell \cap F \ne \emptyset$, $\ell \cap R \ne \emptyset$
c_2	let $C' = (R_t^{-f}, F)$; $\forall\, \ell \in SemiAxes^f(C')$, if $\ell \cap R \ne \emptyset$ then $\ell \cap R_t \ne \emptyset$
e_0	in $C = (R, F)$ all robots in R_t are equivalent, i.e. $\forall\, r, r' \in R_t, \exists\, \varphi$ isometry of C s. t. $\varphi(r) = r'$
e_1	in $C' = (R_t, F)$ all robots are equivalent, i.e. $\forall\, r, r' \in R_t, \exists\, \varphi$ isometry of C' s. t. $\varphi(r) = r'$
e_2	in $C' = (R_t^{-f}, F)$ all robots are equivalent, i.e. $\forall\, r, r' \in R_t^{-f}, \exists\, \varphi$ isometry of C' s. t. $\varphi(r) = r'$
f	on each $\ell \in Rays(F)$ there exists at most one fixed-point f s. t. $f \notin R$; if such a point f exists on ℓ, then: (1) $d(cg(F), f) > d(cg(F), f')$ for each $f' \in (F \setminus \{f\}) \cap \ell$, and (2) there exists $r \in (R \setminus F) \cap \ell$ s. t. there are neither robots nor fixed-points between f and r
i_1	(1) $\exists r \in R_t$ s. t. $r \notin \bigcup_\ell P_{1/2}^\ell$, and (2) $\forall\, r \in R_t, \exists P_{1/2}^\ell = \{p, q\}$ s. t. r lies on the the smallest arc $[p, q]$ of O_t
i_2	(1) $\exists r \in R_t$ s. t. $r \notin \bigcup_\ell P_1^\ell$, and (2) $\forall\, r \in R_t, \exists P_1^\ell = \{p, q\}$ s. t. r lies on the smallest arc $[p, q]$ of O_t
i_3	$\forall r \in R_t, r \in \bigcup_\ell P_1^\ell$
m_0	(1) $\mu : R_t \to F$ is injective and $\mu(R_t) \cap R = \emptyset$, and (2) $R \setminus R_t \subseteq F$
p	$\forall r_1, r_2 \in R_t^{-f}$, let ℓ_1, ℓ_2 be the half-lines s. t. $\mu(r_1) \in \ell_1$ and $\mu(r_2) \in \ell_2$, and let p_1, p_2 be the points in $P_1^{\ell_1}$ and $P_1^{\ell_2}$ closest to r_1, r_2, respectively. Then in $(\{p1, p2\}, F)$, predicate $\neg c_0$ holds
s_0	let $\lambda : R_t \to \bigcup_{\ell \in SemiAxes(F)} \{p_0^\ell\}$ s. t. $\lambda(r)$ is the point closest to r: (1) $C^* = (R \setminus R_t \cup \lambda(R_t), F) \in \mathcal{I} \setminus \mathcal{U}$, and (2) in C^* the predicate $a_0 \wedge b \wedge e_1$ is true
s_1	let $\lambda : R_t \to \bigcup_{\ell \in Rays(F)} \{p_0^\ell\}$ s. t. $\lambda(r)$ is the point closest to r: (1) $C^* = ((R \setminus R_t) \cup \lambda(R_t), F)$ does not contain any multiplicity, and (2) in C^* the predicate f is true
w	$R = F$: EPF solved, see phase $\mathcal{G}$

3.2 Extended Example

In order to better describe the used predicates and the defined phases, we now provide an extended example. Figure 3.i shows a configuration belonging to phase $\mathcal{C}$. This is inferred by the fact that the configuration is asymmetric and hence is not in $\mathcal{U}$; predicates a_0 and a_1 are false since $\rho_{t-1} < \rho_F$, and hence C is not in $\mathcal{A}1_s, \mathcal{A}1_d, \mathcal{A}2_s, \mathcal{B}1, \mathcal{B}2, \mathcal{D}, \mathcal{E}$; predicate b is false, and hence $C \notin \mathcal{A}2_d$; predicate f is false, and hence $C \notin \mathcal{F}$.

Table 2. Composed Boolean variables used to define the phases' invariants.

Var	Definition	Comment
r_0	$(i_1 \lor i_2) \land s_0$	Necessary conditions for rotating possible guards
r_1	$a_0 \land i_1 \land s_0$	Rotation of guards toward $\alpha/2$, see phase $B1$
r_2	$a_0 \land i_2 \land s_0$	Rotation of guards toward α, see phase $B2$
r_3	$a_0 \land i_3 \land s_0$	Rotation of guards completed, see phase D
g_0	$c_0 \land c_1 \land e_2 \land \neg r_0$	Possible guards pulling along axes, see phases $A1$ and $A2$
g_1	$a_0 \land b \land e_1$	Possible guards are on axes ready to rotate, see phase $B1$
g_2	$a_0 \land \neg b \land \neg c_0 \land e_1$	Possible guards are positioned, see phase D
m_1	$\neg c_0 \land m_0$	Distmin-approach completed, see phase E

Table 3. Algorithm for EPF. The first column specifies a different phase to which a configuration belongs to. Then, for each phase, in the upper (shaded) side it is specified the invariant that the configuration satisfies at the beginning of the phase (start), once some robots have started moving (during), and at the end of the phase (end). In the lower side, it is specified the corresponding move performed by the algorithm, and on the last column the possible phases that can be reached.

phase	start	during	end
$A1$	$a_0 \land \neg b \land \neg c_2 \land e_1 \land g_0$	$\neg a_0 \land a_1 \land \neg b \land \neg c_2 \land g_0$	$a_0 \land \neg b \land c_2 \land \neg e_1 \land g_0$
		m_1	$A2_s$
$A2$	$a_0 \land \neg b \land c_2 \land \neg e_1 \land g_0$	$\neg a_1 \land b \land \neg f$	$\neg f \land g_1$
	m_2	m_3	$B1$
$B1$		$\neg m_1 \land r_1$	$\neg m_1 \land r_2$
		m_4	$B2$
$B2$		$\neg m_1 \land r_2$	$\neg m_1 \land r_3$
		m_5	$A1_s, C, D$
C		remaining conf's	$(a_0 \lor \neg b) \land a_1 \land e_0 \land \neg f$
		m_3	$A1_s, A1_d, B1, B2, D, E$
D		$g_2 \land \neg m_1 \land \neg r_0$	$g_2 \land m_1 \land s_1$
		m_6	E
E		$a_0 \land \neg b \land m_1 \land p \land s_1$	f
		m_7	F
F		f	w
		m_8	G

According to our algorithm, move m_3 is applied, that is procedure SIMULATE is invoked. It outputs four robots to move. In fact, it considers the more external robots contained in between the current O_{t-1} and O_t, and looks for a potential symmetric configuration from which C could have been obtained if a subset or all the considered robots are moved radially further from $cg(F)$.

Move m_3 allows the four robots to reach the current O_t and from there they are moved toward O_{t+1}. This is repeated until they all occupy O_t and $\mathbf{a_0}$ holds, that is, the annulus between O_t and O_{t-1} does not contain robots and $\rho_{t-1} > \rho_F$. The reached configuration shown in Fig. 3.ii is stationary and belongs to $\mathcal{A}1$, since it is symmetric and there are fixed-points on axes.

Move m_1 is then applied which pulls guards along axes. It means that the robots currently on O_t cannot serve as guards, since $(R \cap O_t, F)$ induces axes with fixed-points, and we have already observed from Fig. 2.ii why this should be avoided. The two robots on the axis are first moved toward O_t. As long as they both do not reach O_t, the configuration belongs to $\mathcal{A}1_s$ or $\mathcal{A}1_d$, but in either case m_1 is applied. Once all robots reach O_t, the configuration is stationary and belongs to $\mathcal{A}2_s$, see Fig. 3.iii. Move m_2 is then applied. It involves all equivalent robots from the axis of symmetry and residing on O_t, of minimum view.

In our example the two robots on the axis are equivalent and they both move toward O_{t+1}. As soon as one robot moves, the configuration belongs to $\mathcal{A}2_d$, from where move m_3 is applied. In this switch from $\mathcal{A}2_s$ to $\mathcal{A}2_d$, the configuration is not stationary (and in fact the phase has not changed) but m_3 guarantees to move the same set of robots allowed to move by m_2 toward the same targets. Similarly as before, the two robots are moved until $\mathbf{a_0}$ holds again.

The reached configuration depicted in Fig. 3.iv is stationary and belongs to $\mathcal{B}1$, and the candidate guards (the two robots on O_t) are rotated along O_t of an angle $\alpha = \frac{2\pi}{2n^2}$ according to arbitrary directions. The value of α is chosen so that the final point of each moving robot assures that, in case such robots will be the final guards, the function $\mu : G \to F$ that associates each guard to its closer fixed-point is injective. The rotation is made in two steps: first the robots rotate of $\alpha/2$ (reaching a stationary configuration in $\mathcal{B}2$) and then they start again to complete the rotation. This is done for ensuring that all the rotating robots leave the axes before starting the next step.

Once guards are positioned, see Fig. 3.v, the configuration is stationary and belongs to $\mathcal{D}$. Here guards ensure that any movement of all other robots cannot induce axes of symmetry with fixed-points, that is unsolvable configurations cannot be generated. Now, the distmin-approach is applied, that is guards are associated to the closest fixed-points according to function μ, and all other robots are moved according to the minimal view toward the closest (and not occupied) fixed-points excluding those associated to the guards. After, a stationary configuration in phase $\mathcal{E}$ is reached, see Fig. 3.vi. From here, guards are moved toward the associated fixed-points. Again the movement is done in two steps in order to distinguish it from that of phases $\mathcal{B}1$ and $\mathcal{B}2$. First each guard rotates toward the closest axis of F with the associated fixed-point, and a stationary configuration

Table 4. Description of the moves performed by the algorithm.

Move name	Move
m_1	Let $C' = (R_t^{\neg f}, F)$, and $\ell \in SemiAxes^f(C')$. The robot on ℓ (if any) furthest from $cg(F)$ moves toward the point at $\ell \cap O_t$
m_2	Each robot with minimum view in R_t^f moves toward the point at $\ell \cap O_{t+1}$, where ℓ is the axis where the robot lies
m_3	If SIMULATE$(C) = \emptyset$, then each robot with minimum view in R_t moves radially toward O_{t+1}, else each robot in SIMULATE(C) moves radially toward O_t
m_4	Each robot in R_t rotates along O_t toward a closest point in $\bigcup_{\ell \in SemiAxes(F)} P_{1/2}^\ell$
m_5	Each robot in R_t rotates along O_t toward a closest point in $\bigcup_{\ell \in SemiAxes(F)} P_1^\ell$
m_6	Each robot in $R \setminus R_t$ executes Procedure DISTMIN
m_7	Each robot in R_t rotates along O_t toward the closest half-line in $Rays(F)$
m_8	Each robot not on a fixed-point moves along the half-line in $Rays(F)$ where it resides toward the closest fixed-point not occupied by a robot

belonging to $\mathcal{F}$ is reached. Then, they move along the axes toward the assigned fixed-points hence obtaining the required pattern, that is phase $\mathcal{G}$.

4   Conclusion

Starting from [12], we have studied a new branch of investigation about the so-called Embedded Pattern Formation problem. Anonymous and oblivious robots moving in the plane operate in the Look-Compute-Move model without any orientation capability nor randomness feature. Starting from different locations, robots must form the pattern provided by fixed-points in the plane. We design a new deterministic distributed algorithm that solves the EPF problem for all initial configurations but those proved to be unsolvable. The used techniques, as well as the methodology, applied to formalize our algorithm might open intriguing directions for further research. For instance, can our algorithm be exploited to solve the Pattern Formation problem without chirality in a similar way the one proposed in [10] has been used in [12]?

References

1. Bramas, Q., Tixeuil, S., Announcement, B.: Probabilistic asynchronous arbitrary pattern formation. In: Proceedings of the 35th ACM Symposium on Principles of Distributed Computing (PODC) (2016)

2. Chaudhuri, S.G., Ghike, S., Jain, S., Mukhopadhyaya, K.: Pattern formation for asynchronous robots without agreement in chirality. CoRR, abs/1403.2625 (2014)
3. Cicerone, S., Di Stefano, G., Navarra, A.: Minimum-traveled-distance gathering of oblivious robots over given meeting points. In: Gao, J., Efrat, A., Fekete, S.P., Zhang, Y. (eds.) ALGOSENSORS 2014. LNCS, vol. 8847, pp. 57–72. Springer, Heidelberg (2015)
4. Cieliebak, M., Flocchini, P., Prencipe, G., Santoro, N.: Distributed computing by mobile robots: gathering. SIAM J. Comput. 41(4), 829–879 (2012)
5. Courtieu, P., Rieg, L., Tixeuil, S., Urbain, X.: Impossibility of gathering, a certification. Inf. Process. Lett. 115(3), 447–452 (2015)
6. Courtieu, P., Rieg, L., Tixeuil, S., Urbain, X., Announcement, B.: Certified universal gathering in R^2 for oblivious mobile robots. In: Proceedings of the 35th ACM Symposium on Principles of Distributed Computing (PODC) (2016)
7. Das, S., Flocchini, P., Santoro, N., Yamashita, M.: Forming sequences of geometric patterns with oblivious mobile robots. Dist. Comp. 28(2), 131–145 (2015)
8. Flocchini, P., Prencipe, G., Santoro, N., Viglietta, G.: Distributed computing by mobile robots: solving the uniform circle formation problem. In: Aguilera, M.K., Querzoni, L., Shapiro, M. (eds.) OPODIS 2014. LNCS, vol. 8878, pp. 217–232. Springer, Heidelberg (2014)
9. Flocchini, P., Prencipe, G., Santoro, N., Widmayer, P.: Arbitrary pattern formation by asynchronous, anonymous, oblivious robots. Theoret. Comput. Sci. 407(1–3), 412–447 (2008)
10. Fujinaga, N., Ono, H., Kijima, S., Yamashita, M.: Pattern formation through optimum matching by oblivious CORDA robots. In: Lu, C., Masuzawa, T., Mosbah, M. (eds.) OPODIS 2010. LNCS, vol. 6490, pp. 1–15. Springer, Heidelberg (2010)
11. Fujinaga, N., Yamauchi, Y., Kijima, S., Yamashita, M.: Asynchronous pattern formation by anonymous oblivious mobile robots. In: Aguilera, M.K. (ed.) DISC 2012. LNCS, vol. 7611, pp. 312–325. Springer, Heidelberg (2012)
12. Fujinaga, N., Yamauchi, Y., Ono, H., Kijima, S., Yamashita, M.: Pattern formation by oblivious asynchronous mobile robots. SIAM J. Comput. 44(3), 740–785 (2015)
13. Ghike, S., Mukhopadhyaya, K.: A distributed algorithm for pattern formation by autonomous robots, with no agreement on coordinate compass. In: Janowski, T., Mohanty, H. (eds.) ICDCIT 2010. LNCS, vol. 5966, pp. 157–169. Springer, Heidelberg (2010)
14. Millet, L., Potop-Butucaru, M., Sznajder, N., Tixeuil, S.: On the synthesis of mobile robots algorithms: the case of ring gathering. In: Felber, P., Garg, V. (eds.) SSS 2014. LNCS, vol. 8756, pp. 237–251. Springer, Heidelberg (2014)
15. Yamauchi, Y., Uehara, T., Kijima, S., Yamashita, M.: Plane formation by synchronous mobile robots in the three dimensional euclidean space. In: Moses, Y., et al. (eds.) DISC 2015. LNCS, vol. 9363, pp. 92–106. Springer, Heidelberg (2015). doi:10.1007/978-3-662-48653-5_7
16. Yamauchi, Y., Yamashita, M.: Randomized pattern formation algorithm for asynchronous oblivious mobile robots. In: Kuhn, F. (ed.) DISC 2014. LNCS, vol. 8784, pp. 137–151. Springer, Heidelberg (2014)

Polynomial Lower Bound for Distributed Graph Coloring in a Weak LOCAL Model

Dan Hefetz[1,2], Fabian Kuhn[3], Yannic Maus[3(✉)], and Angelika Steger[4]

[1] Hebrew University, Jerusalem, Israel
danny.hefetz@gmail.com
[2] Tel Aviv University, Tel Aviv, Israel
[3] University of Freiburg, Freiburg im Breisgau, Germany
{kuhn,yannic.maus}@cs.uni-freiburg.de
[4] ETH Zurich, Zürich, Switzerland
steger@inf.ethz.ch

Abstract. We show an $\Omega\left(\Delta^{\frac{1}{3}-\frac{\eta}{3}}\right)$ lower bound on the runtime of any deterministic distributed $\mathcal{O}(\Delta^{1+\eta})$-graph coloring algorithm in a weak variant of the LOCAL model.

In particular, given a network graph $G = (V, E)$, in the weak LOCAL model nodes communicate in synchronous rounds and they can use unbounded local computation. The nodes have no identifiers, but instead, the computation starts with an initial valid vertex coloring. A node can **broadcast** a **single** message of **unbounded** size to its neighbors and receives the **set of messages** sent to it by its neighbors.

The proof uses neighborhood graphs and improves their understanding in general such that it might help towards finding a lower (runtime) bound for distributed graph coloring in the standard LOCAL model.

Keywords: Lower bound · Distributed graph coloring · Color reduction · Neighborhood graphs · LOCAL model · Distributed symmetry breaking

1 Introduction

In the distributed message passing model, an n-node communication network is represented as a graph $G = (V, E)$. Each node hosts a processor and processors communicate through the edges of G. In the standard LOCAL model, time is divided into synchronous rounds and in each round, simultaneously, each node $v \in V$ performs an unbounded amount of local computations, sends a single message of unbounded size to each of its neighbors and receives the messages sent to it by its neighbors. The time complexity of an algorithm is measured by the total number of rounds.

A full version of this paper with all proofs is avalaible on arXiv.org [1].

F. Kuhn and Y. Maus—Supported by ERC Grant No. 336495 (ACDC).

C. Gavoille and D. Ilcinkas (Eds.): DISC 2016, LNCS 9888, pp. 99–113, 2016.
DOI: 10.1007/978-3-662-53426-7_8

This paper deals with lower bounds on the time complexity of distributed graph coloring algorithms. A c-(vertex)-coloring of a graph $G = (V, E)$ is a function $\varphi : V \to \{1, \ldots, c\}$ such that $\varphi(u) \neq \varphi(v)$ for all $\{u, v\} \in E$. Coloring a graph with the minimum number of colors is one of Karp's 21 NP-complete problems [2] and the problem is even hard to approximate within a factor $n^{1-\varepsilon}$ for any constant $\varepsilon > 0$ [3]. A simple centralized greedy coloring algorithm which sequentially colors the nodes with the smallest available color guarantees a coloring with at most $\Delta + 1$ colors, where Δ denotes the maximum degree of the graph. In the distributed setting, one is usually interested in competing with this greedy algorithm and to therefore find a coloring with $\Delta + 1$ or more colors [4].

In this paper we consider deterministic *color reduction algorithms*, where before the start of the algorithm the graph is equipped with an m-coloring (usually $m \gg \Delta$). Apart from their initial color, nodes are indistinguishable and therefore, in particular, nodes do not have unique IDs. However, unique IDs in the range $\{1, \ldots, N\}$ for some $N \geq n$ are a special instance of the problem because they form an N-coloring. All recent deterministic coloring algorithms (e.g., [4–6]) begin with the seminal $\mathcal{O}(\log^* n)$-round algorithm by Linial which computes an $\mathcal{O}(\Delta^2)$-coloring [7].[1] Afterwards none of the algorithms make use of the unique IDs again and even Linial's algorithm does not require unique IDs but only an initial coloring of the nodes, i.e., the algorithms fit in the framework of color reduction algorithms. A lower bound for color reduction algorithms is thus almost as relevant as a lower bound for unique IDs.

More specifically, we consider color reduction algorithms in a weak variant of the standard **LOCAL** model, which we name the **SET-LOCAL** model. In each round, each node can send an arbitrarily large message to its neighbors. However, instead of receiving one message from each neighbor, each node only receives the set of messages sent to it by its neighbors. That is, if two or more neighbors send the same message to a node u, u only receives this message once.[2] When assuming unique IDs, there is no difference in power between the **SET-LOCAL** model and the standard **LOCAL** model. Every node can just add its ID to all its messages and each node can then always easily distinguish between the messages sent to it by different neighbors. However, when considering color reduction algorithms, neighbors with the same inital color might send the same message even when including their color or any other local knowledge in their messages.

Contributions: As our main result, we prove the following polynomial (in the maximum degree Δ) lower bound on the time required by color reduction algorithms in the **SET-LOCAL** model (for a formal definition of color reduction and of the **SET-LOCAL** model, see Sect. 2).

Theorem 1 (Color Reduction Lower Bound). *Let $0 \leq \eta < 1$ and $C > 0$ be two constants and assume that $m \geq 2C\Delta^{1+\eta}$. Any deterministic color reduction algorithm which, given an initial m-coloring, computes a coloring with at most*

---

[1] The function $\log^* x$ denotes the number of iterated logarithms needed to obtain a value at most 1, that is, $\forall x \leq 1 : \log^* x = 0$, $\forall x > 1 : \log^* x = 1 + \log^* \log x$.

[2] A similar model, but for completely anonymous graphs, has been studied in [8].

$C\Delta^{1+\eta}$ colors in graphs with maximum degree at most Δ in the SET-LOCAL model requires $\Omega(\Delta^{\frac{1-\eta}{3}})$ rounds.
Thus, in particular, any color reduction algorithm for computing a $(\Delta + 1)$-coloring needs at least $\Omega(\Delta^{\frac{1}{3}})$ rounds.

Note that the theorem in particular implies that the time required for computing a $\Delta^{2-\varepsilon}$-coloring for any constant $\varepsilon > 0$ is at least polynomial in Δ when using color reduction algorithms in the SET-LOCAL model. In a d-defective coloring each color class induces a graph with maximum degree d. A modification of our proofs yield that any one round d-defective color reduction algorithm in the standard LOCAL model needs $\Omega(\Delta^2/(d+1)^2)$ colors if $m \geq 2\Delta^2$. In order to establish that there are non-trivial color reduction algorithms in the SET-LOCAL model, we show that an existing distributed coloring algorithm from [9] works in this setting. For space reasons, the discussion of the lower bound for d-defective coloring and the following theorem appears in [1].

Theorem 2 (Color Reduction Upper Bound). *In graphs with maximum degree at most Δ and an initial m-coloring, there is a deterministic distributed color reduction algorithm in the SET-LOCAL model which computes a $(\Delta + 1)$-coloring in $\mathcal{O}(\Delta \log \Delta + \log^* m)$ rounds.*

Related Work: Distributed coloring has been identified as one of the prototypical problems to understand the problem of breaking symmetries in distributed and parallel systems. In the following, we discuss the work which is most relevant in the context of this paper. For a more general overview of the research on distribted coloring, we refer to the monograph of Barenboim and Elkin [4].

In a classic paper, Cole and Vishkin showed that a ring network can be 3-colored in $\mathcal{O}(\log^* N)$ synchronous rounds, where N is the size of the space of possible node IDs [10]. Most relevant in the context of this work is the seminal paper by Linial [7], where he in particular shows that the $\mathcal{O}(\log^* N)$ algorithm of [10] is asymptotically optimal and that in $\mathcal{O}(\log^* N)$ rounds, it is possible to color arbitrary graphs with $\mathcal{O}(\Delta^2)$ colors. All the above algorithms are deterministic and at the core, they are all based on iterative color reduction schemes where a given valid vertex coloring is improved in a round-by-round manner. A different approach is taken in [11,12], where it is shown how to compute a $(\Delta+1)$-coloring in $2^{\mathcal{O}(\sqrt{\log n})}$ rounds (n is the number of nodes) based on first computing a decomposition of the network into clusters of small diameter. When measuring the time as a function of n, this is still the best known deterministic distributed $(\Delta + 1)$-coloring algorithm for general graphs.

There has been significant recent progress on developing faster deterministic distributed coloring algorithms, particularly for graphs with moderately small maximum degree Δ. In [9], it was shown that combined with a simple iterative color reduction scheme, the algorithm of [7] can be turned into a $\mathcal{O}(\Delta \log \Delta + \log^* N)$-time $(\Delta+1)$-coloring algorithm. By decomposing a graph into subgraphs with small maximum degree, an improved time complexity of $\mathcal{O}(\Delta + \log^* N)$ was achieved in [13]. The basic ideas of [13] were extended and generalized in [14], where in particular it was shown that an $\mathcal{O}(\Delta^{1+o(1)})$-coloring can be computed in time $\mathcal{O}(\Delta^{o(1)}+\log^* N)$. The time complexity for $(\Delta+1)$-colorings was recently improved in [5,6], where upper bounds of $\widetilde{\mathcal{O}}(\Delta^{3/4})+\log^* N$ and $\widetilde{\mathcal{O}}(\sqrt{\Delta})+\log^* N$ rounds were shown. Both algorithm also work for the more general list coloring problem.[3]

While the best deterministic algorithms for distributed $(\Delta+1)$-coloring have time complexities which are polynomial in Δ or exponential in $\sqrt{\log n}$, much faster randomized algorithms are known. Based on the distributed maximal independent set algorithm of [15,16] and a reduction described in [7], by using randomizatiion, a $(\Delta+1)$-coloring can be computed in $\mathcal{O}(\log n)$ rounds. This has recently been improved in [17], where it was shown that a $(\Delta+1)$-coloring can be computed in time $\mathcal{O}(\log \Delta) + 2^{\mathcal{O}(\sqrt{\log\log n})}$ and in [18], where the current best time bound of $\mathcal{O}(\sqrt{\log \Delta}) + 2^{\mathcal{O}(\sqrt{\log\log n})}$ was proven. Closing or understanding the gap between the distributed complexities of randomized and deterministic algorithms for $(\Delta+1)$-coloring and other basic symmetry breaking tasks is one of the main open problems in the area of distributed graph algorithms. Even though we are dealing with a weaker, non-standard communication model, we hope that the present paper contributes in this direction. Note that for Δ-coloring trees with max. degree at most Δ, an exponential separation between randomized and deterministic algorithms has been shown in [19].

Although there has been steady progress on developing upper bounds for distributed coloring, much less is known about lower bounds. While by now there exist many distributed time lower bounds for related graph problems in the LOCAL model (e.g., [20–24]), the $\Omega(\log^* n)$ lower bound for coloring rings with $\mathcal{O}(1)$ colors by Linial [7] is still the only time lower bound for the standard distributed coloring problem. Linial's lower bound is based on the fundamental insight that for a given $r \geq 1$, the minimum number of colors which any r-round coloring algorithm needs to use can be expressed as the chromatic number of a graph Linial names the *neighborhood graph*. Linial then shows that the chromatic number of the r-round neighborhood graph for n-node rings is $\Omega(\log^{(2r)} n)$, where $\log^k x$ is the k-times iterated log-function. For a more detailed discussion of how to use neighborhood graphs for proving distributed coloring lower bounds, we refer to Sect. 3. Using neighborhood graphs, a combination of techniques of [7,25] also shows that coloring d-regular trees with less than $o(\log d/\log\log d)$ colors requires $\Omega(\log d/\log\log d)$ rounds; [26] uses this result to show that $\mathcal{O}(a)$-coloring graphs with arboricity a takes $\Omega(\log(n)/\log(a))$ rounds. Further, in [9,27], neighborhood graphs were used to show that in a single round, when starting with an m-coloring with m sufficiently large, in graphs with maximum degree at most Δ, the number of colors cannot be reduced to fewer than $\Omega(\Delta^2)$ colors. Similar, slightly weaker results were before already proven in [28]. In [20], it has been shown that coloring d-regular graphs with d colors requires at least $\Omega(\log\log n)$ rounds. In addition, in [29], it was shown that $\Omega(\log n/\log\log n)$ rounds are needed to compute a $(\Delta + 1)$-coloring where in the end, each node has the smallest possible color which is consistent with the colors chosen by its neighbors.

---

[3] The algorithm of [6] works for the even more general conflict coloring problem and $\widetilde{\mathcal{O}}$ ignores polylog factors in $\log \Delta$.

2   Model and Problem Statement

Mathematical Notation: For a graph $G = (V, E)$ and a node $v \in V$, $\Gamma_G(v)$ denotes the set of neighbors of v in G. Sometimes we write $\Gamma(v)$ if the graph G is clear from the context. Given a graph G, we use $\Delta(G)$ to denote the maximum degree of G and $\chi(G)$ to denote the chromatic number of G (i.e., the number of colors of a minimum valid vertex coloring). We sometimes abuse notation and identify a set of nodes S of G with the subgraph induced by S. For example, we might write $S \subseteq G$, where S denotes a subset of the nodes of G and also the subgraph induced by S. By $[m]$ we denote the set of integers $\{1, \ldots, m\}$.

The Color Reduction Problem: In the distributed color reduction problem, we are given a network graph $G = (V, E)$ of max. degree at most Δ. Each node $v \in V$ is equipped with an initial color $\varphi(v) \in [m]$ such that the coloring φ provides a valid vertex coloring of G. At the start, nodes can only be distinguished by their initial color and thus at the beginning, except for the value of their initial color, all nodes start in the same state. The goal of a color reduction algorithm is to compute a new color $\varphi'(v)$ for each $v \in V$ such that the coloring φ' also provides a valid vertex coloring of G, but such that the colors $\varphi'(v)$ are from a much smaller range. We say that a color reduction algorithm computes a c-coloring of G if $\varphi'(v) \in [c]$ for all $v \in V$.

Communication Model: We work with an adapted version of the LOCAL model [7,30], which we call the SET-LOCAL model. A communication network is modeled as an n-node graph $G = (V, E)$, where the nodes of G can use unbounded local computation and communicate through the edges of G in synchronized rounds. In each round, a node can **broadcast** a **single** message of **unbounded** size to its neighbors and each node receives the **set of messages** sent to it by its neighbors. That is, if two or more neighbors of a node $v \in V$ send the same message to v, v will receive the message only a single time. Thus, without any further knowledge, v cannot know whether a message was sent by only one or more than one neighbor. Note that a node which broadcasts a single message of arbitrary size can send different messages to different neighbors by indicating which part of the message is for which neighbor. However, to do so it is necessary that the node can already distinguish its neighbors by some property, e.g., by the use of (different) messages received from them previously. In [8], different weak variants of the LOCAL model were studied for problems where the network nodes are completely anonymous without any initial labeling. The SET-LOCAL model corresponds to the SB model in the hierarchy of models discussed in [8].

When running a distributed color reduction algorithm in the SET-LOCAL model, we assume that all nodes are aware of the parameters m and Δ and of the number of nodes n of G. Note that since our main focus is proving a lower bound, this assumption only makes the results stronger.

The Role of Randomness: Generally, there is a large gap between the best known randomized and deterministic distributed coloring algorithms and understanding whether this large gap is inherent or to what extent it can be closed is one of the major open problems in the area of distributed graph algorithms. When considering color reduction algorithms as introduced above, randomness can only help if either an upper bound on n is known or if the running time can depend on n. To see this, assume that we have a randomized color reduction algorithm which computes a $c(m, \Delta)$-coloring in $T(m, \Delta)$ rounds. To have an algorithm which cannot be derandomized trivially, the algorithm must either fail to terminate in $T(m, \Delta)$ rounds with positive probability $\varepsilon > 0$ or it must fail to compute a valid c-coloring with positive probability $\varepsilon > 0$. Let G be a graph on which the algorithm fails in one of the two ways with a positive probability $\varepsilon > 0$. Consider a graph H_k which consists of k identical disjoint copies of G. As the randomness in the k copies has to be independent, when running the algorithm, one of the k copies fails with probability at least $1 - (1 - \varepsilon)^k$. Note that the parameters m and Δ are the same for the two graphs G and H_k. For sufficiently large k, this failure probability becomes arbitrarily close to 1.

3   Neighborhood Graphs to Prove Lower Bounds

Neighborhood graphs were introduced by Linial in his seminal paper [7] in which he uses them to derive his $\Omega(\log^* n)$ lower bound for 3-coloring rings. We quickly recall his main ideas: In the LOCAL model, w.l.o.g., one can assume that an r-round algorithm first collects all data, which it can learn in r rounds, and only then decides on its output. The data, which a synchronous r-round distributed algorithm running at a node v can learn in this model, consists of the IDs and the topology of all nodes in distance at most r, except for edges between nodes in distance exactly r. This is called the r-view of a node and corresponds exactly to the knowledge a node obtains if every node forwards everything it knows (i.e., its current state) to all neighbors in every round, which it can do due to unbounded message size. If the number of IDs $\hat{n}$, the maximum degree Δ, and the number of rounds r are fixed, there are finitely many r-views and an r-round c-coloring algorithm is a function from those r-views to $[c]$. Neighborhood graphs formalize the neighborhood relation between r-views. The neighborhood graph $\mathcal{N}_r^{\mathsf{LOC}}(n, \Delta)$ for the LOCAL model has a node for each feasible r-view and there is an edge between two such nodes if the corresponding r-views can occur at neighboring nodes in some n-node graph with max. degree Δ.

Neighborhood graphs are extensively useful when studying distributed graph coloring because any (correct) r-round c-coloring algorithm yields a c-coloring of the r-round neighborhood graph $\mathcal{N}_r^{\mathsf{LOC}}$ and vice versa, [7,9]. Thus the existence of an r-round c-coloring algorithm reduces to the question whether the chromatic number of $\mathcal{N}_r^{\mathsf{LOC}}(n, \Delta)$ is smaller than or equal to c. Particularly, Linial showed $\chi\big(\mathcal{N}_r^{\mathsf{LOC}}(n, 2)\big) \in \Omega\big(\log^{(2r)} n\big)$ which yields his lower bound of $\Omega(\log^* n)$ rounds.

3.1   Neighborhood Graphs in the SET-LOCAL Model

In the same way as in the LOCAL model we obtain the data a node v can learn in an r-round algorithm of the SET-LOCAL model if every node forwards its knowledge to all neighbors in every round. After 0 rounds a node knows nothing but its own color, after one round it knows its own color and the **set of colors** of its neighbors, and so on. Definition 1 formalizes the data which a node can learn in r rounds in the SET-LOCAL model. A node cannot detect cycles unless unique IDs are given (this holds in the SET-LOCAL model and in the standard LOCAL model). The r-views are thus not formed by the actual topology of the neighborhood, but by the tree unfolding of the neighborhood. Thus for color reduction algorithms, w.l.o.g., we can restrict our attention to the case of trees.

Definition 1 (r-Neighborhood). *Let $G = (V, E)$ be a tree with maximum degree at most Δ and an initial m-coloring $\varphi : V \to \{1, \ldots, m\}$. We define*

$$\mathcal{S}_0^G(v) := \varphi(v) \qquad\qquad \textit{(0-round view)}.$$
$$\mathcal{S}_{r+1}^G(v) := \left(\mathcal{S}_r^G(v), \{\mathcal{S}_r^G(u) \mid u \in \Gamma_G(v)\}\right) \qquad \textit{($r+1$-round view)},$$

where $r \geq 0$ and $\mathcal{S}_r^G(v)$ equals the data which a node $v \in V$ can learn in an r-round distributed algorithm (r-view of v) in the SET-LOCAL model.

The r-view $\mathcal{S}_r^G(v)$ depends on the tree G, the coloring φ, and the node v. If we fix the number of initial colors m, the maximum degree Δ, and the number of rounds r, the number of feasible r-views which can occur at any node in any tree with maximum degree Δ and initial m-coloring is finite. The following definition adapts the neighborhood graphs of the LOCAL model to the SET-LOCAL model.

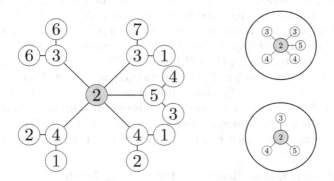

Fig. 1. Left: An extract of a tree graph. Images in Fig. 2 correspond to views of the gray node for two rounds in different models. **Right top:** The 1-round view in the SET-LOCAL model of the gray node in the left image. **Right bottom:** The 1-round view in the LOCAL model of the gray node in the left image. In [9, Lemma 3.1] the authors prove that $\chi(\mathcal{N}_1^{\text{LOC}}(m, D)) = \chi(\widetilde{\mathcal{N}}_1(m, D))$ holds.

Definition 2 (Neighborhood Graph in the SET-LOCAL Model). *Let m, Δ, and $r \geq 0$ be fixed. Consider the following finite graph $\mathcal{N}_r^{\text{SL}}(m, \Delta)$*

$$V(\mathcal{N}_r^{\text{SL}}) := \left\{ \mathcal{S}_r^G(v) \mid \exists\ m\text{-colored tree } G : \Delta(G) \leq \Delta \text{ and } v \in V(G) \right\},$$
$$E(\mathcal{N}_r^{\text{SL}}) := \left\{ \{\mathcal{S}_r^G(v), \mathcal{S}_r^G(u)\} \mid \exists\ m\text{-colored tree } G : \Delta(G) \leq \Delta,\ \{u, v\} \in E(G) \right\}.$$

Just as in the LOCAL model, any r-round c-coloring algorithm in the SET-LOCAL model with an initial m-coloring can be transformed into an equivalent algorithm in which every node first collects its r-neighborhood and then decides on its output. Such an algorithm is a function $f : V(\mathcal{N}_r^{\mathsf{SL}}) \rightarrow \{1, \ldots, c\}$ such that $f(x) \neq f(y)$ for all $\{x, y\} \in E(\mathcal{N}_r^{\mathsf{SL}})$, that is, f is a c-coloring of the graph $\mathcal{N}_r^{\mathsf{SL}}$. A proof of the following lemma can be found in the full version of the paper [1].

Lemma 1. *Any deterministic r-round distributed algorithm in the SET-LOCAL model, which correctly c-colors any intially m-colored graph with maximum degree Δ, yields a feasible c-coloring of $\mathcal{N}_r^{\mathsf{SL}}(m, \Delta)$ and vice versa.*

Thus a lower bound $\chi(\mathcal{N}_r^{\mathsf{SL}}(m, \Delta) > c$ on the chromatic number implies that there is no r-round color reduction algorithm in the SET-LOCAL model which (correctly) c-colors all initially m-colored graphs with maximum degree Δ.

4   Lower Bound Proof

We begin with a lower bound of $\Omega(\Delta^2)$ on the number of colors for any one-round color reduction algorithm in the standard LOCAL model (Sect. 4.1), i.e., $\chi(\mathcal{N}_1^{\mathsf{LOC}}) \in \Omega(\Delta^2)$. This result was shown before in [27], but our proof is much simpler and we believe that it is also instructive as it contains the core idea for the subsequent general lower bound proof for the SET-LOCAL model.

Afterwards, the goal is to device a lower bound on the chromatic number of $\mathcal{N}_r^{\mathsf{SL}}$. For this purpose, we (recursively) define graphs $\mathcal{N}_r$ and $\widetilde{\mathcal{N}}_r$. The recursive structure of the graph $\mathcal{N}_r$ is simpler than the one of $\mathcal{N}_r^{\mathsf{SL}}$ such that the repetitive application of the ideas of Sect. 4.1 amplify to a lower bound on $\chi(\mathcal{N}_r)$ (Sect. 4.2). Any graph homomorphism $h : G \rightarrow H$ implies $\chi(G) \leq \chi(H)$ and in Sect. 4.3, we show that for the correct choice of parameters there is a chain of homomorphisms $\mathcal{N}_r \longrightarrow \widetilde{\mathcal{N}}_r \longrightarrow \mathcal{N}_r^{\mathsf{SL}}$. Hence the lower bound on $\chi(\mathcal{N}_r)$ translates into a lower bound on $\chi(\mathcal{N}_r^{\mathsf{SL}})$. In Sect. 4.4 we combine all results to compute a runtime lower bound on any distributed color reduction algorithm in the SET-LOCAL model. All omitted proofs in this part can be found in the full version of the paper [1].

4.1   One-Round Lower Bound in the LOCAL Model

For a set S let $A \sqsubseteq S$ denote that A is a multiset consisting of elements of S. For integers $\Delta \geq 2$ and $m > \Delta$, we define the one-round neighborhood graph

$$V\left(\mathcal{N}_1^{\mathsf{LOC}}(m, \Delta)\right) := \{(x, A)|x \in [m], A \sqsubseteq [m], |A| \leq \Delta, x \notin A\}.$$

There is an edge between nodes $(x, A), (y, B) \in \mathcal{N}_1^{\mathsf{LOC}}(m, \Delta)$ if $x \in B$ and $y \in A$.

The above definition is the most general version of one-round neighborhood graphs in the LOCAL model; however, in [9, Lemma 3.1] the authors show that for a single round it is sufficient (i.e., to obtain a corresponding version of Lemma 1) to let A be a simple subset of $[m]$ (not a multiset) having exactly Δ elements. After all, we do not know whether multisets are necessary when extending the definition for more than a single round.

Theorem 3. *For all $\Delta \geq 2$ and $m \geq \frac{\Delta^2}{4} + \frac{\Delta}{2} + 1$, we have $\chi(\mathcal{N}_1^{\mathsf{LOC}}(m, \Delta)) > \frac{\Delta^2}{4}$.*

The following proof captures the main idea of the constructions of Sect. 4.2 in a simpler setting. In particular, it contains the main idea for the proof of Lemma 4. Additionally, it provides an alternative characterization of the terms *source* and *non-source* (cf. Definition 4). We believe that this characterization gives a deeper understanding of subsequent proofs.

Proof. Let $I \subseteq V(\mathcal{N}_1^{\mathsf{LOC}})$ be an independent set of $\mathcal{N}_1^{\mathsf{LOC}}(m, \Delta)$. Then I induces an *orientation* D_I of the edges of the complete graph K_m on the vertices $[m]$ in the following way: For each $x, y \in [m]$, if there exists a node $(x, A) \in I$ for which $y \in A$, we say that the edge $\{x, y\}$ of K_m is oriented from x to y ($x \rightarrow_I y$). As I is an independent set, it is not possible that an edge $\{x, y\}$ is oriented in both directions. If I does not lead to an orientation of an edge $\{x, y\}$, we orient it arbitrarily. We say that an independent set *covers* a node (x, A) if $x \rightarrow_I y$ holds for all $y \in A$. Clearly, I covers all nodes with $(x, A) \in I$.

For a set $W \subseteq K_m$ we say that $x \in K_m$ is a W-*source* of I if for all $y \in W \setminus \{x\}$ we have $x \rightarrow_I y$. If $W = K_m$ we simply call x a *source*.

Now assume for contradiction that we are given a vertex coloring of the graph $\mathcal{N}_1^{\mathsf{LOC}}(m, \Delta)$ that uses $c = \Delta^2/4$ colors. For each of the colors $k \in [c]$, the nodes I_k colored with color k form an independent set of $\mathcal{N}_1^{\mathsf{LOC}}(m, \Delta)$. The given c-coloring therefore also induces c orientations $D_1, \ldots, D_c$ of K_m such that for every $(x, A) \in V(\mathcal{N}_1^{\mathsf{LOC}})$, one of the c orientations covers (x, A).

Let $S \subseteq [m]$ be the set of nodes of K_m, which are a source of some orientation $D_k, k \in [c]$. Note that every orientation has at most 1 source and therefore $|S| \leq c$. For the remainder of the proof, we restrict our attention to integers in $\bar{S} = [m] \setminus S$. We first fix an arbitrary set $T \subseteq \bar{S}$ of size $|T| = \lfloor \Delta/2 \rfloor + 1$. Because $m \geq \Delta^2/4 + \Delta/2 + 1$, such a set T exists. Clearly, each orientation D_k can have at most one T-source. By the pigeonhole principle there exists an $x \in T$ such that x is a T-source for at most $c/|T|$ orientations. W.l.o.g., assume that $x \in T$ is a T-source for orientations $D_1, \ldots, D_q$, where $q \leq c/|T|$.

Now, we construct a set A such that the node $(x, A) \in V(\mathcal{N}_1^{\mathsf{LOC}})$ is not covered by any of the c orientations $D_1, \ldots, D_c$. First, we add all $\lfloor \Delta/2 \rfloor$ elements of $T \setminus \{x\}$ to A. Because x is a T-source only for orientations $D_1, \ldots, D_q$, none of the remaining $c - q$ orientations can cover (x, A). We have to add additional elements to A in order to make sure that the orientations $D_1, \ldots, D_q$ also do not cover (x, A). As T only consists of elements that are not sources of any of the orientations, for each orientation D_k, $k \in [c]$, there is an element $y_k \in [m]$ such that the edge $\{y_k, x\}$ of K_m is oriented from y_k to x. For each orientation $D_k \in \{D_1, \ldots, D_q\}$, we pick such an element y_k and add y_k to A. We obtain a node (x, A) that is not covered by any of the orientations $D_1, \ldots, D_q$. The size of A is

$$|A| \leq |T| - 1 + q \leq \left\lfloor \frac{\Delta}{2} \right\rfloor + \frac{c}{|T|} < \frac{\Delta}{2} + \frac{c}{\Delta/2} = \Delta$$

and thus, (x, A) is a node of $\mathcal{N}_1^{\mathsf{LOC}}(m, \Delta)$ which is not covered by any independent set. In particular, it does not have a color, a contradiction.

4.2   Recursive Structure of the Neighborhood Graph

In this section we study the recursive structure of $\mathcal{N}_r^{\mathsf{SL}}$ (the graph $\mathcal{N}_r^{\mathsf{SL}}$ can be built from $\mathcal{N}_{r-1}^{\mathsf{SL}}$). We define two recursively defined sequences of graphs, $(\mathcal{N}_0, \mathcal{N}_1, \ldots)$ and $(\widetilde{\mathcal{N}}_0, \widetilde{\mathcal{N}}_1, \ldots)$. The graphs $\mathcal{N}_0$ and $\widetilde{\mathcal{N}}_0$ are equal to the m-node clique on the nodes $[m]$. The nodes of the remaining graphs of the sequences are built according to the following recursive procedure: For $i \geq 0$, in each of the two sequences, a node of the $(i+1)$-st graph is created by a node x of the i-th graph and a subset A of its neighbors in the i-th graph. The sequences differ in the way which combinations of x's neighbors are allowed to form the set A.

To specify this we need to introduce some notation: For $i \geq 0$ each node of the graph $\mathcal{N}_{i+1}$ (or $\widetilde{\mathcal{N}}_{i+1}$) will be of the form (x, A), where $x \in \mathcal{N}_i$ (or $\widetilde{\mathcal{N}}_i$) and $A \subseteq \Gamma(x)$. Define the *center* of a node (x, A) as $z((x, A)) = x$ and the *types* of a node as $R((x, A)) = A$. For any set of nodes A let $z(A) = \{z(a) \mid a \in A\}$. For $x \in \mathcal{N}_0$ (or $\widetilde{\mathcal{N}}_0$) we define $z(x) = \bot$ and $R(x) = \{\bot\}$.

Definition 3. *Let m, D and r be fixed. $\mathcal{N}_0(m, D) := \widetilde{\mathcal{N}}_0(m, D) := K_m$, i.e., the clique on the nodes $[m]$. For $0 \leq i < r$ we have the following recursive definitions*

$$V(\mathcal{N}_{i+1}(m, D)) := \{(x, A) \mid x \in V(\mathcal{N}_i(m, D)), A \subseteq \Gamma(x), |A| \leq D\},$$
$$V(\widetilde{\mathcal{N}}_{i+1}(m, D)) := \{(x, A) \mid x \in V(\widetilde{\mathcal{N}}_i(m, D)), A \subseteq \Gamma(x), |A| \leq D, R(x) = z(A)\}.$$

There is an edge between $(x, A), (y, B) \in \mathcal{N}_{i+1}$ (or $\widetilde{\mathcal{N}}_{i+1}$) if $x \in B$ and $y \in A$.

We denote $\mathcal{N}_{i+1}(m, D)$ and $\widetilde{\mathcal{N}}_{i+1}(m, D)$ simply as $\mathcal{N}_{i+1}$ and $\widetilde{\mathcal{N}}_{i+1}$ whenever m and D are clear from the context. There is no restriction on the set $A \subseteq \Gamma_{\mathcal{N}_i}(x)$ to build a node of $\mathcal{N}_{i+1}(m, D)$ as long as the size of A is at most D. For a node $(x, A) \in \widetilde{\mathcal{N}}_{i+1}(m, D)$ the set A needs at least one fitting element for every type of x (cf. Fig. 2). For neighborhood graphs in the standard LOCAL model this restriction is even tighter. Then A, $R(x)$ and $z(A)$ need to be multisets and A needs exactly one fitting element for every type of x. We are not aware of a computational model which motivates the sequence $(\mathcal{N}_0, \mathcal{N}_1, \mathcal{N}_2, \ldots)$.

In the proof of the lower bound on $\chi(\mathcal{N}_r)$ we assume that we have a proper c-coloring of $\mathcal{N}_r$ which implies (partial) c-colorings of the graphs $\mathcal{N}_i, i < r$, cf. Lemma 2 and Corollary 1. If c is too small, we can use these partial colorings to construct an uncolored node $(x, A) \in \mathcal{N}_r$, i.e., a contradiction. The partial coloring of $\mathcal{N}_0$ yields an uncolored clique in $\mathcal{N}_0$, which implies a smaller uncolored clique in $\mathcal{N}_1$ and then a smaller uncolored clique in $\mathcal{N}_2$ and so on until we reach an uncolored node in $\mathcal{N}_r$. The construction of a single uncolored node of $\mathcal{N}_{i+1}$, denoted as (x, A), is similar to the proof in Sect. 4.1: For its construction we pick a suitable center node x from the uncolored clique of $\mathcal{N}_i$ and then (carefully) select up to D neighbors to form the set A which will ensure that the resulting node is uncolored. To iterate the argument we slightly modify this procedure to obtain an uncolored clique in $\mathcal{N}_{i+1}$.

A center x is suitable for the above process (this corresponds to a non-source in Sect. 4.1) if for every color there exists a neighbor which, if contained in A,

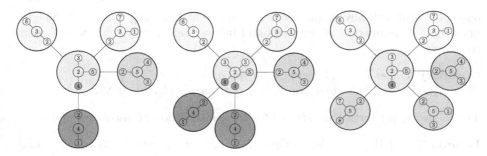

Fig. 2. Images (from left to right) explain the recursive structure of $\widetilde{\mathcal{N}}_2$, $\mathcal{N}_2^{\mathsf{LOC}}$ and $\mathcal{N}_2$, respectively. The colors indicate types. The left image is the 2-round view of the gray node in Fig. 1 in the SET-LOCAL model. Here, after a single round node 2 only knows that its degree is at least 3, after the second round it learned that its degree is at least 4 as it can now distinguish two neighbors with color 3. In the second image there is a neighbor of every type of the center with the corresponding multiplicity. For feasible nodes of $\mathcal{N}_2$ the combination of neighbors is arbitrary w.r.t. to types of the center, e.g., in the third image there is no node for type 4, i.e., no red node. We are not aware of a computational model to motivate $\mathcal{N}_2$. (Color figure online)

implies that (x, A) does not have this color. The (partial) c-coloring of $\mathcal{N}_i$ induced by the (partial) c-coloring of $\mathcal{N}_{i+1}$ is formed by all unsuitable centers (sources). The following definitions and lemmata make this more precise.

Definition 4 (W-source, source). *For any set $I \subseteq \mathcal{N}_{i+1}$ and any set $W \subseteq \mathcal{N}_i$, a node $x \in \mathcal{N}_i$ is called a W-source of I if*

$$\forall w \in W \cap \Gamma_{\mathcal{N}_i}(x) : \exists (x, A) \in I \text{ with } w \in A.$$

If $W = \mathcal{N}_i$ we call x simply a source of I.

Here, we define *sources* without the orientations from Sect. 4.1 to shorten proofs and we hope that this version is easier to be generalized in order to obtain a lower bound in the standard LOCAL model. Another intuition for sources is the following: Given a c-coloring of $\mathcal{N}_{i+1}$ one realizes that c can only be small if many nodes with the same center have the same color and nodes with the same center can never be adjacent. A natural approach would not consider a center x if x already uniquely determines the color of (x, A), independently of A. However, this is too restrictive and sources generalize this approach.

In the following we show how a c-coloring of $\mathcal{N}_r$ implies partial c-colorings of $\mathcal{N}_i$, $i < r$. For a set $I \subseteq \mathcal{N}_r$ set $S_r(I) := I$ and for $i = r - 1, \ldots, 0$ inductively define $S_i(I) := \{x \in \mathcal{N}_i \mid x \text{ is source of } S_{i+1}(I)\}$.

Lemma 2. *Let I be an independent set of $\mathcal{N}_r$.*
Then for all $i = 0, \ldots, r$ the set $S_i(I)$ is an independent set of $\mathcal{N}_i$.

Each color class of a c-coloring is an independent set. Thus any (partial) c-coloring corresponds to c (disjoint) independent sets. Vice versa any c independent sets induce a partial c-coloring though a node might have more than one color. But still any of those colors is different from any color of its neighbors. This identification of colorings and independent sets yields the following corollary.

Corollary 1. *Let $I_1, \ldots, I_c$ be a c-coloring of $\mathcal{N}_r$.*
Then $S_i(I_1), \ldots, S_i(I_c)$ corresponds to a (partial) c-coloring of $\mathcal{N}_i$.

The following properties are needed for the construction of uncolored nodes.

Lemma 3. *Let $W \subseteq \mathcal{N}_i$ be a clique, $I_1, \ldots, I_c$ independent sets of $\mathcal{N}_{i+1}$ and $k \in [c]$.*

(a) *If $x \in \mathcal{N}_i$ is not a source of I_k there exists $w \in \Gamma_{\mathcal{N}_i}(x)$ such that $(x, A) \notin I_k$, whenever $w \in A$.*
(b) *There is at most one W-source of I_k within W.*
(c) *There exists a node $x \in W$ which is a W-source for at most $\frac{c}{|W|}$ of the independent sets $I_1, \ldots, I_c$. Furthermore, for any choice of A with $W \setminus \{x\} \subseteq A$ we have $(x, A) \notin I_k$ for all but $\frac{c}{|W|}$ many independent sets.*

For $I_1, \ldots, I_c \subseteq \mathcal{N}_r$ we call $T \subseteq \mathcal{N}_i$ *uncolored* if we have $\forall k \in [c] : T \cap S_i(I_k) = \emptyset$.

Lemma 4. *Let p, c, d be in $\mathbb{N}$ and $I_1, \ldots, I_c$ independent sets of $\mathcal{N}_r$ with $p + d - 1 + \frac{c}{d} \leq D$. Any uncolored clique $T \subseteq \mathcal{N}_i$ of size $p + d$ implies an uncolored clique $T' \subseteq \mathcal{N}_{i+1}$ of size p.*

Proof. We inductively determine nodes $t_1, \ldots, t_p \in T$ which will form the centers of the clique nodes in $\mathcal{N}_{i+1}$. Assume that nodes $t_1, \ldots, t_{j-1} \in T$ are already determined and let T_j be any subset of $T \setminus \{t_1, \ldots, t_{j-1}\}$ with size d. Such a set exists because $|T \setminus \{t_1, \ldots, t_{j-1}\}| \geq p + d - (j - 1) \geq d$.

T_j is a clique in $\mathcal{N}_i$ and by Lemma 2 the sets $S_{i+1}(I_1), \ldots, S_{i+1}(I_c)$ are independent sets in $\mathcal{N}_{i+1}$. Hence there exists a node in T_j which is a T_j-source for at most $q \leq \frac{c}{|T_j|} = \frac{c}{d}$ independent sets by Lemma 3 (c). Denote this node by t_j and continue with determining the node t_{j+1}.

After determining $t_1, \ldots, t_p$ construct the uncolored clique of $\mathcal{N}_{i+1}$ as follows: For $j = 1, \ldots, p$ let $x_j := (t_j, A_j) = (t_j, (T \setminus \{t_j\}) \cup B_j)$, where B_j will be constructed later. Regardless of the choice of the B_j's the nodes $x_1, \ldots, x_p$ form a clique because $t_{j'} \in A_j$ and $t_j \in A_{j'}$ for $j \neq j'$.

We argue how to choose the set B_j such that x_j is uncolored in $\mathcal{N}_{i+1}$. Due to the choice of t_j and $T_j \setminus \{t_j\} \subseteq A_j$ all but q independent sets do not contain x_j and we eliminate each of those one-by-one with the choice of B_j. W.l.o.g. let the remaining independent sets be $S_{i+1}(I_1), \ldots, S_{i+1}(I_q)$. Because $t_j \in T$ is uncolored in $\mathcal{N}_i$ it is not a source for any of the independent sets $S_{i+1}(I_k), k \in [q]$. Hence via Lemma 3 (a) there exist $b_1, \ldots, b_q \in \Gamma_{\mathcal{N}_i}(t_j)$ such that (t_j, A_j) is not contained in any of the independent sets $S_{i+1}(I_k), k \in [q]$, whenever $B_j := \{b_1, \ldots, b_q\} \subseteq A_j$. Hence x_j is uncolored. The node x_j is a valid node of $\mathcal{N}_{i+1}$ (cf. Definition 3), as $A_j \subseteq \Gamma_{\mathcal{N}_i}(t_j)$ and $|A_j| = |T \setminus \{t_j\} \cup B_j| \leq p + d - 1 + \frac{c}{d} \leq D$. Hence $x_1, \ldots, x_p$ is an uncolored clique of $\mathcal{N}_{i+1}$.

An identical proof for the neighborhood graphs in the LOCAL model fails in the last step because the newly constructed node might not be a node of $\mathcal{N}_{i+1}^{\mathsf{LOC}}$ due to mismatching types (cf. the comment after Definition 3).

Theorem 4. *Let* $m \geq \frac{D^2}{4r} + \frac{D}{2} + 1$. *Then we have* $\chi(\mathcal{N}_r(m, D)) > \frac{D^2}{4r}$.

Proof (sketch). A full proof can be found in [1]. We assume for contradiction that a coloring of $\mathcal{N}_r(m, D)$ with $c = \frac{D^2}{4r}$ colors exists. Let $d = \frac{D}{2r}$. In $\mathcal{N}_0$ at most c nodes are colored and thus the size of m implies an uncolored clique in $\mathcal{N}_0$ of size $rd + 1$. Repeated applications of Lemma 4 yield uncolored cliques in $\mathcal{N}_i, i = 0, \ldots, r$ of size $rd - id + 1$, until we reach an uncolored node in $\mathcal{N}_r$.

4.3   Graph Homomorphisms

The existence of a graph homomorphism from $\widetilde{\mathcal{N}}_r(m, D)$ to $\mathcal{N}_r^{\mathsf{SL}}(m, D)$ is intuitive as the recursive structure of both graphs is exactly the same.

Lemma 5. *There is a graph homomorphism* $h_r : \widetilde{\mathcal{N}}_r(m, D) \to \mathcal{N}_r^{\mathsf{SL}}(m, D)$.

Lemma 6. *There is a graph homomorphism* $f_r : \mathcal{N}_r(m, D) \to \widetilde{\mathcal{N}}_r(m, (r+1)D)$.

4.4   Proof of Theorem 1

Any graph homomorphism $f : G \to H$ implies $\chi(G) \leq \chi(H)$ and we devised

$$\mathcal{N}_r(m, D) \xrightarrow{f_r} \widetilde{\mathcal{N}}_r(m, (r+1)D) \xrightarrow{h_r} \mathcal{N}_r^{\mathsf{SL}}(m, (r+1)D) \xrightarrow{h} \mathcal{N}_r^{\mathsf{SL}}(m, 2rD).$$

The existence of h is trivial and with Theorem 4 this implies $\chi\left(\mathcal{N}_r^{\mathsf{SL}}(m, 2rD)\right) > \frac{D^2}{4r}$ for $m \geq \frac{D^2}{4r} + \frac{D}{2} + 1$. To prove Theorem 1 assume an r-round $(C\Delta^{1+\eta})$-coloring algorithm. Set the parameter $D := \left(2C\Delta^{2+\eta}\right)^{\frac{1}{3}}$. Then the condition on m is satisfied for Δ sufficiently large. With $r := \left(\frac{1}{16C}\Delta^{1-\eta}\right)^{\frac{1}{3}}$, this implies the contradiction $\chi\left(\mathcal{N}_r^{\mathsf{SL}}(m, \Delta)\right) > C\Delta^{1+\eta}$. Theorem 1 follows with Lemma 1. $\square$

References

1. Hefetz, D., Kuhn, F., Maus, Y., Steger, A.: A polynomial lower bound for distributed graph coloring in a weak LOCAL model. CoRR, abs/1607.05212 (2016)
2. Karp, R.M.: Reducibility among combinatorial problems. In: Proceedings of the Symposium on Complexity of Computer Computations, pp. 85–103 (1972)
3. Zuckerman, D.: Linear degree extractors and the inapproximability of max clique and chromatic number. Theory Comput. **3**(1), 103–128 (2007)
4. Barenboim, L., Elkin, M.: Distributed Graph Coloring: Fundamentals and Recent Developments. Morgan & Claypool Publishers (2013)
5. Barenboim, L.: Deterministic $(\Delta + 1)$-coloring in sublinear (in Δ) time in static, dynamic and faulty networks. In: Proceedings of the 34th ACM Symposium on Principles of Distributed Computing (PODC), pp. 345–354 (2015)

6. Fraigniaud, P., Heinrich, M., Kosowski, A.: Local conflict coloring. CoRR, abs/1511.01287 (2015)
7. Linial, N.: Locality in distributed graph algorithms. SIAM J. Comput. **21**(1), 193–201 (1992)
8. Hella, L., Järvisalo, M., Kuusisto, A., Laurinharju, J., Lampiäinen, T., Luosto, K., Suomela, J., Virtema, J.: Weak models of distributed computing, with connections to modal logic. Distrib. Comput. **28**(1), 31–53 (2015)
9. Kuhn, F., Wattenhofer, R.: On the complexity of distributed graph coloring. In: Proceedings of the 25th ACM Symposium on Principles of Distributed Computing (PODC), pp. 7–15 (2006)
10. Cole, R., Vishkin, U.: Deterministic coin tossing with applications to optimal parallel list ranking. Inf. Control **70**(1), 32–53 (1986)
11. Awerbuch, B., Goldberg, A.V., Luby, M., Plotkin, S.A.: Network decomposition and locality in distributed computation. In: Proceedings of the 30th Symposium on Foundations of Computer Science (FOCS), pp. 364–369 (1989)
12. Panconesi, A., Srinivasan, A.: On the complexity of distributed network decomposition. J. Algorithms **20**(2), 581–592 (1995)
13. Barenboim, L., Elkin, M., Kuhn, F.: Distributed (Delta+1)-coloring in linear (in Delta) time. SIAM J. Comput. **43**(1), 72–95 (2015)
14. Barenboim, L., Elkin, M.: Deterministic distributed vertex coloring in polylogarithmic time. In: Proceedings of the 29th Symposium on Principles of Distributed Computing (PODC) (2010)
15. Alon, N., Babai, L., Itai, A.: A fast and simple randomized parallel algorithm for the maximal independent set problem. J. Algorithms **7**(4), 567–583 (1986)
16. Luby, M.: A simple parallel algorithm for the maximal independent set problem. SIAM J. Comput. **15**, 1036–1053 (1986)
17. Barenboim, L., Elkin, M., Pettie, S., Schneider, J.: The locality of distributed symmetry breaking. In Proceedings of the 53rd Symposium on Foundations of Computer Science (FOCS) (2012)
18. Harris, S.G., Schneider, J., Su, H.-H.: Distributed $(\Delta + 1)$-coloring in sublogarithmic rounds. In: Proceedings of the 48th Symposium on the Theory of Computing (STOC) (2016)
19. Chang, Y.-J., Kopelowitz, T., Pettie, S.: An exponential separation between randomized and deterministic complexity in the LOCAL model. CoRR, abs/1602.08166 (2016)
20. Brand, S., Fischer, O., Hirvonen, J., Keller, B., Lempiäinen, T., Rybicki, J., Suomela, J., Uitto, J.: A lower bound for the distributed Lovász local lemma. In: Proceedings of the 48th Symposium on the Theory of Computing (STOC) (2016)
21. Göös, M., Suomela, J.: No sublogarithmic-time approximation scheme for bipartite vertex cover. Distrib. Comput. **27**(6), 435–443 (2014)
22. Göös, M., Hirvonen, J., Suomela, J.: Linear-in-Delta lower bounds in the LOCAL model. In: Proceedings of the 33rd Symposium on Principles of Distributed Computing (PODC), pp. 86–95 (2014)
23. Kuhn, F., Moscibroda, T., Wattenhofer, R.: What cannot be computed locally! In: Proceedings of the 23rd Symposium on Principles of Distributed Computing (PODC), pp. 300–309 (2004)
24. Kuhn, F., Moscibroda, T., Wattenhofer, R.: Local computation: lower and upper bounds. J. ACM **63**(2) (2016). http://dl.acm.org/citation.cfm?id=2742012. Article No. 17

25. Alon, N.: On constant time approximation of parameters of bounded degree graphs. In: Goldreich, O. (ed.) Property Testing. LNCS, vol. 6390, pp. 234–239. Springer, Heidelberg (2010)
26. Barenboim, L., Elkin, M.: Sublogarithmic distributed MIS algorithm for sparse graphs using nash-williams decomposition. Distr. Comput. **22**(5), 363–379 (2010)
27. Kuhn, F.: Local multicoloring algorithms: computing a nearly-optimal TDMA schedule in constant time. In: Proceedings of Symposium on Theoretical Aspects of Computer Science (STACS), pp. 613–624 (2009)
28. Szegedy, M., Vishwanathan, S.: Locality based graph coloring. In: Proceedings of the 25th ACM Symposium on Theory of Computing (STOC), pp. 201–207 (1993)
29. Gavoille, C., Klasing, R., Kosowski, A., Kuszner, Ł., Navarra, A.: On the complexity of distributed graph coloring with local minimality constraints. Technical report 6399, INRIA (2007)
30. Peleg, D.: Distributed Computing: A Locality-Sensitive Approach. SIAM (2000)

Optimal Consistent Network Updates
in Polynomial Time

Pavol Černý[1], Nate Foster[2], Nilesh Jagnik[1(✉)], and Jedidiah McClurg[1]

[1] University of Colorado Boulder, Boulder, USA
[2] Cornell University, Ithaca, USA
{nilesh.jagnik,jedidiah.mcclurg}@colorado.edu

Abstract. Software-defined networking (SDN) enables controlling the
behavior of a network in software, by managing the forwarding rules
installed on switches. However, it can be difficult to ensure that certain
properties are preserved during periods of reconfiguration. The widely-
accepted notion of *per-packet consistency* requires every packet to be
forwarded using the new configuration or the old configuration, but not
a mixture of the two. A (partial) order on switches is a *consistent order
update* if updating the switches in that order guarantees per-packet consistency. A consistent order update is *optimal* if it allows maximal parallelism, where switches may be updated in parallel if they are incompa-
rable in the order. This paper presents a polynomial-time algorithm for
computing optimal consistent order updates. This contrasts with other
recent results, which show that for other properties (e.g., loop-freedom
and waypoint enforcement), the optimal update problem is NP-complete.

1 Introduction

Software-defined networking (SDN) replaces conventional network management
interfaces with higher-level APIs. SDN can be used to build a variety of applications, but it can be difficult for operators to *correctly* and *efficiently* reconfigure
the network—i.e., update the global set of forwarding rules installed on switches
(known as a *configuration*). Even if the initial and final configurations are correct, naïvely updating individual switches (known as *switch-updates*) can lead
to incorrect transient behaviors such as forwarding loops, blackholes, bypassing a firewall, etc. Switch-updates can often be parallelized, but this too can
cause incorrect behavior. Hence, we need a partial order on switch-updates which
ensures that correctness properties hold before, during, and after the update.

Consistent order updates. This paper investigates the problem of computing
a *consistent order update*. Given an initial and final network configuration, a
consistent order update is a partial order on switch-updates, such that if the
switches are updated according to this order, an important consistency property
called *per-packet consistency* [16] is guaranteed throughout the update process.
This property guarantees that each packet traversing the network will follow

C. Gavoille and D. Ilcinkas (Eds.): DISC 2016, LNCS 9888, pp. 114–128, 2016.
DOI: 10.1007/978-3-662-53426-7_9

a single global configuration: either the initial one, or the final one, but not a mixture of the two. In particular, this means that if the initial and the final configurations are loop-free and blackhole-free, prevent bypassing a firewall, etc., then so do all of the intermediate configurations.

Optimal consistent order updates. In implementing a consistent order update, we would generally prefer to use one that is optimal. A consistent order update is *optimal* if it allows the most parallelism among all consistent order updates. Formally, recall that a consistent order update is a partial order on switch-updates—an optimal partial order is one where the length of the longest chain in the order is the smallest among all possible correct partial orders. Intuitively, this means the update can be performed in the smallest number of "rounds," where rounds are separated by waiting for in-flight packets to exit the network and by waiting for all the switch updates from the previous rounds to finish.

Single flow vs. multiple flows. A *flow* is a restriction of a network configuration to packets of a single type, corresponding to values in packet headers. A packet type might include the destination address, protocol number (TCP vs. UDP), etc. We show that if we consider flows to be *symbolic* (i.e., represented by predicates over packet headers, potentially matching multiple flows), then the problem is CO-NP-hard. In this paper, we focus on the problem of updating an *individual* flow—i.e., we are interested in the situation where the flows to be updated can be enumerated. Furthermore, as we are looking for efficient consistent order updates, we focus on the case where each switch can be updated at most once, from its initial to its final configuration.

Main result. Our main result is that for updating a single flow, there is a polynomial-time algorithm, with $O(n^2(n+m))$ complexity where n is the number of switches and m the number of links. The result is interesting both theoretically and practically. On the theoretical side, recent papers have presented complexity results for network updates. However, for many other consistency properties (loop-freedom, waypoint enforcement) and network models, the optimal network update problem is NP-hard [4,6,9–12]. The same is true for results that study these problems with a model which is the same as ours (single flows, update every switch at most once). In contrast, we provide a *positive* result that there exists a polynomial-time algorithm for optimal order updates for a single flow, with respect to the per-packet consistency property. The consistency properties studied in these papers (loop-freedom and waypoint enforcement) are weaker than per-packet consistency, which offers a trade-off: enforcing only (for instance) loop-freedom allows more updates to be found, but it is an (exponentially) harder problem. In practice, network operators might wish to update only a small number of flows, and here our polynomial-time algorithm would be advantageous. A potential limitation is that if many flows are considered separately, it could lead to large forwarding tables.

Algorithm. Our algorithm models a network configuration as a directed graph with unlabeled edges, and an update from an initial configuration to a final configuration as a sequence of individual switch-updates—i.e., updating the outgoing edges at each switch. In order to determine whether a switch n can be updated while properly respecting the per-packet consistency property, we define a set of conditions on the paths *upstream* and *downstream* from n. We show that these conditions can be checked in $O(n(n+m))$ time. In this way, the algorithm produces a partial order on switches, representing the consistent order update (if such an order does not exist, our algorithm reports a failure). Additionally, we show that if the partial order is constructed greedily (i.e., all nodes that can be updated are immediately updated in parallel), it results in an *optimal* consistent order update. The challenging part of the proof is to show that this algorithm is complete (i.e., always finds a consistent order update if one exists) and optimal.

2   Overview

This section presents a number of simple examples to help develop further intuition about the consistent order updates problem and the challenges that any solution must address.

Consistent order updates. Consider Fig. 1. In the initial configuration C_i (denoted by *solid* edges), the forwarding-table rules (outgoing edges) on each switch are set up such that host H_1 is sending packets to H_2 along the path $H_1 \rightarrow A \rightarrow C \rightarrow B \rightarrow H_2$. Let us assume that switch C is scheduled for maintenance, meaning we must first transition to configuration C_f (denoted by the *dashed* edges). Note that the two configurations differ only for nodes A and D. If the node A is updated before node D, packets from H_1 will be dropped at D. On the other hand, updating D before A leads to a consistent order update. Note that since we model networks as graphs, we will use the terms *switch* and *node* interchangeably based on the context, and similarly for the terms *edge* and *forwarding rule*. *Path* will be used to describe a sequence of adjacent edges.

In Fig. 2, regardless of the order in which we update nodes, there will always be inconsistency. Note that here the nodes A and D can be updated first, but a problem arises due to nodes H_1 and C. Specifically, if C is updated before H_1,

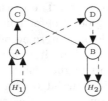

Fig. 1. Trivial update.

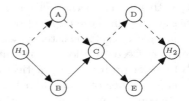

Fig. 2. Double diamond: no consistent update order exists.

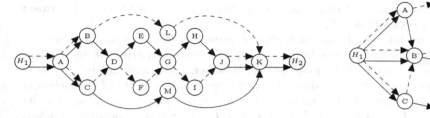

Fig. 3. Removable double diamond.   **Fig. 4.** Wait example.

then the network is in a configuration containing a path $H_1 \to B \to C \to D \to H_2$, which is not in either C_i or C_f. In other words, H_1 cannot be updated unless the (downstream) path from C to H_2 is first updated. On the other hand, C cannot be updated unless the (upstream) path from H_1 to C is first updated. We refer to this case as a *double diamond*. If we consider the notion of dependency graphs [13], where there is an edge from a node x to node y if the update of y can only be executed after the update of x, then our double diamond example corresponds to a cyclic dependency graph between H_1 and C.

Unfortunately, the presence of a double diamond (cyclic dependency) does not necessarily indicate that there cannot be a solution. Consider Fig. 3, where there is a double diamond between D and J. Updating B removes the old traffic to D, and then after updating B, the nodes D, E, G, F, H, I, J have no incoming traffic. At this point, these nodes can be updated without violating per-packet consistency. Thus, the circular dependency has been eliminated, allowing a valid update order such as $[A, H_1, K, L, B, D, E, F, G, H, I, J, C, M]$. This shows that an approach (such as [7,18]) based on a static dependency graph might miss some cases where a consistent order update exists—this is a limitation that is not exhibited by our algorithm.

Waits. As mentioned, it may be impossible to parallelize certain updates—we may need to make sure that some node x is updated before another node y. In other words, we may need to *wait* during the sequence of switch-updates to ensure that such updates are executed one after the other. This requirement can arise because when updating a node, we may need to ensure that (1) all of the previous switch-updates have been completed, and (2) all of the packets that were in the network since before the previous update have exited the network. The former type we call a *switch-wait*, and the latter a *packet-wait*.

In Fig. 3, we see that L must be updated before updating B. To ensure that edges outgoing from L are ready, we must wait after sending the update command to L, in order to ensure that its forwarding rules have been fully installed. In other words, we say that there is a *switch-wait* required between updates of L and B. After updating B, the switch D becomes disconnected, but there may still be some packets in transit on the $B \to D$ path. Before updating D, we must ensure that packets along these old removed paths have been flushed from the network. For this reason, we say that a *packet-wait* is needed between updates of nodes D and B.

If we are interested only in finding a correct sequence of updates, we can wait (for an amount of time larger than the maximum switch-wait and packet-wait duration) after every node update. However, waits may not be necessary after every update if we update switches from separate parts of the network. For the Fig. 3 example, the correct sequence with a *minimal* number of waits is $[A, H_1, K, L, ⓢ, B, ⓟ, D, E, F, G, H, I, J, ⓢ, C, M]$, where ⓟ denotes a packet-wait and ⓢ denotes a switch-wait. In this example, nodes A, H_1, K, L can be updated in parallel. Similarly, nodes D, E, F, G, H, I can be updated in parallel, etc. There are three waits, meaning this consistent order update requires *four* switch-update *rounds*.

The example in Fig. 4 highlights the relationship between switch-waits and packet-waits. Observing that the configurations are roughly symmetrical, let us examine the relationship between nodes A, B, C. The correct order of updates between these nodes is $H_1, A, ⓟ, B, ⓢ, C$. This is because there must be a *switch-wait* between the updates of B and C, due to the presence of a C_f path $C \dashrightarrow B$. There must be a *packet-wait* between updates of switches A and B, due to the presence of a C_i path $A \rightarrow B$.

As is common in various other works (e.g., [9]), in this paper, we do not distinguish between packet-waits and switch-waits, and only use the term *wait*—our goal is to maximize the parallelism of switch-updates, i.e., minimize the number of switch-update rounds.

3   Network Model

Network and Configurations. A topology of a network is a graph $G = (N, E)$, where N is a set of nodes, and E is a set of directed edges. A configuration $C \in \mathcal{P}(E)$ is a subset of edges in E. A *proper* configuration is one that (a) has one source H_1, and (b) is acyclic. Here, a source is a designated node with no incoming edges, representing the point where packets enter the network. Note that cycles in a configuration are undesirable, as this would mean that traffic might loop forever in the network. We first consider the case with one source, and in Sect. 6, we describe a simple reduction for the case of multiple sources. Our goal is to transition from an initial configuration C_i to a final configuration C_f by updating individual nodes. We will consider C_i and C_f to be fixed throughout the paper, and assume that both are proper.

Updates. Let u be a node, and let C be a configuration. We define a function $out(C, u)$ which returns the set of edges from C whose source is u. The function $upd_1(C, u)$ returns the configuration C' such that $C' = (C \setminus out(C_i, u)) \cup out(C_f, u)$, that is, node u is updated to the final configuration in C'. Let R be the set of all sequences of nodes in N without repetition. We extend upd_1 to sequences of nodes by defining the function upd that, given a configuration C and a sequence of nodes S, returns a configuration $C' = upd(C, S)$.

The function upd is defined by $upd(C, \varepsilon) = C$ (where ε is the empty sequence), and $upd(C, uS) = upd(upd_1(C, u), S)$. We consider sequences without repetition, because our goal is to find sequences that update every node at most once.

Paths. Given a configuration C, a C-path is a directed path (finite or infinite) whose edges are in C. For a path p, we write $p \in C$ if p is a C-path. A C_i-only path is one which is in C_i and not in C_f. Similarly, a C_f-only path is in C_f but not C_i. The function *nodes* takes a path q as an argument and returns a set Q of all nodes on a path. Let s and t be two nodes, and let C be a configuration. The function $paths(s, t, C)$ returns the set of all paths between s and t in configuration C. A path p in a configuration C is *maximal* if it is either (a) finite, and its last node has no outgoing edges in C, or (b) infinite. The function $maxpaths(s, C)$ returns the set of all maximal paths starting at node s in configuration C.

Path and Configuration Consistency. We say that a path p is *consistent* if and only if $p \in maxpaths(H_1, C_i) \vee p \in maxpaths(H_1, C_f)$, and a configuration C is *consistent* if and only if $\forall p \in maxpaths(H_1, C)$ we have that p is consistent. Intuitively, all maximal paths starting at H_1 are maximal paths in either the old configuration or the new configuration— this corresponds to per-packet consistency [16]. If C_i and C_f are proper, then so is every consistent configuration.

Waits. Let $U = u_1 u_2 \cdots u_k$ be a sequence of node updates. Let $C_j = upd(C_i, U_j)$ be the configuration reached after updating a sequence $U = u_1 u_2 \cdots u_j$ for $1 \le j \le k$, and let $C_0 = C_i$. For l, u such that $0 \le l \le u \le k$, let C_l^u be the configuration obtained as a union of configurations $C_l \cup \cdots \cup C_u$. We say that a *wait is needed* between u_j and u_k in U if and only if the configuration C_{j-1}^k is not consistent. To illustrate, let us return to the example in Fig. 4 (note that we no longer distinguish between packet-waits and switch-waits). As mentioned, after updating H_1 and A, we need a wait before updating B. Let the configuration C_v be the union of all the intermediate configurations until after the update to B. Then C_v has the path $H_1 \to A \to B \to$, where we take the solid edge from A to B and a dashed outgoing edge from B, meaning a wait is needed. In this case, using the union of the configurations captures the reason for the wait.

Consistent update sequence. For any set of nodes S, let $\pi(S)$ be the set of sequences that can be formed by nodes in S, without repetition. Let $Z = S_1 S_2 \cdots S_k$ be a sequence such that each S_i is a subset of N. Let $\pi(Z)$ be the set of sequences defined by $\{r_1 r_2 \cdots r_k \mid r_1 \in \pi(S_1) \wedge r_2 \in \pi(S_2) \wedge \cdots \wedge r_k \in \pi(S_k)\}$.

The sequence $Z = S_1 S_2 \cdots S_k$ is a *consistent update sequence* if and only if

1. The sets $S_1, S_2, \cdots, S_k$ partition the set of nodes N. This ensures that $\forall U \in \pi(Z)$, we have $upd(C_i, U) = C_f$, i.e., after updating u, we are in C_f.
2. $\forall U \in \pi(Z)$, for every prefix U' of U, $C = upd(C_i, U')$ is a consistent configuration.
3. $\forall U \in \pi(Z)$, let $U' = u_1 u_2 \cdots u_j$ and $U'' = u_1 u_2 \cdots u_k$ be prefixes of u, s.t. $k > j$, then if a wait is needed between u_j, u_k in U, then u_j, u_k are in different sets S and S'.

Consistent Order Update Problem. Given an initial configuration C_i and the final configuration C_f, the *consistent order update problem* is to find a consistent update sequence if there exists one.

Optimal Consistent Order Update Problem. Given C_i and C_f, if a consistent update sequence exists, the *optimal consistent update problem* is to find a consistent update sequence of minimal length.

4   OrderUpdate Algorithm

This section presents an algorithm (Algorithm 1) that solves the consistent order update problem. It works by repeatedly finding and updating a node that can be updated without violating consistency. For clarity, we focus first on correctness. Section 5 presents an improved version that finds an optimal update.

Correct Sequence. A *correct* sequence of node updates $T = t_1 t_2 \cdots t_{|N|}$ refers to a consistent update sequence of singleton sets $Z = S_1 S_2 \cdots S_{|N|}$ s.t. $\forall j \in [1, |N|] : S_j = \{t_j\}$. Algorithm 1 uses a subroutine at Line 6 (in this section, the subroutine is Algorithm 2—in Sect. 5 we will replace it with Algorithm 3 to achieve optimality) to find a correct update sequence. It takes C_i and C_f as inputs and returns two sequences of nodes, R and R_w. Sequence R is the solution to the consistent order update problem (a sequence of singleton sets). Sequence R_w contains information about the placement of waits, which will be the same as R in this section, since we initially wait after every node update.

4.1   Necessary Conditions for Updating a Node

To determine which node updates lead to consistent configurations, we assume the network is in a consistent configuration C_c, and identify a set of necessary conditions that must hold for the update to preserve consistency. We classify nodes into five categories based on the types of paths that are incoming to them from H_1. The classification is given in the left-hand side of Fig. 5.

Upstream Paths and Candidate Nodes. Paths from source H_1 to a node s are called *upstream* paths to s (in some configuration). The condition on these paths is called the upstream condition. If a node satisfies the upstream condition for one of the five categories/types, it is known as a *candidate* of that type.

Downstream Paths and Valid Nodes. Downstream paths from a node s are maximal paths starting at s (in some configuration). For each of the upstream conditions, there is a downstream condition which must be satisfied, in order to ensure that all maximal paths starting from H_1 in $upd(C_c, s)$ through s are consistent. If a candidate node satisfies the corresponding downstream condition, it is called *valid*. A node which is not valid is called *invalid*. Note that upstream paths to s are the same in C_c and $upd(C_c, s)$.

	Upstream (Condition for $paths(H_1, s, C_c)$)	Downstream (Condition for $maxpaths(s, C_c)$)
A	$Y_a(s) = \nexists\, p \in paths(H_1, s, C_c)$	$Z_a^\dagger(s) = (out(s, C_f) = \varnothing)\, \vee$ $\forall p \in maxpaths(s, upd(C_c, s)):$ $p \in maxpaths(s, C_f)$
B	$Y_b(s) = \neg Y_a(s) \wedge \forall p \in paths(H_1, s, C_c):$ $p \in paths(H_1, s, C_i)$ $\wedge\, p \in paths(H_1, s, C_f)$	$Z_b(s) = \forall p \in maxpaths(s, upd(C_c, s)):$ $p \in maxpaths(s, C_i)$ $\vee\, p \in maxpaths(s, C_f)$
C	$Y_c(s) = \neg Y_a(s) \wedge \neg Y_b(s)$ $\wedge\, \forall p \in paths(H_1, s, C_c):$ $p \in paths(H_1, s, C_f)$	$Z_c(s) = \forall p \in maxpaths(s, upd(C_c, s)):$ $p \in maxpaths(s, C_f)$
D	$Y_d(s) = \neg Y_a(s) \wedge \neg Y_b(s)$ $\wedge\, \forall p \in paths(H_1, s, C_c):$ $p \in paths(H_1, s, C_i)$	$Z_d(s) = \forall p \in maxpaths(s, upd(C_c, s)):$ $p \in maxpaths(s, C_i)$
E	$Y_e(s) = \neg Y_a(s) \wedge \neg Y_b(s)$ $\wedge\, \neg Y_c(s) \wedge \neg Y_d(s)$	$Z_e(s) = \forall p \in maxpaths(s, upd(C_c, s)):$ $p \in maxpaths(s, C_i)$ $\wedge\, p \in maxpaths(s, C_f)$

Fig. 5. Necessary conditions for updating a node s in current configuration C_c

Lemma 1. In a consistent configuration C_c, if a valid node s is updated, then $upd(C_c, s)$ is consistent.

Proof Sketch. Figure 5 identifies nodes as Types A–E based on upstream conditions. The upstream conditions are exhaustive and mutually exclusive, meaning each node is a candidate of exactly one of the types. For each type described in Fig. 5, our downstream condition ensures that updating preserves consistency. Upstream paths to a node may be fully contained in C_i or C_f (Type C and Type D respectively). For these cases, we need to ensure that downstream paths are also contained in C_i and C_f respectively. They may be in $C_i \cap C_f$ or $C_i \cup C_f$ (Type B and Type E respectively). For these cases, we need to ensure that downstream paths are in $C_i \cup C_f$ (for Type B) and $C_i \cap C_f$ (for Type E). Type A is a special case, as nodes of this type (also referred to as *disconnected nodes*) do not have any upstream paths. These nodes can be updated without the requirement of a downstream condition. However, we enforce a downstream condition (denoted $Z_a^\dagger$ in the table) in order to streamline the proofs. □

The proof of this and other theorems/lemmas are in the extended version [3]. Using Lemma 1, each node updated by OrderUpdate leads to a valid intermediate configuration. So, we change from C_i to C_f without going through an inconsistent state, and since we wait between all updates, we obtain a consistent sequence.

Theorem 1. Any sequence R of nodes produced by Algorithm 1 (using subroutine Algorithm 2) is correct.

Algorithm 1. *OrderUpdate*

Input: set of all nodes (N), initial configuration (C_i), final configuration (C_f)
Result: consistent order of node updates (R), updates before which there are
waits (R_w)

```
1  R = Rw = P0 ← ∅; k ← 1              // initialize R, Rw, P0 and k
2  Cc ← Ci                            // Cc starts with the initial value of Ci
3  while Cc ≠ Cf do                   // stop when Cc and Cf are equal
4  |   U ← {s | s ∈ N ∧ ((Ya(s) ∧ Za(s)) ∨ (Yb(s) ∧ Zb(s)) ∨
   |        (Yc(s) ∧ Zc(s)) ∨ (Yd(s) ∧ Zd(s)) ∨ (Ye(s) ∧ Ze(s)))}  // valid nodes
5  |   if U = ∅ then EXIT             // no consistent order of updates exists
6  |   s = PickAndWait()              // by default, use Algorithm 2
7  |   Cc ← (Cc ∖ out(s, Ci)) ∪ out(s, Cf)              // update Cc
8  |_  N ← N − {s}                    // remove updated nodes from node list
9  return (R, Rw)
```

Algorithm 2. *SequentialPickAndWait*

```
1  s = Pick(U)                        // pick any valid node
2  Rw ← Rw.s         // by default, there is a wait after every update
3  R ← R.s                            // append s to the end of result R
```

4.2 Careful Sequences

Previously, we said that Type A candidates (disconnected nodes) do not require a downstream condition to be updated. However, Algorithm 1 imposes a downstream condition on disconnected nodes for them to be valid and updated. We refer to sequences that respect this downstream condition (i.e., update only valid nodes) as *careful* sequences. Let s be a node and C be a configuration, and define $valid_1(C, s)$ to be *true* if and only if s in valid in configuration C. We extend $valid_1$ to a sequence of nodes by defining *valid* as $valid(\varepsilon, C) = true$ (where ε is the empty sequence) and $valid(C, uS) = valid(upd(C, u), S) \wedge valid_1(C, u)$.

Careful Sequence. A *careful* sequence $T = t_1 t_2 \cdots t_{|N|}$ is a correct sequence of nodes s.t. $\forall l \in [1, |N|] : valid(upd(C_i, t_1 t_2 \cdots t_{l-1}), t_l)$.

Theorem 2. If a correct sequence of updates exists, then a careful sequence also exists.

4.3 Completeness of the OrderUpdate Algorithm

The OrderUpdate Algorithm (with the SequentialPickAndWait subroutine) is complete, i.e., if there exists any correct sequence, we find one. We can observe that if two nodes a and b are both valid in configuration C_c, then $upd(C_c, ab)$ and $upd(C_c, ba)$ are both consistent configurations. This property holds for any number of nodes and for all *careful* sequences, but not for all *correct* sequences.

Algorithm 3. *OptimalPickAndWait*

---

1 if $k = 1$ then   `// we do not need a wait before first node`
2    $\lfloor$ $P_0 \leftarrow U$ `// all nodes initially valid are` P_0

3 if $P_0 = \varnothing$ then   `// we have to pick a lower priority node`
4    $|$ $P_0 \leftarrow U$ `// all nodes in` U `become` P_0 `after waiting.`
5    $|$ $s = Pick(P_0); R \leftarrow R.s; R_w \leftarrow R_w.s; k \leftarrow k + 1;$ `// pick` P_0 `node, append` s
     $\lfloor$ to result R, add wait, increment number of rounds k

6 else
7    $\lfloor$ $s = Pick(P_0); R \leftarrow R.s$ `// pick any` P_0 `node, add` s `to result` R

We prove this behavior in the following lemma, which is the key to confirming completeness of the OrderUpdate Algorithm.

Lemma 2. If $T = UVnY$ is a careful sequence, and $valid(upd(C_i, U), n)$, then $T' = UnVY$ is also careful.

In other words, Lemma 2 shows that if there are multiple valid nodes in some configuration C, then these nodes can be updated in any order. This is because once a node becomes valid, it does not become invalid. This is why we introduced careful sequences, because this lemma is not true for arbitrary correct sequences. Using this lemma, we can prove the completeness of Algorithm 1 (with the Algorithm 2 subroutine).

Theorem 3. Algorithm 1, using subroutine Algorithm 2, generates a correct order of updates R if one exists, and otherwise fails (in Line 5).

Running Time. Let $|V|$ be the number of nodes and $|E|$ be the number of edges in G. In each iteration of its outer loop, Algorithm 1 using *SequentialPickAndWait* (Algorithm 2) as a subroutine, makes a list of valid nodes and picks one to update. The set of valid nodes U in Line 4 can be found using a graph search on C_c for each node, which takes $O(|V|(|V| + |E|))$ steps. The loop runs $|V|$ times and updates each node, so the overall runtime is $O(|V|^2(|V| + |E|))$. This analysis relies on the fact that the graph search is implemented in a way that goes through each edge and node a constant number of times. Once a node has been visited, it is marked F, I, or B, based on whether the maximal paths downstream from it are maximal paths starting from it in C_i, C_f, or both. This ensures that we avoid visiting the node (and its outgoing edges) again.

5 Optimal OrderUpdate Algorithm

Thus far, we solved the consistent order update problem by generating a consistent sequence with only singleton sets. This corresponds to requiring a wait at every step of the update sequence, which does not allow any parallelism.

However, we have seen in Sect. 2 that some nodes can be updated in parallel. In Sect. 3, we defined when a wait is needed in the sequence of updates. In this section, we provide a sequence of updates where there is a wait if and only if it is needed, solving the optimal version of the problem. We use Algorithm 1, but replace the subroutine *SequentialPickAndWait* (Algorithm 2) with *OptimalPickAndWait* (Algorithm 3). The algorithm returns a solution for the optimal consistent update problem in the following format.

Correct Waited Sequence. A correct waited sequence is a tuple (T, W) of node sequences without repetition, where W is a subsequence of T and $(T, W) = (t_1 t_2 \cdots t_{|N|}, w_1 w_2 \cdots w_{k-1})$, such that a consistent update sequence $S_1 S_2 \cdots S_k$ can be formed by taking $S_1 = \{t_1, \cdots, t_m\}$ where $t_{m_1} = w_1$, $\forall i \in (1, k) : S_i = \{t_{l_i}, \cdots, t_{m_i}\}$ where $t_{l_i} = w_{i-1}$ and $t_{m_i} = w_i$, and $S_k = \{t_{l_k}, \cdots, t_{|N|}\}$ where $t_{l_k} = w_{k-1}$.

Intuitively, T specifies a correct sequence of updates, with some waits, while W specifies the nodes, immediately before which a wait is placed. If we simply group the nodes between i-th and $(i + 1)$-st waits into a set S_{i+1} we obtain the consistent update sequence of Sect. 3. Considering solutions to the problem in the form of a sequence of nodes and waits simplifies the arguments we use to prove correctness and optimality.

Minimal Correct Waited Sequence. A *minimal correct waited sequence* is a correct waited sequence (T, W) such that $|W|$ is minimal. Since we always pick valid nodes, we need to prove that if a minimal correct waited sequence exists, then there exists a minimal correct waited sequence that updates only valid nodes.

Careful Waited Sequence. A *careful waited sequence* of updates $(T, W) = (t_1 t_2 \cdots t_{|N|}, w_1 w_2 \cdots w_{k-1})$ is a correct waited sequence s.t. $\forall j \in [1, |N|]$: *valid* $(upd(C_i, t_1 \cdots t_{j-1}), t_j)$ A *minimal careful waited sequence* is a careful waited sequence (T, W) s.t. $|W|$ is minimal. We prove the following for such sequences.

Theorem 4. If a minimal correct waited sequence exists, then a minimal careful sequence exists as well.

5.1 Condition for Waits

Partial Careful Waited Sequence. Given careful waited sequence $Z = (T = t_1 \cdots t_{|N|}, W = w_1 \cdots w_{k-1})$, a partial careful waited sequence is $Z' = (T' = t_1 \cdots t_r, W' = w_1 \cdots w_s)$ such that T' is a prefix of T and W' is a prefix of W. We start with a partial careful waited sequence with no nodes, and at every step adds a node while ensuring that the obtained sequence is a partial careful waited sequence, i.e., can be extended to a careful waited sequence.

Wait Condition. Consider a function *wait* that takes a partial careful waited sequence $S = (t_1 t_2 \cdots t_r, w_1 w_2 \cdots w_s)$ and node n s.t. $valid(C_i, U t_1 \cdots t_r)$ as an argument and returns *true* if there needs to be a wait before its update. Specifically: $wait(n, S) = true$ if and only if node $\exists x \in [1, r] : \neg valid(upd(C_i, t_1 \cdots t_x), n) \wedge$

$\neg(\exists y \in [1,s], \exists z \in (x,r] : w_y = t_z)$, i.e., in the partial careful waited sequence, there must be a wait before updating a valid node n if and only if it was not valid until its dependencies were updated, and there was no wait after their update. In this case, n must be updated in a new round, after a wait.

We now show *completeness* of the wait condition, i.e., if a wait is needed (as defined in Sect. 3) after updating S and before updating n, then $wait(n, S)$ is true.

Lemma 3. If (1) n is the node picked for update, and (2) the partial careful waited sequence built before updating n is $S = (t_1 t_2 \cdots t_r, w_1 w_2 \cdots w_s)$, and (3) $w_s = t_y$ for some $y \in [1,r]$, and (4) we define $\forall x \in [1,r] : C_{t_x} = upd(C_i, t_1 \cdots t_x)$, and then $wait(n, S) \leftrightarrow C_{t_y} \cup \cdots \cup C_{t_r} \cup upd(C_{t_r}, n)$ is inconsistent.

5.2 Algorithm for Optimal Consistent Order Updates

The *OptimalPickAndWait* (Algorithm 3) subroutine minimizes waits, solving the optimal consistent update problem. We minimize waits by assigning priority P_0 (higher priority) or P_1 (lower priority) to nodes. Let S be a partial sequence. A node is in P_0 if and only if $\neg wait(n, S)$, i.e., P_0 nodes do not require waiting before update. A node is in P_1 if and only if $wait(n, S)$, i.e., we must wait before updating a P_1 node. We greedily update P_0 nodes first.

Correctness and optimality follow from the correctness argument in the previous section, and from Lemma 3. Intuitively, updating a node in P_0 which does not need a wait allows the P_1 list to build up. This means we need to place a single wait for as many P_1 nodes as possible. When we place a wait in the partial careful waited sequence, every valid node that was in P_1 moves to P_0. The last key property needed for the following theorems is that once a node acquires priority P_0, it retains priority P_0.

Theorem 5. Algorithm 1 with Algorithm 3 as its subroutine on Line 6 produces a correct waited sequence.

Theorem 6. Algorithm 1 with Algorithm 3 as its subroutine on Line 6 produces a correct and optimal waited sequence of updates, if one exists.

Running Time. The OrderUpdate Algorithm with the *OptimalPickAndWait* subroutine has the same time complexity that it had with the *SequentialPickAndWait* subroutine. The *OptimalPickAndWait* subroutine introduces a priority-based node selection mechanism— after every wait, it simply moves nodes from the valid set U to the higher priority list P_0, which requires only $O(|N|)$ additional steps in each iteration.

6 Discussion

Multiple hosts and sinks. We can extend our single-source approach to a network with multiple sources $H_A, H_B, H_C, \cdots$. To do this, we assume that there is a master source H_1, and every actual source is connected to H_1, as shown in Fig. 6. This approach works because we update every node only once, meaning we cannot artificially disable and then re-enable some sources and keep others.

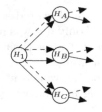

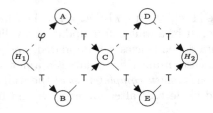

Fig. 6. Multiple sources.   **Fig. 7.** Double diamond with symbolic
                                        forwarding rules.

Multiple packet types. Our approach can be applied when there are multiple
(discrete) packet types, as long as each forwarding rule matches on a *single*
packet type—in this case, we compute an update for each packet type, and
perform these (rule-granularity) updates independently. In the more realistic
case with *symbolic* forwarding rules (i.e., matching based on *first-order formulae
over packet header fields*), deciding whether a consistent update exists is CO-
NP-hard. Specifically, there is a reduction from SAT to this problem. We can
consider each edge in a configuration as being labeled by a formula, and only
packets whose header fields satisfy this formula can be forwarded along that
edge. Consider a double diamond (Fig. 7) with one edge labelled by φ, and all
other edges labelled with *true* ($\top$). We have seen that a consistent update for this
double diamond example is not possible in the situation where packets (of any
type) can flow along all of the edges, so we can see that *there exists a consistent
update if and only if φ is unsatisfiable.* This completes the reduction.

7   Related Work

Consistency. Our core problem is motivated by earlier work by Reitblatt et al.
[16] that proposed *per-packet consistency* and provided basic update mechanisms.

Exponential Search-Based Network Update Algorithms. There are various
approaches for producing a sequence of switch updates guaranteed to respect
certain path-based consistency properties (e.g., properties representable using
temporal logic, etc.). For example, McClurg et al. [15] use counter-example
guided search and incremental LTL model checking, FLIP [17] uses integer linear
programming, and CCG [19] uses custom reachability-based graph algorithms.
Other works such as Dionysus [7], zUpdate [8], and Luo et al. [12], seek to perform updates with respect to quantitative properties.

Complexity results. Mahajan and Wattenhofer [13] propose dependency-graphs
as a representation for network updates, and propose properties that can be
solved using this general approach, including loop freedom, which is handled in
a minimal way. Yuan et al. [18] detail general algorithms for building dependency
graphs and using these graphs to perform a consistent update. Förster et al. [6]

show that for *blackhole-freedom*, computing an update with a minimal number of rounds is NP-hard (assuming memory limits on switches). They also show NP-hardness results for rule-granular loop-free updates with maximal parallelism. Per-packet consistency in our problem is stronger than loop and blackhole freedom, but we consider solutions where each switch is updated *once*, and where a switch update replaces the entire old forwarding table with the new one.

Förster and Wattenhofer [5] examine loop-freedom, showing that maximizing the number for forwarding rules updated simultaneously is NP-hard. Ludwig et al. [10] show how to minimize the number of update rounds with respect to loop-freedom. They show that deciding whether a k-round schedule exists is NP-complete, and they present a polynomial algorithm for computing a weaker variant of loop-freedom. Amiri et al. [1] present an NP-hardness result for greedily updating a maximal number of forwarding rules in this context. Additionally, Ludwig et al. [9] investigate optimal updates with respect to a stronger property, namely *waypoint enforcement* in addition to loop freedom. They produce an update sequence with a minimal number of waits, using mixed-integer programming. Ludwig et al. [11] show that the decision problem is NP-hard.

Mattos et al. [14] propose a relaxed variant of per-packet consistency, where a packet may be processed by several subsequent configurations (rather than a *single* one), and present a polynomial graph-based algorithm for computing updates. Dudycz et al. [4] show that simultaneously computing *two* network updates while minimizing the number of switch updates ("touches") is NP-hard. Brandt et al. [2] give a polynomial algorithm to decide if a congestion-free update is possible when flows are "splittable" and/or not restricted to be integer.

8 Conclusion

We presented a polynomial-time algorithm to find a consistent update order for a single packet type. We then described a modification to the algorithm which finds a consistent update order with a minimal number of waits. Finally, we proved that this modification is correct, complete, and optimal.

References

1. Amiri, S.A., Ludwig, A., Marcinkowski, J., Schmid, S.: Transiently consistent SDN updates: being greedy is hard. In: SIROCCO (2016)
2. Brandt, S., Förster, K.-T., Wattenhofer, R.: On consistent migration of flows in SDNs. In: INFOCOM (2016)
3. Černý, P., Foster, N., Jagnik, N., McClurg, J.: Updates, optimal consistent network in polynomial time (extended version). arXiv:1607.05159 (2016)
4. Dudycz, S., Ludwig, A., Schmid, S.: This, can't touch: consistent network updates for multiple policies. In: DSN (2016)
5. Förster, K.-T., Wattenhofer, R.: The power of two in consistent network updates: hard loop freedom, easy flow migration. In: ICCCN (2016)
6. Förster, K.-T., Mahajan, R., Wattenhofer, R.: Consistent updates in software defined networks: on dependencies, loop freedom, and blackholes. In: IFIP (2016)

7. Jin, X., Liu, H.H., Gandhi, R., Kandula, S., Mahajan, R., Zhang, M., Rexford, J., Wattenhofer, R.: Dynamic scheduling of network updates. In: SIGCOMM (2014)
8. Liu, H.H., Xin, W., Zhang, M., Yuan, L., Wattenhofer, R., Maltz, D.: zUpdate: updating data center networks with zero loss. In: SIGCOMM (2013)
9. Ludwig, A., Rost, M., Foucard, D., Schmid. S.: Good network updates for bad packets: waypoint enforcement beyond destination-based routing policies. In: HotNets (2014)
10. Ludwig, A., Marcinkowski, J., Schmid, S.: Updates, scheduling loop-free network: it's good to relax! In: PODC (2015)
11. Ludwig, A., Dudycz, S., Rost, M., Schmid, S.: Transiently secure network updates. In: SIGMETRICS (2016)
12. Luo, S., Yu, H., Luo, L., Li, L.M.: Arrange your network updates as you wish. In: IFIP (2016)
13. Mahajan, R., Wattenhofer, R.: On consistent updates in software defined networks. In: HotNets (2013)
14. Mattos, D.M.F., Duarte, O.C.M.B., Pujolle, G.: Reverse update: a consistent policy update scheme for software defined networking. IEEE Commun. Lett. **20**(5), 886–889 (2016)
15. McClurg, J., Hojjat, H., Černý, P., Foster, N.: Efficient synthesis of network updates. In: PLDI (2015)
16. Reitblatt, M., Foster, N., Rexford, J., Schlesinger, C., Walker, D.: Abstractions for network update. In: SIGCOMM (2012)
17. Vissicchio, S., Cittadini, L.: FLIP the (Flow) table: Fast LIghtweight Policy-preserving SDN updates. In: INFOCOM (2016)
18. Yuan, Y., Ivančić, F., Lumezanu, C., Zhang, S., Gupta, A.: Generating consistent updates for software-defined network configurations. In: HotSDN (2014)
19. Zhou, W., Jin, D., Croft, J., Caesar, M., Brighten Godfrey, P.: Enforcing customizable consistency properties in software-defined networks. In: NSDI, May 2015

Distributed Construction of Purely Additive Spanners

Keren Censor-Hillel[1], Telikepalli Kavitha[2], Ami Paz[1(✉)], and Amir Yehudayoff[3]

[1] Department of Computer Science, Technion, Haifa, Israel
{ckeren,amipaz}@cs.technion.ac.il
[2] Tata Institute of Fundamental Research, Mumbai, India
kavitha@tcs.tifr.res.in
[3] Department of Mathematics, Technion, Haifa, Israel
amir.yehudayoff@gmail.com

Abstract. This paper studies the complexity of distributed construction of purely additive spanners in the CONGEST model. We describe algorithms for building such spanners in several cases. Because of the need to simultaneously make decisions at far apart locations, the algorithms use additional mechanisms compared to their sequential counterparts.

We complement our algorithms with a lower bound on the number of rounds required for computing pairwise spanners. The standard reductions from set-disjointness and equality seem unsuitable for this task because no specific edge needs to be removed from the graph. Instead, to obtain our lower bound, we define a new communication complexity problem that reduces to computing a sparse spanner, and prove a lower bound on its communication complexity using information theory. This technique significantly extends the current toolbox used for obtaining lower bounds for the CONGEST model, and we believe it may find additional applications.

1 Introduction

A graph *spanner* is a sparse subgraph that guarantees some bound on how much the original distances are stretched. Graph spanners, introduced in 1989 [43,44], are fundamental graph structures which are central for many applications, such as synchronizing distributed networks [44], information dissemination [13], compact routing schemes [14,45,50], and more.

Due to the importance of spanners, the trade-offs between their possible sparsity and stretch have been the focus of a huge amount of literature. Moreover, finding time-efficient constructions of spanners with optimal guarantees has been a major goal for the distributed computing community, with ingenious algorithms given in many studies. One particular type of spanners are *purely additive spanners*, in which the distances are promised to be stretched by no

---

Keren Censor-Hillel and Ami Paz were Supported by ISF individual research grant 1696/14. Part of this work was done while Ami Paz was visiting TIFR, Mumbai.

C. Gavoille and D. Ilcinkas (Eds.): DISC 2016, LNCS 9888, pp. 129–142, 2016.
DOI: 10.1007/978-3-662-53426-7_10

more than an additive term. However, distributed constructions of such spanners have been scarce, with the only known construction being a $(+2)$-additive spanner construction with $O(n^{3/2} \log n)$ edges in $O(\sqrt{n} \log n + D)$ rounds in a network of size n and diameter D [38] (also follows from [34]).

The absence of distributed constructions of purely additive spanners is explicitly brought into light by Pettie [47], and implicitly mentioned in [20].

This paper remedies this state of affairs, by providing a study of the complexity of constructing sparse purely additive spanners in the synchronous CONGEST model [41], in which each of n nodes can send an $O(\log n)$-bit message to each of its neighbors in every round. Our contribution is twofold: first, we provide efficient constructions of several spanners with different guarantees, and second, we present new lower bounds for the number of rounds required for such constructions, using tools that are not standard in this context.

1.1   The Challenge

A subgraph H of an undirected unweighted graph $G = (V, E)$ is called a purely additive spanner with stretch β if for every every pair $(u, v) \in V \times V$, we have $\delta_H(u, v) \le \delta_G(u, v) + \beta$, where $\delta_H(u, v)$ is the u-v distance in H and $\delta_G(u, v)$ is the u-v distance in G. The goal in spanner problems is to construct a subgraph H that is as sparse as possible with β as small as possible, i.e., we seek a sparse subgraph of G which approximates all distances with a small stretch.

The problem of computing sparse spanners with small stretch β is well-studied and we know how to construct sparse purely additive spanners for $\beta = 2, 4, 6$. These have sizes $O(n^{3/2})$ [3], $\tilde{O}(n^{7/5})$ [15], and $O(n^{4/3})$ [6], respectively. In a very recent breakthrough, it was shown that there is *no* purely additive spanner of size at most $n^{4/3}/2^{O(\sqrt{\log n})}$ [1].

In a bid to get sparser subgraphs than all-pairs spanners with the same stretch, the following relaxation of *pairwise spanners* has attracted recent interest. Here we are given $\mathcal{P} \subseteq V \times V$: these are our "relevant pairs" and we seek a sparse subgraph which approximates distances between all pairs in $\mathcal{P}$ with a small stretch. That is, for every pair $(u, v) \in \mathcal{P}$, the graph H should satisfy $\delta_H(u, v) \le \delta_G(u, v) + \beta$ and for pairs (u, v) outside $\mathcal{P}$, the value $\delta_H(u, v)$ could be arbitrarily large. Such a subgraph H is called a $(+\beta)$-pairwise spanner. We use $\tau(\mathcal{P})$ to denote the number of nodes appearing in $\mathcal{P}$, i.e. $\tau(\mathcal{P}) = |\{u \mid \exists v : \{u, v\} \in \mathcal{P}\}|$.

The problem of constructing sparse pairwise spanners was first studied by Coppersmith and Elkin [16] who showed sparse subgraphs where distances for pairs in $\mathcal{P}$ were *exactly preserved*; these subgraphs were called *pairwise preservers*. A natural case for $\mathcal{P}$ is when $\mathcal{P} = S \times V$, where $S \subseteq V$ is a set of *source* nodes — here we seek for a sparse subgraph that well-approximates s-v distances for all $(s, v) \in S \times V$. Such pairwise spanners are called *sourcewise spanners*. Another natural setting is when $\mathcal{P} = S \times S$ and such pairwise spanners are called *subsetwise spanners*.

Purely additive spanners are usually built in three steps: first, building clusters which contain all high-degree nodes and adding all the edges of the unclustered nodes; second, building BFS trees which $(+2)$-approximate all the paths with many missing edges; and third, adding more edges to approximate the other paths.

While our constructions follow the general outline of known sequential constructions of pairwise additive spanners [35,36], their techniques cannot be directly implemented in a distributed setting. In the sequential setting, the *clustering* phase is implemented by repeatedly choosing a high-degree node and adding some of its edges to the spanner; these neighbors are marked and ignored in the rest of the phase. In the distributed setting, going over high degree nodes one by one, creating clusters and updating the degrees is too costly. Instead, we choose the cluster centers at random, as done by Thorup and Zwick [51], Baswana and Sen [9], and Chechik [15] (see also Aingworth et al. [3] for an earlier use of randomization for the a dominating set problem).

Sources for BFS trees are carefully chosen in the sequential setting by approximately solving a set-cover problem, in order to cover all paths with many missing edges. Once again, this cannot be directly implemented in the distributed setting, as the knowledge of all paths cannot be quickly gathered in one location, so we choose the BFS sources randomly [15]. In both the clustering and BFS phases, the number of edges increases by a multiplicative $\log^c n$ factor, for $c < 1$.

The main challenge left is to choose additional edges to add to the spanner in order to approximate the remaining paths well. To this end, we make heavy use of the parallel-BFS technique of Holzer and Wattenhofer [34], which allows to construct BFS trees rooted at s different nodes in $O(s + D)$ rounds. We use this technique to count edges in a path, to count missing edges in it, and to choose which edges to add to the spanner. Yet, interestingly, we are unable to match the guarantee on the number of edges of more sophisticated algorithms [6,35,53]. Some of these algorithms use the *value* of a path, which is roughly the number of pairs of cluster that get closer if the path is added to the spanner. We are not able to measure this quantity efficiently in the distributed setting, and this is one of the reasons we are unable to introduce (+6)-all-pairs spanner matching the sequential constructions.

1.2   Our Contribution

We provide various spanner constructions in the CONGEST model, as summarized in Tables 1 and 2.

The distributed spanner construction algorithms we present have three main properties: stretch, number of edges, and running time. All three properties hold w.h.p. (with high probability). That is, the algorithm stops in the desired time, with the desired number of edges and the spanner produced has the desired stretch with probability $1 - n^{-c}$, where c is constant of choice. However, we can trade the properties and guarantee two of the three to always hold: if the spanner is too dense or the stretch is too large, we can repeat the algorithm; if the running time exceeds some threshold, we can stop the execution and output the whole graph to get 0 stretch, or output an empty graph to get the desired number of edges. The edges of the constructed spanner can be counted over a BFS tree in G within $O(D)$ rounds. In sourcewise, subsetwise and pairwise spanners, the stretch is measured by running BFS from the relevant nodes (nodes of S of appearing in $\mathcal{P}$) for $O(D)$ rounds in G and again in H; in all-pairs spanners,

Table 1. The number of edges in our new constructions versus prior, sequential work. Due to space limitations, most of our results are only stated here, and their proofs appear in the full version of the article. We compare our (+4)-subsetwise with a sequential construction of a (+2)-subsetwise spanner, and our (+8)-all-pairs spanner with a (+6)-all-pairs spanner.

Spanner type	Number of edges — distributed		Number of edges — sequential	
(+2)-sourcewise	$O\left(n^{5/4}\,|S|^{1/4}\log^{3/4} n\right)$	(Theorem 1)	$O\left(n^{5/4}\,|S|^{1/4}\log^{1/4} n\right)$	[36]
(+2)-pairwise	$O\left(n\,|\mathcal{P}|^{1/3}\log^{2/3} n\right)$		$O\left(n\,|\mathcal{P}|^{1/3}\right)$	[2]
(+4)-pairwise	$O\left(n\,|\mathcal{P}|^{2/7}\log^{6/7} n\right)$		$O\left(n\,|\mathcal{P}|^{2/7}\log^{3/7} n\right)$	[35]
(+4)-all-pairs	$O\left(n^{7/5}\log^{4/5} n\right)$		$O\left(n^{7/5}\log^{1/5} n\right)$	[15]
(+8)-all-pairs	$O\left(n^{15/11}\log^{10/11} n\right)$		$O\left(n^{4/3}\right)$	[6]
(+2)-subsetwise	$O\left(n\,|S|^{2/3}\log^{2/3} n\right)$		$O\left(n\,|S|^{1/2}\right)$	[17,46]
(+4)-subsetwise	$O\left(n\,|S|^{4/7}\log^{6/7} n\right)$		$O\left(n\,|S|^{1/2}\right)$	[17,46]

Table 2. Running time: algorithms versus lower bounds, for number of edges as in Table 1. Due to space limitations, most of our results are only stated here, and their proofs appear in the full version of the article. $\tilde{\Omega}$ hides polylogarithmic factors.

Spanner Type	Number of Rounds		Lower Bounds	
(+2)-sourcewise	$O\left(|S| + D\right)$	(Thm. 1)	$\min\left\{\tilde{\Omega}\left(\frac{n^{3/8}}{|S|^{1/8}}\right), \Omega\left(D\right)\right\}$	[47]
(+2)-pairwise	$O\left(\tau(\mathcal{P}) + D\right)$		$\min\left\{\tilde{\Omega}\left(\frac{n^{1/2}}{|\mathcal{P}|^{1/6}}\right), \Omega\left(D\right)\right\}$	[47]
			$\Omega\left(\frac{|\mathcal{P}|}{n\log n}\right)$	(Thm. 3)
(+4)-pairwise	$O\left(\tau(\mathcal{P}) + D\right)$		$\min\left\{\tilde{\Omega}\left(\frac{n^{1/2}}{|\mathcal{P}|^{1/7}}\right), \Omega\left(D\right)\right\}$	[47]
			$\Omega\left(\frac{|\mathcal{P}|}{n\log n}\right)$	
(+4)-all-pairs	$O(n^{3/5}\log^{1/5} n + D)$		$\min\left\{\tilde{\Omega}\left(n^{3/10}\right), \Omega\left(D\right)\right\}$	[47]
(+8)-all-pairs	$O(n^{7/11}\log^{1/11} n + D)$		$\min\left\{\tilde{\Omega}\left(n^{7/22}\right), \Omega\left(D\right)\right\}$	[47]
(+2)-subsetwise	$O(|S| + D)$		$\min\left\{\tilde{\Omega}\left(\frac{n^{1/2}}{|S|^{1/3}}\right), \Omega\left(D\right)\right\}$	[47]
(+4)-subsetwise	$O(|S| + D)$		$\min\left\{\tilde{\Omega}\left(\frac{n^{1/2}}{|S|^{2/7}}\right), \Omega\left(D\right)\right\}$	[47]

the stretch is measured by measuring the stretch of the underlying sourcewise or subsetwise spanner.

We complement our algorithms with some lower bounds for the CONGEST model. We show that any algorithm that constructs an additive (+2)-pairwise spanner with m edges on $p \leq m$ pairs must have at least $\Omega(p/(n \log n))$ rounds, as long as $m \leq n^{3/2}$. For example, a CONGEST construction of a $(+2)$-pairwise spanner must take $\tilde{\Omega}(\sqrt{n})$ rounds. We also prove lower bounds for (α, β)-pairwise spanners (i.e., for which $\delta_H(u, v) \leq \alpha \, \delta_G(u, v) + \beta$). We show that any algorithm that constructs an (α, β)-pairwise spanner with m edges on $p \leq m$ pairs must have at least $\Omega(p/(n \log n))$ rounds, as long as $m \leq n^{1 + \frac{4}{9\alpha + 3\beta - 10}}$, where the constant in the Ω notation depends on α, β.

We believe the difficulty in obtaining this lower bound arises from the fact that standard reductions from set-disjointness and equality are unsuitable for this task. At a high level, in most standard reductions the problem boils down to deciding the existence of an edge (which can represent, e.g., the intersecting element between the inputs); when constructing spanners, no specific edge needs to be added to the spanner or omitted from it, so the solution is allowed a considerable amount of slack that is not affected by any particular edge alone.

Instead, to obtain our lower bound, we define a new communication complexity problem that reduces to computing a sparse spanner, and prove a lower bound on its communication complexity using information theory. In this new problem, which we call PART-COMP$_{m,p}$, Alice has a set $x \subseteq \{1, \ldots, m\}$ of size $|x| = p$, and Bob has to output a set $y \subseteq \{1, \ldots, m\}$ of size $|y| = m/2$ so that $x \cap y = \emptyset$. We show that any protocol that solves PART-COMP$_{m,p}$ must convey $\Omega(p)$ bits of information about the set x. This technique significantly extends the current toolbox used for obtaining lower bounds for the CONGEST model. As such, we believe it may find additional applications, especially in obtaining lower bounds for computing in this model.

Roadmap. We conclude this section with a further discussion of related work. Section 2 contains the definition of the model and some basic routines. In Sect. 3 we present distributed algorithms for computing the various types of spanners discussed above. In Sect. 4 we present our new lower bounds, and we conclude with a short discussion in Sect. 5.

1.3 Related Work

Sparse spanners with a small multiplicative stretch are well-understood: Althöfer et al. [4] in 1993 showed that any weighted graph G on n vertices has a spanner of size $O(n^{1+1/k})$ with multiplicative stretch $2k - 1$, for every integer $k \geq 1$. Since then, several works [9,23,26,29,37,46,48,49,52] have considered the problem of efficiently constructing sparse spanners with small stretch and have used spanners in the applications of computing approximate distances and approximate shortest paths efficiently.

For unweighted graphs, one seeks spanners where the stretch is purely additive and as mentioned earlier, an almost tight bound of $n^{4/3}$ is known for how sparse a purely additive spanner can be. Bollobás et al. [11] were the first to study a variant of pairwise preservers called *distance preservers*, where the set of relevant pairs is $\mathcal{P} = \{(u, v) : \delta_G(u, v) \geq d\}$, for a given parameter d. Coppersmith and Elkin [16] showed pairwise preservers of size $O(n\sqrt{|\mathcal{P}|})$ and $O(n + |\mathcal{P}|\sqrt{n})$

for any $\mathcal{P} \subseteq V \times V$. For $|P| = \omega\left(n^{3/4}\right)$, the bound of $O(n\sqrt{|\mathcal{P}|})$ for pairwise preservers has very recently been improved to $O(n^{2/3}|\mathcal{P}|^{2/3} + n|\mathcal{P}|^{1/3})$ by Bodwin and Williams [10].

The problem of designing sparse pairwise spanners was first considered by Cygan et al. [17] who showed a tradeoff between the additive stretch and size of the spanner. The current sparsest pairwise spanner with purely additive stretch has size $O(n|\mathcal{P}|^{1/4})$ and additive stretch 6 [35]. Woodruff [53] and Abboud and Bodwin [1,2] showed lower bounds for additive spanners and pairwise spanners. Parter [40] showed sparse *multiplicative* sourcewise spanners and a lower bound of $\Omega(n|S|^{1/k}/k)$ on the size of a sourcewise spanner with additive stretch $2(k-1)$, for any integer $k \geq 1$.

Distributed construction of sparse spanners with multiplicative stretch was addressed in several studies [6,9,19–21,25,47]. Constructions of (α,β)-spanners were addressed in [6,22,47]. Towards the goal of obtaining purely additive spanners, for which $\alpha = 1$, Elkin and Peleg [29] introduced nearly-additive spanners, for which $\alpha = 1 + \epsilon$. Additional distributed constructions of nearly-additive spanners are given in [22,26,30,47]. Finally, somewhat related, are constructions of various spanners in the streaming model, and in dynamic settings, both centralized and distributed [5,7,8,27,28].

In his seminal paper, Pettie [47] presents lower bounds for the number of rounds needed by distributed algorithms in order to construct several families of spanners. Specifically, it is shown that computing an all-pair additive β-spanner with size $n^{1+\rho}$ in expectation, for a constant β, requires $\Omega\left(n^{(1-\rho)/2}\right)$ rounds of communication. Because this is an indistinguishability-based lower bound, it holds even for the less restricted LOCAL mode, where message lengths can be unbounded.

The lower bound is obtained by showing an n-node graph with diameter $D = \Theta\left(n^{(1-\rho)/2}\right)$ where, roughly speaking, removing *wrong* edges induces a stretch that is too large, and identifying these wrong edges takes $\Omega(D)$ rounds. This gives a lower bound of $\min\left\{\Omega\left(n^{(1-\rho)/2}\right), \Omega(D)\right\}$ rounds. Examining the construction in detail, it is not hard to show it works for other types of spanners as well: even for a single pair of nodes, or a set S of size 2, at least $\Omega(D)$ rounds are necessary in order to avoid removing wrong edges.

2   Preliminaries

The Model. The distributed model we assume is the well-known CONGEST model [41]. Such a system consists of a set of n computational units, who exchange messages according to an undirected *communication graph* $G = (V, E)$, $|V| = n$, where nodes represent the computational units and edges the communication links. Each node has a unique identifier which can be encoded using $O(\log n)$ bits. The diameter of G is denoted by D.

When the computation starts, each node knows its own identifier and the identifiers of its neighbors; when there is a set S of nodes or a set $\mathcal{P}$ of node-pairs involved in the computation, it also knows if it belongs to S, or all the pairs in $\mathcal{P}$ it belongs to. The computation proceeds in rounds, where in each round each node sends an $O(\log n)$-bits message to each of its neighbors, receives a message from each neighbor, and performs a computation. We use the number of rounds as our complexity measure, while ignoring the local computation time; however, in our algorithms all local computations take polynomial time. When the computation ends, each node knows which of its neighbors is also its neighbor in the new graph $H = (V, E')$ generated. We do not assume that the global structure of H is known to any of the nodes.

Clustering and BFS. The first building block in all of our algorithms is *clustering*. A *cluster* C_i around a *cluster center* c_i is a subset of $\Gamma_G(c_i)$, the set of neighbors of c_i in G (which does not include c_i itself). A node belonging to a cluster is *clustered*, while the other nodes of G are *unclustered*. We use $\mathcal{C}$ to denote the set of cluster centers and $\hat{\mathcal{C}}$ to denote the set of clusters.

In the *clustering* phase of our algorithms we divide some of the nodes into clusters. We create a new graph containing all the edges connecting a clustered node to its cluster center, and all the edges incident on unclustered nodes.

Another building block is *BFS trees.* A BFS tree in a graph G, rooted at a node r, consists of shortest paths from r to all other nodes in G. The process of creating a BFS tree, known as BFS search, is well-known in the sequential setting. In the distributed setting, a single BFS tree can be easily constructed by a techniques called *flooding* (see, e.g. [41, Sect. 3]), and a celebrated result of Holzer and Wattenhofer [34] asserts that multiple BFS trees, rooted at a set S of nodes, can be constructed in $O(|S| + D)$ rounds. Here, D denotes the diameter of the graph, i.e. the maximal distance between two nodes. We use this technique to add BFS trees to the spanner we construct, and to measure distances in the original graph.

3   Building Spanners

In this section we discuss the distributed construction of $(+2)$-sourcewise spanners. We first present an algorithm and analyze the constructed spanner in terms of stretch and number of edges, and then discuss the implementation of this algorithm in the CONGEST model and analyze its running time. Other families of spanners, and their construction, are discussed in the full version of this article.

In a nutshell, our algorithms have three steps: first, each node tosses a coin to decide if it will serve as a cluster center; second, each cluster center tosses another coin to decide if it will serve as a root of a BFS tree; third, add to the current graph edges that are part of certain short paths. The parameters of the coins and the meaning of "short" are carefully chosen, depending on the input to the problem and the desired stretch.

Proving that the algorithms perform well is about analyzing the probability of failure. This analysis uses the graph structure as well as standard concentration bounds. In all of our algorithms, c is a constant that can be chosen according to the desired exponent of $1/n$ in the failure probability.

3.1   A (+2)-Sourcewise Spanner

Our first algorithm constructs a (+2)-sourcewise spanner. Given a set $S \subseteq V$, the algorithm returns a subgraph H of G satisfying $\delta_H(s, v) \leq \delta_G(s, v) + 2$ for all $(s, v) \in S \times V$, with guarantees as given in the following theorem.

Theorem 1. *Given a graph G with n nodes and a set S of source nodes, a (+2)-sourcewise spanner with $O(n^{5/4} |S|^{1/4} \log^{3/4} n)$ edges can be constructed in $O(|S| + D)$ rounds in the CONGEST model w.h.p.*

This is only a factor $O(\log^{1/2} n)$ more than the number of edges given by the best sequential algorithm known for this type of spanners [36]. We first present a sequential algorithm achieving the desired size and stretch, and then discuss its distributed implementation.

Algorithm 2S. Input: a graph $G = (V, E)$; a set of source nodes $S \subseteq V$
Output: a subgraph H
Initialization: $n = |V|$, $h = (n |S|)^{1/4} \log^{3/4} n$, and $H = (V, \emptyset)$

Clustering. Pick each node as a *cluster center* w.p. $\frac{c \log n}{h}$, and denote the set of selected nodes by $\{c_1, c_2, \ldots\}$. For each node $v \in V$, choose a neighbor c_i of v which is a cluster center, if such a neighbor exists, add the edge (v, c_i) to H, and add v to C_i; if none of the neighbors of v is a cluster center, add to H all the edges v belongs to.

BFS. Pick each cluster center as a *root* of a BFS tree w.p. $\frac{h^2}{cn \log n}$, and add to H a BFS tree rooted at each chosen root.

Path Buying. For each source-cluster pair $(s, C_i) \in S \times \hat{C}$: build a temporary set of paths, containing a single, arbitrary shortest path from s to each $x \in C_i$; omit from the set all paths with more than $\frac{2c^2 n \log^2 n}{h^2}$ missing edges (i.e. edges in G but not in H); if any paths are left, add to H the shortest among them.

Analysis of Algorithm 2S. There are $O(n^{5/4} |S|^{1/4} \log^{3/4} n)$ edges in the spanner w.h.p.: in the clustering phase, all nodes of degree at least h are clustered, so unclustered nodes add $O(nh)$ edges; in the BFS phase, the number of BFS trees is at most $4h$, for another $O(nh)$ edges; finally, $|\mathcal{C}| = O\left(\frac{n \log n}{h}\right)$ for another $O\left(\frac{|S| n^2 \log^3 n}{h^3}\right)$ edges. The choice of h gives the stated size of the spanner.

The stretch of each path form $s \in S$ to $v \in V$ is at most $+2$ w.h.p.: a paths with more than $\frac{2c^2 n \log^2 n}{h^2}$ missing edges has a source of a BFS tree adjacent to it, and the BFS tree gives the $+2$ approximation; for a path with fewer missing edges, let u be first unclustered node on the path when traversing it from v, so the algorithm buys a shortest path from s to some node u' in the cluster of u, and the path $s - u' - u - v$ gives a (+2)-approximation of the original path.

Implementing Algorithm 2S in the CONGEST Model

Lemma 1. *Algorithm* 2S *can be implemented in* $O(|S|+D)$ *rounds in the CONGEST model, w.p. at least* $1 - o(n^{-c})$.

Proof (sketch). We sketch distributed implementations for each of the phases in Algorithm 2S, and analyze their running time.

Preprocessing. The parameters $|S|$ and n are gathered along a BFS tree rooted at a predetermined node, and then spread to all the nodes over the same tree, in $O(D)$ rounds.

Clustering. Each node becomes a cluster center w.p. $\frac{c \log n}{h}$ and inform its neighbors; each node that gets at least one message joins a cluster of one of its neighbors arbitrarily; finally, the rest of the nodes and add all their incident edges to the graph. The round complexity of this phase is constant.

BFS. Each cluster center becomes a root of a BFS tree w.p. $\frac{ch^2}{n \log n}$, without communication. The number of BFS trees is $O(h)$ w.p. $1 - o(n^{-c})$, and this number of BFS searches is run in parallel in $O(D+h)$ rounds, using an algorithm of Holzer and Wattenhofer [34, Sect. 6.1].

Path Buying. This phase starts with measuring all the distances between pairs of nodes in $S \times V$, and the number of missing edges in each shortest path measured. To this end, we run a BFS search from each $s \in S$ in parallel in $O(|S|+D)$ rounds, as before, where each BFS also counts the missing edges on each path.

Each node $x \in V$, upon receiving a BFS message initiated in s, knows its distance form s and the number of missing edges on a path from S; we henceforth only consider this specific path. After all BFS searches are over, x reports these parameters to its cluster center; this sub-phase takes $O(|S|)$ rounds to complete.

Each cluster center c_i now chooses, for each $s \in S$, the shortest among all paths with at most $\frac{2c^2 n \log^2 n}{h^2}$ missing edges from s to some $x' \in C_i$; this path is added to H by sending a "buy" message from x' and up the BFS tree of s. This sub-phase requires $O(|S| + D)$ rounds.

In total, the running time of the algorithm is $O(h + |S| + D)$, w.h.p. If $h = \Omega(|S|)$, we replace the algorithm by a simpler algorithm that returns the union of BFS trees rooted at all nodes of S; this exactly preserves all distances and comply with the size and time restrictions.

4 Lower Bounds

In this section we prove lower bounds on the number of rounds that are needed for constructing spanners in the CONGEST model. All previous lower bounds for the distributed construction of spanners [47] use an indistinguishability argument: while many edges should be omitted from the graph in order to create a sparse spanner, there are few edges that must not be omitted. However, in order to distinguish these few edges from the rest, some nodes must learn a considerable part of the graph. In a nutshell, the heart of the proof is that information must travel a constant portion of the diameter D, yielding an $\Omega(D)$ lower bound.

The lower bounds from [47] apply also to the LOCAL model, where the message sizes are unbounded. Here, we present the first lower bound that is specific for the CONGEST model. As in previous lower bounds for the CONGEST model, our proof uses a reduction from a communication complexity problem. However, previous lower bounds used reductions either from the equality problem [42] or from set-disjointness, e.g., [12,18,24,31–33]. These seem unsuitable for our purposes, and hence we diverge from this approach and define a new communication complexity problem we call *partial complement*. We bound the communication complexity of this problem from below, using information theory.

Here, we prove a lower bound for the construction of a $(+2)$-pairwise spanner. In the full version of this paper, we generalize this lower bound for the construction of an (α, β)-pairwise spanner, where $\alpha \geq 1$ and $\beta \geq 0$ are constants.

4.1   A Communication Complexity Problem

Let m, p be two positive integers so that $p \leq m/3$. The *partial complement* communication problem, denoted $\text{PART-COMP}_{m,p}$, is defined as follows: Alice has a set $x \subseteq \{1, \ldots, m\}$ of size $|x| = p$, and Bob has to output a set $y \subseteq \{1, \ldots, m\}$ of size $|y| = m/2$ so that $x \cap y = \emptyset$. Note that the goal of this communication problem is to compute a relation, not a function. In the full version of this paper we prove that the randomized communication complexity of the partial complement problem is high.

Theorem 2. *If π is a $(1/3)$-error randomized protocol computing $\text{PART-COMP}_{m,p}$ then the length of π is at least $p/100$.*

4.2   A Lower Bound for Constructing a $(+2)$-Pairwise Spanner

Theorem 3. *There is a constant $c > 0$ so that the following holds. Any distributed protocol for the CONGEST model with success probability at least $2/3$ which, given a graph with n nodes and a set of $p \leq cn^{3/2}$ pairs of nodes, outputs a $(+2)$-pairwise spanner with at most $cn^{3/2}$ edges, must take $\Omega(\frac{p}{n \log n})$ rounds to complete. The lower bound holds even for graphs with constant diameter.*

The theorem implies a lower bound of $\Omega(\sqrt{n}/\log n)$ on the number of rounds needed for an algorithm in the CONGEST model to output a $(+2)$-pairwise spanner, when $|\mathcal{P}| = \Theta(n^{3/2})$. For comparison, the time for constructing such a spanner using Algorithm 2P can (roughly) vary between $n^{3/4}$ and n, depending on the structure of $\mathcal{P}$.

The graph G for which the lower bound is proved is defined as follows. Let n be such that there is a finite projective plane with $n/4$ points and $n/4$ lines. Let G' be the point-line incidence graph with $n/2$ nodes (see e.g. [39, Sect. 4.5]). The graph G' has $\Theta(n^{3/2})$ edges, girth 6 and diameter 3.[1] We denote the nodes of G' by $V_B = \{v'_1, \ldots, v'_{n/2}\}$. The graph G consists of G', an additional $n/2$ nodes denoted $V_A = \{v_1, \ldots, v_{n/2}\}$, and an additional $n/2$ edges of the form (v_i, v'_i).

In the pairwise spanner we construct, we wish to approximately preserve distances between pairs of nodes in V_A, i.e. $\mathcal{P} \subseteq V_A \times V_A$. The main observation is that, since the girth of G' is 6, if $e' = \{v'_i, v'_j\}$ is an edge of G' then the following holds. If $(v_i, v_j) \in \mathcal{P}$ then any $(+2)$-pairwise spanner must contain the edge e', as otherwise the distance is stretched from 3 to 7, which exceeds the required $+2$ stretch. On the other hand, if $(v_i, v_j) \notin \mathcal{P}$ then the edge e' can be safely omitted from the spanner.

Proof (of Theorem 3). Fix a distributed protocol σ for constructing a $(+2)$-pairwise spanner with at most $m/2$ edges. Let G be the graph described above, and denote the edges of G' by $e_1, \ldots, e_m$.

We describe a reduction from $\text{PART-COMP}_{m,p}$ to σ. Assume Alice has a set $x \subseteq \{1, \ldots, m\}$ of size p, and Bob has to output a set $y \subseteq \{1, \ldots, m\}$ of size $m/2$ satisfying $x \cap y = \emptyset$. Alice and Bob simulate σ on the graph G with the set of pairs

$$\mathcal{P} = \left\{ (v_i, v_j) : \exists k \in x \; e_k = \{v'_i, v'_j\} \right\}.$$

That is, a pair (v_i, v_j) is in $\mathcal{P}$ if the corresponding pair (v'_i, v'_j) is an edge e_k whose index k is in x. Alice simulates the nodes in V_A, and Bob simulates the nodes V_B and the edges among them. To simulate communication on edges of the form (v_i, v'_i), Alice and Bob communicate. Note that $\mathcal{P}$ contains only pairs of nodes that are simulated by Alice.

The spanner constructed is a subgraph H of G with at most $m/2$ edges, satisfying $\delta_H(v_i, v_j) \leq \delta_G(v_i, v_j) + 2$ for all $(v_i, v_j) \in \mathcal{P}$. For each such pair, by definition of $\mathcal{P}$, we have $\delta_G(v_i, v_j) = 3$, which implies $\delta_H(v_i, v_j) \leq 5$ and $\delta_H(v'_i, v'_j) \leq 3$. The fact that G' has girth 6 implies that the edge $\{v'_i, v'_j\}$ must be in H. Let

$$y = \{k : e_k \in E_G \setminus E_H\}.$$

The spanner size implies $|y| \geq m/2$, while the above discussion implies $x \cap y = \emptyset$. Thus, Bob can output a subset of y of size $m/2$, solving the communication complexity problem.

By the communication complexity lower bound, Alice and Bob must communicate $\Omega(p)$ bits during the simulation. The number of edges they simulate together is $n/2$, and $O(\log n)$ bits are sent over each edge at each round. Thus, the protocol must take $\Omega\left(\frac{|\mathcal{P}|}{n \log n}\right)$ rounds to complete.

5 Discussion

This paper presents various algorithms for computing sparse purely additive spanners in the CONGEST model. Our algorithms exhibit tradeoffs between the

---

[1] The *girth* of a graph is the length of the shortest simple cycle in it.

running time and the sparsity of the constructed spanners. By choosing different values for the parameter h, one can obtain a spanner with the same stretch in a smaller number of rounds but at the expense of increasing the density. This tradeoff is an important direction for future work.

Our lower bound uses a new communication complexity problem, and leverages the distributed nature of the system by using the fact that each node initially only knows the pairs in $\mathcal{P}$ to which it belongs[2]. That is, the topology of the graph used for the lower bound reduction is known completely to both Alice and Bob, regardless of their inputs to the PART-COMP$_{m,p}$ instance, while the uncertainty about the identity of the pairs in $\mathcal{P}$ is what makes the problem hard. While it might be unnatural to assume that other nodes know about these pairs, it is theoretically interesting to ask whether one can design faster distributed constructions given this information.

Finally, we believe that our new lower bound technique can be useful for proving additional lower bounds in the CONGEST model, as it diverges from reducing to the set-disjointness problem.

Acknowledgements. We thank Merav Parter for a helpful discussion on the lower bound, and the anonymous referees for helpful comments.

References

1. Abboud, A., Bodwin, G.: The 4/3 additive spanner exponent is tight. In: ACM SIGACT Symposium on Theory of Computing, STOC (2016)
2. Abboud, A., Bodwin, G.: Error amplification for pairwise spanner lower bounds. In: Annual ACM-SIAM Symposium on Discrete Algorithms, SODA (2016)
3. Aingworth, D., Chekuri, C., Indyk, P., Motwani, R.: Fast estimation of diameter and shortest paths (without matrix multiplication). SIAM J. Comput. **28**(4), 1167–1181 (1999)
4. Althöfer, I., Das, G., Dobkin, D.P., Joseph, D., Soares, J.: On sparse spanners of weighted graphs. Discrete Comput. Geom. **9**, 81–100 (1993)
5. Baswana, S.: Streaming algorithm for graph spanners - single pass and constant processing time per edge. Inf. Process. Lett. **106**(3), 110–114 (2008)
6. Baswana, S., Kavitha, T., Mehlhorn, K., Pettie, S.: Additive spanners and (alpha, beta)-spanners. ACM Trans. Algorithms **7**(1), 5 (2010)
7. Baswana, S., Khurana, S., Sarkar, S.: Fully dynamic randomized algorithms for graph spanners. ACM Trans. Algorithms **8**(4), 35 (2012)
8. Baswana, S., Sarkar, S.: Fully dynamic algorithm for graph spanners with polylogarithmic update time. In: ACM-SIAM Symposium on Discrete Algorithms, SODA (2008)
9. Baswana, S., Sen, S.: A simple and linear time randomized algorithm for computing sparse spanners in weighted graphs. Random Struct. Algorithm **30**(4), 532–563 (2007)
10. Bodwin, G., Williams, V.V.: Better distance preservers and additive spanners. In: ACM-SIAM Symposium on Discrete Algorithms, SODA, pp. 855–872 (2016)

---

[2] In fact, our lower bound holds even if all nodes in pairs in $\mathcal{P}$ know all of $\mathcal{P}$.

11. Bollobás, B., Coppersmith, D., Elkin, M.: Sparse distance preservers and additive spanners. SIAM J. Discrete Math. **19**(4), 1029–1055 (2005)
12. Censor-Hillel, K., Ghaffari, M., Kuhn, F.: Distributed connectivity decomposition. In: ACM Symposium on Principles of Distributed Computing, PODC (2014)
13. Censor-Hillel, K., Haeupler, B., Kelner, J.A., Maymounkov, P.: Global computation in a poorly connected world: fast rumor spreading with no dependence on conductance. In: Symposium on Theory of Computing Conference, STOC, 2012
14. Chechik, S.: Compact routing schemes with improved stretch. In: ACM Symposium on Principles of Distributed Computing, PODC (2013)
15. Chechik, S.: New additive spanners. In: ACM-SIAM Symposium on Discrete Algorithms, SODA (2013)
16. Coppersmith, D., Elkin, M.: Sparse sourcewise and pairwise distance preservers. SIAM J. Discrete Math. **20**(2), 463–501 (2006)
17. Cygan, M., Grandoni, F., Kavitha, T.: On pairwise spanners. In: Symposium on Theoretical Aspects of Computer Science, STACS (2013)
18. Das Sarma, A., Holzer, S., Kor, L., Korman, A., Nanongkai, D., Pandurangan, G., Peleg, D., Wattenhofer, R.: Distributed verification and hardness of distributed approximation. SIAM J. Comput. **41**(5), 1235–1265 (2012)
19. Derbel, B., Gavoille, C.: Fast deterministic distributed algorithms for sparse spanners. Theor. Comput. Sci. **399**(1–2), 83–100 (2008)
20. Derbel, B., Gavoille, C., Peleg, D.: Deterministic distributed construction of linear stretch spanners in polylogarithmic time. In: Pelc, A. (ed.) DISC 2007. LNCS, vol. 4731, pp. 179–192. Springer, Heidelberg (2007)
21. Derbel, B., Gavoille, C., Peleg, D., Viennot, L.: On the locality of distributed sparse spanner construction. In: ACM Symposium on Principles of Distributed Computing, PODC, pp. 273–282 (2008)
22. Derbel, B., Gavoille, C., Peleg, D., Viennot, L.: Local computation of nearly additive spanners. In: Keidar, I. (ed.) DISC 2009. LNCS, vol. 5805, pp. 176–190. Springer, Heidelberg (2009)
23. Dor, D., Halperin, S., Zwick, U.: All-pairs almost shortest paths. SIAM J. Comput. **29**(5), 1740–1759 (2000)
24. Drucker, A., Kuhn, F., Oshman, R.: On the power of the congested clique model. In: ACM Symposium on Principles of Distributed Computing, PODC (2014)
25. Dubhashi, D.P., Mei, A., Panconesi, A., Radhakrishnan, J., Srinivasan, A.: Fast distributed algorithms for (weakly) connected dominating sets and linear-size skeletons. J. Comput. Syst. Sci. **71**(4), 467–479 (2005)
26. Elkin, M.: Computing almost shortest paths. ACM Trans. Algorithm **1**(2), 283–323 (2005)
27. Elkin, M.: A near-optimal distributed fully dynamic algorithm for maintaining sparse spanners. In: ACM Symposium on Principles of Distributed Computing, PODC, pp. 185–194 (2007)
28. Elkin, M.: Streaming and fully dynamic centralized algorithms for constructing and maintaining sparse spanners. In: Arge, L., Cachin, C., Jurdziński, T., Tarlecki, A. (eds.) ICALP 2007. LNCS, vol. 4596, pp. 716–727. Springer, Heidelberg (2007)
29. Elkin, M., Peleg, D.: (1+epsilon, beta)-spanner constructions for general graphs. SIAM J. Comput. **33**(3), 608–631 (2004)
30. Elkin, M., Zhang, J.: Efficient algorithms for constructing (1+epsilon, beta)-spanners in the distributed and streaming models. Distrib. Comput. **18**(5), 375–385 (2006)

31. Frischknecht, S., Holzer, S., Wattenhofer, R.: Networks cannot compute their diameter in sublinear time. In: ACM-SIAM Symposium on Discrete Algorithms, SODA, pp. 1150–1162 (2012)
32. Ghaffari, M., Kuhn, F.: Distributed minimum cut approximation. In: Afek, Y. (ed.) DISC 2013. LNCS, vol. 8205, pp. 1–15. Springer, Heidelberg (2013)
33. Holzer, S., Pinsker, N.: Approximation of distances and shortest paths in the broadcast congest clique. CoRR, abs/1412.3445 (2014)
34. Holzer, S., Wattenhofer, R.: Optimal distributed all pairs shortest paths and applications. In: ACM Symposium on Principles of Distributed Computing, PODC (2012)
35. Kavitha, T.: New pairwise spanners. In: Symposium on Theoretical Aspects of Computer Science, STACS, pp. 513–526 (2015)
36. Kavitha, T., Varma, N.M.: Small stretch pairwise spanners. In: International Colloquium on Automata, Languages, and Programming, ICALP (2013)
37. Knudsen, M.B.T.: Additive spanners: a simple construction. In: Ravi, R., Gørtz, I.L. (eds.) SWAT 2014. LNCS, vol. 8503, pp. 277–281. Springer, Heidelberg (2014)
38. Lenzen, C., Peleg, D.: Efficient distributed source detection with limited bandwidth. In: ACM Symposium on Principles of Distributed Computing, PODC (2013)
39. Matousek, J.: Lectures on Discrete Geometry. Springer, New York (2002)
40. Parter, M.: Bypassing Erdős' girth conjecture: hybrid stretch and sourcewise spanners. In: International Colloquium on Automata, Languages and Programming, ICALP (2014)
41. Peleg, D.: Distributed Computing: A Locality-Sensitive Approach. SIAM Monographs on Discrete Mathematics and Applications. Society for Industrial and Applied Mathematics, Philadelphia (2000)
42. Peleg, D., Rubinovich, V.: A near-tight lower bound on the time complexity of distributed MST construction. In: Symposium on Foundations of Computer Science, FOCS, pp. 253–261 (1999)
43. Peleg, D., Schäffer, A.A.: Graph spanners. J. Graph Theory 13(1), 99–116 (1989)
44. Peleg, D., Ullman, J.D.: An optimal synchronizer for the hypercube. SIAM J. Comput. 18(4), 740–747 (1989)
45. Peleg, D., Upfal, E.: A trade-off between space and efficiency for routing tables. J. ACM 36(3), 510–530 (1989)
46. Pettie, S.: Low distortion spanners. ACM Trans. Algorithms 6(1) (2009)
47. Pettie, S.: Distributed algorithms for ultrasparse spanners and linear size skeletons. Distrib. Comput. 22(3), 147–166 (2010)
48. Roditty, L., Thorup, M., Zwick, U.: Deterministic constructions of approximate distance oracles and spanners. In: Caires, L., Italiano, G.F., Monteiro, L., Palamidessi, C., Yung, M. (eds.) ICALP 2005. LNCS, vol. 3580, pp. 261–272. Springer, Heidelberg (2005)
49. Roditty, L., Zwick, U.: On dynamic shortest paths problems. Algorithmica 61(2), 389–401 (2011)
50. Thorup, M., Zwick, U.: Compact routing schemes. In: ACM Symposium on Parallel Algorithms and Architectures, SPAA, pp. 1–10 (2001)
51. Thorup, M., Zwick, U.: Approximate distance oracles. J. ACM 52(1), 113–116 (2005)
52. Thorup, M., Zwick, U.: Spanners and emulators with sublinear distance errors. In: ACM-SIAM Symposium on Discrete Algorithms, SODA, pp. 802–809 (2006)
53. Woodruff, D.P.: Additive spanners in nearly quadratic time. In: Abramsky, S., Gavoille, C., Kirchner, C., Meyer auf der Heide, F., Spirakis, P.G. (eds.) ICALP 2010. LNCS, vol. 6198, pp. 463–474. Springer, Heidelberg (2010)

Optimal Fair Computation

Rachid Guerraoui and Jingjing Wang[✉]

EPFL, IC, Station 14, 1015 Lausanne, Switzerland
{rachid.guerraoui,jingjing.wang}@epfl.ch

Abstract. A computation scheme among n parties is *fair* if no party obtains the computation result unless all other $n - 1$ parties obtain the same result. A fair computation scheme is *optimistic* if n honest parties can obtain the computation result without resorting to a trusted third party. We prove, for the first time, a tight lower-bound on the message complexity of optimistic fair computation for n parties among which $n-1$ can be malicious in an asynchronous network. We do so by relating the optimal message complexity of optimistic fair computation to the length of the shortest permutation sequence in combinatorics.

1 Introduction

In *fair* computation [1,2], n parties possess n pieces of information and need to output a function of these n pieces of information (the inputs) *atomically*. Namely, a party obtains the output of the function if and only if the other $n - 1$ parties obtain the same output. A prominent example is auctions: after n parties offer a price for some item, they wish to determine the highest price and the winner without ambiguity, e.g., when more than one party claims to win the item. A solution is the fair computation of the n bids (prices).

The difficulty of fair computation stems from the fact that a party might be *malicious* (dishonest) and try to obtain other parties' inputs, twist other parties' outputs, or arbitrarily delay other parties from obtaining an output. Still, honest parties should eventually obtain an output in a fair manner: they should all obtain the function of the n inputs, or all obtain a specific value $\perp$ (denoted *abort* in [1]). In fact, (deterministic) fair computation is in general impossible without a trusted third party [3]. Yet, this third party is not needed in every execution of a (deterministic) fair computation protocol.

Optimistic (deterministic) fair computation stipulates that the third party does not need to be invoked if all n parties are honest [1,2,4]. An execution where n honest parties output without invoking the third party is called an *optimistic* execution [1,4]. Given that cheating is seldom and the third party is considered a bottleneck, optimism is practically appealing. To claim true practicality, however, optimistic executions should be efficient. To be specific, the number of messages exchanged among n honest parties (which compute the function without resorting to the third party) should not be prohibitive. Until the present paper, the optimal number of messages was unknown.

© Springer-Verlag Berlin Heidelberg 2016
C. Gavoille and D. Ilcinkas (Eds.): DISC 2016, LNCS 9888, pp. 143–157, 2016.
DOI: 10.1007/978-3-662-53426-7_11

We prove in this paper that $\ell + 2n - 3$ is the optimal number of messages that an optimistic execution of optimistic fair computation may achieve in the presence of $n - 1$ potentially malicious parties in an asynchronous network, where ℓ is the length of the shortest sequence that contains all permutations of n symbols as subsequences [5]. Given recent results in combinatorics [6–9], the optimal number of messages for optimistic fair computation is 4 for $n = 2$, $n^2 + 1$ for $3 \leq n \leq 7$, and asymptotically $\Theta(n^2)$ for $n \geq 8$.[1]

The main idea behind our proof of the $\ell + 2n - 3$ lower-bound is the identification of a *decision propagation* pattern according to which the n parties reach an agreement when any of the parties decides to *stop* the computation. Such ability of a party to stop at any time without jeopardizing *fairness* has been called *timely termination* [1]. It prevents an honest party from waiting forever and is crucial in an asynchronous context. The *decision propagation* pattern is between at least two parties P and Q. To get an intuition, consider an optimistic execution E, let event E_P ="P does not receive message m_P" and let event E_Q ="Q does not receive message m_Q". An honest party P's stop is a result of E_P. However, a malicious P's stop can impose an honest Q's stop: if when P and Q complete E, $\bar{E}_P$ (the complement of E_P) occurs before $\bar{E}_Q$ and Q does not receive any message between $\bar{E}_P$ and $\bar{E}_Q$, then without m_Q, Q is unable to distinguish whether E_P really occurs or not. An immediate result is that malicious P's decision may *propagate* to Q. To prevent *fairness* from being jeopardized by malicious propagation, in the context of possibly $n - 1$ malicious parties, every party should participate in this propagation so that none has a chance to pretend being honest in front of the trusted third party T.

This yields a subsequence of n events E_P (one for each party P) and n messages (whose destinations are the n parties) in E. Clearly, the order of the parties does not matter and therefore, any *permutation* of the n events must occur as a subsequence in E. Hence the relation between the least number of messages of an optimistic execution and ℓ, the length of the shortest sequence that contains all permutations of n symbols as subsequences.

Our lower-bound on the number of messages is tight in the following sense. We present an $(\ell + 2n - 3)$-message optimistic fair computation scheme of some function f given a shortest permutation sequence $\underline{s}$. Our protocol, where the n parties are honest and compute without the third party, consists of three phases: (a) the n parties send *verifiable encryption* [12] of their n inputs respectively, in order to recover those inputs (if needed) in a *non-optimistic* execution, which defines the first n messages; (b) the n parties exchange $\ell - 2$ messages defined by $\underline{s}$; and (c) the n parties exchange the concatenation of the n inputs, which defines the last $n - 1$ messages. The $\ell - 2$ messages $m_1 m_2 \ldots m_{\ell-2}$ in phase (b) have their sources and

---

[1] Newey [6] (and then many others [7–11]) studied the length ℓ of the shortest permutation sequence. Although Newey [6] showed that $\ell = 3$ for $n = 2$, and $\ell = n^2 - 2n + 4$ for $3 \leq n \leq 7$, the exact ℓ for $n \geq 8$ is still considered as an open problem [7,8]. Up until now, the best upper-bound is $\lceil n^2 - \frac{7}{3}n + \frac{19}{3} \rceil$ for $n \geq 7$ [8], while a lower-bound of ℓ is of the form $n^2 - cn^{7/4} + \epsilon$ for some constant c and some $\epsilon > 0$ [9].

destinations defined by the sequence $\underline{s} = s_1 s_2 \ldots s_\ell$ as follows. The party represented by symbol s_j is the source of m_{j-1} for $j = 2, \ldots, \ell-1$, and the destination of m_{j-2} for $j = 3, 4, \ldots, \ell$. (s_1 is the source of the last message m_0 of phase (a) and s_2 is the destination of m_0.) When a party resorts to T in a non-optimistic execution, T uses the decision propagation pattern to decide an output. The pattern is the same as in our proof of the lower-bound so that the number of messages in every optimistic execution is minimal.

As we will explain in Sect. 5, many results have been published on problems related to fair computation [13–18]. None implies our lower-bound. On the other hand, our $(\ell + 2n - 3)$-message optimistic fair computation scheme can be used to implement fair exchange of certain digital signatures (including Schnorr signatures [19], DSS signatures [20], Fiat-Shamir signatures [21], Ong-Schnorr signatures [22], GQ signatures [23]). Thus, our scheme is also a message-optimal optimistic fair exchange scheme [1]. Moreover, combined with our proof of the lower-bound, this optimistic fair exchange scheme of digital signatures also implies that $\ell + 2n - 3$ is the optimal number of messages for optimistic fair contract signing [16]. Finally, our optimal message complexity may be considered as a first step to the optimal (round) complexity. For example, the decision propagation pattern is applicable for any optimistic execution, no matter whether the protocol is in a similar form as our optimal protocol or not.

The rest of this paper is organized as follows. Section 2 presents our general model and defines optimistic fair computation. Section 3 presents our lower-bound on the number of messages. Section 4 presents our $(\ell + 2n - 3)$-message optimistic fair computation scheme. Section 5 discusses related work. For space limitation, we put the details of the proof of our lower-bound and the details of the correctness proof of our message-optimal scheme to our full version [24].

2   Model and Definitions

2.1   The Parties

We consider a set Ω of n parties $P_1, P_2, \ldots, P_n$ (sometimes also denoted by P, Q). These parties are all *interactive* in the sense that they can communicate with each other by exchanging messages. All parties are *computationally-bounded* [25] in the sense that they run in time polynomial in some security parameter s.[2]

In addition to the n parties, we also assume a computationally-bounded trusted third party T. T follows the protocol assigned to it. The communication with T is such that when T is communicating with P, Q needs to wait for Q's turn to communicate with T for any two parties $P, Q \in \Omega$.

At most $n - 1$ parties can be *malicious*. A malicious party could deviate arbitrarily from the protocol assigned to it. A malicious party could interact arbitrarily with the others as well as T. For example, a malicious party may

---

[2] Hereafter, when we say that a probability is negligible, we mean that the probability is a *negligible* function $g(s)$ of the security parameter s; i.e., $\forall c \in \mathbb{N}, \exists C \in \mathbb{N}$ such that $\forall s > C, g(s) < \frac{1}{s^c}$.

drop certain messages. A party that *crashes* at some point in time is considered as a malicious party that drops all the messages from that point. Malicious parties may also collude (e.g., to obtain an output for themselves and to prevent an output to an honest party, i.e., to break *fairness*, which is defined later).

Communication channels do not modify, inject, duplicate or lose messages. Every message sent eventually reaches its destination. Any modified, injected, duplicate, or lost message is considered to be due to malicious parties. The delay on message transmission is finite but unbounded. Messages could be reordered. Communication channels are authenticated and secure such as Transport Layer Security [26]. No party can be masqueraded and no message can be eavesdropped.

2.2 Fair Computation

We consider the problem of optimistic fair computation in the classical sense of [1,2]. The problem involves a deterministic function f to be computed by the n parties. Function f is agreed upon by the n parties in advance. We assume that f takes n strings $x_1 \in \{0,1\}^{\ell_1}, x_2 \in \{0,1\}^{\ell_2}, \ldots, x_n \in \{0,1\}^{\ell_n}$ as inputs and returns $z \in \{0,1\}^{\ell_z}$ as its output.

Definition 1 (Computation). *A computation scheme for f is a collection $(P_1, P_2, \ldots, P_n)$ of n algorithms. The algorithms can carry out two protocols:*[3]

- Compute*: Each party $P_i, i \in \{1, 2, \ldots, n\}$ is initialized with a local input x_i. If P_i finishes this protocol, P_i returns a local output which can take a value in $\{0,1\}^{\ell_z} \cup \{\bot\}$. If Compute is interrupted by Stop (which we introduce below), Compute returns the same output as Stop.*
- Stop*: P_i invokes Stop when P_i wants to stop the computation. P_i can invoke this protocol at any point in time. P_i obtains P_i's status of Compute so far (i.e., the sequence of messages that have arrived at P_i so far) as a local input to Stop. P_i makes a local output which can take a value in $\{0,1\}^{\ell_z} \cup \{\bot\}$.*

In the classical definition of fair computation [2], the problem is defined in the *simulatability paradigm* [27], which basically expresses a solution to fair computation in terms of a simulation of the *ideal process*. We recall the notion of the ideal process in Definition 2, and then fair computation in Definition 3.

Definition 2 (Ideal process [2]). *The ideal process for fair computation of f is a collection $(\bar{P}_1, \bar{P}_2, \ldots, \bar{P}_n, U)$ of $n + 1$ algorithms. Each $\bar{P}_i, i \in \{1, 2, \ldots, n\}$ is initialized with a local input x_i. U is parameterized by f. $\bar{P}_i$ sends message $a_i = x_i$ to U. Messages are delivered instantly. U returns a message m_i to P_i*

---

[3] We consider deterministic protocols here (for Compute and Stop). In this paper, deterministic protocols consists of two classes of protocols: D1 and D2. In any protocol of D1, each party runs a deterministic algorithm and sends deterministic messages; and we define D2 based on D1: for any protocol π_1 in class D1, we can create a protocol π_2 in class D2 such that π_1 and π_2 are the same except for the message contents of π_2 which can be randomized.

according to Eq. (1) as soon as $a_1, a_2, \ldots, a_n$ have arrived at U or one message of $\perp$ has arrived at U. $\bar{P}_i$ outputs whatever U returns to it.

$$\forall i \in \{1, 2, \ldots, n\}, m_i = \begin{cases} f(a_1, a_2, \ldots, a_n) & if\ a_1 \neq \perp, a_2 \neq \perp, \ldots, a_n \neq \perp \\ \perp & if\ \perp \in \{a_1, a_2, \ldots, a_n\} \end{cases}$$

(1)

Definition 3 (Fair computation[4]). *A computation scheme α solves* fair *computation for f [2] if it satisfies the following properties:*

- Fairness: *for any $e \in \mathbb{N}, 1 \leq e \leq n - 1$ and any e malicious parties P_{d_1}, P_{d_2}, $\ldots, P_{d_e}$, for any computationally-bounded algorithm $\mathcal{A}$ that controls the e malicious parties[5], there exists a computationally-bounded algorithm $\mathcal{S}$ that controls $\bar{P}_{d_1}, \bar{P}_{d_2}, \ldots, \bar{P}_{d_e}$[6] such that for any $x_1, x_2, \ldots, x_n$, $O_{P_1, P_2, \ldots, P_n, \mathcal{A}}(x_1, x_2, \ldots, x_n)$ and $O_{\bar{P}_1, \bar{P}_2, \ldots, \bar{P}_n, \mathcal{S}}(x_1, x_2, \ldots, x_n)$ are computationally indistinguishable [28, 29];*
- Termination: *If an honest party P_i invokes Stop, then P_i eventually outputs.*
- Completeness: *$\forall x_1, x_2, \ldots, x_n$, if $P_1, P_2, \ldots, P_n$ are honest and none invokes Stop, then all parties output $z = f(x_1, x_2, \ldots, x_n)$; if $P_1, P_2, \ldots, P_n$ are honest and some invokes Stop, then either all parties output $z = f(x_1, x_2, \ldots, x_n)$, or all parties output $\perp$.*
- Non-triviality: *There is at least one execution in which $P_1, P_2, \ldots, P_n$ are honest and none invokes Stop.*

W.l.o.g., we assume that $P_{d_1}, P_{d_2}, \ldots, P_{d_e}$ output nothing but $\mathcal{A}$ may output arbitrarily, and similarly, $\bar{P}_{d_1}, \bar{P}_{d_2}, \ldots, \bar{P}_{d_e}$ output nothing but $\mathcal{S}$ may output arbitrarily; we denote by $O_{P_1, P_2, \ldots, P_n, \mathcal{A}}(x_1, x_2, \ldots, x_n)$, the joint output of $P_1, P_2, \ldots, P_n, \mathcal{A}$ when running α for inputs $x_1, x_2, \ldots, x_n$, and denote by $O_{\bar{P}_1, \bar{P}_2, \ldots, \bar{P}_n, \mathcal{S}}(x_1, x_2, \ldots, x_n)$, the joint output of $\bar{P}_1, \bar{P}_2, \ldots, \bar{P}_n, \mathcal{S}$ when running the ideal process for inputs $x_1, x_2, \ldots, x_n$.

Definition 4 (Optimistic fair computation). *A fair computation scheme is* optimistic *[1] if it satisfies the following property.*

- Optimism: *If $P_1, P_2, \ldots, P_n$ are honest and none invokes Stop, then all parties output without interacting with T.*

---

[4] The original definition in [2] is ambiguous when all parties are honest: (1) if an algorithm $\mathcal{A}$ delays every message, then to ensure termination, every honest party should output $\perp$ at some point in time; however, by the original definition, all honest parties output z, except with negligible probability, which yields a contradiction; and (2) if in a protocol, all parties send no message and only outputs $\perp$, then this protocol also matches the ideal process, which however is a trivial protocol.

[5] $\mathcal{A}$ also plays the role of the asynchronous network as defined in Sect. 2.1.

[6] In the ideal process, $\mathcal{S}$ sees $x_{d_1}, x_{d_2}, \ldots, x_{d_e}$, may change $a_{d_1}, a_{d_2}, \ldots, a_{d_e}$ and also sees $m_{d_1}, m_{d_2}, \ldots, m_{d_e}$ but $\mathcal{S}$ cannot see other messages from or to U, or U's internal state (which makes U *universally trusted* and the process *ideal*).

When $P_1, P_2, \ldots, P_n$ are honest and none invokes Stop, $P_1, P_2, \ldots, P_n$ carry out Compute only. Thus, an optimistic execution is an execution of Compute.

We focus on the class $\mathcal{C}$ of function f such that for any $x_1 \in \{0,1\}^{\ell_1}, x_2 \in \{0,1\}^{\ell_2}, \ldots, x_n \in \{0,1\}^{\ell_n}$, no computationally-bounded algorithm is able to output $f(x_1, x_2, \ldots, x_n)$ using only $n-1$ out of the n strings, except with negligible probability.[7] For a function f in the complement of $\mathcal{C}$, a protocol that solves optimistic fair computation can still be vulnerable to the following attack: a subset of parties colludes, leaves with the evaluation of f immediately but an honest party outputs $\bot$. In the literature [30,31], fair protocols for the complement of $\mathcal{C}$ are considered, but they ensure fairness different from Definitions 2 and 3, and are not the focus here. We also assume that T does not have prior knowledge of $x_1, x_2, \ldots, x_n$, and therefore no computationally-bounded algorithm, even with the help of T, is able to compute z from any $n - 1$ out of the n inputs of $P_1, P_2, \ldots, P_n$. We call this assumption *no prior knowledge of* T.

3 Lower Bound

In this section, we prove our lower-bound on the number of messages exchanged during an optimistic execution. We express our lower-bound in terms of n and ℓ, the length of the shortest sequence that contains all permutations of n symbols as subsequences.

Theorem 1 (Message complexity). *For any function $f \in \mathcal{C}$, for any optimistic fair computation scheme for f (for n parties, among which $n - 1$ can be malicious), the n parties exchange at least $\ell + 2n - 3$ messages in every optimistic execution.*

Proof sketch. (The full proof is in our full version [24].)

To prove Theorem 1, we view every optimistic execution E as a sequence of messages ordered according to when they reach their destinations respectively. We first pinpoint two necessary messages in E, and then show that between these two messages, there must exist certain patterns of messages.

Intuitively, when starting E, no party knows anything about other parties' inputs; there is a border-line message m_1^* such that, after m_1^* reaches its destination, one and only one party knows something about all the other parties' inputs. If any honest party P_i stops before m_1^* arrives at its destination, then P_i is unable to output $z = f(x_1, x_2, \ldots, x_n)$ with non-negligible probability by *no prior knowledge of* T.

By the end of E, every party receives sufficient messages to compute z by the *optimism* property; there is another border-line message m_2^* such that, after m_2^* reaches its destination, one and only one party has sufficient messages to compute z. If any honest party P_i stops after m_2^* arrives at its destination, P_i outputs z by the *completeness* property. Figure 1a illustrates the two messages.

---

[7] For example, $f = x_1 \cdot x_2 \cdots x_n$ is not in $\mathcal{C}$ (since if one of the values is 0, the output is 0 with probability 1) while $f = x_1 + x_2 + \cdots + x_n$ is.

(a) P_i outputs $\perp$ if P_i stops before m_1^*; and z if P_i stops after m_2^*.

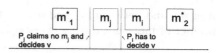

(b) P_i decides the same value v after P_j if P_i stops between m_1^* and m_2^*.

Fig. 1. The output of P_i if P_i stops at some point in execution E

What P_i should output if it stops between m_1^* and m_2^* requires a closer look. Suppose that when P_i wants to stop, P_i has not received some message m_i. (We clarify some terminology here. When we say that P_i has not received or does not receive some message m_i, we mean that P_i has not received m_i but received every message with destination P_i before m_i in E.) When P_i wants to stop, either no other party has decided an output (and then P_i can easily decide), or some party $P_j, j \neq i$ has decided. If P_j claims that it has not received message m_j and m_i is the first message with destination P_i after m_j in E, then P_i must adopt P_j's decision, or in other words, P_j's decision *propagates* to P_i. Because $n-1$ parties can be malicious, P_i is unable to distinguish whether P_j's claim is honest or not and then P_i has to decide the same output as P_j, except with negligible probability, by the *fairness* property. Figure 1b illustrates this agreement.

This agreement between two parties induces a *decision propagation* pattern, which gives rise to a certain pattern of messages in E: after a message m_j with destination P_j, there must exist a message m_i with destination P_i so that P_j could enforce P_i on the same output if (a) P_j does not receive m_j, (b) P_j invokes Stop and outputs $\perp$, and (c) P_i does not receive m_i and invokes Stop.

We use this decision propagation pattern to build the following scenario. Suppose one party P_1 stops before m_1^* arrives at its destination and then the other $n-1$ parties stop following the decision propagation pattern above: for $k = 1$, we denote by m_1 the message which P_1 has not received when P_1 stops; then for $k = 2, 3, \ldots, n$, if there is a message m_k in E that is the first message with destination P_k between m_{k-1} and m_2^*, then P_k stops when P_k has not received m_k, and if not, P_k stops after m_2^* arrives at its destination.

Clearly, if the pattern of the n messages whose destinations are $P_1, P_2, \ldots, P_n$ does not exist between m_1^* and m_2^* in E, then P_n would output z by the property of m_2^*. However, P_1, as well as other parties $P_2, P_3, \ldots, P_k$ for which messages $m_2, m_3, \ldots, m_k$ exist, would output $\perp$ by the property of m_1^* and decision propagation. This would violate the *fairness* property. Therefore, the pattern of the n messages whose destinations are n parties, or in fact any permutation of the n parties must exist as a subsequence of E between between m_1^* and m_2^*.

Thus, the number of messages between m_1^* and m_2^* (inclusive) of E is at least ℓ. In the meantime, in E, before m_1^*, there are at least $n-1$ messages to meet the definition of m_1^* and after m_2^*, there are at least $n-2$ messages to meet the definition of m_2^*. We add together the minimum numbers of messages before m_1^*, after m_2^* and between m_1^* and m_2^*, and then have $\ell + 2n - 3$ as the final minimum number of messages during every optimistic execution.

4   An Optimal Protocol

To show that $\ell + 2n - 3$ is a tight lower-bound, we describe in this section an $(\ell + 2n - 3)$-message optimistic fair computation scheme for the function that implements fair exchange of n inputs. Our optimal protocol relies on a publicly verifiable *transcript*. I.e., each destination can verify in any execution whether previous messages have arrived at their destinations correctly. This is realized by adding digital signatures [25,32]. To help T recover the n inputs when some party invokes Stop, the n parties exchange *verifiable encryption* [12] of the n inputs in Compute. Section 4.1 recalls the basics of digital signatures and verifiable encryption before describing our optimal protocol.

4.1   Preliminaries

We denote a digital signature on message m by $\sigma = Sig_{sk}(m)$, and the verification algorithm by $Ver_{pk}(\sigma, m)$, where pk is a public key and sk is the corresponding secret key. We denote the signature of party $P_i, i \in \{1, 2, \ldots, n\}$ simply by $Sig_i(m)$. A digital signature scheme is secure if no adversary is able to forge a signature even after seeing polynomially many valid signatures. See [25,32] for a discussion on digital signature schemes and their levels of security.

A verifiable encryption scheme is a recovery algorithm D and a two-party protocol between prover P and verifier V [12]. To run the protocol, P and V's common inputs are public key vk, public value x, condition κ and binary relation R. P takes witness w as an extra input. At the end of the protocol, if $(x, w) \notin R$, V rejects and outputs $\perp$; if V accepts, then V also obtains string α such that $D(sk, \kappa, \alpha) = w$ and $(x, w) \in R$. We denote an instance of verifiable encryption by $VE(vk, \kappa, w, x, R)$. A verifiable encryption scheme is secure if no malicious verifier is able to learn w without sk and no malicious prover is able to make V accept $\hat{\alpha}$ which gives $\hat{w}$ by D but $(x, \hat{w}) \notin R$ except with negligible probability. See [12] for a formal definition of security for verifiable encryption schemes. A prominent example of verifiable encryption is Asokan et al.'s non-interactive constructions of verifiable encryption for a list of digital signature schemes, which includes Schnorr signatures, DSS signatures, Fiat-Shamir signatures, Ong-Schnorr signatures and GQ signatures [1].

4.2   Protocol Description

We show the tightness of our lower-bound of $\ell + 2n - 3$ messages in a constructive way: given *any* sequence $\underline{i}$ that contains all the permutations of $\{1, 2, \ldots, n\}$, we build a $(l + 2n - 3)$-message Compute π (Algorithm 1) with Stop μ (Algorithm 2), where l is the length of $\underline{i}$, as an $(l + 2n - 3)$-message optimistic fair computation

---

Algorithm 1. Compute π

Require: a sequence $\underline{i}$ of length l that contains all the permutations of $\{1, 2, \ldots, n\}$

Ensure: $(l + 2n - 3)$-message Compute π

1: Build sequence $\underline{j}$: $j_1, j_2, \ldots, j_{n-2}, \underline{i}, j_{n+l-1}, j_{n+l}, \ldots, j_{l+2n-3}$, where (a) $j_1, j_2, \ldots, j_{n-2}, i_1$ are $n - 1$ different symbols; and (b) $i_l, j_{n+l-1}, j_{n+l}, \ldots, j_{l+2n-3}$ are n different symbols.

2: Set $j_0 = \{1, 2, \ldots, n\} \backslash \{i_1, j_1, j_2, \ldots, j_{n-2}\}$.

3: In π, $P_{j_{k-1}}$ sends a message m_{k-1} to P_{j_k} upon receiving m_{k-2} for $k = 1, 2, \ldots, l + 2n - 3$ (except P_{j_0} who sends $m_0 = VE_{j_0}$ upon initialization) where

$$
m_{k-1} = \begin{cases} m_{k-2} || VE_{j_{k-1}} || Sig_{j_{k-1}}(m_{k-2} || VE_{j_{k-1}}) & 2 \leq k \leq n \\ m_{k-2} || Sig_{j_{k-1}}(m_{k-2}) & n+1 \leq k \leq end_{j_{k-1}} \\ m_{k-2} || x_{j_{k-1}} || Sig_{j_{k-1}}(m_{k-2} || x_{j_{k-1}}) & end_{j_{k-1}} + 1 \leq k \leq l+n-2 \\ (x_1, x_2, \ldots, x_n) & l+n-1 \leq k \leq l+2n-3 \end{cases}
\tag{2}
$$

and

$$
VE_{j_{k-1}} = VE(vk_T, \kappa, x_{j_{k-1}}, a_{j_{k-1}}, R_{j_{k-1}});
$$

$$
\kappa = (a_1, R_1), (a_2, R_2), \ldots, (a_n, R_n), \text{ which identifies the intended } x_1, x_2, \ldots, x_n;
$$

$$
end_{j_{k-1}} = \max_{K \in \{1, 2, \ldots, l\}} \{K | i_K = j_{k-1}\} + n - 2
$$

4: $P_1, P_2, \ldots, P_n$ output $z = (x_1, x_2, \ldots, x_n)$.

---

scheme for the following function (of which the correctness proof is in our full version [24]):

$$
f(x_1, x_2, \ldots, x_n) = \begin{cases} (x_1, x_2, \ldots, x_n) & (a_i, x_i) \in R_i \text{ for } i = 1, 2, \ldots, n \\ \bot & \text{otherwise} \end{cases}
\tag{3}
$$

where $R_1, R_2, \ldots, R_n$ are n relations that allow non-interactive construction of verifiable encryption and $a_1, a_2, \ldots, a_n$ are n public values.[8] $R_1, R_2, \ldots, R_n, a_1, a_2, \ldots, a_n$ are included in the public description of f.

Theorem 2. *Given a sequence $\underline{i}$ of length l that contains all the permutations of $\{1, 2, \ldots, n\}$, the protocol consisting of π and μ is an $(l + 2n - 3)$-message optimistic fair computation scheme for function f in Eq. (3) in an asynchronous network with $n - 1$ potentially malicious parties.*

The one-time setup is not included in Algorithm 1 or Algorithm 2. Before π and μ are carried out, a one-time setup (a) distributes necessary keys: T's public key vk_T and secret key sk_T, n parties' public and secret keys; (b) distributes the public description of f; and (c) executes the one-time setup of the verifiable

---

[8] We also assume that for $i \in \{1, 2, \ldots, n\}$, given a_i, any computationally-bounded algorithm outputs x_i with negligible probability, and given (a_i, x_i) such that $(a_i, x_i) \in R_i$, any computationally-bounded algorithm outputs $y_i, y_i \neq x_i$ such that $(a_i, y_i) \in R_i$ with negligible probability.

Algorithm 2. Stop μ

Require: sequence j of length $l + 2n - 3$ built for π
Ensure: Stop μ that accompanies π

1: For any $k \in \{0, 1 \ldots, l + 2n - 3\}$, P_{j_k} invokes μ when P_{j_k} wants to stop in π; otherwise, if π has not started, the n parties output $\perp$, or if π has finished, the n parties output $(x_1, x_2, \ldots, x_n)$.

2: For $k = 0$, when invoking μ, if P_{j_k} has not sent m_k, P_{j_k} quietly leaves π and μ and outputs $\perp$. For $1 \leq k \leq n - 1$, when invoking μ, if P_{j_k} has not received m_{k-1} correctly, then P_{j_k} quietly leaves π and μ, and P_{j_k} outputs $\perp$.

3: For $n \leq k \leq l + 2n - 3$, let $I_k = \{ix | j_{ix} = j_k, ix \in \{1, 2, \ldots, k - 1\}\}$, let $last_k = \max I_k$ when $I_k \neq \emptyset$ and let $last_k = 0$ when $I_k = \emptyset$, and define m_{-1} as an empty string. Then, for $n \leq k \leq l + 2n - 3$, when invoking μ, if P_{j_k} has not received m_{k-1} correctly and has received m_{last_k-1}, then P_{j_k} sends to T message $req_k = m_{last_k}$. By sending req_k, P_{j_k} claims that P_{j_k} does not receive m_{k-1}.

4: T verifies that req_k is consistent with P_{j_k}'s claim; and T calculates response

$$resp = \begin{cases} \text{``aborted''} & \text{if } req_k \text{ and } P_{j_k}\text{'s claim are not consistent} \\ & \text{or } P_{j_k} \text{ has sent a request before} \\ z = (x_1, x_2, \ldots, x_n) & \text{else if variable } z \text{ (initialized to } \perp) \text{ is not } \perp \\ \text{``aborted''} & \text{else if } req_k \text{ does not contain } VE_1, VE_2, \ldots, VE_n \\ z \leftarrow (x_1, x_2, \ldots, x_n) & \text{else if } k > \min_{ix \in \{prog+1, \ldots, l+2n-3\}} \{ix | j_{ix} = j_k\} \\ & \text{and } x_i \leftarrow D(sk_T, \kappa, VE_i) \text{ for } i = 1, 2, \ldots, n \\ z \leftarrow (x_1, x_2, \ldots, x_n) & \text{else if } k \geq l + n - 1 \\ & \text{and } x_i \leftarrow D(sk_T, \kappa, VE_i) \text{ for } i = 1, 2, \ldots, n \\ \text{``aborted''} & \text{otherwise} \end{cases}$$

T updates $prog$ (which is initialized to 0) to k if $k > prog$, req_k and P_{j_k}'s claim are consistent and P_{j_k} has not sent a request before. T then sends $resp$ to P_{j_k}.

5: P_{j_k} outputs $\perp$ if $resp = $ "aborted"; and P_{j_k} outputs z if $resp = z$.

encryption. (If implemented, a trusted party Certificate Authority [33] can do this one-time setup.)

Some remarks on μ are in order: (a) as each part of the request message is publicly verifiable, T is able to verify efficiently whether a party P's request and P's claim are consistent by following Eq. (2); and (b) P may invoke Stop at any point in time, e.g., when a message received by P in π is incorrect, or when P is impatient while waiting for some message. Our protocol allows P to define its own strategy of invoking Stop, independent of the other $n - 1$ parties, but if messages are delivered correctly and instantly, P does not invoke Stop.

Given a shortest permutation sequence, π and μ together form an $(\ell + 2n - 3)$-message optimistic fair computation scheme. Combined with Theorem 1, $\ell + 2n - 3$ is indeed a tight lower-bound on the number of messages for optimistic fair computation. Now that f implements fair exchange among n parties for items $x_1, x_2, \ldots, x_n$ that satisfy relations $R_1, R_2, \ldots, R_n$, Algorithms 1 and 2 also form a compiler that can transform a shortest permutation sequence into an $(\ell + 2n - 3)$-message optimistic fair exchange scheme. An application is a message-optimal optimistic fair exchange scheme of digital signatures [1].[9]

5 Related Work

5.1 Optimistic Fair Computation

Cachin and Camenisch [2] formalized optimistic fair computation for two parties and a third party T (that can also be malicious). Asokan et al. [1] formalized optimistic fair exchange of digital signatures between two parties and T (where T is honest). In this paper, we assume that T is honest. We briefly compare here the two definitions above. Cachin and Camenisch [2] formalized fair computation using the *simulatability paradigm* [27], while Asokan et al. [1] formalized fair exchange through games [25]. As the former can provide stronger security guarantee, we follow the definition of fair computation in [2]. Both formalizations consider the *termination* property in an asynchronous setting. We model this property using Stop, which is equivalent to the signal of termination in [1]. Asokan et al. [1] also defined the *completeness* property regarding the case where all parties are honest, while there is an ambiguity regarding this case in [2]. We adapt the definition of the *completeness* property from [1]. The *optimism* property was defined differently in [1, 2]. In [2], the trusted party does not communicate with the n parties when n parties are honest and messages are delivered instantly, whereas in [1], the trusted party does not communicate with the n parties, when n parties are honest but the asynchronous network is allowed to deliver messages arbitrarily. We adopt the *optimism* property from [1], as it provides a stronger guarantee. In addition, we include the *non-triviality* property to rule out trivial protocols that send no message and abort all the time. (Our proof of the lower-bound is based on the existence of at least one optimistic execution guaranteed by *non-triviality* and *optimism*, but our fair computation scheme, on the other hand, allows arbitrarily many optimistic executions.)

5.2 Optimistic Fair Exchange

For two parties, Asokan et al. [1] proposed a 4-message optimistic fair exchange scheme that ensures termination. Since $\ell = 3$ for two parties, our Theorem 1 shows that 4-message fair exchange schemes are optimal for two parties. This implies that a 3-message fair exchange scheme does not meet all of the required properties. For example, the optimistic fair exchange scheme proposed in [4] was criticized by Asokan et al. [1] as not ensuring *termination*. Another example is Ateniese's 3-message optimistic fair exchange scheme [34], which also does not ensure termination as noted by the author himself [34]. A recent follow-up work [35] has the same drawback. To the best of our knowledge, up to this paper (and our fair computation scheme), no message-optimal optimistic fair exchange or optimistic fair computation scheme among n parties for an arbitrary n (with $n - 1$ potentially malicious parties) has been proposed.

---

[9] In the application of fair exchange of digital signatures, R_i is an homomorphism θ depending on the given digital signature scheme [1]; each of the first n messages of π is appended with an image of θ such that its pre-image produces a correct signature.

5.3   Optimal Optimistic Schemes

We explain here the relation between the optimal efficiency of optimistic schemes of related problems and our optimal message efficiency. Pfitzmann, Schunter, and Waidner (PSW) [16] determined the optimal efficiency of fair two-party contract signing, Schunter [17] determined the optimal efficiency of fair two-party certified email, whereas Dashti [18] determined the optimal efficiency of two-party fair exchange in the crash-recovery model with no amnesia [36]. None of these results implies our Theorem 1, even only for $n = 2$. For PSW's result as well as Schunter's result, this is because there is no reduction of the problem of fair computation to the problem of fair contract signing[10] or fair certified email; for Dashti's result, this is because our model can be considered as the Byzantine failure model [36], and is thus stronger than the model considered by Dashti. Our proof of the lower-bound, together with our message-optimal scheme, can be applied to prove that $\ell + 2n - 3$ is the optimal message efficiency of fair n-party contract signing in the model of PSW. The special case where $n = 2$ can be used to prove PSW's result, while PSW's proof was, unfortunately, flawed.

5.4   The Shortest Permutation Sequence

Mauw, Radomirović and Dashti (MRD) [13] proved that the optimal number of messages of *totally-ordered* fair contract signing schemes falls between $\ell + n - 1$ and $\ell + 2n - 3$. Later, Mauw and Radomirović (MR) [15] generalized the result of MRD to *DAG-ordered* fair contract signing schemes. Both [13] and [15] considered fair contract signing as fair exchange of digital signatures. They use a model different from PSW, and fall within the coverage of our Theorem 1. Neither MRD's result nor MR's result implies our Theorem 1. Neither allows arbitrarily interleaved messages as our Theorem 1; instead, they assume that communication steps are either totally ordered or ordered following a directed acyclic graph (DAG). In addition, both results [13,15] propose a range of the optimal efficiency for fair exchange, instead of a concrete lower-bound for fair computation in general (as does our Theorem 1).

It is important to note that our Theorem 1 is not a generalization of MRD's result nor of MR's result. What MRD or MR counts are the messages sent from some signer. This makes their proof difficult to extend: after a message m leaves its source s, due to the asynchronous network, m does not help s's knowledge about other parties' possible states. Thus m should not help s reach an agreement if s wants to stop after sending m, unless the messages after m are defined and ordered in advance (as MRD and MR assume). On the contrary, what we count throughout our proof are the messages received (or not) at a destination d, which affects d's stop event. This is key to requiring no ordering.

Another crucial concept in MRD is the *idealized* protocol. An *idealized* protocol is informally defined as a totally-ordered fair exchange protocol of which

---

[10] The main difference is that contract signing outputs a proof which binds a contract agreed in advance, while computation usually does not require such binding.

the number of messages in an optimistic execution is optimal [13]. At the *end* phase of the *idealized* protocol, each of the n signers is supposed to send exactly one message [13]. However, it is not clear yet whether the assumption can be justified or not: the main theorem in [13] relates the end of the *idealized* protocol with the end of the shortest permutation sequence; however, (the form of the end of) the shortest permutation sequence is still open for a large n [5]. This also leads to a non-optimal fair exchange protocol in [13] and a non-optimal protocol compiler in [14] which generates a protocol specification of an optimistic fair contract signing scheme given a shortest permutation sequence.[11] Compared with MRD's *idealized* protocol, our proof of Theorem 1 shows that, at the end of an optimal protocol, each of the n parties may receive exactly one message, and moreover, the end of an optimal protocol is *not* related to the shortest permutation sequence.

Acknowledgements. We are very grateful to the second author of [16] for the time devoted to understanding our argument and for his fairplay in recognizing the mistake. This work has been supported in part by the European ERC Grant 339539 - AOC.

References

1. Asokan, N., Shoup, V., Waidner, M.: Optimistic fair exchange of digital signatures. Sel. Areas Commun. IEEE J. **18**(4), 593–610 (2000)
2. Cachin, C., Camenisch, J.L.: Optimistic fair secure computation. In: Bellare, M. (ed.) CRYPTO 2000. LNCS, vol. 1880, pp. 93–111. Springer, Heidelberg (2000)
3. Cleve, R.: Limits on the security of coin flips when half the processors are faulty. In: STOC 1986, pp. 364–369 (1986)
4. Micali, S.: Simple and fast optimistic protocols for fair electronic exchange. In: PODC (2003)
5. Knuth, D.E.: Open problems with a computational flavor, mimeographed notes for a seminar on combinatorics (1971)
6. Newey, M.C.: Notes on a problem involving permutations as subsequences. Technical Report (1973)
7. Zălinescu, E.: Shorter strings containing all k-element permutations. Inf. Process. Lett. **111**(12), 605–608 (2011)
8. Radomirović, S.: A construction of short sequences containing all permutations of a set as subsequences. Electron. J. Comb. **19**(4) (2012). Paper 31
9. Kleitman, D., Kwiatkowski, D.: A lower bound on the length of a sequence containing all permutations as subsequences. J. Comb. Theor. Ser. A **21**(2), 129–136 (1976)
10. Adleman, L.: Short permutation strings. Discrete Math. **10**(2), 197–200 (1974)
11. Koutas, P., Hu, T.: Shortest string containing all permutations. Discrete Math. **11**(2), 125–132 (1975)

---

[11] Although [14] proved that the resulting protocol needs at least $\ell + 2n - 3$ messages in an optimistic execution, the number of messages exchanged during every optimistic execution is actually strictly larger than $\ell + 2n - 3$ for $n \geq 3$, and is thus not optimal.

12. Camenisch, J.L., Damgård, I.B.: Verifiable encryption, group encryption, and their applications to separable group signatures and signature sharing schemes. In: Okamoto, T. (ed.) ASIACRYPT 2000. LNCS, vol. 1976, pp. 331–345. Springer, Heidelberg (2000)

13. Mauw, S., Radomirović, S., Dashti, M.: Minimal message complexity of asynchronous multi-party contract signing. In: CSF (2009)

14. Kordy, B., Radomirović, S.: Constructing optimistic multi-party contract signing protocols. In: CSF (2012)

15. Mauw, S., Radomirović, S.: Generalizing multi-party contract signing. In: Focardi, R., Myers, A. (eds.) POST 2015. LNCS, vol. 9036, pp. 156–175. Springer, Heidelberg (2015)

16. Pfitzmann, B., Schunter, M., Waidner, M.: Optimal efficiency of optimistic contract signing. In: PODC 1998, pp. 113–122 (1998)

17. Schunter, M.: Optimistic fair exchange. Ph.D. dissertation, Universität des Saarlandes (2000). http://scidok.sulb.uni-saarland.de/volltexte/2004/233

18. Dashti, M.T.: Efficiency of optimistic fair exchange using trusted devices. ACM Trans. Auton. Adapt. Syst. 7(1), 3:1–3:18 (2012)

19. Schnorr, C.: Efficient signature generation by smart cards. J. Cryptology 4(3), 161–174 (1991)

20. Kravitz, D.: Digital signature algorithm. US Patent 5,231,668 (1993)

21. Fiat, A., Shamir, A.: How to prove yourself: practical solutions to identification and signature problems. In: Odlyzko, A.M. (ed.) CRYPTO 1986. LNCS, vol. 263, pp. 186–194. Springer, Heidelberg (1987)

22. Ong, H., Schnorr, C.-P.: Fast signature generation with a fiat shamir-like scheme. In: Damgård, I.B. (ed.) EUROCRYPT 1990. LNCS, vol. 473, pp. 432–440. Springer, Heidelberg (1991)

23. Guillou, L.C., Quisquater, J.-J.: A "paradoxical" indentity-based signature scheme resulting from zero-knowledge. In: Goldwasser, S. (ed.) Advances in Cryptology — CRYPTO'88. LNCS, vol. 403, pp. 216–231. Springer, Heidelberg (2000)

24. Guerraoui, R., Wang, J.: Optimal fair computation. Technical Report (2016). http://infoscience.epfl.ch/record/219171

25. Oded, G.: Foundations of Cryptography. Basic Applications, vol. 2. Cambridge University Press, New York (2009)

26. Dierks, T.: The transport layer security (tls) protocol version 1.2 (2008)

27. Canetti, R.: Security and composition of multiparty cryptographic protocols. J. Cryptology 13(1), 143–202 (2000)

28. Goldwasser, S., Micali, S.: Probabilistic encryption. J. Comput. Syst. Sci. 28(2), 270–299 (1984)

29. Yao, A.C.: Theory and application of trapdoor functions. In: SFCS 1982, pp. 80–91 (1982)

30. Gordon, S.D., Katz, J.: Complete fairness in multi-party computation without an honest majority. In: Reingold, O. (ed.) TCC 2009. LNCS, vol. 5444, pp. 19–35. Springer, Heidelberg (2009)

31. Gordon, S.D., Hazay, C., Katz, J., Lindell, Y.: Complete fairness in secure two-party computation. J. ACM

32. Menezes, A.J., Vanstone, S.A., Oorschot, P.C.V.: Handbook of Applied Cryptography. CRC Press Inc., Boca Raton (1996)

33. I. 9594-8. Information technology - open systems interconnection - the directory: Authentication framework (1995). (equivalent to ITU-T Recommendation X.509, 1993)

34. Ateniese, G.: Efficient verifiable encryption (and fair exchange) of digital signatures. In: CCS 1999, pp. 138–146 (1999)
35. Alaraj, A.M.: Simple and efficient contract signing protocol. CoRR, vol. abs/1204.1646 (2012). http://arxiv.org/abs/1204.1646
36. Guerraoui, R., Rodrigues, L.: Introduction to Reliable Distributed Programming. Springer, New York (2006)

Near-Optimal Low-Congestion Shortcuts on Bounded Parameter Graphs

Bernhard Haeupler[1]([✉]), Taisuke Izumi[2], and Goran Zuzic[1]([✉])

[1] Carnegie Mellon University, Pittsburgh, PA, USA
{haeupler,gzuzic}@cs.cmu.edu
[2] Nagoya Institute of Technology, Gokiso-cho, Showa-ku, Nagoya, Aichi, Japan
t-izumi@nitech.ac.jp

Abstract. We show that many distributed network optimization problems can be solved much more efficiently in structured and topologically simple networks.

It is known that solving essentially any global network optimization problem in a general network requires $\Omega(\sqrt{n})$ rounds in the CONGEST model, even if the network diameter is small, e.g., logarithmic. Many networks of interest, however, have more structure which allows for significantly more efficient algorithms. Recently Ghaffari, Haeupler, Izumi and Zuzic [SODA'16,PODC'16] introduced low-congestion shortcuts as a suitable abstraction to capture this phenomenon. In particular, they showed that graphs with diameter D embeddable in a genus-g surface have good shortcuts and that these shortcuts lead to $\tilde{O}(gD)$-round algorithms for MST, Min-Cut and other problems.

We generalize these results by showing that networks with pathwidth or treewidth k allow for good shortcuts leading to fast $\tilde{O}(kD)$ distributed optimization algorithms. We also improve the dependence on genus g from $\tilde{O}(gD)$ to $\tilde{O}(\sqrt{g}D)$. Lastly, we prove lower bounds which show that the dependence on k and g in our shortcuts is optimal. Overall, this significantly refines and extends the understanding of how the complexity of distributed optimization problems depends on the network topology.

Keywords: Distributed algorithm · CONGEST model · Treewidth · Pathwidth · Bounded-genus graph · Minimum spanning tree · Minimum cut

1 Introduction

We show that many distributed network optimization problems can be solved much more efficiently in pathwidth bounded, treewidth bounded and bounded genus graphs.

Consider the problem of finding the minimum spanning tree (MST) on a distributed network with n independent processing nodes. The network is

This work was supported in part by KAKENHI No. 15H00852 and 16H02878 as well as NSF grants CCF-1527110 and CCF-1618280.

© Springer-Verlag Berlin Heidelberg 2016
C. Gavoille and D. Ilcinkas (Eds.): DISC 2016, LNCS 9888, pp. 158–172, 2016.
DOI: 10.1007/978-3-662-53426-7_12

abstracted as a graph $G = (V, E)$ with n nodes and diameter D. The nodes communicate by synchronously passing $O(\log n)$-bit messages to each of its direct neighbors. The goal is to design the algorithms (protocols) that minimize the number of synchronous rounds before the nodes collaboratively solve the optimization problem. The setting we described is a standard message passing model called CONGEST [12].

Kutten and Peleg [8] describe a protocol for the MST problem in $\tilde{O}(\sqrt{n} + D)$ CONGEST rounds and. Moreover, and perhaps more surprisingly, there is no faster algorithm for general graphs. Specifically, there are graphs in which one cannot do any better than $\tilde{\Omega}(\sqrt{n} + D)$ rounds. To make matters worse, this lower bound was shown to be far reaching. It applies to a multitude of important network optimization problems including MST, Min-Cut, weighted shortest-path, connectivity verification, and so on [13].

However, the authors believe that in practice one should not be stifled by this lower bound as networks often exhibit special properties. However, very little progress has been done on this topic. In this paper we exploit the structure that pathwidth, treewidth and genus bounded networks provide to circumvent the $\tilde{\Omega}(\sqrt{n} + D)$ lower bound.

The main tool we use to obtain these results is the **low-congestion shortcut** framework. It is a general abstraction for designing distributed algorithms [4]. On a high level, if we can always find good-quality shortcuts in a graph, then we can efficiently solve network optimization problems on it. An important construction result states that if a special class of shortcuts (called **tree-restricted shortcuts**) are known to exist in a graph, then we can always find them efficiently [6]. This enables us to convert a purely existential graph-theoretic problem into a practical algorithm: if we can prove that good tree-restricted shortcuts exist in a certain family of graphs, we can effectively design efficient distributed algorithms for various network optimization problems.

This paper is roughly structured as follows: we first give a high-order view of shortcuts in the next section and then give a run-down of related work, mostly focusing on shortcuts. Next, we formally define a different kind of shortcuts and give important prior results such as their construction and application theorems. We then show the existence of good shortcuts for pathwidth, treewidth and genus bounded graphs. Finally, we present nearly tight lower bounds on the quality of shortcuts, implying that one cannot do much better using our techniques.

1.1 Low-Congestion Shortcuts

We now give a short introduction of the low-congestion shortcuts [4]. Consider the following scenario, which is a recurring theme throughout distributed approaches for many network optimization problems:

A graph G is partitioned into a number of disjoint individually-connected
parts *$P_1, P_2, ..., P_N$, and we need to compute a (typically simple) function for each of the parts in isolation.*

A classical example for such a scenario is the 1926 algorithm of Boruvka for computing Minimum Spanning Tree (MST): starting with a trivial partition of each node being its own part, in every iteration each part computes the minimum-weighted outgoing edge and merges with the part incident to this edge. After $O(\log n)$ iterations, we arrive at the MST, where n is the number of nodes of G.

A key concern in designing a distributed version of Boruvka's algorithm is finding good communication schemes that allow each part to collaborate with other nodes inside the same part and without interference from other parts. While a natural solution would be to allow communication only inside the same part, this could take a long time. The problem appears when the diameter of a part in isolation is much larger than the diameter D of the original graph G. The low-congestion shortcut is one of the promising frameworks to overcome this issue: each part P_i is given a subgraph of extra edges H_i that it can use to more efficiently communicate within itself. More precisely, each part P_i is associated with a **shortcut subgraph** H_i and is permitted to use $G[P_i] + H_i$ for communication, where $G[P_i]$ means the subgraph induced by P_i and operator $+$ represents the union of two graphs.

To measure the quality of a shortcut, we define two quality parameters: **congestion** and **dilation**. A shortcut has congestion c and dilation d if *(i)* the diameter of every $G[P_i] + H_i$ is at most d, and *(ii)* every edge is assigned to at most c different subgraphs $G[P_i] + H_i$. Ghaffari and Haeupler [4] also show that, given a shortcut with congestion c and dilation d, we can solve several fundamental problems such as MST and Min-Cut approximation in $\tilde{O}(c + d)$ rounds. Therefore, designing an distributed algorithm can be reduced to finding good-quality shortcuts.

We now state a formal definition of shortcuts. Note that with a small abuse of notation, H_i will indicate both a subgraph and an edge set.

Definition 1. *Let $G = (V, E_G)$ be an undirected graph with nodes subdivided into **disjoint and connected** subsets $\mathcal{P} = (P_1, P_2, ..., P_N), P_i \subseteq V$. In other words, $G[P_i]$ is connected and $P_i \cap P_j = \emptyset$ for $i \neq j$. We call these subsets P_i **parts**. We define a **shortcut** $\mathcal{H}$ as a tuple of N **shortcut subgraphs** $(H_1, H_2, ..., H_N), H_i \subseteq G$. A shortcut is characterized by the following parameters: (i) $\mathcal{H}$ has congestion c if each edge $e \in E_G$ is used in at most c different subgraphs $G[P_i] + H_i$, i.e. $\forall e \in E_T : |\{i : e \in H_i\}| \leq c$; (ii) $\mathcal{H}$ has dilation d if the diameter of any subgraph $G[P_i] + H_i$ is at most d.*

2   Related Work

The complexity theoretic issues in the design of distributed graph algorithms for the CONGEST model have received much attention in the last decade, and got an extensive progress for many problems: Minimum-Spanning Tree [8], Maximum flow [5], Minimum Cut [11], Diameter [10], and so on. Most of those problems have $\tilde{\Theta}(\sqrt{n} + D)$-round upper and lower bounds for some sort of approximation guarantee [13]. The notion of low-congestion shortcuts is invented as a framework of circumventing these lower bounds [4]. Specifically, their ideas can be turned into a very short and clean $O((D + \sqrt{n}) \log n)$ round MST algorithm for general graphs, as well as provide a simple heuristical reasoning why the lower bounds of $\tilde{\Omega}(D + \sqrt{n})$ rounds are pervasive in many distributed optimization problems.

Not much work has been done on circumventing this lower bound problems like MST and Min-Cut. A $\tilde{O}(D)$-round algorithm is known for planar graphs [4]. Their methods could in principle be used to achieve a similar result for genus bounded graphs, but their presented algorithms have a major technical obstacle: they require a surface embedding of the planar/genus bounded graph. While computing a distributed embedding for planar graphs has a complex $O(D \log^{O(1)} D)$-round solution [3], this remains an open problem for genus bounded graphs [4].

In a subsequent advancement, a slightly different version of shortcuts called **tree-restricted shortcuts** are proposed. They offer a distinct advantage as they can be simply and efficiently constructed [6]. In particular, there is a distributed algorithm that finds universally near-optimal tree-restricted shortcuts in any graph G that admits them. The algorithm is completely oblivious to the intricacies of the underlying topology and only requires that a good tree-restricted shortcut exists. This approach can be used to design a $\tilde{O}(gD)$-round algorithm for genus-g networks.

To the best of our knowledge, the work initiating the shortcut notion [4] is the first attempt at considering a non-trivial graph class for global optimization problems. For local problems such as maximal independent set, vertex cover, and coloring there are a number of results focusing on some specific graph class: planar graphs [9], unit-disk graphs [7], and so on.

3   Preliminaries

3.1   CONGEST Model

We work in the classical CONGEST model [12], i.e., a network is given as a connected undirected graph $G = (V, E_G)$ with diameter D. Initially, nodes only know their immediate neighbors and they collaborate to compute some global function of the graph like the MST. Communication occurs in synchronous rounds; during a round each node can send $O(\log n)$ bits to each of its neighbors[1]. The nodes always correctly follow the protocol and never fail. The goal is to design protocols that minimize the number of rounds before the nodes compute the solution.

We now precisely formalize what does solving a problem in this model exactly mean, e.g. how are the input and output given. We specifically formalize the MST problem, but other problems are completely analogous. All nodes synchronously wake up in the first round and start executing some given protocol. Every node initially only knows its immediate neighbors and the weight of each of its incident

---

[1] Note that the nodes also know some polynomially tight bound on n, otherwise sending $O(\log n)$ bits does not make sense.

edges. After a specific number of rounds, all nodes must simultaneously output *(i)* the weight of the computed MST τ *(ii)* for each edge e incident to it, a 0/1 bit indicating if $e \in \tau$.

3.2 Tree-Restricted Shortcuts

Tree-restricted shortcuts are shortcuts with the additional property that any shortcut subgraph H_i is restricted to some spanning tree T. The user of the shortcut can typically fix any tree T, so a cogent choice would be the BFS tree because of its optimal depth.

Definition 2 (Tree-restricted shortcuts [6]). *Let $G = (V, E_G)$ be a graph with a shortcut $\mathcal{H}$ with respect to the parts $\mathcal{P} = (P_i)_{i=1}^N$. Given a rooted spanning tree $T = (V, E_T) \subseteq G$ we say that a shortcut $\mathcal{H}$ is T-restricted if for each $i \in [N], H_i \subseteq E_T$ i.e. every edge of H_i is a tree edge of T.*

Congestion and dilation are still well-defined for tree-restricted shortcuts. However, it is more convenient to use an alternative **block parameter** in place of dilation. The block parameter upper-bounds the number of connected components of each H_i that intersects P_i. Note that H_i is not connected if we consider it in isolation, regardless of the fact that $G[P_i]$ (and therefore $G[P_i] + H_i$) is connected is isolation. Also, note that the intersection property ensures that *(i)* we only count components that have vertices in P_i *(ii)* we penalize isolated vertices in $G[P_i] + H_i$.

Definition 3. *Let $\mathcal{H} = (H_1, H_2, ..., H_N)$ be a T-restricted shortcut on the graph $G = (V, E_G)$. Fix a part P_i and consider the connected components of the spanning subgraph (V, H_i). If such a connected component intersects P_i we call it a* **block component.** *Furthermore, we define the* **block parameter** *b of $\mathcal{H}$ to be any upper bound to the number of block components for all parts.*

A block parameter implies a bound on dilation, hence the block parameter can be seen as a stronger measure of quality. Lemma 1 argues that a block parameter of b implies the dilation of $O(b \cdot \operatorname{depth}(T))$. It also suggests that it's often beneficial to fix T to a BFS tree of G.

Lemma 1. *Let T be a spanning tree with depth D and let $\mathcal{H} = (H_i : i \in [N])$ be a T-restricted shortcut with congestion c and block parameter b with respect to parts $\mathcal{P} = (P_i : i \in [N])$. Then the dilation of $\mathcal{H}$ is at most $b(2D + 1)$.*

Proof. Fix $i \in [N]$. If we contract every block component of H_i into a supernode and remove all other nodes, supergraph will contain $b' \leq b$ supernodes and will be connected (because $G[P_i]$ is connected). Hence its diameter is $b' - 1 \leq b - 1$. Every supernode consists of a block component of diameter $2D$, so the diameter of H_i is at most $2bD + b - 1 < b(2D + 1)$.

The graphs of interest typically have the property that for any partition and any spanning tree we can find good-quality shortcuts. We formalize this notion in the following definition.

Definition 4. *A graph G **admits** tree-restricted shortcuts with congestion c and block parameter b if for all spanning trees T and all node partitions $\mathcal{P} = (P_1, ..., P_N)$ there exists a T-restricted shortcut with the given parameters.*

3.3   Construction and Application of Tree-Restricted Shortcuts

The usefulness of shortcuts can be primarily summarized by the following two theorems:

Construction Theorem provides an efficient construction framework of tree-restricted shortcuts for graph classes that admit them.

Theorem 1 ([6])**.** *Let G be a graph that admits a tree-restricted shortcut with congestion c and block parameter b. Given a spanning tree T with depth D, there is a distributed algorithm that finds a T-restricted shortcut with congestion $O(c \log N)$ and block parameter 3b w.h.p. This shortcut can be found in $O(D \log n \log N + bD \log N + bc \log N)$ rounds.*

MST Application Theorem certifies the existence of efficient distributed algorithms for graphs that admit tree-restricted shortcuts. It uses the Construction Theorem and extends it to a full-fledged MST algorithm.

Theorem 2 ([6])**.** *Let G be a graph with n nodes and diameter D that admits a tree-restricted shortcut with congestion c and block parameter b. There is an distributed algorithm that finds the MST in $O(D \log^3 n + bD \log^2 n + bc \log^2 n)$ CONGEST rounds.*

We also note a different variation of the application theorem for low-congestion shortcuts that relies on an external black box construction of shortcuts.

Theorem 3 ([4])**.** *Given an oracle that finds low-congestion shortcuts with dilation d and congestion c for any partition $\mathcal{P}$, there is a MST algorithm that runs in $\tilde{O}(d + c)$ CONGEST rounds.*

For example, planar graphs admit tree-restricted shortcuts with congestion $O(D \log D)$ and block parameter $O(\log D)$ [4,6]. Then the Theorem 2 implies a $\tilde{O}(D)$ MST algorithm for planar graphs.

4   Summary of Technical Results

The contribution of this paper is to show the existence of good-quality tree-restricted shortcuts for multiple classes of graphs: bounded pathwidth, bounded treewidth and bounded genus graphs. These results, using Theorem 2, imply the first distributed MST algorithm that circumvents the $\tilde{\Omega}(\sqrt{n})$ lower bound for pathwidth and treewidth bounded graphs.

Furthermore, we show that by using the low-congestion shortcut framework, one cannot hope to do much better. Specifically, we prove a lower bound on $d + c$ for any low-congestion shortcut with dilation d and congestion c on pathwidth

Table 1. Upper and lower bounds for shortcuts

Graph Family	Tree-restricted Shortcut Quality			Lower Bound
	Block	Congestion	$O(bD + c)$	$\Omega(d + c)$
Pathwidth k	$O(k)$	$O(k)$	$O(kD)$	$\Omega(kD)$
Treewidth k	$O(k)$	$O(k \log n)$	$O(kD + k \log n)$	$\Omega(kD)$
Genus g Graphs	$O(\sqrt{g})$	$O(\sqrt{g}D \log D)$	$O(\sqrt{g}D \log D)$	$\Omega(\frac{\sqrt{g}D}{\log g})$
Planar Graphs [4]	$O(\log D)$	$O(D \log D)$	$O(D \log D)$	$\Omega(D \frac{\log D}{\log \log D})$

bounded and genus bounded graphs. These lower bounds almost match (within logarithmic factors) the proved upper bounds. Those two lower bounds show that one typically does not lose any power by restricting oneself from low-congestion shortcuts to tree-restricted shortcuts and that the algorithms achieved by using Theorem 3 cannot be made significantly faster. The results and lower bound are summarized in Table 1. Note that $O(bD + c)$ is the analogue of $O(d + c)$ for the tree-restricted case.

We note here one important technical difficulty that applies to distributed algorithms on genus bounded graphs. While we prove that optimal $\tilde{O}(\sqrt{g}D)$ congestion and $\tilde{O}(\sqrt{g})$ block parameter shortcuts do exist, their construction via Theorem 1 takes $\tilde{O}(gD)$ rounds. To mitigate this, it is possible to tweak the Construction Theorem to produce the same quality shortcuts in $\tilde{O}(bD + c)$ rounds, giving a $\tilde{O}(\sqrt{g}D)$ construction for optimal genus bounded shortcuts. However, this is currently an unpublished result that we will expand upon in the journal version of [6].

5   Pathwidth Bounded Graphs

In this section we show that k-pathwidth graphs admit tree-restricted shortcuts with congestion $O(k)$ and block parameter $O(k)$. As noted before, this enables us to leverage the Construction Theorem 1 to design efficient algorithms for pathwidth bounded graphs.

Given a graph $G = (V, E_G)$, a **path decomposition** of G is a sequence of subsets $\mathcal{PD} = (X_1, X_2, ..., X_{|\mathcal{PD}|}), X_i \subseteq V$ with the following properties: *(i)* (X_i) form a partition of V; *(ii)* For all $\{v, w\} \in E_G$ there exists i such that $u \in X_i, v \in X_i$; *(iii)* For all $v \in V$ there exists $1 \leq s_v \leq t_v \leq |\mathcal{PD}|$ such that $v \in X_i \iff i \in [s_v, t_v]$. We call the subsets X_i **bags**. The width of the path decomposition $\mathcal{PD}$ is $k := \max_i |X_i| - 1$. The minimal possible width of a path decomposition of G is called the **pathwidth** of G.

For $v \in V$ let $I(v)$ be the set of indices of bags that contain v. Note that property *(iii)* implies that $I(v)$ is an interval of integers. Similarly, for a set $P \subseteq V$ we define $I(P)$ as $\bigcup_{v \in P} I(v)$. Note that for a connected vertex set P (such as any part), $I(P)$ is also an interval of integers.

Lemma 2. *Let $\mathcal{PD}$ be a k-width path decomposition of a graph $G = (V, E_G)$. For any rooted spanning tree $T = (V, E_T) \subseteq G$, there exists a T-restricted shortcut with congestion $O(k)$ and block parameter $O(k)$.*

Proof. Denote the parts as $\mathcal{P} = (P_1, P_2, ..., P_N)$ and fix a part P_i. Call a node $v \in V$ **admissible** if $I(v) \subseteq I(P_i)$, i.e. if the interval of the node if a subset of the partwise interval. Let A_i be the set of all admissible nodes.

The shortcut subgraphs H_i can be constructed in the following way: H_i contains all tree edges $\{a, b\} \in E_T$ (where a is closer to the root) iff $b \in A_i$.

We first prove that congestion of this tree-restricted shortcut is $O(k)$. Fix an edge $e = \{a, b\} \in E_T$ as before and denote by L_b the lowest-numbered bag containing b. If a shortcut subgraph $H_i \ni e$ then by construction there exist a node $v \in P_i$ that is contained in L_b. Hence the number of shortcut subgraphs that contain e is at most $|L_b| = O(k)$.

To bound the block parameter, fix a part P_i. Call a node $v \in V$ **absorbing** if it is contained in either the lowest-numbered or highest-numbered bag of $I(P_i)$. Denote all absorbing nodes by B_i and note that $|B_i| \leq 2k + 2 = O(k)$. To upper bound the number of block components of part i, we will count the number of nodes that can be the root of a block component (each block component can be bijectively represented by its root). Since every block component of part i must intersect P_i, we can generate the set of roots in the following manner: start with a node $v \in P_i$ and travel along its T-parent edges while the edge exists and is in H_i. The process clearly ends in the root of the block component r_{bc}. It is sufficient to prove that either r_{bc} is the root of T or $r_{bc} \in B_i$, hence there can be $O(k)$ different possibilities for r_{bc} and, consequently, $O(k)$ block components.

We start the process in some $v \in P_i$. By construction, $v \in A_i \implies v \in A_i \cup B_i$. In each step it holds that either: *(i)* v is the root of T, in which case we are done; *(ii)* $v \in B_i$, in which case $r_{bc} = v$ and we are done. Note that its parent is not in H_i; *(iii)* $v \in A_i$, in which case we move to its T-parent v'. Note that, by construction, $v' \in A_i \cup B_i$. Hence by induction we can prove that we always end in the root of T or B_i, which proves the claim. ∎

6   Treewidth Bounded Graphs

In this section we show that k-treewidth graphs with n nodes admit tree-restricted shortcuts with congestion $O(k \log n)$ and block parameter $O(k)$.

Given a graph $G = (V, E_G)$, a **tree decomposition** of G is a tree $\mathcal{TD} = (\mathcal{X}, E_T)$. The nodes of $\mathcal{TD}$, $\mathcal{X} = (X_1, ..., X_{|\mathcal{X}|})$ are called **bags**. Each bag corresponds to a subset of V, the nodes of the original graph G. For the sake of presentation, we will identify the bag X_i and this corresponding subset of nodes. The tree decomposition has to satisfy these properties: *(i)* the union of all sets X_i equals V and they are pairwisely disjoint, i.e. $\mathcal{X}$ is a partition of V; *(ii)* for each $v \in V$ the bags containing vertex v form a connected subtree of $\mathcal{TD}$; *(iii)* for every edge $\{a, b\} \in E_G$ there is a bag X_i that contains both a and b. The **width** of the tree decomposition $\mathcal{TD}$ is $k := \max_i |X_i| - 1$. The minimal possible width of a tree decomposition of G is called the **treewidth** of G.

Lemma 3. *Let TD be a k-width tree decomposition of a graph $G = (V, E_G)$ rooted in an arbitrary bag such that its depth is D_{TD}. For any rooted spanning tree $T = (V, E_T) \subseteq G$ there exists a T-restricted shortcut with congestion $O(kD_{TD})$ and block parameter $O(k)$.*

Proof Sketch. Due to space constraints we will only sketch the construction and the proof. Fix a part P_i and identify all the bags that intersect P_i. Let their lowest common ancestor (in the tree decomposition TD) be the bag L_i. We now define the shortcut subgraph H_i to be composed of all edges $\{a, b\} \in E_T$ (a is closer to the root of T) such that b is not contained in L_i and there exist a TD-descendent of L_i that contains b.

The congestion of this T-restricted shortcut is $O(kD_{TD})$ because each part P_i that contains some fixed $\{a, b\}$ can only have one of $O(D_{TD})$ possible lowest common ancestor bags, each of which contains only $O(k)$ nodes.

The number of block components is determined in the same way as in the pathwidth construction proof - by starting from $v \in P_i$ and walking up the T-tree until hitting a block component root. We can prove that this process will either end in the root of T or in L_i. This proves that the block parameter is $O(k)$.

Corollary 1. *Given a n-node graph G with treewidth k and a spanning tree $T \subseteq G$, there exist a T-restricted shortcut with congestion $O(k \log n)$ and block parameter $O(k)$.*

Proof. By Bodlaender and Hagerup [1], for a graph with treewidth k there exists a $O(k)$-width tree decomposition with depth $O(\log n)$. Applying Lemma 3 finishes the argument.

7   Lower Bound for Pathwidth Bounded Graphs

In this section we prove a lower bound for general low-congestion shortcuts for pathwidth bounded graphs. In particular, we prove that there exists a family of pathwidth bounded graphs $\mathcal{G}_P(\Gamma, w, \delta)$ for which any low-congestion shortcut either must have large congestion or large dilation. More precisely, we exhibit a k-pathwidth graph family such that for any shortcut with dilation d and congestion c it must hold that $d + c = \Omega(kD)$. Note that this result also implies a lower bound for treewidth bounded graphs as k-pathwidth graphs are also k-treewidth graphs.

We now describe the graph family $\mathcal{G}_P(\Gamma, w, \delta)$ in detail, depicted in Fig. 1. All parameters of the graph Γ, w, δ are positive integers. Furthermore, $\Gamma \geq 2, w \geq 2, \delta \geq 2$ and w is a power of 2.

The construction consists of two main parts: Γ different **lanes** and a **tree** $\mathcal{T}$. The lanes are denoted by $\{L^1, L^2, ..., L^\Gamma\}$. Each lane L^l is constructed in two steps: first we take a path consisting of w **named nodes** $v_0^l, v_1^l, ..., v_{w-1}^l$ connected by single edges, and then we subdivide each edge by adding $2\delta - 1$ **unnamed nodes** in its interior.

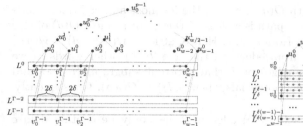

Fig. 1. Graph $\mathcal{G}_P(\Gamma, w, \delta)$ **Fig. 2.** Graph $\mathcal{G}_G(w, \delta)$

The tree $\mathcal{T}$ is a perfect binary tree with w leaves (note again that w is a power of 2). $\mathcal{T}$ has $p = 1 + \log_2 w$ different levels (depths) where the root is on level $p - 1$ and the leaves are on level 0. The tree nodes on level l are denoted by $u_0^l, u_1^l, ..., u_{2^l-1}^l$. Finally, the tree and the lanes are connected: each named node on the lane v_i^l is connected by a **cross edge** to the leaf u_i^0 in the tree.

Claim. The graph $\mathcal{G}_P(\Gamma, w, \delta)$ has $\Theta(\Gamma w \delta)$ nodes. Its diameter is $\Theta(\log w + \delta)$ and pathwidth is $O(w)$.

Proof. The only non-trivial part is the pathwidth. We construct a $O(w)$-width path decomposition of $\mathcal{G}_P$. First, construct a $O(1)$-width path decomposition of each lane L^l in isolation. Next, to each bag in a decomposition of the lane L^l we add all w named nodes of that lane. Next, concatenate the path decompositions together and obtain a $O(w)$ path decomposition of the union of all lanes. Next, add all the nodes of the tree $\mathcal{T}$ to each bag in every lane (there are $O(w)$ nodes that are added). Finally, we have a valid $O(w)$-width path decomposition of $\mathcal{G}_P$.

Lemma 4. *There exists a node partition on $\mathcal{G}_P(\Gamma, w, \delta)$ such that the (general) shortcut for this partition either has dilation $\Omega(w\delta)$ or congestion $\Omega(\frac{\Gamma}{\log w})$.*

Proof. We let each lane L^l be its own part $P_l, l \in [\Gamma]$, as depicted by a red box in Fig. 1. There are Γ parts in total.

In order to prove that a shortcut subgraph for a part either has large dilation or has to congested edges of $\mathcal{T}$, we define **potential** on all of the edges in $\mathcal{G}_P(\Gamma, w, \delta)$ in the following way:

- every cross edge is assigned a potential of 0
- every edge between two nodes on a lane is assigned a potential of 1
- every tree edge between u_i^l and u_j^{l+1} is assigned a potential of $\delta 2^l$

Define the **potential of a path** as the sum of potentials of the edges on that path. Observe that the potential of any path between any leftmost node of a lane v_0^l and rightmost node of the same lane v_{w-1}^l is at least $(w-1)2\delta = \Omega(w\delta)$. Also, note that the sum of potentials of all edges in $\mathcal{T}$ is $O(\delta w \log w)$.

For the sake of contradiction assume that there exists a shortcut $\mathcal{H}$ with dilation $d = o(w\delta)$ and congestion c. Then for each part (i.e. lane) P_l there exists a path in $\mathcal{G}_P[P_i] + H_l$ of length $O(d)$ between the leftmost and rightmost node in its lane. The potential of that path is at least $\Omega(w\delta)$, but at most $O(d)$ of this potential can come from edges from a lane. Hence, at least $\Omega(w\delta - d) = \Omega(w\delta)$ of the potential has to come from edges on the tree $\mathcal{T}$. In other words, if we define T_l as the subset of tree edges of $\mathcal{T}$ that shortcut subgraph H_l uses and define $\phi(T_l)$ as the sum of their potentials, then $\phi(T_l) = \Omega(w\delta)$. Consequently, $\sum_{i=0}^{\Gamma-1} \phi(T_l) = \Omega(\Gamma w\delta)$.

But on the other hand, each (tree) edge in $\mathcal{T}$ can only be contained in c different shortcut subgraphs, so $\sum_{i=0}^{\Gamma-1} \phi(T_l) = O(c\delta w \log w)$ since the sum of potentials of all tree edges in $\mathcal{T}$ is $O(\delta w \log w)$. If follows that $c = \Omega(\frac{\Gamma}{\log w})$, as required.

Corollary 2. *Given $k \geq 2, D = \Omega(\log k)$ and a sufficiently large n, there exists a graph with $O(n)$ nodes that has (i) pathwidth $O(k)$, (ii) diameter $\Theta(D)$, (iii) there exists a node partition $\mathcal{P}$ such that any (general) shortcut for that partition must have either dilation $\Omega(kD)$ or congestion $\Omega(\frac{n}{Dk \log k})$.*

Proof. This corollary follows directly from Lemma 4 by taking the graph $\mathcal{G}_P(\Gamma, w, \delta)$ with $\Gamma = \frac{n}{kD}, \delta = D$ and $w = \Theta(k)$ (note that we can always find a power of 2 within a constant factor of any k).

8   Genus Bounded Graphs

The main idea of our construction for bounded genus graphs is a reduction from the planar-graph case: We first construct another planar graph J related to the original genus-g graph G, and compute a good shortcut for J. Then, we map each shortcut subgraph in J to a subgraph in G as a shortcut in G. We first introduce the general framework of this "mapping" strategy.

8.1   Graph Extension

Definition 5. *A graph J is an extension of a graph G if G is obtained from J by deleting edges or contracting vertex pairs (contracting pair may not be adjacent, and multiedges caused by a contraction is merged into a single edge).*

Throughout this section we use notation $V(G)$ and $E(G)$ to indicate the sets of vertices and edges in G respectively. Node contraction maps several nodes in J to a node in G. The mapping is denoted by $f : V(J) \to V(G)$. Let $\overline{E}$ be the set of deleted edges. By the definition of contraction, for any two nodes $v, u \in V(J)$ such that $f(v) \neq f(u)$, if $(v, u) \in E(J) \setminus \overline{E}$ holds, $(f(v), f(u)) \in E(G)$ also holds. That is, there exists a mapping from $E(J) \setminus \overline{E}$ to $E(G)$. We commonly use function f to indicate this edge mapping. We define, we define $f^{-1}(v) = \{v' \in V(J) | f(v') = v\}$ for any $v \in V(G)$, and define $f^{-1}(e)$ for edge $e \in E(G)$ similarly. The cardinality of $f^{-1}(e)$ for edge $e \in E(G)$ is called the *multiplicity* of e. The maximum multiplicity of all edges in G are denoted by μ. The mappings f and f^{-1} are also extended for the set of vertices or edges. For example, for $U \in V(G)$, we define $f^{-1}(U) = \cup_{u \in U} f^{-1}(u)$. All other cases are defined similarly. Let $\lambda = |V(J)| - |V(G)|$ for short.

A hurdle of converting a shortcut in J to G is that given a connected component U in G, $G[f^{-1}(U)]$ is not necessarily connected (i.e., each part in G is fragmented into several subparts in J). The following lemma states the bound on the number of fragments.

Lemma 5. *Let G be a graph and J be its extension. Given a node subset $U \subset V(G)$ such that the subgraph of G induced by U is connected, the subgraph of J induced by $f^{-1}(U)$ consists of at most $|f^{-1}(U)| - |U| + 1$ connected components.*

Proof. (Omitted due to space constraints)

Now consider a part P_i in G, which is separated into $\gamma(i)$ connected components (say subparts) in J. In the construction of shortcuts in J, each subpart must be treated as an indepentdent part. Thus when mapping the shortcuts augmented with those subparts into the shortcut for P_i in G, the number of blocks is multiplied by $\gamma(i)$. That is, if each subpart in J achieves a shortcut with b block components, their mapping into G yields a shortcut with $b\gamma(i)$ block components. Thus a part P_i with high $\gamma(i)$ suffers a high block parameter. To overcome that matter, we additionally adopt the second strategy: If $\gamma(i)$ is so large, every edge in T is augmented with P_i as a shortcut edge. While it causes the increase of the congestion, by a careful analysis, we can bound the extra congestion derived from the second strategy by a moderately small value. The argument above is summarized by the following lemma:

Lemma 6. *Let G be a graph, J be its extension, T be a spanning tree of G, T^{-1} be a spanning tree of J, and $\nu = |E(T^{-1}) \setminus f^{-1}(T)|$. If J has a T^{-1}-restricted shortcut with congestion c and block parameter b, then G has a T-restricted shortcut with congestion $\mu c + \alpha$ and block parameter $(\lambda b + \nu c)/\alpha + 1$ for any $\alpha \geq 1$.*

Proof. (Omitted due to space constraints)

8.2   Optimal Shortcut for Genus-g Graphs

The core of the proof for genus-g graphs is the following lemma.

Lemma 7. *Let G be any graph of genus g and diameter D. Then there exists an extension J of G satisfying the following conditions: (i) J is planar, (ii) There exists a spanning tree T^{-1} with depth at most $2D + 1$, and (iii) $\mu = 2$, $\lambda \leq 12gD$, and $\nu \leq 12g$ for T^{-1}.*

To explain how this lemma is proved, we prepare several notions related to graph embeddings on surfaces: Let G be a graph of genus g. In the following argument we assume that G is 2-cell embedded in an orientable surface of genus

g, which is denoted by $\Sigma_g{}^2$. A loop on a surface Σ is a continuous function $f : [0,1] \rightarrow \Sigma$ satisfying $f(0) = f(1)$. For any spanning tree T of G and an edge e not contained in T, graph $G + e$ contains exactly one simple cycle. We denote it by $loop(T, e)$. We also use the notation $loop(T, e)$ as the loop on surface Σ if G is embedded in Σ. A key tool of our proof is the following theorem.

Theorem 4 (Eppstein [2]). *Let G be a graph of genus g and consider its arbitrary 2-cell embedding on Σ_g. Given any node $v_x \in V$, let T be the shortest path tree of G rooted by v_x. Then there exists a set B of $2g$ edges $= \{e'_1, e'_2, \ldots, e'_{2g}\}$ such that a set of loops $loop(T, e'_1), loop(T, e'_2), \ldots, loop(T, e'_{2g})$ generates the fundamental group of the surface Σ_g whose base point is v_x.*

Let G' be the subgraph of G induced by the set of edges $\cup_{i=1}^{2g} E(loop(T, e'_i))$, and T' be a subtree of T obtained from G' by removing all edges in B. Then the following lemma holds:

Lemma 8. *Given any 2-cell embedding of G into Σ_g, we remove all edges and vertices in $G - G'$. After the removal, we obtain a embedding of G' into Σ_g. This embedding is still a 2-cell embedding and the number of faces is one.*

Proof. It is obvious that the embedding of G' stated by the lemma is 2-cell embedding: If it has a face not topologically isomorphic to a disk, by cutting and capping all the boundaries in that face by disks, we can obtain an embedding of G' on a surface with genus $g - 1$ or less, which contradicts the fact that G' is the union of the generators of Σ_g. The number of faces is obtained by applying Euler's formula. Since $E(G')$ consists of a subtree T' of T spanning G' and $2g$ edges not in T but whose endpoints are both in T'. Thus the total number of the edges is $|V(G')| - 1 + 2g$. Since G' is 2-cell embedded in Σ_g, by applying Euler's formula, we can conclude that the number of faces for that embedding is one.

This lemma implies that by "cutting" Σ_g along the (embedded) edges in $E(G')$, it becomes topologically equivalent to a disk. In other words, if we embed some graph on Σ_g without crossing $\cup_{i=1}^{2g} loop(T, e'_i)$, it becomes a planar embedding. The proof of lemma 7 is to identify a graph J which is an extension of G and planarly embeddable on Σ_g in the sense above (the proof details are omitted due to lack of space).

It is known that any planar graph has a T-restricted shortcut for congestion $O((D_T \log D_T))$ and block parameter $O(\log D_T)$ [4,6], where D_T is the depth of T. Combining that fact with Lemmas 6 and 7 with $\alpha = \sqrt{g}D \log D$, we obtain the main theorem.

Theorem 5. *Any graph with genus g has a T-restricted shortcut with congestion $(O\sqrt{g}D \log D)$ and block parameter $O(\sqrt{g})$ for any spanning tree T with diameter D.*

---

[2] 2-cell embedding is the embedding where every face on Σ is topologically isomorphic to an open disk.

8.3 Lower Bounds for Genus Bounded Graphs

In this section we state a low-congestion shortcuts lower bound for genus bounded graphs. However, due to space constraints we will omit the details because of their similarity to the lower bound for pathwidth bounded graphs (Sect. 7). The graph family $\mathcal{G}_P(\Gamma, w, \delta)$ that entails this lower bound is depicted in Fig. 2.

Corollary 3. *Given $g \geq 2, D = \Omega(\log g)$ and a sufficiently large n, there exists a graph with $O(n)$ nodes that has (i) genus $O(g)$, (ii) diameter $\Theta(D)$, (iii) there exists a node partition $\mathcal{P}$ such that any (general) shortcut for that partition must have either dilation $\Omega(\sqrt{g}D)$ or congestion $\Omega(\frac{\sqrt{g}D}{\log g})$.*

Acknowledgments. We are thankful to the Center for Exploring the Limits of Computation (ELC) and the Japan Society for the Promotion of Science for funding a three-week collaborative research visit. We also thank Mohsen Ghaffari for discussions and contributions at the beginning of this project and the DISC reviewers of this paper for their helpful comments.

References

1. Bodlaender, H.L., Hagerup, T.: Parallel algorithms with optimal speedup for bounded treewidth. SIAM J. Comput. **27**(6), 1725–1746 (1998)
2. Eppstein, D.: Dynamic generators of topologically embedded graphs. In: Proceedings of the ACM-SIAM Symposium on Discrete Algorithms (SODA), pp. 599–608 (2003)
3. Ghaffari, M., Haeupler, B.: Distributed algorithms for planar networks I: Planar embedding. Manuscript (2015)
4. Ghaffari, M., Haeupler, B.: Distributed algorithms for planar networks II: Low-congestion shortcuts, mst, and min-cut. In: Proceedings of ACM-SIAM Symposium on Discrete Algorithms (SODA), pp. 202–219. SIAM (2016)
5. Ghaffari, M., Karrenbauer, A., Kuhn, F., Lenzen, C., Patt-Shamir, B.: Near-optimal distributed maximum flow: Extended abstract. In: The Proceedings of the Int'l Symposium on Prince of District Company (PODC), pp. 81–90 (2015)
6. Haeupler, B., Izumi, T., Zuzic, G.: Low-congestion shortcuts without embedding. In: Proceedings of the 2016 ACM Symposium on Principles of Distributed Computing. ACM (2016)
7. Kuhn, F., Moscibroda, T., Wattenhofer, R.: On the locality of bounded growth. In: The Proceedings of the Int'l Symposium on Prince of District Company (PODC), pp. 60–68 (2005)
8. Kutten, S., Peleg, D.: Fast distributed construction of k-dominating sets and applications. In: The Proceedings of the Int'l Symposium on Prince of District Company (PODC), pp. 238–251 (1995)
9. Lenzen, C., Oswald, Y.A., Wattenhofer, R.: What can be approximated locally?: case study: dominating sets in planar graphs. In: The Proceedings of the Symposium on Parallel Algorithms and Architectures, pp. 46–54 (2008)
10. Lenzen, C., Patt-Shamir, B.: Fast partial distance estimation and applications. In: The Proceedings of the Int'l Symposium on Prince of District Company (PODC), pp. 153–162 (2015)

11. Nanongkai, D., Su, H.-H.: Almost-tight distributed minimum cut algorithms. In: Kuhn, F. (ed.) DISC 2014. LNCS, vol. 8784, pp. 439–453. Springer, Heidelberg (2014)
12. Peleg, D.: Distributed Computing: A Locality-sensitive Approach. Society for Industrial and Applied Mathematics, Philadelphia (2000)
13. Sarma, A.D., Holzer, S., Kor, L., Korman, A., Nanongkai, D., Pandurangan, G., Peleg, D., Wattenhofer, R.: Distributed verification and hardness of distributed approximation. SIAM J. Comput. 41(5), 1235–1265 (2012)

Anonymity-Preserving Failure Detectors

Zohir Bouzid and Corentin Travers[✉]

LaBRI, U. Bordeaux, Bordeaux, France
{zohir.bouzid,corentin.travers}@labri.fr

Abstract. The paper investigates the consensus problem in anonymous, failures prone and asynchronous shared memory systems. It introduces a new class of failure detectors, called *anonymity-preserving* failure detectors suited to anonymous systems. As its name indicates, a failure detector in this class cannot be relied upon to break anonymity. For example, the anonymous perfect detector AP, which gives at each process an estimation of the number of processes that have failed belongs to this class.

The paper then determines the weakest failure detector among this class for consensus. This failure detector, called C, may be seen as a loose failures counter: (1) after a failure occurs, the counter is eventually incremented, and (2) if two or more processes are non-faulty, it eventually stabilizes.

1   Introduction

Anonymous computing. The vast majority of the literature about distributed computing assumes that each process is provided with a unique identifier. We consider in this work *anonymous computing* in which processes have no identifiers and are programmed identically. Besides intellectual curiosity, anonymous computing might be of practical interest [23]. For example, for privacy reasons, a set of distributed processes may be willing to compute some function on their inputs without revealing their identity. Alternatively, the distributed computation might be performed on top of an anonymous communication system [14], and thus using ids is forbidden.

Specifically, we consider the *totally anonymous shared memory model* of distributed computing. The shared memory consists only in basic shared objects, namely read/write registers. We assume that there is no way to uniquely assign registers to the processes as this would provide a way to differentiate them. Previous works [5,23] have shown that the lack of unique identifiers limits the computational power of the shared memory model. Similarly, starting from the pioneering work of Angluin [1], the computational power of anonymous message passing system in the failure-free case has been investigated for particular or general graph topologies, e.g., [6,25].

This work has been carried out with financial support from the French State, managed by the French National Research Agency (ANR) in the frame of the "Investments for the future" Program IdEx Bordeaux - CPU (ANR-10-IDEX-03-02).

© Springer-Verlag Berlin Heidelberg 2016
C. Gavoille and D. Ilcinkas (Eds.): DISC 2016, LNCS 9888, pp. 173–186, 2016.
DOI: 10.1007/978-3-662-53426-7_13

Consensus, failure and asynchrony. Besides the unavailability of unique identifiers, a major difficulty is coping with failures and asynchrony. Many simple distributed tasks cannot be solved in asynchronous and failures-prone distributed system. A prominent example is *consensus*, which is a cornerstone task in fault-tolerant distributed computing. Informally, the processes, each starting with a private value, are required to agree on one value chosen among their initial values. Even if processes have unique identifiers, it is well known that asynchronous fault tolerant consensus is impossible as soon as at least one process may fail by crashing [24]. This impossibility trivially extends to anonymous systems.

Failure detectors. A popular approach to circumvent impossibilities stemming from asynchrony and failures is to use *failure detectors* [13]. A failure detector is a distributed device that provides each processes with perhaps unreliable information about which other processes have crashed. In systems with identities, several classes of failure detectors have been defined [18]. In many cases, their specification involves processes identities. For example, the *perfect detector* P provides each process with a list of the identities of some of the processes that have crashed. The list is eventually complete in the sense that it eventually includes the identity of each crashed process. The *leader* failure detector Ω eventually outputs the same identity at every process, which is the identity of a non-faulty process.

Given a distributed task T, a natural question is to determine the *weakest failure detector* for T, that is a failure detector D which is both *sufficient* to solve the task – there is an asynchronous, fault tolerant protocol that uses D to solve T – and *necessary*, in the sense that any failure detector D' that can be used to solve T can also be used to emulate D. For example, it is well-known that Ω is the weakest failure detector for consensus [12] in shared memory systems with identities.

Failure detectors in anonymous systems. The study of failure detectors in anonymous message passing systems was initiated in [8]. In particular, *identity-free* counterparts of classical failure detectors including Ω and P are identified. $A\Omega$, an identity-free failure detector equivalent to Ω, outputs a Boolean value at each process such that eventually true is output only at a unique correct process. A consensus protocol that uses $A\Omega$ was also presented. In the shared memory model, an anonymous $A\Omega$-based protocol can be found in [15]. Bonnet and Raynal left open the following question: "Consensus in anonymous distributed systems: is there a weakest failure detector?" [7]. We answer this question positively.

Contributions of the paper. Although the definition of the failure detector $A\Omega$ is useful for anonymous systems, as it does not involve processes identities, it can be used to (eventually) break symmetry, as it eventually singles out one process. We are interested in failure detectors that preserve anonymity in the following sense: for any process p and any sequence of failure detector outputs at process p, the same sequence might be output at every process without violating the specification of the failure detector. An example of such a failure detector is AP which provides each process with an eventually accurate estimation of the number of faulty processes. Within this framework, we identify the weakest failure detector for consensus in the shared memory model. In more details, the paper makes the following contributions:

1. It first defines (Sect. 3) the class of anonymity-preserving failure detectors and a new failure detector denoted C. Failure detector C might be seen as a shared loose failure counter. It guarantees that after a failure occurs the counter is eventually incremented, and in case two or more processes are non-faulty, the counter eventually stabilizes. Let us notice that even if several failures occur, the counter might be incremented only once. C is thus far from providing an accurate tally of failures.
2. The paper shows that C is strong enough to solve consensus while tolerating any number of failures (Sect. 4). Striving to not reinvent the wheel, the protocol relies on standard shared memory constructs, namely adopt-commit [19] and safe-agreement [10] objects.
3. It is then shown that C can be emulated using any anonymity-preserving failure detector powerful enough to solve consensus (Sect. 5). The extraction protocol reuses in part the techniques developed by Zieliński [26] for proving a statement of this type in the shared memory model when processes are not anonymous. Interestingly, the proof does not rely on the specifics of the impossibility of fault-tolerant consensus but rather on the fact this task cannot be solved non-anonymously wait-free among two processes.

Due to space constraints, some proofs and additional results have been omitted. See [11] for a complete report on this work.

2   Computational Model

We consider an *asynchronous* and *crash-prone* shared-memory system consisting in a set $\Pi = \{p_1, \ldots, p_n\}$ of $n \geq 2$ processes, i is the *index* of p_i. Processes are *anonymous* in the sense that they run the same code and are not aware of their index. They communicate via a *shared memory* that consists in an unbounded number of *multi-writer/multi-reader atomic registers*. For modeling purposes we assumed the existence of global clock not accessible to the processes and whose range is the integers.

A *failure pattern* is a function $\mathcal{F} : \mathbb{N} \to 2^{\Pi}$ that specifies the set of processes that have failed at each time $\tau \in \mathbb{N}$. $\mathsf{faulty}(\mathcal{F}) = \bigcup_{\tau \geq 0} \mathcal{F}(\tau)$ denotes the set of processes that fail in $\mathcal{F}$. A process p is *faulty* in $\mathcal{F}$ if it belongs to $\mathsf{faulty}(\mathcal{F})$ and *correct* otherwise, that is $p \in \mathsf{correct}(\mathcal{F}) = \Pi \setminus \mathsf{faulty}(\mathcal{F})$. We assume the *wait-free environment* that contains every failure pattern in which at least one process is correct. A *failure detector* D with range $\mathcal{R}$ is a distributed device that provides each process with information about the failure pattern [13]. A *failure detector history* is a function $H : \Pi \times \mathbb{N} \to \mathcal{R}$ that maps each pair (process index, time) to a value in the failure detector range. The value returned by the failure detector at process p_i at time τ is $H(p_i, \tau)$. D associates a non-empty set of histories $D(\mathcal{F})$ with each failure pattern $\mathcal{F}$.

A *protocol* consists in n copies of a local algorithm $\mathcal{A}$, one per process. In a *step* a process (1) queries the failure detector or (2) reads or (3) writes a shared register, and then performs some local computation. A *run of a protocol* $\mathcal{A}$ *using failure detector* D is a tuple $e = (\mathcal{F}, H, I, S, T)$ where $\mathcal{F}$ is a failure pattern, $H \in D(\mathcal{F})$, I and S are respectively an initial configuration and a sequence of steps of $\mathcal{A}$ and T a non-decreasing sequence of times. S is called a *schedule* and the ith step $S[i]$ of S takes place at time $T[i]$. $e = (\mathcal{F}, H, I, S, T)$ represents an execution of $\mathcal{A}$ if and only if (1) S and T are both infinite or $|S| = |T|$, (2) no processes take a step after it has crashed, (3) if step $S[i]$ is a failure detector query by process p that returns d, then $d = H(p, T[i])$, (4) the steps taken in S are consistent with $\mathcal{A}$, (5) the timings of read and write steps, together with the values written or read in these steps are consistent with the atomic semantic of the shared registers and, (6) if S is infinite, every correct process takes infinitely many steps in S.

In the *consensus* task, each process starts with a value taken from some set $\mathcal{V}$ and is required to *decide* a value subject to the following requirements: (*Validity*) any decided value is the initial value of some process, (*Agreement*) no two distinct values are decided and (*Termination*) every non-faulty process decides.

A failure detector D is said to be *as least as weak as* a failure detector D', denoted $D \leq D'$ if there is a protocol $T_{D' \to D}$ that *emulates* D using D'. Failure detector D is said to be the *weakest failure detector* for a task T if (1) there is a protocol that solves T using D in $\mathcal{E}$ and (2) for every failure detector D' that can be used to solve T, $D \leq D'$. In systems with identities, Ω is the weakest failure detector for consensus [12].

3   Anonymity-Preserving Failure Detectors

The class of anonymity-preserving failure detectors Intuitively, a failure detector is anonymity preserving if it cannot be relied upon to break symmetry among the processes. A failure detector history H is *anonymity-preserving* if for every time τ and every processes indexes i, j, $H(p_i, \tau) = H(p_j, \tau)$. That is, two queries at the same time by different processes return the same value. Hence, in such history, the value output by the failure detector only depends on the time at which the failure detector is queried, and does not depend on the querying process. An anonymity preserving history is thus a function $H : \mathbb{N} \to \mathcal{R}$ that maps time to values in the failure detector range.

A failure detector is *anonymity preserving* if for every failure pattern $\mathcal{F}$, for every $p_i \in \Pi$ and every history $H \in D(\mathcal{F})$, the anonymity-preserving history H': $\forall p_j \in \Pi, \forall \tau, H'(p_j, \tau) = H(p_i, \tau)$ also belongs to $D(\mathcal{F})$. Intuitively, any sequence of values output by the failure detector at process p_i may have been returned at every other process. That is, if $d = d_1, d_2, \ldots$ is a legal sequence of output for process p_i for some failure pattern $\mathcal{F}$, then d is also a valid sequence for process $p_j \neq p_i$, for the same failure pattern $\mathcal{F}$.

For instance, the failure detector $A\Omega$ [8] eventually distinguishes a unique correct process. It provides to each process a single bit whose value eventually is 0 except for one correct process. $A\Omega$ is thus not an anonymity-preserving failure detector. An example of an anonymity-preserving failure detector is the identity-free variant of the perfect failure detector, denoted AP in [8]. The range of AP is $\mathbb{N}$ and, for any failure pattern $\mathcal{F}$ the history $H : \Pi \times \mathbb{N} \to \mathbb{N}$ belongs to $AP(\mathcal{F})$ if and only if: (*Accuracy*) For every time τ and every process p_i, $H(p_i, \tau) \leq |\mathcal{F}(\tau)|$, and (*Completeness*) there exists a time τ such that for all $\tau' \geq \tau$, $H(p_i, \tau') = |\mathcal{F}(\tau')|$. AP is an anonymity-preserving failure detector. If for failure pattern $\mathcal{F}$ the sequence of outputs $f_1, f_2, \ldots$ is valid for process p_i, so is it for any process $p_j \neq p_i$.

Failure detector C. Failure detector C might be seen as an unreliable variant of the *signaling failure* detector $\mathcal{FS}$ [22]. The range of failure detector $\mathcal{FS}$ is $\{green, red\}$. While no failures occur, the output of $\mathcal{FS}$ is *green*. Once a failure occurs, and only if it does, the failure detector must eventually output *red* at every correct process.

The range of failure detector C is the integers. At each process, the sequence of integers output by C is non-decreasing, and after each new failure, the output of the failure detector is eventually increased. Moreover, when at least two processes are correct in the underlying failure pattern, C output eventually stabilizes. That is, after some time, every query to C by process p_i returns the same value, for each process p_i. More formally, for every failure pattern $\mathcal{F}$, history $H : \Pi \times \mathbb{N} \to \mathbb{N}$ belongs to $C(\mathcal{F})$ if and only if:

1. *Monotonicity.* For every process p_i, for every times $\tau \leq \tau'$, $H(p_i, \tau) \leq H(p_i, \tau')$;
2. *Signaling.* For every times $\tau, \tau' : \tau < \tau'$, for every processes p_i, p_j, if $|\mathcal{F}(\tau)| < |\mathcal{F}(\tau')|$, there exists a time $\tau'', \tau' \leq \tau''$ such that $H(p_i, \tau) < H(p_j, \tau'')$;
3. *Convergence.* If $|\mathsf{correct}(\mathcal{F})| > 1$, there exists a time τ : for every process p_i, $\forall \tau' : \tau \leq \tau'$, $H(p_i, \tau) = H(p_i, \tau')$.

4   A *C*-based Consensus Protocol

This section presents a consensus protocol (Protocol 1) based on failure detector C. To simplify the presentation, we concentrate on *binary consensus* in which the set of possible inputs is $\{0, 1\}$. Besides registers, it relies on standard shared memory constructs, namely adopt-commit [19] and safe agreement [9,10] objects, that we describe next.

Base objects. An *adopt-commit* object has a single operation denoted propose(v) where v is a value from some finite set $\mathcal{V}$. Such an operation returns a couple (b, u) where b is either *adopt* or *commit* and u is a value in $\mathcal{V}$, subject to the following requirements [3, 19]: (*Validity*) If an operation returns (d, v) then v is the input of a propose() operation; (*Agreement*) If an operation returns (*commit*, v) then each output is either (*adopt*, v) or (*commit*, v); (*Convergence*) If the input of every operation is v, then every output is $(commit, v)$; (*Termination*) Each operation by a non-faulty process produces an output.

A shared-memory implementation of an adopt-commit object that tolerates an arbitrary number of crash-failures can be found in [3]. The implementation ([3], Algorithm 2) uses two multi-writer/multi-reader registers and a *conflict-detector*, which in turn can be implemented in a wait-free manner using only $\text{fact}^{-1}(|\mathcal{V}|)$ multi-writer/multi-reader registers ([3], Algorithm 3). These algorithms do not use identities, and are thus suitable for the anonymous shared-memory model.

The *safe agreement* object, introduced by Borowsky and Gafni in [9] allows processes to propose values and to agree on a single value. It is at the heart of the BG-simulations [9] in which it is used by simulators to agree on each step of the simulated processes. Different specifications of a safe agreement object can be found in the literature, e.g., [4,10]. Our specification below closely follows [4].

A safe agreement object supports two operations propose(v) where v is a value in $\{0, 1\}^1$ and read(). Both operations return either a value $u \in \{0, 1\}$ or $\bot$. Each process can invoke propose() at most once, while read() can be invoked arbitrarily many times. We say that a propose() operation is *successful* if it returns a value $\neq \bot$. An execution is *well-formed* if (1) each process calls propose() at most once and, (2) no processes start a read() or propose() operation before its previous operation (if any) has returned. It is required that in any well-formed execution, the following properties are satisfied: (*Validity*) If an operation returns a value $v \neq \bot$, v is the input of a propose() operation; (*Agreement*) If values $v, v' \in \{0, 1\}$ are returned by some operation, $v = v'$; (*Termination*) Every operation performed by a non-faulty process terminates; (*Consistent reads*) Any read() operation that terminates and starts after a successful propose() operation has completed returns a non-$\bot$ value; (*Non-triviality*) Not every propose() operation returns $\bot$.

Observe that the non-triviality property is satisfied in executions in which a process fails while performing a propose() operation. In the case in which no processes fail while performing propose(), it follows from the termination and non-triviality properties that at least one propose() operation is successful. Nevertheless, it is not guaranteed that every propose() operation is successful. However, the consistent reads property implies that if, after its propose() operation has returned, a process keeps reading the object, it eventually gets back a non-$\bot$ value.

In systems with identities, safe agreement objects can be implemented with registers, e.g., [9]. In anonymous systems, a safe agreement object implementation can be obtained by slightly modifying an anonymous binary consensus protocol by Attiya, Gorbach and Moran [5] designed for the asynchronous shared memory model with no failures.

---

[1] More generally, v may belong to any finite set. Restricting to binary inputs is sufficient for our purpose, namely using failure detector C to solve binary consensus.

Protocol 1. C-based binary consensus.

```
 1: init SA[1,...], AC[1,...], D ← ⊥         ▷ Arrays of safe agreement, adopt-commit
      objects and decision register
 2: function propose(v)                                              ▷ v ∈ {0,1}
 3:     est ← v; start tasks T1, T2;
 4: task T1:
 5:     for r = 1, 2, ... do
 6:         repeat d ← C-query() until d ≥ r end repeat
 7:         aux ← SA[r].propose(est)                              ▷ aux ∈ {0, 1, ⊥}
 8:         if aux = ⊥ then
 9:             repeat aux ← SA[r].read(); d ← C-query()
10:             until (d > r) ∨ (aux ≠ ⊥)
11:         end if
12:         (b, u) ← AC[r].propose(aux)        ▷ b ∈ {adopt, commit}, u ∈ {0, 1, ⊥}
13:         case b = commit ∧ u ∈ {0, 1} then D ← u; return
14:              b = adopt  ∧ u ∈ {0, 1} then est ← u
15:              default             then nop                        ▷ u = ⊥
16:         end case
17:     end for
18: task T2:
19:     repeat u ← D until u ≠ ⊥ end repeat
20:     stop task T1; return u
```

Description of the protocol. Protocol 1 consists in two tasks denoted T1 and T2, launched in parallel at each process p (line 3). In task T2, process p keeps reading a shared register D, whose initial value is $\perp$, until it sees some non-$\perp$ value u. u is then decided by p (line 20).

In task T1, processes proceed in asynchronous rounds aiming at writing a single non-$\perp$ value to D. An adopt-commit object and a safe agreement object denoted respectively $AC[r]$ and $SA[r]$ are associated with each round r. Following a standard design pattern, e.g., [2,20], the processes that enter round r first try to reach agreement by accessing the safe agreement object $SA[r]$ (line 7) and then check whether agreement has been achieved using the adopt-commit object $AC[r]$ (line 12).

In more details, each process p maintains an estimate est that contains the value it currently favors. In round r, process p proposes its estimate to $SA[r]$ (line 7) and, if its operation is unsuccessful (line 8), it enters a loop in which it repeatedly reads the object (line 9). If no processes that enter round r fail, at least one of the invocations of propose() on $SA[r]$ is successful (non-triviality and termination properties of safe agreement) and thus by keeping reading the object, a process eventually obtains a non-$\perp$ value (consistent reads property of safe agreement). Hence, in the case in which no processes entering round r fail, every process that enters that round eventually obtains a non-$\perp$ value, either because its propose() operation is successful, or as a result of a read() operation. Note that this value is the same for every process (agreement property of safe agreement).

However, some of the processes that enter round r may fail. In this case, each propose() operation may be unsuccessful, and every read() operation may return $\perp$. We rely on failure detector C to ensure progress as follows:

- A process is allowed to enter a round r only if its local failure detector module output is larger than or equal to r (line 6);
- A process exits the loop in which it is trying to obtain a non-$\perp$ value by performing read() operations on $SA[r]$ when its local failure detector output is strictly larger than d_c (line 10).

This simple mechanism prevents processes from getting stuck in any round r in which a failure occurs. Indeed, a process p failing in round r must have obtained from C a value $d_c \geq r$ (line 5). Then, following the crash of p, due to the signaling property of C, C eventually outputs at every non-faulty processes values strictly larger than d_C, allowing these processes to exit the loop in which the safe agreement object $SA[r]$ is read (lines 9-10).

To reconcile processes that have obtained a non-$\perp$ value form $SA[r]$ and those to which C has signaled a failure, we use the adopt-commit object $AC[r]$ (line 12). Each process p keeps in its local variable aux the result of its operations (at lines 7 and 9) on $SA[r]$, e.g., $\perp$ or some value $v \in \{0, 1\}$. In the second part of round r, process p proposes the value stored in aux to $AC[r]$ (line 12). If it gets back $(adopt, u)$, where $u \neq \perp$ it changes its estimate to u (line 14). A process that receives $(commit, u)$ can thus safely write u to the decision register D, as it follows from the agreement of adopt-commit that every propose() operation returns $(commit, u)$ or $(adopt, u)$. Hence, every process either writes u to D or changes its estimate to u, thus preventing any value $u' \neq u$ to be written to D in subsequent rounds. Finally, if a process p receives $(*, \perp)$, then no process writes to D in the current round r, and p leaves its estimate unchanged (line 15).

As for termination, a process decides as soon as it reads a non-$\perp$ value from D (task T2). Let us observe that this happens if there is a round r in which (1) enters only one process, and this process is correct or (2) enter only correct processes, and at each of these processes, the largest output of C is r. Clearly, if only one process p enters round r, its propose() operation on $SA[r]$ returns a non-$\perp$ value u (non-triviality property of safe agreement). u is then the only value proposed to $AC[r]$. p thus receives $(commit, u)$ from $AC[r]$ (convergence property of adopt-commit) and then writes u to D. Condition (1) is satisfied in executions in which there is only one correct process.

For the second condition, if only correct processes enter round r, at least one of the propose() operations on $SA[r]$ is successful. Moreover, no process can exit the reading loop (lines 9-10) without having obtained a non-$\perp$ value from $SA[r]$, as C never outputs a value larger than r to those processes. Since all non-$\perp$ values returned by operations on $SA[r]$ are the same, only one value is proposed to $AC[r]$, from which we conclude that only $(commit, v)$, where $v \neq \perp$, is returned by each propose() operation performed on $AC[r]$ (convergence property of $AC[r]$.). Hence a value is written to D in round r. Condition (2) is met in every execution in which there are at least two correct processes, since in that case the output of C eventually stabilizes at every correct process, and the stabilization value is larger than every value output at faulty processes. The proof of correctness can be found in the full version [11].

5 C Is Necessary to Solve Consensus

Let X be an anonymity-preserving failure detector, and assume that there is a protocol $\mathcal{A}$ that solves consensus using X. We present (Protocol 1) a protocol $\mathcal{T}_{X \to C}$ that emulates C using X in the wait-free environment.

Overview. As in previous protocols [12,16,21,26] that emulate weakest failure detectors, in $\mathcal{T}_{X \to C}$ each process locally simulates many possible runs of protocol $\mathcal{A}$. According to the output of these runs, information on the failure pattern is inferred and the desired weakest failure detector emulated.

Let $\mathcal{F}$ denote the failure pattern underlying the execution of $\mathcal{T}_{X \to C}$. In order to simulate valid runs of $\mathcal{A}$, e.g., runs indistinguishable from reals runs of $\mathcal{A}$, samples from the underlying failure detector X have to be collected. Those samples are then used in the simulation of each step in which a query to failure detector X occurs. Hence, each process p must collect samples from its failure detector module, but also from other processes. Precedence relationships between samples should also be maintained to order to simulate valid runs of $\mathcal{A}$. For example, the simulation must avoid using a sample from some faulty process q if a sample taken after the failure of q has already been used. In systems with identities, this is usually achieved by maintaining a DAG, where each vertex v contains a failure detector sample d and a process id, and for any successor v' of v, the sample d' associated with v' has been taken after d. In the anonymous shared memory model, the lack of identifiers make tracking precedence relationships difficult and the standard technique [12] does not apply. However, in the case of anonymity-preserving failure detectors, the samples taken by each process p from its local failure detector module are sufficient to simulate runs of $\mathcal{A}$, even with more than one participating process. This is because the sequence of samples obtained by p might have been also obtained by every other processes in some execution with the same failure pattern $\mathcal{F}$.

Each process p simulates executions of $\mathcal{A}$ in which at most two processes, denoted q_0 and q_1, participate with input 0 and 1 respectively. On the one hand, for such an execution e by adding *clones* of q_0 and q_1 one may construct an indistinguishable execution e' in which the number of participating processes matches the number of correct processes in $\mathcal{F}$. It thus can be shown that, from the point of view of q_0 and q_1, execution e is indistinguishable from some real execution of $\mathcal{A}$ with failure pattern $\mathcal{F}$. On the other hand, there must exist an interleaving of the steps of q_0 and q_1 such that the corresponding emulated execution of $\mathcal{A}$ does not decide. Otherwise, protocol $\mathcal{A}$ together with the sequence of failure detector samples collected by p can be used to solve binary consensus wait-free and without failure detector by two non-anonymous processes q_0 and q_1, contradicting the impossibility of consensus.

Operationally, process p explores every possible two-processes schedules of $\mathcal{A}$ in a particular, *corridor*-based order, as in [21,26]. Whenever a decision occurs in

---

Protocol 2. $\mathcal{T}_{X \to C}$, where X can be used to solve consensus.

1: **init** $A[1 \ldots] \leftarrow [\bot, \ldots]$ ▷ Array of registers with initial value $\bot$

2: **procedure** C-emulation

3:     $x[1 \ldots] \leftarrow [\bot, \ldots]$ ▷ Array for storing outputs of X

4:     $c_0 \leftarrow$ initial configuration: $q_i, i \in \{0,1\}$ input is i, MEM is initialized as prescribed by $\mathcal{A}'$

5:     $P_0 \leftarrow \{q_0, q_1\}$; $\lambda_0 \leftarrow \epsilon$; OUT-$C \leftarrow 0$; *start* tasks T and T' where task T' is explore(λ_0, c_0, P_0);

6: **function** explore(λ, c, P)

7:     **let** U be the set of processes still undecided in c

8:     **for each** $P' \subseteq P \cap U$ in an order consistent with $\subseteq$ **do**

9:        **for each** $q_i \in P'$ **do**

10:           **let** *step* be the next step of q_i in configuration c according to $\mathcal{A}'$ ▷ simulate next step of q_i

11:             **case** *step* = read() from ℓth register **then** read $c.MEM[\ell]$

12:                  *step* = write(v) to ℓth register **then** write v to $c.MEM[\ell]$

13:                  *step* = X-query() **then** take $x[\ell]$ as the output of X, where ℓ is the value of η in $c.s_i$;

14:             **end case**

15:             perform local computation; update $c.s_i$

16:             **if** q_i has decided in c **then let** $m \leftarrow \min\{\ell : A[\ell] = \bot\}$; $A[m] \leftarrow \top$; C-OUT $\leftarrow m$

17:             **end if**   ▷ update (emulated) failure detector C output

18:             $\lambda \leftarrow \lambda \cdot i$; explore($\lambda, c, P'$)

19:        **end for**

20:     **end for**

21: **task** T: **for** $i = 1, 2, \ldots$ **do** $x[i] \leftarrow X$-query() **end for**   ▷ f.d. X sampling

---

the execution simulated by p, a shared counter is incremented, and the output of C at p is set to the new value of the counter. We prove that (1) following any (real) process failure, p eventually simulates an execution of $\mathcal{A}$ in which a decision occurs, and due to the order in which schedules are explored, that (2) eventually p keeps simulating one infinite execution in which no processes decide. The correctness of the emulation C then follows from (1) and (2).

Protocol $\mathcal{A}'$. Let MEM denote the (not necessarily finite) array of registers used by $\mathcal{A}$. Recall that in a step of $\mathcal{A}$, a process performs a read() or write() operation on some register $MEM[\ell]$ or a query() operation to the underlying failure detector X. It may then perform some local computation. Instead of simulating runs of $\mathcal{A}$, we are going to simulate runs of a slightly modified version of $\mathcal{A}$, called $\mathcal{A}'$, defined as follows. The purpose of the modification is to help tracking causality relations between steps of the protocols.

In protocol $\mathcal{A}'$, each process has an extra local counter η whose initial value is 1. Each register $MEM[\ell]$ is divided in two fields, *data* and *ctr*. $MEM[\ell].data$ is initialized as specified by $\mathcal{A}$ while the initial value of $MEM[\ell].ctr$ is 0. For each integer ℓ and value v, each operation $MEM[\ell].write(v)$ in $\mathcal{A}$ is replaced in

$\mathcal{A}'$ by $MEM[\ell]$.write($\langle v, \eta \rangle$), i.e., v and the current value of the local variable η are written to the $data$ and ctr components, respectively, of $MEM[\ell]$. Similarly, each instruction of the form $v \leftarrow MEM[\ell]$.read() in $\mathcal{A}$ is replaced in $\mathcal{A}'$ by $\langle v, \eta' \rangle \leftarrow MEM[\ell]$.read(); $\eta \leftarrow \max(\eta, \eta' + 1)$. Finally, after each write(), read() or query() operation η is incremented ($\eta \leftarrow \eta + 1$). For each step s of the modified protocol $\mathcal{A}'$, we define $\eta(s)$ as the value of η immediately before it is incremented (e.g., immediately before $\eta \leftarrow \eta + 1$ is performed). Obviously, these modifications do not affect the correctness of $\mathcal{A}'$, i.e., $\mathcal{A}'$ solves consensus using X.

Causality. Let r be a run of $\mathcal{A}'$ with two processes q_0, q_1, where the input of $q_i, i \in \{0, 1\}$ is i. Note that in these particular executions, although the processes are anonymous, we can assume that the values written are unique, as they can be tagged with the process input and a sequence number. For any two steps s, s' in r, s *causally precedes* s', denoted $s \preceq s'$ if and only if (1) s and s' are performed by the same process in that order or, (2) in s a value v is written to some register $MEM[\ell]$, and in s' v is read from $MEM[\ell]$ or, (3) there exists a step s'' such that $s \preceq s''$ and $s'' \preceq s'$. The following Lemma follows from the management of the variables η in $\mathcal{A}'$.

Lemma 1. *Let r be a run of $\mathcal{A}'$ by two processes q_0, q_1 with input 0 and 1 respectively. For every steps s, s' of r, $s \preceq s' \implies \eta(s) < \eta(s')$.*

Collecting failure detector X samples. As X is anonymity-preserving, for any failure pattern $\mathcal{F}$ and any finite or infinite sequence $x = x_1, x_2, \ldots$ of outputs of X collected by some process p in a run with failure pattern $\mathcal{F}$, there is a run with the same failure pattern in which every process see the same sequence x of outputs of X. Therefore, in order to provide failure detector values for the simulation of runs of $\mathcal{A}'$, p simply builds an ever growing sequence of failure detector outputs $x[1], x[2], \ldots$ by repeatedly querying its local failure detector module.

Induced schedules of $\mathcal{A}'$. Each process p simulates runs of $\mathcal{A}'$ in which at most two processes, denoted q_0 and q_1, take steps with initial values 0 and 1 respectively. We next describe how a binary sequence (specifying the order in which q_0 and q_1 takes steps) and a sequence of failure detector X outputs induce a schedule S of $\mathcal{A}'$, that is a sequence of steps of $\mathcal{A}'$.

Let x denote a sequence of failure detector outputs, obtained from X at increasing times, and let λ denote a binary sequence. Intuitively, λ describes in which order processes take steps in S and x supplies failure detector outputs for simulating query(). A difficulty is to choose an output in x for each query() step of S in such a way that there is a real execution of $\mathcal{A}'$ indistinguishable from S to both q_0 and q_1.

Schedule S is defined inductively. Recall that a configuration c, in the context of a two processes schedule consists in a triplet (s_0, s_1, MEM) where $s_i, i \in \{0, 1\}$ is the local state of q_i and the array MEM contains the current value of each register used by $\mathcal{A}'$. In the initial configuration c_0 of S, $c_0.s_i, i \in \{0, 1\}$ reflects the fact that the initial value of q_i is i and $c_0.MEM$ is initialized as specified by

$\mathcal{A}'$. The ith step of S is taken by process $q_{\lambda[i]}$ and is deduced from $\mathcal{A}'$ applied to the local state of $q_{\lambda[i]}$ in configuration c_{i-1}. If this step is a read() or write() step, it is simulated by reading or writing a value to/from MEM. If the step is a query() operation, it is simulated by taking $x[\eta_{\lambda[i]}]$ as its result, where $\eta_{\lambda[i]}$ is the value of the variable η at process $q_{\lambda[i]}$ in configuration c_{i-1}. Configuration c_i is then derived from c_{i-1} in the obvious way.

The choice of output for each simulated query() preserves causality in the following sense: Let s and s' be steps of S in which X is queried and assume that $s \preceq s'$. Let j, j' the indices in x of the values returned by these queries in the simulation. Then $x[j]$ is obtained from X before $x[j']$, i.e., $j < j'$, as one would expect. Indeed, let q_i and $q_{i'}$ be respectively the processes that perform s and s', and let $\eta(s)$ and $\eta(s')$ be the value of η at process q_i and $q_{i'}$ in the configurations that immediately precede s and s', respectively. The results of the queries in s and s' are $x[\eta(s)]$ and $x[\eta(s')]$. By Lemma 1, as $s \preceq s'$, $\eta(s) < \eta(s')$.

Indistinguishability of induced schedules from real runs. Given a binary sequence λ and a sequence x of outputs of X, the schedule $S_{\lambda,x}$ induced by λ and x may not correspond to a real execution of $\mathcal{A}'$. More precisely, for the simulation of S to be meaningful, we need that there exists a real run r of $\mathcal{A}'$ that is indistinguishable from S to q_0 and q_1. The schedule in r may differ from S, but the successive states of q_i must be the same in S and r, for each $i \in \{0, 1\}$. Next Lemma establishes the existence of r.

Lemma 2. *Let λ be a binary sequence. Let x denote a (finite or infinite) sequence of outputs of X and let S denote the schedule induced by λ and x. Assume that there exists a failure pattern $\mathcal{F}$, a history $H \in X(\mathcal{F})$ and an increasing sequence of times $\tau_1 < \tau_2 < \ldots$ such that for every $i, x[i] = H(p, \tau_i)$ for some process p. If for every $i, |\mathcal{F}(\tau_i)| \leq n-2$, there exists a run of $\mathcal{A}$ indistinguishable from S to q_0 and q_1.*

Run r may however not be fair. A infinite run $r = (\mathcal{F}, H, I, S, T)$ is *fair* if every process in correct$(\mathcal{F})$ take infinitely many steps in r. Given an infinite binary sequence λ, let $inf(\lambda) \subseteq \{0, 1\}$ be the bits that appear infinitely often in λ. Next Lemma expresses a sufficient condition for the existence of a fair run indistinguishable to q_0 and q_1 from the schedule induced by a binary sequence and a sequence of failure detector outputs λ, x.

Lemma 3. *Let λ, x be infinite sequences of respectively bits and failure detector X outputs. Suppose that there exists a failure pattern $\mathcal{F}$, a sequence of times $\tau_1 < \tau_2 < \ldots$ and a history $H \in X(\mathcal{F})$ such that for every $i \geq 1, x[i] = H(p, \tau)$ for some process p. If $|$correct$(\mathcal{F})| \geq 2$ and $\inf(\lambda) = \{0, 1\}$ then the schedule $S_{\lambda,x}$ induced by λ, x is indistinguishable from the schedule in a fair run r of $\mathcal{A}$.*

In the induced schedule $S_{\lambda,x}$, only two processes take step. However, more than two processes may be correct in the failure pattern $\mathcal{F}$. We resolve this difficulty by adding clones of q_0 and q_1. A *clone* [17] of process q_i is a process that has the same input and the same code as q_i. p is scheduled in lock-step with

q_i: it reads and writes the same values as p, and each of its queries to X returns the same output as the queries by p. The latter is made possible by the fact that X is anonymity-preserving. The outputs of X at q_i are also valid outputs at any other processes.

C emulation. Protocol 2 emulates failure detector C from any anonymity preserving failure detector X that can be used to solve consensus. It closely follows the emulation technique of Zieliński [26]. At each process p, the emulation consists in two tasks T and T' that run in parallel. In task T, p collects outputs of X by querying its local failure detector module. The outputs are stored in the array x. In task T', p recursively simulates every possible schedule of $\mathcal{A}'$ (lines 8-18). An infinite array A of registers is used to implement a weak shared counter. Each register $A[i]$ initial value is $\perp$. The counter is incremented by changing to $\top$ the value of the register with the smallest index containing $\perp$. The value of the counter is thus the largest index i of A such that $A[i] = \top$. Each time a process decides in a simulated schedule, the counter is incremented and the output of C is set to the counter new value (line 16).

For any arbitrary run of protocol 2 with failure pattern $\mathcal{F}$, we first show (see [11]) that each correct process p simulates at least one schedule in which a decision occurs after the time of the last crash. Consequently, the output of C at p is incremented at least once after the last time a process fails, as required by the signaling property. We then establish that if $|\mathsf{correct}(\mathcal{F})| \geq 2$, the exploration procedure is eventually stuck simulating a non-deciding schedule. As the output of C is modified each time a simulated schedule decides, the output of C eventually stabilizes at each process, hence,

Theorem 1. *Protocol 2 emulates C.*

6   Conclusion

The paper has defined the class of anonymity-preserving failure detectors and has shown that within this class, at least for consensus a weakest failure C exists in the anonymous shared-memory model.

In the full version [11], a natural generalization denoted C_k of failure detector C is introduced and a C_k-based protocol for k-set agreement is presented. Questions for future work include (dis)proving that C_k is the weakest anonymity preserving failure detector for k-set agreement and extending weakest failure detector results in anonymous systems outside the domain of anonymity preserving failure detectors.

References

1. Angluin, D.: Local and global properties in networks of processors (extended abstract). In: STOC 1980, pp. 82–93. ACM (1980)
2. Aspnes, J.: A modular approach to shared-memory consensus, with applications to the probabilistic-write model. Distributed Comput. **25**(2), 179–188 (2012)

3. Aspnes, J., Ellen, F.: Tight bounds for adopt-commit objects. Theor. Comput. Syst. **55**(3), 451–474 (2014)
4. Attiya, H.: Adapting to point contention with long-lived safe agreement. In: Flocchini, P., Gasieniec, L. (eds.) SIROCCO 2006. LNCS, vol. 4056, pp. 10–23. Springer, Heidelberg (2006)
5. Attiya, H., Gorbach, A., Moran, S.: Computing in totally anonymous asynchronous shared memory systems. Inf. Comput. **173**(2), 162–183 (2002)
6. Attiya, H., Snir, M.: Better computing on the anonymous ring. J. Algorithms **12**(2), 204–238 (1991)
7. Bonnet, F., Raynal, M.: Consensus in anonymous distributed systems: Is there a weakestfailure detector? In: AINA 2010, pp. 206–213. IEEE (2010)
8. Bonnet, F., Raynal, M.: Anonymous asynchronous systems: the case of failure detectors. Distributed Comput. **26**(3), 141–158 (2013)
9. Borowsky, E., Gafni, E.: Generalized FLP impossibility result for t-resilient asynchronouscomputations. In: PODC 1993, pp. 91–100. ACM (1993)
10. Borowsky, E., Gafni, E., Lynch, N.A., Rajsbaum, S.: The BG distributed simulation algorithm. Distributed Comput. **14**(3), 127–146 (2001)
11. Bouzid, Z., Travers, C.: Anonymity preserving failure detectors. Technical Report, LaBRI, July 2016. https://hal.archives-ouvertes.fr/hal-01344446
12. Chandra, T.D., Hadzilacos, V., Toueg, S.: The weakest failure detector for solving consensus. J. ACM **43**(4), 685–722 (1996)
13. Chandra, T.D., Toueg, S.: Unreliable failure detectors for reliable distributed systems. J. ACM **43**(2), 225–267 (1996)
14. Danezis, G., Diaz, C.: A survey of anonymous communication channels. Technical Report, MSR-TR-2008-35, Microsoft Research (2008)
15. Delporte-Gallet, C., Fauconnier, H.: Two consensus algorithms with atomic registers and failure detector Ω. In: Garg, V., Wattenhofer, R., Kothapalli, K. (eds.) ICDCN 2009. LNCS, vol. 5408, pp. 251–262. Springer, Heidelberg (2008)
16. Delporte-Gallet, C., Fauconnier, H., Guerraoui, R.: Tight failure detection bounds on atomic object implementations. J. ACM **57**(4), 22:1–22:32 (2010)
17. Fich, F.E., Herlihy, M., Shavit, N.: On the space complexity of randomized synchronization. J. ACM **45**(5), 843–862 (1998)
18. Freiling, F.C., Guerraoui, R., Kuznetsov, P.: The failure detector abstraction. ACM Comput. Surv. **43**(2), 9 (2011)
19. Gafni, E.: Round-by-round fault detectors: Unifying synchrony and asynchrony (extended abstract). In: PODC 1998, pp. 143–152. ACM (1998)
20. Gafni, E.: The extended BG-simulation and the characterization of t-resiliency. In: STOC 1909, pp. 85–92. ACM (1990)
21. Gafni, E., Kuznetsov, P.: On set consensus numbers. Distributed Comput. **24**(3–4), 149–163 (2011)
22. Guerraoui, R., Hadzilacos, V., Kuznetsov, P., Toueg, S.: The weakest failure detectors to solve quittable consensus and nonblocking atomic commit. SIAM J. Comput. **41**(6), 1343–1379 (2012)
23. Guerraoui, R., Ruppert, E.: Anonymous and fault-tolerant shared-memory computing. Distributed Comput. **20**(3), 165–177 (2007)
24. Loui, M., Abu-Amara, H.: Memory requirements for agreement among unreliable asynchronous processes. Adv. Comput. Res. **4**, 163–183 (1987)
25. Yamashita, M., Kameda, T.: Computing on anonymous networks: Part I-characterizing the solvable cases. Trans. Parallel Distrib. Syst. **7**(1), 69–89 (1996)
26. Zieliński, P.: Anti-Ω: the weakest failure detector for set agreement. Distributed Comput. **22**(5–6), 335–348 (2010)

Certified Universal Gathering in $\mathbb{R}^2$ for Oblivious Mobile Robots

Pierre Courtieu[1], Lionel Rieg[2], Sébastien Tixeuil[3], and Xavier Urbain[4,5(✉)]

[1] CÉDRIC – Conservatoire national des arts et métiers, 75141 Paris, France
[2] Collège de France, 75006 Paris, France
[3] UPMC Sorbonne Universités, LIP6-CNRS 7606,
Institut Universitaire de France, Paris, France
[4] ENSIIE, 91025 Évry, France
[5] LRI, CNRS UMR 8623, Université Paris-Sud,
Université Paris-Saclay, 91405 Orsay, France
xavier.urbain@lri.fr

Abstract. We present a unified formal framework for expressing mobile robots models, protocols, and proofs, and devise a protocol design/proof methodology dedicated to mobile robots that takes advantage of this formal framework.

As a case study, we present the first formally certified protocol for oblivious mobile robots evolving in a two-dimensional Euclidean space. In more details, we provide a new algorithm for the problem of universal gathering mobile oblivious robots (that is, starting from any initial configuration that is not bivalent, using any number of robots, the robots reach in a finite number of steps the same position, not known beforehand) without relying on a common orientation nor chirality. We give very strong guaranties on the correctness of our algorithm by *proving formally* that it is correct, using the CoQ proof assistant.

This result demonstrates both the effectiveness of the approach to obtain new algorithms that use as few assumptions as necessary, and its manageability since the amount of developed code remains human readable.

1 Introduction

Networks of mobile robots captured the attention of the distributed computing community, as they promise new applications (rescue, exploration...) in potentially dangerous (and harmful) environments. Since its initial presentation [20], this computing model has grown in popularity[1] and many refinements have been proposed (see [15] for a recent state of the art). From a theoretical point

---

A preliminary version of this work appears as a 3-page-long Brief Announcement in PODC'16.

[1] The 2016 SIROCCO Prize for Innovation in Distributed Computing was awarded to Masafumi Yamashita for this line of work.

© Springer-Verlag Berlin Heidelberg 2016
C. Gavoille and D. Ilcinkas (Eds.): DISC 2016, LNCS 9888, pp. 187–200, 2016.
DOI: 10.1007/978-3-662-53426-7_14

of view, the interest lies in characterising the exact conditions for solving a particular task.

In the model we consider, robots operate in Look-Compute-Move cycles. In each cycle a robot "Looks" at its surroundings and obtains (in its own coordinate system) a snapshot containing some information about the locations of all robots. Based on this visual information, the robot "Computes" a destination location (still in its own coordinate system) and then "Moves" towards the computed location. When the robots are oblivious, the computed destination in each cycle depends only on the snapshot obtained in the current cycle (and not on the past history of execution). The snapshots obtained by the robots are not necessarily consistently oriented in any manner. The execution model significantly impacts the solvability of collaborative tasks. Three different levels of synchronisation have been considered. The strongest model [20] is the fully synchronised (FSYNC) model where each stage of each cycle is performed simultaneously by all robots. On the other hand, the asynchronous model [15] (ASYNC) allows arbitrary delays between Look, Compute and Move stages, and the movement itself may take an arbitrary amount of time, possibly a different amount for each robot. We consider in this paper the semi-synchronous (SSYNC) model [20], lying somewhere between the two extreme models. In the SSYNC model, time is discretised into rounds and in each round an arbitrary subset of the robots are active. The active robots in a round perform exactly one atomic Look-Compute-Move cycle in that round. The scheduler (seen as an adversary) is assumed to be fair in the sense that it guarantees that in any configuration, any robot is activated within a finite number of steps.

Designing and proving mobile robot protocols is notoriously difficult. The diversity of model variants makes it extremely onerous to check whether a particular property of a robot protocol holds in a particular setting. Even worse, checking whether a property that holds in a particular setting also holds in another setting that is not strictly contained in the first one often requires a completely new proof, even if the proof argument is very similar. The lack of proof reusability between model variants is a major problem for investigating the viability of new solutions or implementations of existing protocols (that are likely to execute in a more concrete execution model). Also, oblivious mobile robot protocols are mostly based on observing geometric constructions and deriving invariants from those observations. As the protocols are typically written in an informal high level language, assessing whether they conform to a particular model setting is particularly cumbersome, and may lead to hard to find mismatches. Hence, solely relying on handcrafted protocols, models and proofs is likely to introduce subtle errors that eventually lead to catastrophic failures when the system is actually deployed. Formal methods encompass a long-lasting path of research that is meant to overcome errors of human origin. Not surprisingly, this mechanised approach to protocol correctness was successively used in the context of mobile robots [2,3,5,8,12,13,18].

Related Work. Model-checking proved useful to find bugs in existing literature [3] and assess formally published algorithms [3,13], in a simpler setting where robots evolve in a *discrete space* where the number of possible positions is finite. Automatic program synthesis (for the problem of perpetual exclusive exploration in a ring-shaped discrete space) is due to Bonnet *et al.* [5], and can be used to obtain automatically algorithms that are "correct-by-design". The approach was refined by Millet *et al.* [18] for the problem of gathering in a discrete ring network. As all aforementioned approaches are designed for a discrete setting where both the number of positions and the number of robots are known, they cannot be used in the continuous space where robots positions take values in a set that is not enumerable, and they cannot permit to establish results that are valid for any number of robots. The use of a mechanical proof assistants like COQ[2] allows for more genericity as this approach is not limited to *particular instances* of algorithms. Castéran *et al.* [9] use COQ and their libray Loco to prove positive and negative results about subclasses of LC systems. Developed for the COQ proof assistant, the Pactole[3] framework enabled the use of high-order logic to certify impossibility results [2] for the problem of convergence: for any positive ε, robots are required to reach locations that are at most ε apart. Another classical impossibility result that was certified using the Pactole framework is the impossibility of gathering starting from a bivalent configuration [12]. While the proof assistant approach seems a sensible path for establishing certified results for mobile robots that evolve in a continuous space, until this paper there exists no *positive* certified result in this context. Expressing mobile robot protocols in a formal framework that permits certification poses a double challenge: how to express the protocol (which can make use of complex geometric abstractions that must be properly defined within the framework), and how to write the proof?

Other formal models exist, the most famous ones being TLA+ and process algebras. These are not very suited to our setting because they do not easily take into account the spatial location of robots, which is critical here. Furthermore, a dedicated framework allows to hard-wire some necessary properties while still being flexible enough to encompass most of the models.

Our contribution. Our first contribution is a unified formal framework for expressing mobile robots models, protocols, and proofs. This framework is motivated by the fact that many of the observed errors in published papers come from a mismatch between the advertised model and the model that is actually used for writing the proofs. For example, some dining philosophers protocols were expressed and proved in a high-level atomicity model, but advertised as working in a lower-level atomicity model, revealed to be incorrect in the lower-level atomicity model (see the work of Adamek *et al.* [1] and references herein). Sometimes, the mismatch between the proof and the advertised model is more subtle: a perpetual exclusive exploration protocol the proof of which did not consider all possible behaviours in the advertised model ASYNC was used to exhibit a counter example in such a setting (See the work of Berard *et al.* [3] and references therein). A unified formalisation whose consistency can be mechanically

---

[2] http://coq.inria.fr.

[3] Available at http://pactole.lri.fr.

assessed is a huge asset for designing correct solutions, whose correctness can be certified. As we used a subset of the same framework for certifying impossibility results [2,12], consistency between negative and positive results is also guaranteed. Our second contribution is a protocol design/proof methodology dedicated to mobile robots. We advocate the joint development of both the mobile robot protocol and its correctness proof, by taking advantage of the CoQ proof assistant features. The proof assistant is typically able to check whether the proof of a particular theorem/lemma/corollary is valid. So replacing particular clauses of those theorems/lemmas/corollaries statements makes the proof assistant check whether the proof still is acceptable for the new statement. We used this feature to lift a preliminary version of this paper (uni-dimensional setting [11]) to a Euclidean bi-dimensional space: the proof assistant checked which arguments were still valid in the new setting. This feature also proved useful when slightly changing parts of the algorithm: the impact of the changes on the proofs were immediate. Also, it becomes easy to remove or weaken hypotheses from the protocol, as the proof assistant makes it obvious if they are not used in the proof arguments. Finally, our methodology includes a formal way to guarantee whether the "global" view of the system (as seen from the protocol prover point of view) is effectively realisable given the hypotheses assumed in the model. We instantiate our framework and methodology to actually design and prove correct a new protocol for oblivious mobile robot universal gathering problem. The mobile robot gathering problem is a benchmarking problem in this context and can be informally defined as follows: robots have to reach in a finite number of steps the same location, not known beforehand. In more details, we present a new gathering algorithm for robots operating in a continuous space that *(i)* can start from any configuration that is not bivalent (that is, the robots are not initially equally placed in exactly two locations, since gathering is impossible in this case), *(ii)* does not put restriction on the number of robots, *(iii)* does not assume that robots share a common chirality (no common notion of "left" and "right"). To our knowledge, this is the first certified positive (and constructive) result in the context of oblivious mobile robots. Our bottom-up approach permits to lay sound theoretical foundations for future developments in this domain. The sources package is available at http://pactole.lri.fr, as well as its online html documentation.

2   A Formal Model to Prove Robot Protocols

To certify results and to guarantee the soundness of theorems, we use CoQ, a Curry-Howard-based interactive proof assistant enjoying a trustworthy kernel. The (functional) language of CoQ is a very expressive λ-calculus: the *Calculus of Inductive Constructions* (CIC) [10]. In this context, datatypes, objects, algorithms, theorems and proofs can be expressed in a unified way, as terms.

The reader will find in [4] a very comprehensive overview and good practices with reference to CoQ. Developing a proof in a proof assistant may nonetheless be tedious, or require expertise from the user. To make this task easier, we are actively developing (under the name Pactole) a formal model, as well as lemmas and theorems, to specify and certify results about networks of autonomous mobile robots. It is designed to be robust and flexible enough to express most of the variety of assumptions in robots network, for example with reference to the considered space: discrete or continuous, bounded or unbounded... We want to stress that the framework eases the developer's task. The notations and definitions we give hereafter should be simply read as typed functional expressions.

The Pactole model has been sketched in [2,12]; we recall here its main characteristics. We use two important features of COQ: a formalism of *higher-order* logic to quantify over programs, demons, etc., and the possibility to define *inductive* and *coinductive* types [19] to express inductive and coinductive datatypes and properties. Coinductive types are of invaluable help to express infinite behaviours, infinite datatypes and properties on them, as we shall see with demons. Robots are anonymous, however we need to identify some of them in the proofs. Thus, we consider given a finite set of *identifiers*, isomorphic to a segment of N. We hereafter omit this set G unless it is necessary to characterise the number of robots. The full model is also able to handle byzantine faults (as done in [2]) but this is not necessary here and will be omitted for simplicity. Robots are distributed in space, at places called *locations*. We call a *configuration* a *function* from the set of identifiers to the space of locations. From that definition, there is information about identifiers contained in configurations, notably, equality between configurations does *not* boil down to the equality of the multisets of inhabited locations. If we are under the assumption that robots are anonymous and indistinguishable, we have to make sure that those identifiers are not used by the embedded algorithm.

Spectrum. The computation of any robot's target location is based on the perception they get from their environment, that is, in an SSYNC execution scheme, from a configuration. The result of this observation may be more or less accurate, depending on sensors' capabilities. A robot's perception of a configuration is called a *spectrum*. To allow for different assumptions to be studied, we leave abstract the type *spectrum* (Spect.t) and the notion of spectrum of a position. *Robograms*, representing protocols, will then output a location when given a spectrum (instead of a configuration), thus guaranteeing that assumptions over sensors are fulfilled. For instance, the spectrum for anonymous robots with *weak* global multiplicity detection could be the set of inhabited locations, i.e. without any multiplicity information. In a *strong* global multiplicity setting, the multiset of inhabited locations is a suitable spectrum. In the following we will distinguish a *demon* configuration (resp. spectrum), expressed in the global frame of reference, from a *robot* configuration (resp. spectrum), expressed in the robot's own frame of reference. At each step of the distributed protocol (see definition of round below) the demon configuration and spectrum are transformed (recentered, rotated and scaled) into the considered robots ones before being given as parameters to the robogram. Depending on assumptions, zoom and rotation factors may be constant or chosen by the demon at each step, shared by all robots or not, etc.

Demon. Rounds in this SSYNC setting are characterised with set of oblivious robots receiving their new frame of reference, if activated. We call *demonic action* this operation together with the logical properties ensuring, for example, that new frames of reference make sense. *Demons* are streams of demonic actions. As such, they are naturally defined in COQ as a coinductive construct. Synchrony constraints (e.g. fairness) may be defined as coinductive properties on demons, as detailed in [2,12].

Robogram. Robograms may be defined in a *completely abstract manner*, without any concrete code, in our COQ model. They consist of an actual algorithm pgm that represents the considered protocol, taking a spectrum as input and returning a location, and a compatibility property pgm_compat stating that target locations are the same if equivalent spectra are given (for some equivalence on spectra).

```
Record robogram := {
  pgm :> Spect.t → Location.t;
  pgm_compat : Proper (Spect.eq ⇒ Location.eq) pgm }.
```

3 Case Study: A Universal Gathering for Mobile Oblivious Robots

The gathering problem is one of the benchmarking tasks in mobile robot networks, and has received a considerable amount of attention (see [15] and references herein). The gathering tasks consists in all robots (considered as dimensionless points in a Euclidean space) reaching a single point, not known beforehand, in finite time. A foundational result [20] shows that in the SSYNC model, no oblivious deterministic algorithm can solve gathering for two robots without additional assumptions [17]. This result can be extended [12] to the bivalent case, that is when an even number of robots is initially evenly split in exactly two locations. On the other hand, it is possible to solve gathering if $n > 2$ robots start from initially distinct positions, provided robots are endowed with multiplicity detection: that is, a robot is able to determine the number of robots that occupy a given position.

While probabilistic solutions [16,20] can cope with arbitrary initial configuration (including bivalent ones), most of the deterministic ones in the literature [15] assume robots always start from distinct locations (that is, the initial configuration contains no multiplicity points). Some recent work was devoted to relaxing this hypothesis in the deterministic case. Dieudonné and Petit [14] investigated the problem of gathering from *any* configuration (that is, the initial configuration can contain arbitrary multiplicity points): assuming that the number of robots is odd (so, no initial bivalent configuration can exist), they provide a deterministic algorithm for gathering starting from any configuration. Bouzid *et al.* [6] improved the result by also allowing an even number of robots to start from configurations that contain multiplicity points (albeit the initial bivalent configuration is still forbidden due to impossibility results in this case).

In that sense, the algorithm of Bouzid *et al.* [6] is *universal* in the sense that it works for all gatherable configurations, including those with multiplicity points. The assumption that robots have a common chirality was removed in a context where robots may fail-stop in an unexpected manner [7].

A general description on how to characterise a solution to the problem of gathering has been given in [12]. We specialise it here to take into account that an initial configuration is not bivalent. This is straightforward: any robogram r is a solution w.r.t. a demon d if for every configuration cf that is not bivalent (that is ¬ forbidden), there is a point pt to which all robots will eventually gather (and stay) in the execution defined by r and d, and starting from cf.

We present a new gathering algorithm for robots operating in a continuous space that *(i)* can start from any configuration that is not bivalent, *(ii)* does not put restriction on the number of robots, *(iii)* does not assume that robots share a common chirality. We give very strong guarantees on the correctness of our algorithm by *proving formally* that it is correct, using the CoQ proof assistant.

Definition solGathering (r : robogram) (d : demon) :=
  ∀ cf, ¬ forbidden cf →
  ∃ pt : R2, WillGather pt (execute r d cf).

3.1 Setting and Protocol

We consider a set of nG anonymous robots that are oblivious and equipped with global strong multiplicity detection (i.e., they are able to count the number of robots that occupy any given position). The demon is supposed to be fair, and the execution model is SSYNC. The space in which robots move (the set of locations) is the real plane $\mathbb{R}^2$; they do not share any common direction, nor any chirality. Any initial configuration is accepted as long as it is not bivalent (including those with multiplicity points).

Protocol. The protocol we propose is presented in Fig. 1. It uses multiplicity to build the set of towers of maximal height. If there is a unique tower of maximal height, i.e., a unique location of highest multiplicity, this location is the destination of each activated robot. Otherwise, the inhabited locations on the smallest enclosing circle (SEC) are taken into account to define a *target*.

Our robots enjoy strong global multiplicity detection: as noticed in Sect. 2, the spectrum of a configuration is the multiset of all its robots' locations. It is *clean* if inhabited locations are either on the SEC or at target. When it is not clean (*dirty*), robots on SEC (or at target) stay where they are, the others move to the target, thus cleaning the spectrum. In a clean spectrum, activated robots move to the target. A configuration is said to be clean if and only if its spectrum is clean.

The important operation is thus to define a convenient target. Our target depends on how many inhabited locations are on the SEC. If there is only one, the whole spectrum is reduced to a single location and all robots are already gathered. When the number of towers on the SEC is not equal to 3, the target is the center of the SEC. Critical situations occur when towers on the SEC define a triangle. If it is *equilateral*, we cannot break the symmetry between its vertices and the target is the center of the SEC (which is also the triangle's barycenter). On the contrary, in all other cases we can break the symmetry and select a particular vertex as the target. If the triangle is *isosceles* and not equilateral, the target is the vertex opposite to its base. Finally if the triangle is *scalene*, the target is the vertex opposite to its longest side. Let us rephrase that description in informal pseudo-code. See Sect. 2 for its formal version, that is the COQ definition of our algorithm. For a spectrum s, let support(s) be the set of locations in s, let max(s) be the set of locations of maximal multiplicity in s, and let SEC(s) be the smallest enclosing circle of s. Let *dest* be the destination to be computed. Remember that $(0,0)$ is always the location of a robot in its own frame of reference.

> **if** max(s) $= \emptyset$ **then** *dest* := $(0,0)$
> **else if** max(s) $= \{p\}$ **then** *dest* := p
> **else begin**
>   **if** support(s) $\cap$ SEC(s) $= \emptyset$ **then** *dest* := $(0,0)$
>   **else if** support(s) $\cap$ SEC(s) $= \{p\}$ **then** *target* := p
>   **else if** support(s) $\cap$ SEC(s) $= \{p_1, p_2, p_3\}$ **then**
>   **if** equilateral(p_1, p_2, p_3) **then** *target* := barycenter(p_1, p_2, p_3)
>   **else if** isosceles(p_1, p_2, p_3) **then** *target* := opposite of base(p_1, p_2, p_3)
>   **else** *target* := opposite of longest(p_1, p_2, p_3)
>   **else** *target* := center(SEC(s));
>   **if** $\forall p \in s, p \in$ SEC(s) **or** $p = target$ **then** *dest* := *target*
>   **else if** $(0,0) \in$ SEC(s) **or** $(0,0) = target$ **then** *dest* := $(0,0)$
>   **else** *dest* := *target*
> **end**

Fig. 1. Gathering protocol.

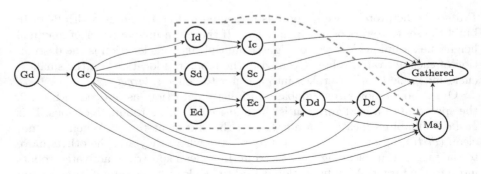

Fig. 2. Reachability graph for the categories of spectra. For clarity's sake, self loops are omitted. The boxed area contains the triangle cases, all linked to Maj.

Phases of the algorithm. We characterise several cases of the protocol, called *phases*, which depend on what is perceived from the configuration, and which are mutually exclusive in an execution: Gathered robots, the Majority case where there is a unique tower of maximal height, the three triangle cases (Equilateral, Isosceles, Scalene), and finally the General case. To ease the proof of termination, we chose to consider differently an instance of the general case, namely the Diameter case where support(s) $\cap$ SEC(s) contains exactly two points (in which case they are a diameter of the SEC).

For all cases that need the computation of a target, we moreover distinguish between clean and dirty situations. Note that from any dirty version of a case, the only two other reachable cases are its clean version and Majority. This leaves us with twelve phases: Gathered (the success situation), Majority (Maj), Diameter clean (Dc) and dirty (Dd), Equilateral, Isosceles, Scalene clean (Ec, Ic, Sc) and dirty (Ed, Id, Sd), and General clean (Gc) and dirty (Gd). Figure 2 summarises the reachability relation between cases.

3.2   Formal Description, and Key Points to Prove Correctness

Coq implementation of the algorithm. The type of locations is $\mathbb{R}^2$ (noted R2.t and defined as R*R from the type R of the Coq library on axiomatic reals). The robogram as described in Sect. 3.1 is:

```
Definition gatherR2_pgm (s : Spect.t) : R2.t :=
  match Spect.support (Spect.max s) with    (* max height towers?*)
  | nil ⇒ (0, 0)                 (* None? only happens when no robot *)
  | pt :: nil ⇒ pt               (* Unique highest tower? go there *)
  | _ :: _ :: _ ⇒                                  (* Otherwise *)
    if is_clean s then target s else      (* All on SEC/target ? *)
    if (0, 0) ∈ (SECT s) then (0, 0) else target s
  end.
```

Target is defined as follows, in critical situations where exactly three inhabited positions are on the SEC target depends on the shape of the triangle (here isosceles *excludes* equilateral):

```
Function target_triangle (pt1 pt2 pt3 : R2.t) : R2.t :=
  match classify_triangle pt1 pt2 pt3 with (* Kind of triangle? *)
  | Equilateral ⇒ barycenter_3_pts pt1 pt2 pt3 (* To barycenter *)
  | Isosceles p ⇒ p
  | Scalene ⇒ opposite_of_max_side pt1 pt2 pt3
  end.
```

```
Function target (s : Spect.t) : R2.t :=
  match on_SEC (Spect.support s) with (* inhabited loc. on SEC?*)
  | nil ⇒ (0, 0)                                      (* None? *)
  | pt :: nil ⇒ pt             (* Unique loc. on SEC? ⇒ gathered! *)
  | pt1 :: pt2 :: pt3 :: nil ⇒ target_triangle pt1 pt2 pt3
  | _ ⇒ center (SEC 1)            (* Gen. case: center of SEC *)
  end.
```

Note that this is almost exactly an actual robot code. The instantiated robogram (in the sense of Sect. 2) binding together this code and its compatibility property is defined under the name gatherR2.

Some properties are fundamental in our proof that the algorithm actually solves Gathering. Namely, that robots move towards the same location, that a legal configuration cannot evolve into a forbidden (that is: bivalent) one, and finally that the configuration is eventually reduced to a single inhabited location.

Expressing the robogram in the global frame of reference. The first step towards reasoning about a robogram is to leave the robots local frames of reference and rephrase the robogram in the demon global frame of reference. This step is always left implicit in pen-and-paper proofs but it is actually not trivial: it relies on the fact that the protocol uses only geometrical concepts that are invariant under the allowed changes of frame, here scaling, rotation, and translation. Using a formal framework ensures that this overlooked proof is indeed done and correct. This in turn gives a global version of the round function and creates a global view of the configuration after one round, expressed by Lemma round_simplify.

Robots that move go to the same location. Note that by robots "that move" we explicitly mean robots that change location during the round, *not* robots that are activated (some of which may not move). Robots enjoy global strong multiplicity detection, hence they all detect the number of highest towers, they share the same notion of SEC, and they all compute the same number of towers on the SEC. Moreover, in both non-equilateral triangle cases, pointing out the longest side or the base side is not ambiguous as relative distances compare the same way for all robots. Hence, cleanliness and targets are the same for all activated robots, which means that computed destinations are the same.

Further note that we actually just showed that all moving robots are in the same phase of the protocol, and that the resulting destination does not depend on the frame of reference of the robot. This is formalised by Theorem same_destination which states that two robots id_1 and id_2 whose locations change during the round (moving) compute the same destination location (in the demon's frame of reference). The 20 line long formal proof is developed by case on the robogram phases, and on the code structure; it uses round_simplify.

Theorem same_destination : ∀ da cf id1 id2,
  In id1 (moving gatherR2 da cf)
  → In id2 (moving gatherR2 da cf)
  → round gatherR2 da cf id1 = round gatherR2 da cf id2.

Bivalent positions are unreachable. We require that the initial configuration does not consist of exactly two towers with the same multiplicity. One of the key points ensuring this algorithm's correctness is that there is no way to reach a position that is bivalent from a position that is *not* bivalent. Consider two configurations C_0 and C_1, C_1 being bivalent and resulting from C_0 by some round. Let us denote by $|x|_0$ (resp. $|x|_1$) the multiplicity of location x in C_0 (resp. in C_1). By definition,

C_1 consists of two locations l_1 and l_2 such that $|l_1|_1 = |l_2|_1 = \frac{nG}{2}$. As all moving robots go to *the same location*, we can assume without loss of generality that robots moved to, say, l_1, adding to its original multiplicity $|l_1|_0$ (which might have been 0). Since the configuration is now bivalent, this means that l_2 was inhabited in C_0 and such that $|l_2|_0 \geq \frac{nG}{2}$ (some robot in l_2 might have moved to l_1). There cannot have been only one inhabited location l distinct from l_2 before the round because either $|l|_0 = |l_2|_0 = \frac{nG}{2}$ but we supposed the configuration was not bivalent, or $|l|_0 < \frac{nG}{2} < |l_2|_0$ but then by phase Majority robots would have moved to l_2 and not l_1. Hence C_0 consisted of l_2 and several inhabited l_i ($i \neq 2$) amongst which the robots not located in l_2 were distributed, but then none of the l_i could have held more than $\frac{nG}{2} - 1$ robots, hence phase Majority should have applied and robots should have moved to l_2, a contradiction. Interestingly, this argument makes no reference to the dimension of the space. Hence we were able to reuse the CoQ script developed earlier for [11] (and thus in our libraries) to prove this statement. Theorem `never_forbidden` says that for all demonic action da and configuration cf, if cf is not bivalent (*i.e.* not `forbidden`), then the configuration after the round is not bivalent.

Theorem `never_forbidden`:
  $\forall$ `da cf`, $\neg$`forbidden cf` $\rightarrow$ $\neg$`forbidden (round gatherR2 da cf)`.

Eventually no-one moves. Termination of the algorithm is ensured by exhibiting a measure that decreases at each round involving a moving robot for a well-founded ordering. We then conclude using the assumption that the demon is fair.

To define the measure, we associate a weight to each of the protocol's phases (see Sect. 3.1) as follows: Maj $\mapsto$ 0, Dc $\mapsto$ 1, Dd $\mapsto$ 2, Ec, Ic, Sc $\mapsto$ 3, Ed, Id, Sd $\mapsto$ 4, Gc $\mapsto$ 5, Gd $\mapsto$ 6. Note that these weights decrease along the arcs of Fig. 2. We may now map any configuration C_i to a $(p_i, m_i^{p_i}) \in \mathbb{N} \times \mathbb{N}$ such that p_i is the weight of the phase for the moving robots, and:

- m_i^0 is the number of robots that are *not at* the unique location of maximal multiplicity, and
- $m_i^{p_i > 0}$ is $\begin{cases} \text{- }\sharp\text{robots that are } not \, at \text{ target if } C_i \text{ is clean, or} \\ \text{- }\sharp\text{robots that are } neither \text{ at target } nor \text{ on SEC if } C_i \text{ is dirty.} \end{cases}$

Let $>_\mathbb{N}$ be the usual ordering on natural numbers, the relevant ordering $\succ$ is defined as the lexicographic extension of $>_\mathbb{N}$ on pairs: $(p, m) \succ (p', m')$ iff either $p >_\mathbb{N} p'$, or $p =_\mathbb{N} p'$ and $m >_\mathbb{N} m'$. It is well-founded since $>_\mathbb{N}$ is well-founded.

We show that for any round on a configuration C_k resulting in a *different* configuration C_{k+1} (that is, some robots have moved), $(p_k, m_k^{p_k}) \succ (p_{k+1}, m_{k+1}^{p_{k+1}})$, hence proving that eventually there is no more change in successive configurations. We name `lt_config` this ordering relation on configurations, and prove that it is well-suited:

Theorem `round_lt_config`: $\forall$ `da conf`, $\neg$ `forbidden conf`
  $\rightarrow$ `moving gatherR2 da conf` $\neq$ `nil`
  $\rightarrow$ `lt_config (round gatherR2 da conf) conf`.

The theorem stating the correctness of our robogram is then simply: for all demon d that is fair, gatherR2 is a solution with reference to d.

Theorem Gathering_in_R2: ∀ d, Fair d → solGathering gatherR2 d.

The proof is led by well-founded induction on the lt_config relation. If all robots are gathered, then it is done. If not, by fairness some robots will have to move, thus a robot will be amongst the first to move. (Formally, this is an induction using fairness.) We conclude by using the induction hypothesis (of our well-founded induction) as this round decreases the measure on configurations. This proof of the main theorem is interestingly small as it is only 20 lines long. The whole file dedicated to specification and certification of our algorithm (Algorithm.v) consists of 478 lines of definitions, specification and intermediate lemmas, and 2836 lines of actual proof.

4   Discussion and Perspectives

The Distributed Computing community is known to have fundamental algorithms tightly coupled with their proof of correctness. The mobile robot setting is no exception, as the minimal hypotheses a protocol must make to solve a given problem are extremely difficult to identify without actually writing the corresponding correctness proofs (that is, an intuitive approach is often detrimental to the correctness of the result to be established, as recent errors found in the literature proved [1]). In a formal proof approach to obtain mechanically certified protocols, our framework and methodology clearly contributes to two main phases in a verified development. Firstly the *specification* phase, where all objects, definitions, algorithms, statements and expected properties are expressed without any ambiguity, in a higher order type theoretic functional environment. The lack of ambiguity is a key feature to enable the early detection of inconsistencies between the problem specification, the algorithmic proposal, and the execution model. Secondly the *proof* phase, where properties are proved to hold for the relevant executions. This phase is of course more demanding on the expertise side, so our goal when constructing the framework was to provide useful libraries and proof techniques that can be reused in other contexts, enabling more automation to the protocol designer. Considering reusability, useful assets brought by the current work are the notions of gathering, SSYNC demons, etc., developments on geometry in $\mathbb{R}^2$ and smallest enclosing circles, and the proof of never_forbidden [11]. Those will most likely prove useful in future developments. When developing the protocol for our case study, we decided to modify the protocol code several times, either to fix a newly discovered bug, or to ease the writeup of the proofs. In such a setting, correcting the algorithm amounts to modifying the algorithm definition, and replaying the proofs certification process after adapting the proof scripts written previously. The mechanised verification of the proofs makes this process fast and trustworthy, compared to a purely handcrafted approach.

Perspectives. A next step would be to add more dimensions to the considered Euclidean space. As the framework is highly parametric, specifying another space in which robots move is not a dramatic change: the type of locations is a parameter, it is left abstract throughout the majority of the formalism, in which a concrete instance is not needed. Another interesting evolution would be to take into account the more general ASYNC model, that is when Look-Compute-Move cycles and stages are not atomic anymore. However, describing ASYNC behaviours in CoQ may nonetheless add to the intricacy of formal proofs because of abitrary interleaving, and relevant libraries to ease the task of the developer will have to be provided accordingly.

References

1. Adamek, J., Nesterenko, M., Tixeuil, S.: Evaluating and optimizing stabilizing dining philosophers. In: 11th European Dependable Computing Conference, EDCC 2015, Paris, France, September 7–11, pp. 233–244. IEEE (2015)
2. Auger, C., Bouzid, Z., Courtieu, P., Tixeuil, S., Urbain, X.: Certified impossibility results for byzantine-tolerant mobile robots. In: Higashino, T., Katayama, Y., Masuzawa, T., Potop-Butucaru, M., Yamashita, M. (eds.) SSS 2013. LNCS, vol. 8255, pp. 178–190. Springer, Heidelberg (2013)
3. Berard, B., Millet, L., Potop-Butucaru, M., Thierry-Mieg, Y., Tixeuil, S.: Formal verification of Mobile Robot Protocols. Technical report, LIP6, LINCS, IUF, May 2013
4. Bertot, Y., Castéran, P.: Interactive Theorem Proving and Program Development. Coq'Art: the calculus of inductive constructions. Springer, Heidelberg (2004)
5. Bonnet, F., Défago, X., Petit, F., Potop-Butucaru, M., Tixeuil, S.: Discovering and assessing fine-grained metrics in robot networks protocols. In: 33rd IEEE International Symposium on Reliable Distributed Systems Workshops, SRDS Workshops 2014, Nara, Japan, October 6–9, 2014, pp. 50–59. IEEE (2014)
6. Bouzid, Z., Das, S., Tixeuil, S.: Gathering of mobile robots tolerating multiple crash faults. In: ICDCS, pp. 337–346. IEEE Computer Society, Philadelphia, Pennsylvania, USA, July 2013
7. Bramas, Q., Tixeuil, S.: Wait-free gathering without chirality. In: Scheideler, C. (ed.) Structural Information and Communication Complexity. LNCS, vol. 9439, pp. 313–327. Springer, Heidelberg (2015). doi:10.1007/978-3-319-25258-2_22
8. Bérard, B., Courtieu, P., Millet, L., Potop-Butucaru, M., Rieg, L., Sznajder, N., Tixeuil, S., Urbain, X., Methods, F.: Formal method for mobile robots: current results and open problems. Int. J. Inf. Soci. **7**(3), 101–114 (2015). Invited Paper
9. Castéran, P., Filou, V.: Tasks, types and tactics for local computation systems. Stud. Inf. Univers. **9**(1), 39–86 (2011)
10. Coquand, T., Paulin, C.: Inductively defined types. In: Martin-Löf, P., Mints, G. (eds.) COLOG-88. LNCS, vol. 417, pp. 50–56. Springer, Heidelberg (1990)
11. Courtieu, P., Rieg, L., Tixeuil, S., Urbain, X.: A Certified Universal Gathering Algorithm for Oblivious Mobile Robots. CoRR, abs/1506.01603 (2015)
12. Courtieu, P., Rieg, L., Tixeuil, S., Urbain, X.: Impossibility of gathering, a certification. Inf. Process. Lett. **115**, 447–452 (2015)
13. Devismes, S., Lamani, A., Petit, F., Raymond, P., Tixeuil, S.: Optimal grid exploration by asynchronous oblivious robots. In: Richa, A.W., Scheideler, C. (eds.) SSS 2012. LNCS, vol. 7596, pp. 64–76. Springer, Heidelberg (2012)
14. Dieudonné, Y., Petit, F.: Self-stabilizing gathering with strong multiplicity detection. Theor. Comput. Sci. **428**, 47–57 (2012)

15. Flocchini, P., Prencipe, G., Santoro, N.: Distributed Computing by Oblivious Mobile Robots. Synthesis Lectures on Distributed Computing Theory. Morgan & Claypool Publishers, San Rafeal (2012)
16. Izumi, T., Izumi, T., Kamei, S., Ooshita, F.: Feasibility of polynomial-time randomized gathering for oblivious mobile robots. IEEE Trans. Parallel Distrib. Syst. **24**(4), 716–723 (2013)
17. Izumi, T., Souissi, S., Katayama, Y., Inuzuka, N., Défago, X., Wada, K., Yamashita, M.: The gathering problem for two oblivious robots with unreliable compasses. SIAM J. Comput. **41**(1), 26–46 (2012)
18. Millet, L., Potop-Butucaru, M., Sznajder, N., Tixeuil, S.: On the synthesis of mobile robots algorithms: the case of ring gathering. In: Felber, P., Garg, V. (eds.) SSS 2014. LNCS, vol. 8756, pp. 237–251. Springer, Heidelberg (2014)
19. Sangiorgi, D.: Introduction to Bisimulation and Coinduction. Cambridge University Press, Cambridge, UK (2012)
20. Suzuki, I., Yamashita, M.: Distributed anonymous mobile robots: formation of geometric patterns. SIAM J. Comput. **28**(4), 1347–1363 (1999)

Non-local Probes Do Not Help
with Many Graph Problems

Mika Göös[1], Juho Hirvonen[2], Reut Levi[3(✉)], Moti Medina[3],
and Jukka Suomela[2]

[1] Department of Computer Science, University of Toronto, Toronto, Canada
mika.goos@mail.utoronto.ca
[2] Helsinki Institute for Information Technology HIIT,
Department of Computer Science, Aalto University, Espoo, Finland
{juho.hirvonen,jukka.suomela}@aalto.fi
[3] MPI for Informatics, Saarbrücken, Germany
{rlevi,mmedina}@mpi-inf.mpg.de

Abstract. This work bridges the gap between distributed and centralised models of computing in the context of sublinear-time graph algorithms. A priori, typical centralised models of computing (e.g., parallel
decision trees or centralised local algorithms) seem to be much more
powerful than distributed message-passing algorithms: centralised algorithms can directly probe any part of the input, while in distributed
algorithms nodes can only communicate with their immediate neighbours. We show that for a large class of graph problems, this extra
freedom does not help centralised algorithms at all: efficient stateless
deterministic centralised local algorithms can be simulated with efficient
distributed message-passing algorithms. In particular, this enables us to
transfer existing lower bound results from distributed algorithms to centralised local algorithms.

1 Introduction

A lot of recent work on efficient graph algorithms for massive graphs can be
broadly classified in one of the following categories:

1. *Probe-query models* [1,3,6–8,15,20,25]: Here typical applications are related
   to *large-scale network analysis*: we have a huge storage system in which the
   input graph is stored, and a computer that can access the storage system.
   The user of the computer can make *queries* related to the properties of the
   graph. Conceptually, we have two separate entities: the input graph and a
   computer. Initially, the computer is unaware of the structure of the graph,
   but it can *probe* it to learn more about the structure of the graph. Typically,
   the goal is to answer queries after a *sublinear number of probes*.

The full version of this paper can be found in http://arxiv.org/abs/1512.05411.

© Springer-Verlag Berlin Heidelberg 2016
C. Gavoille and D. Ilcinkas (Eds.): DISC 2016, LNCS 9888, pp. 201–214, 2016.
DOI: 10.1007/978-3-662-53426-7_15

2. *Message-passing models* [5,12,13,17,18,21,23,26]: In message-passing models, typical applications are related to *controlling large computer networks*: we have a computer network (say, the Internet) that consists of a large number of network devices, and the devices need to collaborate to solve a graph problem related to the structure of the network so that each node knows *its own part of the solution* when the algorithm stops.

Conceptually, each node of the input graph is a computational entity. Initially, the nodes are only aware of their own identity and the connections to their immediate neighbours, but the nodes can *exchange messages* with their neighbours in order to learn more about the structure of the graph. Typically, the goal is to solve graph problems in a *sublinear number of communication rounds*.

Example: Vertex Colouring. Using the task of finding a proper vertex colouring as an example, the external behaviour of the algorithms can be described as follows:

1. *Probe-query models:* The user can make queries of the form "what is the colour of node v?" The answers have to be consistent with some fixed feasible solution: for example, if we query the same node twice, the answer has to be the same, and if we query two adjacent nodes, their colours have to be different.
2. *Message-passing models:* The local output of node v is the colour of node v. The local outputs constitute some feasible solution: the local outputs of two adjacent nodes have to be different.

Message-Passing Models and Locality. From our perspective, the key difference between probe-query models and message-passing models is that the structure of the graph constrains the behaviour of message-passing algorithms, but not probe-query algorithms:

1. *Probe-query models:* Given any query v, the algorithm is free to probe any parts of the input graph. In particular, it does not need to probe node v or its immediate neighbours.
2. *Message-passing models:* Nodes can only exchange messages with their immediate neighbours. For example, in 1 communication round, a node can only learn information related to its immediate neighbours. More generally, after t communication rounds, in any message-passing algorithm, each node can only be aware of information that was initially available in its radius-t neighbourhood.

In essence, efficient message-passing algorithms have a high *locality*: if the running time of a message-passing algorithm is t, then the local output of a node v can only depend on the information that was available within its radius-t neighbourhood in the input graph.

1.1   Trivial: From Message-Passing to Probe-Query

One consequence of locality is that we can fairly easily *simulate efficient message-passing algorithm in probe-query models* (at least for deterministic algorithms).

If we have a message-passing algorithm A with a running time of t for, say, graph colouring, we can turn it easily into a probe-query algorithm A' for the same problem: to answer a query v, algorithm A' simply gathers the radius-t neighbourhood of node v and simulates the behaviour of A in this neighbourhood.

In particular, if t is a constant, and the maximum degree of the input graph is bounded by a constant, the probe complexity of A' is also bounded by a constant.

1.2   Impossible: From Probe-Query to Message-Passing

At first, it would seem that the converse cannot hold: probe-query algorithms can freely probe remote parts of the network, and therefore they cannot be simulated with efficient message-passing algorithms.

Indeed, it is easy to construct *artificial* graph problems that are trivial to solve in probe-query models in constant time and that take linear time to solve in the message-passing models. Consensus-like problems provide a simple example.

In the *binary consensus* problem, the nodes of the network are labeled with inputs 0 and 1, all nodes have to produce the same output, and the common output has to be equal to the input of at least one node. In a probe-query algorithm, we can simply always follow the local input of node number 1: regardless of the query v, we will probe node 1, check what was its local input, and answer accordingly. It is straightforward to see that any message-passing algorithm requires linear time (consider three cases: a path with inputs $00\ldots0$, a path with inputs $11\ldots1$, and a path with inputs $00\ldots011\ldots1$).

1.3   Our Contribution: Remote Probes Are of Little Use

While the consensus problem demonstrates that the possibility to probe remote parts of the network makes probe-query models strictly stronger than message-passing models, there seem to be few *natural* graph problems in which remote probes would help.

In this work, we formalise this intuition. We show that for a large class of graph problems, remote probes do not give probe-query algorithms any advantage over message-passing algorithms.

Among others, we will show that for a large family of problems which also includes the so-called *locally checkable problems* (LCL) [21], probe-query algorithms in Rubinfeld et al.'s model [25] can be efficiently simulated with message-passing algorithms in Linial's model [17].

Corollary: Probe-Query Lower Bounds. While lower-bound results in probe-query models are scarce, there is a lot of prior work on lower-bound results in message-passing models. Indeed, the very concept of locality makes it relatively easy to derive lower-bound results for message-passing models: a problem cannot be solved in time t if there is at least one graph in which the output of some node necessarily depends on information that is not available in its radius-t neighbourhood.

Our simulation result makes it now possible to take existing lower bounds for message-passing models and use them to derive analogous lower bounds for probe-query models.

1.4 Related Work

While both message-passing models and probe-query models have been studied extensively, it seems that there is little prior work on their connection. The closest prior work that we are aware of is the 1990 paper by Fich and Ramachandran [10]. They show a result similar to our main theorem for one graph problem—graph colouring in cycles—with problem-specific arguments. While our techniques are different, our main result can be seen as a generalisation of their work from a single graph problem to a broad family of graph problems.

On the side of probe-query algorithms, our main focus is on the CentLOCAL model [25]. Algorithms in the CentLOCAL model are abundant, and include algorithms for various graph problems such as *maximal matching, approximated maximum matching*[1], *approximated maximum weighted matching, graph colouring, maximal independent set, approximated maximum independent set, approximated minimum dominating set*, and *spanning graphs* [1,3,4,6–9,14–16,19,20,24,25]. However, lower bounds in this model are almost nonexistent. In fact, the only lower bound shown directly in the centralised local model is for the spanning graph problem in which the CentLOCAL algorithm computes a "tree-like" subgraph of a given bounded degree graph [14,15].

1.5 Overview

We start this work by introducing the models of computing that we study (Sect. 2). The key models are the LOCAL model, which is a message-passing model introduced by Linial [17], and the CentLOCAL model (centralised local model, a.k.a. local computation algorithms), which is a probe-query model introduced by Rubinfeld et al. [25]. We will also use parallel decision trees as an intermediate model. In Sect. 3 we show our main result, a simulation between the LOCAL model and parallel decision trees. In Sect. 4 we show that query-order-oblivious deterministic CentLOCAL algorithms are equivalent to parallel decision trees. By applying our main result we provide several new lower bounds in the CentLOCAL model. In Sect. 5 we give an explicit simulation which transfers CentLOCAL algorithms (that are allowed to probe anywhere in the graph)

---

[1] We note that in [16] the algorithm for approximated maximum matching takes the advantage of remote probes. However, since in this algorithm there is an underlying assumption that the input graph is connected, our simulation result cannot be applied in order to eliminate the remote probes.

into CentLOCAL algorithms which, on each query, are allowed to probe the graph only in a limited local neighborhood.

2 Preliminaries

In this section we describe the various models we discuss in this paper. We focus on *problems over labeled graphs* defined as follows. Let $\mathcal{P}$ denote a computational problem over labeled graphs. A solution for problem $\mathcal{P}$ over a labeled graph G is a function of which the domain and range depend on $\mathcal{P}$ and G. For example, in the maximal independent set problem, a solution is an indicator function $I \colon V \to \{0, 1\}$ of a maximal independent set in G. Let $\mathrm{sol}(G, \mathcal{P})$ denote the set of solutions of problem $\mathcal{P}$ over the labeled graph G.

2.1 LOCAL: Message-Passing Algorithms

We use the standard LOCAL model [17,23] as our starting point. The nodes communicate in synchronous rounds, exchanging messages with all neighbours and doing local computation. Since we are comparing the power of non-local probes, we assume that the size of the graph is known to the nodes, as it usually is in the probe models.

The LOCAL model can be defined by the fact that in t communication rounds a node can learn exactly its radius-t neighbourhood. A distributed algorithm with running time t is then a function from the set of possible local neighbourhoods to the set of outputs.

2.2 ParallelDecTree: Parallel Decision Trees

We use parallel decision trees, a simple probe model, to connect the LOCAL model and the CentLOCAL model.

Fix an n. Our unknown input graph $G = (V, E)$ will have n nodes, labelled with $V = [n] := \{1, 2, \dots, n\}$. We also refer to the labels as identifiers. Let $N(v) \subseteq V$ denote the set of neighbours of node v. For our purposes, a *decision tree* $\mathcal{T}$ of depth t is an algorithm that can make at most t *probes*: for each probe $v \in V$, tree $\mathcal{T}$ will learn $N(v)$. In words, a decision tree can point at any node of G and ask for a list of its neighbours. After t probes, tree $\mathcal{T}$ produces an output; we will write $\mathcal{T}(G)$ for the output of decision tree $\mathcal{T}$ when we apply it to graph G.

We study graph problems in which the goal is to find a feasible labelling $f \colon V \to L$ of the nodes of our input graph G. We say that a graph problem $\mathcal{P}$ can be solved with $t(n)$ *probes in parallel* if there are decision trees $\mathcal{T}_1, \mathcal{T}_2, \dots, \mathcal{T}_n$ of depth $t(n)$ such that $f \colon v \mapsto \mathcal{T}_v(G)$ is a feasible solution to problem $\mathcal{P}$ for any input graph G. That is, we have n parallel decision trees such that tree $\mathcal{T}_v$ computes the output for node v and each tree makes at most $t(n)$ probes.

The *probe complexity* of problem $\mathcal{P}$ is the smallest $t(n)$ such that $\mathcal{P}$ can be solved with $t(n)$ probes in parallel.

2.3 CentLOCAL: Centralised Local Algorithms

We adopt the definition of the centralised local model (CentLOCAL) as formalised in [25]. In this paper we focus on graph computation problems in which the algorithm is given a probe access to the input graph G through a graph oracle $\mathcal{O}^G$. A *probe* to $\mathcal{O}^G$ is an identifier of a vertex $v \in V$, in turn, $\mathcal{O}^G$ returns a list of the identifiers of the neighbors of v. We assume that for a graph of size $|V| = n$, the set of identifiers is $[n]$.

A CentLOCAL *algorithm* $\mathcal{A}$ for a computation problem $\mathcal{P}$ is a (possibly randomised) algorithm $\mathcal{A}$ with the following properties. Algorithm $\mathcal{A}$ is given probe access to the adjacency list oracle $\mathcal{O}^G$ for the input graph G, tape of random bits, and local read-write computation memory. When given an input (query) x, algorithm $\mathcal{A}$ returns the answer for x. This answer depends only on x, G, and the random bits. The answers given by $\mathcal{A}$ to all possible queries must be consistent; namely, all answers constitute some valid solution to $\mathcal{P}$.

The *probe complexity* is the maximum number of probes that $\mathcal{A}$ makes to G in order to compute an answer for any query. The *seed length* is the length of the random tape. The *space complexity* is the local computation memory used by $\mathcal{A}$ over all queries (not including the seed length). The *success probability* is the probability that $\mathcal{A}$ consistently answers all queries.

We say that a CentLOCAL algorithm is *stateless* if its space complexity is zero. We say that a CentLOCAL algorithm is *state-full* if it is not stateless. With this terminology, we can characterise parallel decision trees as follows:

Fact 1. *The deterministic stateless* CentLOCAL *model is identical to the deterministic parallel decision tree model* [2].

2.4 NICE Graph Problems

We say that a problem $\mathcal{P}$ defined over labeled graphs is NICE if the following holds:

1. There is a bound on the maximum degree $\Delta = o(\log n)$.
2. The problem remains invariant under permutation of the labels. Namely, the set of solutions $\text{sol}(G, \mathcal{P})$ is the same for any permutation of the labels of $V(G)$.
3. For every $f \in \text{sol}(G, \mathcal{P})$ and every connected component C (maximal connected graph) of G, f restricted to C is in $\text{sol}(C, \mathcal{P})$.

We note the family of NICE problems includes the so-called *LCL problems* (locally checkable labellings) on bounded-degree graphs [21].

---

[2] One can also consider a randomised ParallelDecTree model in which every tree has access to an independent source of randomness. We note that the randomised stateless CentLOCAL model is stronger than this model since the algorithm has access to the same random seed throughout its entire execution.

Examples of NICE problems include minimum spanning forest, maximal independent sets, minimal dominating sets, minimal vertex covers, and vertex colouring with $\Delta + 1$ colours. With a straightforward generalisation, we can also consider problems in which the goal is to label edges (e.g., maximal matchings and edge colourings) and problems in which the input graph is labeled (e.g., stable matchings).

3 Simulating Probes in the LOCAL Model

In this section we prove the following theorem.

Theorem 1 (ParallelDecTree to LOCAL). *Any* NICE *problem that can be solved in the parallel decision tree model with probe complexity $t(n)$ can be solved in time $t(N)$ in the* LOCAL *model, where $N = \Theta(n^{\log n})$, provided that $t(n) = o(\sqrt{\log n})$.*

Overview of the Proof. Fix an input size $n \in \mathbb{N}$. In order to solve the graph problem on an n-node graph G in the LOCAL model we simulate the decision tree $\mathcal{T}$ *not* on G directly, but on a much larger graph $G \cup H$ that is the disjoint union of G and some *virtual* graph H. The structure of the virtual graph H is agreed upon ahead of time by all the nodes participating in the simulation. Before we invoke the decision tree on $G \cup H$, however, we first *reshuffle* its identifiers randomly. The key idea is to show that this reshuffling trick fools the decision tree: if we simulate $\mathcal{T}$ on a node v and $\mathcal{T}$ probes some node outside of v's local neighbourhood, then the probe lands in H with overwhelming probability. Since all nodes in G know the structure of H, they can answer such "global" probes consistently. Finally, we argue that there is some fixed choice of randomness that makes the simulation succeed on all graphs on n nodes and degree bounded by Δ. This makes the simulation deterministic.

Proof (Proof of Theorem 1.) Let H be any graph on the vertex set $[N] \setminus [n]$ with degree bounded by Δ. This graph remains fixed and does not depend on the n-node input graph G. In this sense, all the nodes in the simulation know the structure of H. Let $\pi\colon [N] \to [N]$ be a random permutation. Again, all the nodes in the simulation are assumed to agree on the same π. (The simulation can be thought of as being defined with respect to the outcomes of some public random coins.)

During the simulation we will always present the decision tree with a relabelled version of the graph $G \cup H$ where a node v has identifier $\pi(v)$. That is, when $\mathcal{T}$ probes an identifier w, the simulation interprets this as probing $\pi^{-1}(w)$ and when we respond to $\mathcal{T}$ with a node v we relabel its identifier as $\pi(v)$. Note that each node in G, knowing π, can perform this translation locally.

A node $v \in V(G)$ starts its simulation by invoking the decision tree on $\pi(v)$ with the hope of answering its $t(N)$ probes based on the $t(N)$-neighbourhood of v in G and knowledge of H. During this attempt we maintain a set of *discovered nodes* Q that contains all the nodes whose relabelled versions have been sent back to $\mathcal{T}$ in response to a probe. Note that $|Q| \leq k$ where $k \triangleq 1 + (\Delta + 1) \cdot t(N)$ is an upper bound on the total number of inspections of π performed by the simulation. Initially $Q = \{v\}$, so that only v is discovered. We will ensure that the following invariant holds throughout the simulation: After the s-th step every member of Q is either in H or at most at distance s from v. Suppose T probes a relabelled identifier w corresponding to a node $u = \pi^{-1}(w)$. We have two cases:

Local probe, $u \in Q$. In this case we are always successful: by the invariant, the neighbours of u are known to v so we can add them to Q and return their relabelled versions to T.

Global probe, $u \notin Q$. Two sub-cases depending on whether $u \in V(H)$:

- $u \in V(H)$: Success! The structure of H is known to v so we can add the neighbours of u to Q and return their relabelled versions to T.
- $u \notin V(H)$: Here we simply say that the simulation has *failed* and we terminate the simulation. (Note that by this convention we may fail even if u is in the $t(N)$-neighbourhood of v; however this convention helps us maintain the invariant.)

When the decision tree returns an output for $\pi(v)$, we simply return the same output for v.

Next, we analyse the probability that our simulation fails when invoked on a particular node and a particular input graph G. Suppose we need to respond to a global probe sometime in our simulation. That is, the probe is to a node whose relabelled identifier is w and the node has not been discovered yet, i.e., $w \notin \pi(Q)$. By the principle of deferred decisions, we can think of the node $u = \pi^{-1}(w)$ as being uniformly distributed among the undiscovered nodes $[N] \smallsetminus Q$. Hence the failure probability (conditioned on any outcome of $\pi(Q)$) is $\Pr[u \in V(G)] = \frac{|V(G) \smallsetminus Q|}{|[N] \smallsetminus Q|} \leq \frac{n}{N-k}$. Consequently, by the union bound the probability that the simulation fails at some probe step is at most $k \cdot \frac{n}{N-k}$, which is at most $\frac{n^2}{N}$ for any $k \leq n/2$.

Let $\mathcal{G}_\Delta$ denote the set of all n-node graphs with degree bounded by Δ. We argue next that there is a fixed choice for π that makes the simulation succeed on all graphs $G \in \mathcal{G}_\Delta$. To this end, we note that on any simulation of T, the final output of T depends on the query v and on at most $t(N)$ nodes and their adjacency relations in $G \cup H$. Fix H, π and the query v and observe that any probe in $V(H)$ has a fixed outcome (for all possible input graphs $G \in \mathcal{G}_\Delta$). On the other hand, if we probe $V(G)$, then the number of possible outcomes is at most n^Δ. Let $\mathcal{H}$ denote the set of possible probe-answer transcripts when simulating $T(v)$. Then, by the above, $|\mathcal{H}| \leq n^{\Delta \cdot t(N)}$. Executing our simulation on each node (n choices), the probability that some simulation fails (each fails with probability $\leq n^2/N$) is at most $n \cdot n^{\Delta \cdot t(N)} \cdot n^2/N = n^{-\Omega(\log n)} = o(1)$, by yet another union bound. Thus, we can find a fixed outcome of π for which the simulation succeeds simultaneously on all $G \in \mathcal{G}_\Delta$.

It remains to point out that the output labelling f produced by the simulation constitutes a feasible solution to the graph problem under consideration. Here it suffices to assume that the graph problem satisfies the following property: if f is a feasible solution for a graph G and $C \subseteq G$ is a connected component of G, then the restriction of f to $V(C)$ is a feasible solution for C and that this remains so under any relabelling of the identifiers. In particular, all NICE problems satisfy this property.

Remark 1 (Simulation for Approximation Algorithms). We note that for the correctness we used a weaker property than property (3) of NICE problems. In fact the correctness applies to any problem $\mathcal{P}$ such that for all n there exists a graph H on n vertices and with maximum degree at most Δ such that for every $f \in \mathrm{sol}(H \cup G, \mathcal{P})$ we have that f restricted to G is in $\mathrm{sol}(G, \mathcal{P})$. By taking H to be the graph with no edges we obtain that Theorem 1 can be generalised to, for example, $(1 - \varepsilon)$-approximated maximum (weighted) matching and approximation of vertex covers.

4   Centralised Local Model and Parallel Decision Trees

In this section we observe that one can simulate query-order-oblivious CentLOCAL algorithms by stateless algorithms. Recall that a deterministic stateless CentLOCAL algorithm is a ParallelDecTree algorithm (Fact 1). Hence, the simulation result (Theorem 1) applies to the CentLOCAL model w.r.t. query-order-oblivious deterministic algorithms. We then summarise the obtained lower bounds and show the optimality of several known algorithms.

4.1   Query-Order-Oblivious vs. Stateless CentLOCAL Algorithms

We say that a CentLOCAL algorithm is *query-order-oblivious* if the (global) solution that the algorithm computes does not depend on the input sequence of queries. Even et al. [6] state that a stateless CentLOCAL algorithm is also query-order-oblivious. We observe that the converse is also true, as stated next.

Observation 1. *For every query-order-oblivious CentLOCAL algorithm C there is a stateless CentLOCAL algorithm S that simulates C. Moreover, the probe complexities of C and S are equal.*

In order to verify the correctness of Observation 1, consider a stateless algorithm S which simply invokes C with its initial state and the same random seed for every input query.

In the full version of this paper we show a separation between stateless and stateful CentLOCAL algorithms. Specifically, we prove that there is a linear gap in the probe complexity between a CentLOCAL with (only) logarithmic state and a stateless algorithm that computes a leader in a variant of the leader election problem.

4.2   CentLOCAL vs. LOCAL

Parnas and Ron [22] observed that given a deterministic LOCAL algorithm D that performs r rounds of communication, there is a CentLOCAL algorithm C that simulates D with probe complexity which is $O(\Delta^r)$. On the other hand, as indicated in Even et al. [6], if a deterministic CentLOCAL algorithm C probes in an r-neighborhood of each queried vertex, then there is a deterministic LOCAL algorithm D that simulates C in r communication rounds. Theorem 1 implies that for some CentLOCAL algorithms there is a LOCAL (implicit) simulation such that the number of communication rounds is asymptotically equal to the probe complexity, even though the CentLOCAL algorithm probes outside of the r-neighborhood of a queried vertex. This argument allows carrying lower bounds to the CentLOCAL model from the LOCAL model. Specifically, Theorem 1 combined with Fact 1 and Observation 1 implies the following theorem.

Theorem 2 (CentLocal to LOCAL). *For every query-order-oblivious (or stateless) deterministic CentLOCAL algorithm D that solves a problem $\mathcal{P} \in$ NICE with probe complexity $t(n) = o(\sqrt{\log n})$, there is LOCAL algorithm that solves $\mathcal{P}$ by simulating D, and for which the number of rounds is at most $t(N)$ where $N = \Theta(n^{\log n})$.*

As mentioned in Remark 1, the simulation also applies to several optimization problems. In Table 1 we summarise (1) the known CentLOCAL algorithms, their probe complexities as well as the obtained approximation ratios, and (2) corresponding LOCAL lower bounds. By Theorem 2 all stated lower bounds apply to deterministic, query-order-oblivious CentLOCAL algorithms.

Table 1. MIS denotes maximal independent set, MM denotes maximal matching, $(\Delta + 1)$-COLOUR denotes $\Delta + 1$ vertex colouring, $(1 - \varepsilon)$-MCM denotes $(1 - \varepsilon)$-approximated maximum cardinality matching, and $(1 - \varepsilon)$-MWM denotes $(1 - \varepsilon)$-approximated maximum weighted matching. All the upper bounds presented in this table are of algorithms which are deterministic and stateless. All the upper bounds are presented under the assumption that $\Delta = O(1)$ and $\varepsilon = O(1)$. For weighted graphs, the ratio between the maximum to minimum edge weight is denoted by Γ.

Problem	CentLOCAL upper bounds (deterministic, 0-space) # probes		LOCAL lower bounds # rounds	
MIS	$O(\log^* n)$	[6]	$\Omega(\log^* n)$	[17]
MM	$O(\log^* n)$	[6]	$\Omega(\log^* n)$	[17]
$(\Delta + 1)$-COLOUR	$O(\log^* n)$	[6]	$\Omega(\log^* n)$	[17]
$(1 - \varepsilon)$-MCM	$\mathrm{poly}(\log^* n)$	[6]	$\Omega(\log^* n)$	[5,13]
$(1 - \varepsilon)$-MWM	$\mathrm{poly}(\min\{\Gamma, n/\varepsilon\} \cdot \log^* n)$	[6]	$\Omega(\log^* n)$	[5,13]

5   Localizing Stateless CentLocal Algorithms

In this section we give a constructive, polynomial blow-up, randomised CentLOCAL simulation (see Theorem 3). For many graph problems this simulation enables us to design a CentLOCAL algorithm that only performs "close" probes. In the CentLOCAL model an explicit simulation is possible, since, unlike the LOCAL and ParallelDecTree models, a CentLOCAL algorithm uses the same random seed for all queries. So while this simulation brings closer the two models of CentLOCAL and LOCAL, the single source of randomness that a CentLOCAL algorithm possesses keeps the advantage to the CentLOCAL model.

Recall that the simulation in Sect. 3 simulates a ParallelDecTree algorithm via a distributed LOCAL algorithm. In order to prove Theorem 3 we consider a similar simulation with the difference that now both the simulation and the simulated algorithm are in CentLOCAL. However, the simulation has the property that it is limited to query $\mathcal{O}^G$ only on Q (as defined in Sect. 3). Since a CentLOCAL is equipped with a random seed we can use a randomised simulation and consequently the blow-up in the probe-complexity will be significantly smaller. In particular, in this section we consider $N = O(n^4)$, that is, the size of the augmented graph $G \cup H$ is polynomial in the size of the input graph G. Additionally, we show that the additional random seed that is required for the simulation is small.

This random seed is a costly resource and we try to minimize its length. Known randomised implementations of greedy algorithms in the CentLOCAL domain require explicit random ordering constructions [3,24] over the vertices or edges [3,19,20,24]. In our implementation of the simulation we use a permutation over the labels, which is a stronger requirement than a random ordering. This requirement comes from the fact that in the simulation each vertex has a unique identifier and that the set of identifiers is assumed to be known. In what follows we build on techniques by [2,11].

Theorem 3 (Explicit CentLOCAL to CentLOCAL). *Let A be a query-order-oblivious CentLOCAL algorithm that solves a NICE problem $\mathcal{P}$ with probe-complexity $t(n) = O(n^{1/4}/\Delta)$ and seed length $s(n)$. Then, there is a query-order-oblivious CentLOCAL algorithm B that solves $\mathcal{P}$ by simulating algorithm A. Algorithm B has a probe-complexity of $t(n^4)$ and a seed length of $s(n^4) + O(t(n^4) \cdot \Delta \cdot \log n)$ and the property that it probes within a radius of $t(n^4)$; moreover the subgraph induced on the probes of B is connected. The error probability of B equals to the error probability of A plus $O(1/n)$.*

5.1 Preliminaries

Definition 1 (Statistical Distance). *Let D_1, D_2 be distributions over a finite set Ω. The statistical distance between D_1 and D_2 is $\|D_1 - D_2\| = \frac{1}{2} \sum_{\omega \in \Omega} |D_1(\omega) - D_2(\omega)|$. Alternatively, $\|D_1 - D_2\| = \max_{A \subseteq \Omega} \left| \sum_{\omega \in A} D_1(\omega) - \sum_{\omega \in A} D_2(\omega) \right|$. We say that D_1 and D_2 are ϵ-close if $\|D_1 - D_2\| \leq \epsilon$.*

Let S_n denote the set of all permutations on $[n]$.

Definition 2. *Let $n, k \in \mathbb{N}$, and let $\mathcal{F} \subseteq S_n$ be a multiset of permutations. Let $\varepsilon \geq 0$. The multiset $\mathcal{F}$ is k-wise ε-dependent if for every k-tuple of distinct elements $(x_1, \ldots, x_k) \in [n]^k$, the distribution $(f(x_1), f(x_2), \ldots, f(x_k))$, when $f \sim_{u.a.r.} \mathcal{F}$ is ε-close to the uniform distribution over all k-tuples of distinct elements of $[n]$.*

As a special case, a multiset of permutations is k-wise independent if it is k-wise 0-dependent.

We shall use the following results from previous work in the proof of Theorem 3. The following theorem is an immediate corollary of a theorem due to Alon and Lovett [2, Theorem 1.1].

Theorem 4. *Let μ be a distribution taking values in S_n which is k-wise ϵ-dependent. Then there exists a distribution μ' over permutations which is k-wise independent, and such that the statistical distance between μ and μ' is at most $O(\epsilon n^{4k})$.*

Additionally, we build on the following construction in our CentLOCAL simulation SIM. This construction enables accesses to a uniform random permutation from a k-wise ϵ-dependent family of permutations by using a seed of length $O(k \cdot \log n + \log(1/\epsilon))$.

Theorem 5 ([11, Theorem 5.9]). *There exists $\mathcal{F} \subseteq S_n$, such that $\mathcal{F}$ is k-wise ϵ-dependent. $\mathcal{F}$ has description length $O(k \cdot \log n + \log(1/\epsilon))$, and time complexity $\mathsf{poly}(\log n, k, \log(1/\epsilon))$.*

5.2 Proof of Theorem 3

Let A be as in Theorem 3 and let SIM denote its simulation on $G \cup H$ as described above. Since the size of $G \cup H$ is N the size of the random seed required by A is $s(N)$. For a fixed random seed $r \in \{0,1\}^{s(N)}$, a fixed query $q \in V(G)$ and a fixed permutation $\pi \in S_N$ let $\mathrm{SIM}(G, r, \pi, q)$ be the indicator variable for the event that the simulation succeeds in simulating A with random seed r on input q where π is the permutation which is used to relabel the vertices in $G \cup H$.

Let $\mathcal{F}$ be a family of k-wise independent permutations over $[N]$ where $k \triangleq 1 + (\Delta + 1) \cdot t(N)$.

Lemma 1. *For every $q \in V(G)$ and $r \in \{0,1\}^{s(N)}$,*

$$\Pr_{\pi \sim_{u.a.r.} \mathcal{F}}(\mathrm{SIM}(G, r, \pi, q) = 0) \leq \frac{kn}{N - k}$$

Proof. Fix $r \in \{0,1\}^{s(N)}$, $\pi \in S_N$ and $q \in V(G)$. As in the proof of Theorem 1 we have that $\Pr_{\pi \sim_{u.a.r.} S_N}(\mathrm{SIM}(G, r, \pi, q) = 0) \leq \frac{kn}{N-k}$. Thus it suffices to show that $\Pr_{\pi \sim_{u.a.r.} \mathcal{F}}(\mathrm{SIM}(G, r, \pi, q) = 0) = \Pr_{\pi \sim_{u.a.r.} S_N}(\mathrm{SIM}(G, r, \pi, q) = 0)$. Recall that the simulation relabels the vertices by accessing both to π and π^{-1}. Now consider the sequence of inspections the simulation makes to π and π^{-1} by the order they occurred.[3] The first inspection to π is $\pi(q)$. Then, according to the decisions of A and the answers from $\mathcal{O}^G$, the simulation continues to inspect both π and π^{-1} on at most $k - 1$ locations.

Let $(v, u, b) \in N \times N \times \{-1, 1\}$ represent a single inspection and answer as follows: If $b = 1$ then the interpretation is that the simulation inspects π at index v and the answer is u and if $b = -1$ then the interpretation is that the simulation inspects π^{-1} at v and the answer is u.

---

[3] The construction stated in Theorem 5 computes $\pi(v)$ for some v in time $\mathsf{poly}(\log n, k, \log(1/\epsilon))$. This construction does not describe a time efficient way to access π^{-1}. As time complexity is not the focus of this paper, we implement the inverse access in a straightforward manner.

For a fixed G, r, π and q the sequence of (possibly adaptive) inspections and answers is fixed. Let it be denoted by $\sigma = (v_1, u_1, b_1), \ldots, (v_\ell, u_\ell, b_\ell)$ where $\ell \leq k$. We say that a permutation π agrees with the sequence σ iff $\pi^{b_i}(v_i) = u_i$ for every $i \in [\ell]$. Clearly, we can replace π with any permutation π' which agrees with σ and the outcome (failure or success) remains unchanged, that is $\mathrm{SIM}(G, r, \pi, q) = \mathrm{SIM}(G, r, \pi', q)$. We say that σ is *positive* if $b_i = 1$ for every $i \in [\ell]$. We say that a pair of sequences σ and σ' are *equal* if any permutation that agrees with σ also agrees with σ' and vice versa. Observe that from any sequence σ we can obtain an equal sequence, σ', which is positive by performing the following replacements: If there exists j such that $b_j = -1$ (this means that $\pi^{-1}(v_j) = u_j$ which is equivalent to $v_j = \pi(u_j)$) then replace $(v_j, u_j, -1)$ with $(u_j, v_j, 1)$. Therefore we obtain that S_N can be partitioned into equivalence classes where in each class C: (1) all the permutations agree with some positive sequence Q of length at most k, and (2) $\mathrm{SIM}(G, r, \pi, q)$ is fixed when π is taken from C. Since for every positive sequence σ we have $\Pr_{\pi \sim_{\mathrm{u.a.r.}} \mathcal{F}}[\pi \text{ agrees with } \sigma] = \Pr_{\pi \sim_{\mathrm{u.a.r.}} S_N}[\pi \text{ agrees with } \sigma]$, we obtain the desired result.

Corollary 1. *For a fixed graph G and a fixed random seed $r \in \{0,1\}^{s(N)}$, the probability that the simulation succeeds when $\pi \sim_{u.a.r.} \mathcal{F}$ is at least $1 - O(1/n)$.*

Let $\mathcal{F}'$ be a k-wise ϵ-dependent family of permutations.

Corollary 2. *For a fixed graph G and a fixed random seed $r \in \{0,1\}^{s(N)}$, the probability that the simulation succeeds when $\pi \sim_{u.a.r.} \mathcal{F}'$ is at least $1 - O(1/n) - O(\epsilon N^{4k})$.*

Proof (Proof of Theorem 3). In the simulation we shall use the construction from Theorem 5 to obtain a random access to a permutation π over $[N]$ where $N = n^4$, using a random seed of length $O(k \cdot \log N + \log \gamma)$ where $\gamma = O(nN^{4k})$ and access time $\mathsf{poly}(\log N, k, \log \gamma)$. By Corollary 2 the simulation succeeds with probability at least $1 - O(1/n)$ as desired.

References

1. Alon, N.: On constant time approximation of parameters of bounded degree graphs. In: Goldreich, O. (ed.) Property Testing. LNCS, vol. 6390, pp. 234–239. Springer, Heidelberg (2010)
2. Alon, N., Lovett, S.: Almost k-Wise vs. k-wise independent permutations, and uniformity for general group actions. Theor. Comput. **9**(15), 559–577 (2013)
3. Alon, N., Rubinfeld, R., Vardi, S., Xie, N.: Space-efficient local computation algorithms. In: Proceedings of SODA, pp. 1132–1139. SIAM (2012)
4. Campagna, A., Guo, A., Rubinfeld, R.: Local reconstructors and tolerant testers for connectivity and diameter. In: Raghavendra, P., Raskhodnikova, S., Jansen, K., Rolim, J.D.P. (eds.) RANDOM 2013 and APPROX 2013. LNCS, vol. 8096, pp. 411–424. Springer, Heidelberg (2013)
5. Czygrinow, A., Hańćkowiak, M., Wawrzyniak, W.: Fast distributed approximations in planar graphs. In: Taubenfeld, G. (ed.) DISC 2008. LNCS, vol. 5218, pp. 78–92. Springer, Heidelberg (2008)

6. Even, G., Medina, M., Ron, D.: Best of Two Local Models: Local Centralized and Local Distributed Algorithms (2014). arXiv:1402.3796
7. Even, G., Medina, M., Ron, D.: Deterministic stateless centralized local algorithms for bounded degree graphs. In: Schulz, A.S., Wagner, D. (eds.) ESA 2014. LNCS, vol. 8737, pp. 394–405. Springer, Heidelberg (2014)
8. Even, G., Medina, M., Ron, D.: Distributed maximum matching in bounded degree graphs. In: Proceedings of ICDCN, pp. 1–19. ACM (2014)
9. Feige, U., Mansour, Y., Schapire, R.E.: Learning and Inference in the Presence of Corrupted Inputs. In: Proceedings of the 28th Conference on Learning Theory, vol. 40, pp. 637–657. J. Mach. Learn. Res. (2015)
10. Fich, F.E., Ramachandran, V.: Lower bounds for parallel computation on linked structures. In: Proceedings of SPAA, pp. 109–116. ACM Press (1990)
11. Kaplan, E., Naor, M., Reingold, O.: Derandomized constructions of k-wise (almost) independent permutations. Algorithmica **55**(1), 113–133 (2009)
12. Kuhn, F., Moscibroda, T., Wattenhofer, R.: What cannot be computed locally! In: Proceedings of PODC, pp. 300–309. ACM Press (2004)
13. Lenzen, C., Wattenhofer, R.: Leveraging Linial's locality limit. In: Taubenfeld, G. (ed.) DISC 2008. LNCS, vol. 5218, pp. 394–407. Springer, Heidelberg (2008)
14. Levi, R., Moshkovitz, G., Ron, D., Rubinfeld, R., Shapira, A.: Constructing near spanning trees with few local inspections. Random Struct. Algorithms (2016)
15. Levi, R., Ron, D., Rubinfeld, R.: Local algorithms for sparse spanning graphs. In: Proceedings of APPROX/RANDOM, pp. 826–842. Schloss Dagstuhl-Leibniz-Zentrum fuer Informatik (2014)
16. Levi, R., Rubinfeld, R., Yodpinyanee, A.: Local computation algorithms for graphs of non-constant degrees. In: Proceedings of SPAA, pp. 59–61. ACM Press (2015)
17. Linial, N.: Locality in distributed graph algorithms. SIAM J. Comput. **21**(1), 193–201 (1992)
18. Lynch, N.A.: Distributed Algorithms. Morgan Kaufmann Publishers, San Francisco (1996)
19. Mansour, Y., Rubinstein, A., Vardi, S., Xie, N.: Converting online algorithms to local computation algorithms. In: Czumaj, A., Mehlhorn, K., Pitts, A., Wattenhofer, R. (eds.) ICALP 2012, Part I. LNCS, vol. 7391, pp. 653–664. Springer, Heidelberg (2012)
20. Mansour, Y., Vardi, S.: A local computation approximation scheme to maximum matching. In: Raghavendra, P., Raskhodnikova, S., Jansen, K., Rolim, J.D.P. (eds.) RANDOM 2013 and APPROX 2013. LNCS, vol. 8096, pp. 260–273. Springer, Heidelberg (2013)
21. Naor, M., Stockmeyer, L.: What can be computed locally? SIAM J. Comput. **24**(6), 1259–1277 (1995)
22. Parnas, M., Ron, D.: Approximating the minimum vertex cover in sublinear time and a connection to distributed algorithms. Theor. Comput. Sci. **381**(1–3), 183–196 (2007)
23. Peleg, D.: Distributed Computing: A Locality-sensitive Approach. SIAM Monographs on Discrete Mathematics and Applications. Society for Industrial and Applied Mathematics, Philadelphia (2000)
24. Reingold, O., Vardi, S.: New Techniques and Tighter Bounds for Local Computation Algorithms (2014). arXiv:1404.5398
25. Rubinfeld, R., Tamir, G., Vardi, S., Xie, N.: Fast local computation algorithms. In: Proceedings of the ICS (2011)
26. Suomela, J.: Survey of local algorithms. ACM Comput. Surv. **45**(2), 24:1–24:40 (2013)

Are Byzantine Failures Really Different from Crash Failures?

Damien Imbs[1](✉), Michel Raynal[2,3], and Julien Stainer[4]

[1] Department of Mathematics, University of Bremen, Bremen, Germany
imbs@uni-bremen.de
[2] Institut Universitaire de France, Paris, France
[3] IRISA, Université de Rennes, 35042 Rennes, France
[4] École Polytechnique Fédérale de Lausanne, Lausanne, Switzerland

Abstract. When considering n-process asynchronous systems, where up to t processes can fail, and communication is by read/write registers or reliable message-passing, are (from a computability point of view) Byzantine failures "different" from crash failures? This is the question addressed in this paper, which shows that the answer is "no" for systems where $t < n/3$.

To this end, the paper presents a new distributed simulation whose core is an extended BG simulation suited to asynchronous message-passing systems. More precisely, assuming $t < \min(n', n/3)$, it describes a signature-free algorithm that simulates a system of n' processes where up to t may crash, on top of a basic system of n processes where up to t may be Byzantine. In addition to extending (in a modular and direct way) the basic BG simulation to Byzantine message-passing systems this simulation also allows crash-tolerant algorithms, designed for asynchronous read/write systems, to be executed on top of asynchronous message-passing systems prone to Byzantine failures.

1 Introduction

Let us assume that we have a distributed algorithm A that solves a problem P on top of an asynchronous system made up of n processes among which up to t may crash. Do we have to design a new algorithm from scratch when the problem P has to be solved in a failure context where up to t processes can commit Byzantine failures instead of crash failures?

The paper answers this question for the class of problems known under the name *decision tasks*. Assuming $t < \min(n', n/3)$, and an algorithm A that solves such a problem P in an n'-process asynchronous (read/write or message-passing) distributed system in which up to t processes may crash, the paper presents an algorithm that allows to simulate A on top of an asynchronous message-passing system made up of n processes among which up to t can be Byzantine.

To attain this goal, the paper considers an approach based on the BG simulation [3] (other approaches could be envisaged, e.g. [5][1]). The BG simulation

---

[1] Independently from our work, a concurrent work by Dolev and Gafni [5] (based on a totally different approach) shows a result similar to ours, namely, a system

© Springer-Verlag Berlin Heidelberg 2016
C. Gavoille and D. Ilcinkas (Eds.): DISC 2016, LNCS 9888, pp. 215–229, 2016.
DOI: 10.1007/978-3-662-53426-7_16

allows $(t + 1)$ processes (simulators) to simulate a large number n' of asynchronous processes that communicate through read/write registers, and collectively solve a decision task, in the presence of at most t crashes. Each of the $(t + 1)$ simulators simulates the n' processes. These $(t+1)$ simulators cooperate through underlying objects that allow them to agree on a single output for each of the non-deterministic statements issued by every simulated process. (These underlying objects, called safe agreement objects, can be built of top of read/write atomic registers.)

On the BG simulation. Let BG(RW,C) denote the basic BG simulation algorithm [3] (RW stands for "read/write communication", and C stands for "crash failures"). The simulation BG(RW,C) is "symmetric" in the sense that each of the n' processes is simulated by every simulator, and the $(t + 1)$ simulators are "equal" with respect to each simulated process, namely, (1) every simulator fairly simulates all the processes, and (2) the crash of a simulator entails the crash of at most one simulated process. This symmetry allows BG(RW,C) to be suited to colorless tasks (i.e., distributed computing problems where the value decided by a process can be decided by any process).

Content of the paper: on the simulation side. The paper extends the BG-simulation in two directions. The first is the communication model, namely, it considers that processes cooperate by sending and receiving messages via asynchronous reliable channels. The second direction is related to the type of failures; more precisely, it considers two types of failures: process crash failures, and the more severe process Byzantine failures.

Hence, an important contribution of the paper is an algorithm, denoted BG(MP,B), which simulates the execution of a colorless task running in an asynchronous message-passing system of n' processes, where up to t may crash, on top of an asynchronous message-passing system of n processes where up to t may be Byzantine [9]. This simulation requires $t < n/3$ (according to the task which is simulated, additional constraint on t may be needed, see [6]; see also Sect. 5). While the number of simulated processes n' can be any integer, for the simulation to be non-trivial we consider that $t < n'$. This algorithm has two noteworthy features: it is the first BG simulation algorithm that considers Byzantine failures, and it allows to run a crash-tolerant algorithm solving a colorless task on top of an asynchronous system prone to Byzantine failures. Moreover, the algorithm BG(MP,B) is *genuine* in the sense that it does not rely on the simulation of an underlying shared memory.

While the full-information algorithm presented in [10] can be used to decide when there is a simulation between two models, the present paper is the first

---

with $t < n/3$ Byzantine processes can neutralize the Byzantine processes to appear as a t-resilient system (with respect to crash failures). Hence, both papers show that "the difficulty of distributed computing is captured solely by crash failures". Consequently, according to an implicit suggestion appearing in a referee report, the title of the current proceedings version has been modified (with respect to the title of the submitted version [8]) to emphasize this important observation.

(to our knowledge) that allows the direct execution in the presence of Byzantine failures of any crash-tolerant algorithm that solves a colorless task. BG(MP,B) provides an algorithmic approach which complements the topology-based simulation framework of [10], and may also be of practical interest. It has the interesting property that the simulation of a message only requires a polynomial number of messages in the base system, and the increase in size of these messages, when compared to the size of the simulated message, is also polynomial. Additionally, differently from early works on Byzantine failures, it does not use any cryptography-based mechanism.

Content of the paper: on the safe agreement objects side. The core of the previous algorithm lies in a new underlying safe agreement object, which allows the n simulators to agree on the next operation executed by each of the n' simulated processes. Such a safe agreement object ensures that all the simulators produce the very same simulation. At the operational level, a safe agreement object provides processes with two operations, denoted propose() and decide(), which are invoked in this order by each correct process. The termination property associated with a safe agreement object SA is the following: if no simulator commits a failure while executing SA.propose(), then any invocation of SA.decide() by a non-faulty simulator terminates. Moreover, no two correct processes decide differently.

On the algorithmic side, a novelty of the paper lies in the algorithm implementing this new safe agreement object. Differently from its read/write memory counterpart, it is not based on underlying atomic snapshot objects. Instead, it relies heavily on message communication patterns inspired from reliable broadcast algorithms. This object is the core of the simulation when one wants to execute asynchronous read/write crash-tolerant algorithms on top of asynchronous message-passing systems prone to Byzantine failures.

Existing simulations considering Byzantine failures. Simulations of crash failures in a Byzantine system have been addressed in the context of synchronous systems (e.g. [2,11,12]. The only articles we are aware of concerning such a simulation in asynchronous systems are [4,7,10]: [4] considers a restricted class of round-based deterministic algorithms; [10] considers a full-information asynchronous crash-tolerant algorithm in an asynchronous Byzantine system; [7] considers an agent/host model and focuses mainly on reliable broadcast.

Due to page limitations, all the proofs and some developments are omitted. They can be found in the companion tech report [8] (along with a simpler simulation that only considers crash failures).

2   Computation Models and Tasks

The system is made up of a set Π of n sequential processes, denoted p_1, p_2, ..., p_n. These processes are asynchronous in the sense that each process progresses at its own speed, which can be arbitrary and always remains unknown to the other processes. Processes may deviate from their specification; such processes are said to be *faulty*. Other processes are *correct* (or *non-faulty*). The model parameter t denotes the maximal number of processes that can be faulty in a given execution.

Communication happens through a complete network of asynchronous reliable channels, which means that each process p_i can directly send a message to any process p_j (including itself) without loss, corruption, or creation of messages, and that there is no upper bound on message transit times.

The macro-operation "broadcast TYPE(m)", where TYPE is a message type and m is its content, is a shortcut for the following statement: "send TYPE(m) to each process (including itself)".

The crash failure model. In the crash failure model, a process may prematurely stop its execution. A process executes correctly its algorithm until it possibly crashes. Once crashed, a process remains crashed forever. It is assumed that at most t processes may crash. If there is no specific constraint on t, this model is denoted $\mathcal{CAMP}_{n,t}[t < n]$.

The Byzantine failure model. A Byzantine process is a process that behaves arbitrarily: it may crash, fail to send or receive messages, send arbitrary messages, start in an arbitrary state, perform arbitrary state transitions, etc. Hence, a Byzantine process, which should send the same message m to all the processes, can send a message m_1 to some processes, a different message m_2 to another subset of processes, and no message at all to the other processes. Moreover, while Byzantine processes can collude to "pollute" the computation, they cannot control the network: when a process receives a message, it can unambiguously identify its sender. As previously, t denotes the upper bound on the number of processes that may commit Byzantine failures. When it is assumed that at most $t < n/3$ processes may be faulty, the corresponding model is denoted $\mathcal{BAMP}_{n,t}[t < n/3]$.

Decision Tasks. The problems we are interested in are called *decision tasks*. In every run, each process proposes a value and the proposed values define an input vector I, where $I[j]$ is the value proposed by process p_j. Let $\mathcal{I}$ denote the set of allowed input vectors. Each process has to decide a value. The decided values define an output vector O, such that $O[j]$ is the value decided by p_j. Let $\mathcal{O}$ be the set of the output vectors.

A decision task is a binary relation Δ from $\mathcal{I}$ into $\mathcal{O}$. A task is *colorless* if, when a value v is proposed by a process p_j (i.e., $I[j] = v$), then v can be proposed by any number of processes and, when a value v' is decided by a process p_j (i.e., $O[j] = v'$), then v' can be decided by any number of processes. Consensus, and more generally k-set agreement, are colorless tasks. Otherwise the task is *colored*. Symmetry breaking and renaming are colored tasks.

3   Structure of the Simulation Algorithms

Aim. Let A be an algorithm that solves a colorless decision task among n' processes in the system model $\mathcal{CAMP}_{n',t}[t < n']$. The aim is to design an algorithm that simulates A in the system model $\mathcal{BAMP}_{n,t}[t < n/3]$.

Notation. A simulated process is denoted p_j, where $1 \leq j \leq n'$. Similarly, a simulator process ("simulator" in short') is denoted q_i, where $1 \leq i \leq n$. The set Π denote the set of the simulator indexes, i.e., $\Pi = \{1, ..., n\}$. The safe agreement objects, build in the simulation and used by the simulators, are identified with upper case letters, e.g., *SA*. The variables local to simulator q_j are identified with lower case letters, and the resulting identifiers are subscripted with j.

Behavior of a simulator q_i. Each simulator is given the code of all the simulated processes p_1, ..., $p_{n'}$. It manages n' threads, one associated with each simulated process, and executes them in a fair way.

The code of a simulated process p_j contains local statements, send statements, and receive statements. It is assumed that the behavior of a simulated process p_j is deterministic in the sense it is entirely defined from its local input (as defined by the task instance), and the order in which p_j receives messages.

The simulation has to ensure that (1) all correct simulators simulate the same behavior of the set of simulated processes, and (2) f faulty simulators entail the failure of at most f simulated processes.

4   BG in the Byzantine Message-Passing Model

This section presents the algorithm BG(MP,B). As previously indicated, this algorithm implements the BG simulation in the Byzantine asynchronous message-passing model $\mathcal{BAMP}_{n,t}[t < n/3]$. To this end, an appropriate safe agreement object is first built, and then used by the simulation algorithm. A simpler simulation BG(MP,C), implementing the BG simulation in the crash failure-prone asynchronous message-passing model $\mathcal{CAMP}_{n,t}[t < n/2]$, is presented in the full version of the paper. It is based on the same general mechanism as BG(MP,B) and may be used as an introduction to it. Due to page limitations, it is not presented here.

From Byzantine Behaviors to Crash Failures. The aim is to obtain a simulation algorithm that copes with Byzantine simulators. To this end, the main issues that have to be solved are the following.

- The simulators need a mechanism to control the validity of the inputs to the safe agreement objects. (See below for the notion of a valid value.)
- The simulators must be able to check if a given simulator q_i is participating in more than one operation propose() at the same time (on the same or several safe agreement objects). If it is the case, q_i is faulty and its definitive stop can block forever several simulated processes. Hence, such a faulty simulator has to be ignored.

To solve these issues, differently from the original BG simulation, each safe agreement object may no longer be considered as a separate abstraction: each new instance depends on the previous ones. This is captured in the following specification customized to the Byzantine model, and, at the operational level, in the predicate valid() used in the algorithm implementing the operation propose().

4.1 Safe Agreement in $\mathcal{BAMP}_{n,t}[t < n/3]$: Definition

To cope with the previous observations, the fact that a faulty process may decide an arbitrary value, and the fact that the safe agreement objects are used to solve specific problems (a simulation in our case), the specification of the safe agreement object is reshaped as follows.

A value proposed by a process to a safe agreement object must be *valid*. At each correct simulator q_i, the validity of a value is captured by a predicate denoted $\mathsf{valid}_i(j, v)$ where v is the value and q_j the simulator that proposed it. This predicate is made up of two parts (defined in Sects. 4.2 and 4.3, respectively). If q_j is correct, the predicate $\mathsf{valid}_i(j, v)$ eventually returns *true* at p_i. If q_j is faulty, $\mathsf{valid}_i(j, v)$ returns *true* at p_i only if (a) the value v could have been proposed by a correct simulator and (b) to q_i's knowledge, q_j does not participate concurrently in several invocations of propose().

- Validity. If a correct simulator q_i decides the value v, there is a correct simulator q_j such that $\mathsf{valid}_j(-, v)$. (v was validated by a correct simulator.)
- Agreement. No two correct simulators decide distinct values.
- Propose-Termination. Any invocation of propose() by a correct simulator terminates.
- Decide-Termination. The invocations by all the correct simulators of decide() on all the safe agreement objects terminate, except for at most t of them.

4.2 Safe Agreement in $\mathcal{BAMP}_{n,t}[t < n/3]$: Algorithm

An algorithm implementing a safe agreement object in $\mathcal{BAMP}_{n,t}[t < n/3]$ is described in Figs. 1 and 2.

Local data structures. Each simulator q_i, $1 \leq i \leq n$, manages four local data structures, namely, the arrays $values_i[1..n]$, $my\_view_i[1..n]$, $all\_views_i[1..n]$, all initialized to $[\bot, ..., \bot]$, where $\bot$ denotes a default value that cannot be proposed to the safe agreement object by the simulators, and $answers_i[1..n][1..n][1..n]$, all entries of which are initialized to a default value "?" that cannot be the content of a message.

- The aim of $values_i[x]$ is to contain, as currently known by q_i, the value proposed to the safe agreement object by the simulator q_x.
- The aim of $my\_view_i[x]$ is to contain, as known by q_i, the value proposed to the safe agreement object by the simulator q_x, as witnessed by strictly more than $\frac{n}{2}$ distinct simulators (i.e., at least a correct process).
- The aim of $all\_views_i[x]$ is to contain what q_i knows about the view of q_x.
- The meaning of "$answers_i[k][j][x] = v$" (where v is a proposed value or $\bot$) is the following: to the knowledge of q_i, the simulator q_k answered value v when it received the message READ(j, x) sent by q_j. (A simulator q_j broadcasts such a message when it needs to know the value proposed by the simulator q_x; $\bot$ means that q_k does not know this value yet.) This means that, from q_i's point of view, the value proposed by q_x, as known by q_k when it received the request by q_j, is v.

```
operation propose (v_i) is
(B01)   broadcast VALUE (i, v_i);
(B02)   wait (VALUE'ACK (i, v_i) received from > (n+t)/2 different simulators);
(B03)   for each x ∈ [1..n] do broadcast READ (i, x) end for;
(B04)   for each x ∈ [1..n] do
(B05)       wait (((|{k : answers_i[k][i][x] = ⊥}| > (n+t)/2) ∨
(B06)           ( ∃ w : VALUE'ACK (x, w) received from > (n+t)/2 different simulators));
(B07)       if (predicate of line B06 satisfied)
(B08)           then my_view_i[x] ← w
(B09)           else  my_view_i[x] ← ⊥
(B10)       end if
(B11)   end for;
(B12)   broadcast VIEW (i, my_view_i);
(B13)   wait (VIEW'ACK (i, my_view_i) received from > (n+t)/2 different simulators);
(B14)   return().
operation decide () is
(B15)   wait (∃ a non-empty set σ ⊆ Π: ∀ y ∈ σ :
(B16)       [(all_views_i[y] ≠ ⊥) ∧ (∀ z ∈ Π : (all_views_i[y][z] ≠ ⊥) ⇒ (z ∈ σ))]);
(B17)   let min_σ_i be the set σ of smallest size;
(B18)   let res be min({values_i[y] : y ∈ min_σ_i});
(B19)   return(res).
```

Fig. 1. Safe agreement object in $\mathcal{BAMP}_{n,t}[t < n/3]$: client side of simulator q_i

Lemma 1. *Any two sets of simulators Q_1 and Q_2 of more than $\frac{n+t}{2}$ elements have at least one correct simulator in their intersection.*

The fact that, despite Byzantine processes, the intersection of any two simulator sets of size greater than $\frac{n+t}{2}$ have at least one correct simulator in common, is used in many places in the algorithm. This property is used in the proof to show that the local views of the correct processes are mutually consistent.

The operation propose(). The client side of the algorithm implementing the operation propose() is described in Fig. 1; its server side is described in Fig. 2. This algorithm is made up of three parts.

First part: messages VALUE, VALUE'VALID, VALUE'WITNESS *and* VALUE'ACK When a simulator q_i invokes the operation propose(v_i), it first broadcasts the message VALUE (i, v_i), and waits for $\frac{n+t}{2}$ acknowledgments (messages VALUE'ACK(i, v_i), lines B01-B02). Then, it builds its local view of the values proposed to the safe agreement object (lines B03-B11). Finally, it sends its local view to all other simulators (lines B12-B13).

On its server side, when a simulator q_i receives a message VALUE (j, v), it first checks if this message is valid (line B20). If the message is valid, q_i broadcasts (echoes) the message VALUE'VALID (j, v) to inform the other simulators that it agrees to take into account the pair (j, v) (line B20).

when the message VALUE (j, v) **is received from** q_j **for the first time:**
(B20) **wait** $(\text{valid}_i(j, v))$; broadcast VALUE'VALID (j, v).
when the message VALUE'VALID (j, v) **is received:**
(B21) **if** ((VALUE'VALID (j, v) received from $> \frac{n+t}{2}$ different simulators)
(B22) $\wedge$ (VALUE'WITNESS $(j, -)$ never broadcast))
(B23)   **then** broadcast VALUE'WITNESS (j, v) **end if.**
when the message VALUE'WITNESS (j, v) **is received:**
(B24) **if** ((VALUE'WITNESS (j, v) received from $t + 1$ different simulators)
(B25) $\wedge$ (VALUE'WITNESS (j, v) never broadcast))
(B26)   **then** broadcast VALUE'WITNESS (j, v) **end if**;
(B27) **if** (VALUE'WITNESS (j, v) received from $> \frac{n+t}{2}$ different simulators)
(B28)   **then** $values_i[j] \leftarrow v$; broadcast VALUE'ACK (j, v) **end if.**

---

when the message READ (j, x) **is received from** q_j **for the first time:**
(B29) **wait** (VALUE'ACK (j, v) received from $> \frac{n+t}{2}$ different simulators);
(B30) $values_i[j] \leftarrow v$; broadcast VALUE'ACK (j, v);
(B31) broadcast READ'ANSWER $(j, x, values_i[x])$.
when the message READ'ANSWER (j, x, v) **received from** q_k **for the first time:**
(B32) **if** (READ'ANSWER'WITNESS $(k, j, x, -)$ never broadcast)
(B33)   **then** broadcast READ'ANSWER'WITNESS (k, j, x, v) **end if.**
when the message READ'ANSWER'WITNESS (k, j, x, v) **is received:**
(B34) **if** ((READ'ANSWER'WITNESS (k, j, x, v) received from $t + 1$ diff. simulators)
(B35) $\wedge$ (READ'ANSWER'WITNESS (k, j, x, v) never broadcast))
(B36)   **then** broadcast READ'ANSWER'WITNESS (k, j, x, v) **end if**;
(B37) **if** (READ'ANSWER'WITNESS (k, j, x, v) received from $> \frac{n+t}{2}$ diff. simulators)
(B38)   **then** $answers_i[k][j][x] \leftarrow v$ **end if.**

---

when the message VIEW $(j, view)$ **is received from** q_j **for the first time:**
(B39) **if** ((VIEW'WITNESS $(j, -)$ never broadcast) $\wedge$ $(view[j] \neq \perp)$) **then**
(B40)   **for** $x \in [1..n]$ **do**
(B41)   **if** $(view[x] \neq \perp)$
(B42)   **then wait** (VALUE'ACK $(x, view[x])$ rec. from $> \frac{n+t}{2}$ diff. simulators)
(B43)   **else wait** $(|\{k \ : \ answers_i[k][j][x] = \perp\}| > \frac{n+t}{2})$ **end if end for**;
(B44)   broadcast VIEW'WITNESS $(j, view)$ **end if.**
when the message VIEW'WITNESS $(j, view)$ **is received:**
(B45) **if** ((VIEW'WITNESS $(j, view)$ received from $t + 1$ different simulators)
(B46) $\wedge$ (VIEW'WITNESS $(j, view)$ never broadcast))
(B47)   **then** broadcast VIEW'WITNESS $(j, view)$ **end if**;
(B48) **if** (VIEW'WITNESS $(j, view)$ received from $> \frac{n+t}{2}$ different simulators)
(B49)   **then** $all\_views_i[j] \leftarrow view$; send VIEW'ACK $(j, view)$ to q_j **end if.**

Fig. 2. Safe agreement object in $\mathcal{BAMP}_{n,t}[t < n/3]$: server side of simulator q_i

When the simulator p_i has received the message VALUE'VALID (j, v) from more than $\frac{n+t}{2}$ simulators, it broadcasts the message VALUE'WITNESS (j, v) to inform the other processes that at least $\frac{n+t}{2} - t = \frac{n-t}{2} \geq t + 1$ correct simulators, have validated the pair (j, v).

When q_i has received the message VALUE'WITNESS (j, v) from $(t + 1)$ simulators (i.e., from at least one correct simulator) it broadcasts this message, if not yet done (lines B24-B26). This is to prevent invocations of propose() from blocking forever (while waiting VALUE'ACK (j, v) messages at line B02, B06, B29 or B42), because not enough VALUE'WITNESS (j, v) messages have been broadcast. Then, if q_i has received the message VALUE'WITNESS (j, v) from more than $\frac{n+t}{2}$ simulators, it takes v into account (writes it into $values_i[j]$) and sends an acknowledgment to q_j (lines B27-B28). The corresponding message VALUE'ACK (j, v) broadcast by q_i will also inform the other simulators that q_i took into account the value v proposed by q_j. Hence, this message will help q_j progress at line B02, and all correct simulators progress at line B06.

First part of the predicate valid$_i(j, v)$ As already indicated, the aim of this predicate is to help a simulator q_i detect if the value v proposed by the simulator q_j is valid. It is always satisfied when q_j is correct, and it can return *true* or *false* when q_j is faulty. It is made up of two sub-predicates $P1$ and $P2$.

- The first sub-predicate $P1$ checks if, for the messages VALUE $(j, -)$ (from q_j) and VALUE'VALID $(j, -)$ (from more than $t+1$ different simulators) that q_i has received for other safe agreement objects, q_i has also received the associated messages VIEW'WITNESS $(j, -)$ from at least $(n - t)$ different simulators. This allows q_i to check if the simulator q_j is not simultaneously participating in other invocations of propose() on other safe agreement objects.
- The aim of the second sub-predicate $P2$ (defined in Sect. 4.3 and used in the simulation) is to allow the simulators to check that the simulation is consistent. As the present section considers safe agreement objects independently from its use in the simulation, we consider, for now, that $P2$ is always satisfied.

If the full predicate valid$_i(j, v)$ is never satisfied, q_i will, collectively with the other correct simulators, prevent the faulty simulator q_j from progressing with respect to the corresponding safe agreement object.

Second part: messages READ, READ'ANSWER *and* READ'ANSWER'WITNESS After the value v_i it proposes to the safe agreement object has been taken into account by $\frac{n+t}{2}$ simulators, q_i builds a local view of all the values proposed (array $my\_view_i[1..n]$). To this end, for each simulator q_x, q_i broadcasts the message READ (i, x) (line B03). It then waits until either $|\{k \quad : \quad answers_i[k][i][x] = \bot\}| > \frac{n+t}{2}$ is satisfied (line B05) or there is a value w such that it has received VALUE'ACK (x, w) from more than $\frac{n+t}{2}$ processes (line B06). The predicate $|\{k \quad : \quad answers_i[k][i][x] = \bot\}| > \frac{n+t}{2}$ states that more than $\frac{n+t}{2}$ simulators answered $\bot$ to the request message READ (i, x) broadcast by q_i, i.e., they did not know the value proposed by q_x when they received the read request.

When q_i receives the message READ (j, x) from the simulator q_j, it first waits until it knows that the value proposed by q_j is known by more than $\frac{n+t}{2}$ simulators (line B29). This is to check that q_j broadcast its proposed value before reading the other simulator values used to build its own view. When this occurs, q_i answers the message READ (j, x) by broadcasting the message READ'ANSWER $(j, x, values_i[x])$ to inform all the simulators on what it currently knows on the value proposed by q_x (line B31).

When it receives READ'ANSWER (j, x, v) from a simulator q_k, if not yet done, q_i broadcasts READ'ANSWER'WITNESS (k, j, x, v). The lines B32-B36 implement a reliable broadcast, i.e., the message READ'ANSWER'WITNESS (k, j, x, v) is received by all correct processes or none of them, and is always received if the sender is correct. The reliable reception of this message entails the assignment of $answer_i[k, j, x]$ to v (line B38).

Third part: messages VIEW, VIEW'WITNESS *and* VIEW'ACK Finally, the simulator q_i broadcasts its local view of proposed values to all simulators, waits until more than $\frac{n+t}{2}$ of them sent back an acknowledgment, and returns from the invocation of propose() (lines B12-B14).

When q_i receives for the first time the message VIEW $(j, view)$, it realizes an enriched reliable broadcast whose aim is to assign $view$ to $all\_view_i[j]$. Let us first observe that if $view[j] = \bot$, then q_j is Byzantine. If it has not yet broadcast the message VIEW'WITNESS $(j, view)$ and if $view[j] \neq \bot$ (line B39), q_i first checks if all the values in $view[1..n]$ are consistent. From its point of view, this means that, for each simulator q_x, (a) if $view[x] = v$, it must receive messages VALUE'ACK (x, v) from more than $\frac{n+t}{2}$ simulators, and (b) if $view[x] == \bot$, the same predicate as in line B05 must become satisfied. This consistency check is realized by the lines B40-B43.

Finally, when q_i receives a message VIEW'WITNESS $(j, view)$, it does the following. First, if it has received this message from at least one correct simulator, and has not yet broadcast it, q_i does it (lines B45-B47). This part of the reliable broadcast is to prevent the correct simulators from blocking forever. Then, if it has received VIEW'WITNESS $(j, view)$ from more than $\frac{n+t}{2}$ simulators and has not yet assigned a value to $all\_view_i[j]$, q_i does it and sends the acknowledgment VIEW'ACK $(j, view)$ to q_j to inform it that it knows its view (lines B48-B49).

Algorithm: the operation decide() The algorithm implementing the operation decide() is described at lines B15-B19. It consists in a "closure" computation. A simulator q_i waits until it knows a non-empty set of simulators σ such that (a) it knows their views, and (b) this set is closed under the relation "has in its published view the value of" which means that the processes whose values appear in a view of a process of σ are also in σ (lines B15-B16).

Let us observe that it is possible that, locally, several sets satisfy this property. If it is the case, q_i selects the smallest of them. Let min_σ_i be this set of simulators (lines B17). The value that is returned by q_i is then the smallest value among the the values proposed by the simulators in min_σ_i (lines B18-B19).

Theorem 1. *The algorithms described in Figs. 1 and 2 implement a safe-agreement object in* $\mathcal{BAMP}_{n,t}[t < n/3]$.

4.3   Simulation Algorithm in $\mathcal{BAMP}_{n,t}[t < n/3]$

The algorithm takes as input a distributed algorithm A solving a (colorless) task in the system model $\mathcal{CAMP}_{n',t}[t < n']$, and simulates it in $\mathcal{BAMP}_{n,t}[t < n/3]$. Each simulator q_i, $1 \leq i \leq n$, is given a copy of the n' processes of A, and a private input vector $input_i[1..n']$, with one input per simulated processes p_j.

The simulation consists in a fair simulation by each of the correct simulators q_i of the n' simulated processes p_j. To that end, each simulator manages n' threads (each simulating a process p_j), and the n threads associated with the simulation of a process p_j cooperate through safe agreement objects.

Objects shared by the simulators. To produce a consistent simulation, for each simulated process p_j, the correct simulators have to agree on the same sequence of the messages received by p_j. To that end, they use an array of safe agreement objects, denoted $SA[1..n', -]$, such that $SA[j, sn]$ allows them to agree on the sn-th message received by the n' threads simulating p_j at each simulator q_i.

Objects managed by each simulator q_i. Each simulator manages the following data structures, with respect to each simulated process p_j.

- $input_i[j]$ contains the input of the simulated process p_j, proposed by the simulator q_i. (Simulators are allowed to propose different input vectors for the simulated processes).
- $sn_i[j]$ is the sequence number (from the simulation point of view) of the next message received by the simulated process p_j.
- $sent_i[j]$ is a sequence containing messages sent by the simulated processes to the simulated process p_j. It is assumed that the n' threads of q_i access $sent_i[j]$ in mutual exclusion (when they add messages to or withdraw messages from this sequence). The symbol $\oplus$ is used to add messages at the end of a sequence. Sometimes $sent_i[j]$ is used as a set.
- $received_i[j]$ is a set containing the messages received by p_j (init. $\emptyset$).
- $state_i[j]$ contains the current local state of p_j. $input_i[j]$ is a part of $state_i[j]$. It is assumed that the behavior of each simulated process p_j is described by a deterministic transition function $\delta_j()$, such that $\delta_j(state_i[j], msg)$ (a) simulates p_j until its next message reception, and (b) returns a pair. This pair is made up of the new local state of p_j plus an array $msgs[1..n']$ where $msgs[x]$ contains messages sent by p_j to the simulated process p_x.

In addition to the previous local data, each simulator q_i uses a starvation-free mutual exclusion lock, whose operations are denoted $\mathsf{mutex\_in}_i()$ and $\mathsf{mutex\_out}_i()$. This lock is used to ensure that, at any time, at most one of the n' threads of q_i access a safe agreement object. Because correct simulators never invoke two $\mathsf{propose}()$ operations concurrently, a Byzantine simulator can be prevented from blocking forever more than one safe agreement object, by forcing it to simulate a correct behavior and to finish its participation in such an object before it can participate in another one (sub-predicate $P1$ of $\mathsf{valid}_i(j, v)$).

```
(01)   mutex_in_i(); SA[j, 0].propose(input_i[j]); mutex_out_i();
(02)   input_i[j] ← SA[j, 0].decide();
(03)   ⟨state_i[j], msgs[1..n']⟩ ← δ_j(state_i[j], ∅);
(04)   for each x ∈ {1, ..., n'} do sent_i[x] ← sent_i[x] ⊕ msgs[x] end for;
(05)   sn_i[j] ← 0;
(06)   repeat forever
(07)       sn_i[j] ← sn_i[j] + 1;
(08)       wait ((sent_i[j] \ received_i[j]) ≠ ∅);
(09)       msg ← oldest message in sent_i[j] \ received_i[j];
(10)       mutex_in_i(); SA[j, sn_i[j]].propose.(msg); mutex_out_i();
(11)       rec_msg ← SA[j, sn_i[j]].decide();
(12)       received_i[j] ← received_i[j] ∪ {rec_msg};
(13)       ⟨state_i[j], msgs[1..n']⟩ ← δ_j(state_i[j], rec_msg);
(14)       for each x ∈ {1, ..., n'} do sent_i[x] ← sent_i[x] ⊕ msgs[x] end for;
(15)       if (no value yet decided by p_j ∧ state_i[j] allows p_j to decide a value v)
(16)           then the simulated process p_j decides v end if end repeat.
```

Fig. 3. Thread of the simulator q_i, $1 \leq i \leq n$, simulating the process p_j, $1 \leq j \leq n'$

The simulation algorithm. The algorithm describing the simulation of a process p_j by the associated thread of the correct simulator q_i is presented in Fig. 3.

The simulators first have to agree on the same input for process p_j. To this end, they use the safe agreement object $SA[j, 0]$ (lines 01-02). Moreover, when considering all the simulated processes, it follows from the mutual exclusion lock that, whatever the number of simulated processes, a correct simulator q_i is engaged in at most one invocation of propose() at a time. Then, according to the decided input of p_j, q_i locally simulates p_j until it invokes a message emission (lines 03-04).

After this initialization, each correct simulator q_i enters a loop whose aim is to locally simulate p_j. To this end, q_i first determines the message that p_j will receive; this message is saved in rec_msg and added to $received_i[j]$ (lines 07-12). When this message has been determined, q_i simulates the behavior of p_j until its next message reception (lines 13-14). Finally, if $state_i[j]$ allows p_j to decide a value with respect to the simulated decision task, this value is decided (lines 15-17).

Sub-predicate P2. As far as $P2$ is concerned we have the following. Let us consider the simulator q_i that invokes $valid_i(j, v)$, with respect to the simulation of a process p_x. In the simulation algorithm, the parameter v is the message msg that q_j proposes to a safe agreement object from which will be decided the next message to be received by the simulated process p_x (lines 08-09 of Fig. 3). $P2$ checks, from q_i's local point of view, that the message v has been sent in the simulation and that it has not yet been consumed, i.e., $(v \in sent_i[x]) \wedge (v \notin received_i[x])$.

Theorem 2. *Let A be an algorithm solving a decision task in $\mathcal{CAMP}_{n',t}[t < n']$. The algorithm described in Fig. 3, in which Byzantine-tolerant safe agreement objects are used, is a correct simulation of A in $\mathcal{BAMP}_{n,t}[t < n/3]$.*

The reader can easily check that simulating a message only requires a polynomial number of messages in the base system, and the increase in size of these messages, when compared to the size of the simulated message, is also polynomial.

5   Implications of the Simulation

From Byzantine-failures to crash failures in message-passing systems. The signature-free simulation presented here allows the execution of a t-resilient crash-tolerant algorithm in an asynchronous message-passing system where up to t processes may be Byzantine. A feature that is sometimes required from a Byzantine-tolerant algorithm solving a task (not usually considered in the crash failure case) is that the value decided by any correct process should be based only on inputs of correct processes. This prevents Byzantine processes from "polluting" the computation with their inputs. A way to guarantee that an input has been proposed by a correct process is to check that it has been proposed by at least $(t + 1)$ different processes. Assuming that in any execution at most m values are proposed, this constraint translates as $n - t > mt$ [6,10].

In the case of the simulation presented in Sect. 4, this requirement can easily be satisfied by adding a first step of computation before the start of the simulation. Simulators first broadcast their input. They then echo every value that they receive from more than $t + 1$ different simulators, and consider these values (and only these values) as valid inputs. An input considered valid by a correct simulator is then eventually considered valid by all correct simulators, and the only inputs allowed in the simulation are inputs of correct simulators. Because we consider colorless tasks, the choice of output is done in the same way as in the original BG-simulation: a simulator can adopt the output of any simulated process that has decided a value.

The possible Byzantine behaviors are restrained by the underlying Byzantine-tolerant safe agreement objects used in the simulation. Surprisingly, this shows that, from the point of view of the computability of colorless tasks and assuming $n > (m + 1)t$ (this requirement always implies $n > 3t$ when at least two different values can be proposed), Byzantine failures are equivalent to crash-failures. This provides us with a new understanding of Byzantine failures and shows that their impact can be restricted to the much simpler crash-failure case.

From wait-free shared memory to message-passing. The proposed simulation can be combined with previous works to further extend the scope of the result.

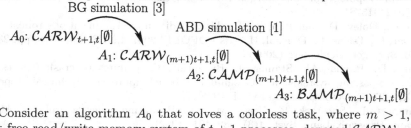

Consider an algorithm A_0 that solves a colorless task, where $m > 1$, in a wait-free read/write memory system of $t + 1$ processes, denoted $\mathcal{CARW}_{t+1,t}[\emptyset]$.

Using the basic BG-simulation [3], this algorithm can be transformed into an algorithm A_1 that works in the t-resilient read/write memory system of $(m + 1)t + 1$ processes, in which at most t can crash. This model is denoted $\mathcal{CARW}_{(m+1)t+1,t}[\emptyset]$. Using an implementation of a read/write memory in a crash-prone message-passing system in which a majority of processes are correct [1], we obtain an algorithm A_2 which work in $\mathcal{CAMP}_{(m+1)t+1,t}[\emptyset]$ (message-passing system of $(m+1)t+1$ processes, in which at most t can crash; notice that $m > 0 \Rightarrow (m+1)t+1 > 2t$). Finally, using the simulation presented in this paper, we obtain a Byzantine-tolerant algorithm A_3 which works in $\mathcal{BAMP}_{(m+1)t+1,t}[\emptyset]$ (message-passing system of $(m + 1)t + 1$ processes, of which at most t can be Byzantine; notice that $m > 1 \Rightarrow (m + 1)t + 1 > 3t$).

These transformations show that, as far as the computability of colorless tasks that admit up to $m > 1$ different input values is concerned, an n-process Byzantine-prone message-passing system, in which up to $t < n/(m + 1)$ processes can be Byzantine, is equivalent to a wait-free shared memory system of $t + 1$ processes, which at most commit crash failures. Differently from the full-information algorithm presented in [10], the simulation presented in the present paper (along with [3] and [1]) allows a *direct* transformation of any wait-free shared-memory algorithm that solves a colorless task into a message-passing Byzantine-tolerant algorithm.

References

1. Attiya, H., Bar-Noy, A., Dolev, D.: Sharing memory robustly in message passing systems. J. ACM **42**(1), 121–132 (1995)
2. Bazzi, R., Neiger, G.: Optimally simulating crash failures in a byzantine environment. In: Toueg, S., Spirakis, P.G., Kirousis, L. (eds.) Distributed Algorithms. LNCS, vol. 579, pp. 108–128. Springer, Heidelberg (1991)
3. Borowsky, E., Gafni, E.: Generalized FLP impossibility results for t-resilient asynchronous computations. In: Proceedings 25th ACM STOC, pp. 91–100. ACM Press (1993)
4. Coan, B.A.: A compiler that increases the fault-tolerance of asynchronous protocols. IEEE Trans. Comput. **37**(12), 1541–1553 (1988)
5. Dolev, D., Gafni, E.: Some garbage in - some garbage out,: asynchronous t-Byzantine as asynchronous benign t-resilient system with fixed t-Trojan horse inputs. Tech Report, arXiv, 14 p., July 2016. arXiv:1607.01210
6. Herlihy, M.P., Kozlov, D., Rajsbaum, S.: Distributed Computing through Combinatorial Topology, p. 336. Morgan Kaufmann/Elsevier, New York (2014). (ISBN 9780124045781)
7. Ho, C., Dolev, D., van Renesse, R.: Making distributed applications robust. In: Tovar, E., Tsigas, P., Fouchal, H. (eds.) OPODIS 2007. LNCS, vol. 4878, pp. 232–246. Springer, Heidelberg (2007)
8. Imbs, D., Raynal, M., Stainer, J., Byzantine, F.: Failures to crash failures in message-passing systems: a BG simulation-based approach. Technical Report, arXiv, 27 p., October 2015. arXiv:1510.09119
9. Lamport, L., Shostack, R., Pease, M.: The Byzantine generals problem. ACM Trans. Program. Lang. Syst. **4**(3), 382–401 (1982)

10. Mendes, H., Tasson Ch., Herlihy, M.: Distributed computability in Byzantine asynchronous systems. In: Proceedings 46th STOC, pp. 704–713. ACM Press (2014)
11. Neiger, G., Toueg, S.: Automatically increasing the fault-tolerance of distributed algorithms. J. Algorithms **11**(3), 374–419 (1990)
12. Srikanth, T.K., Toueg, S.: Simulating authenticated broadcasts to derive simple fault-tolerant algorithms. Distributed Comput. **2**(2), 80–94 (1987)

Sublinear-Space Distance Labeling Using Hubs

Paweł Gawrychowski[1], Adrian Kosowski[2], and Przemysław Uznański[3(✉)]

[1] Institute of Informatics, University of Warsaw, Warsaw, Poland
[2] Inria Paris and IRIF, Université Paris Diderot, Paris, France
[3] Department of Computer Science, ETH Zürich, Zürich, Switzerland
przemyslaw.uznanski@inf.ethz.ch

Abstract. A distance labeling scheme is an assignment of bit-labels to the vertices of an undirected, unweighted graph such that the distance between any pair of vertices can be decoded solely from their labels. We propose a series of new labeling schemes within the framework of so-called hub labeling (HL, also known as landmark labeling or 2-hop-cover labeling), in which each node u stores its distance to all nodes from an appropriately chosen set of hubs $S(u) \subseteq V$. For a queried pair of nodes (u, v), the length of a shortest u–v-path passing through a hub node from $S(u) \cap S(v)$ is then used as an upper bound on the distance between u and v.

We present a hub labeling which allows us to decode exact distances in sparse graphs using labels of size sublinear in the number of nodes. For graphs with at most n nodes and average degree Δ, the tradeoff between label bit size L and query decoding time T for our approach is given by $L = \mathcal{O}(n \log \log_\Delta T / \log_\Delta T)$, for any $T \leq n$. Our simple approach is thus the first sublinear-space distance labeling for sparse graphs that simultaneously admits small decoding time (for constant Δ, we can achieve any $T = \omega(1)$ while maintaining $L = o(n)$), and it also provides an improvement in terms of label size with respect to previous slower approaches.

By using similar techniques, we then present a 2-additive labeling scheme for general graphs, i.e., one in which the decoder provides a 2-additive-approximation of the distance between any pair of nodes. We achieve almost the same label size-time tradeoff $L = \mathcal{O}(n \log^2 \log T / \log T)$, for any $T \leq n$. To our knowledge, this is the first additive scheme with constant absolute error to use labels of sublinear size. The corresponding decoding time is then small (any $T = \omega(1)$ is sufficient).

We believe all of our techniques are of independent value and provide a desirable simplification of previous approaches.

1 Introduction

Distance labeling schemes, popularized by Gavoille et al. [16], are among the most fundamental distributed data structures for graph data. The design problem combines two major challenges. First of all, distance labelings serve the role of a *distance oracle*, i.e., a data structure which for a given undirected graph

© Springer-Verlag Berlin Heidelberg 2016
C. Gavoille and D. Ilcinkas (Eds.): DISC 2016, LNCS 9888, pp. 230–242, 2016.
DOI: 10.1007/978-3-662-53426-7_17

$G = (V, E)$ can answer queries of the form: "what is the distance between the nodes $s, t \in V$?". Throughout most of this paper, we will assume that G is an unweighted graph with n nodes and m edges. The efficiency of a distance oracle is measured by the interplay between the *space* requirement of the data structure representation, the *encoding time* required to set up the oracle for a given graph, and perhaps more importantly, its *decoding time*, that is, the time of processing a $s - t$ distance query. Moreover, a distance labeling scheme is defined more restrictively than a distance oracle, as an assignment of a binary string (label) label(u) to each node $u \in V$, so that the graph distance between u and v is uniquely determined by the pair of labels: label(u) and label(v). The *size* of a distance labeling scheme is now the maximum length of a node label in the graph. In this way, distance labelings add an extra layer of complexity to the graph distance decoding problem, by imposing a distributed representation of information in the labels (label(u) : $u \in V$). Whereas the concatenation of all n labels in a distance labeling forms a centralized distance oracle, distance labelings can also be applied in a distributed setting, in which the label of each node is stored at a distinct location in the network. This is the case, for instance, in applications in compact routing protocols, where the goal is to find a shortest path from a source node to a target node with a known label [12].

An interesting characteristic of the problem of distance oracle design for sparse graph is its inherent link to an underlying set intersection task. On the side of lower bounds, this is most clearly observed, following Pătraşcu and Roditty [21], when we consider a pair of vertices belonging to the same partition of a bipartite graph. The distance between them is 2 if and only if the sets of their neighbors intersect, and at least 4 otherwise. Consequently, assuming a plausible conjecture on the space required to decide intersection of a set of small sets, it follows that any oracle for graphs with $\widetilde{O}(1)$ maximum degree, which admits constant decoding time, requires $\widetilde{\Omega}(n^2)$ space. (Here, the $\widetilde{O}$ and $\widetilde{\Omega}$ notation disregards polylogarithmic factors in n.) By contrast, many efficient algorithms for answering distance queries in real-world scenarios rely on the premise that the distance between a pair of nodes can be computed using an intersection-type query on a pair of small sets. In the basic framework of hub labelings, see [1], (introduced in [13] under the name of 2-hop covers, and also referred to as landmark labelings [3]), each node $u \in U$ stores the set of its distances to some subset $S(u) \subseteq V$ of other nodes of the graph. Then, the computed distance value $\delta'(u, v)$ for a queried pair of nodes $u, v \in V$ is returned as:

$$\delta'(u, v) := \min_{w \in S(u) \cap S(v)} \delta(u, w) + \delta(w, v), \tag{1}$$

where δ denotes the shortest path distance function between a pair of nodes. The computed distance between all pairs of nodes u and v is exact if set $S(u) \cap S(v)$ contains at least one node on some shortest $u-v$ path. This property of the family of sets $(S(u) : u \in V)$ is known as *shortest path cover*. The hub-based method of distance computation is in practice effective for two reasons. First of all, for transportation-type networks it is possible to show bounds on the sizes of sets S, which follow from the network structure. Notably, Abraham et al. [2] introduce the notion of highway dimension h of a network, which is presumed to be a small constant e.g. for road networks, and show that an appropriate cover of all shortest paths in the graph can be achieved using sets S of size $\widetilde{\mathcal{O}}(h)$. Moreover, the order in which elements of sets $S(u)$ and $S(v)$ is browsed when performing the minimum operation is relevant, and in some schemes, the operation can be interrupted once it is certain that the minimum has been found, before probing all elements of the set. This is the principle of numerous heuristics for the exact shortest-path problem, such as contraction hierarchies and algorithms with arc flags [9,18].

In this work, we make use of the hub set techniques to obtain better (distributed) distance labelings. Whereas $\Omega(n)$ is a lower bound of the size of a hub set for general graphs, we provide hub-based schemes using smaller sets for specific case, leading to labels which can be encoded on $o(n)$ bits. Our scheme provides a shortest-path cover in the class of sparse graphs (with average degree $\Delta = 2m/n$ subpolynomial in n). This construction is overviewed in more detail in Sect. 1.2.

The implications of our result can be seen as twofold. First of all, our approach directly leads to labeling of smaller size (and smaller decoding time) for exact distance queries in sparse graphs than all previous distance labeling approaches. Additionally, an corollary of our result concerns the case of k-*additive* approximate distance labeling, in which the distance decoder is required to return an upper bound on the shortest path length which is within an additive factor of at most k from the optimum. So far, no way to construct k-additive distance labels using labels of sublinear size in n was known for any constant $k > 0$. (This question was considered previously in, e.g., [7]). We provide a way to construct a 2-additive distance labeling in general graphs using distance labels of size $o(n)$. (This result is essentially the best possible, since a 1-additive distance labeling requires distance labels of size at least $n/4$ already on the class of bipartite graphs.)

In our approaches, the size of the obtained distance labels for the considered cases is improved with respect to the state-of-the-art by up to a logarithmic multiplicative factor. Rather than seeing this as "gaining" a logarithm, we rather see this as "not losing" a logarithm. Indeed, the basic ingredient of the hub sets in previous approaches was a subset of nodes, sampled independently at random from V [6,10]. The constructions then relied on the probabilistic method to guarantee that the hubs would have the shortest-path cover properties, based on the premise that for each pair of nodes the constructed hubs provide a shortest path cover with sufficiently high probability. The derandomization of this process resulted in a loss of a logarithmic factor in the analysis of the size of labels. Our approach shows how to avoid this issue: when constructing labelings for sparse graphs, we do away with randomization altogether, relying on simple structural results to replace the random subset of nodes.

1.1   Related Work

Distance Labelings. The distance labeling problem in undirected graphs was first investigated by Graham and Pollak [17], who provided the first labeling scheme with labels of size $\mathcal{O}(n)$. The decoding time for labels of size $\mathcal{O}(n)$ was subsequently improved to $\mathcal{O}(\log\log n)$ by Gavoille et al. [16] and to $\mathcal{O}(\log^* n)$ by Weimann and Peleg [25]. Finally, Alstrup et al. [7] present a scheme for general graphs with decoding in $\mathcal{O}(1)$ time using labels of size $\frac{\log 3}{2} n + o(n)$ bits.[1] This matches up to low order terms the space of the currently best known distance oracle with $\mathcal{O}(1)$ time and $\frac{\log 3}{2} n^2 + o(n^2)$ total space in a *centralized* memory model, due to Nitto and Venturini [19].

The notion of D-preserving distance labeling, first introduced by Bollobás et al. [10], describes a labeling scheme correctly encoding every distance that is at least D. [10] presents such a D-preserving scheme of size $\mathcal{O}(\frac{n}{D} \log^2 n)$. This was recently improved by Alstrup et al. [6] to a D-preserving scheme of size $\mathcal{O}(\frac{n}{D} \log^2 D)$. Together with an observation that all distances smaller than D can be stored directly, this results in a labeling scheme of size $\mathcal{O}(\frac{n}{R} \log^2 R)$, where $R = \frac{\log n}{\log \frac{m+n}{n}}$. For sparse graphs, this is $o(n)$.

For specific classes of graphs, Gavoille et al. [16] described a $\mathcal{O}(\sqrt{n} \log n)$ distance labeling for planar graphs, together with $\Omega(n^{1/3})$ lower bound for the same class of graphs. Additionally, $\mathcal{O}(\log^2 n)$ upper bound for trees and $\Omega(\sqrt{n})$ lower bound for sparse graphs were given.

Distance Labeling with Hub Sets. For a given graph G, the computational task of minimizing the sizes of hub sets $(S(u) : u \in V)$ for exact distance decoding is relatively well understood. A $\mathcal{O}(\log n)$-approximation algorithm for minimizing the average size of a hub set having the sought shortest path cover property was presented in Cohen et al. [13], whereas a $\mathcal{O}(\log n)$-approximation for minimizing the largest hub set at a node was given more recently in Babenko et al. [8]. Rather surprisingly, the structural question of obtaining bounds on the size of such hub sets for specific graph classes is wide open. For example, for the class of graphs of constant maximum degree, there is a large gap between the hub sets in our construction (of size $\mathcal{O}(n/\log n)$) and the generic lower bound of $\widetilde{\Omega}(\sqrt{n})$.

Distance Oracles. A centralized version of distance labeling problem is *distance oracle* problem, where one asks for a centralized data structure allowing for querying a distance between pair of vertices. There usually one asks for what type of tradeoffs are possible between size of the structure, time of the query and allowed error (multiplicative stretch). Sommer et al. [23] proved that any constant time, constant stretch oracle must be superlinear in n. Thorup and Zwick [24] proved that distance oracles of stretch 2 require $\Omega(n^2)$ space, and of stretch 3 require $\Omega(n^{3/2})$ space. Pătraşcu and Roditty [21] strengthened the lower bound for stretch 2, proving a lower bound of $\Omega(n\sqrt{m})$ on the size of oracles with constant query time. For general weighted graphs, Thorup and Zwick [24] designed a distance oracle of size $\mathcal{O}(kn^{1+1/k})$, stretch-$(2k-1)$ and $\mathcal{O}(k)$ time. The query time has been improved to $\mathcal{O}(\log k)$ time by Wulff-Nilsen [26], and to constant time in Chechik [11]. The size of the distance oracle from [24] is optimal assuming girth-conjecture. For sparse graphs, [21] design distance oracle of size

---

[1] For the sake of sanity of the notation, we define $\log x = \max(1, \log_2(x))$.

$\mathcal{O}(n^{4/3}m^{1/3})$ and stretch 2 in constant time. Also in [21], a conditional lower bound of $\tilde{\Omega}(n^2)$ bits for a constant time distance oracle is provided. Cohen and Porat [14] extended this result to sparse graphs. An up-to-date survey of results on approximate distance oracles is provided in [22].

1.2 Our Results and Organization of the Paper

We start by introducing the necessary conventions in Sect. 2. We also describe the basic building block for encoding distance labels, namely, an efficient method of storing the hub set of a node, together with corresponding distances, in its distance label.

In Sect. 3, we show how to construct an exact distance labeling scheme for graphs of bounded maximum degree. This relies on hub sets which consist, for a vertex u of the union of all nodes from a small ball around vertex u, and all nodes from a selection of equally-spaced levels of the breadth-first-search tree of u. We then apply a trick, known from the previous work of [4], to reduce the problem of constructing a labeling scheme for a graph with bounded average degree to that of constructing a labeling scheme for a bounded-degree graph on twice as many nodes. For graphs with at most n nodes and average degree Δ, the tradeoff between label bit size L and query decoding time T for our approach is given by $L = \mathcal{O}(n \log \log_\Delta T / \log_\Delta T)$, for any $T \leq n$. In particular, setting $T = n$, we obtain labels of size $\mathcal{O}(\frac{n}{R} \log R)$, which improves previously best result [6] by a factor of $\log R$, keeping the $\tilde{\mathcal{O}}(n)$ decoding time. On the other end, setting $T = \log n$ we obtain first sublinear size distance labeling that achieves almost-constant decoding time.

In Sect. 4, we adapt our approach to general graphs, using a variant of the proposed labeling scheme for sparse graphs to achieve 2-additive approximation of distances. As before, we achieve a tradeoff between label size L and time T of the form $L = \mathcal{O}(n \log^2 \log T / \log T)$, for any $T \leq n$. This 2-additive distance labeling scheme can be easily transformed into an exact one, by encoding the difference between the estimation and the true distances. Since this difference is always from $\{0, 1, 2\}$, we achieve labels of size $\frac{\log 3}{2} n + o(n)$ (with any $\omega(1)$ decoding time), or of size $(\frac{\log 3}{2} + \varepsilon)n$ (with $\mathcal{O}(1)$ decoding time), for any $\varepsilon > 0$. Our approach almost matches the size of the best known distance labeling schemes [7], which make use of labels of size $\frac{\log 3}{2} n + o(n)$ to achieve $\mathcal{O}(1)$ decoding time. Arguably, our approach may be considered simpler.

We remark that all our results apply to unweighted graphs, in which each edge has unit length. For sparse graphs, in which each edge has an integer weight from some interval $[1, W]$, we can use the same hub sets with an appropriately modified encoding to achieve a time-label tradeoff of $L = \mathcal{O}(n \log \log_\Delta T \log W / \log_\Delta T)$. For the additive scheme, by subdividing each edge of length $w \in [1, W]$ into a chain of unweighted edges (of length 1), we achieve a conversion of the 2-additive distance labeling scheme into a $(2W)$-additive-distance scheme for weighted graphs.

2   Preliminaries

Notation and Conventions. Even though we are mainly interested in unweighted graphs, for technical reasons in Sects. 3 and 4 we will work in a more general setting where every edge of a graph has a fixed cost from the set $\{0, 1\}$. $\delta(u, v)$ denotes the cost of a cheapest path connecting a pair of nodes u and v, and $\ell(u, v)$ denotes the smallest number of edges on such a path. We will require the constructed distance labeling to return the value of $\delta(u, v)$. The degree of a node v is denoted by $\deg(v)$. When analyzing the complexity of the decoding, we assume standard word RAM with logarithmic word size, where we are allowed to access $\log n$ consecutive bits of the stored binary string in constant time.

From now on, we assume that the graph is connected. This is enough because we can always include the identifier of its connected component in the label of every node, and return ∞ if u and v belong to different connected components; this only induces additive $\log n$ overhead to the label size.

Encoding Distances and Identifiers. The basic procedure for encoding a hub set in a label exploits some ideas from [7]; we provide a self-contained exposition for completeness. We fix an arbitrary spanning tree of the graph and assign preorder numbers in the tree to the nodes, i.e., node numbered 1 corresponds to the root and so on. The preorder number of a node u is denoted by name(u). Such a numbering has the following useful property.

Lemma 1. *Let $v_1, v_2, \ldots, v_n$ be the preorder sequence of all nodes. Then, for any node u, $\sum_{i=2}^{n} |\delta(u, v_{i-1}) - \delta(u, v_i)| \leq 2n$.*

Proof. Consider an Euler tour corresponding a traversal of the chosen spanning tree. Every node is visited at least once there, and the total length of the tour is at most $2n$. Consequently, we can cut the tour into paths connecting node v_{i-1} with node v_i, for every $i = 2, 3, \ldots, n$. The total length of all these paths is at most $2n$ and the claim follows. $\qquad\square$

The following lemma is used for encoding a hub set S using $\mathcal{O}(|S| \log(n/|S|))$ bits.

Lemma 2. *For a fixed v and set S such that $|S| \leq \frac{n}{x}$, set S and all of the distances $\delta(v, u)$ for $u \in S$ can be stored in $\mathcal{O}(\frac{n}{x} \log x)$ bits. For any constant $t > 0$, the representation can be augmented with $\mathcal{O}(\frac{n}{\log^t n})$ additional bits so that all elements of S can be extracted one-by-one in $\mathcal{O}(|S|)$ total time and given any u we can check if $u \in S$ (and if so, extract $\delta(u, v)$) in $\mathcal{O}(1)$ time.*

Proof. Let $S = (v_1, \ldots, v_{|S|})$, where name$(v_1)$ < name(v_2) < $\ldots$ < name$(v_{|S|})$. We store name(v_1) and then the differences name(v_2) − name$(v_1), \ldots,$ name$(v_{|S|})$ − name$(v_{|S|-1})$. Every difference is encoded using the Elias γ code (see Elias [15]), and the encodings are concatenated to form one binary string. We are storing up to $\frac{n}{x}$ integers whose absolute values sum up to at most n, so by Jensen's inequality this takes $\mathcal{O}(\frac{n}{x} \log x)$ bits in total. Similarly, we store $\delta(u, v_1)$ and then the differences $\delta(u, v_2) - \delta(u, v_1), \ldots, \delta(u, v_{|S|}) -$

$\delta(u, v_{|S|-1})$. By Lemma 1 we are again storing up to $\frac{n}{x}$ numbers whose absolute values sum up to at most $2n$, which takes $\mathcal{O}(\frac{n}{x} \log x)$ bits.

All v_i can be extracted one-by-one in $\mathcal{O}(1)$ time each with standard bitwise operations. To facilitate checking if $x \in S$ in $\mathcal{O}(1)$ time, we observe that it is enough to store a bit-vector $B[1..n]$, where the name(v_i)-th bit is set to 1, for every $i = 1, 2, \ldots, |S|$. Then checking if $x \in S$ reduces to two rank$_1$ queries. A rank$_1$ query counts 1s in the specified prefix of the bit-vector and a select$_1$ query returns the position of the k-th 1 in the bit-vector. By the result of Pătraşcu [20], for any constant $t > 0$, a bit-vector of length n containing $\frac{n}{x}$ 1s can be stored using

$$\log \binom{n}{\frac{n}{x}} + \mathcal{O}(\frac{n}{\log^t n}) = \mathcal{O}(\frac{n}{x} \log x) + \mathcal{O}(\frac{n}{\log^t n})$$

bits so that any rank or select query can be answered in $\mathcal{O}(t)$ time. This allows us to check if $u \in S$ and calculate i such that $u = v_i$ in $\mathcal{O}(t)$ time. To retrieve $\delta(u, v_i)$, we store two additional bit-vectors B_+ and B_-. Each of them contains exactly $\frac{n}{x}$ 1s and up to $2n$ 0s. The bit-vectors are defined as follows. For each $i = 2, 3, \ldots, n$ we consider the difference $\eta = \delta(u, v_i) - \delta(u, v_{i-1})$. If $\eta \geq 0$, we append $0^\eta 1$ to B_+ and 1 to B_-. Otherwise, we append 1 to B_+ and $0^{-\eta} 1$ to B_-. By Lemma 1, each of these two bit-vectors contains at most $2n$ 0s, so they can be stored using $\mathcal{O}(\frac{n}{x} \log x + \frac{n}{\log^t n})$ bits so that any rank or select query can be answered in $\mathcal{O}(t)$ time. To recover $\delta(u, v_i)$, we need to sum up all the differences. This reduces to summing up all positive and all negative differences separately, which can be done using the corresponding bit-vector with one rank$_1$ and one select$_0$ query in $\mathcal{O}(t)$ total time.   □

We remark that the above encoding and decoding scheme is efficient for sets of size $|S| = \widetilde{\mathcal{O}}(n)$. For smaller sets, we will simply use an explicit encoding of all distances in S, requiring $\mathcal{O}(|S| \log n)$ bits.

3   Exact Distance Labeling in Sparse Graphs

3.1   Graphs of Bounded Maximum Degree

In this subsection, we assume that $\deg(u) \leq \Delta$ for every node u. We consider distance labeling schemes characterized by a time parameter T. Intuitively, in the construction, $R = \frac{\log T}{\log \Delta}$ will be a threshold parameter, distinguishing small distances from large distances in the graph — a node will be able to afford to explicitly store the distances and identifiers of all nodes up to some distance $\mathcal{O}(R)$ from itself in its distance label. Although this case is of independent interest, we are considering it as a building block for construction of labeling in graphs of bounded average degree. Thus graphs considered here are weighted with edge weights from $\{0, 1\}$, for the reason explained in Sect. 3.2.

The rest of this subsection is devoted to the proof of the following Theorem.

Theorem 1. *Fix any value $\Delta \leq T \leq n$ and let $R = \log_\Delta T$. In bounded-degree graphs, there is a labeling scheme of size $\mathcal{O}(\frac{n}{R} \log R)$ and decoding time $\mathcal{O}(T)$.*

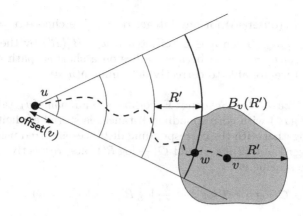

Fig. 1. Shortest path from u to v goes through w which belongs to both $B_v(R')$ and $L_u(\mathsf{offset}(u))$.

Let us denote $R' = \lfloor R \rfloor$. Since $R' \geq 1$, we can bound $R \geq R' \geq \frac{1}{2}R$. Consider a node u. The ball of radius r centered at u, denoted $B_u(r)$, is the set of nodes which can be reached from u by following at most r edges. Because the degrees of all nodes are bounded by Δ, $|B_u(r)| = \mathcal{O}(\Delta^r)$. The k-th layer centered at u, denoted $L_u(k)$, consists of all nodes v such that $\ell(u, v) = k \pmod{R}'$. Because the layers are disjoint, there exists an $\mathsf{offset}(u) \in \{0, 1, \ldots, R' - 1\}$ such that $|L_u(\mathsf{offset}(u))| \leq \frac{n}{R'}$.

Definition of the Labeling. We define the hub set of node u, to which it stores all its distances, as $S(u) := B_u(R') \cup L_u(\mathsf{offset}(u))$, see Fig. 1. Formally, the label of u consists of the following:

1. n and $\mathsf{name}(u)$,
2. $\mathsf{name}(v)$ and $\delta(u, v)$ for every $v \in B_u(R')$,
3. $\mathsf{name}(v)$ and $\delta(u, v)$ for every $v \in L_u(\mathsf{offset}(u))$.

Computing $\delta(u, v)$. For reasons of efficiency, we will not perform the distance decoding following Eq. (1) directly, but we will treat the two components of the hub set of each node separately. Given $\mathsf{name}(u)$ and $\mathsf{name}(v)$, we can determine $\delta(u, v)$ as follows. First we check if $v \in B_u(R')$ and if so return the stored $\delta(u, v)$. Otherwise, we iterate through all nodes $w \in B_u(R')$ and check if $w \in L_v(\mathsf{offset}(v))$. If so, we know $\delta(u, w) + \delta(w, v)$. We return the smallest such sum.

For the proof of correctness of the distance decoder, it is clear that $\delta(u, w) + \delta(w, v) \geq \delta(u, v)$ for any w, so it remains to argue that either $v \in B_u(R')$ or there exists $w \in B_u(R')$ such that $w \in L_v(\mathsf{offset}(v))$ and $\delta(u, w) + \delta(w, v) = \delta(u, v)$. Consider a shortest path $(p_0, p_1, p_2, \ldots p_\ell)$ where $v = p_0$ and $u = p_\ell$ such that $\ell = \ell(u, v)$. If $\ell \leq R'$, $v \in B_u(R')$ and there is nothing to prove, so we can assume that $\ell > R'$. Observe that for any $i = 0, 1, \ldots, \ell$, $\ell(v, p_i) = i$, so in particular

$p_{\alpha \cdot R' + \mathsf{offset}(v)} \in L_v(\mathsf{offset}(v))$ for any integer $\alpha \geq 0$. We choose $\alpha = \left\lfloor \frac{\ell - \mathsf{offset}(v)}{R'} \right\rfloor$ and $w = p_{\alpha \cdot R' + \mathsf{offset}(v)}$. Then $w \in L_v(\mathsf{offset}(v))$, $w \in B_u(R')$ by the choice of α, and $\delta(u, w) + \delta(w, v) = \delta(u, v)$ because w lies on a shortest path connecting u and v, so indeed we are able to correctly determine $\delta(u, v)$.

Encoding and Size of the Scheme. Encoding n and $\mathsf{name}(u)$ takes $\mathcal{O}(\log n)$ bits. The set $B_u(R')$ with corresponding distances is stored explicitly, while set $L_u(\mathsf{offset}(u))$ together with the corresponding distances is stored using Lemma 2, using $\mathcal{O}(\Delta^{R'} \log n) = \mathcal{O}(T \log n)$ and $\mathcal{O}(\frac{n}{R'} \log R')$ bits, respectively. Hence the total size of the scheme is

$$\mathcal{O}(\log n + T \log n + \frac{n}{R'} \log R') = \mathcal{O}(\frac{n}{R} \log R),$$

where we have used the fact that for any $T = \mathrm{poly}(n)$ the claimed label size is the same, thus we can assume $T = o(n/\mathrm{polylog}(n))$.

Complexity of the Decoding. Checking if $v \in B_u(R')$ and retrieving the encoded $\delta(u, v)$ takes $\mathcal{O}(T)$ time. Similarly, iterating through all $w \in B_u(R')$, checking if $w \in L_v(\mathsf{offset}(v))$ and if so retrieving the encoded $\delta(v, w)$, takes, by Lemma 2, $\mathcal{O}(1)$ time per single w, thus $\mathcal{O}(|B_u(R')|) = \mathcal{O}(T)$ total time. All in all, we can compute $\delta(u, v)$ in $\mathcal{O}(T)$ total time.   □

Smaller values of T. For the sake of completeness, we consider the special case of $T < \Delta$. Consider labeling where the label of a node u consists of n, $\mathsf{name}(u)$, and all values $\delta(u, v)$ for $v \in V$ stored using Lemma 2. This takes $\mathcal{O}(n)$ bits, with $\mathcal{O}(1)$ decoding time, and matches claimed bounds from Theorem 1.

We also observe that our result applies not only to distance labels, but also as a size upper bound of hub sets for sparse graphs. Indeed, by fixing $T = n$, and observing that $|B_u(R')| + |L_u(\mathsf{offset}(u))| \leq \frac{n}{R'}$, we have the following:

Corollary 1. *In bounded-degree graphs, there is a hub set construction of size $\mathcal{O}(\frac{n}{\log_\Delta n})$ vertices per node.*

3.2   Graphs of Bounded Average Degree

We now allow for bounded average degree by reduction to the approach from Subsect. 3.1. Given a graph G, let $\Delta = \frac{m+n}{n}$. We will create a new graph by splitting nodes of high degree. Following the formulation from [4, Lemma 4.2] (cf. Fig. 2), we can obtain a graph G' on at most $2n$ nodes and at most $m + n$ edges, such that the degree of every node is bounded by $\lceil \frac{m}{n} \rceil + 2 \leq \Delta + 2$ and the distance between two nodes in the original graph G is exactly the same as the distance between their corresponding nodes in the new graph G'. We can now directly apply the scheme from Theorem 1 to graph G', and exactly the same

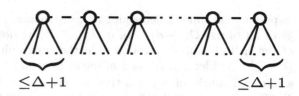

Fig. 2. Example of subdividing of a large degree node (on the left) into a family of nodes of small degree, connected by edges of weight 0 (dashed edges).

distance labels will work for the corresponding nodes of graph G. In this way, we obtain a scheme of size:

$$\mathcal{O}(\frac{n}{R}\log R + \frac{m}{n}) = \mathcal{O}(\frac{n}{R}\log R), \text{ where } R = \mathcal{O}(\frac{\log T}{\log \Delta}).$$

which returns $\delta(u,v)$ in $\mathcal{O}(T)$ time given the labels of u and v. The correctness of the this reduction is guaranteed by the fact that Theorem 1 allows for edge weights from $\{0, 1\}$.

Theorem 2. *Fix any $T \leq n$ and Δ, and let $R = \frac{\log T}{\log \Delta}$. There exists an exact distance labeling for graphs with average degree Δ using labels of size $\mathcal{O}(\frac{n}{R}\log R)$ and a corresponding decoding scheme requiring time $\mathcal{O}(T)$.* □

It is easy to see that this reduction preserves bounds on the size of hub sets, so we have the following:

Corollary 2. *In graphs with average degree Δ, there is a hub set construction of size $\mathcal{O}(\frac{n}{\log_\Delta n})$ vertices per node.*

4   2-Additive Distance Labeling in General Graphs

We will apply a similar distance labeling scheme as for sparse graphs, obtaining a 2-additive approximation of the distance between any pair of with label sizes of $o(n)$ per node. In this approximate scheme, the hub sets will have the following property. The label of each node $u \in V$ will provide an encoding of the node identifiers of a subset $S(u) \subseteq V$ and of the distances from u to all elements of $S(u)$. The sets $S(u)$ will be defined so that for any pair u, v, there exists a node $w \in S(u) \cap S(v)$, such that either w or a neighbor of w lies on the shortest path from u to v in G. We will decode the approximate distance as before, using Eq. (1); clearly, $\delta'(u, v) \in \delta(u, v) + \{0, 1, 2\}$.

The construction of sets $S(u)$ is performed as follows. Let $\tau < \frac{1}{2}\log n$ be an threshold value of vertex degree, to be chosen later. Let $V' = \{v \in V : \deg(v) > \tau\}$, and let $S' \subseteq V$ be a minimal dominating set for V', i.e., a subset of V with the property: $\forall_{w \in V'} B_w(1) \cap S' \neq \emptyset$. By a straightforward application of the probabilistic method (cf. [5, proof of Theorem 1.2.2]), we have that there is S' such that $|S'| \leq \frac{1+\ln(\tau+1)}{\tau+1}n < \frac{2\ln\tau}{\tau}n$, and it can be easily constructed in polynomial time (a deterministic construction by a folklore greedy algorithm gives set of size $\mathcal{O}(\frac{\ln \tau}{\tau}n)$). For every $u \in V$, we define $B'_u(r)$ as the set of nodes of the ball of radius r around u in the subgraph $G[V \backslash V']$. Finally, we define $R = \frac{\tau}{\log \tau}$ and let L_u, R', and $\mathsf{offset}(u)$ be defined as in Sect. 3.1, and let S'_u be a minimal subset of S' such that for every $w \in V'$ adjacent the boundary of $B'_u(R')$, i.e. $B_w(1) \cap B'_u(R') \neq \emptyset$, we have $B_w(1) \cap S'_u \neq \emptyset$. Such S'_u can be easily constructed in polynomial time, and moreover, since there are at most $\tau^{R'+1}$ vertices adjacent to the boundary, we have $|S'_u| = 2^{\mathcal{O}(\tau)}$.

The approximate distance label of u now consists of the following elements:

1. n and $\mathsf{name}(u)$,
2. $\mathsf{name}(v)$ and $\delta(u,v)$ for every $v \in B'_u(R')$,
3. $\mathsf{name}(v)$ and $\delta(u,v)$ for every $v \in L_u(\mathsf{offset}(u))$.
4. $\mathsf{name}(v)$ and $\delta(u,v)$ for every $v \in S'_u$,
5. $\mathsf{name}(v)$ and $\delta(u,v)$ for every $v \in S' \backslash S'_u$.

The separation of S' into S'_u and $S' \backslash S'_u$ in the label is done to allow efficient decoding.

Computing $\delta(u,v)$. To show the correctness of this approximate labeling scheme, fix a pair of vertices $u, v \in V$. If there exists a vertex $w \in B'_u(R')$ lying on a fixed shortest path P between u and v such that $w = v$ or $w \in L_v(\mathsf{offset}(v))$, then the labeling scheme finds the shortest path distance between u and v as in Sect. 3.1. Otherwise, let y be the nearest vertex to u lying in $P \backslash B'_u(R')$; it follows from the construction that $y \in V'$. Then, there exists $w \in B_y(1)$ such that $w \in S'_u \subseteq S'$. In this case, the distance $\delta(u,w) + \delta(v,w)$ is a 2-additive approximation of $\delta(u,v)$.

Size of the Scheme. The size of the label of a node u in the scheme can be bounded as follows: $|B'_u(R')| \leq \tau^{R'} \leq 2^\tau$, $|L_u(\mathsf{offset}(u))| \leq \frac{n}{R}$, $S' < \frac{2\ln \tau}{\tau}n$. Overall, the total size is $|B'_u(R') \cup L_u(\mathsf{offset}(u)) \cup S'| = \mathcal{O}(\frac{\log \tau}{\tau}n)$, thus using Lemma 2 to store the sets and the corresponding distances we obtain labels of size $\mathcal{O}(n \frac{\log^2 \tau}{\tau})$.

Complexity of the Decoding. To perform the distance decoding, for a given pair $u, v \in V$, it suffices to minimize $\delta(u,w) + \delta(v,w)$ over all w belonging to $B'_u(R') \cup S'_u$ which are also encoded in the label of v. Hence, distance decoding is possible in time $2^{\mathcal{O}(\tau)}$. Overall, setting $T := 2^{\mathcal{O}(\tau)}$, we obtain the following main result of the section.

Theorem 3. *There is a 2-additive distance labeling scheme for general graphs, which achieves decoding time T using labels of size $\mathcal{O}(n \frac{\log^2 \log T}{\log T})$, for any $T \leq n$.* $\square$

Finally, we remark on some implications of our result. By a standard argument, converting a 2-additive approximate distance labeling into an exact one requires an additional label of size $\frac{\log_2 3}{2}n$ bits per node (and an additional $\mathcal{O}(\frac{n}{\log n})$ overhead in the space, which is negligible), with each node u encoding the difference between the approximate and real distance value, $\delta'(u, v) - \delta(u, v)$, for all $v \in \{(u + 1) \bmod n, \ldots, (u + \lfloor \frac{n}{2} \rfloor) \bmod n\}$. The time overhead of the corresponding decoding is $\mathcal{O}(1)$. In an analogous manner, converting a 2-additive approximate distance labeling into an 1-additive approximate one requires an additional label of size $\frac{1}{2}n$ bits per node. Thus we convert our scheme into an exact distance labeling scheme or 1-additive scheme achieving T decoding time using labels of size respectively $\frac{\log_2 3}{2}n + \mathcal{O}(n\frac{\log^2 \log T}{\log T})$ or $\frac{1}{2}n + \mathcal{O}(n\frac{\log^2 \log T}{\log T})$, for any $T \le n$.

Thus, setting τ as an arbitrarily small increasing function of n, for any desired decoding time $T = \omega(1)$ we can make use of labels of size $o(n)$, $\frac{1}{2}n + o(n)$ and $\frac{\log_2 3}{2}n + o(n)$ respectively for 2-additive, 1-additive and exact distances. Moreover, using this scheme, $\mathcal{O}(1)$ decoding time can be achieved for labels of size εn, $(\frac{1}{2} + \varepsilon) \cdot n$ and $(\frac{\log_2 3}{2} + \varepsilon) \cdot n$, for any absolute constant $\varepsilon > 0$.

While a slightly stronger in terms of decoding time schemes were presented in Alstrup et al. [7] (achieving $\mathcal{O}(1)$ decoding time and labels of size $\frac{\log_2 3}{2}n + o(n)$ and $\frac{1}{2}n + o(n)$ for exact and 1-additive distances), we believe that presented here schemes are of independent value due to the simplification of the construction.

Acknowledgments. Most of the work was done while PU was affiliated to Aalto University, Finland. Research partially supported by the National Science Centre, Poland - grant number 2015/17/B/ST6/01897.

References

1. Abraham, I., Delling, D., Goldberg, A.V., Werneck, R.F.: Hierarchical hub labelings for shortest paths. In: Epstein, L., Ferragina, P. (eds.) ESA 2012. LNCS, vol. 7501, pp. 24–35. Springer, Heidelberg (2012)
2. Abraham, I., Fiat, A., Goldberg, A.V., Werneck, R.F.: Highway dimension, shortest paths, and provably efficient algorithms. In: Proceedings of the Twenty-First Annual ACM-SIAM Symposium on Discrete Algorithms, SODA 2010, Austin, Texas, USA, January 17-19, pp. 782–793 (2010). http://dx.doi.org/10.1137/1.9781611973075.64
3. Abraham, I., Gavoille, C.: On approximate distance labels and routing schemes with affine stretch. In: Peleg, D. (ed.) Distributed Computing. LNCS, vol. 6950, pp. 404–415. Springer, Heidelberg (2011)
4. Agarwal, R., Godfrey, P.B.: Distance oracles for stretch less than 2. In: Khanna, S., (ed.) Proceedings of the Twenty-Fourth Annual ACM-SIAM Symposium on Discrete Algorithms (SODA 2013), New Orleans, Louisiana, USA, 6–8 January 2013, pp. 526–538. SIAM (2013)
5. Alon, N., Spencer, J.H.: The Probabilistic Method, 2nd edn. Wiley, New York (2000)
6. Alstrup, S., Dahlgaard, S., Knudsen, M.B.T., Porat, E.: Sublinear distance labeling for sparse graphs. CoRR, abs/1507.02618 (2015)
7. Alstrup, S., Gavoille, C., Halvorsen, E.B., Petersen, H.: Simpler, faster and shorter labels for distances in graphs. In: Krauthgamer, R., (ed) Proceedings of the Twenty-Seventh Annual ACM-SIAM Symposium on Discrete Algorithms (SODA 2016), Arlington, VA, USA, 10–12 January 2016, pp. 338–350. SIAM (2016)

8. Babenko, M., Goldberg, A.V., Gupta, A., Nagarajan, V.: Algorithms for hub label optimization. In: Fomin, F.V., Freivalds, R., Kwiatkowska, M., Peleg, D. (eds.) ICALP 2013, Part I. LNCS, vol. 7965, pp. 69–80. Springer, Heidelberg (2013)
9. Bauer, R., Delling, D.: SHARC: fast and robust unidirectional routing. J. Exp. Algorithmics 14, 4: 2.4-4–4: 2.29 (2010)
10. Bollobás, B., Coppersmith, D., Elkin, M.: Sparse distance preservers and additive spanners. SIAM J. Discrete Math. 19(4), 1029–1055 (2005)
11. Chechik, S.: Approximate distance oracles with constant query time. In: Proceedings of the 46th Annual ACM Symposium on Theory of Computing (STOC 2014), pp. 654–663, New York, NY, USA. ACM (2014)
12. Chepoi, V., Dragan, F.F., Estellon, B., Habib, M., Vaxès, Y., Xiang, Y.: Additive spanners and distance and routing labeling schemes for hyperbolic graphs. Algorithmica 62(3–4), 713–732 (2012)
13. Cohen, E., Halperin, E., Kaplan, H., Zwick, U.: Reachability and distance queries via 2-hop labels. SIAM J. Comput. 32(5), 1338–1355 (2003)
14. Cohen, H., Porat, E.: On the hardness of distance oracle for sparse graph. CoRR, abs/1006.1117 (2010)
15. Elias, P.: Universal codeword sets and representations of the integers. IEEE Trans. Inf. Theory 21(2), 194–203 (1975)
16. Gavoille, C., Peleg, D., Pérennes, S., Raz, R.: Distance labeling in graphs. J. Algorithms 53(1), 85–112 (2004)
17. Graham, R., Pollak, H.: On embedding graphs in squashed cubes. In: Alavi, Y., Lick, D., White, A. (eds.) Graph Theory and Applications. Lecture Notes in Mathematics, vol. 303, pp. 99–110. Springer, Berlin Heidelberg (1972)
18. Köhler, E., Möhring, R.H., Schilling, H.: Fast point-to-point shortest path computations with arc-flags. In: 9th DIMACS Implementation Challenge (2006)
19. Nitto, I., Venturini, R.: On compact representations of all-pairs-shortest-path-distance matrices. In: Ferragina, P., Landau, G.M. (eds.) CPM 2008. LNCS, vol. 5029, pp. 166–177. Springer, Heidelberg (2008)
20. Pătraşcu, M.: Succincter. In: 49th Annual IEEE Symposium on Foundations of Computer Science (FOCS), 25–28 October 2008, Philadelphia, PA, USA, pp. 305–313. IEEE Computer Society (2008)
21. Pătraşcu, M., Roditty, L.: Distance oracles beyond the Thorup-Zwick bound. SIAM J. Comput. 43(1), 300–311 (2014)
22. Roditty, L.: Distance oracles for sparse graphs. In: Kao, M.-Y. (ed.) Encyclopedia of Algorithms, pp. 1–3. Springer, New York (2014)
23. Sommer, C., Verbin, E., Yu, W.: Distance oracles for sparse graphs. In: 50th IEEE Symposium on Foundations of Computer Science (FOCS), pp. 703–712. IEEE (2009)
24. Thorup, M., Zwick, U.: Compact routing schemes. In: Proceedings of the Thirteenth Annual ACM Symposium on Parallel Algorithms and Architectures (SPAA 2001), pp. 1–10, New York, NY, USA. ACM (2001)
25. Weimann, O., Peleg, D.: A note on exact distance labeling. Inf. Process. Lett. 111(14), 671–673 (2011)
26. Wulff-Nilsen, C.: Approximate distance oracles with improved query time. In: Proceedings of the Twenty-Fourth Annual ACM-SIAM Symposium on Discrete Algorithms, pp. 539–549 (2013)

Online Balanced Repartitioning

Chen Avin[1], Andreas Loukas[2], Maciej Pacut[3], and Stefan Schmid[2,4(✉)]

[1] Ben Gurion University of the Negev, Beersheba, Israel
[2] TU Berlin, Berlin, Germany
[3] University of Wroclaw, Wroclaw, Poland
[4] Aalborg University, Aalborg, Denmark
schmiste@gmail.com, schmiste@cs.aau.dk

Abstract. Distributed cloud applications, including batch processing, streaming, and scale-out databases, generate a significant amount of network traffic and a considerable fraction of their runtime is due to network activity. This paper initiates the study of deterministic algorithms for collocating frequently communicating nodes in a distributed networked systems in an online fashion. In particular, we introduce the *Balanced RePartitioning* (BRP) problem: Given an arbitrary sequence of pairwise communication requests between n nodes, with patterns that may change over time, the objective is to dynamically partition the nodes into ℓ clusters, each of size k, at a minimum cost. Every communication request needs to be served: if the communicating nodes are located in the same cluster, the request is served locally, at cost 0; if the nodes are located in different clusters, the request is served remotely using inter-cluster communication, at cost 1. The partitioning can be updated dynamically (i.e., repartitioned), by *migrating* nodes between clusters at cost α per node migration. The goal is to devise online algorithms which find a good trade-off between the communication and the migration cost, i.e., "rent" or "buy", while maintaining partitions which minimize the number of inter-cluster communications. BRP features interesting connections to other well-known online problems. In particular, we show that scenarios with $\ell = 2$ generalize online paging, and scenarios with $k = 2$ constitute a novel online version of maximum matching. We consider settings both with and without cluster-size augmentation. Somewhat surprisingly (and unlike online paging), we prove that any deterministic online algorithm has a competitive ratio of at least k, *even with augmentation*. Our main technical contribution is an $O(k \log k)$-competitive deterministic algorithm for the setting with (constant) augmentation. This is attractive as, in contrast to ℓ, k is likely to be small in practice. For the case of matching ($k = 2$), we present a constant competitive algorithm that does not rely on augmentation.

Keywords: Dynamic graphs · Clustering · Graph partitioning · Algorithms · Competitive analysis · Cloud computing

Research supported by the German-Israeli Foundation for Scientific Research (GIF) Grant I-1245-407.6/2014 and by the Polish National Science Centre grant DEC-2013/09/B/ST6/01538. We thank Marcin Bienkowski for many inputs and feedback on this paper.

C. Gavoille and D. Ilcinkas (Eds.): DISC 2016, LNCS 9888, pp. 243–256, 2016.
DOI: 10.1007/978-3-662-53426-7_18

1   Introduction

Graph partitioning problems, like minimum graph bisection and maximum matching, are among the most fundamental problems in Theoretical Computer Science. Due to their numerous practical applications (e. g., communication networks, data mining, social networks, etc. [4,15,27]), partitioning problems are also among the most intensively studied problems. Interestingly however, not much is known today about how to dynamically partition nodes which interact or communicate in a time-varying fashion.

This paper initiates the study of a natural model for *online* graph partitioning. We are given a set of n nodes with time-varying pairwise communication patterns, which we have to partition into ℓ clusters of equal size k. Intuitively, we would like to minimize inter-cluster links by mapping frequently communicating nodes to the same cluster. Since communication patterns change over time, partitions should be dynamically readjusted, that is, the nodes should be *repartitioned*, in an online manner, by *migrating* them between clusters. The objective is to jointly minimize inter-cluster communication and reconfiguration costs, defined respectively as the number of communication requests served remotely and the number of times nodes are migrated from one cluster to another.

One practical motivation for our problem arises in the context of server virtualization in datacenters. Distributed cloud applications, including batch processing applications such as MapReduce, streaming applications such as Apache Flink or Apache Spark, and scale-out databases and key-value stores such as Cassandra, generate a significant amount of network traffic and a considerable fraction of their runtime is due to network activity [25]. For example, traces of jobs from a Facebook cluster reveal that network transfers on average account for 33 % of the execution time [14]. In such applications, it is desirable that frequently communicating virtual machines are *collocated*, i.e., mapped to the same physical server, since communication across the network (i.e., inter-server communication) induces network load and latency. However, migrating virtual machines between servers also comes at a price: the state transfer is bandwidth intensive, and may even lead to short service interruptions. Therefore the goal is to design online algorithms which find a good trade-off between the inter-server communication cost and the migration cost, similar in spirit to classical ski rental and rent-or-buy problems.

Formally we define the *Balanced RePartitioning* (BRP) problem as follows. The inputs to BRP are:

1. A set V of $n = |V|$ nodes (e.g., the virtual machines), initially distributed arbitrarily across ℓ clusters $\mathcal{C} = \{C_1, \ldots, C_\ell\}$ (e.g., the physical servers, interconnected by a top-of-the-rack switch [2]), each of size k (e.g., the number of cores or slots for virtual machines).
2. An arbitrary and possibly infinite sequence σ of $|\sigma|$ communication requests, $\sigma = \{u_1, v_1\}, \{u_2, v_2\}, \{u_3, v_3\}, \ldots, \{u_{|\sigma|}, v_{|\sigma|}\}$. For any t, $\sigma_t = \{u_t, v_t\}$ denotes a communication request: at time t, nodes $u_t, v_t \in V$ exchange (a fixed amount of) data. Intuitively, every request σ_t can be thought of as an

edge of the communication graph which appears at time t and then disappears at $t + 1$.

At any time t, each node $v \in V$ is assigned to a cluster, which we will refer to by $C_t(v) \in \mathcal{C}$. If the time t is clear from the context or irrelevant, we simply write $C(v)$. We call two nodes $u, v \in V$ *collocated* if they are in the same cluster: $C(u) = C(v)$. We consider two settings:

1. *Without augmentation:* The nodes fit perfectly into the clusters, i.e., $n = k \cdot \ell$.
2. *With augmentation:* The online algorithm has access to additional space in each cluster. We say that an algorithm is δ-augmented if the size of each cluster is $k' = \delta \cdot k$, whereas the total number of nodes remains $n = k \cdot \ell < k' \cdot \ell$. As usual, in the competitive analysis, the augmented online algorithm is compared to the optimal offline algorithm without augmentation.

At each time t, the online algorithm needs to serve the communication request $\{u_t, v_t\}$, but can also repartition the nodes into new clusters before serving the request. We assume that a communication request between two nodes located in different clusters costs 1, a communication request between two nodes collocated in the same cluster costs 0, and migrating a node from one cluster to another costs $\alpha \geq 1$. Note that in a setting without augmentation, due to cluster size constraints, a node can never be migrated alone, but it must be swapped with another node at a cost of (at least) 2α.

As it turns out, BRP features some interesting connections to other well-known graph and online problems: (i) The static version (without migration) is the minimum balanced graph partitioning problem (where ℓ is the number of components). (ii) For $\ell = 2$, BRP can be shown to be a generalization of online paging, where the first cluster simulates the cache (the small but fast memory) and the second the slow but large memory. (iii) For $k = 2$, BRP is a novel online version of maximum matching. In the static case, maximum matching is a special case of minimum balanced graph partitioning with $n/2$ components.

The cost of an algorithm ALG for a given sequence of communication requests σ is

$$\mathrm{ALG}(\sigma) = \sum_{t=1}^{|\sigma|} \mathrm{mig}(\sigma_t; \mathrm{ALG}) + \mathrm{com}(\sigma_t; \mathrm{ALG}), \tag{1}$$

where $\mathrm{mig}(\sigma_t; \mathrm{ALG})$ is the migration cost at time t (α or 0) and $\mathrm{com}(\sigma_t; \mathrm{ALG})$ is the communication cost of σ_t (1 or 0). Let $\mathrm{ON}(\sigma)$ and $\mathrm{OFF}(\sigma)$ be the cost induced by σ on an online algorithm ON and an optimal offline algorithm OFF, respectively. In contrast to ON, which learns the requests one-by-one as it serves them, OFF has a complete knowledge of the entire request sequence σ ahead of time. We are in the realm of online algorithms and competitive analysis: We want to design online repartitioning algorithms which provide conservative (worst-case) guarantees, and minimize the (strict) competitive ratio:

$$\rho(\mathrm{ON}) = \max_\sigma \frac{\mathrm{ON}(\sigma)}{\mathrm{OFF}(\sigma)}. \tag{2}$$

To be competitive, an online repartitioning algorithm has to define a strategy for each of the following questions:

(A) *Serve remotely or migrate ("rent or buy")?* If a communication pattern is short-lived, it may not be worthwhile to collocate the nodes: the migration cost cannot be amortized.

(B) *Where to migrate, and what?* If nodes should be collocated, the question becomes where. Should u_t be migrated to $C(v_t)$, v_t to $C(u_t)$, or should both nodes be migrated to a new cluster? Moreover, an algorithm may be required to pro-actively migrate (resp. swap) additional nodes.

(C) *Which nodes to evict?* There may not exist sufficient space in the desired destination cluster. In this case, the algorithm needs to decide which nodes to evict, to free up space.

Our Contributions. This paper introduces the online balanced repartitioning problem. We consider deterministic algorithms and make the following technical contributions:

1. *Online Rematching:* For the special case of online rematching ($k = 2$, but arbitrary ℓ), Theorem 1 presents a greedy online algorithm which is almost optimal: it is 7-competitive and we prove a lower bound of 3.

2. *Lower Bounds:* While in a setting without augmentation, a $k - 1$ lower bound for the competitive ratio of any online algorithm follows from a simulation of online paging, in Theorem 2, we show a lower bound which is strictly larger than k, for any $\alpha > 0$. Intriguingly, we show that the online repartitioning problem remains hard even with augmentation. In particular, in Theorem 3 we prove that no augmented online algorithm can achieve a competitive ratio below k, as long as it cannot solve the problem trivially by placing all nodes into a single cluster. In contrast, online paging is known to become constant competitive with constant augmentation [29].

3. *Online Balanced Repartitioning:* Our main technical contribution stated in Theorem 4 is a non-trivial $O(k \log k)$-competitive algorithm for the setting with 4-augmentation.

Observe that none of our bounds depends on ℓ. This is interesting, as for example, in our motivating virtual machine collocation problem, k is likely to be small: a server typically hosts a small number of virtual machines (e.g., related to the constant number of cores on the server).

Paper Organization. The remainder of this paper is organized as follows. After reviewing related work in Sect. 2, we start by discussing the special case of matchings ($k = 2$) in Sect. 3. We consider lower bounds for the general setting with and without augmentation in Sect. 4. Section 5 is then devoted to the presentation and analysis of CREP, an augmented deterministic algorithm. We conclude in Sect. 6. Due to space constraints, some technical details and proofs only appear in our technical report [6].

2   Related Work

Our work assumes a new perspective on several classic algorithmic problems. The static version of our problem (without migration) is the minimum balanced graph partitioning problem (where ℓ is the number of components). This problem is known to be NP-complete, and cannot even be approximated within any finite factor [4]. The static variant where $k = 2$ corresponds to a maximum matching problem, which is polynomial-time solvable. The static variant where $\ell = 2$ corresponds to the minimum bisection problem [17] and can be approximated within a factor of $O(\log^{1.5} n)$ from the minimum cost [20]. The concept of cluster-size augmentation is inspired by offline *bicriteria* approximations to graph partitioning, in particular the (ℓ, δ)-balanced graph partitioning problem [4], where the graph has to be partitioned in ℓ components of size less than $\delta \cdot \frac{n}{\ell}$, as well as by the concept of c-balanced cuts used by Arora, Rao, and Vazirani [5], where both partitioned components should be of size at least $c \cdot n$.

In terms of online algorithms, the subproblem of finding a good trade-off between serving requests remotely (at a low but repeated communication cost) or migrating nodes together (entailing a potentially high one-time cost α), is essentially a ski rental or rent-or-buy problem [21,22]. A similar tradeoff also arises in the context of online page and server migration problems [9,10], where requests appear in a metric space [11] or graph [7] over time, and need to be served by one [10] or multiple [19] servers. However, in BRP, the number of possible node-cluster configurations is large, rendering it difficult to cast the problem into an online metrical task system. Moreover, in contrast to most online migration problems, which typically optimize the placement of a page or server with respect to the request locations, in our model, *both* end-points of a communication request are subject to optimization. A second difference to the usual models studied in the literature (where requests appear at specific locations in the metric space) is that in our problem a request only reveals partial and binary information about the optimal location (resp. configuration) to serve it: the request can be served at cost zero whenever the communicating are collocated.

Our model can be seen as a generalization of online paging [18,23,24,30], sometimes also referred to as online caching, where requests for data items arrive over time and need to be served from a cache of finite capacity, and where the number of cache misses must be minimized. The online caching and paging problem was first analyzed in the framework of the competitive analysis by Sleator and Tarjan [29], who presented a $kALG/(kALG - kOPT + 1)$-competitive algorithm, where $kALG$ is the cache size of the online and $kOPT$ the cache size of the offline algorithm. The authors also proved that no deterministic online algorithm can beat this ratio. In the classic caching model and its variants [12,13,24], items need to be put into the cache upon each request, and the problem usually boils down to finding a smart eviction strategy, such as Least Recently Used (LRU) or Flush-When-Full (FWF). In contrast, in our setting, requests can be served remotely. In this light, our model is reminiscent of caching models *with bypassing* [1,16]. In fact, it is easy to see that in a scenario with $\ell = 2$ clusters, online paging can be simulated: in this simulation, one cluster can be used as the cache and the other cluster as the slow memory; by the corresponding problem reduction we also obtain a $k - 1$ lower bound for our problem without augmentation. However, in general, in our model, the "cache" is *distributed*: requests occur *between* nodes and *not to* nodes, and costs can be saved by collocation.

BRP also has connections to online packing problems, where items of different sizes arriving over time need to be packed into a minimal number of bins [26,28]. In contrast to these problems, however, in our case the objective is not to minimize the number of bins but rather the number of "links" between bins, given a fixed number of bins.

Finally, our model also connects to recent work on online clique and correlation clustering [3,8,15,27]. In this prior work, nodes and/or links can appear over time, but the underlying communication graph remains invariant.

3   Online Rematching

Let us first consider the special case where clusters are of size two ($k = 2$, arbitrary ℓ). This is essentially an online maximal (re)matching problem: clusters of size two host (resp. "match") exactly one pair of nodes, and maximizing pairwise communication within each cluster is equivalent to minimizing inter-cluster communication. In a $k = 2$ scenario, the question of which node to evict is trivial: there is simply no choice. The problem can also be seen from a ski-rental perspective: one has to identify a good tradeoff between serving requests remotely ("renting") and migrating the communicating nodes together ("buy").

A natural greedy online algorithm GREEDY to solve this problem proceeds as follows: For each cluster C_i, hosting nodes u_i, v_i, we count the total number of inter-cluster requests over time for its nodes. After 3α requests occur between nodes inside any cluster C_1 to nodes outside the cluster, we identify the cluster C_2 with which C_1 communicated most frequently in this time period. We then collocate u_1 with the single node in C_2 (v_2 or u_2) with which it communicated the most—ties broken arbitrarily and without involving any other clusters in the repartitioning. Afterwards, we reset all pairwise communication counters involving nodes from (old) clusters C_1 and C_2 (i.e., u_1, u_2, v_1, v_2).

Theorem 1. GREEDY *is 7-competitive. No deterministic online algorithm achieves a competitive ratio below 3 when* $|\sigma| \to \infty$.

4   Lower Bounds for Online Balanced Repartitioning

Our problem is generally hard to approximate online. While it is easy to see that a lower bound of $k - 1$ follows by simulating online paging (using only two servers), in the following we prove a strictly larger lower bound (cf. Theorem 2). In fact, we observe that, even with augmentation, our problem is hard to approximate online: as long as the augmentation is less than what would be required to solve the partitioning problem trivially, by putting all nodes into the same cluster (i. e., $\delta < \ell$), no deterministic online algorithm can achieve a competitive ratio better than k (cf. Theorem 3). This highlights an intriguing difference from online paging, where the competitive ratio becomes constant under augmentation [29]. Our lower bounds are independent of the initial configuration: both OFF and ON start off having the nodes placed identically in clusters.

Theorem 2. *No deterministic online algorithm can achieve a competitive ratio smaller than* $k + \frac{k-2}{2\alpha}$, *independently of* ℓ.

Interestingly, an adversary can outwit any online algorithm, even in the setting with augmentation. In the following, we consider online algorithms which, compared to OFF, have δ-times more space in each cluster.

Theorem 3. *No* δ-*augmented deterministic online algorithm can achieve a competitive ratio smaller than* k, *as long as* $\delta < \ell$.

5   CREP Algorithm: An $O(k \log k)$ Upper Bound

The main technical contribution of this paper is an online *Component-based REPartitioning algorithm (CREP)* which achieves an almost tight upper bound matching the k lower bound of Theorem 3 with augmentation at least 4. Intuitively, it helps to think of a 4-augmented algorithm as one that can use twice as many clusters, each having twice as much space (though this is a special case of the definition of augmentation). Formally, we claim:

Theorem 4. *With augmentation at least 4,* CREP *is* $O(k \log k)$-*competitive.*

CREP is summarized in Algorithm 1. The algorithm is non-trivial and relies on the following basic ideas:

1. *Communication components.* CREP groups nodes which have recently communicated into *components*. Once the cumulative communication cost of a group of nodes distributed across two or more components exceeds a certain threshold, CREP merges them into a single component, by collocating them in the same cluster. That is, we maintain a logical, time-varying weighted component graph $G_t = (\Phi_t, E_t, w_t)$, where Φ_t is the set of components immediately after request t has been issued, the edges E_t connect components which communicated at least once during this epoch, and w_t is the number of communication requests between the corresponding two nodes in this epoch. In other words, an edge $(i, j) \in E$ between two components $\phi_i, \phi_j \in \Phi_t$ indicates that the two components (resp. the corresponding nodes in ϕ_i and those in ϕ_j) were involved in $w_{ij} > 0$ requests. Although the graph G_t changes over time (when components are merged or split according to CREP), when the time is clear from the context, we drop the time-index and simply write $G = (\Phi, E, w)$. Edges disappear (and their weights are reset) when the components are merged. For a *component set* $X = \{\phi_i, \phi_j, \dots\} \subseteq \Phi$, let $|X|$ denote the number of components in X. We call $\mathrm{vol}(X) = \sum_{\phi \in X} |c|$ the *volume* of the set and $\mathrm{com}(X) = \sum_{\phi_i, \phi_j \in X} w_{ij}$ the *communication cost* among the members of X.

2. *Component epochs.* We analyze CREP in terms of component-wise epochs. A component epoch starts with the first request between two individual nodes (singleton components), and ends when: (i) the size of the component (the number of nodes in the component) exceeds k and (ii) the accumulated communication between the components exceeds a certain threshold. CREP maintains the invariant that components are never split during an epoch, that is, once two nodes of the same component epoch are placed together in a cluster, they will remain in the same cluster in the remainder of the epoch (but they may possibly be migrated together to a new cluster). As such, when a component set X is merged into a new component (Line 7), CREP tries to migrate all the components to the cluster of the largest component (ties broken arbitrarily). If there is not enough reserved space in the cluster, then all components are migrated to a new cluster. If on the other hand $\mathrm{vol}(X)$ exceeds k, the component-epoch ends, and all $\phi \in X$ are reset to singleton components (Line 19). More specifically, according to Algorithm 1, *two* termination criteria have to be fulfilled for a component set Y to end an epoch: $\mathrm{vol}(Y) > k$ *and* $\mathrm{com}(Y) \geq \mathrm{vol}(Y) \cdot \alpha$. This non-trivial criterion is critical, to keep the migration cost competitive. An epoch that ends as a result of a set Y is referred to as a Y-epoch.

3. *Space reservations.* In order to keep the number of migrations low, CREP performs space reservations in clusters. Whenever CREP migrates a component ϕ into a cluster, it reserves additional space $\mathrm{reserve}(\phi) = \min\{k - |\phi|, |\phi|\}$. As we will prove, these proactive space reservations can ensure that a component has to be migrated again only after its size doubles. For a cluster s, let $\mathrm{reserved}(s), \mathrm{occupied}(s)$ and $\mathrm{spare}(s)$ denote the reserved, occupied and spare (unreserved) space in s, where always $\mathrm{reserved}(s) + \mathrm{occupied}(s) + \mathrm{spare}(s) = 2k$. Similarly, for a component ϕ let $\mathrm{reserved}(\phi)$ denote the amount of its reserved space that is still available in its current cluster.

The remainder of this section is devoted to the proof of Theorem 4. The proof unfolds in a number of observations and lemmas. We first observe, in Property 1, that indeed, it is always possible to find a cluster where the to-be-merged components fit. We then derive an upper bound on CREP's cost per component epoch and a lower bound on the optimal offline cost per component epoch. Finally, we show that the competitive ratio is also bounded with respect to incomplete epochs.

We start by observing that there always exists a cluster which can host the entire merged component, including the required reserved space without any evacuation, i.e., its spare space is at least k.

Property 1. At any point in time, a cluster exists having at least k spare space.

So indeed, CREP can always place a merged component greedily into clusters—no global component rearrangement is necessary. On the other hand, augmenting the cluster size allows CREP to reserve additional space for migrated components. As we show in the following, this ensures that each node

---

Algorithm 1. CREP with 4 Augmentation

1: Construct graph $G = (\Psi, E, w)$ with singleton components: one component per node. Set $w_{ij} = 0$ for all $\{v_i, v_j\} \in \binom{V}{2}$. For each component ϕ_i, reserve space reserve$(\phi_i) = 1$.

2: **for** each new request $\{u_t, v_t\}$ **do**
$\qquad\qquad\qquad\qquad\qquad\qquad\qquad\qquad\qquad$ ▷ Keep track of communication cost.
3: $\qquad$ Let $\phi_i = \Phi(u_t)$ and $\phi_j = \Phi(v_t)$ be the two components that communicated.
4: $\qquad$ **if** $\phi_i \neq \phi_j$ **then**
5: $\qquad\qquad$ $w_{ij} \leftarrow w_{ij} + 1$
6: $\qquad$ **end if**
$\qquad\qquad\qquad\qquad\qquad\qquad\qquad\qquad\qquad\qquad\qquad$ ▷ Merge components.
7: $\qquad$ Let X be the largest cardinality set with vol$(X) \leq k$ and com$(X) \geq (|X| - 1) \cdot \alpha$

8: $\qquad$ **if** $|X| > 1$ **then**
9: $\qquad\qquad$ Let $\phi_0 = \bigcup_{\phi_i \in X} \phi_i$ and for all $\phi_j \in \Phi \backslash X$ set $w_{0j} = \sum_{\phi_i \in X} w_{ij}$.
10: $\qquad\qquad$ Let $\phi \in X$ be the component having the largest reserved space.
11: $\qquad\qquad$ **if** reserved$(\phi) \geq$ vol$(X) - |\phi|$ **then**
12: $\qquad\qquad\qquad$ Migrate ϕ_0 to the cluster hosting ϕ
13: $\qquad\qquad\qquad$ Update reserved$(\phi_0) =$ reserved$(\phi) - ($vol$(X) - |\phi|)$
14: $\qquad\qquad$ **else**
15: $\qquad\qquad\qquad$ Migrate ϕ_0 to a cluster s with spare$(s) \geq \min(k, 2|\phi_0|)$
16: $\qquad\qquad\qquad$ Set reserved$(\phi_0) = \min(k - |\phi_0|, |\phi_0|)$
17: $\qquad\qquad$ **end if**
18: $\qquad$ **end if**
$\qquad\qquad\qquad\qquad\qquad\qquad\qquad\qquad\qquad\qquad\qquad$ ▷ End of a Y-epoch.
19: $\qquad$ Let Y be the smallest components set with vol$(Y) > k$ and , $Y \geq$ vol$(Y) \cdot \alpha$
20: $\qquad$ **if** $Y \neq \emptyset$ **then**
21: $\qquad\qquad$ Split every $\phi_i \in Y$ into ϕ_i singleton components and reset the weights of all edges involving at least one newly created component. Reserve one additional space for each newly created component. If necessary, migrate at most vol$(Y)/2 + 1$ singletons to clusters with spare space.
22: $\qquad$ **end if**
23: **end for**

---

is migrated at most $\log k$ times (rather than k) during the formation of a component.

Upper bound on CREP's costs. The online algorithm's cost during each epoch consists of the *communication cost*, which amounts to the number of communication requests that were served remotely, and the *migration cost*, which is equal to the number of node migrations. The following properties provide upper bounds for both kinds of costs for a single component:

Property 2. At any point in time, consider a component c induced by the communication pattern in this epoch, then:

1. The communication cost between nodes in ϕ is, in this epoch, at most $(|\phi| - 1) \cdot \alpha$.
2. The migration cost of nodes in ϕ is, in this epoch, at most $(|\phi| \log |\phi|) \cdot \alpha$.

Proof (Proof of Property 2). The two properties are proved in turn.

Property 2.1. We prove this property by induction on the *merging sequence*, i.e., the sequence of merges that includes all the nodes in ϕ from the time when they were singletons, ordered by time. To establish the base case, consider the first merge of nodes in ϕ, where X was a set of singletons (Line 7) and $|X|$ singleton components were combined into a new component $\phi_0 = \cup_{\phi_i \in X} \phi_i$. By CREP's merging condition, the cost up to this point is equal to $(|X| - 1) \cdot \alpha = (|\phi_0| - 1) \cdot \alpha$. For the inductive step, consider again that X' is merged into ϕ_0 and suppose that the communication cost paid for each component $\phi' \in X'$ is $(|\phi'| - 1) \cdot \alpha$. After the merge, CREP's total communication cost is equal to

$$(|X'| - 1) \cdot \alpha + \sum_{\phi_i \in X'} (|\phi_i| - 1) \cdot \alpha = \left(\sum_{\phi_i \in X'} |\phi_i| \right) \cdot \alpha - \alpha = (|\phi_0| - 1) \cdot \alpha \text{ and}$$

the induction holds.

Property 2.2. First observe that any node u which belongs to ϕ is migrated at most $\log |\phi|$ times during an epoch. To see this, suppose that u was just migrated into a cluster and that the size of u's current component is $|\phi'|$. From Property 1, we know that u will not be migrated as a consequence of a merge that does not involve u's component (i.e., it will never be evicted). Furthermore, due to the existence of reserved space, u will stay in the same cluster as long as the size of its current component ϕ' remains smaller or equal to $2|\phi'|$. Since the size of u's component between any consecutive migrations doubles, the total migrations can be at most $\log |\phi|$. This implies the total number of migrations pertaining to all nodes in ϕ is at most $|\phi| \log |\phi|$.

Using Property 2, we can bound the migration and communication cost of a Y-epoch:

Lemma 1. *Consider the end of a Y-epoch (Line 19). CREP migrates at most $\sum_{\phi_i \in Y} |\phi_i| \log |\phi_i| \leq vol(Y) \cdot \log k$ nodes and serves at most $2 \, vol(Y) \cdot \alpha$ remote requests during this epoch for nodes in Y.*

The proof of Lemma 1 follows directly from Property 2 and is omitted.
Lower bound on Off's cost. Having derived an upper bound on CREP's cost, we next compute a lower bound of OFF's cost.

Lemma 2. *By the end of a Y-epoch, OFF pays at least $vol(Y)/k \cdot \alpha$ communication cost (during this epoch) for nodes in Y.*

To establish the above lower bound, we will need two useful properties.

Property 3. Consider any component ϕ in the current epoch and *any* partition of ϕ into two non-empty disjoint sets B and W, with $B \cup W = \phi$. During the creation of ϕ (by merging), there were at least α communication requests between nodes in B and W.

Proof (Proof of Property 3). Consider the tree T which describes how component ϕ merged from singletons into ϕ during the current epoch. The leafs of the tree are the nodes in ϕ and each internal node corresponds to a component set X that was found in Line 7 of the algorithm, and entails a merge to a new component ϕ_0. Now color the leafs of the tree according to W and B. Since both sets are non-empty there must exist an internal node τ in T, whose descendant leafs in the subtree are not colored identically. Let $B' = \{b_1, b_2, \ldots, b_p\}$ be the child components of τ which are in B, and let $W' = \{w_1, w_2, \ldots, w_q\}$ be the components which are children of τ and which are in W. Let X be the set corresponding to the descendant leafs of τ and note that $X = B' \cup W'$ and $|X| = p + q$. Since neither B' nor W' were merged earlier, the total communication cost among B' (resp. W') is at most $(p-1)\alpha$ (resp. $(q-1)\alpha$), which sums up to at most $(p+q-2)\alpha$. But since X is witnessing a communication cost of at least $(|X|-1)\alpha = (p+q-1)\alpha$, there must have occurred at least $(p+q-1)\alpha - (p+q-2)\alpha = \alpha$ communication cost between the nodes in B and the nodes in W during the current epoch.

Property 4. Consider *any* two non-empty disjoint subsets of components $U, V \subset Y$ s.t. $U \cup V = Y$ and $\mathrm{vol}(U) < k$ (i.e., U's components fit in one cluster). The inter-communication cost between U and V is at least α during the Y-epoch.

Proof (Proof of Property 4). The proof follows from the minimality of Y and because no merge involving components happened in Y. From the Y-epoch termination condition, we have $\mathrm{com}(Y) = \mathrm{com}(U) + \mathrm{com}(V) + \mathrm{inter}(U, V) \geq \mathrm{vol}(Y) \cdot \alpha$, where $\mathrm{inter}(U, V)$ is the inter-communication cost between U and V. Assume for the sake of contradiction that $\mathrm{inter}(U, V) < \alpha$. Recall that $\mathrm{vol}(U) \leq k$ and, since the components in U have not been merged yet, $\mathrm{com}(U) \leq (|U| - 1) \cdot \alpha \leq (\mathrm{vol}(U) - 1) \cdot \alpha$ (the equality holds when $|U| = 1$). We therefore have

$$\mathrm{com}(V) = \mathrm{com}(Y) - \mathrm{com}(U) - \mathrm{inter}(U, V)$$
$$> \mathrm{vol}(Y) \cdot \alpha - (\mathrm{vol}(U) - 1) \cdot \alpha - \alpha = \mathrm{vol}(V) \cdot \alpha.$$

We obtain the desired contradiction by distinguishing between two cases: (i) If $\mathrm{vol}(V) > k$, then $V \subset Y$ meets both termination conditions of a component epoch (Line 19), and thus the minimality of set Y is contradicted. (ii) Next, consider that $\mathrm{vol}(V) \leq k$ and notice that it must hold that $|V| > 1$ (otherwise $\mathrm{com}(V) = 0$). Since the components in V have not been merged yet, $\mathrm{com}(V) \leq (|V| - 1) \cdot \alpha \leq (\mathrm{vol}(V) - 1) \cdot \alpha \leq \mathrm{vol}(V) \cdot \alpha$, which is again a contradiction.

Proof (Proof of Lemma 2). We now use Properties 3 and 4 to lower bound OFF's cost. First, it follows from Property 3 that OFF cannot gain by splitting any component $\phi \in Y$ between different clusters (which would only increase its cost). The question is then, how much can OFF reduce the inter-communication cost by arranging $\phi \in Y$ more efficiently? Let R_{intra} be the number of inter-communication requests (of CREP) OFF did not pay by placing the components in an optimal way. Furthermore, denote by s the number of clusters OFF used and by $b_j \leq k$ the number of nodes OFF placed in each cluster $j = 1, \ldots, s$. Consider any cluster j. In the best case for OFF, each of the b_j nodes in the cluster is a singleton component which CREP placed in a different cluster. It follows that OFF's saved cost cannot be greater than $(b_j - 1)\alpha$: otherwise CREP would have merged the b_j components into a single component. Observe also that, although OFF aims to put the components in as few possible clusters, by a simple pigeonhole argument, s must be at least $\text{vol}(Y)/k$. Combining the above, the number of requests R_{inter} OFF serves remotely (assuming that no node was migrated during the Y-epoch) is

$$R_{inter} = \text{vol}(Y) \cdot \alpha - R_{intra} \geq \text{vol}(Y) \cdot \alpha - \sum_{j=1}^{s}(b_j - 1) \cdot \alpha$$

$$= \left(\text{vol}(Y) - \sum_{j=1}^{s} b_j + \sum_{j=1}^{s} 1\right) \cdot \alpha \geq \sum_{j=1}^{\text{vol}(Y)/k} 1 = \frac{\text{vol}(Y)}{k} \cdot \alpha,$$

where the last step follows from the fact that $\sum_{j=1}^{s} b_j = \text{vol}(Y)$.

It remains to show that OFF cannot decrease R_{inter} any further by swapping nodes during the Y-epoch. From Property 4, the nodes in each cluster j communicated at least α times with clusters $i \neq j$. Since any swap that OFF performs between two clusters costs at least 2α, a swap between the involved clusters can only be beneficial to ON. Considering that there are at least $s \geq \text{vol}(Y)/k$ clusters, even with migrations, OFF's cost will be at least $\text{vol}(Y)/k \cdot \alpha$.

Incomplete Component Epoch. So far, we have quantified the cost that CREP and OFF pay *at the end of each epoch*. It remains to account for the costs that CREP accumulates in incomplete epochs.

First, let us observe that the edge weights w of incomplete epochs in the component graph are naturally bounded: at some point, the edge will cause a merge, or end the epoch. By dividing the edges of the component graph G into *light edges* and *heavy edges*, we can claim the following:

Property 5. For every edge (ϕ_i, ϕ_j) in the component graph, at any given time:

1. If $|\phi_i| + |\phi_j| \leq k$ (we call this a *light edge*), the edge has cost at most α.
2. If $|\phi_i| + |\phi_j| > k$ (we call this a *heavy edge*), the edge cost is at most $(|\phi_i| + |\phi_j|)\alpha \leq (2k)\alpha$

The claim is implied by the definition of CREP. In the first case, if the (ϕ_i, ϕ_j) edge cost was larger than α, CREP would have merged ϕ_i and ϕ_j into a new component. Similarly, in the second case, if the edge (ϕ_i, ϕ_j) cost was larger than $(|\phi_i| + |\phi_j|)\alpha$, CREP would have ended the epoch.

Let us consider the request sequence σ at some time t. Recall that at the end of an epoch, we reset all involved edge weights, and charge OFF for them. So at time t, we have not taken into account yet the communication requests that were not reset. For any two nodes u and v, we consider all their communication requests since the last time they belonged to the same Y, at the end of a Y-epoch. All these requests belong to what we call the *last epoch*. Note that σ may not contain any complete epochs at all. But every request $\{u, v\} \in \sigma$ must belong to some Y-epoch or to the last epoch. Using Property 5 we obtain:

Lemma 3. *The competitive ratio of CREP for communication requests which belong to the* last *epoch, is bounded by $O(k \log k)$.*

The competitive ratio of CREP follows from Lemmas 1, 2, and 3.

6 Conclusion

This paper initiated the study of a natural dynamic partitioning problem which finds applications, e.g., in the context of virtualized distributed systems subject to changing communication patterns. We derived different upper and lower bounds, both for the general case as well as for a special case describing a matching problem. While the derived competitive ratios are sometimes linear or even super-linear in k, they do not depend on ℓ: We believe that this is attractive in practice: for example, while the number of servers in a datacenter (i.e., ℓ) can be large, the number of virtual machines hosted per server (e.g., the number of cores) is usually small. The main open question raised by our work regards the optimality of our upper bound: currently, the upper and lower bounds are off by a logarithmic factor. Moreover, it will be interesting to explore randomized settings: While we have some early positive results on the potential of randomization for special problem instances, the feasibility of $o(k)$-competitive randomized algorithms remains an open problem.

References

1. Adamaszek, A., Czumaj, A., Englert, M., Räcke, H.: An O(log k)-competitive algorithm for generalized caching. In: Proceedings of 23rd SODA, pp. 1681–1689 (2012)
2. Al-Fares, M., Loukissas, A., Vahdat, A.: A scalable, commodity data center network architecture. ACM SIGCOMM CCR **38**(4), 63–74 (2008)
3. Andreev, K., Räcke, H.: Balanced graph partitioning. In: Proceedings of 16th Annual ACM Symposium on Parallelism in Algorithms and Architectures (SPAA) (2004)
4. Andreev, K., Räcke, H.: Balanced graph partitioning. Theory Comput. Syst. **39**(6), 929–939 (2006)
5. Arora, S., Rao, S., Vazirani, U.: Expander flows, geometric embeddings and graph partitioning. J. ACM (JACM) **56**(2), 5 (2009)
6. Avin, C., Loukas, A., Pacut, M., Schmid, S.: Online balanced repartitioning. arXiv https://arxiv.org/abs/1511.02074 (2016)
7. Awerbuch, B., Bartal, Y., Fiat, A.: Competitive distributed file allocation. Inf. Comput. **185**(1), 1–40 (2003)
8. Bansal, N., Blum, A., Chawla, S.: Correlation clustering. Mach. Learn. **56**(1–3), 89–113 (2004)

9. Bartal, Y., Charikar, M., Indyk, P.: On page migration and other relaxed task systems. Theor. Comput. Sci. **268**(1), 43–66 (2001). Also appeared in Proceedings of the 8th SODA, pp. 43–52 (1997)
10. Bienkowski, M., Feldmann, A., Grassler, J., Schaffrath, G., Schmid, S.: The wide-area virtual service migration problem: a competitive analysis approach. IEEE/ACM Trans. Netw. **22**(1), 165–178 (2014)
11. Borodin, A., Linial, N., Saks, M.E.: An optimal on-line algorithm for metrical task system. J. ACM **39**(4), 745–763 (1992). Also appeared in Proceedings of the 19th STOC, pp. 373–382 (1987)
12. Brehob, M., Enbody, R.J., Torng, E., Wagner, S.: On-line restricted caching. J. Sched. **6**(2), 149–166 (2003)
13. Buchbinder, N., Chen, S., Naor, J.S.: Competitive algorithms for restricted caching and matroid caching. In: Schulz, A.S., Wagner, D. (eds.) ESA 2014. LNCS, vol. 8737, pp. 209–221. Springer, Heidelberg (2014)
14. Chowdhury, M., Zaharia, M., Ma, J., Jordan, M.I., Stoica, I.: Managing data transfers in computer clusters with orchestra. SIGCOMM CCR **41**(4), 98–109 (2011)
15. Ding, C.H.Q., He, X., Zha, H., Gu, M., Simon, H.D.: A min-max cut algorithm for graph partitioning and data clustering. In: Proceedings of IEEE International Conference on Data Mining (ICDM), pp. 107–114 (2001)
16. Epstein, L., Imreh, C., Levin, A., Nagy-György, J.: Online file caching with rejection penalties. Algorithmica **71**(2), 279–306 (2015)
17. Feige, U., Krauthgamer, R.: A polylogarithmic approximation of the minimum bisection. SIAM J. Comput. **31**(4), 1090–1118 (2002)
18. Fiat, A., Karp, R.M., Luby, M., McGeoch, L.A., Sleator, D.D., Young, N.E.: Competitive paging algorithms. J. Algorithms **12**(4), 685–699 (1991)
19. Fiat, A., Rabani, Y., Ravid, Y.: Competitive k-server algorithms. J. Comput. Syst. Sci. **48**(3), 410–428 (1994)
20. Krauthgamer, R., Feige, U.: A polylogarithmic approximation of the minimum bisection. SIAM Rev. **48**(1), 99–130 (2006)
21. Kumar, A., Gupta, A., Roughgarden, T.: A constant-factor approximation algorithm for the multicommodity rent-or-buy problem. In Proceedings of 43rd Symposium on Foundations of Computer Science (FOCS) (2002)
22. Lotker, Z., Patt-Shamir, B., Rawitz, D.: Rent, lease or buy: randomized algorithms for multislope ski rental. In: Proceedings of the 25th Symposium on Theoretical Aspects of Computer Science (STACS), pp. 503–514 (2008)
23. McGeoch, L.A., Sleator, D.D.: A strongly competitive randomized paging algorithm. Algorithmica **6**(6), 816–825 (1991)
24. Mendel, M., Seiden, S.S.: Online companion caching. Theor. Comput. Sci. **324**(2–3), 183–200 (2004)
25. Mogul, J.C., Popa, L.: What we talk about when we talk about cloud network performance. ACM SIGCOMM CCR **42**, 44–48 (2012)
26. Ramanan, P.V., Brown, D.J., Lee, C.C., Lee, D.T.: On-line bin packing in linear time. J. Algorithms **10**(3), 305–326 (1989)
27. Schaeffer, S.E.: Graph clustering. Comput. Sci. Rev. **1**(1), 27–64 (2007)
28. Seiden, S.S.: On the online bin packing problem. J. ACM **49**(5), 640–671 (2002)
29. Sleator, D.D., Tarjan, R.E.: Amortized efficiency of list update and paging rules. Commun. ACM **28**(2), 202–208 (1985)
30. Young, N.E.: On-line caching as cache size varies. In: Proceedings of the 2nd ACM-SIAM Symposium on Discrete Algorithms (SODA), pp. 241–250 (1991)

Lower Bound on the Step Complexity
of Anonymous Binary Consensus

Hagit Attiya[1]($\boxtimes$), Ohad Ben-Baruch[2]($\boxtimes$), and Danny Hendler[2]($\boxtimes$)

[1] Department of Computer Science, Technion, Haifa, Israel
hagit@cs.technion.ac.il
[2] Department of Computer-Science,
Ben-Gurion University of the Negev, Beer-Sheva, Israel
bbohad@gmail.com, hendlerd@cs.bgu.ac.il

Abstract. *Obstruction-free* consensus, ensuring that a process running solo will eventually terminate, is at the core of practical ways to solve consensus, e.g., by using randomization or failure detectors. An obstruction-free consensus algorithm may not terminate in many executions, but it must terminate whenever a process runs solo. Such an algorithm can be evaluated by its *solo step complexity*, which bounds the worst case number of steps taken by a process running alone, from any configuration, until it decides.

This paper presents a lower bound of $\Omega(\log n)$ on the solo step complexity of obstruction-free binary anonymous consensus. The proof constructs a sequence of executions in which more and more distinct variables are about to be written to, and then uses the *backtracking covering* technique to obtain a single execution in which many variables are accessed.

1 Introduction

Consensus is an essential coordination mechanism for distributed systems: processes start with inputs from some domain and have to decide on the same output value, which is the input of some process. In asynchronous distributed systems, a consensus algorithm cannot ensure termination regardless of the way processes' steps are interleaved. It is possible, however, to solve *obstruction-free* consensus, ensuring that a process running solo will eventually terminate. This progress property is at the core of practical ways to solve consensus, e.g., by using randomization or failure detectors.

The feasibility and usefulness of obstruction-free consensus raise the important question of the resources, especially in terms of space and time, needed for solving it. An obstruction-free consensus algorithm may not terminate in many executions, and therefore, its worst-case time complexity—measured over

---

This work is supported by the Israel Science Foundation (grant 1749/14). The second and third authors are also supported by the Lynne and William Frankel Center for Computing Science at Ben-Gurion University.

© Springer-Verlag Berlin Heidelberg 2016
C. Gavoille and D. Ilcinkas (Eds.): DISC 2016, LNCS 9888, pp. 257–268, 2016.
DOI: 10.1007/978-3-662-53426-7_19

all executions—is unbounded. However, since an obstruction-free consensus algorithm terminates whenever a process runs *solo*, i.e., without interleaving of steps by other processes, it makes sense to evaluate its time complexity by counting the worst case number of steps taken by a process running alone, *from any configuration*, until it decides. This measure, called the *solo step complexity* [3], is formally defined in Sect. 2.

Our Contribution: Our main result is a lower bound of $\Omega(\log n)$ on the solo step complexity of obstruction-free *binary* anonymous consensus, where the domain of input values is $\{0, 1\}$. The first part of the proof is a construction of a sequence of executions in which more and more distinct variables are about to be written to.[1] Each of these variables must be read in some execution in the sequence, but not necessarily all in the same execution. To obtain a single solo execution in which many variables are accessed, we employ the *backtracking covering* technique [1,3,6] to get an $\Omega(\log n)$ lower bound for the solo step complexity of obstruction-free anonymous binary consensus.

This is the first lower bound on the step complexity of a one-shot problem with inputs from a domain of constant size. As we show, the lower bound also holds for *solo-fast* algorithms [3,10], in which a process only reads and writes when it runs solo, but may resort to any other primitives, including *compare & swap* or even general *read-modify-write* operations, when it encounters contention.

Related Work: Attiya et al. [3] define solo step complexity and solo-fast algorithms and prove an $\Omega(\log n)$ lower bound for the space and solo step complexity of solo-fast implementations of *perturbable* objects. These proofs also employ the backtracking covering technique. However, the proofs hold for *long-lived* objects, while our lower bound is for the *one-shot* consensus problem. On the other hand, they do not assume that the implementation is anonymous.

Adopt-Commit objects capture an inherent part of obstruction-free and randomized consensus. Aspnes and Ellen [2] prove an $\Omega(\min\{n, \frac{\log m}{\log \log m}\})$ lower bound on the space and solo step complexity of anonymous Adopt-Commit objects, with input domain of size m. Since a consensus algorithm implies an implementation of an Adopt-Commit object, the same lower bounds hold for anonymous m-valued consensus. However, the bounds degenerate for binary consensus, leaving open the question of the step complexity for binary consensus, with or without an anonymity assumption. Our paper gives the first answer to this question.

Aspnes and Ellen [2] also present an anonymous Adopt-Commit algorithm whose solo step complexity is in $O(\min\{n, \frac{\log \log m}{\log m}\})$, matching their lower bound. This implies an $O(1)$ upper bound for the solo step complexity of binary Adopt-Commit.

---

[1] A by-product of this part is a very simple proof of an $\Omega(\sqrt{n})$ lower bound for the space complexity of obstruction-free anonymous binary consensus [7,11] (now obsolete, due to [12]).

Table 1. Lower and upper bounds for the solo step complexity of adopt-commit and consensus.

Problem	Lower bound	Upper bound
m-valued adopt-commit	$\Omega(\min\{\frac{\sqrt{\log n}}{\log\log n}, \frac{\log m}{\log\log m}\})$ [2]	$O(n)$
Anonymous m-valued adopt-commit	$\Omega(\min\{\sqrt{n}, \frac{\log m}{\log\log m}\})$ [2,5]	$O(\min\{\sqrt{n}, \frac{\log m}{\log\log m}\})$ [2,5]
Anonymous obstruction-free m-valued consensus	Follows from above	$O(n)$ [3]
Obstruction-free anonymous binary consensus	$\Omega(\log n)$ (this paper)	Follows from above

Recent work by Capdevielle et al. [5] improves these results to bound the *solo write complexity* of binary anonymous consensus, i.e., the number of writes executed when a process runs solo. They show a lower bound of $\Omega(\min\{\sqrt{n}, \frac{\log\log m}{\log m}\})$ on the solo write complexity of anonymous m-valued consensus. They present algorithms with a matching solo write complexity.

An obstruction-free consensus algorithm with $O(n)$ solo step complexity is implied by the results of [3]. A solo-fast consensus algorithm is presented in [10]. The *Janus* algorithm [4] solves obstruction-free anonymous consensus with $O(\sqrt{n})$ writes and $O(n)$ accesses to shared variables on the solo path, regardless of the number of possible values, m.

Table 1 compares our results and known results.

Organization: The model we use and required definitions are provided in Sect. 2. Our lower bound proofs appear in Sect. 3, and we conclude with a short discussion in Sect. 4.

2   Model of Computation

We use a standard model of an anonymous asynchronous shared memory system. A set **P** of $n > 1$ *processes* $p_0, \ldots, p_{n-1}$ communicate by applying primitive operations (*primitives*), e.g., reads, writes and read-modify-write, to shared variables. No bound is assumed on the size of a shared variable (i.e., the number of distinct values it can take).

An *algorithm* is a collection of deterministic state machines, one for each process. The algorithm also assigns initial values to the shared variables. Processes are *anonymous*, that is, they do not have access to process-identifiers and consequently, the steps they perform when executing their algorithms depend only on their initial inputs and on the responses they receive from the operations they apply.

A *configuration* specifies the value of each shared variable and the state of each process. In an *initial configuration*, all shared variables have their initial values and all processes are in their initial states. Each step of process p_i consists of some local computation and one shared memory *event*, which is a primitive applied to a shared variable and the corresponding response. A *block write* is a contiguous sequence of write events, each by a different process.

An *execution fragment* is a (possibly infinite) sequence of events, that results from interleaving the steps taken by processes, according to their state machines. For any finite execution fragment α and any execution fragment α', the execution fragment $\alpha\alpha'$ is the concatenation of α and α'; in this case α' is called an *extension* of α.

An *execution* is an execution fragment that starts from an initial configuration; the configuration at the end of the execution is reached by applying the events of the execution one by one starting from the initial configuration. If C is the configuration at the end of an execution α, we say that α *leads to* C. If another execution α' starts from C, we sometimes write that α' starts from α instead of writing that it starts from C. We denote the configuration reached after executing α starting from C by $C\alpha$. Two executions are *indistinguishable* to a process p, if p issues the same sequence of events and gets the same responses from these events in both executions. We denote by $\alpha|p$ the sequence of events issued by p in α.

Let α be an execution and let p_i, p_j be two processes. We say that p_i, p_j are *clones in* α (or simply *clones* if α is understood from the context) if they start with the same input and if $\alpha|p_i = \alpha|p_j$.

An execution fragment α is Q-*solo*, for a non-empty set of processes $Q \subset \mathbf{P}$, if only processes in Q have events in α. If $Q = \{q\}$, we say that α is q-*solo* instead of $\{q\}$-solo. Unless stated otherwise, a q-solo extension from an execution α (for some process q) refers to the q-solo extension of α in which q completes its operation.

A *consensus* object supports a single *decide* operation that receives an input value from some domain $\mathcal{D}$. In this work, we consider *binary consensus* objects, for which $\mathcal{D} = \{0, 1\}$. Decide operations by different processes must *return* the same output value, which must be one of the inputs.

A process p *participates* in an execution fragment α if p has an event in α. We say that α is *step-contention free for* p if the events of $\alpha|p$ are contiguous in α. Also, α is *step-contention free* if α is step-contention free for all processes. A process p is *eventually step-contention free in* α, if either p returns in α or if some suffix of α is p-solo.

An algorithm is *obstruction-free* if every process that is eventually step-contention free eventually returns [9]. This requirement is equivalent to *solo termination* [7].

Assume that p is eventually step-contention free in an execution α of an obstruction-free algorithm. Then p's *solo step complexity* in α is the number of steps p performs in the p-solo suffix of α until it returns. Since the algorithm is obstruction-free, this number is well-defined. The *solo step complexity* of the algorithm is the supremum of this number over all processes and executions.

An algorithm is *solo-fast* if processes only apply reads and writes in step-contention free executions but can apply additional primitives in other executions.

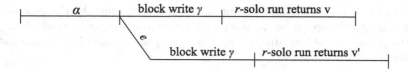

Fig. 1. An (α, γ)-modifying event e.

3   Lower Bound Proof

The lower bound on the solo step complexity of obstruction-free consensus is proved by constructing a sequence of executions. In these executions, events applied by an operation of one process influence the response of an operation of another process. Roughly speaking, since the latter process needs to return a different value, it must be able to distinguish between the different executions, implying that it must read an increasing number of variables.

Throughout the proof, p denotes a process with input 0 that has yet to run; such a process exists as long as not all of the processes participate in the execution. In addition, for any execution α, we can extend α by letting a clone of p run in order to obtain β, and then we can let another clone of p run starting from β. Although in both cases we use a clone of p, we run different processes, one starting from α with input 0, and one starting from β with input 0, where in both cases, these are processes that did not participate in the execution before.

Our proofs generalize the notion of a modifying event, introduced in [8]. Let α be an execution and q be a process participating in α. We define q's solo-valency after α to be the response returned by q in a q-solo execution that extends α and ends when q completes its decide operation. We let $\mathcal{S}(\alpha, p)$ denote this response.

Definition 1. *Let γ be a set of write events about to be applied by a set of processes R after an execution α. Let $r, q \notin R$ be two processes participating in α and let e denote the event that q is about to apply after α. We say that e is an (α, γ)-modifying event for r if $\mathcal{S}(\alpha\gamma, p) \neq \mathcal{S}(\alpha e\gamma, p)$. We say that e is an (α, γ)-visible event for r if the sequences of events performed in the r-solo executions from $\alpha\gamma$ and from $\alpha e\gamma$ differ.*

We say that e is a γ-modifying event for r (a γ-visible event for p) when α can be understood from the context.

Figure 1 illustrates the effect of a modifying event e. Informally, an event is an (α, γ)-modifying event for p if, when executed after α, it changes the response of a p-solo execution that follows the block write γ. An event is an (α, γ)-visible event for p if, when executed after α, p reads a different value from some variable in a solo execution that follows γ, but p's response may or may not change.

Observation 1. *An (α, γ)-visible event for p is a write event applied to a variable other than those to which the events of γ are applied, which is read in a p-solo extension of $\alpha e\gamma$.*

Proof. Let e be an (α, γ)-visible event. If e is not as specified by the observation, then p cannot distinguish between $\alpha\gamma$ and $\alpha e\gamma$ in a solo execution, which implies that the p-solo executions after $\alpha\gamma$ and after $\alpha e\gamma$ are identical. This contradicts Definition 1. □

Observation 2. *A modifying event is a visible event.*

Proof. If e is not a visible event then, from Definition 1, the sequences of events performed in the p-solo extensions of $\alpha\gamma$ and of $\alpha e\gamma$ are identical. In particular, p returns the same responses in these two executions. This contradicts Definition 1. □

We now define the notion of a visible sequence of executions $\{\alpha_i\gamma_i\}_{i=1}^{L}$, which is central to our proof. The i'th execution ends with a block write γ_i, to i distinct variables. The key requirement is that, for all i and $u \in \{0,1\}$, there is an extension of α_i in which a process $q_i^u \neq p$ returns u while γ_i is still pending. Letting v denote p's solo-valency after $\alpha_i\gamma_i$, this allows us to construct the next sequence execution by deploying $q_i^{\overline{v}}$ until it is about to perform a γ_i-visible event for p.

Definition 2. *A visible sequence of length L is a sequence of executions $\{\alpha_i\gamma_i\}_{i=1}^{L}$ such that the following requirements hold:*

1. *At most $\frac{1}{2}i(i+1)$ processes participate in α_i.*
2. *γ_i is a block write by i different processes to i different variables.*
3. *For $v \in \{0,1\}$, there exists a process $q_i^v \neq p$ and a block write $\gamma_i^v \subseteq \gamma_i$, such that $\mathcal{S}(\alpha_i\gamma_i^v, q_i^v) = v$.*

Moreover, the $(i+1)$'th visible execution is constructed from the i'th visible execution as follows: Let $\mathcal{S}(\alpha_i\gamma_i, p) = v$ and let q_i and $\gamma \subseteq \gamma_i$ be such that $\mathcal{S}(\alpha_i\gamma, q_i) = \overline{v}$. Let β denote the q_i-solo extension from $\alpha_i\gamma$ (in which q_i returns $\overline{v}$) and let $\beta = \beta'e_i\beta''$, where e_i is the first γ_i-visible event for p in β. Then $\alpha_{i+1} = \alpha_i\gamma\beta'$ and $\gamma_{i+1} = e_i\gamma_i$, where the events of γ are re-issued in γ_{i+1} by new clone processes.

Figure 2 illustrates the manner in which execution $\alpha_{i+1}\gamma_{i+1}$ is constructed from $\alpha_i\gamma_i$.

We now prove that any anonymous consensus algorithm has a visible sequence of length approximately $\sqrt{n}$. This sequence will be used in order to obtain the step complexity lower bound, using the backtracking covering technique.

Lemma 1. *Let $\mathcal{A}$ be an obstruction-free anonymous binary consensus algorithm, then $\mathcal{A}$ has a visible sequence of length $\Omega(\sqrt{n})$.*

Proof. The construction of the visible sequence is inductive. In the i'th step of the induction, we construct execution $\alpha_i\gamma_i$. Throughout the proof, we fix process p to be some process with input 0. We assume that at least $\lfloor n/2 \rfloor$ of the processes have input 0 and at least $\lfloor n/2 \rfloor$ of them have input 1.

Let C_0 be an initial configuration. For the base case, let q_1^1 be a process with input 1. Let α denote a q_1^1-solo execution starting from C_0. Clearly, q_1^1 must write in the course of α to a variable that is read by a p-solo execution from C_0. Let α_1 denote the prefix of α up until q_1^1's first such write event, denoted e. Let $\gamma_1 = e$, then γ_1 is a block write of size 1. Let $q_1^0 \neq p$ be a process with input 0. Process q_1^0 is a clone of p in C_0. By setting γ_1^0 to be the empty sequence of events, a q_1^0-solo extension from $\alpha_1 \gamma_1^0$ returns 0 (as would a p-solo execution), whereas by setting $\gamma_1^1 = \{e\}$, a q_1^1-solo extension from $\alpha_1 \gamma_1^1$ returns 1, implying that Requirements 2 and 3 of Definition 2 hold. In addition, exactly one process participates in α_1, implying that Requirement 1 also holds for the base case.

For the induction step, consider an execution $\alpha_i \gamma_i$ that satisfies Requirements 1–3 of Definition 2. Let $C_i = C_0 \alpha_i$ and let $\mathcal{S}(\alpha_i \gamma_i, p) = v$. From Requirement 3 of the induction hypothesis, there exist $q_i^{\overline{v}}$ (which will play the role of q_i in the construction of Definition 2) and $\gamma_i^{\overline{v}} \subseteq \gamma_i$ (which will play the role of γ) such that $\mathcal{S}(\alpha_i \gamma_i^{\overline{v}}, q_i^{\overline{v}}) = \overline{v}$. Let β denote the $q_i^{\overline{v}}$-solo extension of $\alpha_i \gamma_i^{\overline{v}}$. Since the algorithm is anonymous, we can use clones after α_i for processes in $\gamma_i^{\overline{v}}$ so that the block write γ_i can be performed after the $\gamma_i^{\overline{v}}$ block write. Process p returns v in a p-solo extension of $\alpha_i \gamma_i^{\overline{v}} \gamma_i$ (which is indistinguishable to p from $\alpha_i \gamma_i$) but returns $\overline{v}$ in a p-solo extension of $\alpha_i \gamma_i^{\overline{v}} \beta \gamma_i$, hence, $q_i^{\overline{v}}$ must perform a γ_i-modifying event e' for p in β. Consequently, from Observation 2, $q_i^{\overline{v}}$ performs a γ_i-visible event for p in β. Thus, the γ_i-visible event e_i specified by Definition 2 exists. As specified by Definition 2, let $\beta = \beta' e_i \beta''$, $\alpha_{i+1} = \alpha_i \gamma_i^{\overline{v}} \beta'$ and $\gamma_{i+1} = e_i \gamma_i$. Since e_i is a γ_i-visible event, from Observation 1, it is a write event to a variable not covered by γ_i. Hence, γ_{i+1} is a block write by $i + 1$ different processes to $i + 1$ different variables. Therefore, Requirement 2 holds.

A $q_i^{\overline{v}}$-solo extension of $\alpha_{i+1} e_i$ returns $\overline{v}$ (as this is a continuation of $\alpha_i \gamma_i^{\overline{v}} \beta' e_i$), thus by taking $q_{i+1}^{\overline{v}} = q_i^{\overline{v}}$ and $\gamma_{i+1}^{\overline{v}} = \{e_i\}$, we get that $q_{i+1}^{\overline{v}}$ returns $\overline{v}$ when running solo after $\alpha_{i+1} \gamma_{i+1}^{\overline{v}}$. Let $q_{i+1}^v \neq p$ be a process with input 0 that does not participate in $\alpha_{i+1} \gamma_{i+1}$. q_{i+1}^v is a clone of p in α_i. Hence, a q_{i+1}^v-solo extension of

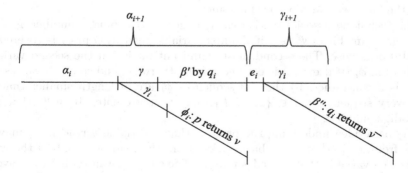

Fig. 2. The inductive execution construction of Definition 2. Process q_i is designated as $q_{i+1}^{\overline{v}}$ with corresponding $\gamma_{i+1}^{\overline{v}} = \{e_i\}$; a clone of p is designated as q_{i+1}^v with corresponding $\gamma_{i+1}^v = \gamma_i$ (see the proof of Lemma 1).

$\alpha_{i+1}\gamma_i$ returns v (as would a p-solo execution). Thus, by taking $\gamma^v_{i+1} = \gamma_i$ we get that q^v_{i+1} returns v when running solo after $\alpha_{i+1}\gamma^v_{i+1}$. Therefore, Requirement 3 holds.

Since $|\gamma^{\overline{v}}_i| \leq i$, we employ at most $i+1$ new clones in order to extend α_i and obtain α_{i+1}. By the induction hypothesis, at most $\frac{1}{2}i(i+1)$ processes participate in α_i, and hence, at most $\frac{1}{2}(i+1)(i+2)$ processes participate in α_{i+1}. Even if all the processes that participate in α_i have the same input, as long as $i < \sqrt{\lfloor n/2 \rfloor}$ there is a sufficient number of processes to construct $\alpha_{i+1}\gamma_{i+1}$. It follows that our construction may proceed for at least $\sqrt{n/2}$ iterations.   □

Since every obstruction-free anonymous binary consensus algorithm has a visible sequence of length $\Omega(\sqrt{n})$, Requirement 2 of Definition 2 implies:

Corollary 1. *Let $\mathcal{A}$ be an obstruction-free read/write anonymous binary consensus algorithm, then $\mathcal{A}$ uses $\Omega(\sqrt{n})$ distinct shared variables.*

To conclude the lower bound proof, we now show that any algorithm with a visible sequence of length L has an execution that reaches a configuration C, such that a solo run by process p starting at C reads at least $\log_2 L$ different variables. Let $\mathcal{A}$ be an algorithm that has a visible sequence $\{\alpha_i\gamma_i\}^L_{i=1}$. Let e_i denote the event used in Definition 2 to construct the $(i+1)$'th visible execution, that is, $\gamma_{i+1} = e_i\gamma_i$. Also, let ϕ_i denote the p-solo extension from $\alpha_i\gamma_i$. Our goal is to prove that in one of the solo extensions ϕ_i, p reads a large set of variables.

Let π_i denote the sequence of distinct variables read by p in ϕ_i, in the order of their first read in ϕ_i. If all the variables read in ϕ_i are always read also in ϕ_{i+1}, then, since we know that e_i writes to a variable not covered by γ_i that is read in the course of ϕ_{i+1}, the size of π_i is always at least i, so that π_L is of size at least L. However, this is not necessarily the case, as it may happen that reading the value written by e_i causes p to "backtrack" and avoid reading some of the variables of π_i, thus making π_{i+1} shorter than π_i. The *backtracking covering* technique [1,3,6] is used to derive a step complexity lower bound even when the latter scenario occurs for some i.

The technique associates with each sequence π_i a binary number Ψ_i. The most significant bit of Ψ_i is 1 if the first variable read by p in ϕ_i is covered by γ_i and 0 otherwise. The second most significant bit is 1 if the second variable read by p in ϕ_i (if it exists) is covered and 0 otherwise, and so on. If we assume (towards a contradiction) that all sequences ϕ_i are of length smaller than L, then every sequence $\pi_i, i \in \{1, \ldots, L\}$, may be represented by a Ψ_i that is a $\log_2 L$-digit number.

The basic idea underlying the proof is that a variable v read in π_i may be absent from π_{i+1} (that is, p "backtracks" from the read of v) only if the write in e_i is to a variable that precedes v in π_i. The simple intuition is that p avoids reading v in ϕ_{i+1} although it reads it in ϕ_i, only if it reads from some variable v' *that precedes v in ϕ_i* different values in ϕ_i and ϕ_{i+1}.

In terms of the values of Ψ, this implies that a less significant bit of Ψ may be flipped from 1 to 0 only if a more significant bit of Ψ is flipped from 0 to 1.[2] If no digits are flipped, then all the variables read in ϕ_i are read also in ϕ_{i+1} (that is, there is no backtracking) but a variable not covered by γ_i is covered be e_i, hence the value of Ψ grows as well. It follows that function Ψ is monotonically increasing. Since it increases L times, it cannot be that all sequences π_i are represented by numbers with fewer than $\log_2 L$ binary bits, hence, at least one of the executions ϕ_i reads at least $\log_2 L$ variables. We formalize these arguments in the proof of the following lemma.

Lemma 2. *Let $\mathcal{A}$ be an algorithm that has a visible sequence of executions of length L. Then $\mathcal{A}$ has an execution in which some process accesses at least $\log_2 L$ different variables in the course of a solo execution.*

Proof. We prove that one of the p-solo execution fragments ϕ_i accesses at least $\log_2 L$ different variables. For simplicity, and without loss of generality, we assume that L is an integral power of 2 and let $s = \log_2 L - 1$.

We define a monotone increasing progress function Ψ_i as follows: Ψ_i is a $(\log_2 L)$-bit number, where the j'th bit is 1 if and only if ϕ_i accesses at least j variables and the j'th variable (in the order of first variable-accesses) is covered by γ_i. Thus, the j'th bit of Ψ_i is 0 if either ϕ_i accesses fewer than j variables or, otherwise, if the j'th variable accessed in ϕ_i is not covered by γ_i.

If there exists an i such that $|\pi_i| > s$ then we are done. Otherwise $|\pi_i| \leq s$ for all i, hence, for all $i \in \{1, \ldots, L\}$, every variable of π_i has a corresponding bit of Ψ_i. Recall the construction of α_{i+1} from α_i by Lemma 1. The construction was done by extending α_i with write steps to some of the variables covered by γ_i (while keeping these variables covered by clone processes). The construction then proceeded by a q_i-solo execution until q_i was about to perform a write step e_i to an uncovered variable. In terms of the value of Ψ, event e_i may flip some of the bits of Ψ_i from 1 to 0, if the corresponding variables are not accessed in ϕ_{i+1}. However, this may happen only if e_i covers an earlier variable, that is, if e_i covers a variable that corresponds to a more significant bit of Ψ, and thus $\Psi_{i+1} > \Psi_i$.

To proceed with the corresponding formal argument, let $\Psi_i[j]$ denote the j'th (in left to right order) bit of Ψ_i:

$$\Psi_i = \sum_{j=0}^{s} 2^{s-j} \cdot \Psi_i[j].$$

We now show that $\Psi_{i+1} > \Psi_i$ for all $i \in \{1, \ldots, L-1\}$. To see this, recall that the $i+1$ sequence execution is constructed by extending α_i with execution fragment $\gamma \beta' e_i$, where $\beta' e_i$ is a q_i-solo execution such that e_i is its first γ_i-visible event for p. From Definition 1, e_i is the first write step by q_i to a variable u not

---

[2] Note that once a variable becomes covered in the executions we construct for our proofs, it remains covered, so a bit of Ψ may be flipped from 1 to 0 only if the corresponding variable was read in ϕ_i and is no longer read in ϕ_{i+1}.

covered by γ_i that is accessed in the course of a solo execution by p after $\alpha_i \gamma_i$. Hence, u appears in π_i. Let k be the index of u in π_i. Variable u was not covered before by γ_i, therefore $\Psi_i[k] = 0$. For every $j < k$, $\Psi_i[j] = \Psi_{i+1}[j]$ because e_i is the first write by q_i to a variable not covered by γ_i, and therefore, e_i does not change any of the bits corresponding to the variables that precede u in π_i: if any such variable was covered by γ_i, then it is also covered by γ_{i+1}. Moreover, e_i causes bit k of Ψ_i to flip from 0 to 1, since it covers the k'th variable accessed in ϕ_i (which is also the k'th variable accessed in ϕ_{i+1}). We get:

$$
\begin{aligned}
\Psi_{i+1} &= \sum_{j=0}^{s} 2^{s-j} \cdot \Psi_{i+1}[j] \\
&= \sum_{j=0}^{k-1} 2^{s-j} \cdot \Psi_{i+1}[j] + 2^{s-k} + \sum_{j=k+1}^{s} 2^{s-j} \cdot \Psi_{i+1}[j] \\
&\geq \sum_{j=0}^{k-1} 2^{s-j} \cdot \Psi_{i+1}[j] + 2^{s-k} \\
&> \sum_{j=0}^{k-1} 2^{s-j} \cdot \Psi_{i+1}[j] + \sum_{j=k+1}^{s} 2^{s-j} \\
&\geq \Psi_i
\end{aligned}
$$

Using the last inequality and the fact that $\Psi_1 > 0$ (as γ_1 covers a variable accessed in ϕ_1) we conclude that $\Psi_L \geq L$. However, Ψ is a $(\log L)$-bit number and therefore cannot exceed $L - 1$. This is a contradiction. Thus, there must be an i such that $|\pi_i| > s$, as required.   □

Theorem 1. *The solo step complexity of any read/write obstruction-free anonymous consensus algorithm is $\Omega(\log n)$.*

Proof. From Lemma 1, any read/write obstruction-free anonymous algorithm for binary consensus has a visible sequence of executions of length $\Omega(\sqrt{n})$. The theorem now follows from Lemma 2.   □

Unlike read/write algorithms, solo-fast algorithms are allowed to perform stronger synchronization operations (such as compare-and-swap or fetch-and-add) in the face of step contention. We now strengthen Theorem 1 by showing that it holds also for solo-fast implementations. This would have been immediate if the executions we construct to prove Theorem 1 were step-contention free, but this is not the case. To see this, consider the construction of α_{i+1} in Definition 2. A new process q_i runs solo after $\alpha_i \gamma$ until about to perform its first γ_i-visible event e_i, which is used to extend the block write. If and when e_i is eventually executed (as part of a block write γ associated with some later process $q_j, j > i$), the execution may have already been extended by steps of processes other than q_i, making q_i's execution non step-contention free.

Though not step-contention free, it is easy to show that all the events of the executions in a visible sequence are issued by processes that are unaware of step contention. It follows that these executions may be constructed also for solo-fast implementations. A formal proof follows.

Let α' be a step-contention free execution for some process p and let α be an execution that is indistinguishable to p from α'. Let e be the event that p is about to perform after α, then we say that e *is issued while p is unaware of step contention*. This notion was defined in [3].

Lemma 3. *Let $\alpha = \alpha_i \gamma_i$ be an execution of a visible sequence, then all the events of α are issued by processes that are unaware of step contention.*

Proof (Sketch). We consider the events performed by processes that participate in α. The proof proceeds by case analysis on the sets of participating processes.

1. Processes deployed by the inductive construction. Let q be a process that is deployed in the i'th step of the inductive construction as q_i (see Definition 2). When q first joins the execution (either as process q_1^1 in the base case or as a clone of process p named q_{i+1}^v, see the proof of Lemma 1), it runs solo until about to perform a γ_i-visible event, e_i. If e_i is not a modifying event, then q is designated as $q_{i+1}^{\overline{v}}$ and e_i is designated as $\gamma_{i+1}^{\overline{v}}$ (see the proof of Lemma 1). Process q is then deployed also in the next inductive construction step, after its step e_i is executed (as part of γ_{i+1}, see Definition 2). Eventually, either the construction terminates or there is a step $j > i$ of the inductive construction when q (now called q_j in Definition 2) is about to execute a visible event, e_j, which is also a modifying event. This is the last event executed by q in the construction. Apart from clone processes that run in lockstep with q, no events by other processes are interleaved within its steps. Thus, all the events of this set of processes are issued when they are unaware of step contention.
2. Clones for processes that execute an event in $\gamma_i^{\overline{v}}$ (see the proof of Lemma 1), for $1 \le i < L$. Each clone runs in lockstep with its respective "original process" (and possibly also with the steps of additional clones) and performs exactly the same steps, until the original process executes an event e_i which is part of $\gamma_i^{\overline{v}}$, for some $1 \le i < L$ and $v \in \{0, 1\}$. Then, the clone's last event (which is identical to e_i) becomes part of γ_{i+1}. Hence, also the events of these processes are issued when they are unaware of step contention.

It follows from the above case analysis that all participating processes run solo or in lockstep with their clones until they are about to perform their last event, hence they all issue their events when they are unaware of step contention. $\square$

Corollary 2. *Let $\mathcal{A}$ be a solo-fast obstruction-free anonymous binary consensus algorithm. Then the solo step complexity of $\mathcal{A}$ is $\Omega(\log n)$.*

Proof. A visible sequence of executions of $\mathcal{A}$ can be constructed as prescribed by Lemma 1 as long as all processes may only perform reads and writes. From

Lemma 3, all the events in these executions are by processes that are unaware of step contention, hence they may only perform reads and writes. Process p itself runs solo as it executes ϕ_i after visible execution i (see the proof of Lemma 1), for $i \in \{1, \ldots, L\}$, hence it encounters no step contention.   □

4   Discussion

This paper presents the first lower bound, of $\Omega(\log n)$, for the solo step complexity of obstruction-free anonymous binary consensus. Previously, there were no nontrivial lower bounds on the time complexity of obstruction-free *binary* consensus. This improves our understanding of the time complexity of obstruction-free consensus, which has been lagging behind our understanding of its space complexity. Recently, the question of the space complexity of binary obstruction-free consensus (with solo termination) has been largely settled, showing that $\Omega(n)$ shared variables are necessary [12].

An obvious open question is to remove the anonymity assumption, possibly exploiting ideas from the recent lower bound on the space complexity of consensus [12]. Another direction is to improve the lower bound, with or without the anonymity assumption, or to find a matching upper bound.

References

1. Aspnes, J., Attiya, H., Censor-Hillel, K., Hendler, D.: Lower bounds for restricted-use objects. In: SPAA, pp. 172–181 (2012)
2. Aspnes, J., Ellen, F.: Tight bounds for adopt-commit objects. Theor. Comput. Syst. **55**(3), 451–474 (2013)
3. Attiya, H., Guerraoui, R., Hendler, D., Kuznetsov, P.: The complexity of obstruction-free implementations. J. ACM **56**(4), 444–468 (2009)
4. Bouzid, Z., Sutra, P., Travers, C.: Anonymous agreement: the janus algorithm. In: Fernàndez Anta, A., Lipari, G., Roy, M. (eds.) OPODIS 2011. LNCS, vol. 7109, pp. 175–190. Springer, Heidelberg (2011)
5. Capdevielle, C., Johnen, C., Kuznetsov, P., Milani, A.: Brief announcement: on the uncontended complexity of anonymous consensus. In: Moses, Y. (ed.) DISC 2015. LNCS, vol. 9363, pp. 667–668. Springer, Heidelberg (2015)
6. Ellen, F., Hendler, D., Shavit, N.: On the inherent sequentiality of concurrent objects. SIAM J. Comput. **41**(3), 519–536 (2012)
7. Fich, F., Herlihy, M., Shavit, N.: On the space complexity of randomized synchronization. J. ACM **45**(5), 843–862 (1998)
8. Hendler, D., Shavit, N.: Solo-valency and the cost of coordination. Distrib. Comput. **21**(1), 43–54 (2008)
9. Herlihy, M., Luchangco, V., Moir, M.: Obstruction-free synchronization: double-ended queues as an example. In: ICDCS, pp. 522–529 (2003)
10. Luchangco, V., Moir, M., Shavit, N.N.: On the uncontended complexity of consensus. In: Fich, F.E. (ed.) DISC 2003. LNCS, vol. 2848, pp. 45–59. Springer, Heidelberg (2003)
11. Zhu, L.: Brief announcement: tight space bounds for memoryless anonymous consensus. In: Moses, Y. (ed.) DISC 2015. LNCS, vol. 9363, pp. 665–666. Springer, Heidelberg (2015)
12. Zhu, L.: A tight space bound for consensus. In: STOC (2016, to appear)

Opacity vs TMS2: Expectations and Reality

Sandeep Hans[✉], Ahmed Hassan, Roberto Palmieri,
Sebastiano Peluso, and Binoy Ravindran

Virginia Tech, Blacksburg, USA
sandeep.hans@vt.edu

Abstract. Most of the popular Transactional Memory (TM) algorithms
are known to be safe because they satisfy opacity, the well-known correctness criterion for TM algorithms. Recently, it has been shown that
they are even more conservative, and that they satisfy TMS2, a strictly
stronger property than opacity. This paper investigates the theoretical
and practical implications of relaxing those algorithms in order to allow
histories that are not TMS2. In particular, we present four impossibility results on TM implementations that are not TMS2 and are either
opaque or strictly serializable, and one practical TM implementation
that extends TL2, a high-performance state-of-the-art TM algorithm, to
allow non-TMS2 histories. By matching our theoretical findings with the
results of our performance evaluation, we conclude that designing and
implementing TM algorithms that are not TMS2, but safe, has inherent
costs that limit any possible performance gain.

1 Introduction

Transactional Memory (TM) [14] is a programming abstraction that ease the
development of concurrent applications. Most of the popular TM algorithms
(e.g., TL2 [4], NOrec [3], and LSA [19]) are proved to be correct because they do
not violate opacity [11], the well-known criterion that requires each transaction
(even a non-committed one) to (*i*) read only committed values, and (*ii*) behave
as atomically executed at a single point between its beginning and its completion.
However Doherty *et al.* [6] showed that most of the TM implementations that
aim at satisfying opacity actually guarantee a strictly stronger correctness criterion, known as TMS2. In practice, TMS2 implementations reject executions that
would not violate opacity while seeking for a tradeoff between the performance
and complexity of the concurrency control implementation.

In this paper, we evaluate the costs and implications of having TM implementations that guarantee weaker conditions than TMS2, such as opacity. In
particular, we focus on the simple execution pattern used in [6] to distinguish
between TMS2 and opaque TM implementations. We name this execution pattern as *reverse-commit anti-dependency* (*RC-anti-dependency* in short). Intuitively, we say that a TM implementation allows RC-anti-dependency if it accepts
the execution in Fig. 1, where there is an anti-dependency between two committed update transactions T_1 and T_2 (i.e., T_2 overwrites T_1's previous read) and

© Springer-Verlag Berlin Heidelberg 2016
C. Gavoille and D. Ilcinkas (Eds.): DISC 2016, LNCS 9888, pp. 269–283, 2016.
DOI: 10.1007/978-3-662-53426-7_20

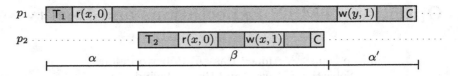

Fig. 1. An execution with RC-anti-dependency: $r(x, 0)$ denotes the read operation on x, $w(x, 1)$ denotes the write operation on x; C denotes a successful commit operation.

their commit order is reversed with respect to the anti-dependency (i.e., T_2 starts its commit phase and completes it before T_1 does).

Designing a TM implementation that includes RC-anti-dependency looks appealing because, on the one hand, the execution pattern looks simple to accept, and on the other hand, performance is likely to improve thanks to the possibility of committing transactions that otherwise would abort due to a read invalidation. That is why embracing this pattern was one of the goals of previous attempts to increase the number of accepted executions, such as permissive TMs [9,16], and TWM [5]. However, none of those attempts isolated the advantages and limitations of allowing RC-anti-dependency in a TM implementation. Specifically, permissive TMs aims at allowing all the possible schedules of execution within a certain correctness guarantee; and the latter relies on a class of input-acceptance [8] that mixes anti-dependency with multi-versioning and non-blocking read-only transactions. This paper is the first one that isolates RC-anti-dependency in order to assess the need of designing TM implementations that are not TMS2. Specifically, we provide a set of impossibility results on allowing RC-anti-dependency, and one possibility result, which is a concrete TM implementation, built on top of TL2, that allows RC-anti-dependency and confirms our theoretical claims.

We prove that in any strictly serializable [18] minimally progressive [11] TM implementation that allows RC-anti-dependency: *(i)* read operations of update transactions must be visible; *(ii)* either read-only transactions or the read-only prefix (i.e., all read operations before the first write) of update transactions must be visible. We also prove that if a strictly serializable TM that allows RC-anti-dependency has obstruction-free [13] read-only transactions, they must be visible. Finally, we prove that if we consider opacity rather than strict serializability, the visibility of read operations must be immediate and cannot be deferred to the commit phases of transactions. Table 1 summarizes our results. Due to space constraints, we defer the formal proofs to [12].

As a possibility result, we present the design and implementation of a TM, named TL2-RCAD, which allows executions that are not TMS2, including the one in Fig. 1, and limits the overhead of making visible reads by deploying specific algorithmic optimization. Evaluating TL2-RCAD we found that, contrary to expectations, the overall percentage of potential RC-anti-dependency executions is small. Thus the performance gain (if any) of allowing them is very limited in

Table 1. Summary of the impossibility results presented in the paper.

	Consistency	Progress	Impossibility
Theorem 1	Strict Serializability	Minimal Progressiveness	Invisible Read Operations (update transactions)
Theorem 2	Strict Serializability	Minimal Progressiveness	Invisible Read-only Transactions Invisible Read Executions
Theorem 3	Strict Serializability	Obstruction-freedom (read-only transactions)	Invisible Read-only Transactions
Theorem 4	Opacity	Minimal Progressiveness	Invisible Read Executions

all the tested scenarios that include STAMP [17], the standard benchmark suite for TM, and even customized micro-benchmarks.

The paper is organized as follows. In Sect. 2, we introduce our basic model definitions. In Sect. 3, we present our impossibility results. TL2-RCAD's design is presented in Sect. 4, and its performance results are analyzed in Sect. 5. Section 6 overviews the related work, and Sect. 7 concludes the paper.

2 Preliminaries

System and Transaction Execution Model. We consider an asynchronous shared memory system composed of N processes $p_1, \ldots, p_N$ that communicate by executing transactions on shared objects, which we call transactional objects, and may be faulty by crashing (i.e., slow down or block indefinitely). We use the term *transactional objects*, or equivalently *objects*, to distinguish them from *base objects*, which are used to encapsulate any information (data and metadata) associated with transactional objects.

Each transaction is a sequence of accesses, reading from and writing to the set of objects. In particular a transaction T_j accesses objects with *operations* $op_{ij} \in \{read, write, begin, tryAbort, tryCommit\}$, each being a matching pair of *invocation* $Inv_{op_{ij}}$ and *response* $Res_{op_{ij}}$ actions. For a more compact representation of both the invocation and the response of an operation, we also use the notation $T_j.op_{ij} \rightarrow val$, where val is the value returned by its response action.

The specification of all possible operations of a transaction T_j is the following: $T_j.read(x) \rightarrow val$ is a read operation by T_j of an object x, which returns either a value in some domain V or a special value aborted $\notin V$; $T_j.write(x,v) \rightarrow val$ is a write operation by T_j on an object x with a value $v \in V$, which returns either *ok* or aborted; $T_j.begin() \rightarrow val$ is the begin operation by T_j, which returns either *ok* or aborted; $T_j.tryAbort() \rightarrow val$ is the request of an abort by T_j, which returns aborted; $T_j.tryCommit() \rightarrow val$ is the request of a commit by T_j, which returns either committed $\notin V \cup \{aborted\}$ or aborted. We also use the following notation: T_j.read(x), to indicate T_j.read(x) $\rightarrow$ val, with val $\neq$ aborted; T_j.write(x, v), to indicate T_j.write(x, v) $\rightarrow$ ok; T_j.begin(), to indicate T_j.begin() $\rightarrow$ ok; T_j.abort(), to indicate T_j.tryAbort() $\rightarrow$ aborted; and T_j.commit(), to indicate T_j.tryCommit() $\rightarrow$ committed.

Histories and implementations. A *history* $\mathcal{H}$ of a TM implementation is a (possibly infinite) sequence of invocation and response actions of operations. Let tx($\mathcal{H}$) denote the set of transactions in $\mathcal{H}$. A history $\mathcal{H}$ is *well-formed* if for all $T \in$ tx($\mathcal{H}$): *(i)* T begins with an invocation of begin(); *(ii)* every invocation in T is followed by a matching response; *(iii)* T has no actions after a response has returned either aborted or committed; and *(iv)* T cannot invoke more than one begin operation. For simplicity, we assume that all histories are well-formed. Two histories $\mathcal{H}$ and $\mathcal{H}'$ are *equivalent* if tx($\mathcal{H}$) = tx($\mathcal{H}'$), and for every process p, $\mathcal{H}|p = \mathcal{H}'|p$, where $\mathcal{H}|p$ denote the projection of actions of process p in $\mathcal{H}$.

The *read-set* of a transaction T in history $\mathcal{H}$, denoted as rset(T), is the set of objects that T reads in $\mathcal{H}$; the *write-set* of T in history $\mathcal{H}$, denoted as wset(T), is the set of objects that T writes to in $\mathcal{H}$. T is an *update* transaction if wset(T) $\neq \emptyset$; otherwise, T is a *read-only* transaction.

A *TM implementation* (TM for short), denoted by $\mathcal{T}$, provides processes with algorithms for implementing read, write, begin, tryCommit and tryAbort of a transaction. $\mathcal{T}$ is defined as a set of well-formed histories, which are the histories that are produced by $\mathcal{T}$. We denote by $\mathcal{H}_1 \cdot \mathcal{H}_2$, the concatenation of histories $\mathcal{H}_1$ and $\mathcal{H}_2$, $T_1 \cdot T_2$, the concatenation of transactions T_1 and T_2, and $op_{ij} \cdot op_{zk}$, the concatenation of operations op_{ij} and op_{zk}.

Complete histories and real-time precedence. A transaction $T \in$ tx($\mathcal{H}$) is *complete* if T ends with abort or committed in $\mathcal{H}$. A transaction T is *pending* in $\mathcal{H}$ if the last action of T is the invocation of tryCommit. A transaction T is *committed* (resp., *aborted*) in $\mathcal{H}$ if the return value of the last operation of T is committed (resp., aborted). A transaction T is *live* in $\mathcal{H}$ if it is neither pending nor completed. The history $\mathcal{H}$ is *complete* if all transactions in tx($\mathcal{H}$) are complete.

Given two transactions T_j and T_k, and two operations op_{ij} and op_{zk} in $\mathcal{H}$ by T_j and T_k, respectively, we say that op_{ij} *precedes* op_{zk} in the *real-time order* of $\mathcal{H}$, denoted $op_{ij} \prec_{\mathcal{H}} op_{zk}$, if the response action $Res_{op_{ij}}$ precedes the invocation action $Inv_{op_{zk}}$ in $\mathcal{H}$. Otherwise, if neither $op_{ij} \prec_{\mathcal{H}} op_{zk}$ nor $op_{zk} \prec_{\mathcal{H}} op_{ij}$, then op_{ij} and op_{zk} are *concurrent* in $\mathcal{H}$. We overload the notation and say, for transactions $T_j, T_k \in$ tx($\mathcal{H}$), that T_j *precedes* T_k in the *real-time order* of $\mathcal{H}$, denoted $T_j \prec_{\mathcal{H}} T_k$, if T_j is complete in $\mathcal{H}$ and the last action of T_j precedes the first action of T_k in $\mathcal{H}$. If neither $T_j \prec_{\mathcal{H}} T_k$ nor $T_k \prec_{\mathcal{H}} T_j$, then T_j and T_k are *concurrent* in $\mathcal{H}$. A history $\mathcal{H}$ is *sequential* if there are no concurrent transactions in $\mathcal{H}$.

For simplicity, we assume that each history $\mathcal{H}$ begins with a complete transaction T_0 that writes initial values to all objects and commits before any other transaction begins in $\mathcal{H}$. A read operation T.read(x) in a complete and sequential history $\mathcal{H}$ is *legal* if it returns the latest value written by T, if T writes on x before T.read(x), otherwise it returns the latest value written by a committed transaction. A complete and sequential history $\mathcal{H}$ is *legal* if every read operation in $\mathcal{H}$, which does not return aborted, is legal.

Configuration, Step, and Execution. A *configuration* is a tuple characterizing the status of each process, and of the base objects at some point in time. On the other hand, a *step* ϕ_τ performed by a process encompasses a local computation, the application of a primitive operation (e.g., CAS) to a base object, and a possible change to the status of the process. Any step ϕ_τ is executed atomically, and it is generated by an operation op_{ij} of a transaction T_j, hence also denoting the step as $\phi_\tau^{op_{ij}}$. In general, an operation op_{ij} of a transaction can generate one or more steps $\phi_\tau^{op_{ij}}$, such that, for each op_{ij}, τ, one of the following conditions is true: $\phi_\tau^{op_{ij}}$ is the invocation $Inv_{op_{ij}}$; $\phi_\tau^{op_{ij}}$ is the response $Res_{op_{ij}}$; $\phi_\tau^{op_{ij}}$ is executed after $Inv_{op_{ij}}$ and before $Res_{op_{ij}}$.

An *execution interval* is a sequence $\Psi_\tau \cdot \phi_\tau \cdot \Psi_{\tau+1} \cdot \phi_{\tau+1} \cdots$ that alternates configurations Ψ_τ and steps ϕ_τ, where $\Psi_\tau \cdot \phi_\tau$ generates the configuration $\Psi_{\tau+1}$. A step ϕ_τ by process p_k is *legal* if its primitive operation applied to a base object follows the object's sequential specification [15]. Moreover, a configuration Ψ_τ is *quiescent* if, for any transaction T_i, Ψ_τ is not after the first operation of T_i and before its completion.

We define an *execution* E as an execution interval starting from an initial configuration Ψ_0. We also say that two executions are *indistinguishable* to a process p_k if *(i)* p_k performs the same sequence of steps in both the executions, and *(ii)* the steps by p_k are legal.

Since an execution E is actually a low-level history of configurations and steps that are generated by operations of transactions in a history $\mathcal{H}$, we may also want to derive a history $\mathcal{H}$ from one of the possible executions, say E. In particular, given an execution E, we define $E|\mathcal{H}$ as the history derived from E, where $\forall i, j, k$, we remove all the configurations and the steps $\phi_k^{op_{ij}}$ such that $\phi_k^{op_{ij}} \neq Inv_{op_{ij}} \wedge \phi_k^{op_{ij}} \neq Res_{op_{ij}}$.

Invisible Transactions. Given an execution E and a set S of steps in E, we use the notation $E \setminus S$ to indicate the execution derived from E by removing only the steps in S and all the configurations generated by those steps. Also, given an execution E, and an operation op_{ij} by transaction T_j, we define $S_E^{op_{ij}}$ as the set $\{\phi_\tau^{op_{ij}} | \phi_\tau^{op_{ij}} \in E\}$. Given an execution E and a process p_k that executes a transaction T_j in E, we say that a set of operations Q of T_j is *invisible* in E if the executions E and $E \setminus (\bigcup_{op_{ij} \in Q} S_E^{op_{ij}})$ are indistinguishable to every process $p_{h \neq k}$ that takes steps in E. Therefore, we define a read-only transaction T_j as *invisible* if, for any possible execution E, the set of *all* the operations of T_j are invisible in E. Analogously, we say that a transaction has *invisible read operations* if, for any possible execution E, the set of the read operations of T_j are invisible in E. Moreover, we say that a transaction has an *invisible read execution* if it is a live transaction, and it has invisible read operations.

Consistency. Serializability [18] requires that for a history $\mathcal{H}$ to be serializable, there must exist a complete and sequential legal history S that is equivalent to all the committed transactions in $\mathcal{H}$, and strict-serializability requires S to preserve the real-time order in $\mathcal{H}$. Opacity [10,11], informally, requires that for a history $\mathcal{H}$ to be opaque, there must exist a complete and sequential legal history S which is equivalent to a completion of $\mathcal{H}$, and preserves the real-time order in $\mathcal{H}$. *Transactional Memory Specification 2 (TMS2)* [6] is a stronger condition than opacity, and requires S to preserve the order of non-concurrent commit operations of committed update transactions. *Transactional Memory Specification 1 (TMS1)* [1,6] is weaker than opacity, and requires $\mathcal{H}$ to be strictly serializable, and for each operation in $\mathcal{H}$, there must exist an equivalent legal history, and restricts this history to include all the committed transaction preceding the transaction of the operation in real-time order.

Progress guarantees. We say that a process p_i runs with no *step contention* in an execution interval α if α contains steps by p_i, and there are no other processes different from p_i that take steps in α. We also say that a transaction T_k (resp. op_{ik}) that is executed by a process p_i in an execution E does not encounter step contention in E if p_i runs with no *step contention* in the minimal execution interval α that contains all the steps of T_k (resp. op_{ij}) in E. A TM guarantees *obstruction-freedom* [13] if, for every execution E that is generated by the TM, a transaction T_i is forcefully aborted in E only if T_i encounters *step contention* in E. On the other hand, a TM guarantees *minimal progressiveness* [11] if, for every execution E that is generated by the TM, a transaction T_i is forcefully aborted in E only if T_i either encounters *step contention* in E or it does not start from a quiescent configuration. We assume that operations are *obstruction-free*.

3   The Cost of Reverse-Commit Anti-Dependency

We say that a TM implementation $\mathcal{T}$ allows RC-anti-dependency if the history shown in Fig. 1 is a history of $\mathcal{T}$. More formally:

Definition 1. *Let* $\mathcal{H}_{rcad} = \mathcal{H}_\alpha \cdot \mathcal{H}_\beta \cdot \mathcal{H}_{\alpha'}$, *where* $\mathcal{H}_\alpha = T_i.\mathsf{begin}() \cdot T_i.\mathsf{read}(x) \to v_0$, $\mathcal{H}_\beta = T_j.\mathsf{begin}() \cdot T_j.\mathsf{read}(x) \to v_0 \cdot T_j.\mathsf{write}(x, v_j) \cdot T_j.\mathsf{commit}()$, *and* $\mathcal{H}_{\alpha'} = T_i.\mathsf{write}(y, v_i) \cdot T_i.\mathsf{commit}()$, *with* $i \neq j$ *and* $x \neq y$. *We say that a TM implementation* $\mathcal{T}$ *allows RC-anti-dependency iff* $\mathcal{H}_{rcad} \in \mathcal{T}$.

We use $\mathcal{H}_{rcad}$ to prove our impossibility results. Note that $\mathcal{H}_{rcad}$ is accepted by all known non-TMS2 implementations, e.g., TWM, as well as our TL2-RCAD algorithm. Intuitively, any TM implementation that accepts $\mathcal{H}_{rcad}$ is expected to include more histories that are not TMS2.

Our first result shows that allowing RC-anti-dependency in strictly serializable TMs implies an impossibility on having invisible read operations of update transactions.

Theorem 1. *A TM $\mathcal{T}$ that allows RC-anti-dependency cannot guarantee both strict serializability and minimal progressiveness if update transactions have invisible read operations.*

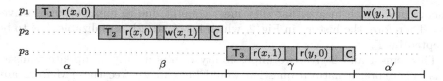

Fig. 2. For the transaction T_1, since read only transactions are invisible, this execution is indistinguishable to p_1 and p_2 from the execution in Fig. 1.

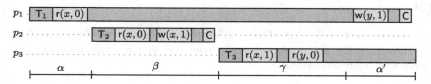

Fig. 3. For the transactions T_1 and T_2, since read operations are invisible, this execution is indistinguishable to p_1 and p_2 from the execution in Fig. 1.

The intuition of the proof can be inferred from Fig. 1. In order to allow RC-anti-dependency in Fig. 1 and to guarantee that the history is strictly serializable, T_2 cannot read any object written by T_1. However, if read operations are invisible, it is impossible for T_1 to know whether such a read exists or not. We show that such a result holds even with a weak progress guarantee, like minimal progressiveness.

This result justifies the design of TM implementations like TWM [5], as well as our TL2-RCAD algorithm, which both allow RC-anti-dependency by making read operations of each update transaction visible at a certain point of the transaction execution. Indeed, in both implementations read operations of update transactions remain invisible until the execution of the transactions' commit phase, and then read operations are forced to be visible during the commit phase. This means, based on our definitions, that both implementations have invisible read executions.

Having invisible read executions is weaker than having invisible read operations, because the former does not prevent a transaction from making its read operations visible after the invocation of either tryCommit or tryAbort. However, this relaxation for update transactions requires having visible read-only transactions, which is implied by our second impossibility result (Theorem 2).

Theorem 2. *A TM $\mathcal{T}$ that allows RC-anti-dependency cannot guarantee both strict serializability and minimal progressiveness if (i) update transactions have invisible read executions, and (ii) read-only transactions are invisible.*

The proof intuition is based on the indistinguishability of the two histories in Figs. 1 and 2, due to the invisibility of the read-only transaction T_3. Specifically, if T_3 is invisible, T_1 has to behave in Fig. 2 as in Fig. 1. Also, the invisible read execution of T_1 gives both T_2 and T_3 the illusion of executing without concurrency, which means that they must commit due to minimal progressiveness. Therefore, the history in Fig. 2, which is not strictly serializable, has to be accepted by $\mathcal{T}$.

Theorems 1 and 2 give two impossibility results mainly on update transactions. Therefore, a natural question would be: can we free the TM from any constraint on the invisibility of read operations of update transactions, and have non-TMS2 implementations that guarantee strict serializability? Theorem 3 shows that the answer is still "no", in case read-only transactions are invisible and obstruction-free.

Theorem 3. *A TM $\mathcal{T}$ that allows RC-anti-dependency cannot guarantee both strict serializability and minimal progressiveness if read-only transactions are invisible and obstruction-free.*

The intuition of the proof is also based on the indistinguishability of the two histories in Figs. 1 and 2, due to the invisibility of the read-only transaction T_3. Specifically, if T_3 is invisible, both T_1 and T_2 must behave in Fig. 2 as they do in Fig. 1. In this case, although the read-only transaction T_3 does not have the illusion of running without concurrency, it has to commit because we assume that read-only transactions are obstruction-free, and T_3 runs without any step contention. Therefore, the history in Fig. 2 has to be accepted by $\mathcal{T}$.

All the previous theorems assume strictly serializable TM implementations. Theorem 4, on the other hand, shows how the impossibility results will change if we rather aim for opacity than strict serializability. Specifically, we show that in order to have TM implementations that guarantee opacity and allow RC-anti-dependency, any read operation of any transaction (whether it is read-only or not) must be visible at the time the operation is executed. Our investigation on the relation between guaranteeing opacity and allowing RC-anti-dependency is motivated by some TM implementations that allow RC-anti-dependency and violate opacity, such as TWM and TL2-RCAD.

Theorem 4. *A TM $\mathcal{T}$ that allows RC-anti-dependency cannot guarantee both opacity and minimal progressiveness if transactions have invisible read executions.*

The intuition of the proof is based on the indistinguishability of the two histories in Figs. 1 and 3, due to the invisibility of the read executions. Specifically, based on the definition of invisible read executions, T_3 is invisible since it is live and it did not execute any write operation yet. Thus, both T_1 and T_2 must behave in Fig. 3 as they do in Fig. 1. Furthermore, the invisible read execution of T_1 gives both T_2 and T_3 the illusion of executing without concurrency, which means that they cannot abort due to minimal progressiveness. As a result, the history in Fig. 3 has to be accepted by $\mathcal{T}$, which violates opacity. Note that T_3 can abort later, in order to preserve strict serializability after T_1 commits. However, aborting T_3 does not make the history opaque.

4   TL2-RCAD: a TM implementation that allows RC-anti-dependency

In the previous section, we showed a set of impossibility results on allowing RC-anti-dependency in a TM implementation. In this section, we show a possibility result: a modified version of TL2 [4], named TL2-RCAD, that allows RC-anti-dependency and therefore deploys visible read operations. Algorithm 1 shows the main procedures of TL2-RCAD. The entire pseudo code is included in [12].

TL2 uses a shared timestamp, which is atomically incremented anytime an update transaction commits and locally copied into the *start timestamp* at the beginning of a transaction execution. This timestamp is used by read operations to decide if the version available of a shared object is compliant with the transaction's history. At commit time, update transactions undergo a two-phase locking on written locations, and modifications are applied to the shared state only if all versions of read locations are still valid. Versions of locations are stored along with locks in a shared ownership record (*orec*) table.

One of the main issues in TL2 is that the live validation (i.e., the one made before returning from a read operation) is conservative: a transaction T_i aborts if the version of the *orec* to be read is greater than T_i's start timestamp. Using such a scheme to build TL2-RCAD would reduce the chance for allowing RC-anti-dependency because only few transactions with a potential RC-anti-dependency would reach the commit phase. Therefore we use a variant of TL2 that extends T_i's starting timestamp by using the technique presented in [19] (lines 17–21).

To the best of our knowledge, all TM algorithms that allow RC-anti-dependency are multi-versioning. Multi-versioning has its own practical limitations (e.g., expensive memory management) that makes it not a candidate in some real applications. TL2-RCAD is the first practical single-version TM algorithm that allows RC-anti-dependency. In Sect. 6, we discuss the differences between TL2-RCAD and TWM [5], a multi-versioning algorithm that allows RC-anti-dependency.

TL2-RCAD Metadata. Based on our impossibility results, a mandatory step to allows RC-anti-dependency and guarantee at least strict serializability is to expose more metadata to make read-only transactions and the read operations of update transactions visible. TL2-RCAD exposes per-*orec* metadata for update transactions and a global flag for read-only transactions.

More in details, each *orec* is enriched with a read version, named *orec.rv*, that is modified at the commit time of only update transactions (hereafter we name TL2's original *orec* versions as write version, or *orec.wv*). As we will show later, adding the read version is enough to detect simple scenarios where there is no read-only transactions and there is only one transaction that allows RC-anti-dependency at a time, like the example in Fig. 1. We also define three shared global metadata: *anti_dep_lock*, *last_ro*, and *last_anti_dep*. Those metadata are used to detect the more complicated scenarios, like the one in Fig. 2, where at least two concurrent transactions attempt to commit and they both allow RC-anti-dependency, or one of them allows RC-anti-dependency and the other

Algorithm 1. TL2-RCAD

```
 1: procedure START()                    23: procedure WRITE(ADDR, VALUE)
 2:     tx.start = global_timestamp      24:     tx.writeset.add(addr, value)
 3: end procedure                        25: end procedure
 4: procedure READ(ADDR)
 5:     val = tx.write-set.find(addr)    26: procedure COMMITRW()
 6:     if val != NULL then              27:     LockAbortIfLockedNotByMe(tx.writeset)
 7:         return val                   28:     for each (r_orec) in tx.readset do
 8:     orec = getOrec(addr)             29:         if LockedNotByMe(r_orec) then
 9:     while true do                    30:             Abort()
10:         val = *addr                  31:     for each (r_orec) in tx.readset do
11:         o = orec                     32:         if r_orec.wv > tx.start then
12:         if o.lock then               33:             CheckAntiDep()
13:             continue                 34:             break
14:         if o.wv ≤ tx.start then      35:     WriteBack(tx.writeset)
15:             tx.readset.append(orec)  36:     tx.end = AtomicInc(global_timestamp)
16:             return val               37:     UpdateVersions()
17:         new_start = global_timestamp 38:     Unlock(tx.writeset)
18:         for each (orec) in tx.readset do  39: end procedure
19:             if orec.wv > tx.start then
20:                 Abort()              40: procedure COMMITRO
21:         tx.start = new_start         41:     AntiDepHandle()
22: end procedure                        42: end procedure
```

is read-only. Note that *last_ro*, and *last_anti_dep*, and the read versions of the *orecs* should be monotonically increasing, which is not guaranteed if transactions overwrite their values without checking the old values. Hereafter we use the term *monotonic update* to refer to the correct action that considers this requirement. The detailed pseudo code of this monotonic update is in [12].

TL2-RCAD Commit Procedure. Now we show how we modify the commit procedure of TL2 to allow RC-anti-dependency. We structured the pseudocode in Algorithm 1 so that the difference between TL2 and TL2-RCAD, in addition to the new metadata, lies only in the three functions at lines 33, 37, and 41. For each function, we show how TL2 implements it, and how TL2-RCAD extends that. The detailed pseudocode for both TL2 and TL2-RCAD is in [12].

The first function is *CheckAntiDep*. TL2-RCAD allows RC-anti-dependency at commit time by enriching TL2's validation procedure. In TL2 each transaction T_i iterates over all the *orecs* of its read-set and checks if the write version of each *orec* is higher than the start timestamp of T_i, which is the condition for RC-anti-dependency. At this point, TL2 conservatively aborts T_i, while TL2-RCAD tries to commit T_i if allowing RC-anti-dependency does not result in executions that violate strict serializability. To do so, the *CheckAntiDep* function in TL2-RCAD is implemented as follows: it first acquires the *anti_dep_lock* to guarantee that no other transaction will concurrently allow RC-anti-dependency. Then, it checks if T_i's start timestamp is less than: (*i*) *last_ro*, (*ii*) *last_anti_dep*, and (*iii*) both the read versions and the write versions of all T_i's write-set entries. Interestingly, all those steps use only information saved in T_i's read-set and do not require any accurate knowledge about dependencies of other transactions.

The second function is *UpdateVersions*. In this function, TL2 only modifies the write version of the write-set entries. In addition to that, TL2-RCAD modifies the read version of the read-set entries. Also, if committing the transaction generates RC-anti-dependency (i.e., it calls *CheckAntiDep*), *last_anti_dep* is monotonically updated to be the new value of the shared timestamp (after being atomically incremented in line 36), then *anti_dep_lock* is released. The third function is *AntiDepHandle*, which is an empty function in TL2. In TL2-RCAD a read-only transaction T_r monotonically updates *last_ro* to be the current value of the shared timestamp. Then, it checks if *anti_dep_lock* is acquired or *last_anti_dep* is greater than or equal to T_r's start timestamp, which indicates a concurrent transaction that allowed or is trying to allow RC-anti-dependency. In that case, T_r conservatively aborts.

Considering Theorem 4, TL2-RCAD violates opacity because it makes read operations visible only during the commit phase. However, as we prove in Theorem 5 (proof is in [12]), TL2-RCAD guarantees strict serializability, and this does not contradict the other impossibility results presented in Sect. 3, because read operations and read-only transactions are visible in TL2-RCAD. In fact, Theorem 5 proves that TL2-RCAD guarantees TMS1 [6], which is stronger than strict serializability. Interestingly, to the best of our knowledge, TL2-RCAD is the first TM implementation that has TMS1 guarantee.

Theorem 5. *TL2-RCAD guarantees TMS1.*

5   Evaluation

In this section, we evaluate TL2-RCAD, mainly to understand how allowing RC-anti-dependency and weakening TMS2 affects performance. To do so, we compare three variants of the TL2 algorithm: the TL2 implementation (TL2), the TL2 implementation with the extension of the transaction start timestamp (TL2-Extend), and TL2-RCAD. We evaluated the algorithms using the STAMP benchmark suite [17]. The testbed consists of an AMD server equipped with 64 CPU-cores. Each datapoint is the average of 5 runs. We use two metrics during the evaluation: throughput (in Fig. 4) and the commit/abort ratio normalized to the total number of executions of TL2 (in Fig. 5). Due to space constraints, we show the most significant plots here and we refer to [12] for the others.

Our main observation is that aborts occur because of two main reasons other than for RC-anti-dependency: finding an inconsistent state by a live transaction, and failing in acquiring locks at commit time. That is why, the results in Fig. 4 show only a marginal performance improvement in one application (kmeans), and a performance similar to or worse than the other versions of TL2 in all other applications. Roughly, the results split STAMP benchmarks into four categories based on the level of contention and the size of transactions read-sets. This is because contention level is an indicator of the potential gain of allowing RC-anti-dependency; and the size of the read-set indicates the overhead of allowing RC-anti-dependency in TL2-RCAD given the need of updating the read versions.

The first category includes ssca2 and labyrinth. In ssca2, transactions are non-conflicting and have small read-sets, while in labyrinth transactions

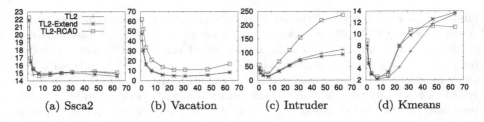

Fig. 4. Performance using STAMP. X-axis: number of threads; Y-axis: Time (s).

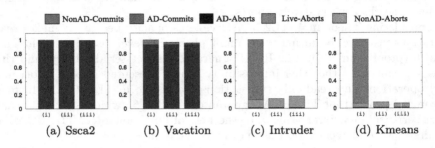

Fig. 5. Commit/abort ratios in STAMP. *(i)* TL2; *(ii)* TL2-Extended; *(iii)* TL2-RCAD.

have dominating non-transactional work. That is why in both scenarios allowing RC-anti-dependency causes neither a degradation nor an improvement in performance. Figure 4(a) confirms that by showing similar performance for all competitors. The second category (`vacation` and `genome`) represents workloads with non-conflicting transactions and large read-sets. In this case, the overhead of allowing RC-anti-dependency increases due to large read-sets, but it does not provide any benefit because most of the transactions already commit even using the original TL2. That is why the performance of TL2-RCAD is constantly worse than other competitors, as shown in Fig. 4(b), which reflects the overhead of allowing RC-anti-dependency. The third category is represented by `intruder`, which is the worst case for TL2-RCAD. Performance degradation is higher than all the other benchmarks, as shown in Fig. 4(c). This is mainly because transactions have large read-sets, which adds a significant overhead that increases the overall commit time. `Kmeans` (Fig. 4(d)) represents the forth category, where transactions have small read-sets but they are more conflicting than the previous applications. Due to the small read-sets, TL2-RCAD does not generally perform worse than its competitors. However, we also observe no gain from allowing RC-anti-dependency, as detailed below.

Figure 5 shows, for each version of TL2, the percentage of committed read-only and update transactions that never called *CheckAntiDep* (*NonAD-Commits*); committed update transactions that called *CheckAntiDep* (*AD-Commits*); aborted transactions that called either *CheckAntiDep* or *AntiDepHandle* (*AD-Aborts*); aborted live transactions (*Live-Aborts*); and aborted update transactions due to failing in locking an *orec* at commit (*NonAD-Aborts*). The sum of *AD-Commits* and *AD-Aborts* represents all the potential executions for RC-anti-dependency, while *Live-Aborts* and *NonAD-Aborts* represent the two reasons for aborting transactions other than observing RC-anti-dependency. Unfortunately, although we can save some *Live-Aborts* by spinning until the location is unlocked, which is the case of both TL2-Extend and TL2-RCAD (line 13), spinning at commit time in order to save some *NonAD-Aborts* can result in deadlock.

Figure 5 assesses that the overall percentage of potential RC-anti-dependency is small, which clarifies the reason of limited performance improvement (or degradation). More in details, Figs. 5(a) and (b) confirm our analysis in ssca2 and vacation by showing that *NonAD-Commits* is dominating. Labyrinth cannot be interpreted due to its dominating non-transactional work. In intruder (Fig. 5(c)), *NonAD-Aborts* of TL2-RCAD are higher than TL2-Extend. This is a direct implication of holding locks for a longer time at commit time, due to the longer validation process and the time spent in writing the read versions. Finally, in kmeans (Fig. 5(d)) the number of RC-anti-dependency observed is very limited, which results in a slight performance improvement only for the cases of 48/64 threads. Note that, although both TL2-Extend and TL2-RCAD save most of live aborts in both kmeans and intruder, the impact of that in performance is not reflected. This is mainly because preventing aborts in those cases come with an additional cost of incrementally validating the whole read-set.

We also ran micro-benchmarks (shown in [12]) seeking for a favorable configuration that allows RC-anti-dependency. Results confirmed a limited performance improvement. As a summary, although we cannot claim that more favorable workloads do not exist, our evaluation study assesses that, even with a hand-tuned micro-benchmark, it is hard to find workloads where allowing RC-anti-dependency in a single-version TM enhances performance noticeably.

6   Related Work

We classify the previous works that allow RC-anti-dependency into two categories: permissive algorithms, and multi-versioning algorithms. Interestingly, both of them confirm our impossibility results by adopting techniques that make both read-only transactions and the reads of update transactions visible.

Permissive algorithms need to track all dependencies in the system [9,16], and/or acquire locks for read operations [2], and both these techniques are known to have a significant negative impact on performance. That is why, unlike TL2-RCAD, all those solutions in this regard aimed at proving theoretical possibility results rather than assessing practical implications.

Multi-versioning algorithms have a major benefit: allowing read-only transactions to progress (usually non-blocking), and, generally, read operations to complete without aborting the enclosing transaction. That is easy to achieve because, thanks to the multi-versioned memory, transactions can always find a consistent version to read. That is why even multi-versioning algorithms that do not allow

RC-anti-dependency, such as LSA [19] or JVSTM [7], have this positive effect. We believe that the advantages of allowing RC-anti-dependency have a limited gain compared to the potential gain of having non-blocking read-only transactions. We justify this claim by briefly analyzing TWM [5], an algorithm that uses multi-versioning and allows RC-anti-dependency. In the evaluation of TWM, all the workloads that show a significant improvement have long and mostly read-only transactions. Here TWM mainly benefits from the strong progress of read operations. Those scenarios are not favorable for TL2-RCAD because, without multi-versioning, it is hard to improve the progress of read operations, and also those workloads add significant overhead due to their long read-sets.

Theoretically, our results are inspired by a research trend that aims at identifying the cost of accepting more histories in TM. For example, both *online permissiveness* [16] and *input-acceptance* [8] introduce similar impossibility results on the visibility of read and write operations when the TM accepts some sets of histories. Our results, however, are stronger since they are based on the assumption that TM accepts only one history. Also, we selected that history as it is the one used for identifying TMS2, which allows, for the first time, understanding the cost and limitations of relaxing TMS2 while still being safe.

7   Conclusion

In this paper we investigated the inherent costs and limitations of allowing RC-anti-dependency in TM implementations. The major outcome of our findings is that, the mandatory costs of allowing RC-anti-dependency (e.g., having visible read operations) is not reflected in noticeable performance improvement.

Acknowledgements. This work is partially supported by Air Force Office of Scientific Research (AFOSR) under grant FA9550-14-1-0187.

References

1. Attiya, H., Gotsman, A., Hans, S., Rinetzky, N.: Safety of live transactions in transactional memory: TMS is necessary and sufficient. In: Kuhn, F. (ed.) DISC 2014. LNCS, vol. 8784, pp. 376–390. Springer, Heidelberg (2014)
2. Attiya, H., Hillel, E.: A single-version STM that is multi-versioned permissive. Theory Comput. Syst. **51**(4), 425–446 (2012)
3. Dalessandro, L., Spear, M.F., Scott, M.L.: NOrec: streamlining STM by abolishing ownership records. In: PPOPP, pp. 67–78 (2010)
4. Dice, D., Shalev, O., Shavit, N.N.: Transactional locking II. In: Dolev, S. (ed.) DISC 2006. LNCS, vol. 4167, pp. 194–208. Springer, Heidelberg (2006)
5. Diegues, N., Romano, P.: Time-warp: lightweight abort minimization in transactional memory. In: PPoPP, pp. 167–178 (2014)
6. Doherty, S., Groves, L., Luchangco, V., Moir, M.: Towards formally specifying and verifying transactional memory. Formal Aspects Comput. **25**(5), 769–799 (2013)
7. Fernandes, S.M., Cachopo, J.P.: Lock-free and scalable multi-version software transactional memory. In: PPOPP, pp. 179–188 (2011)

8. Gramoli, V., Harmanci, D., Felber, P.: On the input acceptance of transactional memory. Parallel Process. Lett. **20**(1), 31–50 (2010)

9. Guerraoui, R., Henzinger, T.A., Singh, V.: Permissiveness in transactional memories. In: Taubenfeld, G. (ed.) DISC 2008. LNCS, vol. 5218, pp. 305–319. Springer, Heidelberg (2008)

10. Guerraoui, R., Kapalka, M.: On the correctness of transactional memory. In: PPOPP, pp. 175–184 (2008)

11. Guerraoui, R., Kapalka, M.: Principles of Transactional Memory. Synthesis Lectures on Distributed Computing Theory. Morgan and Claypool, Williston (2011)

12. Hans, S., Hassan, A., Palmieri, R., Peluso, S., Ravindran, B.: Opacity vs TMS2: expectations and reality. Technical report, Virginia Tech (2016). http://www.ssrg.ece.vt.edu/papers/disc16-TR.pdf

13. Herlihy, M., Luchangco, V., Moir, M., Scherer III, W.N.: Software transactional memory for dynamic-sized data structures. In: PODC, pp. 92–101 (2003)

14. Herlihy, M., Moss, J.E.B.: Transactional memory: architectural support for lock-free data structures. In: ISCA, pp. 289–300 (1993)

15. Herlihy, M., Wing, J.M.: Linearizability: a correctness condition for concurrent objects. ACM Trans. Program. Lang. Syst. **12**(3), 463–492 (1990)

16. Keidar, I., Perelman, D.: On avoiding spare aborts in transactional memory. In: SPAA, pp. 59–68 (2009)

17. Minh, C.C., Chung, J., Kozyrakis, C., Olukotun, K.: STAMP: stanford transactional applications for multi-processing. In: IISWC, pp. 35–46 (2008)

18. Papadimitriou, C.H.: The serializability of concurrent database updates. J. ACM **26**, 631–653 (1979)

19. Riegel, T., Felber, P., Fetzer, C.: A lazy snapshot algorithm with eager validation. In: Dolev, S. (ed.) DISC 2006. LNCS, vol. 4167, pp. 284–298. Springer, Heidelberg (2006)

On Composition and Implementation of Sequential Consistency

Matthieu Perrin[✉], Matoula Petrolia, Achour Mostéfaoui, and Claude Jard

LINA – University of Nantes, Nantes, France
{matthieu.perrin,stamatina.petrolia,
achour.mostefaoui,claude.jard}@univ-nantes.fr

Abstract. To implement a linearizable shared memory in synchronous message-passing systems it is necessary to wait for a time linear to the uncertainty in the latency of the network for both read and write operations. Waiting only for one of them suffices for sequential consistency. This paper extends this result to crash-prone asynchronous systems, proposing a distributed algorithm that builds a sequentially consistent shared snapshot memory on top of an asynchronous message-passing system where less than half of the processes may crash. We prove that waiting is needed only when a process invokes a read/snapshot right after a write.

We also show that sequential consistency is composable in some cases commonly encountered: (1) objects that would be linearizable if they were implemented on top of a linearizable memory become sequentially consistent when implemented on top of a sequential memory while remaining composable and (2) in round-based algorithms, where each object is only accessed within one round.

Keywords: Asynchronous message-passing system · Crash-failures · Sequential consistency · Composability · Shared memory · Snapshot

1 Introduction

A distributed system is abstracted as a set of entities (nodes, processes, agents, etc.) that communicate through a communication medium. The two most used communication media are communication channels (message-passing system) and shared memory (read/write operations). Programming with shared objects is generally more convenient as it offers a higher level of abstraction to the programmer, therefore facilitates the work of designing distributed applications. A natural question is the level of consistency ensured by shared objects. An intuitive property is that shared objects should behave as if all processes accessed the same physical copy of the object. *Sequential consistency* [1] ensures that all the operations in a distributed history appear as if they were executed sequentially, in an order that respects the sequential order of each process (*process order*).

Unfortunately, sequential consistency is not composable: if a program uses two or more objects, despite each object being sequentially consistent individually, the set of all objects may not be sequentially consistent. *Linearizability* [2]

© Springer-Verlag Berlin Heidelberg 2016
C. Gavoille and D. Ilcinkas (Eds.): DISC 2016, LNCS 9888, pp. 284–297, 2016.
DOI: 10.1007/978-3-662-53426-7_21

overcomes this limitation by adding constraints on real time: each operation appears at a single point in time, between its start event and its end event. As a consequence, linearizability enjoys the locality property [2] that ensures its composability. Because of this composability, much more effort has been focused on linearizability than on sequential consistency so far. However, one of our contributions implies that in asynchronous systems where no global clock can be implemented to measure real time, a process cannot distinguish between a linearizable and a sequentially consistent execution, thus the connection to real time seems to be a worthless—though costly—guarantee.

In this paper we focus on message-passing distributed systems. In such systems a shared memory is not a physical object; it has to be built using the underlying message-passing communication network. Several bounds have been found on the cost of sequential consistency and linearizability in synchronous distributed systems, where the transit time for any message is in a range $[d - u, d]$, where d and u are called respectively the *latency* and the *uncertainty* of the network. Let us consider an implementation of a shared memory, and let r (resp. w) be the worst case latency of any read (resp. write) operation. Lipton and Sandberg proved in [3] that, if the algorithm implements a sequentially consistent memory, the inequality $r + w \geq d$ must hold. Attiya and Welch refined this result in [4], proving that each kind of operations could have a 0-latency implementation for sequential consistency (though not both in the same implementation) but that the time duration of both kinds of operations has to be at least linear in u in order to ensure linearizability.

Therefore the following questions arise. Are there applications for which the lack of composability of sequential consistency is not a problem? For these applications, can we expect the same benefits in weaker message-passing models, such as asynchronous failure-prone systems, from using sequentially consistent objects rather than linearizable objects?

To illustrate the contributions of the paper, we also address a higher level operation: a snapshot operation [5] that allows to read in a single operation a whole set of registers. A sequentially consistent snapshot is such that the set of values it returns may be returned by a sequential execution. This operation is very useful as it has been proved [5] that linearizable snapshots can be wait-free implemented from single-writer/multi-reader registers. Indeed, assuming a snapshot operation does not bring any additional power with respect to shared registers. Of course this induces an additional cost: the best known simulation needs $O(n \log n)$ basic read/write operations to implement each of the snapshot operations and the associated update operation [6]. Such an operation brings a programming comfort as it reduces the "noise" introduced by asynchrony and failures [7] and is particularly used in round-based computations [8] we consider for the study of the composability of sequential consistency.

Contributions. We present three major contributions. (1) We identify two contexts that can benefit from the use of sequential consistency: round-based algorithms using a different shared object for each round, and asynchronous shared-memory systems, where programs can not distinguish a sequentially consistent memory from a linearizable one. (2) We propose an implementation of a sequentially consistent memory where waiting is only required when a write is immediately followed by a read. This extends the result presented in [4] about synchronous failure-free systems, to failure-prone asynchronous systems. (3) The proposed algorithm also implements a sequentially consistent snapshot operation the cost of which compares very favorably with the best existing linearizable implementation to our knowledge (the stacking of the snapshot algorithm of Attiya and Rachman [6] over the ABD simulation of linearizable registers)

Outline. The remainder of this article is organized as follows. In Sect. 2, we define more formally sequential consistency, and we present special contexts in which it becomes composable. In Sect. 3, we present our implementation of shared memory and study its complexity. Finally, Sect. 4 concludes the paper.

2   Sequential Consistency and Composability

2.1   Definitions

In this section we recall the definitions of the most important notions we discuss in this paper: two consistency criteria, sequential consistency (SC, Definition 2, [1]) and linearizability (L, Definition 3, [2]), as well as composability (Definition 4). A consistency criterion associates a set of admitted *histories* to the *sequential specification* of each given object. A history is a representation of an execution. It contains a set of operations, that are partially ordered according to the sequential order of each process, called *process order*. A sequential specification is a language, i.e. a set of sequential (finite and infinite) words. For a consistency criterion C and a sequential specification T, we say that an algorithm implements a $C(T)$-consistent object if all its executions can be modelled by a history that belongs to $C(T)$, that contains all returned operations and only invoked operations. Note that this implies that if a process crashes during an operation, then the operation will appear in the history as if it was complete or as if it never took place at all.

Definition 1 (Linear extension). *Let H be a history and T be a sequential specification. A linear extension $\leq$ is a total order on all the operations of H, that contains the process order, and such that each event e has a finite past $\{e' : e' \leq e\}$ according to the total order.*

Definition 2 (Sequential Consistency). *Let H be a history and T be a sequential specification. The history H is sequentially consistent regarding T, denoted $H \in SC(T)$, if there exists a linear extension $\leq$ such that the word composed of all the operations of H ordered by $\leq$ belongs to T.*

Definition 3 (Linearizability). *Let H be a history and T be a sequential specification. The history H is linearizable regarding T, denoted $H \in L(T)$, if there exists a linear extension $\leq$ such that (1) for two operations a and b, if operation a returns before operation b begins, then $a \leq b$ and (2) the word formed of all the operations of H ordered by $\leq$ belongs to T.*

Let T_1 and T_2 be two sequential specifications. We define the *composition* of T_1 and T_2, denoted by $T_1 \times T_2$, as the set of all the interleaved sequences of a word from T_1 and a word from T_2. An interleaved sequence of two words l_1 and l_2 is a word composed of the disjoint union of all the letters of l_1 and l_2, that appear in the same order as they appear in l_1 and l_2. For example, the words ab and cd have six interleaved sequences: *abcd, acbd, acdb, cabd, cadb* and *cdab*.

A consistency criterion C is composable (Def. 4) if the composition of a $C(T_1)$-consistent object and a $C(T_2)$-consistent object is a $C(T_1 \times T_2)$-consistent object. Linearizability is composable, and sequential consistency is not.

Definition 4 (Composability). *For a history H and a sequential specification T, let H_T be the sub-history of H containing only the operations belonging to T.*

A consistency criterion C is composable *if, for all sequential specifications T_1 and T_2 and all histories H containing only events on T_1 and T_2, $(H_{T_1} \in C(T_1)$ and $H_{T_2} \in C(T_2))$ imply $H \in C(T_1 \times T_2)$.*

2.2 From Linearizability to Sequential Consistency

Software developers usually abstract the complexity of their system gradually, which results in a layered software architecture: at the top level, an application is built on top of several objects specific to the application, themselves built on top of lower levels. Such an architecture is represented in Fig. 1a. The lowest layer usually consists of one or several objects provided by the system itself, typically a shared memory. The system can ensure sequential consistency globally on all the provided objects, therefore composability is not required for this level. Proposition 1 expresses the fact that, in asynchronous systems, replacing a linearizable object by a sequentially consistent one does not affect the correctness of the programs running on it circumventing the non composability of sequential consistency. This result may have an impact on parallel architectures, such as modern multi-core processors and, to a higher extent, high performance supercomputers, for which the communication with a linearizable central shared memory is very costly, and weak memory models such as cache consistency [9] make the writing of programs tough. The idea of the proof is that in any sequentially consistent execution (Fig. 1b), it is possible to associate a local clock to each process such that, if these clocks followed real time, the execution would be linearizable (Fig. 1c). In an asynchronous system, it is impossible for the processes to distinguish between these clocks and real time, so the operations of the objects of the upper layers are not affected by the change of clock. The complete proof of this proposition can be found in [10].

Proposition 1. *Let A be an algorithm that implements an $SC(Y)$-consistent object when it is executed on an asynchronous system providing an $L(X)$-consistent object. Then A also implements an $SC(Y)$-consistent object when it is executed in an asynchronous system providing an $SC(X)$-consistent object.*

An interesting point about Proposition 1 is that it allows sequentially consistent—but not linearizable—objects to be composable. Let A_Y and A_Z

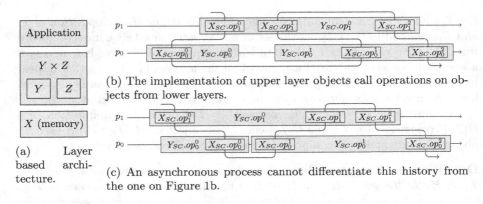

(a) Layer based architecture.

(b) The implementation of upper layer objects call operations on objects from lower layers.

(c) An asynchronous process cannot differentiate this history from the one on Figure 1b.

Fig. 1. In layer based program architecture running on asynchronous systems, local clocks of different processes can be distorted such that it is impossible to differentiate a sequentially consistent execution from a linearizable execution.

be two algorithms that implement $L(Y)$-consistent and $L(Z)$-consistent objects when they are executed on an asynchronous system providing an $L(X)$-consistent object, like on Fig. 1a. As linearizability is stronger than sequential consistency, according to Proposition 1, executing A_Y and A_Z on an asynchronous system providing an $SC(X)$-consistent object would implement sequentially consistent—yet not linearizable—objects. However, in a system providing the linearizable object X, by composability of linearizability, the composition of A_Y and A_Z implements an $L(Y \times Z)$-consistent object. Therefore, by Proposition 1 again, in a system providing the sequentially consistent object X, the composition also implements an $SC(Y \times Z)$-consistent object. In this example, the sequentially consistent versions of Y and Z derive their composability from an anchor to a *common time*, given by the sequentially consistent memory, that can differ from *real time*, required by linearizability.

2.3   Round-Based Computations

Even at a single layer, a program can use several objects that are not composable, but that are used in a fashion so that the non-composability is invisible to the program. Let us illustrate this with round-based algorithms. The synchronous distributed computing model has been extensively studied and well-understood leading the researchers to try to offer the same comfort when dealing with asynchronous systems, hence the introduction of synchronizers [11]. A synchronizer slices a computation into phases during which each process executes three steps: send/write, receive/read and then local computation. This model has been extended to failure prone systems in the round-by-round computing model [8] and to the Heard-Of model [12] among others. Such a model is particularly interesting when the termination of a given program is only eventual. Indeed, some problems are undecidable in failure prone purely asynchronous systems. In

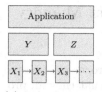

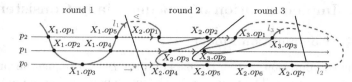

(a) Round-based program architecture

(b) As the ordering between different objects follows the process order, that is contained into the serialization order of each object, no loop can appear.

Fig. 2. The composition of sequentially consistent objects used in different rounds is sequentially consistent.

order to circumvent this impossibility, eventually or partially synchronous systems have been introduced [13]. In such systems the termination may hold only after some finite but unbounded time, and the algorithms are implemented by the means of a series of asynchronous rounds each using its own shared objects.

In the round-based computing model the execution is sliced into a sequence of asynchronous rounds. During each round, a new data structure (usually a single-writer/multi-reader register per process) is created and it is the only shared object used to communicate during the round. At the end of the round, each process destroys its local accessor to the object, so that it can no more access it. Note that the rounds are asynchronous: the processes do not necessarily start and finish their rounds at the same time. Moreover, a process may not terminate a round and keep accessing the same shared object forever or may crash during this round and stop executing. A round-based execution is illustrated in Fig. 2b.

In Proposition 2, we prove that sequentially consistent objects of different rounds behave well together: as the ordering added between the operations of two different objects always follows the round numbering, that is consistent with the program order already contained in the linear extension of each object, the composition of all these objects cannot create loops (Fig. 2b). The complete proof of this proposition can be found in [10]. Putting together this result and Proposition 1, all the algorithms that use a round-based computation model can benefit of any improvement on the implementation of an array of single-writer/multi-reader register that sacrifices linearizability for sequential consistency. Note that this remains true whatever is the data structure used during each round. The only constraint is that a sequentially consistent shared data structure can be accessed during a unique round. If each object is sequentially consistent then the whole execution is consistent.

Proposition 2. *Let $(T_r)_{r \in \mathbb{N}}$ be a family of sequential specifications and $(X_r)_{r \in \mathbb{N}}$ be a family of shared objects such that, for all r, X_r is $SC(T_r)$-consistent. Let H be a history that does not contain two operations $X_r.a$ and $X_{r'}.b$ with $r > r'$ such that $X_r.a$ precedes $X_{r'}.b$ in the process order. Then H is sequentially consistent with respect to the composition of all the T_r.*

3 Implementation of a Sequentially Consistent Memory

3.1 Computation Model

The computation system consists of a set Π of n sequential processes, denoted $p_0, p_1, \ldots, p_{n-1}$. The processes are asynchronous, in the sense that they all proceed at their own speed, not upper bounded and unknown to all other processes.

Among these n processes, up to t may crash (halt prematurely) but otherwise execute correctly the algorithm until the moment of their crash. We call a process *faulty* if it crashes, otherwise it is called *correct* or *non-faulty*. In the rest of the paper we will consider the above model restricted to the case $t < \frac{n}{2}$.

The processes communicate with each other by sending and receiving messages through a complete network of bidirectional channels. A process can directly communicate with any other process, including itself (p_i receives its own messages instantaneously), and can identify the sender of the message received. Each process is equipped with two operations: **send** and **receive**.

The communication channels are reliable (no losses, no creation, no duplication, no alteration of messages) and asynchronous (finite time needed for a message to be transmitted but there is no upper bound). We also assume the channels are FIFO: if p_i sends two messages to p_j, p_j will receive them in the order they were sent. As stated in [14], FIFO channels can always be implemented on top of non-FIFO channels. Therefore, this assumption does not bring additional computational power to the model, but it allows us to simplify the writing of the algorithm. Process p_i can also use the macro-operation **FIFO broadcast**, that can be seen as a multi-send that sends a message to all processes, including itself. Hence, if a faulty process crashes during the broadcast operation some processes may receive the message while others may not, otherwise all correct processes will eventually receive the message.

3.2 Single-Writer/Multi-Reader Registers and Snapshot Memory

The shared memory considered in this paper, called a *snapshot memory*, consists of an array of shared registers denoted REG[1..n]. Each entry REG[i] represents a single-writer/multi-reader (SWMR) register. When process p_i invokes REG.update(v), the value v is written into the SWMR register REG[i] associated with process p_i. Differently, any process p_i can read the whole array REG by invoking a single operation namely REG.snapshot(). According to the sequential specification of the snapshot memory, REG.snapshot() returns an array containing the most recent value written by each process or the initial default value if no value is written on some register. Concurrency is possible between snapshot and writing operations, as soon as the considered consistency criterion, namely linearizability or sequential consistency, is respected. Informally in a sequentially consistent snapshot memory, each snapshot operation must return the last value written by the process that initiated it, and for any pair of snapshot operations, one must return values at least as recent as the other for all registers.

Compared to read and write operations, the snapshot operation is a higher level abstraction introduced in [5] that eases program design without bringing additional power with respect to shared registers. Of course this induces an additional cost: the best known simulation, above SWMR registers proposed in [6], needs $O(n \log n)$ basic read/write operations to implement each of the snapshot and the associated update operations.

Since the seminal paper [15] that proposed the so-called ABD simulation that emulates a linearizable shared memory over a message-passing distributed system, most of the effort has been put on the shared memory model given that a simple stacking allows to translate any shared memory-based result to the message-passing system model. Several implementations of linearizable snapshot have been proposed in the literature some works consider variants of snapshot (e.g. immediate snapshot [16], weak-snapshot [17], one scanner [18]) others consider that special constructions such as test-and-set (T&S) [19] or load-link/store-conditional (LL/SC) [20] are available, the goal being to enhance time and space efficiency. In this paper, we propose the first message-passing sequentially consistent (not linearizable) snapshot memory implementation directly over a message-passing system (and consequently the first sequentially consistent array of SWMR registers), as traditional read and write operations can be immediately deduced from snapshot and update with no additional cost.

3.3 The Proposed Algorithm

Algorithm 1 proposes an implementation of the sequentially consistent snapshot memory data structure presented in Sect. 3.2. The complete proof of correctness of this algorithm can be found in the technical report [10]. Process p_i can write a value v in its own register $REG[i]$ by calling the operation $REG.\text{update}(v)$ (lines 6–9). It can also call the operation $REG.\text{snapshot}()$ (lines 10–11). Roughly speaking, the principle of this algorithm is to maintain, on each process, a local view of the object that reflects a set of *validated* update operations. To do so, when a value is written, all processes label it with their own timestamp. The order in which processes timestamp two different update operations define a *dependency relation* between these operations. For two operations a and b, if b depends on a, then p_i cannot validate b before a.

More precisely, each process p_i maintains five local variables:

- $\mathsf{X}_i \in \mathbb{N}^n$ is the array of most recent validated values written on each register.
- $\mathsf{ValClock}_i \in \mathbb{N}^n$ represents the timestamps associated with the values stored in X_i, labelled by the process that initiated them.
- $\mathsf{SendClock}_i \in \mathbb{N}$ is an integer clock used by p_i to timestamp all the update operations. $\mathsf{SendClock}_i$ is incremented each time a message is sent, which ensures all timestamps from the same process are different.
- $\mathsf{G}_i \subset \mathbb{N}^{3+n}$ encodes the dependencies between update operations that have not been validated yet, as known by p_i. An element $g \in \mathsf{G}_i$, of the form $(g.\mathsf{v}, g.\mathsf{k}, g.\mathsf{t}, g.\mathsf{cl})$, represents the update operation of value $g.\mathsf{v}$ by process $p_{g.\mathsf{k}}$ labelled by process $p_{g.\mathsf{k}}$ with timestamp $g.\mathsf{t}$. For all $0 \leq j < n$, $g.\mathsf{cl}[j]$

contains the timestamp given by p_j if it is known by p_i, and ∞ otherwise.

All updates of a history can be uniquely represented by a pair of integers (k, t), where p_k is the process that invoked it, and t is the timestamp associated to this update by p_k. Considering a history and a process p_i, we define the dependency relation $\rightarrow_i$ on pairs of integers (k, t), by $(k, t) \rightarrow_i (k', t')$ if for all g, g' ever inserted in G_i with $(g.\mathtt{k}, g.\mathtt{t}) = (k, t)$, $(g'.\mathtt{k}, g'.\mathtt{t}) = (k', t')$, we have $|\{j : g'.\mathtt{cl}[j] < g.\mathtt{cl}[j]\}| \leq \frac{n}{2}$ (i.e. the dependency does not exist if p_i knows that a majority of processes have seen the first update before the second). Let $\rightarrow_i^*$ denote the transitive closure of $\rightarrow_i$.

- $V_i \in \mathbb{N} \cup \{\bot\}$ is a buffer register used to store a value written while the previous one is not yet validated. This is necessary for validation (see below).

The key of the algorithm is to ensure the inclusion between sets of validated updates on any two processes at any time. Remark that it is not always necessary to order all pairs of update operations to implement a sequentially consistent snapshot memory: for example, two update operations on different registers commute. Therefore, instead of validating both operations on all processes in the exact same order (which requires Consensus), we can validate them at the same time to prevent a snapshot to occur between them. Thus, it is sufficient to ensure that, for all pairs of update operations, there is a dependency agreed by all processes (possibly in both directions). This is expressed by Lemma 1.

lemma 1. *Let p_i, p_j be two processes and t_i, t_j be two time instants, and let us denote by $\mathsf{ValClock}_i^{t_i}$ (resp. $\mathsf{ValClock}_j^{t_j}$) the value of $\mathsf{ValClock}_i$ (resp. $\mathsf{ValClock}_j$) at time t_i (resp. t_j). We have either, for all k, $\mathsf{ValClock}_i^{t_i}[k] \leq \mathsf{ValClock}_j^{t_j}[k]$ or for all k, $\mathsf{ValClock}_j^{t_j}[k] \leq \mathsf{ValClock}_i^{t_i}[k]$.*

This is done by the mean of messages of the form $\mathtt{message}(\mathsf{v}, \mathsf{k}, \mathsf{t}, \mathsf{cl})$ containing four integers: v the value written, k the identifier of the process that initiated the update, t the timestamp given by p_k and cl the timestamp given by the process that sent this message. Timestamps of successive messages sent by p_i are unique and totally ordered, thanks to variable $\mathsf{SendClock}_i$, that is incremented each time a message is sent by p_i. When process p_i wants to submit a value v for validation, it FIFO-broadcasts a message $\mathtt{message}(\mathsf{v}, i, \mathsf{SendClock}_i, \mathsf{SendClock}_i)$ (lines 8 and 28). When p_i receives a message $\mathtt{message}(\mathsf{v}, \mathsf{k}, \mathsf{t}, \mathsf{cl})$, three cases are possible. If p_i has already validated the corresponding update ($\mathsf{t} > \mathsf{ValClock}_i[\mathsf{k}]$), the message is simply ignored. Otherwise, if it is the first time p_i receives a message concerning this update (G_i does not contain any piece of information concerning it), it FIFO-broadcasts a message with its own timestamp and adds a new entry $g \in G_i$. Whether it is its first message or not, p_i records the timestamp cl, given by p_j, in $g.\mathtt{cl}[j]$ (lines 14 or 19). Note that we cannot update $g.\mathtt{cl}[\mathsf{k}]$ at this point, as the broadcast is not causal: if p_i did so, it could miss dependencies imposed by the order in which p_k saw concurrent updates. Then, p_i tries to validate update operations: p_i can validate an operation a if it has received messages from a majority of processes, and there is no operation $b \rightarrow_i^* a$ that cannot be validated. For that, it creates the set G' that initially contains all

---

Algorithm 1. Implementation of a sequentially consistent memory (for p_i)

```
    /* Local variable initialization                                         */
1   X_i ← [0, ..., 0];                  // X_i[j] ∈ ℕ: last validated value written by p_j
2   ValClock_i ← [0, ..., 0];           // ValClock_i[j] ∈ ℕ: stamp given by p_j to X_i[j]
3   SendClock_i ← 0;                     // used to stamp all the updates
4   G_i ← ∅;                             // contains a g = (g.v, g.k, g.t, g.cl) per non-val. update
5   V_i ← ⊥;                             // V_i ∈ ℕ ∪ {⊥}: stores postponed updates

    operation update(v) /* v ∈ ℕ: written value; no return value            */
6   │ if ∀g ∈ G_i : g.k ≠ i then         // no non-validated update by p_i
7   │   │  SendClock_i++;
8   │   │  FIFO broadcast message(v, i, SendClock_i, SendClock_i);
9   └ else V_i ← v;                       // postpone the update

    operation snapshot() /* return type: ℕⁿ                                  */
10  │  wait until V_i = ⊥ ∧ ∀g ∈ G_i : g.k ≠ i ;    // make sure p_i's updates are validated
11  └  return X_i;

    when a message message(v, k, t, cl) is received from p_j
       // v ∈ ℕ: written value, k ∈ ℕ: writer id, t ∈ ℕ: stamp by p_k, cl ∈ ℕ: stamp by p_j
12  │ if t > ValClock_i[k] then          // update not validated yet
13  │  │ if ∃g ∈ G_i : g.k = k ∧ g.t = t then     // update already known
14  │  │  │  g.cl[j] ← cl;
15  │  │ else                            // first message for this update
16  │  │  │ if k ≠ i then
17  │  │  │  │  SendClock_i++ ;           // forward with own stamp
18  │  │  │  └  FIFO broadcast message(v, k, t, SendClock_i);
19  │  │  │ var g ← (g.v = v, g.k = k, g.t = t, g.cl = [∞, ..., ∞]); g.cl[j] ← cl;
20  │  └  └  G_i ← G_i ∪ {g};            // create an entry in G_i for the update

21  │ var G' = {g ∈ G_i : |{l : g'.cl[l] < ∞}| > n/2};     // G' contains validable updates
22  │ while ∃g ∈ G_i \ G', g' ∈ G' : |{l : g'.cl[l] < g.cl[l]}| ≠ n/2 do  G' ← G' \ {g'};
23  │ G_i ← G_i \ G';                    // validate updates of G'
24  │ for g ∈ G' do
25  │  └  if ValClock_i[g.k] < g.t then ValClock_i[g.k] = g.t; X_i[g.k] = g.V;

26  │ if V_i ≠ ⊥ ∧ ∀g ∈ G_i : g.k ≠ i then    // start validation process for
27  │  │  SendClock_i++ ;                // postponed update if any
28  │  │  FIFO broadcast message(V_i, i, SendClock_i, SendClock_i);
29  └  └  V_i ← ⊥;
```

---

the operations that have received enough messages, and removes all operations with unvalidatable dependencies from it (lines 21–22), and then updates X_i and $ValClock_i$ with the most recent validated values (lines 23–25).

This mechanism is illustrated in Fig. 3a. Processes p_0 and p_4 initially call operation REG.update(1). Messages that have an impact in the algorithm are depicted by arrows and messages that do not appear are received later. The simplest case is process p_3 that received three messages concerning a (from p_4, p_3 and p_2, with $3 > \frac{n}{2}$) before its first message concerning b, allowing it to validate a. The case of p_4 is similar: even if it knows that process p_1 saw b before a, it received messages concerning a from three *other* processes, which allows it to ignore the message from p_1. The situation of p_0 and p_1 may look similar to this of p_4, but the message they received concerning a and one of the messages they received concerning b are from the same process p_2, forcing them to respect the dependency $a \rightarrow_0 b$. The same situation occurs for p_2 so even if a was validated before b by other processes, p_2 must respect the dependency $b \rightarrow_2 a$.

Sequential consistency requires the total order to contain the process order. Therefore, a snapshot of process p_i must return values at least as recent as its last updated value, i.e. it is not allowed to return from a snapshot between an update and the time of its validation (grey zones in Fig. 3a). This can be done in two ways: either by waiting at the end of each update until it is validated, in which case all snapshot operations are done for free, or by waiting at the beginning of all snapshots that immediately follow an update. This extends the remark of [4] to crash-prone asynchronous systems: to implement a sequentially consistent memory it is necessary and sufficient to wait during either read or write operations. In Algorithm 1, we chose to wait during read/snapshot operations (line 10). This is more efficient for two reasons: first, it is not needed to wait between two consecutive updates, which cannot be avoided in the other case, and second the time between the end of an update and the beginning of a snapshot counts in the validation process, but it can be used for local computations. Note that when two snapshot operations are invoked successively, the second one also returns immediately, which improves the result of [4] according to which waiting is necessary for all the operations of one kind.

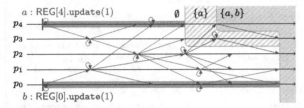 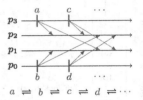

(a) An update is validated by a process when it has received enough messages for this update, and all the other updates it depends of have also been validated.

(b) Infinite chains of dependencies must be avoided to ensure termination.

Fig. 3. Two executions of Algorithm 1

In order to obtain termination of the snapshot operations (and progress in general), we must ensure that all update operations are eventually validated by all processes. This is expressed by Lemma 2. Figure 3b shows such a case. Process p_2 receives a message concerning a and a message concerning c before a message concerning b, while p_1 receives a message concerning b before messages concerning a and c. This may create dependencies $a \rightarrow_i b \rightarrow_i c \rightarrow_i b \rightarrow_i a$ on a process p_i thus forcing p_i to validate a and c at the same time, even if they are ordered by the process order. Fig. 3b shows that it can result in an infinite chain of dependencies, blocking validation of any update operation. To break this chain, we force process p_3 to wait until a is validated locally before it proposes c to validation by storing the value written by c in a local variable V_i until a is validated (lines 6 and 9). When a is validated, we start the same validation process for c (lines 26–29). Note that, if several updates (say c and e) happen before a is validated, the update of c can be dropped as it will eventually be overwritten by e. In this case, c will happen just before e in the final linearization required for sequential consistency.

lemma 2. *If a message $message(v, i, t, t)$ is sent by a correct process p_i, then beyond some time t', for each correct process p_j, $\mathsf{ValClock}_j^{t'}[i] \geq t$.*

We can now prove that all histories admitted by Algorithm 1 are sequentially consistent with respect to the snapshot memory object. The idea is to order snapshot operations according to the order given by Lemma 1 on the value of $\mathsf{ValClock}_i$ when they were made and to insert the update operations at the position where $\mathsf{ValClock}_i$ changes because they are validated. This order can be completed into a linear extension, by Lemma 2, and to show that the execution of all the operations in that order respects the sequential specification of the snapshot memory data structure. The complete proof can be found in [10].

3.4   Complexity

In this section, we analyze the complexity of Algorithm 1 in terms of number of messages and latency for each operation. We compare the complexity of our algorithm with the standard implementation of linearizable registers in [15] with unbounded messages. Note that [15] also proposes an implementation with bounded messages but at a much higher cost in terms of latency, which is the parameter we are really interested in improving in this paper. As our algorithm also implements the snapshot operation, we compare it to the implementation of a snapshot object [6] on top of registers. Fig. 4 sums up these complexities.

We measure the complexity as the length of the longest chain of causally related messages to expect before an operation can complete, e.g. if a process sends a message and then waits for some answers, the complexity will be 2.

Each update generates at most n^2 messages and has latency 0, as update operations return immediately. No message is sent for snapshot operations. In terms of latency, in the worst case a snapshot is called directly after two update operations a and b: the process must wait for acknowledgements for its message for a, and then for acknowledgements for its message for b, which gives a complexity of 4. However, if enough time has elapsed between a snapshot and the last update, the snapshot returns immediately.

In comparison, the ABD simulation uses solely a linear number of messages per operation (reads as well as writes), but waiting is necessary for both kinds of operations. Even in the case of the read operation, our worst case corresponds to the latency of the ABD simulation. Moreover, our solution directly implements the snapshot operation. Implementing a snapshot operation on top of a linearizable shared memory is in fact more costly than just reading each register once. The AR implementation [6], that is (to our knowledge) the implementation of the snapshot that uses the least amount of operations on the registers, uses $\mathcal{O}(n \log n)$ operations on registers to complete both a snapshot and an update operation. As each operation on memory requires $\mathcal{O}(n)$ messages and has a latency of $\mathcal{O}(1)$, our approach leads to a better performance in all cases.

	Read		Write		Snapshot		Update	
	# messages	latency	# messages	latency	# messages	latency	# messages	latency
ABD [15]	$\mathcal{O}(n)$	4	$\mathcal{O}(n)$	2	$\sim$	$\sim$	$\sim$	$\sim$
ABD + AR [15,6]	$\sim$	$\sim$	$\sim$	$\sim$	$\mathcal{O}\left(n^2\log n\right)$	$\mathcal{O}\left(n\log(n)\right)$	$\mathcal{O}\left(n^2\log n\right)$	$\mathcal{O}\left(n\log(n)\right)$
Algorithm 1	0	$0-4$	$\mathcal{O}(n^2)$	0	0	$0-4$	$\mathcal{O}(n^2)$	0

Fig. 4. Complexity of several algorithms to implement a shared memory

Algorithm 1, like [15], uses unbounded integer values to timestamp messages. Therefore, the complexity of an operation depends on the number m of operations executed before it, in the linear extension. All messages sent by Algorithm 1 have a size of $\mathcal{O}\left(log(nm)\right)$. The same complexity is necessary to implement n instances of a register with ABD.

In terms of local memory, due to asynchrony, in some cases G_i may contain an entry g for each value previously written. In that case, the space occupied by G_i may grow up to $\mathcal{O}(mn\log m)$. Remark though that, by Lemma 1, an entry g is eventually removed from G_i (in a synchronous system, after 2 time units if $g.k = i$ or 1 time unit if $g.k \neq i$). Thus, this maximal bound is unlikely to happen. Also, if all processes stop writing (e.g. in the round based model we discussed in Sect. 2.3), eventually $G_i = \emptyset$ and the space occupied by the algorithm drops down to $\mathcal{O}(n\log m)$, which is comparable to ABD. In comparison, the AR implementation keeps a tree containing past values from all registers, in each register which leads to a much higher size of messages and local memory.

4 Conclusion

In this paper, we investigated the advantages of focusing on sequential consistency. We show that in many applications, the lack of composability is not a problem. The first case concerns applications built on a layered architecture and the second example concerns round-based algorithms where processes access to one different sequentially consistent object in each round.

Using sequentially consistent objects instead of their linearizable counterpart can be very profitable in terms of execution time of operations. Whereas waiting is necessary for all operations when implementing linearizable memory, we presented an algorithm in which waiting is only required for read operations when they follow directly a write operation. This extends the result of Attiya and Welch to asynchronous systems with crashes. Moreover, the proposed algorithm implements a sequentially consistent snapshot memory for the same cost.

Exhibiting such an algorithm is not an easy task for two reasons. First, as write operations are wait-free, a process may write before its previous write has been acknowledged by other processes, which leads to "concurrent" write operations by the same process. Second, proving that an implementation is sequentially consistent is more difficult than proving it is linearizable since the condition on real time that must be respected by linearizability highly reduces the number of linear extensions that need to be considered.

Acknowledgments. This work has been partially supported by the Franco-German ANR project DISCMAT under grant agreement ANR-14-CE35-0010-01.

References

1. Lamport, L.: How to make a multiprocessor computer that correctly executes multiprocess programs. IEEE Trans. Comput. **100**(9), 690–691 (1979)
2. Herlihy, M.P., Wing, J.M.: Linearizability: a correctness condition for concurrent objects. ACM Trans. Program. Lang. Syst. (TOPLAS) **12**(3), 463–492 (1990)
3. Lipton, R.J., Sandberg, J.S.: PRAM: a scalable shared memory. Princeton University, Department of Computer Science (1988)
4. Attiya, H., Welch, J.L.: Sequential consistency versus linearizability. ACM Trans. Comput. Syst. (TOCS) **12**(2), 91–122 (1994)
5. Afek, Y., Attiya, H., Dolev, D., Gafni, E., Merritt, M., Shavit, N.: Atomic snapshots of shared memory. J. ACM **40**(4), 873–890 (1993)
6. Attiya, H., Rachman, O.: Atomic snapshots in o(n log n) operations. SIAM J. Comput. **27**(2), 319–340 (1998)
7. Gafni, E.: Distributed Computing: a Glimmer of a Theory. In: Handbook of Computer Science. CRC Press (1998)
8. Gafni, E.: Round-by-round fault detectors: Unifying synchrony and asynchrony (extended abstract). In: Proceedings of the 17th ACM Symposium on Principles of Distributed Computing, PODC 1998, pp. 143–152, Puerto Vallarta (1998)
9. Goodman, J.R.: Cache consistency and sequential consistency. University of Wisconsin-Madison, Computer Sciences Department (1991)
10. Perrin, M., Petrolia, M., Mostefaoui, A., Jard, C.: On Composition and implementation of sequential consistency (extended version). Research report, LINA-University of Nantes, July 2016
11. Awerbuch, B.: Complexity of network synchronization. J. ACM **32**(4), 804–823 (1985)
12. Charron-Bost, B., Schiper, A.: The heard-of model: computing in distributed systems with benign faults. Distrib. Comput. **22**(1), 49–71 (2009)
13. Dwork, C., Lynch, N., Stockmeyer, L.: Consensus in the presence of partial synchrony. J. ACM **35**(2), 288–323 (1988)
14. Birman, K.P., Joseph, T.A.: Reliable communication in the presence of failures. ACM Trans. Comput. Syst. (TOCS) **5**(1), 47–76 (1987)
15. Attiya, H., Bar-Noy, A., Dolev, D.: Sharing memory robustly in message-passing systems. J. ACM (JACM) **42**(1), 124–142 (1995)
16. Borowsky, E., Gafni, E.: Immediate atomic snapshots and fast renaming (extended abstract). In: Proceedings of the Twelth Annual ACM Symposium on Principles of Distributed Computing, pp. 41–51, Ithaca (1993)
17. Dwork, C., Herlihy, M., Plotkin, S.A., Waarts, O.: Time-lapse snapshots. In: Dolev, D., Galil, Z., Rodeh, M. (eds.) ISTCS 1992. LNCS, vol. 601, pp. 154–170. Springer, Heidelberg (1992)
18. Kirousis, L.M., Spirakis, P.G., Tsigas, P.: Reading many variables in one atomic operation: solutions with linear or sublinear complexity. IEEE Trans. Parallel Distrib. Syst. **5**(7), 688–696 (1994)
19. Attiya, H., Herlihy, M., Rachman, O.: Atomic snapshots using lattice agreement. Distrib. Comput. **8**(3), 121–132 (1995)
20. Riany, Y., Shavit, N., Touitou, D.: Towards a practical snapshot algorithm. Theor. Comput. Sci. **269**(1–2), 163–201 (2001)

k-Abortable Objects:
Progress Under High Contention

Naama Ben-David[1], David Yu Cheng Chan[2(✉)], Vassos Hadzilacos[2],
and Sam Toueg[2]

[1] Carnegie Mellon University, Pittsburgh, PA 15213, USA
naama@cmu.edu
[2] University of Toronto, Toronto, ON M5S1A1, Canada
{davidchan,vassos,sam}@cs.toronto.edu

Abstract. In this paper, we define k-abortable objects, the first kind
of abortable objects [2,7] that guarantee some degree of progress *even
under high contention*. The definition is simple and natural: intuitively,
an operation on a k-abortable object can abort only if k operations
from distinct processes succeed during the execution of the aborted
operation. We first show that k-abortable objects can easily implement *k-lock-free* objects, i.e., objects where at least k processes make
progress [5], but in contrast to k-lock-free objects, k-abortable objects
always return control. We then give an efficient universal construction
for wait-free k-abortable objects shared by n processes that takes only
$O(k)$ steps per operation. We also give a $\Omega(\log k)$-steps lower bound
for universal constructions of k-abortable objects shared by $n \geq k$
processes. Since every wait-free k-abortable object can implement its
k-lock-free counterpart, our universal construction also provides a universal construction for k-lock-free objects.

Keywords: Shared memory · Lock-freedom · Wait-freedom · Distributed algorithms · Abortable objects · Liveness conditions · Asynchronous
system

1 Introduction

Motivation and Related Work. We consider asynchronous distributed systems where processes apply operations to linearizable shared objects [10].
A *liveness property* specifies the conditions under which processes make progress,
i.e., the conditions under which the operations that they apply to the shared
objects return a response. A strong liveness property is *wait-freedom* [8], which
guarantees that *all* correct processes make progress. This is an attractive property, but wait-free objects are often difficult and inefficient to implement, and so
several weaker liveness properties have been suggested.

N. Ben-David—Part of this work was done while the author was at the University
of Toronto.

© Springer-Verlag Berlin Heidelberg 2016
C. Gavoille and D. Ilcinkas (Eds.): DISC 2016, LNCS 9888, pp. 298–312, 2016.
DOI: 10.1007/978-3-662-53426-7_22

One such property is *lock-freedom*, which guarantees that *at least one* correct process makes progress (this property is also called *non-blocking*). Many concurrent data structures are implemented in a lock-free manner [4,13]. Bushkov and Guerraoui recently defined *k-lock-freedom* [5], which, roughly speaking, guarantees that *at least k* correct processes make progress. This generalization of lock-freedom is appealing because when k ranges from 1 to n, k-lock-freedom goes from lock-freedom all the way to wait-freedom. Prior to the present paper, for $k > 1$, there was no implementation of any k-lock-free object that was not also wait free.

Another weak liveness property is *obstruction-freedom* [9]: if a process applies an operation to an obstruction-free object, and it eventually runs *alone* for sufficiently many steps, then this operation terminates. One advantage of obstruction-freedom is that any obstruction-free data structure can be implemented purely from registers, so there is no need for stronger, more expensive primitives. But if there are two (or more) processes that take steps concurrently, all of them can be stuck forever "inside" an object. To strengthen obstruction-freedom, Taubenfeld [14] defines *k-obstruction freedom*: if processes apply operations to a k-obstruction-free object, and a group of up to k of them eventually run alone for sufficiently many steps, then the operations of this group terminate.

Note that with k-lock-freedom and k-obstruction freedom, a correct process may get "stuck", i.e., it may apply an operation that never returns.[1] This motivates the idea of *always* returning from an operation at the cost of sometimes returning with an exception. Early work in this direction focused on objects that can be implemented from registers alone: [3] allows concurrent operations to return "pause" (in which case, they must be resumed), and [2] allows concurrent operations to return "abort", in which case they may or may not have taken effect. More recent work [7] introduced a stronger type of abortable objects, called *deterministic abortable* objects, where it is guaranteed that aborted operations do *not* take effect. With such objects, a process that applies an operation that aborts is free to do some other work before *safely* retrying this operation (because it knows that the previous attempt did not have any effect), or to attempt other alternatives if possible.[2]

The abortable objects defined in [2,7], however, have a serious drawback: when processes are concurrently active no progress is guaranteed. This is because an operation op may abort even if it is concurrent with only one other operation op', and, symmetrically, op' may also abort. A similar problem also affects pausable objects [3].

Contributions of this Paper. In this paper, we introduce k-abortable objects, the first kind of abortable objects that guarantee some degree of progress *even*

---

[1] This is akin to entering a bakery and getting stuck inside forever, because other customers keep cutting in line.

[2] This is akin to entering a bakery and being notified that it is currently too busy; the customer is now free to do other errands and come back later, when the bakery may be less busy, or to go to another bakery.

under high contention. This progress guarantee is achieved by strengthening the conditions under which concurrent operations can abort, as follows:

1. An operation *op* can abort only if it is concurrent with at least k other operations; moreover, these k operations must be executed by *distinct* processes.[3] This requirement ensures that if *at most* k processes are active, no operation aborts, and so all the processes make progress. But if more than k processes are active, this property alone does not guarantee any progress because all operations can abort. Thus we also require the following property.
2. The k operations that "cause" an operation *op* to abort must themselves succeed; moreover, they must take effect during *op*'s execution interval.[4] This requirement ensures that if *more than* k processes are active, at least k of them make progress.

Together, the above two requirements can be stated in a more precise and succinct way as follows: *an operation op may abort only if at least k operations by distinct processes do not abort and are linearized within op's execution interval.* As in [7], k-abortable objects also have the property that aborted operations are guaranteed *not* to take effect.

After defining k-abortable objects, we compare them to k-lock-free objects and show that every k-abortable object can implement a k-lock-free object of the same type (so every 1-abortable object can implement its lock-free counterpart).

We then investigate whether, in general, k-abortable objects can be implemented more efficiently than their wait-free counterparts. To do so, we give an efficient universal construction for k-abortable objects shared by n processes that takes only $O(k)$ steps per operation and uses only LL/VL/SC base objects.[5] In contrast, Jayanti has shown a lower bound of $\Omega(\log n)$ steps for universal constructions of *wait-free* objects shared by n processes [11], and this lower bound holds for shared-memory that supports LL/VL/SC, *move* and *swap* operations. Therefore, in such systems, k-abortable objects can be implemented more efficiently than their wait-free counterparts when $k = o(\log n)$. Furthermore, all the known universal constructions of wait-free objects require $\Omega(n)$ steps per operation in the worst case, except for those that make impractical assumptions on the size of registers (such as registers that can hold n operations) [6,11]. Our universal construction of k-abortable objects does not make such assumptions; the effect of these assumptions is further discussed in Sect. 6.

Finally, we show an $\Omega(\log k)$-steps lower bound for universal constructions of k-abortable objects shared by $n \geq k$ processes in systems with LL/VL/SC objects (we do so by using Jayanti's lower bound for wait-free universal constructions). This leaves an interesting open problem, namely closing the gap between the $\Omega(\log k)$ lower bound and the $O(k)$ upper bound given by our universal construction. This mirrors another open problem [11], namely closing the

---

[3] So *op* cannot abort just because it is concurrent with k operations of a fast process.
[4] So they cannot cause operations that start after *op* to abort.
[5] In general, k-abortable objects require strong primitives because they can implement their lock-free counterparts.

gap between the $\Omega(\log n)$ lower bound and the $O(n)$ upper bound for universal constructions of wait-free objects that "do not make impractical assumptions on the size of registers" [11].

An important remark about *adaptive implementations* [1] and their relation to k-abortable implementations is now in order. Afek et al. presented an adaptive wait-free universal construction called "Individual Update" [1] that takes only $O(\ell)$ steps per operation, where ℓ is the number of processes that access the object concurrently. When contention is high, ℓ can increase all the way up to n, and in this case adaptive implementations are just as expensive as conventional wait-free implementations. In contrast, our universal construction for k-abortable objects never takes more than $O(k)$ steps per operation, at the cost of allowing some operations to abort. Note that the concepts of adaptivity and abortability are not mutually exclusive: a k-abortable object could have an *adaptive* implementation that runs in $O(\min(\ell, k))$ time, where ℓ is the number of processes that access the object concurrently. Adaptivity and k-abortability are also compared in Sects. 4 and 6.

In summary, our main contributions are:

1. We define k-abortable objects, the first kind of abortable objects that guarantee some degree of progress even under high contention. The definition is simple and natural: intuitively, an operation on a k-abortable object can abort only if k operations from distinct processes succeed during the execution of the aborted operation.
2. We show that every k-lock-free object can be implemented by a single instance of a k-abortable object of the same type. Recall that, in contrast to k-lock-free objects where some processes may get "stuck", k-abortable objects always return control.
3. We give a universal construction for wait-free k-abortable objects shared by n processes that takes only $O(k)$ steps per operation: for $k = o(\log n)$, this beats the well-known lower bound of $\Omega(\log n)$ steps per operation for universal constructions of wait-free objects [11]. This is also significantly better than the $O(n)$ steps per operation required by known "practical" universal constructions of wait-free objects.
4. Since every k-abortable object can implement its k-lock-free counterpart, our universal construction also provides a universal construction for k-lock-free objects. Prior to our work, for $k > 1$, there was no implementation of any k-lock-free object, except for ones that are also wait free (and therefore incur the cost of achieving wait freedom).
5. Finally, we show that Jayanti's $\Omega(\log n)$-steps lower bound for wait-free universal constructions implies an analogous $\Omega(\log k)$-steps lower bound for universal constructions of k-abortable objects shared by $n \geq k$ processes.

2 Model Sketch

We adopt a standard model for systems with asynchronous processes and shared objects, with a minor extension to describe abortable objects (this model is similar to the one in [7]).

Steps and Histories. Each process p executes *steps*, which are of two kinds: the invocation by p of an operation *op* on an object O, denoted (INV, p, op, O); and the receipt by p of a response *res* from an object O, denoted (RES, p, res, O). A history H of an object is a sequence of invocation and response steps, such that: for each process p, the subsequence of H involving only the steps of p consists of zero or more pairs of invocation and response steps (the two steps of each pair are called *matching*), possibly followed by an invocation step. An *operation execution opx* in a history H of an object is either a pair consisting of an invocation and its matching response in H, in which case we say that *opx* is *complete* in H; or an invocation in H that has no matching response in H, in which case we say that *opx* is *incomplete* or *pending* in H. A history H is *complete* if all operation executions in H are complete. A *completion* of H is a history H' formed by removing invocations or adding responses to every pending operation execution in H, such that H' is complete.

Object Types and Linearizability. Each object has a type that specifies how the object behaves when it is accessed sequentially. Formally, an *object type* T is specified by a tuple (OP, RES, Q, δ), where OP is a set of operations, RES is a set of responses, Q is a set of states, and $\delta \subseteq Q \times OP \times Q \times RES$ is a state transition relation. A tuple (s, op, s', res) in δ means that if type T is in state s when operation $op \in OP$ is invoked, then T can change its state to s' and return the response *res*.

For each type $T = (OP, RES, Q, \delta)$, we define the *abortable counterpart* $T_\perp$ of T.[6] Intuitively, type $T_\perp$ is the same as T, except that every operation is allowed to *abort*, making no change to the state and terminating with a special response $\perp$. More precisely, $T_\perp = (OP, RES^a, Q, \delta^a)$ where $RES^a = RES \cup \{\perp\}$ for some $\perp \notin RES$, and, for every tuple (s, op, s', res) in the state transition relation δ of T, the state transition relation δ^a of $T_\perp$ contains both (s, op, s', res) and $(s, op, s, \perp)$: the first tuple corresponds to *op* completing normally as it does in T, and the second corresponds to *op* aborting without changing the state.

When an object O of type T is accessed concurrently, its behaviour should be *linearizable with respect to* T: every operation on O must appear to take effect instantaneously, at some point during the operation's execution interval, according to type T [10]. More precisely, a *linearization L of a complete history H of an object* is an assignment of a distinct *linearization point* $L(opx)$ to every operation execution *opx* in H such that $L(opx)$ is within the execution interval of *opx* in H. A linearization L of a complete history H of an object *conforms to type T*, if the operation responses in H could be those received when applying these operations sequentially, in the order dictated by L, on an object of type T. *A history H of an object is linearizable with respect to a type T if H has a completion H' and a linearization L' of H' that conforms to type T. An object O is linearizable with respect to a type T if every history H of O is linearizable with respect to type T.*

---

[6] This was originally called the *deterministic abortable* counterpart of a type T in [7].

k-Abortable Objects. Intuitively, O is a k-abortable object of type T if: (1) O behaves like an object of type T except that operations may also abort (aborted operations have no effect), and (2) for each operation opx that aborts, there are k operations from distinct processes that do not abort and take effect within opx's interval. More precisely, an object O is a *k-abortable object of type T* if, for every history H of O, there is a completion H' and a linearization L' of H' such that: (1) the linearization L' of H' conforms to the abortable counterpart $T_\perp$ of T, and (2) for each operation execution opx that aborts in H', there are k operations from distinct processes that do *not* abort in H' and whose linearization point $L'(opx)$ is within the execution interval of opx in H'. Note that in a system with n processes, an n-abortable object of type T is just an object of type T. An (implementation of a) k-abortable object of type T is *wait-free* if a process cannot invoke an operation on O and then take infinitely many steps without receiving a response from O. Henceforth, we consider only wait-free (implementations of) k-abortable objects, and by "k-abortable O" we mean "wait-free k-abortable O". Thus, n-abortable objects are wait-free objects.

3 Relation to k-Lock Freedom

In this section, we relate k-abortability to k-lock-freedom [5] (recall that when k ranges from 1 to n, k-lock-freedom ranges from lock-freedom to wait-freedom). Intuitively, an object O is k-lock-free if it ensures the following: (1) if *at most* k processes access O, then they all make progress, and (2) if *more than* k processes access O, then at least k of

---

Algorithm 1. Implementing a k-lock-free object O of type T

Shared Object:
$O_\perp$: *k-abortable object of type T*

```
1: procedure INVOKE(op)
2:     repeat
3:         res ← O_⊥.INVOKE(op)
4:     until res ≠ ⊥
5:     return res
```

---

them make progress. This is equivalent to the following requirement: a process can get "stuck" while accessing O only if at least k other processes make progress forever. More precisely:

Definition 1. *An object O is k-lock-free if it guarantees the following property: if a process invokes an operation on O and then takes an infinite number of steps without receiving a response from O, then at least k processes complete infinitely many operations on O.*

Algorithm 1 relates k-abortability to k-lock-freedom: for every type T, this algorithm implements O, a k-lock-free object of type T using $O_\perp$, a k-abortable object of type T. The algorithm is trivial: to invoke an operation op on O, a process invokes op on $O_\perp$ until it doesn't abort; it then returns the value that was returned by $O_\perp$. So we have the following theorem, whose proof we defer to the full version of this paper.

Theorem 2. *In an n-process system, for all $1 \leq k \leq n$ and all type T: a k-abortable object of type T can implement a k-lock-free object of type T.*

4   k-Abortable Universal Construction

In this section, we present a k-abortable universal construction that takes $O(k)$ steps per operation. As with many wait-free universal constructions, our construction assumes that the shared state of the implemented object can be stored in a single LL/VL/SC register, and therefore it takes constant time to copy. This assumption is reasonable for 'small' objects; we discuss how to remove it for large objects in Sect. 6.

At a high level, our construction is reminiscent of "Individual Update", the adaptive universal construction presented in [1]. To initiate an operation, a process records the operation in a *Records Array*, which has one entry reserved for each process. It then tries to find an available slot in a separate *Announcements Array*, which determines the order in which operations will be helped. Finally, operations are executed through the use of a shared *Core*, in which all processes agree on the state of the object and the next operation to execute.

However, our announcing procedure is significantly more involved than that of "Individual Update" [1]. The difference in the procedures stems from the difference in requirements. An operation on a k-abortable object must make sure that k operations by distinct processes *succeed within its interval* before it can abort. Adaptive implementations do not confront such a requirement.

In our construction, the Announcements Array has only k slots. If a process succeeds in announcing its operation by securing a slot in the Announcements Array, that operation will not abort; it will get linearized as a successful operation, even if its initiating process is slow or has crashed. On the other hand, if a process fails to find an empty slot, its operation will eventually abort. However, before it does so, it needs to help the announced operations, to ensure that at least k of them get linearized during its interval.

There are three main stages in the execution of an operation by a process:

1. **The Recording Stage**: The process records its intent to execute the operation in its slot in the Records Array. If this operation eventually gets helped by another process in the system, its response will be recorded in this slot as well.
2. **The Announcement Stage**: The process tries to announce its operation by securing a slot in the Announcements Array. This is done by sequentially checking whether each slot in the array is available.
3. **The Helping Stage**: Regardless of whether the process succeeded in announcing its operation, it attempts to help other operations. Only the operations in the Announcements Array are helped. There are two ways in which a process helps operations: (1) it executes the operation by calculating the outcome of applying it to the current state and then updating the object accordingly, and (2) it cleans up operations that have already been executed by relaying their response to their initiating process (by writing it in the appropriate slot in the Records Array).

4.1   Details of the Algorithm

The detailed pseudocode is given in Algorithm 2. In the code, variables starting with g are *global*, and variables starting with l are *local copies* of global variables. Generally, processes that update global variables first get a local copy of the data they intend to change, make the changes locally, and then try to update the global variable accordingly.

Each process keeps track of the number of operations it has executed, and assigns a unique ID (*oid* in the algorithm) for every operation it executes (line 2). The *oid* is an *auxiliary* variable; it is useful for referring to specific operations when discussing the algorithm's execution and the proof, but all appearances of *oid* in Algorithm 2 can be safely removed without affecting the correctness of the universal construction.

The Records Array g_rec contains n slots, one reserved for each process. Each slot contains 3 fields, all initially set to null. To initiate an operation, a process p fills its slot ($g\_rec[p]$) with information about the operation: its *oid*, its operation type *opType*, and a special value $\perp$ in the field *res* (line 17). If the operation is eventually applied, $\perp$ is replaced by the response value from the object. Otherwise, $\perp$ will remain in that slot for the duration of the operation's interval. When this operation terminates, it will return the value written in *res* at that time (line 50).

After recording its intended operation, a process tries to announce it in the Announcements Array g_ann which has only k slots. Each slot of g_ann contains two fields, both initially null. Announcing is critical for the success of the operation: it will abort if and only if it doesn't get announced. The announcing stage involves iterating through g_ann to try to find an available slot (lines 19 to 24). If an available slot is found, the process tries to store its *pid* and its operation's *oid* in it, and thereby claim the slot for its operation.

A slot in g_ann is considered *available* if one of two conditions hold (line 22): either (1) its *pid* value is null, i.e. no process has claimed it, or (2) the process which claimed it has already finished its operation. This second condition is checked by reading the *res* field of the operation record in g_rec. If *res* is not $\perp$, then the operation has already been executed, and no longer needs to occupy the announcement slot. Note that a process will never hold on to a slot in g_ann and use it for subsequent operations: once its current operation is successfully applied, if no other process claims the slot (line 45), the process will unannounce its own operation by resetting the fields of the slot back to null (line 46).

When trying to announce, a process p checks each slot in g_ann *twice* before it moves on to the next (line 20). Intuitively, this is done to ensure that if p does not manage to announce in slot i, then that slot is truly occupied by another operation that needs help. The problem with a single check is that p might fail its SC because of an unannouncing process, which means that the slot could actually be available throughout the entire execution interval of p's operation. Checking each slot twice eliminates this possibility, and this is crucial for correctness of the algorithm. Specifically, it is necessary for proving that within the execution interval of each operation that aborts, k operations by distinct processes succeed.

Algorithm 2. k-Abortable Universal Construction for Objects of Type T

Shared Objects:

$g\_rec[1..n]$: Records Array. LL/SCs containing $\{oid$: int, $opType$: operation type, res: a response$\}$; all set to null.

$g\_ann[1..k]$: Announcements Array. LL/VL/SCs containing $\{oid$: int, pid: int$\}$; all set to null.

g_core: LL/VL/SC containing $\{state$: a state, aid: int, oid: int, pid: int, res: a response$\}$; set to $\{s_0, 1, \text{null}, \text{null}, \text{null}\}$.

Code performed by process p:

```
1:  procedure UNIVERSAL(my_opType)
2:      my_Oid ← my_Oid + 1              ▷ Auxiliary persistent variable denoting the operation's ID
3:      RECORD(my_opType)                ▷ To start operation, record it in the Records Array
4:      my_Aid ← ANNOUNCE()                          ▷ Try to announce the operation
5:      if my_Aid ≠ null then               ▷ Successfully announced; will not abort
6:          repeat
7:              my_res ← g_rec[p].LL().res              ▷ Check if my operation is done
8:              HELP()
9:          until my_res ≠ ⊥
10:         UNANNOUNCE(my_Aid)           ▷ Clear my slot in the Announcements Array
11:     else                             ▷ Failed to announce. Will abort after helping
12:         loop k + 2 times
13:             HELP()                   ▷ Help linearize at least k operations
14:     return UNRECORD()                ▷ Clear record of operation before terminating

15: procedure RECORD(my_opType)          ▷ Record your intention to execute the operation.
16:     g_rec[p].LL()
17:     g_rec[p].SC((my_Oid, my_opType, ⊥))          ▷ This SC always succeeds.

18: function ANNOUNCE()
19:     for j : 1 . . . k do   ▷ Go over array sequentially, trying to announce in each slot in turn
20:         loop 2 times       ▷ Trying each slot twice ensures that failure is justified
21:             temp_Pid ← g_ann[j].LL().pid
22:             if temp_Pid = null or g_rec[temp_Pid].LL().res ≠ ⊥ then       ▷ If slot is free
23:                 if g_ann[j].SC((my_Oid, p)) then      ▷ Try to announce there
24:                     return j          ▷ If successful, return the index of the slot
25:     return null                       ▷ If the entire array was occupied, return with failure

26: procedure HELP()
27:     l_core ← g_core.LL()                ▷ Create a local copy of the Core
28:     if l_core.pid ≠ null then    ▷ Clean up the previous operation (if it has not yet been
    cleaned).
29:         l_rec ← g_rec[l_core.pid].LL()  ▷ Check if the response should be relayed to the Record
30:         if ¬g_core.VL() then return     ▷ Ensure that the local Core is still up to date
31:         if l_rec.res = ⊥ then     ▷ The response entry is blank, so the operation needs help
32:             l_rec.res ← l_core.res      ▷ Copy the response from the Core to the process's record
33:             g_rec[l_core.pid].SC(l_rec) ▷ This is the helped operation's linearization point
34:     l_core.aid ← (l_core.aid mod k) + 1     ▷ Determine which announcement to help next
35:     (l_core.oid, l_core.pid) ← (null, null)
36:     l_ann ← g_ann[l_core.aid].LL()                      ▷ Find the operation to help
37:     if l_ann.pid ≠ null then
38:         l_rec ← g_rec[l_ann.pid].LL()       ▷ Check whether the operation needs help
39:         if l_rec.res = ⊥ then
40:             if g_ann[l_core.aid].VL() then    ▷ Ensure that operation is still announced.
41:                 (l_core.oid, l_core.pid) ← (l_ann.oid, l_ann.pid)
42:                 (l_core.state, l_core.res) ← APPLY_T(l_core.state, l_rec.opType)  ▷ Execute locally
43:     g_core.SC(l_core)            ▷ Attempt to replace the Core by its local copy.

44: procedure UNANNOUNCE(my_Aid)         ▷ Remove yourself from the Announcements Array.
45:     if g_ann[my_Aid].LL().pid = p then
46:         g_ann[my_Aid].SC((null, null))

47: function UNRECORD()                  ▷ Read the response and clear your Record.
48:     my_res ← g_rec[p].LL().res
49:     g_rec[p].SC((null, null, null))          ▷ This SC always succeeds.
50:     return my_res
```

Whether a process succeeds or fails to announce its operation, it proceeds to help some announced operations using the HELP procedure. The execution of HELP begins by performing an LL on g_core to get a local copy l_core (line 27). The Core holds the current state of the object (*state*), and may also hold information about the operation that was most recently executed. In that case, *oid* and *pid* describe the operation and its process, *aid* is the index at which this operation was announced in g_ann, and *res* is the response returned by the object when the operation was applied to it. We say that the operation described by the fields in g_core is the *scheduled* operation. The HELP procedure proceeds in two stages. First, if there is a scheduled operation *op* (line 28), the process helps to copy the response in l_core to *op*'s record if it still has $\perp$ in *res* (line 31). Second, $l\_core.aid$ is moved to the next slot of g_ann, and if the slot is not available, the process helps the announced operation become scheduled. To do so, the helping process applies the operation to $l\_core.state$ to determine the next state and response (line 42). Note that APPLY_T corresponds to the state transition relation δ of type T. At the end of the HELP procedure, the process attempts to finalize all of the changes it has performed on its local copy l_core by copying its contents into g_core via an SC (line 43).

A process that *successfully announces* its operation repeats the HELP procedure until it finds its response in its slot of the Records Array; this will occur after at most $k + 3$ executions of HELP. A process that *fails to announce* its operation executes the HELP procedure $k + 2$ times.

Once a process p receives the response for its operation *op*, p does some cleanup before *op* terminates. Specifically, it executes the HELP procedure one more time (line 8), and calls UNANNOUNCE (line 10) and UNRECORD (line 14). This ensures that this operation will not interfere with its subsequent ones.

4.2 Correctness Proof Sketch

Theorem 3. *Algorithm 2 implements a k-abortable object of type T.*

To show this, we need to prove the following. For every history H of O, there is a completion H' and a linearization L' of H' such that: (1) the linearization L' of H' conforms to $T_\perp$ (2) for each operation *op* that aborts in H', there are k operations from distinct processes that do *not* abort in H' and whose linearization points in L' is within the execution interval of *op* in H'.

Intuitively, each operation whose record gets a response is linearized at that time (line 33), while aborting operations are linearized when they terminate. We leave the construction of H' and L' to the full version of the paper.

Lemma 4. *The linearization L' of history H' conforms to type $T_\perp$.*

In order to show that L' conforms to $T_\perp$, we first need to show that aborted operations don't change the state of the object. Roughly speaking, this is because an operation that aborts does so because it was never announced, and therefore no process applies it. Thus, it does not have any effect on the object. The actual proof is more intricate, since we need to ensure that the HELP procedure indeed only helps operations that are announced, and doesn't accidentally follow outdated pointers to find and help operations that should not be helped. Since $T_\perp$ is the abortable counterpart of type T, we also need to show that, aside from aborts, the object behaves as if it is of type T. Intuitively, g_core holds the state of O, and is only modified when an operation is stored in the Core. Whenever that happens, line 42 applies the operation according to the state transition relation of type T.

Lemma 5. *For each operation op that aborts in H', there are k operations from distinct processes that do not abort in H' and whose linearization points in L' are within the execution interval of op in H'.*

To show Lemma 5, we begin with the following claim, whose proof we defer to the full version of the paper. We say that an operation is *open* at time t if it has been invoked but not linearized by time t.

Claim 6. *An attempt by an operation op to announce at slot i of the Announcements Array only fails if at some time t during the attempt, there is an open operation in slot i.*

Claim 7. *Let t_s^{op} denote the starting time of an operation op. If op fails to announce in slot i at time t_i then at some time t in $[t_s^{op}, t_i]$, there are i other open operations, each announced in some slot $1 \ldots i$ before time t_i.*

Proof. The proof is by induction on i. If op fails to announce in slot 1 at time t_1, Claim 6 asserts that at some time t during op's attempt to announce in slot 1, there is an open operation in slot 1.

Assume that the claim holds for slot $i - 1$. Suppose that op fails to announce in slot i at time t_i. Then by Claim 6, there is an open operation op' announced at slot i at time $t_i' < t_i$. Since operations have to go through the announce array sequentially and try each slot, both op and op' must have tried and failed to announce in slot $i - 1$ at time $t_{i-1} < t_i$ and $t_{i-1}' < t_i' < t_i$, respectively, before attempting to announce in slot i. So, by the induction hypothesis (because op and op' failed to announce in slot $i - 1$), there are times $t \in [t_s^{op}, t_{i-1}]$ and $t' \in [t_s^{op'}, t_{i-1}']$ and sets S_t and $S_{t'}$ of $i - 1$ operations each that are open at times t and t', and are announced in some slot $1 \ldots i - 1$ before time t_{i-1} and t_{i-1}'.

Let $t_{max} = max\{t, t'\}$ and $S_{t_{max}}$ be the corresponding set of $i - 1$ open operations. Since neither op nor op' were announced in any slot $1 \ldots i - 1$, neither of them belong to $S_{t_{max}}$. Furthermore, both op and op' are open at t_{max}. Since $t \in [t_s^{op}, t_{i-1}]$ and $t' \in [t_s^{op'}, t_{i-1}']$ and $t_{i-1} < t_i$ and $t_{i-1}' < t_i$, we have $t_s^{op} < t < t_i$ and $t_s^{op'} < t' < t_i$; thus $t_s^{op} < t_{max} < t_i$. So $S_{t_{max}} \cup \{op'\}$ is a set of i operations, all of which are open at time $t_s^{op} < t_{max} < t_i$, and which were all announced in some slot $1 \ldots i$ before time t_i. Therefore, the claim holds for slot i. $\square$

Suppose an operation op of a process p aborts. Clearly op failed to announce its operation. By Claim 7 (with $i = k$), there is a time within its execution interval during which there are k other open operations. Since each process can only execute one operation at a time, these must be operations by k different processes. In addition, we know that all of these operations get announced before op fails to announce. To complete the proof of Lemma 5, it remains to show that these k operations are linearized before op terminates. To see this, first note that a process that fails to announce its operation executes the HELP procedure $k + 2$ times. The following claim (whose proof we defer to the full version of the paper) immediately implies Lemma 5:

Claim 8. *All operations announced before p starts executing the* HELP *procedure are linearized by the time p finishes executing the* HELP *procedure $k + 2$ times.*

4.3 Running Time

Theorem 9. *Each operation terminates within $O(k)$ steps.*

Proof. The RECORD, UNRECORD, HELP and UNANNOUNCE procedures take constant time. The ANNOUNCE procedure contains one loop, which gets executed at most $2k$ times. Among these procedures, HELP is the only procedure that is called more than once per operation. If a process p fails to announce its operation, it only executes the HELP procedure $k + 2$ times. Otherwise, it executes the HELP procedure until its record has been given a response. Recall that an announced operation is linearized when it receives a response. Claim 8 asserts that after p executes the HELP procedure $k + 2$ times, its operation must be linearized, so p will find its response in the Records Array during the next execution. □

5 Lower Bound

In this section, we show a $\Omega(\log k)$-steps lower bound on wait-free universal constructions of k-abortable objects shared by n processes. This result is a consequence of Jayanti's lower bound in [11].

Theorem 10. *Consider a shared-memory system S that supports only LL, SC, VL (i.e., validate), move, and swap operations. Given any wait-free implementation of a k-abortable fetch&increment shared by $n \geq k$ processes, some operation requires $\Omega(\log k)$ steps.*

Proof [Sketch]. Suppose, for contradiction, that there is a wait-free implementation I of a k-abortable *fetch&increment* shared by $n \geq k$ processes such that all operations take $o(\log k)$ steps in system S. Observe that when at most k processes access the object implemented by I, no operation can abort, so I implements an ordinary, non-abortable *fetch&increment*. Thus, I is also a wait-free implementation of a *fetch&increment* shared by k processes such that all operations take $o(\log k)$ steps in system S. By Theorem 6.2 in [11], however, for every wait-free implementation of a *fetch&increment* shared by k processes in system S, some operation requires $\Omega(\log k)$ steps — a contradiction. □

Corollary 11. *For every wait-free universal construction of k-abortable objects shared by n processes in system S, some operation requires $\Omega(\log k)$ steps.*

6   Concluding Remarks

In Sect. 4, we gave a universal construction of k-abortable objects in which every operation takes at most $O(k)$-steps. As we mentioned before, our construction has similarities with an *adaptive* wait-free universal construction called "Individual Update" given by Afek et al. in [1]: this construction takes $O(\ell)$ steps per operation, where ℓ is the number of processes that access the object concurrently. Under high contention, however, operations may take $O(n)$ steps with the adaptive construction, whereas operations never take more than $O(k)$ steps with our construction, at the cost of sometimes aborting. Another difference between our construction and the adaptive one is how slow or crashed processes affect the performance of other processes. With the adaptive construction, a slow process can in turn slow down other processes: ℓ counts *all* processes accessing the object. For example, if most of the n processes slow down or crash in the middle of an operation, all subsequent operations of the remaining processes may take $O(n)$ steps.[7] In contrast, a process p that slows down or crashes while accessing a k-abortable object does not degrade the performance of other processes; as long as p remains in the object, p (together with $k-1$ other processes) can "cause" each process to abort *at most once*. Note that this property is not a special feature of our universal construction: it is a property inherent in the definition of k-abortability; the k operations that "cause" an operation op to abort are linearized during op's execution, so they cannot cause operations that start after op to abort. Adaptivity and k-abortability are orthogonal concepts: it may be possible to combine their benefits into *adaptive* k-abortable objects, but doing so remains an open problem.

As with many wait-free universal constructions, including the well-known one given by Herlihy in [8], our construction assumes that the shared state of the implemented object can be stored in a single base object. While this assumption may be reasonable for "small" objects, it is not tenable for objects with unbounded state, such as queues and stacks. One method to support such data structures using base objects of small size, called "Agree on Changes", was proposed by Afek et al. in [1]. We can apply the same method to our universal construction so that: (a) it uses LL/VL/SC objects of *bounded* size, and (b) every operation on a k-abortable object O takes $O(kf(s))$-steps, where $f(s)$ is the *sequential complexity* of O, i.e., $f(s)$ is the maximum number of steps required by a sequential algorithm to apply any operation on O when O has size s. For queues and stacks, $f(s) = 1$, and therefore we can implement k-abortable queues or stacks that take $O(k)$ steps per operation, while using only bounded-size LL/VL/SC objects. In contrast, the best wait-free implementation of a queue that we are aware of takes $\Theta(n)$ steps per operation [12].

For some popular data structures, there may be k-abortable implementations that are simpler and more efficient than those given by our universal construction

---

[7] This is not obvious, but it is possible to construct such runs of the adaptive algorithm in [1].

of k-abortable objects. For small values of k, such implementations may prove to be attractive alternatives to lock-free data structures [4,13].

Our $\Omega(\log k)$ lower bound for k-abortable universal constructions was derived from Jayanti's $\Omega(\log n)$ lower bound for wait-free universal constructions [11] in shared-memory systems that support only LL, VL, SC, move, and swap operations. Under the impractical assumption that a LL/VL/SC object can store n operations, Jayanti observed that his lower bound is tight: there is a wait-free universal construction that takes $O(\log n)$ steps per operation. In fact, Fatourou and Kallimanis [6] proved that, with LL/VL/SC *and* Fetch&Add objects of size $\Theta(n)$, one can beat the $\Omega(\log n)$ lower bound: they present a wait-free universal construction that uses such objects and takes only $O(1)$ steps per operation. They note, however, that this construction "is not practical since it employs a large Fetch&Add object", and give a practical version of it that uses only objects of reasonable size but takes $\Omega(n)$ steps per operation. The time complexity of universal constructions for both wait-free and k-abortable objects using only objects of reasonable size is an open question.

References

1. Afek, Y., Dauber, D., Touitou, D.: Wait-free made fast. In: Proceedings of the Twenty-Seventh Annual ACM Symposium on Theory of Computing, pp. 538–547. ACM (1995)
2. Aguilera, M.K., Frolund, S., Hadzilacos, V., Horn, S.L., Toueg, S.: Abortable and query-abortable objects and their efficient implementation. In: Proceedings of the Twenty-Sixth Annual ACM Symposium on Principles of Distributed Computing, pp. 23–32. ACM (2007)
3. Attiya, H., Guerraoui, R., Kouznetsov, P.: Computing with reads and writes in the absence of step contention. In: Fraigniaud, P. (ed.) DISC 2005. LNCS, vol. 3724, pp. 122–136. Springer, Heidelberg (2005)
4. Brown, T., Ellen, F., Ruppert, E.: A general technique for non-blocking trees. In: Proceedings of the 19th ACM SIGPLAN Symposium on Principles and Practice of Parallel Programming, pp. 329–342. ACM (2014)
5. Bushkov, V., Guerraoui, R.: Safety-liveness exclusion in distributed computing. In: Proceedings of the Twenty Fourth Annual ACM Symposium on Principles of Distributed Computing. ACM (2015)
6. Fatourou, P., Kallimanis, N.D.: Highly-efficient wait-free synchronization. Theor. Comput. Syst. **55**(3), 475–520 (2014)
7. Hadzilacos, V., Toueg, S.: On deterministic abortable objects. In: Proceedings of the 2013 ACM Symposium on Principles of Distributed Computing, pp. 4–12. ACM (2013)
8. Herlihy, M.: Wait-free synchronization. ACM Trans. Program. Lang. Syst. (TOPLAS) **13**(1), 124–149 (1991)
9. Herlihy, M., Luchangco, V., Moir, M.: Obstruction-free synchronization: Double-ended queues as an example. In: 23rd International Conference on Distributed Computing Systems, Proceedings, pp. 522–529. IEEE (2003)
10. Herlihy, M.P., Wing, J.M.: Linearizability: a correctness condition for concurrent objects. ACM Trans. Program. Lang. Syst. (TOPLAS) **12**(13), 463–492 (1990)

11. Jayanti, P.: A time complexity lower bound for randomized implementations of some shared objects. In: Proceedings of the Seventeenth Annual ACM Symposium on Principles of Distributed Computing, pp. 201–210. ACM (1998)

12. Kogan, A., Petrank, E.: Wait-free queues with multiple enqueuers and dequeuers. ACM SIGPLAN Not. **46**, 223–234 (2011). ACM

13. Michael, M.M., Scott, M.L.: Simple, fast, and practical non-blocking and blocking concurrent queue algorithms. In: Proceedings of the Fifteenth Annual ACM Symposium on Principles of Distributed Computing, pp. 267–275. ACM (1996)

14. Taubenfeld, G.: Contention-sensitive data structures and algorithms. In: Keidar, I. (ed.) DISC 2009. LNCS, vol. 5805, pp. 157–171. Springer, Heidelberg (2009)

Linearizability of Persistent Memory Objects Under a Full-System-Crash Failure Model

Joseph Izraelevitz[✉], Hammurabi Mendes, and Michael L. Scott

University of Rochester, Rochester, NY 14627-0226, USA
{jhi1,hmendes,scott}@cs.rochester.edu

Abstract. This paper provides a theoretical and practical framework for crash-resilient data structures on a machine with persistent (non-volatile) memory but transient registers and cache. In contrast to certain prior work, but in keeping with "real world" systems, we assume a full-system failure model, in which all transient state (of all processes) is lost on a crash. We introduce the notion of *durable linearizability* to govern the safety of concurrent objects under this failure model and a corresponding relaxed, buffered variant which ensures that the persistent state in the event of a crash is consistent but not necessarily up to date.

At the implementation level, we present a new "memory persistency model," *explicit epoch persistency*, that builds upon and generalizes prior work. Our model captures both hardware buffering and fully relaxed consistency, and subsumes both existing and proposed instruction set architectures. Using the persistency model, we present an automated transform to convert any linearizable, nonblocking concurrent object into one that is also durably linearizable. We also present a design pattern, analogous to linearization points, for the construction of other, more optimized objects. Finally, we discuss generic optimizations that may improve performance while preserving both safety and liveness.

1 Introduction

Current industry projections indicate that nonvolatile, byte-addressable memory (NVM) will become commonplace over the next few years. While the availability of NVM suggests the possibility of keeping persistent data in main memory (not just in the file system), the fact that recent updates to registers and cache may be lost during a power failure means that the data in main memory, if not carefully managed, may not be consistent at recovery time.

Maintaining a consistent state in NVM requires special care to order main memory updates. Several groups have designed libraries to support such ordering using failure atomic updates, via either a transactional memory interface [6,7,20,26] or one inferred from mutex synchronization [5,17]. Others

---

This work was supported in part by NSF grants CCF-0963759, CCF-1116055, CNS-1319417, CCF-1422649, and CCF-1337224, and by support from the IBM Canada Centres for Advanced Study.

© Springer-Verlag Berlin Heidelberg 2016
C. Gavoille and D. Ilcinkas (Eds.): DISC 2016, LNCS 9888, pp. 313–327, 2016.
DOI: 10.1007/978-3-662-53426-7_23

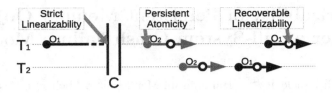

Fig. 1. Linearization bounds for interrupted operations under thread reuse failure model. Displayed is a concurrent abstract (operation-level) history of two threads (T_1 and T_2) on two objects (O_1 and O_2); linearization points are shown as circles. These correctness conditions differ in the deadline for linearization for a pending operation interrupted by a crash (T_1's first operation). *Strict linearizability* [1] requires that the pending operation linearizes or aborts by the crash. *Persistent atomicity* [10] requires that the operation linearizes or aborts before any subsequent invocation by the pending thread on any object. *Recoverable linearizability* [2] requires that the operation linearizes or aborts before any subsequent linearization by the pending thread on that same object; under this condition a thread may have more than one operation pending at a time. O_2 demonstrates the non-locality of persistent atomicity; T_2 demonstrates a program order inversion under recoverable linearizability.

have designed data structures that tolerate power failures (e.g. [25,27]), but the semantics of these structures are typically specified informally; the criteria according to which they are correct remain unclear. Guerraoui and Levy have proposed *persistent atomicity* [10] as a safety condition for persistent concurrent objects. This condition ensures that the state of an object will be consistent in the wake of a crash, but it does not provide *locality*: correct histories of separate objects, when merged, will not necessarily yield a correct composite history. Berryhill et al. have proposed an alternative, *recoverable linearizability* [2], which achieves locality but may sacrifice program order after a crash. Earlier work by Aguilera and Frølund proposed *strict linearizability* [1], which preserves both locality and program order but provably precludes the implementation of some wait-free objects for certain (limited) machine models. These safety conditions are illustrated in Fig. 1.

Interestingly, both the lack of locality in persistent atomicity and the loss of program order in recoverable linearizability stem from the assumption that an individual abstract thread may crash, recover, and then continue execution. While well defined, this *failure model* is more general than is normally assumed in real-world systems. More commonly, processes are assumed to fail together, as part of a "full system" crash. A data structure that survives such a crash may safely assume that subsequent accesses will be performed by different threads. We observe that if we consider only full-system crashes (an assumption modeled as a well-formedness constraint on histories), then persistent atomicity and recoverable linearizability are indistinguishable (and thus local). They are also satisfied by existing persistent structures. We use the term *durable linearizability* to refer to this merged safety condition under the restricted failure model.

Independent of failure model, existing theoretical work typically requires that operations become persistent before they return to their caller. In practice, this requirement is likely to impose unacceptable overhead, since persistent memory, while dramatically faster than disk or flash storage, still incurs latencies of hundreds of cycles. To address the latency problem, we introduce *buffered durable linearizability*, which requires only that an operation be "persistently ordered" before it returns. State in the wake of a crash is still required to be consistent, but it need not necessarily be fully up-to-date. Data structures designed with buffering in mind will typically provide an explicit sync method that guarantees, upon its return, that all previously ordered operations have reached persistent memory; an application thread might invoke this method before performing I/O. Unlike its unbuffered variant, buffered durable linearizability is not local: a history may fail to be buffered durably linearizable even if all of its object sub-histories are. If the buffering mechanism is shared across all objects, however, an implementation can ensure that all *realizable* histories—those that actually emerge from the implementation—will indeed be buffered durably linearizable: the post-crash states of all objects will be mutually consistent.

At the implementation level, prior work has explored the *memory persistency model* (analogous to a traditional *consistency* model) that governs instructions used to push the contents of cache to NVM. Existing persistency models assume that hardware will track dependencies and automatically write dirty cache lines back to NVM as necessary [8, 19, 23]. Unfortunately, real-world ISAs require the programmer to request writes-back explicitly. Furthermore, existing persistency models have been explored only for sequentially consistent (SC) [23] or total-store order (TSO) machines [8, 19]. At the same time, recent persistency models [19, 23] envision functionality not yet supported by commercial ISAs—namely, hardware buffering in an ordered queue of writes-back to persistent memory, allowing *persistence fence* (pfence) ordering instructions to complete without waiting for confirmation from the physical memory device. To accommodate anticipated hardware, we introduce a memory persistency model, *explicit epoch persistency*, that is both buffered and fully relaxed (release consistent).

Just as traditional concurrent objects require not only safety but liveness, so too should persistent objects. We define two optional liveness conditions: First, an object designed for buffered durable linearizability may provide *nonblocking sync*, ensuring that calls to sync complete without blocking. Second, a nonblocking object may provide *bounded completion*, limiting the amount of work done after a crash prior to the completion (if any) of operations interrupted by the crash. As a liveness constraint, bounded completion contrasts with prior art which imposes safety constraints [1, 2, 10] on completion (see Fig. 1).

We also present a simple transform that takes a data-race-free program designed for release consistency and generates an equivalent program in which the state persisted at a crash is guaranteed to represent a consistent cut across the happens-before order of the original program. When the original program comprises the implementation of a linearizable nonblocking concurrent object, extensions to this transform result in a buffered durably or durably linearizable object. (If the original program is blocking, additional machinery—e.g., undo logging—may be required. While we do not consider such machinery here, we note that it still requires consistency as a foundation.)

To enable reasoning about our correctness conditions, we extend the notion of linearization points into persistent memory objects, and demonstrate how such *persist points* can be used to argue a given implementation is correct. We also consider optimizations (e.g. elimination) that may safely be excluded from persistence in order to improve performance. Proofs for our lemmas and theorems can be found in an associated technical report [18].

2   Abstract Models

An *abstract history* is a sequence of *events*, which can be: (i) invocations of an object method, (ii) responses associated with invocations, and (iii) system-wide crashes. We use $O.\text{inv}\langle m \rangle_t(params)$ to denote the invocation of operation m on object O, performed by thread t with parameters $params$. Similarly, $O.\text{res}\langle m \rangle_t(retvals)$ denotes the response of m on O, again performed by t, returning $retvals$. A crash is denoted by C.

Given a history $\mathcal{H}$, we use $\mathcal{H}[t]$ to denote the subhistory of $\mathcal{H}$ containing all and only the events performed by thread t. Similarly, $\mathcal{H}[O]$ denotes the subhistory containing all and only the events performed on object O, plus crash events. We use C_i to denote the i-th crash event, and $\text{ops}(\mathcal{H})$ to denote the subhistory containing all events other than crashes. The crash events partition a history as $\mathcal{H} = \mathcal{E}_0 \, C_1 \, \mathcal{E}_1 \, C_2 \ldots \mathcal{E}_{c-1} \, C_c \, \mathcal{E}_c$, where c is the number of crash events in $\mathcal{H}$. Note that $\text{ops}(\mathcal{E}_i) = \mathcal{E}_i$ for all $0 \le i \le c$. We call the subhistory $\mathcal{E}_i$ the i-th *era* of $\mathcal{H}$.

Given a history $\mathcal{H} = \mathcal{H}_1 \, A \, \mathcal{H}_2 \, B \, \mathcal{H}_3$, where A and B are events, we say that A *precedes* B (resp. B *succeeds* A). For any invocation $I = O.\text{inv}\langle m \rangle_t(params)$ in $\mathcal{H}$, the first $R = O.\text{res}\langle m \rangle_t(retvals)$ (if any) that succeeds I in $\mathcal{H}$ is called a *matching response*. A history $\mathcal{S}$ is *sequential* if $\mathcal{S} = I_0 \, R_0 \ldots I_x \, R_x$ or $\mathcal{S} = I_0 \, R_0 \ldots I_x \, R_x \, I_{x+1}$, for $x \ge 0$, and $\forall 0 \le i \le x, R_i$ is a matching response for I_i.

Definition 1 (Abstract Well-Formedness). *An abstract history $\mathcal{H}$ is said to be* well formed *if and only if $\mathcal{H}[t]$ is sequential for every thread t.*

Note that sequential histories contain no crash events, so the events of a given thread are confined to a single era. (In practice, thread IDs may be re-used as soon as operations of the previous era have completed. In particular, an object with *bounded completion* [Sect. 3.3, Definition 10] can rapidly reuse IDs.)

We consider only well-formed abstract histories. A *completed operation* in $\mathcal{H}$ is any pair (I, R) of invocation I and matching response R. A *pending operation* in $\mathcal{H}$ is any pair $(I, \perp)$ where I has no matching response in $\mathcal{H}$. In this case, I is called a *pending invocation* in $\mathcal{H}$, and any response R such that (I, R) is a completed operation in $\mathcal{H} \, R$ is called a *completing response* for $\mathcal{H}$.

Definition 2 (Abstract Happens-Before). *In any (well-formed) abstract history $\mathcal{H}$ containing events E_1 and E_2, we say that E_1 happens before E_2*

(denoted $E_1 \prec E_2$) if E_1 precedes E_2 in $\mathcal{H}$ and (1) E_1 is a crash, (2) E_2 is a crash, (3) E_1 is a response and E_2 is an invocation, or (4) there exists an event $\hat{E}$ such that $E_1 \prec \hat{E} \prec E_2$. We extend the order to operations: $(I_1, R_1) \prec (I_2, x)$ if and only if $R_1 \prec I_2$.

Two histories $\mathcal{H}$ and $\mathcal{H}'$ are said to be *equivalent* if $\mathcal{H}[t] = \mathcal{H}'[t]$ for every thread t. We use compl($\mathcal{H}$) to denote the set of histories that can be generated from $\mathcal{H}$ by appending completing responses, and trunc($\mathcal{H}$) to denote the set of histories that can be generated from $\mathcal{H}$ by removing pending invocations. As is standard, a history $\mathcal{H}$ is *linearizable* if it is well formed, it has no crash events, and there exists some history $\mathcal{H}' \in \text{trunc(compl}(\mathcal{H}))$ and some legal sequential history $\mathcal{S}$ equivalent to $\mathcal{H}'$ such that $\forall E_1, E_2 \in \mathcal{H}' \ [E_1 \prec_{\mathcal{H}'} E_2 \Rightarrow E_1 \prec_{\mathcal{S}} E_2]$.

Definition 3 (Durable Linearizability). *An abstract history $\mathcal{H}$ is said to be durably linearizable if it is well formed and ops($\mathcal{H}$) is linearizable.*

Durable linearizability captures the idea that operations become persistent before they return; that is, if a crash happens, all previously completed operations remain completed, with their effects visible. Operations that have not completed as of a crash may or may not be completed in some subsequent era. Intuitively, their effects may be visible simply because they "executed far enough" prior to the crash (despite the lack of a response), or because threads in subsequent eras finished their execution for them (for instance, by scanning an "announcement array" in the style of universal constructions [15]). While this approach is simple, it preserves important properties from linearizability, namely *locality* (composability) and *nonblocking progress* [18].

Given a history $\mathcal{H}$ and any transitive order $<$ on events of $\mathcal{H}$, a $<$-*consistent cut* of $\mathcal{H}$ is a subhistory $\mathcal{P}$ of $\mathcal{H}$ where if $E \in \mathcal{P}$ and $E' < E$ in $\mathcal{H}$, then $E' \in \mathcal{P}$ and $E' < E$ in $\mathcal{P}$. In abstract histories, we are often interested in cuts consistent with $\prec$, the happens-before order on events.

Definition 4 (Buffered Durable Linearizability). *A history $\mathcal{H}$ with c crash events is said to be buffered durably linearizable if it is well formed and there exist subhistories $\mathcal{P}_0, \ldots, \mathcal{P}_{c-1}$ such that for all $0 \leq i \leq c$, $\mathcal{P}_i$ is a $\prec$-consistent cut of $\mathcal{E}_i$, and $\mathcal{P} = \mathcal{P}_0 \ldots \mathcal{P}_{i-1} \mathcal{E}_i$ is linearizable.*

The intent here is that events in the portion of $\mathcal{E}_i$ after $\mathcal{P}_i$ were buffered but failed to persist before the crash. Note that since $\mathcal{P}_i = \mathcal{E}_i$ is a valid $\prec$-consistent cut for all $0 \leq i < c$, we can have $\mathcal{P} = \text{ops}(\mathcal{H})$, and therefore any durably linearizable history is buffered durably linearizable. Note also that buffered durable linearizability is not in general local: if an operation does not persist before it returns, we will not in general be able to ensure that it persists before any operation that follows it in happens-before order unless we arrange for the implementations of separate objects to cooperate.

3 Concrete Models

Concurrent objects are typically implemented by code in some computer language. We want to know if this code is correct. Following standard practice, we model implementation behavior as a set of *concrete histories*, generated under some language and machine model assumed to be specified elsewhere. Each concrete history consists of a sequence of events, including not only operation invocations, responses, and crash events, but also load, store, and read-modify-write (RMW—e.g., compare-and-swap [CAS]) events, which access the representation of the object. Let $x.\mathsf{ld}_t(v)$ denote a load of variable x by thread t, returning the value v. Let $x.\mathsf{st}_t(v)$ denote a store of v to x by t.

Given a concrete history $\mathcal{H}$, the *abstract history of* $\mathcal{H}$, denoted abstract($\mathcal{H}$), is obtained by eliding all events other than invocations, responses, and crashes. As in abstract histories, we use $\mathcal{H}[t]$ and $\mathcal{H}[O]$ to denote the thread and object subhistories of $\mathcal{H}$. The concept of *era* from Sect. 2 applies verbatim. We say that an event E *lies between* events A and B in a concrete or abstract history $\mathcal{H}$ if A precedes E and E precedes B in $\mathcal{H}$.

Definition 5 (Concrete Well-Formedness). *A concrete history $\mathcal{H}$ is well-formed if and only if*

1. abstract($\mathcal{H}$) *is well-formed.*
2. *In each thread subhistory of $\mathcal{H}$, each memory event either (a) lies between some invocation and its matching response; (b) lies between a pending invocation I and the first crash that succeeds I in $\mathcal{H}$ (if such a crash exists); (c) succeeds a pending invocation I if no crash succeeds I in $\mathcal{H}$.*
3. *The values returned by the loads and RMWs respect the reads-see-writes relation (Definition 7, below).*

3.1 Basic Memory Model

For the sake of generality, we build our reads-see-writes relation on the highly relaxed *release consistency* memory model [9]. We allow certain loads to be labeled as *load-acquire* (ld_acq) events and certain stores to be labeled as *store-release* (st_rel) events. We treat RMW events as atomic $\langle \mathsf{ld\_acq}, \mathsf{st\_rel} \rangle$ pairs.

Definition 6 (Concrete Happens-Before). *Given events E_1 and E_2 of concrete history $\mathcal{H}$, we say that E_1 is sequenced-before E_2 if E_1 precedes E_2 in $\mathcal{H}[t]$ for some thread t and (a) E_1 is a ld_acq, (b) E_2 is a st_rel, or (c) E_1 and E_2 access the same location. We say that E_1 synchronizes-with E_2 if $E_2 = x.\mathsf{ld\_acq}_{t'}(v)$ and E_1 is the closest preceding $x.\mathsf{st\_rel}_t(v)$ in history order. The happens-before partial order on events in $\mathcal{H}$ is the transitive closure of sequenced-before order with synchronizes-with order. As in abstract histories, we write $E_1 \prec E_2$.*

Note that the definitions of happens-before are different for concrete and abstract histories; which one is meant in a given case should be clear from context.

The release-consistent model corresponds closely to that of the ARM v8 instruction set and can be considered a generalization of Intel's x86 instruction set. Given concrete happens-before, we can define the reads-see-writes relation:

Definition 7 (Reads-See-Writes). *A concrete history* $\mathcal{H}$ *respects the* reads-see-writes *relation if for each load* $R \in \{x.ld_t(v), x.ld\_acq_t(v)\}$, *there exists a store* $W \in \{x.st_u(v), x.st\_rel_u(v)\}$ *such that either (1)* $W \prec R$ *and there exists no store* W' *of* x *such that* $W \prec W' \prec R$ *or (2)* W *is unordered with respect to* R *under happens-before.*

For simplicity of exposition, we consider the initial value of each variable to have been specified by a store that happens before all other instructions in the history. We consider only well-formed concrete histories in this paper. If case (2) in Definition 7 never occurs in a history $\mathcal{H}$, we say that $\mathcal{H}$ is *data-race-free*.

3.2   Extensions for Persistence

The semantics of instructions controlling the ordering and timing under which cached values are pushed to persistent memory comprise a memory *persistency model* [23]. Since any machine with bounded caches must sometimes evict and write back a line without program intervention, the principal challenge for designers of persistent objects is to ensure that a newer write does not persist before an older write (to some other location) when correctness after a crash requires the locations to be mutually consistent.

Under the *epoch persistency* model of Condit et al. [8] and Pelley et al. [23], writes-back to persistent memory (*persist* operations) are *implicit*—they do not appear in the program's instruction stream. When ordering is required, a program can issue a special instruction (which we call a pfence) to force all of its earlier writes to persist before any subsequent writes. Periods between pfences in a given thread are known as *epochs*. As noted by Pelley et al. [23], it is possible for writes-back to be *buffered*. When necessary, a separate instruction (which we call psync) can be used to wait until the buffer has drained.

Unfortunately, implicit write-back of persistent memory is difficult to implement in real hardware [8,19,23]. Instead, manufacturers have introduced explicit *persistent write-back* (pwb) instructions. These are typically implemented in an eager fashion: a pwb starts the write-back process; a psync waits for the completion of all prior pwbs (under some appropriate definition of "prior").

We generalize proposed implicit persistency models [8,19,23] and real world (explicit) persistency ISAs to define our own, new model, which we call *explicit epoch persistency*. Like real-world explicit ISAs, our persistency model requires programmers to use a pwb to force back data into persistence. Like other buffered models, we provide pfence, which ensures that all previous pwbs are ordered with respect to any subsequent pwbs, and psync, which waits until all previous pwbs have actually reached persistent memory. We assume that persists to a given location respect coherence: the programmer need never worry that a newly persisted value will later be overwritten by the write-back of some earlier value. Unlike prior art, which assumes sequential consistency [23] or total store order [8, 19,20], we integrate our instructions into a relaxed (release consistent) model.

Returning to concrete histories, we use $x.\text{pwb}_t$ to denote a pwb of variable x by thread t, pfence_t to denote a pfence by thread t, and psync_t to denote a psync by thread t. We amend our definition of concrete histories to include these *persistence events*. We refer to any non-crash event of a concrete history as an *instruction*.

Definition 8 (Persist Ordering). *Given events E_1 and E_2 of concrete history $\mathcal{H}$, with E_1 preceding E_2 in the same thread subhistory, we say that E_1 is persist-ordered before E_2, denoted $E_1 \lessdot E_2$, if*

(a) $E_1 = pwb$ and $E_2 \in \{pfence, psync\}$;
(b) $E_1 \in \{pfence, psync\}$ and $E_2 \in \{pwb, st, st\_rel\}$;
(c) $E_1, E_2 \in \{st, st\_rel, pwb\}$, and E_1 and E_2 access the same location;
(d) $E_1 \in \{ld, ld\_acq\}$, $E_2 = pwb$, and E_1 and E_2 access the same location; or
(e) $E_1 = ld\_acq$ and $E_2 \in \{pfence, psync\}$.

Finally, across threads, $E_1 \lessdot E_2$ if

(f) $E_1 = st\_rel$, $E_2 = ld\_acq$, and E_1 synchronizes with E_2.

To identify the values available after a crash, we extend the syntax of concrete histories to allow store events to be labeled as "persisted," meaning that they will be available in subsequent eras if not overwritten. Persisted store labels introduce additional well-formedness constraints:

Definition 9 (Concrete Well-Formedness [augments Definition 5]**).** *A concrete history $\mathcal{H}$ is* well-formed *if and only if it satisfies the properties of Definition 5 and*

4. *For each variable x, at most one store of x is labeled as persisted in any given era. We say the $(x, 0)$-persisted store is the labeled store of x in $\mathcal{E}_0$, if there is one; otherwise it is the initialization store of x. For $i > 0$, we say the (x, i)-persisted store is the labeled store of x in $\mathcal{E}_i$, if there is one; otherwise it is the $(x, i - 1)$-persisted store.*
5. *For any (x, i)-persisted store W, there is no store W' of x and psync event P such that $W \lessdot W' \lessdot P$.*
6. *For any (x, i)-persisted store W, there is no store W' of x and (y, i)-persisted store S such that $W \lessdot W' \lessdot S$.*

These rules ensure that persisted stores compose a $\lessdot$-consistent cut of $\mathcal{H}$. To allow loads to see persisted values in the wake of a crash, we augment the definition of happens-before to declare that the (x, i)-persisted store happens before all events of era $\mathcal{E}_{i+1}$. Definition 7 then stands as originally written.

3.3 Liveness

With strict linearizability, no operation is left pending in the wake of a crash: either it has completed when execution resumes, or it never will. With persistent atomicity and recoverable linearizability, the time it may take to complete a pending operation m in thread t can be expressed in terms of execution steps in t's reincarnation (see Fig. 1). With durable linearizability, which admits no reincarnated threads, any bound on the time it may take to complete m must depend on other threads.

Definition 10 (Bounded Completion). *An object O has* bounded completion *if, for each concrete history $\mathcal{H}$ of O that ends in a crash with an operation m on O still pending, there exists a positive integer k such that for all realizable extensions $\mathcal{H}'$ of $\mathcal{H}$ in which some era of $\mathcal{H}' \setminus \mathcal{H}$ contains at least k instructions issued by an arbitrary thread, either (1) for all realizable extensions $\mathcal{H}''$ of $\mathcal{H}'$, $\mathcal{H}'' \setminus \text{inv}\langle m \rangle$ is buffered durably linearizable or (2) for all realizable extensions $\mathcal{H}''$ of $\mathcal{H}'$, if there exists a completed operation n with $\text{inv}\langle n \rangle \in \mathcal{H}'' \setminus \mathcal{H}'$, then there exists a sequential history S equivalent to $\mathcal{H}''$ with $m \prec_S n$.*

Briefly: by k post-crash instructions by any thread, m completes, if it ever will.

It is also desirable to discuss progress towards persistence. Under durable linearizability, every operation persists before it responds, so any liveness property (e.g. lock freedom) that holds for method invocations also holds for persistence. Under buffered durable linearizability, the liveness of persist *ordering* is subsumed in method invocations.

As noted in Sect. 1, data structures for buffered persistence will typically need to provide a sync method that guarantees, upon its return, that all previously ordered operations have reached persistent memory. If sync is not rolled into operations, then buffering (and sync) need to be coordinated across all mutually consistent objects, for the same reason that buffered durable linearizability is not a local property (Sect. 2). The existence of sync impacts the definition of buffered durable linearizability. In Definition 4, all abstract events that precede a sync instruction in their era must appear in $\mathcal{P}$, the sequence of consistent cuts. For a set of nonblocking objects, it is desirable that the shared sync method be wait-free or at least obstruction free—a property we call *nonblocking sync*. (As sync is shared, lock freedom doesn't seem applicable.)

4   Implementations

Given our prior model definitions and correctness conditions, we present an automated transform that takes as input a concurrent multi-object program written for release consistency and transient memory, and turns it into an equivalent program for explicit epoch persistency. Rules (T1) through (T5) of our transform (below) preserve the happens-before ordering of the original concurrent program: in the event of a crash, the values present in persistent memory are guaranteed to represent a $\prec$-consistent cut of the pre-crash history. Additional rules (T6) through (T8) serve to preserve real-time ordering not captured by happens-before but required for durable linearizability. The intuition behind our transform is that, for nonblocking concurrent objects, a cut across the happens-before ordering represents a valid static state of the object [22]. For blocking objects, additional recovery mechanisms (not discussed here) may be needed to move the cut if it interrupts a failure-atomic or critical section [5,7,17,26].

The following rules serve to preserve happens-before ordering into persist-before ordering. Their key observation is that a thread t which issues a $x.\text{st\_rel}_t(v)$ cannot atomically ensure the value's persistence. Thus, the subsequent thread u which synchronizes-with $x.\text{ld\_acq}_u(v)$ shares responsibility for x's persistence.

(T1) Immediately after $x.\mathsf{st}_t(v)$, write back the value by issuing $x.\mathsf{pwb}_t$.

(T2) Immediately before $x.\mathsf{st\_rel}_t(v)$, issue a pfence; immediately afterward, write back the value by issuing $x.\mathsf{pwb}_t$.

(T3) Immediately after $x.\mathsf{ld\_acq}_t(v)$, write back the loaded value by issuing $x.\mathsf{pwb}_t$, then issue a pfence.

(T4) Handle CAS instructions as atomic $\langle x.\mathsf{ld\_acq}_t(v), x.\mathsf{st\_rel}_t(v') \rangle$ pairs: immediately before the pair, issue a pfence; immediately afterward, write back the (potentially modified) value by issuing $x.\mathsf{pwb}_t$, then issue a pfence. (Extensions for other RMW instructions are straightforward.)

(T5) Take no persistence action on loads.

In the wake of a crash, the values present in persistent memory will reflect, by Definition 9, a consistent cut across the (partial) persist ordering ($<$) of the preceding era. We wish to show that in any program created by our transform, it will also reflect a consistent cut across that era's happens-before ordering ($\prec$). Mirroring condition 6 of concrete well-formedness (Definition 9), but with $\prec$ instead of $<$, we can prove [18]:

Lemma 1. *Consider a concrete history $\mathcal{H}$ emerging from our transform. For any location x and (x, i)-persisted store $A \in \mathcal{H}$, there exists no store A' of x, location y, and (y, i)-persisted store $B \in \mathcal{H}$ such that $A \prec A' \prec B$.*

Unfortunately, preservation of happens-before is not enough to give us durable linearizability: we also need to preserve the "real-time" order of non-overlapping operations (Definition 2, clause 3) in different threads. (As in conventional linearizability, "real time" serves as a stand-in for forms of causality—e.g., loads and stores of variables outside of operations—that are not captured in our histories.)

For objects that are (non-buffered) durably linearizable, we simply need to ensure that each operation persists before it returns:

(T6) Immediately before $O.\mathsf{res}\langle m \rangle_t$, issue a psync.

For buffered durably linearizable objects, we leave out the psync and instead introduce a shared global variable G:

(T7) Immediately before $O.\mathsf{res}\langle m \rangle_t$, issue a pfence, then issue $G.\mathsf{st\_rel}_t(g)$, for some arbitrary fixed value g.

(T8) Immediately after $O.\mathsf{inv}\langle m \rangle_t$, issue $G.\mathsf{ld\_acq}_t(g)$, for the same fixed value g, then issue a pfence.

To facilitate our proof of correctness [18], we introduce the notion of an *effective history* for $\mathcal{H}$. This history leaves out both the crashes of $\mathcal{H}$ and, in each era, the suffix of each thread's execution that fails to reach persistence before the crash. We can then prove (Lemma 2) that any effective history of a program emerging from our transform is itself a valid history of that program (and could have happened in the absence of crashes), and (Lemma 3) that the (crash-free) abstract history corresponding to the effective history is identical to some concatenation of $\prec$-consistent cuts of the eras of the (crash-laden) abstract history corresponding to $\mathcal{H}$. These two lemmas then support our main result (Theorem 1).

Definition 11. *Consider a concrete history* $\mathcal{H} = \mathcal{E}_0\, C_1\, \mathcal{E}_1 \dots \mathcal{E}_{c-1}\, C_c\, \mathcal{E}_c$. *For any thread t and era $0 \le i < c$, let E_i^t be the last store in $\mathcal{E}_i[t]$ that either is a persisted store or happens before some persisted store in $\mathcal{E}_i$. Let B_i^t be the last non-store instruction that succeeds E_i^t in $\mathcal{E}_i[t]$, with no stores by t in-between (or, if there is no such instruction, E_i^t itself). Finally, for $0 \le j < c$, let $\mathcal{P}_j$ be the subhistory of $\mathcal{E}_j$ obtained by removing all persistence events and, for each t, all events that follow B_j^t in $\mathcal{E}_j[t]$. The* effective concrete history *of $\mathcal{H}$ at era i, denoted* $\text{effective}_i(\mathcal{H})$, *is the history* $\mathcal{P}_0 \dots \mathcal{P}_{i-1}\mathcal{E}_i$.

Lemma 2. *Consider a nonblocking, data-race-free program* $\mathbb{P}$, *and the transformed program* $\mathbb{P}'$. *For any realizable concrete history* $\mathcal{H}$ *of* $\mathbb{P}'$, *and any* $0 \le i \le c$, $\text{effective}_i(\mathcal{H})$ *is a realizable concrete history of* $\mathbb{P}$.

Lemma 3. *Consider a nonblocking, data-race-free program* $\mathbb{P}$, *and the transformed program* $\mathbb{P}'$. *For any realizable concrete history* $\mathcal{H}$ *of* $\mathbb{P}'$, *and any* $0 \le i \le c$, *the history* $\text{abstract}(\text{effective}_i(\mathcal{H}))$ *is precisely* $\mathcal{P}_0^a \dots \mathcal{P}_{i-1}^a\, \mathcal{E}_i^a$, *where* $\mathcal{E}_i^a$ *is the i-th era of* $\text{abstract}(\mathcal{H})$, *and* $\mathcal{P}_i^a$ *is a $\prec$-consistent cut of* $\mathcal{E}_i^a$.

Theorem 1 (Buffered Durable Linearizability). *If a nonblocking, data-race-free program* $\mathbb{P}$ *is linearizable, the transformed program* $\mathbb{P}'$ *is buffered durably linearizable.*

In addition to the correctness properties of our automated transform, we can characterize other properties of the code it generates. For example, the transformed implementation of a nonblocking concurrent object requires no change to persistent state before relaunching threads—that is, it has a *null recovery procedure*. Moreover, any set of transformed objects will share a wait-free sync method (a single call to psync).

In each operation on a transient linearizable concurrent object, we can identify some instruction within as the operation's *announce point*: once execution reaches the announce point, the operation may linearize without its thread taking additional steps. Wait-free linearizable objects sometimes have announce points that are not atomic with their linearization points. In most nonblocking objects, however, the announce point *is* the linearization point, a property we call *unannounced*. This property results in stronger correctness properties in the persistent version when the object is transformed. The result of transform when applied to an object whose operations are unannounced is strictly linearizable. Perhaps surprisingly, our transform does not guarantee bounded completion, even on wait-free objects. Pending announced operations may be ignored for an arbitrary interval before eventually being *helped* to completion [4] [14, Sect. 4.2.5].

4.1 Persist Points

Linearizability proofs for transient objects are commonly based on the notion of a *linearization point*—an instruction between an operation's invocation and response at which the operation appears to "take effect instantaneously" [16]. In simple objects, linearization points may be statically known. In more complicated cases, one may need to reason retrospectively over a history in order to identify the linearization points, and the linearization point of an operation need not necessarily be an instruction issued by the invoking thread.

The problem for persistent objects is that an operation cannot generally linearize and persist at the same instant. Clearly, it will need to linearize first; otherwise it will not know what values to persist. Unfortunately, as soon as an operation (call it m) linearizes, other operations can see its state, and might, naively, linearize *and persist* before m had a chance to persist. The key to avoiding this problem is for every operation n to ensure that any predecessor on which it depends has persisted (in the unbuffered case) or persist-ordered (with global buffering) before n itself linearizes. To preserve real-time order, n must also persist (or persist-order) before it returns.

Theorem 2 (Persist Points). *Suppose that for each operation m of object O it is possible to identify not only a linearization point l_m between* inv$\langle m \rangle$ *and* res$\langle m \rangle$ *but also a persist point instruction p_m between l_m and* res$\langle m \rangle$ *such that (1) "all stores needed to capture m" are written back to persistent memory, and a pfence issued, before p_m; and (2) whenever operations m and n overlap, linearization points can be chosen such that either $p_m \lessdot l_n$ or l_n precedes l_m. Then O is (buffered) durably linearizable.*

The notion of "all stores needed to capture m" will depend on the details of O. In simple cases (e.g., those emerging from our automated transform), those stores might be all of m's updates to shared memory. In more optimized cases, they might be a proper subset (as discussed below). Generally, a nonblocking persistent object will embody helping: if an operation has linearized but not yet persisted, its successor operation must be prepared to push it to persistence.

4.2 Practical Applications

A variety of standard concurrent data structure techniques can be adapted to work with both durable and strict linearizability and their buffered variants. While our automated transform can be used to create correct persistent objects, judicious use of transient memory can often reduce the overhead of persistence without compromising correctness. For instance, announcement arrays [13] are a common idiom for wait-free helping mechanisms. Implementing a transient announcement array [2] while using our transform on the remainder of the object state will generally provide a (buffered) strictly linearizable persistent object.

Other data structure components may also be moved into transient memory. Elimination arrays [12] might be used on top of a durably or strictly linearizable data structure without compromising its correctness. The flat combining technique [11] is also amenable to persistence. Combined operations can be built together and ordered to persistence with a single pfence, then linked into the main data structure with another, reducing pfence instructions per operation. A transient combining array will generally result in a strictly linearizable object; leaving it persistent memory results in a durably linearizable object.

Several library and run-time systems have already been designed to take advantage of NVM; many of these can be categorized by the presented correctness conditions. Strictly linearizable examples include trees [25,27], file systems [8], and hash maps [24]. Buffered strictly linearizable data structures also exist [21], and some libraries explicitly enable their construction [3,5]. Durably (but not strictly) linearizable data structures are a comparatively recent innovation [17].

5   Conclusion

This paper has presented a framework for reasoning about the correctness of persistent data structures, based on two key assumptions: *full-system crashes* at the level of abstract histories and *explicit write-back and buffering* at the level of concrete histories. For the former, we capture safety as (buffered) *durable linearizability*; for the latter, we capture anticipated real-world hardware with *explicit epoch consistency*, and observe that both buffering and persistence introduce new issues of liveness. Finally, we have presented both an automatic mechanism to transform a transient concurrent object into a correct equivalent object for explicit epoch persistency and a notion of *persist points* to facilitate reasoning for other, more optimized, persistent objects.

References

1. Aguilera, M.K., Frølund, S.: Strict linearizability and the power of aborting. Technical report. HPL-2003-241, HP Labs (2003)
2. Berryhill, R., Golab, W., Tripunitara, M.: Robust shared objects for non-volatile main memory. In: International Conference on Principles of Distributed Systems, Rennes, France (2015)
3. Boehm, H.J., Chakrabarti, D.: Persistence programming models for non-volatile memory. Technical report. HP-2015-59, HP Laboratories (2015)
4. Censor-Hillel, K., Petrank, E., Timnat, S.: Help! In: ACM Symposium on Principles of Distributed Computing, Donostia-San Sebastián, Spain (2015)
5. Chakrabarti, D.R., Boehm, H.J., Bhandari, K.: Atlas: leveraging locks for non-volatile memory consistency. In: 2014 ACM International Conference on Object Oriented Programming Systems Languages & Applications, Portland, OR (2014)
6. Chatzistergiou, A., Cintra, M., Viglas, S.D.: Rewind: recovery write-ahead system for in-memory non-volatile data-structures. Proc. VLDB Endow. **8**(5), 497–508 (2015)
7. Coburn, J., Caulfield, A.M., Akel, A., Grupp, L.M., Gupta, R.K., Jhala, R., Swanson, S.: NV-Heaps: making persistent objects fast and safe with next-generation, non-volatile memories. In: 16th International Conference on Architectural Support for Programming Languages and Operating Systems, Newport Beach, CA (2011)

8. Condit, J., Nightingale, E.B., Frost, C., Ipek, E., Lee, B., Burger, D., Coetzee, D.: Better I/O through byte-addressable, persistent memory. In: 22nd ACM Symposium on Operating Systems Principles, Big Sky, MT (2009)

9. Gharachorloo, K., Lenoski, D., Laudon, J., Gibbons, P., Gupta, A., Hennessy, J.: Memory consistency and event ordering in scalable shared-memory multiprocessors. In: 17th International Symposium on Computer Architecture, Seattle, WA (1990)

10. Guerraoui, R., Levy, R.: Robust emulations of shared memory in a crash-recovery model. In: 24th International Conference on Distributed Computing Systems, Santa Fe, NM (2004)

11. Hendler, D., Incze, I., Shavit, N., Tzafrir, M.: Flat combining and the synchronization-parallelism tradeoff. In: 22nd ACM Symposium on Parallelism in Algorithms and Architectures, Santorini, Greece (2010)

12. Hendler, D., Shavit, N., Yerushalmi, L.: A scalable lock-free stack algorithm. In: 16th ACM Symposium on Parallelism in Algorithms and Architectures, Barcelona, Spain (2004)

13. Herlihy, M.: A methodology for implementing highly concurrent data objects. ACM Trans. Program. Lang. Syst. **15**(5), 745–70 (1993)

14. Herlihy, M., Shavit, N.: The Art of Multiprocessor Programming. Morgan Kaufmann, San Francisco (2008)

15. Herlihy, M.P.: Wait-free synchronization. ACM Trans. Program. Lang. Syst. **13**(1), 124–49 (1991)

16. Herlihy, M.P., Wing, J.M.: Linearizability: a correctness condition for concurrent objects. ACM Trans. Program. Lang. Syst. **12**(3), 463–92 (1990)

17. Izraelevitz, J., Kelly, T., Kolli, A.: Failure-atomic persistent memory updates via JUSTDO logging. In: 21st International Conference on Architectural Support for Programming Languages and Operating Systems, Atlanta, GA (2016)

18. Izraelevitz, J., Mendes, H., Scott, M.L.: Linearizability of persistent memory objects under a full-system-crash failure model. Technical report. 999, Dept. of Computer Science, Univ. of Rochester (2016)

19. Joshi, A., Nagarajan, V., Cintra, M., Viglas, S.: Efficient persist barriers for multicores. In: 48th International Symposium on Microarchitecture, Waikiki, HI (2015)

20. Kolli, A., Pelley, S., Saidi, A., Chen, P.M., Wenisch, T.F.: High-performance transactions for persistent memories. In: 21st International Conference on Architectural Support for Programming Languages and Operating Systems, Atlanta, GA (2016)

21. Moraru, I., Andersen, D.G., Kaminsky, M., Tolia, N., Binkert, N., Ranganathan, P.: Consistent, durable, and safe memory management for byte-addressable non volatile main memory. In: ACM Conference on Timely Results in Operating Systems, Farmington, PA (2013)

22. Nawab, F., Chakrabarti, D.R., Kelly, T., Morrey III., C.B.: Procrastination beats prevention: timely sufficient persistence for efficient crash resilience. In: 18th International Conference on Extending Database Technology, Brussels, Belgium (2015)

23. Pelley, S., Chen, P.M., Wenisch, T.F.: Memory persistency. In: 41st International Symposium on Computer Architecture, Minneapolis, MN (2014)

24. Schwalb, D., Dreseler, M., Uflacker, M., Plattner, H.: NVC-hashmap: a persistent and concurrent hashmap for non-volatile memories. In: 3rd VLDB Workshop on In-Memory Data Management and Analytics, Kohala, HI (2015)

25. Venkataraman, S., Tolia, N., Ranganathan, P., Campbell, R.H.: Consistent and durable data structures for non-volatile byte-addressable memory. In: 9th USENIX Conference on File and Storage Technologies, San Jose, CA (2011)

26. Volos, H., Tack, A.J., Swift, M.M.: Mnemosyne: lightweight persistent memory. In: 16th International Conference on Architectural Support for Programming Languages and Operating Systems, Newport Beach, CA (2011)
27. Yang, J., Wei, Q., Chen, C., Wang, C., Yong, K.L., He, B.: NV-Tree: reducing consistency cost for NVM-based single level systems. In: 13th USENIX Conference on File and Storage Technologies, Santa Clara, CA (2015)

Buffer Size for Routing Limited-Rate Adversarial Traffic

Avery Miller[✉] and Boaz Patt-Shamir[✉]

Tel Aviv University, Tel Aviv, Israel
avery@averymiller.ca, boaz@tau.ac.il

Abstract. We consider the slight variation of the adversarial queuing theory model in which an adversary injects packets with routes into the network subject to the following constraint: For any link e, the total number of packets injected in any time window $[t, t')$ and whose route contains e is at most $\rho(t' - t) + \sigma$, where ρ and σ are non-negative parameters. Informally, ρ bounds the long-term rate of injections and σ bounds the "burstiness" of injection: $\sigma = 0$ means that the injection is as smooth as it can be.

It is known that greedy scheduling of the packets (under which a link is not idle if there is any packet ready to be sent over it) may result in $\Omega(n)$ buffer size even on an n-node line network and very smooth injections ($\sigma = 0$). In this paper, we propose a simple non-greedy scheduling policy and show that, in a tree where all packets are destined at the root, no buffer needs to be larger than $\sigma + 2\rho$ to ensure that no overflows occur, which is optimal in our model. The rule of our algorithm is to *forward a packet only if its next buffer is completely empty*. The policy is centralized: in a single step, a long "train" of packets may progress together. We show that, in some sense, central coordination is required for our algorithm, and even for the more sophisticated "downhill" algorithm in which each node forwards a packet only if its next buffer is less occupied than its current one. This is shown by presenting an injection pattern with $\sigma = 0$ for the n-node line that results in $\Omega(n)$ packets in a buffer if local control is used.

1 Introduction

We study the process of packet routing over networks, where an adversary injects packets at nodes, and the routing algorithm is required to forward the packets along network links until they reach their prescribed destination, subject to link capacity constraints. Our guiding question is the following: assuming that the injection pattern adheres to some given upper bound specification, what is the smallest buffer size that will allow a routing algorithm to deliver all traffic, i.e., that will ensure that there is no overflow at the node buffers?

To bound the injection rate, we follow the classical (σ, ρ) burstiness model of Cruz [9,10]. Specifically, we assume that the number of packets that are injected in any time interval of t time units is at most $\sigma + \rho \cdot t$ for some non-negative

© Springer-Verlag Berlin Heidelberg 2016
C. Gavoille and D. Ilcinkas (Eds.): DISC 2016, LNCS 9888, pp. 328–341, 2016.
DOI: 10.1007/978-3-662-53426-7_24

parameters σ and ρ. Intuitively, ρ represents the maximal long-term injection rate and σ represents the maximal "burstiness" of the injection pattern. We assume that the injection pattern is feasible, in the sense that the total average rate of traffic that needs to cross a link does not exceed its capacity.

Our approach is very close to that of the *adversarial queuing theory* [3, 8] henceforth abbreviated AQT. In the AQT model, packets are injected along with their routes by an adversary. The adversary is limited by the feasibility constraint, which is formalized as follows. Assuming that all links have capacity 1, i.e., a link can deliver at most one packet at a time step, the requirement is that in any time window of length w, the number of injected packets that need to use any link does not exceed $\lceil w\rho \rceil$, where w and ρ are model parameters.[1] The main question in AQT is when a given routing policy is *stable*, i.e., what is the maximum rate that allows the queues to be bounded under the given policy. Furthermore, AQT concerns itself with *local, greedy* policies. Local policies are defined by a rule that can be applied by each node based only on it local information (packets residing in that node and possibly its immediate neighbors). Greedy (a.k.a. *work conserving*) policies are policies under which a link is not fully utilized only when there are not enough packets ready to be transmitted over that link. These restrictions are justified by the results that say that there are local greedy policies that are stable for any feasible injection rate [3]. While stability means that the required buffer size can be bounded, the bounds are usually large (polynomial in the network size). It should be noted that even linear buffer size is not practical in most cases. Furthermore, it is known that in the Internet, big buffers have negative effect on traffic (cf. "bufferbloat" [12]).

In this work, in contrast to AQT, on one hand we are interested in the quantitative question of buffer size, and on the other hand we do not restrict ourselves to local greedy policies. While the interest in buffer size is obvious, we offer the following justification to our liberalism regarding the nature of policies we consider. First, we claim that with the advent of software-defined networks [22], central control over the routing algorithm has become a reality in many networks and should not be disqualified as a show-stopper anymore. Moreover, our results give a strong indication that insisting on strict locality may result in a significant blowup in buffer size. Our second relaxation, namely not insisting on greedy policies, is not new, as it is already known that greedy policies may require large buffers. Specifically, in [23], Rosén and Scalosub show that the buffer size required to ensure no losses in an n-node line network with a single destination is $\Theta(n\rho^2)$, where ρ is the injection rate. Note that this result means that for greedy routing, sublinear buffers can guarantee loss-free routing only if the injection rate is $o(1)$.

We present two sets of results. Our main result is positive: we propose a centralized routing algorithm that requires buffers whose size is independent of the network size. We prove that in the case of tree networks, when packets are

---

[1] This model is almost equivalent to Cruz's (σ, ρ) model (see discussion in [8]). We chose to use the (σ, ρ) model as it allows for simpler expressions to bound the buffer size.

destined to the tree root, if the injection pattern is feasible with injection rate ρ and maximal burstiness σ, then the required buffer space need not exceed $\sigma + 2\rho$ in order not to lose any packet. We provide a matching lower bound to show that this is the optimal buffer size. The routing algorithm, which we believe to be attractive from the practical point of view, says simply "forward a packet to the next hop only if its next buffer is *empty*." The algorithm is centralized in that it may simultaneously forward long "trains" of packets (a train consists of a single packet per node and an empty buffer in front of the leading packet).

Our second set of results is negative. We show that central coordination is necessary, even for the more refined (and non-greedy) *downhill algorithm*. In the downhill algorithm, a packet is forwarded over a link whenever the buffer at the other endpoint is less full than the buffer in its current location. We show that even in the n-node line network, there are feasible injection patterns with 0 burstiness under which the downhill algorithm results in buffer buildup of $\Omega(n)$ packets. Interestingly, as we show, there are certain situations where the downhill algorithm requires buffers of size $\Omega(n)$ while the greedy algorithm only needs buffers of size 1, and other situations where the downhill algorithm needs buffers of size 1 while the greedy algorithm needs buffers of size $\Omega(n)$.

We may note in this context the result of Awerbuch *et al.* [4], where they consider the case of a single destination node in dynamic networks. They show that a certain variant of the downhill algorithm ensures that the number of packets in a buffer is bounded by $O(nS_{\max})$, where $S_{\max}$ is a bound on the number of packets co-residing in the network under an unknown optimal schedule.

1.1 More Related Work

In the *buffer management* model [15,20], a different angle is taken. The idea is to lift all restrictions on the injection pattern, implying that packet loss is possible. The goal is to deliver as many packets as possible at their destination. The buffer management model is usually used to study routing within a single switch, modeled by very simple topologies (e.g., a single buffer [2], a star [16], or a complete bipartite graph [18]). The difficulty in such scenarios may be due to packets with different values or to some dependencies between packets [11]. The tree topology is studied in [17]. The interested reader is referred to [14] for a comprehensive survey of the work in this area.

The idea of the downhill algorithm has been used for various objectives (avoiding deadlocks [21], computing maximal flow [13], multicommodity flow [5,6], and routing in the context of dynamically changing topology [1,4,7,19]). With the exception of [19], the buffer size is usually assumed to be linear in the number of nodes (or in the length of the longest possible simple path in the network). In [19], a buffer's height is accounted for by counters, so that each node needs to hold only a constant number of packets and $O(\log n)$-bit counters.

Organization of the paper. The remainder of the paper is structured as follows. In Sect. 2, we define the network model. Section 3 describes and analyzes our Forward-If-Empty algorithm. Section 4 gives lower bounds for local downhill algorithms.

2   Model

The system. We model the system as a directed graph $G = (V, E)$, where nodes represent hosts or network switches (routers), and edges represent communication links. For a link $u \to v$ (denoted by (u, v)), we say that u is an *in-neighbor* of v, and v is an *out-neighbor* of u. Each edge $e \in E$ has capacity $c(e) \in \mathbb{N}$. We consider static systems, i.e., G is fixed throughout the execution.

Input (a.k.a. adversary). We assume that in every round t, a set of packets is *injected* into the system. Each packet p is injected at a node, along with a complete route that specifies a simple path, denoted by $r(p)$, in G that starts at the node of injection, called the *source*, and ends at the packet's *destination*. The set of all packets injected in the time interval $[t, t']$ is denoted by $P(t, t')$. We use $P(t)$ to denote the set of packets injected in round t. Many packets may be injected in the same node, and the routes may be arbitrary. However, we consider the following type of restriction on injection patterns.

Definition 1. *For any $\sigma, \rho \geq 0$, an injection pattern is said to adhere to a (ρ, σ) bound if, in any time interval $[t, t']$ and for any edge $e \in E$, it holds that $|\{p \in P(t, t') \mid e \in r(p)\}| \leq \rho(t' - t) + \sigma$.*

Executions. A system *configuration* is a mapping of packets to nodes. An execution of the system is an infinite sequence of configurations $C_0, C_1, C_2 \ldots$, where C_i for $i > 0$ is called the configuration after round i, and C_0 is the initial configuration. The evolution of the system from C_i to C_{i+1} consists of a sequence of *ministeps*: 0 or more *injection ministeps* followed by exactly 1 *forwarding ministep*. In particular,

1. There is one injection ministep for each packet $p \in P(i)$, and, in this ministep, p is mapped to the first node in $r(p)$.
2. In the forwarding ministep, for each packet p currently mapped to a node v such that $e = (v, u)$ is an edge in $r(p)$, packet p may be re-mapped to u. In this case we say that v *forwards* p over e to u. If u is the destination of p, then p is said to be *delivered* and is removed from subsequent configurations. The number of packets forwarded over e in one round may not exceed $c(e)$. The choice of which packets to forward is controlled by the *algorithm*.

We use $v[s]$ to refer to node v at the start of ministep s. We view packets mapped to a node as stored by the node's *buffer*, which is an array of *slots*. The *load* of a buffer in a given configuration is the number of packets mapped to it in that configuration. We further assume that in a configuration, each packet mapped to a node is mapped to a particular slot in that node's buffer. The slot's index is called the packet's *position*, denoted $pos(p)$ for a packet p. Note that we do not place explicit restrictions on the buffer sizes, so overflows never occur.

Algorithms. The role of the algorithm is to determine which packets are forwarded in each round. The algorithm must obey the link capacity constraints. We distinguish between two types of algorithms: local and centralized. In a *centralized* algorithm, the decisions of the algorithm may depend, in each round, on the history of complete system configurations at that time. In a *local* algorithm, the decision of which packets should be forwarded from node v may depend only on the packets stored in the buffer of v and the packets stored in the buffers of v's neighbors. Note that both centralized and local algorithms are required to be on-line, i.e., may not make decisions based on future injections.

Target Problem: Information Gathering on Trees. In this paper, we consider networks whose underlying topology is a directed tree where all links have the same capacity c. Furthermore, we assume that the destination of all packets is the root of the tree. We sometimes call the root the *sink* of the system. Injections adhere to a (ρ, σ) bound. To ensure that the injection pattern is feasible, i.e., that finite buffers suffice to avoid overflows, we assume that $\rho \leq c$.

3   The Forward-If-Empty Algorithm

In this section, we describe the Forward-If-Empty (FIE) algorithm and prove that, for any (ρ, σ)-injection pattern, the load of every buffer is bounded above by $\sigma + 2\rho$ during the execution of FIE. We then show that this bound is optimal by proving that, for any algorithm, there is an injection pattern such that the load of some buffer reaches $\sigma + 2\rho$.

3.1   Algorithm

First, we specify how FIE positions packets within each buffer. Each buffer is partitioned into *levels* of c slots each, where level $i \geq 1$ consists of slots $(i - 1)c + 1, \ldots, ic$. For a packet p, its level is given by $\lceil pos(p)/c \rceil$. Suppose that $m \geq 1$ packets are mapped to a node. In the simplest case, i.e., when $c = 1$, the algorithm maps the m packets to slots $1, \ldots, m$ in the node's buffer. In general, the m packets are mapped so that $m \bmod c$ packets are mapped to the first level, while the rest of the packets fill up levels $2, \ldots, \lceil m/c \rceil$. More formally, for $c \geq 1$, the algorithm maps the m packets to positions $\lceil m/c \rceil \cdot c, \ldots, \lceil m/c \rceil \cdot c - m + 1$.

Definition 2. *The height of a node v at ministep s is denoted by $height(v[s])$ and is defined as $\max_p \{level\ of\ packet\ p\ in\ v[s]\}$. The height of the sink is defined to be $-\infty$.*

Next, we specify how the algorithm behaves during each forwarding ministep. Intuitively, we think of the system as having sections of "ground" that consist of connected subgraphs of nodes with height at most 1, and "hills" that consist of connected subgraphs of nodes with height greater than 1. The algorithm works by draining the ground packets "horizontally" towards the sink, and by breaking off some packets from the boundaries of the hills to fall into empty nodes surrounding the hills. Notice that nothing happens in the interior of each hill, e.g., the peak does not get flattened; in each forwarding ministep, only packets from the boundary of the hill get chipped away.

We now describe the algorithm in detail. At the start of every forwarding ministep s, the algorithm computes a maximal set $AP(s)$ of directed paths called *activation paths* for ministep s. All nodes that are contained in paths of $AP(s)$ are considered *activated* for ministep s. In what follows, we say that two paths are *node-disjoint* if their intersection is empty or equal to the sink. To construct $AP(s)$, the algorithm greedily adds maximal directed paths to $AP(s)$ and ensures that all paths in $AP(s)$ are node-disjoint. The paths can be one of three types:

1. *Downhill-to-Sink:* the first node has height greater than 1, the last node is the sink, and all other nodes in the path (if any) have height 1.
2. *Downhill-to-Empty:* the first node has height greater than 1, the last node has height 0, and all other nodes in the path (if any) have height 1.
3. *Flat:* the last node is the sink or has height 0, and all other nodes in the path have height 1.

At the start of ministep s, the algorithm first adds Downhill-to-Sink paths to $AP(s)$ until none remains, then adds Downhill-to-Empty paths to $AP(s)$ until none remains, then adds all Flat paths to $AP(s)$. Each time a path is added to $AP(s)$, the nodes in that path (except the sink) are unusable in the remainder of the construction of $AP(s)$.

In each forwarding ministep, each activated node for that ministep forwards c packets (or all of its packets if it has fewer than c). Since the packets are identical, it does not matter which c packets are forwarded. However, it is convenient for our analysis to assume that the buffers are LIFO, i.e., the forwarded packets are taken from an activated node's highest level and, when received, are stored in the receiving node's highest level. This ensures that the level of a packet can only change when it is forwarded.

3.2   Analysis

We now prove that, for any (ρ, σ)-injection pattern, the load of every buffer is bounded above by $\sigma + 2\rho$ during the execution of FIE. Without loss of generality, we may assume that $\rho = c$, since, if $\rho < c$, we can artificially restrict the edge capacity to ρ when executing the algorithm to get the same result.

The analysis of our algorithm depends crucially on what happens to the loads of connected subsets of nodes that all meet a certain minimum height requirement. Informally, we can think of any configuration of the system as a collection of hills and valleys, and, for a given hill, "slice" it at some level h and look at what happens to all of the packets in that hill above the slice. We call the portion of the hill that has packets above this slice a *plateau*.

Definition 3. *A plateau of height h (or h-plateau) at ministep s is a maximal set of nodes forming a connected subgraph such that each node has a packet at level $h - 1$ and at least one of the nodes has a packet at level h. A plateau P at ministep s will be denoted by $P[s]$, and $height(P[s])$ denotes its height at the start of ministep s.*

Observation 1. *If $P[s], Q[s]$ are plateaus at ministep s, then they are disjoint or one is a subset of the other. If $height(P[s]) = height(Q[s])$ and $P[s] \neq Q[s]$, then $P[s] \cap Q[s] = \emptyset$.*

Plateaus are defined so that every pair of disjoint plateaus is separated by a sufficiently deep "valley". This ensures that a packet forwarded from one plateau does not immediately arrive at another plateau, allowing us to argue about the number of packets in each plateau independently. We measure the "fullness" of a plateau by the number of packets it contains at a given level and higher.

Definition 4. *The k-load of a plateau $P[s]$ is defined to be the number of packets in $P[s]$ at level k or higher. For any plateau $P[s]$, we denote by $load_k(P[s], s')$ the k-load of $P[s]$ at time s'.*

In Definition 4, note that $P[s]$ might not be a plateau at the start of a ministep s', but it still represents a well-defined set of nodes. Note that we may speak of the k-load of an h-plateau for any k and h.

We now proceed to analyze the dynamics of the FIE algorithm. By the choice of activated nodes in each forwarding ministep, whenever a node receives packets during a forwarding ministep, the packets are always placed at level 1 in that node's buffer. In particular, each node receives at most c packets, and, either the receiving node's buffer was empty at the beginning of the forwarding ministep, or, it only had packets at level 1 and it forwarded them all.

Lemma 1. *Let w be a non-sink node. Packets forwarded to w in ministep s are at level 1 in node w's buffer at the start of ministep $s + 1$.*

We now set out to prove that each 2-plateau "loses" $c = \rho$ packets per round due to forwarding, which means that any increase in the load of a plateau is due to the burstiness of injections. Since the network is a directed tree, we know that, from every node, there exists a unique directed path to the sink. So, we can uniquely identify how packets will leave each plateau, which we now formalize.

Definition 5. *Consider any h-plateau $P[s]$ at the start of a forwarding ministep s. The node v in $P[s]$ whose outgoing edge leads to a node whose height is at most $h - 2$ at the start of ministep s is called the* exit node *of $P[s]$ at ministep s and is denoted by $exitNode(P[s], s)$. We define the* landing node *of $P[s]$ at ministep s to be the node at the head of the outgoing edge of $exitNode(P[s], s)$.*

In Fig. 1, we illustrate the definitions and concepts introduced so far by giving an example of how the system evolves in a forwarding step.

We want to show that, for each forwarding ministep s, the 2-load of each 2-plateau shrinks by at least c. The following result shows that this is the case if the exit node of such a plateau is activated during s. This is because exit node z is part of some activation path whose first node v is in the same plateau as z, and, by Lemma 1, v forwards c packets from a level greater than 1 to level 1.

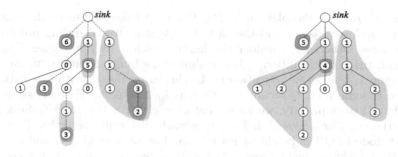

Fig. 1. On the left, the state of a network at the start of some forwarding ministep. Each node is labeled with its load. Dotted lines show the activation paths chosen by the algorithm. On the right, the network immediately after this ministep. Each light grey region is a 2-plateau, and each dark grey region is a subplateau with height greater than 2. In each plateau, the node closest to the sink is the exit node and its parent is the landing node.

Lemma 2. *For any forwarding ministep s and any 2-plateau $P[s]$, we have $load_2(P[s], s + 1) \leq load_2(P[s], s)$. If $exitNode(P[s], s)$ is activated in s, then $load_2(P[s], s + 1) \leq load_2(P[s], s) - c$.*

The next challenge is to deal with the fact that plateaus can merge during a forwarding ministep. For example, an exit node of one plateau might forward packets to a node v that was sandwiched between two disjoint plateaus both with larger height than v, but the increase in v's height results in one large plateau formed by the merging of v with the two plateaus. Figure 1 shows an example of three plateaus merging into one. We want to compare the load of this newly-formed plateau with the loads of the plateaus that merged. To this end, we consider the "pre-image" of a plateau: for each plateau $P[s + 1]$ that exists at the start of ministep $s + 1$, we keep track of the disjoint plateaus at ministep s that were merged together to form $P[s + 1]$.

Definition 6. *Consider any forwarding ministep s and any h-plateau $P[s + 1]$ with $h \geq 2$ that exists immediately after s. The* pre-image *of $P[s + 1]$, denoted by $Pre(P[s + 1])$, is the set of h-plateaus that existed at the start of s that are contained in $P[s + 1]$.*

Observation 2. *For any plateau $P[s+1]$, any plateaus $P_1[s], P_2[s] \in Pre(P[s+1])$ are disjoint. Further, for any two distinct h-plateaus $P_1[s + 1], P_2[s + 1]$ that exist at the start of ministep $s + 1$, we have $Pre(P_1[s + 1]) \cap Pre(P_2[s + 1]) = \emptyset$.*

We now prove that, for any 2-plateau $P[s + 1]$, there always exists a plateau in $Pre(P[s + 1])$ whose exit node is activated during ministep s.

Lemma 3. *For any forwarding ministep s and any 2-plateau $P[s+1]$ that exists at the start of ministep $s + 1$, there exists a $P[s] \in Pre(P[s + 1])$ such that $exitNode(P[s], s)$ is activated in s.*

Proof: Let $P[s]$ be the plateau in $Pre(P[s+1])$ that minimizes the distance between $exitNode(P[s], s)$ and the sink. If $P[s]$ is activated during ministep s, we are done. Otherwise, consider the landing node ℓ of $P[s]$. Since $P[s]$ is a 2-plateau, then, by definition, ℓ is the sink or ℓ's buffer is empty at the start of ministep s. The set of activation paths chosen by the algorithm is maximal, so there is some path Q of nodes with ℓ as its last node. Further, since Flat paths have lowest priority, we know that Q is either a Downhill-To-Sink path (if ℓ is the sink) or a Downhill-To-Empty path (if ℓ isn't the sink). Therefore, the first node in Q has height at least 2, the last node in Q is ℓ, and all other nodes (if any) have height exactly 1. Let $P'[s]$ be the 2-plateau that contains $Q \setminus \{\ell\}$ at the start of ministep s, and note that $exitNode(P'[s], s)$ is activated in ministep s since all nodes in Q are activated. Hence, it is sufficient to show that $P'[s] \in Pre(P[s+1])$. To do so, note that, immediately after the forwarding ministep s, all nodes in $Q \cup \{\ell\}$ have height at least 1, as do all nodes in $P[s]$ (since no nodes in $P[s]$ were activated in ministep s). Therefore, the nodes of $Q \cup P[s] \cup \{\ell\}$ are all contained in the same 2-plateau at the start of ministep $s+1$. Since $P[s] \subseteq P[s+1]$, it follows that $Q \subseteq P[s+1]$, and so the plateau $P'[s]$ containing Q is a subset of $P[s+1]$. This proves that $P'[s] \in Pre(P[s+1])$. $\square$

Next we show that, as plateaus merge during a forwarding ministep, at least c packets are "lost". This follows by applying Lemma 2 to each plateau involved in the merge (which is permitted due to Observation 2), and using Lemma 3 to show that the exit node of at least one of these plateaus is activated.

Lemma 4. *For any forwarding ministep s and any 2-plateau $P[s+1]$, we have*
$$load_2(P[s+1], s+1) \leq load_2(\textstyle\bigcup_{P[s] \in Pre(P[s+1])} P[s], s) - c.$$

We now arrive at the main result, which shows that the buffer loads are always bounded above by $\sigma + 2c$.

Theorem 3. *Consider the execution of Forward-If-Empty in a directed tree network with link capacity c. Suppose that the destination of all injected packets is the root, and that the injection pattern adheres to a (c, σ) bound. For each node v, the number of packets in v's buffer never exceeds $\sigma + 2c$.*

Proof: (Sketch). For any ministep s, let $round(s)$ be the round that contains s. Let $flat(s)$ be the last ministep, up to and including s, such that all nodes have height at most 1 at the start of the ministep. For any ministeps $s_1 \leq s_2$, let $totalinj(s_1, s_2)$ be the total number of packets injected into the system in all ministeps in the range $s_1, \ldots, s_2$. The following invariant, which bounds the total number of packets at level 2 or higher, can be proved by induction on s.

> **Invariant I:** at the start of any ministep s, the sum of 2-loads of all 2-plateaus is bounded above by $totalinj(flat(s) + 1, s) - c \cdot (round(s) - round(flat(s)))$.

To see why Invariant I is sufficient to prove the theorem, note that, at the start of any ministep s, the height of any node v is bounded above by the number of packets at level 1 in v's buffer (i.e., at most c), plus the 2-load of the 2-plateau containing v. Using the invariant, the 2-load of the 2-plateau containing v is bounded above by $totalinj(flat(s)+1,s) - c \cdot (round(s) - round(flat(s)))$. By separately considering the packets injected in the first $(round(s)-round(flat(s)))$ rounds and the packets injected so far in $round(s)$, we get $totalinj(flat(s)+1,s) \leq c \cdot (round(s) - round(flat(s))) + \sigma + c$. Putting together all of these facts, we get that the height of any node v is bounded above by $c \cdot (round(s)-round(flat(s))) + \sigma + c - c \cdot (round(s) - round(flat(s))) + c \leq \sigma + 2c$.   □

3.3   Existential Optimality

In this section, we show that there is no algorithm that can prevent buffer overflows when the buffer size is strictly less than $\sigma + 2c$.

Theorem 4. *Consider the network consisting of nodes $v_1, \ldots, v_n$ such that, for each $i \in \{1, \ldots, n-1\}$, there is a directed edge from v_i to v_{i+1}. Consider any edge capacity $c \geq 1$ and $\sigma \geq 0$. For any algorithm, there is a (c, σ)-injection pattern such that the load of some buffer is at least $\sigma + 2c$ in some configuration of the algorithm's execution.*

Proof: Consider the following injection pattern that injects packets destined for node v_n. In the first round, inject c packets into v_1, and, in each subsequent round i, injects c packets into the node with smallest index that has the maximum load at the start of round i. If the maximum load in round $i-1$ was m_{i-1} at some node v_j, then either v_j or v_{j+1} has load at least $\lceil m_{i-1}/2 \rceil$ after the forwarding ministep of round $i-1$. Therefore, at the start of each round $i > 1$, the load at some node is at least $\lceil \sum_{k=1}^{i-1} c/2^k \rceil$. So, at the start of some round i, some node v has load at least c, at which time $c + \sigma$ packet injections are performed at v. □

4   Local Downhill Algorithms

In this section, we consider downhill algorithms where each node in the network must decide whether or not it will forward packets based only on local information. We show that local downhill algorithms require significantly larger buffer size than the centralized algorithm presented in Sect. 3. We also show that local downhill algorithms may require significantly larger buffer sizes than the GREEDY algorithm where each node always forwards packets if it has any. However, we show that the opposite is also true by providing situations where GREEDY requires significantly larger buffer sizes than local downhill algorithms.

4.1   Local vs. Centralized Algorithms

Recall that in a downhill algorithm, packets may be forwarded only to a lighter-load node. Intuitively, the difficulty faced by local downhill algorithms is that they cannot perform a coordinated move in which all nodes along a path simultaneously forward a packet each. In this case, only the node closest to the sink knows whether or not it will forward a packet (based on the load of its out-neighbour) so, to ensure that no packets are forwarded "uphill", none of the other nodes in the interval can decide to forward a packet. We now set out to show the effects of this limitation on a local version of FIE and on a more sophisticated downhill algorithm.

The bad scenario. We consider a network $v_1, \ldots, v_n$ of nodes (where $n > 2$) such that, for each $i \in \{1, \ldots, n-1\}$, there is a directed edge with capacity 1 from v_i to v_{i+1}. One packet with destination v_n is injected at node v_1 in each round. Note that, under this $(1, 0)$-injection pattern, GREEDY only needs buffers of size 1 to ensure that no overflows occur.

LOCAL-FIE. The LOCAL-FIE algorithm is a local version of Forward-If-Empty described in Sect. 3, defined as follows. Each node forwards a packet if and only if its buffer is non-empty and its out-neighbour has an empty buffer. Under the injection pattern specified above, v_1 receives a packet in every round but only forwards a packet every two rounds. It follows that, in the first R rounds, the load of v_1 is $\lceil R/2 \rceil$. Note that R can be chosen to be arbitrarily large, independently of n. This can be generalized to any injection pattern with $\rho > 1/2$.

Theorem 5. *If $n > 2$, then, for any R and constant $\rho > 1/2$, there is a $(\rho, 1)$-injection pattern of R packets such that LOCAL-FIE requires buffers of size $\Omega(R)$ to prevent overflows.*

LOCAL-DOWNHILL. In LOCAL-DOWNHILL, each node forwards a packet if and only if its buffer is non-empty and the load of its out-neighbour's buffer is strictly less than the load of its own buffer. We set out to show that, after sufficiently many rounds, v_1's load is $\Omega(n)$.

For each $j \geq 1$, let *state* S_j be the sequence of n integers corresponding to the load of each node's buffer immediately after all injections of round j occur. In each state, we focus on what happens between v_1 and the first empty node. More formally, for any sequence S of non-negative integers, the *initial segment* of S, denoted by $init(S)$, is the maximal prefix of non-zero entries in S. In what follows, we assume that n is large enough such that $init(S_j)$ is always a proper subsequence of $v_1, \ldots, v_n$ (we later show that, for an execution of R rounds, $n \geq \sqrt{R} + 2$ suffices.) For each $k \geq 0$, we use $f(k)$ to denote the index of the first state such that v_1's load is at least k. For each $k \geq 1$, we define $\Delta_k = f(k) - f(k-1)$. An intuitive definition of Δ_k is the number of forwarding ministeps that occur between $S_{f(k-1)}$ and $S_{f(k)}$.

To prove the lower bound, we consider the states where the load of v_1 increases and show that the number of rounds between consecutive such states keeps growing by 2. We first illustrate this phenomenon by examining a concrete example. In Fig. 2, we have provided a prefix of the execution of LOCAL-DOWNHILL. Let's consider the number of rounds between S_7 (the state where v_1's load first becomes 3) and S_{13} (the state where v_1's load first becomes 4). Notice that, if we ignore v_1 in states $S_7, \ldots, S_{12}$, the remainder of their initial segments is equal to the initial segments of $S_2, \ldots, S_7$, respectively. Within this interval, notice that $S_3, \ldots, S_7$ is the part of the execution where v_1's load first becomes 2 and then first becomes 3. So we can split up the set of states $S_7, \ldots, S_{13}$ as follows: 4 "middle" rounds corresponding to the states $S_3, \ldots, S_7$, plus the first round and last round. The above example illustrates (and mimics the proof structure of) the following general fact.

Lemma 5. *For every* $k \geq 1$, $\Delta_{k+1} = \Delta_k + 2$.

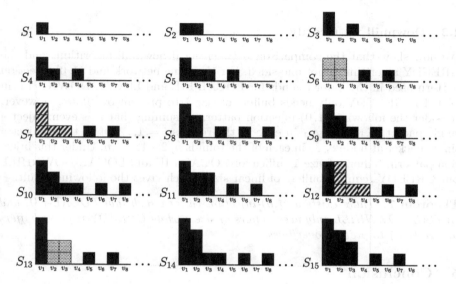

Fig. 2. The first 15 states of LOCAL-DOWNHILL when a packet is injected at v_1 in each round. The dotted packets demonstrate that $tail(S_{f(4)}) = init(S_{f(3)-1})$. The diagonally-hatched packets demonstrate that $tail(S_{f(4)-1}) = init(S_{f(3)})$.

The key to proving Lemma 5 is observing, as we did in the above example, that the initial segments of some states will reappear later as the suffix of others. To describe this phenomenon, we divide the initial segment of each state S into two parts: the first node of the segment is denoted by $front(S)$, and $tail(S)$ is defined to be $init(S)$ without its first entry[2]. The main structural result that is needed to prove Lemma 5 can be stated as follows, and is demonstrated by the patterned packets in Fig. 2.

Lemma 6. *For any positive integer* k, *we have* $tail(S_{f(k+1)}) = init(S_{f(k)-1})$ *and* $tail(S_{f(k+1)-1}) = init(S_{f(k)})$.

We now show that v_1's load is eventually $\Omega(n)$. Lemma 5 implies that, for any positive integer k, we have $f(k) = k^2 - k + 1$. It follows that, by choosing

---

[2] LISP programmers might prefer to use *car* and *cdr* instead of *front* and *tail*!

$k = n - 2$ and executing LOCAL-DOWNHILL on the specified injection pattern for $k^2 - k + 1$ rounds, the buffer at node v_1 will contain $n - 2$ packets in the last round of the execution. An induction argument shows that the width of the initial segment is bounded above by one more than the load of v_1, so, as we assumed, the initial segment is always a proper subsequence of $v_1, \ldots, v_n$. Therefore, we get the following lower bound on the buffer size required by LOCAL-DOWNHILL.

Theorem 6. *There is a (1,0)-injection pattern such that LOCAL-DOWNHILL requires buffers of size $\Omega(n)$ to prevent overflows.*

4.2   Downhill vs. Greedy

We now show that the comparison between local downhill algorithms and the GREEDY algorithm is not one-sided. For the same network and $(1, 0)$-injection pattern used in the lower bounds for LOCAL-FIE and LOCAL-DOWNHILL in Sect. 4.1, GREEDY only needs buffers of size 1 to prevent overflows. However, consider the following $(1, 0)$-injection pattern, assuming that n is even: inject a single packet at node v_{2i-1} in each of the rounds $i = 1, \ldots, n/2$, then, inject a single packet at node v_{n-1} in each of the rounds $n/2 + 1, \ldots, n$. Under this injection pattern, buffers of size 1 suffice for LOCAL-FIE and LOCAL-DOWNHILL but GREEDY requires buffers of linear size, which gives the following result.

Theorem 7. *There exists a (1,0)-injection pattern such that LOCAL-FIE and LOCAL-DOWNHILL only need buffers of size 1 while GREEDY requires buffers of size $\Omega(n)$ to prevent overflows.*

5   Conclusion

In this work, we have shown that an extremely simple algorithm (requiring central coordination) suffices to bound the required buffer size by a function of the burstiness of the injected traffic. In other words, it is possible to design an algorithm that does not increase the inherent burstiness of the traffic. This required the algorithm to be non-greedy and non-local, and this is not coincidental.

In future work, we would like to extend the results to topologies more general than trees, and to multiple destinations. It would also be interesting to determine whether or not there is a more general local algorithm, e.g., that sometimes sends packets 'uphill', whose buffer size requirements depend only on the values of ρ and σ. The semi-local variant is also intriguing: suppose that nodes can coordinate within a certain range. How does this affect packet accumulation?

References

1. Afek, Y., Awerbuch, B., Gafni, E., Mansour, Y., Rosén, A., Shavit, N.: Slide-the key to polynomial end-to-end communication. J. Algorithms **22**(1), 158–186 (1997)
2. Aiello, W.A., Mansour, Y., Rajagopolan, S., Rosén, A.: Competitive queue policies for differentiated services. In: INFOCOM 2000, vol. 2, pp. 431–440 (2000)

3. Andrews, M., Awerbuch, B., Fernández, A., Leighton, T., Liu, Z., Kleinberg, J.: Universal-stability results and performance bounds for greedy contention-resolution protocols. J. ACM **48**(1), 39–69 (2001)
4. Awerbuch, B., Berenbrink, P., Brinkmann, A., Scheideler, C.: Simple routing strategies for adversarial systems. In: 42nd Annual Symposium on Foundations of Computer Science FOCS, pp. 158–167. IEEE Computer Society (2001)
5. Awerbuch, B., Leighton, F.T.: A simple local-control approximation algorithm for multicommodity flow. In: 34th Annual Symposium on Foundations of Computer Science (FOCS), pp. 459–468 (1993)
6. Awerbuch, B., Leighton, T.: Improved approximation algorithms for the multicommodity flow problem and local competitive routing in dynamic networks. In: Proceedings of the 26th Annual ACM Symposium on Theory of Computing (STOC), pp. 487–496 (1994)
7. Awerbuch, B., Patt-Shamir, B., Varghese, G.: Self-stabilizing end-to-end communication. J. High Speed Netw. **5**(4), 365–381 (1996)
8. Borodin, A., Kleinberg, J., Raghavan, P., Sudan, M., Williamson, D.P.: Adversarial queuing theory. J. ACM **48**(1), 13–38 (2001)
9. Le Boudec, J.-Y., Thiran, P. (eds.): Network Calculus. LNCS, vol. 2050. Springer, Heidelberg (2001)
10. Cruz, R.L.: A calculus for network delay, part I: network elements in isolation. IEEE Trans. Inf. Theory **37**(1), 114–131 (1991)
11. Emek, Y., Halldórsson, M.M., Mansour, Y., Patt-Shamir, B., Radhakrishnan, J., Rawitz, D.: Online set packing. SIAM J. Comput. **41**(4), 728–746 (2012)
12. Gettys, J., Nichols, K.: Bufferbloat: dark buffers in the internet. ACM Queue **9**(11) (2011)
13. Goldberg, A.V., Tarjan, R.E.: Finding minimum-cost circulations by successive approximation. Math. Oper. Res. **15**(3), 430–466 (1990)
14. Goldwasser, M.H.: A survey of buffer management policies for packet switches. SIGACT News **41**(1), 100–128 (2010)
15. Kesselman, A., Lotker, Z., Mansour, Y., Patt-Shamir, B., Schieber, B., Sviridenko, M.: Buffer overflow management in QoS switches. SIAM J. Comput. **33**(3), 563–583 (2004)
16. Kesselman, A., Mansour, Y.: Harmonic buffer management policy for shared memory switches. Theoret. Comput. Sci. **324**(2–3), 161–182 (2004)
17. Kesselman, A., Mansour, Y., Lotker, Z., Patt-Shamir, B.: Buffer overflows of merging streams. In: Proceedings of the 15th Annual ACM Symposium on Parallel Algorithms and Architectures (SPAA), pp. 244–245 (2003)
18. Kesselman, A., Rosén, A.: Scheduling policies for CIOQ switches. J. Algorithms **60**(1), 60–83 (2006)
19. Kushilevitz, E., Ostrovsky, R., Rosén, A.: Log-space polynomial end-to-end communication. SIAM J. Comput. **27**(6), 1531–1549 (1998)
20. Mansour, Y., Patt-Shamir, B., Lapid, O.: Optimal smoothing schedules for real-time streams. Distrib. Comput. **17**(1), 77–89 (2004)
21. Merlin, P.M., Schweitzer, P.J.: Deadlock avoidance in store-and-forward networks–I: store and forward deadlock. IEEE Trans. Commun. **28**(3), 345–354 (1980)
22. Open Network Foundation: software-defined networking: the new norm for networks. White paper, April 2012. https://www.opennetworking.org/images/stories/downloads/sdn-resources/white-papers/wp-sdn-newnorm.pdf
23. Rosén, A., Scalosub, G.: Rate vs.buffer size-greedy information gathering on the line. ACM Trans. Algorithms **7**(3, article 32) (2011)

Distributed Testing of Excluded Subgraphs

Pierre Fraigniaud[1], Ivan Rapaport[2], Ville Salo[2], and Ioan Todinca[3(✉)]

[1] CNRS and University Paris Diderot, Paris, France
[2] DIM-CMM (UMI 2807 CNRS), Universidad de Chile, Santiago, Chile
[3] Université d'Orléans, Orléans, France
`ioan.todinca@univ-orleans.fr`

Abstract. We study *property testing* in the context of *distributed computing*, under the classical CONGEST model. It is known that testing whether a graph is triangle-free can be done in a constant number of rounds, where the constant depends on how far the input graph is from being triangle-free. We show that, for every connected 4-node graph H, testing whether a graph is H-free can be done in a constant number of rounds too. The constant also depends on how far the input graph is from being H-free, and the dependence is identical to the one in the case of testing triangle-freeness. Hence, in particular, testing whether a graph is K_4-free, and testing whether a graph is C_4-free can be done in a constant number of rounds (where K_k denotes the k-node clique, and C_k denotes the k-node cycle). On the other hand, we show that testing K_k-freeness and C_k-freeness for $k \geq 5$ appear to be much harder. Specifically, we investigate two natural types of generic algorithms for testing H-freeness, called DFS tester and BFS tester. The latter captures the previously known algorithm to test the presence of triangles, while the former captures our generic algorithm to test the presence of a 4-node graph pattern H. We prove that both DFS and BFS testers fail to test K_k-freeness and C_k-freeness in a constant number of rounds for $k \geq 5$.

1 Introduction

Let $\mathcal{P}$ be a graph property, and let $0 < \epsilon < 1$ be a fixed parameter. According to the usual definition from *property testing* [16], an n-node m-edge graph G is ϵ-far from satisfying $\mathcal{P}$ if applying a sequence of at most ϵm edge-deletions or edge-additions to G cannot result in a graph satisfying $\mathcal{P}$. In the context of property testing, graphs are usually assumed to be stored using an adjacency list[1], and a centralized algorithm has the ability to probe nodes, via queries of

---

Additional support from ANR project DISPLEXITY, Inria project GANG, CONICYT via Basal in Applied Mathematics, Núcleo Milenio Información y Coordinación en Redes ICM/FIC RC130003, Fondecyt 1130061 and Fondecyt 3150552.

[1] Actually, property testing tackles graph problems in both the *dense* model (graphs represented by adjacency matrices) and the *sparse* model (graphs represented by adjacency lists). In this paper, we are interested in property testing in the sparse model.

© Springer-Verlag Berlin Heidelberg 2016
C. Gavoille and D. Ilcinkas (Eds.): DISC 2016, LNCS 9888, pp. 342–356, 2016.
DOI: 10.1007/978-3-662-53426-7_25

the form (i, j) where $i \in \{1, \ldots, n\}$, and $j \geq 0$. The answer to a query $(i, 0)$ is the degree of node i, while the answer to a query (i, j) with $j > 0$ is the identity of the jth neighbor of node i. After a small number of queries, the algorithm must output either accept or reject. An algorithm Seq is a testing algorithm for $\mathcal{P}$ if and only if, for every input graph G,

$$\begin{cases} G \text{ satisfies } \mathcal{P} \implies \Pr[\text{Seq accepts } G] \geq \frac{2}{3}; \\ G \text{ is } \epsilon\text{-far from satisfying } \mathcal{P} \implies \Pr[\text{Seq rejects } G] \geq \frac{2}{3}. \end{cases}$$

(An algorithm is 1-sided if it systematically accepts every graph satisfying $\mathcal{P}$). The challenge in this context is to design testing algorithms performing as few queries as possible.

In the context of *distributed* property testing [6], the challenge is not the number of queries (as all nodes perform their own queries in parallel), but the lack of global perspective on the input graph. The graph models a network. Every node of the network is a processor, and every processor can exchange messages with all processors corresponding to its neighboring nodes in the graph. After a certain number of rounds of computation, every node must output accept or reject. A distributed algorithm Dist is a distributed testing algorithm for $\mathcal{P}$ if and only if, for any graph G modeling the actual network,

$$\begin{cases} G \text{ satisfies } \mathcal{P} \implies \Pr[\text{Dist accepts } G \text{ in all nodes}] \geq \frac{2}{3}; \\ G \text{ is } \epsilon\text{-far from satisfying } \mathcal{P} \implies \Pr[\text{Dist rejects } G \text{ in at least one node}] \geq \frac{2}{3}. \end{cases}$$

The challenge is to use as few resources of the network as possible. In particular, it is desirable that every processor could take its decision (accept or reject) without requiring data from far away processors in the network, and that processors exchange messages of size respecting the inherent bounds imposed by the limited bandwidth of the links. These two constraints are well captured by the CONGEST model. This model is a classical model for distributed computation [27]. Processors are given distinct identities, that are supposed to have values in $[1, n^c]$ in n-node networks, for some constant $c \geq 1$. All processors start at the same time, and then proceed in synchronous rounds. At each round, every processor can send and receive messages to/from its neighbors, and perform some individual computation. All messages must be of size at most $O(\log n)$ bits. So, in particular, every message can include at most a constant number of processor identities. As a consequence, while every node can gather the identities of all its neighbors in just one round, a node with large degree that is aware of all the identities of its neighbors may not be able to send them all simultaneously to a given neighbor. The latter observation enforces strong constraints on distributed testing algorithms in the CONGEST model. For instance, while the LOCAL model allows every node to gather its t-neighborhood in t rounds, even just gathering the 2-neighborhood may require $\Omega(n)$ rounds in the CONGEST model (e.g., in the Lollipop graph, which is the graph obtained by joining a path to a clique). As a consequence, detecting the presence of even a small given pattern in a graph efficiently is not necessarily an easy task.

The presence or absence of a certain given pattern (typically, paths, cycles or cliques of a given size) as a subgraph, induced subgraph, or minor, has a significant impact on graph properties, and/or on the ability to design efficient algorithms for hard problems. This paper investigates the existence of efficient distributed testing algorithms for the H-freeness property, depending on the given graph H. Recall that, given a graph H, a graph G is H-*free* if and only if H is not isomorphic to a subgraph of G, where H is a subgraph of a graph G if $V(H) \subseteq V(G)$, and $E(H) \subseteq E(G)$. Recently, Censor-Hillel et al. [6] established a series of results regarding distributed testing of different graph properties, including bipartiteness and triangle-freeness. A triangle-free graph is a K_3-free graph or, equivalently, a C_3-free graph, where K_k and C_k respectively denote the clique and the cycle on k vertices. The algorithm in [6] for testing bipartiteness (of bounded degree networks) requires $O(\log n)$ rounds in the CONGEST model, and the authors conjecture that this is optimal. However, quite interestingly, the algorithm for testing triangle-freeness requires only a constant number of rounds, $O(1/\epsilon^2)$, i.e., it depends only on the (fixed) parameter ϵ quantifying the ϵ-far relaxation.

In this paper, we investigate the following question: what are the (connected) graphs H for which testing H-freeness can be done in a constant number of rounds in the CONGEST model?

1.1   Our Results

We show that, for every connected 4-node graph H, testing whether a graph is H-free can be done in $O(1/\epsilon^2)$ rounds. Hence, in particular, testing whether a graph is K_4-free, and testing whether a graph is C_4-free can be done in a constant number of rounds. Our algorithm is generic in the sense that, for all 4-node graphs H, the global communication structure of the algorithm is the same, with only a variant in the final decision for accepting or rejecting, which of course depends on H.

In fact, we identify two different natural generic types of testing algorithms for H-freeness. We call the first type DFS tester, and our algorithm for testing the presence of 4-node patterns is actually the DFS tester. Such an algorithm applies to Hamiltonian graphs H, i.e., graphs H containing a simple path spanning all its vertices (the only non-hamiltonian connected graph on 4 vertices is the star $K_{1,3}$, for which the problem is trivial). The DFS tester performs in $|H| - 1$ rounds. Recall that, for a node set A, $G[A]$ denotes the subgraph of G induced by A. At each round t of the DFS tester, at every node u, and for each of its incident edges e, node u pushes a graph $G[A_t]$ (where, initially, A_0 is just the graph formed by u alone). The graph $G[A_t]$ is chosen u.a.r. among the sets of graphs received from the neighbors at the previous round. More specifically, upon reception of every graph $G[A_{t-1}]$ at round $t-1$, node u forms a graph $G[A_{t-1} \cup \{u\}]$, and the graph $G[A_t]$ pushed by u along e at round t is chosen u.a.r. among the collection of graphs $G[A_{t-1} \cup \{u\}]$ currently held by u. By repeating this algorithm $O(1/\epsilon^2)$ times we obtain the desired probability.

We call BFS tester the second type of generic testing algorithm for H-freeness. The algorithm in [6] for triangle-freeness is a simplified variant of the BFS tester, and we prove that the BFS tester can test K_4-freeness in $O(1/\epsilon^2)$

rounds. Instead of guessing a path spanning H (which may actually not exist for H large), the BFS tester aims at directly guessing all neighbors in H simultaneously. The algorithm performs in $D - 1$ rounds, where D is the diameter of H. For the sake of simplicity, let us assume that H is d-regular. At each round, every node u forms groups of d neighboring nodes. These groups may overlap, but a neighbor should not participate to more than a constant number of groups. Then for every edge $e = \{u, v\}$ incident to u, node u pushes all partial graphs of the form $G[A_{t-1} \cup \{v_1, \ldots, v_t\}]$ where $v \in \{v_1, \ldots, v_t\}$, A_{t-1} is chosen u.a.r. among the graphs received at the previous round, and the v_i's will be in charge of checking the presence of edges between them and the other v_j's.

We prove that neither the DFS tester, nor the BFS tester can test K_k-freeness in a constant number of rounds for $k \geq 5$, and that the same holds for testing C_k-freeness (with the exception of a finite number of small values of k). This shows that testing K_k-freeness or C_k-freeness for $k \geq 5$ in a constant number of rounds requires, if at all possible, to design algorithms which explore G from each node in a way far more intricate than just parallel DFSs or parallel BFSs. Our impossibility results, although restricted to DFS and BFS testers, might be hints that testing K_k-freeness and C_k-freeness for $k \geq 5$ in n-node networks does require to perform a number of rounds which grows with the size n of the network.

1.2 Related Work

The CONGEST model has become a standard model in distributed computation [27]. Most of the lower bounds in the CONGEST model have been obtained using reduction to communication complexity problems [8,11,23]. The so-called *congested clique* model is the CONGEST model in the complete graph K_n [10,22,24,26]. There are extremely fast protocols for solving different types of graph problems in the congested clique, including finding ruling sets [20], constructing minimum spanning trees [19], and, closely related to our work, detecting small subgraphs [7,9].

The distributed property testing framework in the CONGEST model was recently introduced in the aforementioned paper [6], inspired from classical property testing [16,17]. Distributed property testing relaxes classical distributed decision [12,13,18], typically designed for the LOCAL model, by ignoring illegal instances which are less than ϵ-far from satisfying the considered property. Without such a relaxation, distributed decision in the CONGEST model requires non-constant number of rounds [8]. Other variants of local decision in the LOCAL model have been studied in [2,3], where each process can output an arbitrary value (beyond just a single bit — accept or reject), and [4,21], where nodes are bounded to perform a single round before to output at most $O(\log n)$ bits. Distributed decision has been also considered in other distributed environments, such as shared memory [14], with application to runtime verification [15], and networks of finite automata [28].

2   Detecting Small Graphs Using a DFS Approach

In this section, we establish our main positive result, which implies, in particular, that testing C_4-freeness and testing K_4-freeness can be done in constant time in the CONGEST model.

Theorem 1. *Let H be a connected graph on four vertices. There is a 1-sided error distributed property-testing algorithm for H-freeness, performing in a constant number of rounds in the* CONGEST *model.*

Proof. All 4-node connected graphs H contain a P_4 (a path on four vertices) as a subgraph, with the only exception of the *star* $K_{1,3}$ (a.k.a. the *claw*). Nevertheless, testing whether a graph G is $K_{1,3}$-free is trivial (every node rejects whenever its degree is at least three). Therefore, we are going to show the theorem by exhibiting a generic distributed testing protocol for testing H-freeness, that applies to any graph H on four vertices containing a P_4 as a subgraph. The core of this algorithm is presented as Algorithm 1. Note that the test $H \subseteq G[u, u', v', w']$ at step 4 of Algorithm 1 can be performed thanks to the bit b that tells about the only edge that node u is not directly aware of. Algorithm 1 performs in just two rounds (if we omit the round used to acquire the identities of the neighbors), and that a single $O(\log n)$-bit message is sent through every edge at each round. Clearly, if G is H-free, then all nodes accept.

Algorithm 1. Testing H-freeness for 4-node Hamiltonian H. Instructions for node u.

---

1 Send $\mathrm{id}(u)$ to all neighbors;
2 For every neighbor v, choose a received identity $\mathrm{id}(w)$ u.a.r., and send $(\mathrm{id}(w), \mathrm{id}(u))$ to v;
3 For every neighbor v, choose a received pair $(\mathrm{id}(w'), \mathrm{id}(u'))$ u.a.r., and send $(\mathrm{id}(w'), \mathrm{id}(u'), \mathrm{id}(u), b)$ to v, where $b = 1$ if w' is a neighbor of u, and $b = 0$ otherwise;
4 For every received 4-tuple $(\mathrm{id}(w'), \mathrm{id}(v'), \mathrm{id}(u'), b)$, check whether $H \subseteq G[u, u', v', w']$;
5 If $H \subseteq G[u, u', v', w']$ for one such 4-tuple then reject else accept.

In order to analyze the efficiency of Algorithm 1 in case G is ϵ-far from being H-free, let us consider a subgraph $G[\{u_1, u_2, u_3, u_4\}]$ of G containing H, such that (u_1, u_2, u_3, u_4) is a P_4 spanning H. Let $\mathcal{E}$ be the event "at step 2, vertex u_2 sends $(\mathrm{id}(u_1), \mathrm{id}(u_2))$ to its neighbor u_3". We have $\Pr[\mathcal{E}] = 1/d(u_2)$. Similarly, let $\mathcal{E}'$ be the event "at step 3, vertex u_3 sends $(\mathrm{id}(u_1), \mathrm{id}(u_2), \mathrm{id}(u_3))$ to its neighbor u_4". We have $\Pr[\mathcal{E}'|\mathcal{E}] = 1/d(u_3)$. Since $\Pr[\mathcal{E} \wedge \mathcal{E}'] = \Pr[\mathcal{E}'|\mathcal{E}] \cdot \Pr[\mathcal{E}]$, it follows that

$$\Pr[H \text{ is detected by } u_4 \text{ while performing Algorithm 1}] \geq \frac{1}{d(u_2)d(u_3)}. \qquad (1)$$

Note that the events $\mathcal{E}$ and $\mathcal{E}'$ only depend on the choices made by u_2 for the edge $\{u_2, u_3\}$ and by u_3 for the edge $\{u_3, u_4\}$, in steps 3 and 4 of Algorithm 1, respectively. Since these choices are performed independently at all nodes, it follows that if H_1 and H_2 are edge-disjoint copies of H in G, then the events $\mathcal{E}_1$ and $\mathcal{E}_2$ associated to them are independent, as well as the events $\mathcal{E}'_1$ and $\mathcal{E}'_2$.

The following result will be used throughout the paper, so we state it as a lemma for further references.

Lemma 1. *Let G be ϵ-far from being H-free. Then G contains at least $\epsilon m/|E(H)|$ edge-disjoint copies of H.*

Proof of Lemma 1. Let $S = \{e_1, \ldots, e_k\}$ be a smallest set of edges whose removal from G results in an H-free graph. We have $k \geq \epsilon m$. Let us then remove these edges from G according to the following process. The edges are removed in arbitrary order. Each time an edge e is removed from S, we select an arbitrary copy H_e of H containing e, we remove all the edges of H_e from G, and we reset S as $S \setminus E(H_e)$. We proceed as such until we have exhausted all the edges of S. Note that each time we pick an edge $e \in S$, there always exists a copy H_e of H containing e. Indeed, otherwise, $S \setminus \{e\}$ would also be a set whose removal from G results in an H-free graph, contradicting the minimality of $|S|$. After at most k such removals, we get a graph that is H-free, and, by construction, for every two edges $e, e' \in S$, we have that H_e and $H_{e'}$ are edge-disjoint. Every step of this process removes at most $|E(H)|$ edges from S, hence the process performs at least $\epsilon m/|E(H)|$ steps before exhausting all edges in S. Lemma 1 follows. $\square$

Let us now define an edge $\{u, v\}$ as *important* if it is the middle-edge of a P_4 in one of the $\epsilon m/|E(H)|$ edge-disjoint copies of H constructed in the proof of Lemma 1. We denote by $I(G)$ the set of all important edges. Let N_0 be the random variable counting the number of distinct copies of H that are detected by Algorithm 1. As a direct consequence of Eq. (1), we get that

$$\mathbf{E}(N_0) \geq \sum_{\{u,v\} \in I(G)} \frac{1}{d(u)d(v)}.$$

Define an edge $\{u, v\}$ of G as *good* if $d(u)d(v) \leq 4m|E(H)|/\epsilon$, and let $g(G)$ denote the set of good edges. Note that if there exists a constant $\gamma > 0$ such that $|I(G) \cap g(G)| \geq \gamma m$, then the expected number of copies of H detected during a phase is

$$\mathbf{E}(N_0) \geq \sum_{\{u,v\} \in I(G) \cap g(G)} \frac{1}{d(u)d(v)} \geq \gamma m \frac{1}{4m|E(H)|/\epsilon} = \frac{\gamma\epsilon}{4|E(H)|}. \tag{2}$$

We now show that the number of edges that are both important and good is indeed at least a fraction γ of the edges, for some constant $\gamma > 0$. We first show that G has at least $(1 - \frac{3}{4|E(H)|}\epsilon)m$ good edges. Recall that $\sum_{u \in V(G)} d(u) = 2m$, and define $N(u)$ as the set of all neighbors of node u. We have

$$\sum_{\{u,v\}\in E(G)} d(u)d(v) = \frac{1}{2}\sum_{u\in V(G)} d(u)\sum_{v\in N(u)} d(v) \le \sum_{u\in V(G)} d(u)\, m \le 2m^2.$$

Thus G must have at least $(1 - \frac{3}{4|E(H)|}\epsilon)m$ good edges, since otherwise

$$\sum_{\{u,v\}\in E(G)} d(u)d(v) \ge \sum_{\{u,v\}\in E(G)\setminus g(G)} d(u)d(v) > \frac{3}{4|E(H)|}\epsilon m\frac{4m|E(H)|}{\epsilon} = 3m^2,$$

contradicting the aforementioned $2m^2$ upper bound. Thus, G has at least $(1 - \frac{3}{4|E(H)|}\epsilon)m$ good edges. On the other hand, since the number of important edges is at least the number of edge-disjoint copies of H in G, there are at least $\epsilon m/|E(H)|$ important edges. It follows that the number of edges that are both important and good is at least $\frac{\epsilon}{4|E(H)|}m$. Therefore, by Eq. (2), we get that

$$\mathbf{E}(N_0) \ge \left(\frac{\epsilon}{4|E(H)|}\right)^2.$$

All the above calculations were made on the $\epsilon m/|E(H)|$ edge-disjoint copies of H constructed in the proof of Lemma 1. Therefore, if $X_i^{(0)}$ denotes the random variable satisfying $X_i^{(0)} = 1$ if the ith copy H is detected, and $X_i^{(0)} = 0$ otherwise, then we have $N_0 = \sum_{i=1}^{\epsilon m/|E(H)|} X_i^{(0)}$, and the variables $X_i^{(0)}$, $i = 1,\ldots,\epsilon m/|E(H)|$, are mutually independent. Let $T = 8\ln 3 \left(\frac{4|E(H)|}{\epsilon}\right)^2$.

By repeating the algorithm T times, and defining $N = \sum_{t=0}^{T-1} N_t$ where N_t denotes the number of copies of H detected at the tth independent repetition, we get $\mathbf{E}(N) \ge 8\ln 3$. In fact, we also have $N = \sum_{t=0}^{T-1}\sum_{i=1}^{\epsilon m/|E(H)|} X_i^{(t)}$ where $X_i^{(t)} = 1$ if the ith copy H is detected at the tth iteration of the algorithm, and $X_i^{(t)} = 0$ otherwise. All these variables are mutually independent, as there is mutual independence within each iteration, and all iterations are performed independently. Therefore, Chernoff bound applies (see Theorem 4.5 in [25]), and so, for every $0 < \delta < 1$, we have $\Pr[N \le (1-\delta)\mathbf{E}[N]] \le e^{-\delta^2\mathbf{E}[N]/2}$.

By taking $\delta = \frac{1}{2}$ we get $\Pr[N \le 4\ln 3] \le \frac{1}{3}$. Therefore, a copy of H is detected with probability at least $\frac{2}{3}$, which completes the proof of Theorem 1. □

3   Limits of the DFS Approach

Algorithm 1 can be extended in a natural way to any k-node graph H containing a Hamiltonian path, as depicted in Algorithm 2. At the first round, every vertex u sends its identifier to its neighbors, and composes the $d(u)$ graphs formed by the edge $\{u, v\}$, one for every neighbor v. Then, during the $k-2$ following rounds, every node u forwards through each of its edges one of the graphs formed a the previous round.

Let $(u_1, u_2, \ldots, u_k)$ be a simple path in G, and assume that $G[\{u_1, u_2, \ldots, u_k\}]$ contains H. If, at each round i, $2 \le i < k$, vertex u_i sends to u_{i+1} the graph $G[\{u_1, \ldots, u_i\}]$, then, when the repeat-loop completes, vertex u_k

---

Algorithm 2. Testing H-freeness: Hamiltonian H, $|V(H)| = k$. Instructions for node u.

1 send the 1-node graph $G[u]$ to every neighbor v;
2 form the graph $G[\{u, v\}]$ for every neighbor v;
3 **repeat** $k - 2$ **times**
4   **for** *every neighbor v* **do**
5   choose a graph $G[A]$ u.a.r. among those formed during the previous round;
6   send $G[A]$ to v;
7   receive the graph $G[A']$ from v;
8   form the graph $G[A' \cup \{u\}]$;

9 **if** $H \subseteq G[A]$ for one of the graphs formed at the last round **then** reject **else** accept.

---

will test precisely the graph $G[\{u_1, u_2, \ldots, u_k\}]$, and thus H will be detected by the algorithm. Theorem 1 states that Algorithm 2 works fine for 4-node graphs H. We show that, $k = 4$ is precisely the limit of detection for graphs that are ϵ-far from being H-free, even for the cliques and the cycles.

Theorem 2. *Let $H = K_k$ for arbitrary $k \geq 5$, or $H = C_k$ for arbitrary odd $k \geq 5$. There exists a graph G that is ϵ-far from being H-free in which any constant number of repetitions of Algorithm 2 fails to detect H, with probability at least $1 - o(1)$.*

For the purpose of proving Theorem 2, we use the following combinatorial result, which extends Lemma 7 of [1], where the corresponding claim was proved for $k = 3$, with a similar proof. The bound on p' is not even nearly optimal in Lemma 2 below, but it is good enough for our purpose[2].

Lemma 2. *Let k be a constant. For any sufficiently large p, there exists a set $X \subset \{0, \ldots, p - 1\}$ of size $p' \geq p^{1 - \frac{\log \log \log p + 4}{\log \log p}}$ such that, for any k elements $x_1, x_2, \ldots, x_k$ of X, $\sum_{i=1}^{k-1} x_i \equiv (k-1)x_k \pmod{p} \implies x_1 = \cdots = x_{k-1} = x_k$.*

Proof. Let $b = \lfloor \log p \rfloor$ and $a = \left\lfloor \frac{\log p}{\log \log p} \right\rfloor$. Take p sufficiently large so that $a < b/k$ is satisfied. X is a set of integers encoded in base b, on a b-ary digits, such that the digits of each $x \in X$ are a permutation of $\{0, 1, \ldots, a - 1\}$. More formally, for any permutation π over $\{0, \ldots, a-1\}$, let $N_\pi = \sum_{i=0}^{a-1} \pi(i)b^i$. Then, let us set $X = \{N_\pi \mid \pi \text{ is a permutation of } \{0, \ldots, a - 1\}\}$. Observe that different permutations π and π' yield different numbers N_π and $N_{\pi'}$ because these numbers have different digits in base b. Hence X has $p' = a!$ elements. Using the inequality $z! > (z/e)^z$ as in [1] (Lemma 7), we get that $a! \geq p^{1 - \frac{\log \log \log p + 4}{\log \log p}}$, as desired.

---

[2] The interested reader can consult [29] for the state-of-the-art on such combinatorial constructions, in particular constructions for $p' \geq p^{1 - c/\sqrt{\log p}}$, for a constant c depending on k.

Now, for any $x \in X$, we have $x \leq p/k$. Indeed, $x < a \cdot b^{a-1} \leq \frac{1}{k}b^a$, and $b^a \leq (\log p)^{\frac{\log p}{\log \log p}} = p$. Consequently, the modulo in the statement of the Lemma becomes irrelevant, and we will simply consider integer sums. Let $x_1, \ldots, x_{k-1}, x_k$ in X, such that $\sum_{l=1}^{k-1} x_i = (k-1)x_k$. Viewing the x_i's as integers in base b, and having in mind that all digits are smaller than b/k, we get that the equality must hold coordinate-wise. For every $1 \leq l \leq k$, let π_l be the permutation such that $x_l = N_{\pi_l}$. For every $i \in 0, \ldots, a-1$, we have $\sum_{l=1}^{k-1} \pi_l(i) = (k-1)\pi_k(i)$. By the Cauchy-Schwarz inequality applied to vectors $(\pi_1(i), \ldots, \pi_{k-1}(i))$ and $(1, \ldots, 1)$, for every $i \in \{0, \ldots, a-1\}$, we also have $\sum_{l=1}^{k-1} (\pi_l(i))^2 \geq (k-1)(\pi_k(i))^2$. Moreover equality holds if and only if $\pi_1(i) = \cdots = \pi_{k-1}(i) = \pi_k(i)$. By summing up the a inequalities induced by the a coordinates, observe that both sides sum to exactly $(k-1)\sum_{i=0}^{a-1} i^2$. Therefore, for every i, the Cauchy-Schwarz inequality is actually an equality, implying that the ith digit is identical in all the k integers $x_1, \ldots, x_k$. As a consequence, $x_1 = \cdots = x_{k-1} = x_k$, which completes the proof. □

Proof of Theorem 2. Assume that $G[\{u_1, u_2, \ldots, u_k\}]$ contains H, where the sequence $(u_1, u_2, \ldots, u_k)$ is a path of G. For $2 \leq i \leq k-1$, let us consider the event "at round i, vertex u_i sends the graph $G[u_1, \ldots, u_i\}]$ to u_{i+1}". Observe that this event happens with probability $\frac{1}{d(u_i)}$ because u_i choses which subgraph to send uniformly at random among the $d(u_i)$ constructed subgraphs. With the same arguments as the ones used to establish Eq. (1), we get

$$\Pr[H \text{ is detected along the path } (u_1, \ldots, u_k)] = \frac{1}{d(u_2)d(u_3)\ldots d(u_{k-1})}. \quad (3)$$

We construct families of graphs which will allow us to show, based on that latter equality, that the probability to detect a copy of H vanishes with the size of the input graph G. We actually use a variant of the so-called *Behrend graphs* (see, e.g., [1,5]), and we construct graph families indexed by k, and by a parameter p, that we denote by $BC(k,p)$ for the case of cycles, and by $BK(k,p)$ for the case of cliques. We prove that these graphs are ϵ-far from being H-free, while the probability that Algorithm 2 detects a copy of H in these graphs goes to 0.

Let us begin with the case of testing cycles. Let p be a large prime number, and let X be a subset of $\{0, \ldots, p-1\}$ of size $p' \geq p^{1 - \frac{\log \log \log p + 4}{\log \log p}}$, where p' is as defined in Lemma 2. Graph $BC(k,p)$ is then constructed as follows. The vertex set V is the disjoint union of an odd number k of sets, $V^0, V^1, \ldots V^{k-1}$, of p elements each. For every l, $0 \leq l \leq k-1$, let u_i^l, $i = 0, \ldots, p-1$ be the nodes in V^l so that $V^l = \{u_i^l \mid i \in \{0, \ldots, p-1\}\}$. For every $i \in \{0, \ldots, p-1\}$ and every $x \in X$, edges in $BC(k,p)$ form a cycle

$$C_{i,x} = (u_i^0, \ldots, u_{i+lx}^l, u_{i+(l+1)x}^{l+1}, \ldots, u_{i+(k-1)x}^{k-1}),$$

where the indices are taken modulo p. The cycles $C_{i,x}$ form a set of pp' edge-disjoint copies of C_k in $BC(k,p)$. Indeed, for any two distinct pairs $(i,x) \neq$

(i', x'), the cycles $C_{i,x}$ and $C_{i',x'}$ are edge-disjoint. Otherwise there exists a common edge e between the two cycles. It can be either between two consecutive layers V^l and V^{l+1}, or between V^0 and V^{k-1}. There are two cases. If $e = \{u_y^l, u_z^{l+1}\}$ we must have $y = i+lx = i'+lx'$ and $z = i+(l+1)x = i'+(l+1)x'$, where equalities are taken modulo p, and, as a consequence, $(i, x) = (i', x')$. If $e = \{u_y^0, u_z^{k-1}\}$ then we have $y = i = i'$ and $z = i + (k-1)x' = i' + (k-1)x'$, and, since p is prime, we also conclude that $(i, x) = (i', x')$.

We now show that any k-cycle has exactly one vertex in each set V^l, for $0 \leq l < k - 1$. For this purpose, we focus on the parity of the layers formed by consecutive vertices of a cycle. The "short" edges (i.e., ones between consecutive layers) change the parity of the layer, and hence every cycle must include "long" edges (i.e., ones between layers 0 and $k - 1$). However, long edges do not change the parity of the layer. Therefore, every cycle contains an odd number of long edges, and an even number of short edges. For this to occur, the only possibility is that the cycle contains a vertex from each layer.

Next, we show that any cycle of k vertices in $BC(k, p)$ must be of the form $C_{i,x}$ for some pair (i, x). Let $C = (u_{y_0}^0, \ldots u_{y_l}^l, u_{y_{l+1}}^{l+1}, \ldots, u_{y_{k-1}}^{k-1})$ be a cycle in $BC(k, p)$. For every $l = 1, \ldots, k - 1$, let $x_l = y_l - y_{l-1} \bmod p$. We have $x_l \in X$ because the edge $\{u_{y_{l-1}}^{l-1}, u_{y_l}^l\}$ is in some cycle C_{i,x_l}. Also set $x_k \in X$ such that the edge $\{u_{y_0}^0, u_{y_{k-1}}^{k-1}\}$ is in the cycle C_{y_0,x_k}. In particular we must have that $y_{k-1} = y_0 + (k-1)x_k$. It follows that $y_{k-1} = y_0 + (k-1)x_k = y_0 + x_1 + x_2 + \cdots + x_{k-1}$. By Lemma 2, we must have $x_1 = \cdots = x_{k-1} = x_k$, so C is of the form $C_{i,x}$.

It follows from the above that $BC(k, p)$ has exactly pp' edge-disjoint cycles of k vertices. Since $BC(k, p)$ has $n = kp$ vertices, and $m = kpp'$ edges, $BC(k, p)$ is ϵ-far from being C_k-free, for $\epsilon = \frac{1}{k}$. Also, each vertex of $BC(k, p)$ is of degree $2p'$ because each vertex belongs to p' edge-disjoint cycles.

Let us now consider an execution of Algorithm 2 for input $BC(k, p)$. As $BC(k, p)$ is regular of degree $d = 2p'$, this execution has probability at most $\frac{2k}{d^{k-2}}$ to detect any given cycle C of k vertices. Indeed, C must be detected along one of the paths formed by its vertices in graph $BC(k, p)$, there are at most $2k$ such paths in C (because all C_k's in $BC(k, p)$ are induced subgraphs, and paths are oriented), and, by Eq. (3), the probability of detecting the cycle along one of its paths is $\frac{1}{d^{k-2}}$. Therefore, applying the union bound, the probability of detecting a given cycle C is at most $\frac{2k}{d^{k-2}}$.

Since there are pp' edge-disjoint cycles, the expected number of cycles detected in one execution of Algorithm 2 is at most $\frac{2kpp'}{(2p')^{k-2}}$. It follows that the expected number of cycles detected by repeating the algorithm T times is at most $\frac{2kpT}{2(2p')^{k-3}}$. Consequently, the probability that the algorithm detects a cycle is at most $\frac{2kpT}{2(2p')^{k-3}}$. Plugging in the fact that, by Lemma 2, $p' = p^{1-o(1)}$, we conclude that, for any constant T, the probability that T repetitions of Algorithm 2 detect a cycle goes to 0 when p goes to ∞, as claimed.

The case of the complete graph is treated similarly. Graphs $BK(k, p)$ are constructed in a way similar to $BC(k, p)$, as k-partite graphs with p vertices in each partition (in particular, $BK(k, p)$ also has $n = kp$ vertices). The difference with $BC(k, p)$ is that, for each pair $(i, x) \in \{0, \ldots, p-1\} \times X$, we do not add a cycle, but a complete graph $K_{i,x}$ on the vertex set $\{u_i^0, \ldots, u_{i+lx}^l, u_{i+(l+1)x}^{l+1}, \cdots, u_{i+(k-1)x}^{k-1}\}$. By the same arguments as for $BC(k,p)$, $BK(k,p)$ contains contains exactly pp' edge-disjoint copies of K_k (namely $K_{i,x}$, for each pair (i,x)). This fact holds even for even values of k, because any k-clique must have a vertex in each layer, no matter the parity of k. Thus, in particular $BK(k,p)$ has $m = \binom{k}{2}pp'$ edges, and every vertex is of degree $d = (k-1)p'$. The graph $BK(k,p)$ is ϵ-far from being K_k-free, for $\epsilon = \frac{2}{k(k-1)}$. The probability that Algorithm 2 detects a given copy of K_k is at most $\frac{k!}{d^{k-2}}$. Indeed, a given K_k has $k!$ (oriented) paths of length k, and, by Eq. (3), the probability that the algorithm detects this copy along a given path is $\frac{1}{d^{k-2}}$. The expected number $\mathbf{E}[N]$ of K_k's detected in T runs of Algorithm 2 is, as for $BC(k,p)$, at most $\frac{k!\,Tpp'}{d^{k-2}} = \frac{k!\,pT}{(k-1)^{k-2}(p')^{k-3}}$. Therefore, since $\Pr[N \neq 0] \leq \mathbf{E}[N]$, we get that the probability that the algorithm detects some K_k goes to 0 as p goes to ∞. It follows that the algorithm fails to detect K_k, as claimed. □

Remark. The proof that Algorithm 2 fails to detect C_k for odd $k \geq 5$, can be extended to all (odd or even) $k \geq 13$, as well as to $k = 10$. The cases of C_6, C_8, are C_{12} are open, although we strongly believe that Algorithm 2 also fails to detect these cycles in some graphs.

4   Detecting Small Graphs Using a BFS Approach

We discuss here another very natural approach, extending the algorithm proposed by Censor-Hillel et al. [6] for testing triangle-freeness. In the protocol of [6], each node u samples two neighbors v_1 and v_2 uniformly at random, and asks them to check the presence of an edge between them. We generalize this protocol as follows. Assume that the objective is to test H-freeness, for a graph H containing a universal vertex (a vertex adjacent to every other). Each node u samples $d(u)$ sets $S_1, \ldots, S_{d(u)}$, of $|V(H)| - 1$ neighbors each. For each $i = 1, \ldots, d(u)$, node u sends S_i to all its neighbors in S_i, asking them to check the presence of edges between them, and collecting their answers. Based on these answers, node u can tell whether $G[S_i \cup \{u\}]$ contains H. We show that this very simple algorithm can be used for testing K_4-freeness.

Theorem 3. *There is a 1-sided error distributed property-testing algorithm for K_4-freeness, performing in a constant number of rounds in the* CONGEST *model.*

Again, we show the theorem by exhibiting a generic distributed testing protocol for testing H-freeness, that applies to any graph H on four vertices with a universal vertex. The core of this algorithm is presented as Algorithm 3 where all calculations on indices are performed modulo $d = d(u)$ at node u. This algorithm is presented for a graph H with k nodes.

At Step 3, node u picks a permutation π u.a.r., in order to compose the $d(u)$ sets $S_1, \ldots, S_{d(u)}$, which are sent in parallel at Steps 4–5. At Step 8, every node u considers separately each of the $k-1$ tuples of size $k-1$ received from each

---

Algorithm 3. Testing H-freeness for H with a universal vertex. Instructions for node u of degree d. We let $k = |V(H)|$.

---

1 send id(u) to all neighbors;
2 index the d neighbors $v_0, \ldots, v_{d-1}$ in increasing order of their IDs;
3 pick a permutation $\pi \in \Sigma_d$ of $\{0, 1, \ldots, d-1\}$, u.a.r.;
4 **for** each $i \in \{0, \ldots, d-1\}$ **do**
5 $\quad\lfloor$ Send $(\mathrm{id}(v_{\pi(i)}), \mathrm{id}(v_{\pi(i+1)}), \ldots, \mathrm{id}(v_{\pi(i+k-2)}))$ to $v_{\pi(i)}, v_{\pi(i+1)}, \ldots, v_{\pi(i+k-2)}$;
6 **for** each $i \in \{0, \ldots, d-1\}$ **do**
7 $\quad$ **for** each of the $k-1$ tuples $(\mathrm{id}(w^{(1)}), \ldots, \mathrm{id}(w^{(k-1)}))$ received from v_i **do**
8 $\quad\quad\lfloor$ Send $(b^{(1)}, \ldots, b^{(k-1)})$ to v_i where $b^{(j)} = 1$ iff $u = w^{(j)}$ or $\{u, w^{(j)}\} \in E$;
9 If $\exists i \in \{0, \ldots, d-1\}$ s.t. $H \subseteq G[u, v_{\pi(i)}, \ldots, v_{\pi(i+k-2)}]$ then reject else accept.

---

of its neighbors, checks the presence of edges between u and each of the nodes in that tuple, and sends back the result to the neighbor from which it received the tuple. Finally, the tests $H \subseteq G[u, v_{\pi(i)}, v_{\pi(i+1)}, \ldots, v_{\pi(i+k-2)}]$ performed at the last step is achieved thanks to the $(k-1)$-tuple of bits received from each of the neighbors $v_{\pi(i)}, v_{\pi(i+1)}, \ldots, v_{\pi(i+k-2)}$, indicating the presence or absence of all the edges between these nodes. Note that exactly $2k-5$ IDs are actually sent through each edges at Steps 4–5, because of the permutation shifts. Similarly, $2k-5$ bits are sent through each edge at Steps 6–8. Therefore Algorithm 3 runs in a constant number of rounds in the CONGEST model. The proof of the following result will appear in a full version of this paper. Among others, it relies on the observation that two disjoint copies of K_4 share at most one vertex (which does not hold for other graphs H).

Lemma 3. *Let G be ϵ-far from being K_4-free. Algorithm 3 for $H = K_4$ rejects G with constant probability.*

5   Limits of the BFS Approach

As it happened with the DFS-based approach, the BFS-based approach fails to generalize to large graphs H. Actually, it already fails for K_5.

Theorem 4. *Let $k \geq 5$. There exists a graph G that is ϵ-far from being K_k-free in which any constant number of repetitions of Algorithm 3 fails to detect any copy of K_k, with probability at least $1 - o(1)$.*

Proof. The family of graphs $BK(k, p)$ constructed in the proof of Theorem 2 for defeating Algorithm 2 can also be used to defeat Algorithm 3. Recall that those graphs have $n = kp$ vertices, $m = \binom{k}{2}pp'$ edges, and every vertex is of degree $d = (k-1)p'$, for $p' = p^{1-o(1)}$. Moreover, they have exactly pp' copies of K_k, which are pairwise edge-disjoint. $BK(k, p)$ is ϵ-far from being K_k-free with $\epsilon = 1/\binom{k}{2}$. For each copy K of K_k, and for every $u \in K$, the probability that u

detects K is $d/\binom{d}{k-1} \le \frac{\alpha}{d^{k-2}}$ for some constant $\alpha > 0$. Therefore, when running the algorithm T times, it follows from the union bound that the expected number of detected copies of K_k is at most $\frac{\alpha k T p p'}{d^{k-2}}$, which tends to 0 when $p \to \infty$, for any $k \ge 5$. Consequently, the probability of detects at least one copy of K_k also tends to 0. $\qquad\square$

6 Conclusion and Further Work

The lower bound techniques for the CONGEST model are essentially based on reductions to communication complexity problems. Such an approach does not seem to apply easily in the context of distributed testing. The question of whether the presence of large cliques (or cycles) can be tested in $O(1)$ rounds in the CONGEST model is an intriguing open problem.

It is worth mentioning that our algorithms generalize to testing the presence of *induced* subgraphs. Indeed, if the input graph G contains at least ϵm edge-disjoint *induced* copies of H, for a graph H on four vertices containing a Hamiltonian path, then Algorithm 1 detects an induced subgraph H with constant probability (the only difference is that, in the last line of the algorithm, we check for an induced subgraph instead of just a subgraph). Moreover, if the input contains ϵm edge-disjoint induced claws (i.e., induced subgraphs $K_{1,3}$), then Algorithm 3 detects one of them with constant probability. Thus, for any connected graph H on four vertices, distinguishing between graphs that do not have H as induced subgraph, and those who have ϵm edge-disjoint induced copies of H can be done in $O(1)$ rounds in the CONGEST model. However, we point out that, unlike in the case of subgraphs, a graph that is ϵ-far from having H as induced subgraph may not have many edge-disjoint induced copies of H.

References

1. Alon, N., Kaufman, T., Krivelevich, M., Ron, D.: Testing triangle-freeness in general graphs. SIAM J. Discrete Math. **22**(2), 786–819 (2008)
2. Arfaoui, H., Fraigniaud, P., Ilcinkas, D., Mathieu, F.: Distributedly testing cycle-freeness. In: Kratsch, D., Todinca, I. (eds.) WG 2014. LNCS, vol. 8747, pp. 15–28. Springer, Heidelberg (2014)
3. Arfaoui, H., Fraigniaud, P., Pelc, A.: Local decision and verification with bounded-size outputs. In: Higashino, T., Katayama, Y., Masuzawa, T., Potop-Butucaru, M., Yamashita, M. (eds.) SSS 2013. LNCS, vol. 8255, pp. 133–147. Springer, Heidelberg (2013)
4. Becker, F., Kosowski, A., Matamala, M., Nisse, N., Rapaport, I., Suchan, K., Todinca, I.: Allowing each node to communicate only once in a distributed system: shared whiteboard models. Distrib. Comput. **28**(3), 189–200 (2015)
5. Behrend, F.A.: On sets of integers which contain no three terms in arithmetical progression. Proc. Natl. Acad. Sci. **32**(12), 331 (1946)
6. Censor-Hillel, K., Fischer, E., Schwartzman, G., Vasudev, Y.: Fast distributed algorithms for testing graph properties. CoRR abs/1602.03718, February 2016

7. Censor-Hillel, K., Kaski, P., Korhonen, J.H., Lenzen, C., Paz, A., Suomela, J.: Algebraic methods in the congested clique. In: Proceedings of PODC 2015, pp. 143–152 (2015)
8. Das-Sarma, A., Holzer, S., Kor, L., Korman, A., Nanongkai, D., Pandurangan, G., Peleg, D., Wattenhofer, R.: Distributed verification and hardness of distributed approximation. SIAM J. Comput. **41**(5), 1235–1265 (2012)
9. Dolev, D., Lenzen, C., Peled, S.: "Tri, Tri Again": finding triangles and small subgraphs in a distributed setting. In: Aguilera, M.K. (ed.) DISC 2012. LNCS, vol. 7611, pp. 195–209. Springer, Heidelberg (2012)
10. Drucker, A., Kuhn, F., Oshman, R.: On the power of the congested clique model. In: Proceedings of PODC 2014, pp. 367–376 (2014)
11. Elkin, M.: An unconditional lower bound on the time-approximation trade-off for the distributed minimum spanning tree problem. SIAM J. Comput. **36**(2), 433–456 (2006)
12. Fraigniaud, P., Göös, M., Korman, A., Suomela, J.: What can be decided locally without identifiers? In: Proceedings of PODC 2013, pp. 157–165 (2013)
13. Fraigniaud, P., Korman, A., Peleg, D.: Local distributed decision. In: Proceedings of FOCS 2011, pp. 708–717 (2011)
14. Fraigniaud, P., Rajsbaum, S., Travers, C.: Locality and checkability in wait-free computing. Distrib. Comput. **26**(4), 223–242 (2013)
15. Fraigniaud, P., Rajsbaum, S., Travers, C.: On the number of opinions needed for fault-tolerant run-time monitoring in distributed systems. In: Bonakdarpour, B., Smolka, S.A. (eds.) RV 2014. LNCS, vol. 8734, pp. 92–107. Springer, Heidelberg (2014)
16. Goldreich, O. (ed.): Property Testing. LNCS, vol. 6390. Springer, Heidelberg (2010)
17. Goldreich, O., Goldwasser, S., Ron, D.: Property testing and its connection to learning and approximation. J. ACM **45**(4), 653–750 (1998)
18. Göös, M., Jukka Suomela, J.: Locally checkable proofs. In: Proceedings of PODC 2011, pp. 159–168 (2011)
19. Hegeman, J.W., Pandurangan, G., Pemmaraju, S.V., Sardeshmukh, V.B., Scquizzato, M.: Toward optimal bounds in the congested clique: graph connectivity and MST. In: Proceedings of PODC 2015, pp. 91–100 (2015)
20. Hegeman, J.W., Pemmaraju, S.V., Sardeshmukh, V.B.: Near-constant-time distributed algorithms on a congested clique. In: Kuhn, F. (ed.) DISC 2014. LNCS, vol. 8784, pp. 514–530. Springer, Heidelberg (2014)
21. Kari, J., Matamala, M., Rapaport, I., Salo, V.: Solving the induced subgraphproblem in the randomized multiparty simultaneous messages model. In: Scheideler, C. (ed.) SIROCCO 2015. LNCS, vol. 9439, pp. 370–384. Springer, Heidelberg (2015)
22. Lenzen, C.: Optimal deterministic routing and sorting on the congested clique. In: Proceedings of PODC 2013, pp. 42–50 (2013)
23. Lotker, Z., Patt-Shamir, B., Peleg, D.: Distributed MST for constant diameter graphs. Distrib. Comput. **18**(6), 453–460 (2006)
24. Lotker, Z., Pavlov, E., Patt-Shamir, B., Peleg, D.: MST construction in $\mathcal{O}(\log \log n)$ communication rounds. In: Proceedings of SPAA 2003, pp. 94–100 (2003)
25. Mitzenmacher, M., Upfal, E.: Probability and Computing: Randomized Algorithms and Probabilistic Analysis. Cambridge University Press, Cambridge (2005)

26. Patt-Shamir, B., Teplitsky, M.: The round complexity of distributed sorting. In: Proceedings of PODC 2011, pp. 249–256 (2011)
27. Peleg, D.: Distributed Computing: A Locality-sensitive Approach. SIAM, Philadelphia (2000)
28. Reiter, F.: Distributed graph automata. In: Proceedings of LICS 2015, pp. 192–201 (2015)
29. Schoen, T., Shkredov, I.D.: Roth's theorem in many variables. Isr. J. Math. **199**(1), 287–308 (2014)

How to Discreetly Spread a Rumor in a Crowd

Mohsen Ghaffari[1] and Calvin Newport[2]([⊠])

[1] MIT CSAIL, Cambridge, MA, USA
`ghaffari@mit.edu`
[2] Georgetown University, Washington, D.C., USA
`cnewport@cs.georgetown.edu`

Abstract. In this paper, we study PUSH-PULL style rumor spreading algorithms in the *mobile telephone model*, a variant of the classical *telephone model* in which each node can participate in at most one connection per round; i.e., you can no longer have multiple nodes pull information from the same source in a single round. Our model also includes two new parameterized generalizations: (1) the network topology can undergo a bounded rate of change (for a parameterized rate that spans from no changes to changes in every round); and (2) in each round, each node can advertise a bounded amount of information to all of its neighbors before connection decisions are made (for a parameterized number of bits that spans from no advertisement to large advertisements). We prove that in the mobile telephone model with no advertisements and no topology changes, PUSH-PULL style algorithms perform poorly with respect to a graph's vertex expansion and graph conductance as compared to the known tight results in the classical telephone model. We then prove, however, that if nodes are allowed to advertise a single bit in each round, a natural variation of PUSH-PULL terminates in time that matches (within logarithmic factors) this strategy's performance in the classical telephone model—even in the presence of frequent topology changes. We also analyze how the performance of this algorithm degrades as the rate of change increases toward the maximum possible amount. We argue that our model matches well the properties of emerging peer-to-peer communication standards for mobile devices, and that our efficient PUSH-PULL variation that leverages small advertisements and adapts well to topology changes is a good choice for rumor spreading in this increasingly important setting.

1 Introduction

Imagine the following scenario. Members of your organization are located throughout a crowded conference hall. You know a rumor that you want to spread to all the members of your organization, but you do not want anyone else in the hall to learn it. To maintain discreetness, communication occurs only through whispered one-on-one conversations held between pairs of nearby members of

This work is supported in part by NSF grant number CCF 1320279.

C. Gavoille and D. Ilcinkas (Eds.): DISC 2016, LNCS 9888, pp. 357–370, 2016.
DOI: 10.1007/978-3-662-53426-7_26

your organization. In more detail, time proceeds in rounds. In each round, each member of your organization can attempt to initiate a whispered conversation with a single nearby member in the conference hall. To avoid drawing attention, each member can only whisper to one person per round. In this paper, we study how quickly simple random strategies will propagate your rumor in this imagined crowded conference hall scenario.

The Classical Telephone Model. At first encounter, the above scenario seems mappable to the well-studied problem of rumor spreading in the classical *telephone model*. In more detail, the telephone model describes a network topology as a graph $G = (V, E)$ of size $n = |V|$ with a computational process (called *nodes* in the following) associated with each vertex in V. In this model, an edge $\{u, v\} \in E$ indicates that node u can communicate directly with node v. Time proceeds in rounds. In each round, each node can initiate a *connection* (e.g., place a telephone call) with a neighbor in G through which the two nodes can then communicate.

There exists an extensive literature on the performance of a random rumor spreading strategy called PUSH-PULL in the telephone model under different graph assumptions; e.g., [2,8–10]. The PUSH-PULL algorithm works as follows: *in each round, each node connects to a neighbor selected with uniform randomness; if exactly one node in the connection is informed (knows the rumor) and one node is uninformed (does not know the rumor), then the rumor is spread from the informed to the uninformed node.* An interesting series of papers culminating only recently established that PUSH-PULL terminates (with high probability) in $\Theta((1/\alpha) \log^2 n)$ rounds in graphs with vertex expansion α [9], and in $\Theta((1/\phi) \log n)$ rounds in graphs with graph conductance ϕ [8]. (see Sect. 3 for definitions of α and ϕ.)

It might be tempting to use these bounds to describe the performance of the PUSH-PULL strategy in our above conference hall scenario—*but they do not apply.* A well-known quirk of the telephone model is that a given node can accept an unbounded number of incoming connections in a single round. For example, if a node u has $n - 1$ neighbors initiate a connection in a given round, in the classical telephone model u is allowed to accept all $n - 1$ connections and communicate with all $n - 1$ neighbors in that round. In our conference hall scenario, by contrast, we enforce the natural assumption that each node can participate in at most one connection per round. (To share the rumor to multiple neighbors at once might attract unwanted attention.) The existing analyses of PUSH-PULL in the telephone model, which depend on the ability of nodes to accept multiple incoming connections, do not carry over to this bounded connection setting.

The Mobile Telephone Model. In this paper, we formalize our conference hall scenario with a variant of the telephone model we call the *mobile telephone model*. Our new model differs from the classical version in that it now limits each node to participate in at most one connection per round. We also introduce two new parameterized properties. The first is *stability*, which is described with an integer $\tau > 0$. For a given τ, the network topology must remain stable for intervals of at least τ rounds before changing. The second property is *tag length*, which is described with an integer $b \geq 0$. For a given b, at the beginning of each round, each node is allowed to publish an *advertisement* containing b bits that is visible to its neighbors. Notice, for $\tau = \infty$ and $b = 0$, the mobile telephone model exactly describes the conference hall scenario that opened this paper.

Our true motivation for introducing this model, of course, is not just to facilitate covert cavorting at conferences. We believe it fits many emerging peer-to-peer communication technologies better than the classical telephone model. In particular, in the massively important space of mobile wireless devices (e.g., smartphones, tablets, networked vehicles, sensors), standards such as Bluetooth LE, WiFi Direct, and the Apple Multipeer Connectivity Framework, all depend on a *scan-and-connect* architecture in which devices scan for nearby devices before attempting to initiate a reliable unicast connection with a single neighbor. This architecture does not support a given device concurrently connecting with many nearby devices. Furthermore, this scanning behavior enables the possibility of devices adding a small number of advertisement bits to their publicly visible identifiers (as we capture with our tag length parameter), and mobility is fundamental (as we capture with our graph stability parameter).

Results. In this paper, we study rumor spreading in the mobile telephone model under different assumptions regarding the connectivity properties of the graph as well as the values of model parameters τ and b. All upper bound results described below hold with high probability in the network size n.

We begin, in Sect. 5, by studying whether α and ϕ still provide useful upper bounds on the efficiency of rumor spreading once we move from the classical to mobile telephone model. We first prove that offline optimal rumor spreading terminates in $O((1/\alpha)\log n)$ rounds in the mobile telephone model in any graph with vertex expansion α. It follows that it is *possible*, from a graph theory perspective, for a simple distributed rumor spreading algorithm in the mobile telephone model to match the performance of PUSH-PULL in the classical telephone model. (The question of whether simple strategies *do* match this optimal bound is explored later in the paper.) At the core of this analysis are two ideas: (1) the size of a maximum matching bridging a set of informed and uninformed nodes at a given round describes the maximum number of new nodes that can be informed in that round; and (2) we can, crucially, bound the size of these matchings with respect to the vertex expansion of the graph. We later leverage both ideas in our upper bound analysis.

We then consider graph conductance and uncover a negative answer. In particular, we prove that offline optimal rumor spreading terminates in $O(\frac{\Delta}{\delta \cdot \phi} \log n)$ rounds in graphs with conductance ϕ, maximum degree Δ, and minimum degree δ. We also prove that there exist graphs where $\Omega(\frac{\Delta}{\delta \cdot \phi})$ rounds are required. These results stand in contrast to the potentially much smaller upper bound of $O((1/\phi)\log n)$ for PUSH-PULL in the classical telephone model. In other words, once we shift from the classical to mobile telephone model, conductance no longer provides a useful upper bound on rumor spreading time.

In Sect. 6, we turn our attention to studying the behavior of the PUSH-PULL algorithm in the mobile telephone model with $b = 0$ and $\tau = \infty$.[1] Our goal is to determine whether this standard strategy approaches the optimal bounds from Sect. 5. For the case of vertex expansion, we provide a negative answer by constructing a graph with constant vertex expansion α in which PUSH-PULL requires $\Omega(\sqrt{n})$ rounds to terminate. Whether there exists *any* distributed rumor spreading algorithm that can approach optimal bounds with respect to vertex expansion under these assumptions, however, remains an intriguing open question. For the case of graph conductance, we note that a consequence of a result from [4] is that PUSH-PULL in this setting comes within a log factor of the (slow) $O(\frac{\Delta}{\delta \cdot \phi} \log n)$ optimal bound proved in Sect. 5. In other words, in the mobile telephone model rumor spreading might be slow with respect to a graph's conductance, but PUSH-PULL matches this slow spreading time.

Finally, in Sect. 7, we study PUSH-PULL in the mobile telephone model with $b = 1$. In more detail, we study the natural variant of PUSH-PULL in this setting in which nodes use their 1-bit tag to advertise at the beginning of each round whether or not they are informed. We assume that informed nodes select a neighbor in each round uniformly from the set of their uninformed neighbors (if any). We call this variant *productive PUSH* (PPUSH) as nodes only attempt to push the rumor toward nodes that still need the rumor.

Notice, in the classical telephone model, the ability to advertise your informed status trivializes rumor spreading as it allows nodes to implement a basic flood (uninformed nodes pull only from informed neighbors)—which is clearly optimal. In the mobile telephone model, by contrast, the power of $b = 1$ is not obvious: a given informed node can only communicate with (at most) a single uninformed neighbor per round, and it cannot tell in advance which such neighbor might be most useful to inform.

Our primary result in this section, which provides the primary upper bound contribution of this paper, is the following: in the mobile telephone model with $b = 1$ and stability parameter $\tau \geq 1$, PPUSH terminates in $O((1/\alpha)\Delta^{\frac{1}{r}} r \log^3 n)$ rounds, where $r = \min\{\tau, \log \Delta\}$. In other words, for $\tau \geq \log \Delta$, PPUSH terminates in $O((1/\alpha) \log^4 n)$ rounds, matching (within log factors) the performance of the optimal algorithm in the mobile telephone model *and* the performance of PUSH-PULL in the classical telephone model. An interesting implication of this result is that the power gained by allowing nodes to advertise whether or not they know the rumor outweighs the power lost by limiting nodes to a single connection per round.

As the stability of the graph decreases from $\tau = \log \Delta$ toward $\tau = 1$, the performance of PPUSH is degraded by a factor of $\Delta^{1/\tau}$. At the core of this result is a novel analysis of randomized approximate distributed maximal matchings in bipartite graphs, which we combine with the results from Sect. 5 to connect the approximate matchings generated by our algorithm to the graph vertex

---

[1] As we detail in Sect. 6, there are several natural modifications we must make to PUSH-PULL for it to operate as intended under the new assumptions of the mobile telephone model.

expansion. We note that it is not *a priori* obvious that mobility makes rumor spreading more difficult. It remains an open question, therefore, as to whether this $\Delta^{1/\tau}$ factor is an artifact of our analysis or a reflection of something fundamental about changing topologies.

Returning to the Conference Hall. The PPUSH algorithm enables us to tackle the question that opens the paper: *What is a good way to discreetly spread a rumor in a crowd?* One answer, we now know, goes as follows. If you know the rumor, randomly choose a nearby member that does not know the rumor and attempt to whisper it in their ear. When you do, also instruct them to make some visible sign to indicate to their neighborhood that they are now informed; e.g., "turn your conference badge upside down". (This signal can be agreed upon in advance or decided by the source and spread along with the rumor.) This simple strategy—which effectively implements PPUSH in the conference hall— will spread the rumor fast with respect to the crowd topology's vertex expansion, and it will do so in a way that copes elegantly and automatically to any level of encountered topology changes. More practically speaking, we argue that in the new world of mobile peer-to-peer networking, something like PPUSH is probably the right primitive to use to spread information efficiently through an unknown and potentially changing network.

2   Related Work

The telephone model described above was first introduced by Frieze and Grimmett [6]. A key problem in this model is *rumor spreading*: a rumor must spread from a single source to the whole network. In studying this problem, algorithmic simplicity is typically prioritized over absolute optimality. The PUSH algorithm (first mentioned [6]), for example, simply has every node with the message choose a neighbor with uniform randomness and send it the message. The PULL algorithm (first mentioned [3]), by contrast, has every node without the message choose a neighbor with uniform randomness and ask for the message. The PUSH-PULL algorithm combines those two strategies. In a complete graph, both PUSH and PULL complete in $O(\log n)$ rounds, with high probability—leveraging epidemic-style spreading behavior. Karp et al. [11] proved that the average number of connections per node when running PUSH-PULL in the complete graph is bounded at $\Theta(\log \log n)$.

In recent years, attention has turned toward studying the performance of PUSH-PULL with respect to graph properties describing the connectedness or expansion characteristics of the graph. One such measure is *graph conductance*, denoted ϕ, which captures, roughly speaking, how well-knit together is a given graph. A series of papers produced increasingly refined results with respect to ϕ, culminating in the 2011 work of Giakkoupis [8] which established that PUSH-PULL terminates in $O((1/\phi) \log n)$ rounds with high probability in graphs with conductance ϕ. This bound is tight in the sense that there exist graphs with this diameter and conductance ϕ. Around this same time, Chierichetti et al. [2] motivated and initiated the study of PUSH-PULL with respect to the graphs vertex expansion number, α, which measures its expansion characteristics. Follow-up work by Giakkoupis and Sauerwald [10] proved that there exist graphs with expansion α where $\Omega((1/\alpha) \log^2 n)$ rounds are necessary for PUSH-PULL to terminate, and that PUSH alone achieves this time in regular graphs. Fountoulakis et al. [5] proved that PUSH performs better—in this case, $O((1/\alpha) \log n)$ rounds—given even stronger expansion properties. A 2014 paper by Giakkoupis [9] proved a matching bound of $O((1/\alpha) \log^2 n)$ for PUSH-PULL in any graph with expansion α.

Recent work by Daum et al. [4] emphasized the shortcoming of the telephone model mentioned above: it allows a single node to accept an unlimited number of incoming connections. They study a restricted model in which each node can only accept a single connection per round. We emphasize that the mobile telephone model with $b = 0$ and $\tau = \infty$ is equivalent to the model of [4].[2] This existing work proves the existence of graphs where PULL works in polylogarithmic time in the classical telephone model but requires $\Omega(\sqrt{n})$ rounds in their bounded variation. They also prove that in any graph with maximum degree Δ and minimum degree δ, PUSH-PULL completes in $O(\mathcal{T} \cdot \frac{\Delta}{\delta} \cdot \log n)$ rounds, where $\mathcal{T}$ is the performance of PUSH-PULL in the classical telephone model. Our work picks up where [4] leaves off by: (1) studying the relationship between rumor spreading and graph properties such as α and ϕ under the assumption of bounded connections; (2) leveraging small advertisement tags to identify simple strategies that close the gap with the classical telephone model results; and (3) considering the impact of topology changes.

Finally, from a centralized perspective, Baumann et al. [1] proved that in a model similar to the mobile telephone model with $b = 1$ and $\tau = \infty$ (i.e., a model where you can only connect with a single neighbor per round but can learn the informed status of all neighbors in every round) there exists no PTAS for computing the worst-case rumor spreading time for a PUSH-PULL style strategy in a given graph.

3   Preliminaries

We will model a network topology with a connected undirected graph $G = (V, E)$. For each $u \in V$, we use $N(u)$ to describe u's neighbors and $N^+(u)$ to describe $N(u) \cup \{u\}$. We define $\Delta = \max_{u \in V}\{|N(u)|\}$ and $\delta = \min_{u \in V}\{|N(u)|\}$. For a given node $u \in V$, define $d(u) = |N(u)|$. For given set $S \subseteq V$, define $vol(S) = \sum_{u \in S} d(u)$ and let $cut(S, V \setminus S)$ describe the number of edges with one endpoint in S and one endpoint in $V \setminus S$. As in [8], we define the *graph*

---

[2] There are some technicalities in this statement. A key property of the model from [4] is how concurrent connection attempts are resolved. They study the case where the successful connection is chosen randomly and the case where it is chosen by an adversary. In our model, we assume the harder case of multiple connections being resolved arbitrarily.

conductance ϕ of a given graph $G = (V, E)$ as follows:

$$\phi = \min_{S \subseteq V, 0 < vol(S) \leq vol(V)/2} \frac{cut(S, V \setminus S)}{vol(S)}.$$

For a given $S \subseteq V$, define the *boundary* of S, indicated ∂S, as follows: $\partial S = \{v \in V \setminus S : N(v) \cap S \neq \emptyset\}$: that is, ∂S is the set of nodes not in S that are directly connected to S by an edge. We define $\alpha(S) = |\partial S|/|S|$. As in [9], we define the *vertex expansion* α of a given graph $G = (V, E)$ as follows:

$$\alpha = \min_{S \subset V, 0 < |S| \leq n/2} \alpha(S).$$

Notice that, despite the possibility of $\alpha(S) > 1$ for some S, we always have $\alpha \in [0, 1]$. Our model defined below sometimes considers a *dynamic graph* which can change from round to round. Formally, a dynamic graph $\mathcal{G}$ is a sequence of static graphs, $G_1 = (V, E_1), G_2 = (V, E_2), \ldots$. When using a dynamic graph $\mathcal{G}$ to describe a network topology, we assume the rth graph in the sequence describes the topology during round r. We define the vertex expansion of a dynamic graph $\mathcal{G}$ to be the minimum vertex expansion over all of $\mathcal{G}$'s constituent static graphs, and the graph conductance of $\mathcal{G}$ to be the minimum graph conductance over $\mathcal{G}$'s static graphs. Similarly, we define the maximum and minimum degree of a dynamic graph to be the maximum and minimum degrees defined over all its static graphs.

Finally, we state a pair of well-known inequalities that will prove useful in several places below:

Fact 1. *For $p \in [0, 1]$, we have $(1 - p) \leq e^{-p}$ and $(1 + p) \geq 2^p$.*

4   Model and Problem

We introduce a variation of the classical telephone model we call the *mobile telephone model*. This model describes a network topology in each round as an undirected connected graph $G = (V, E)$. We assume a computational process (called a *node*) is assigned to each vertex in V. Time proceeds in synchronized rounds. At the beginning of each round, we assume each node u knows its neighbor set $N(u)$. Node u can then select at most one node from $N(u)$ and send a connection proposal. A node that sends a proposal cannot also receive a proposal. However, if a node v does not send a proposal, and at least one neighbor sends a proposal to v, then v can select at most one incoming proposal to accept. (A slightly stronger variation of this model is that the accepted proposal is selected arbitrarily by an adversarial process and not by v. Our algorithms work for this strong variation and our lower bounds hold for the weaker variation.) If node v accepts a proposal from node u, the two nodes are *connected* and can perform an unbounded amount of communication in that round.

We parameterize the mobile telephone model with two integers, $b \geq 0$ and $\tau \geq 1$. If $b > 0$, then we allow each node to select a *tag* containing b bits to advertise at the beginning of each round. That is, if node u chooses tag b_u at the beginning of a round, all neighbors of u learn b_u before making their connection decisions in this round. We also allow for the possibility of the network topology changing, which we formalize by describing the network topology with a dynamic graph $\mathcal{G}$. We bound the allowable changes in $\mathcal{G}$ with a *stability* parameter τ. For a given τ, $\mathcal{G}$ must satisfy the property that we can partition it into intervals of length τ, such that all τ static graphs in each interval are the same.[3] For $\tau = 1$, the graph can change every round. We use the convention of stating $\tau = \infty$ to indicate the graph never changes.

In the mobile telephone model we study the *rumor spreading problem*, defined as follows: A single distinguished source begins with a *rumor* and the problem is solved once all nodes learn the rumor.

5   Rumor Spreading with Respect to Graph Properties

As summarized above, a series of recent papers established that in the classical telephone model PUSH-PULL terminates with high probability in $\Theta((1/\alpha)\log^2 n)$ rounds in graphs with vertex expansion α, and in $\Theta((1/\phi)\log n)$ rounds in graphs with graph conductance ϕ. The question we investigate here is the relationship between α and ϕ and the optimal offline rumor spreading time in the mobile telephone model. That is, we ask: once we bound connections, do α and ϕ still provide a good indicator of how fast a rumor can spread in a graph? The missing proofs for this section can be found in the full version of this paper [7].

5.1   Optimal Rumor Spreading for a Given Vertex Expansion

Our goal is to prove the following property regarding optimal rumor spreading in our model and its relationship to the graph's vertex expansion:

Theorem 1. *Fix some connected graph G with vertex expansion α. The optimal rumor spreading algorithm terminates in $O((1/\alpha)\log n)$ rounds in G in the mobile telephone model.*

In other words, it is at least theoretically possible to spread a rumor in the mobile telephone model as fast (with respect to α) as PUSH-PULL in the easier classical telephone model. In the analysis below, assume a fixed connected graph $G = (V, E)$ with vertex expansion α and $|V| = n$.

Connecting Maximum Matchings to Rumor Spreading. The core difference between our model and the classical telephone model is that now each node

---

[3] Our algorithms work for many different natural notions of stability. For example, it is sufficient to guarantee that in each such interval the graph is stable with constant probability, or that given a constant number of such intervals, at least one contains no changes, etc. The definition used here was selected for analytical simplicity.

can only participate in at most one connection per round. Unlike in the classical telephone model, therefore, the set of connections in a given round must describe a matching. To make this more concrete, we first define some notation. In particular, given some $S \subset V$, let $B(S)$ be the bipartite graph with bipartitions $(S, V \setminus S)$ and the edge set $E_S = \{(u, v) : (u, v) \in E, u \in S, \text{and } v \in V \setminus S\}$. Also recall that the *edge independence number* of a graph H, denoted $\nu(H)$, describes the maximum matching on H. We can now formalize our above claim as follows:

Lemma 1. *Fix some $S \subset V$. The maximum number of concurrent connections between nodes in S and $V \setminus S$ in a single round is $\nu(B(S))$.*

We can connect the smallest such maximum matchings in our graph G to the optimal rumor spreading time. Our proof of the following lemma combines the connection between matchings and rumor spreading captured in Lemma 1, with the same high-level analysis structure deployed in existing studies of rumor spreading and vertex expansion in the classical telephone model (e.g., [9]):

Lemma 2. *Let $\gamma = \min_{S \subset V, |S| \leq n/2} \{\nu(B(S))/|S|\}$. It follows that optimal rumor spreading in G terminates in $O((1/\gamma) \log n)$ rounds.*

Connecting Maximum Matching Sizes to Vertex Expansion. Given Lemma 2, to connect rumor spreading time to vertex expansion in our mobile telephone model, it is sufficient to bound maximum matching sizes with respect to α. In particular, we will now argue that $\gamma \geq \alpha/4$ (the details of this constant factor do not matter much; 4 happened to be convenient for the below argument). Theorem 1 follows directly from the below result combined with Lemma 2.

Lemma 3. *Let $\gamma = \min_{S \subset V, |S| \leq n/2} \{\nu(B(S))/|S|\}$. It follows that $\gamma \geq \alpha/4$.*

Proof. We can restate the lemma equivalently as follows: *for every $S \subset V$, $|S| \leq n/2$, the maximum matching on $B(S)$ is of size at least $(\alpha|S|)/4$.* We will prove this equivalent formulation.

To start, fix some arbitrary subset $S \subset V$ such that $|S| \leq n/2$. Let m be the size of a maximum matching on $B(S)$. Recall that $\alpha \leq \alpha(S) = |\partial S|/|S|$. Therefore, if we could show that $|\partial S| \leq 4m$, we would be done. Unfortunately, it is easy to show that this is not always the case. Consider a partition S in which a single node $u \in S$ is connected to large number of nodes in $V \setminus S$, and these are the only edges leaving S. The vertex expansion in this example is large while the maximum matching size is only 1 (as all nodes in ∂S share u as an endpoint). To overcome this problem, we will, in some instances, instead consider a related smaller partition S' such that $\alpha(S') \geq \alpha$ is small enough to ensure our needed property. In more detail, we consider two cases regarding the size of m:

The *first case* is that $m \geq |S|/2$. By definition, $\alpha \leq 1$. It follows that $m \geq (|S|\alpha)/2$, which more than satisfies our claim.

The *second (and more interesting) case* is that $m < |S|/2$. Let M be a maximum matching of size m for $B(S)$. Let M_S be the endpoints in M in S. We define a smaller partition $S' = S \setminus M_S$. Note, by the case assumption, $|S'| \geq |S|/2$.

We now argue that every node in $\partial S'$ is also in M. To see why, assume for contradiction that there exists some $v \in \partial S'$ that is not in M. Because $v \in \partial S'$, there must exist some edge (u, v), where $u \in S'$. Notice, however, because u is in S' it is not in M. If follows that we could have added (u, v) to our matching M defined on $B(S)$—contradicting the assumption that M is maximum. We have established, therefore, that $|\partial S'| \leq 2m$. It follows:

$$\alpha \leq \alpha(S') \leq 2m/|S'| = 2m/(|S| - m) \overset{(m < |S|/2)}{<} \frac{2m}{|S|/2} = (4m)/|S|,$$

from which it follows that $\alpha|S| < 4m \Rightarrow m > (\alpha|S|)/4$, as needed.

5.2   Optimal Rumor Spreading for a Given Graph Conductance

In the classical telephone model PUSH-PULL terminates in $O((1/\phi)\log n)$ rounds in a graph with conductance ϕ. Here we prove optimal rumor spreading might be much slower in the mobile telephone model. To establish the intuition for this result, consider a star graph with one center node and $n - 1$ points. It is straightforward to verify that the conductance of this graph is constant. But it is also easy to verify that at most one point can learn the rumor per round in the mobile telephone model, due to the restriction that each node (including the center of the star) can only participate in one connection per round. In this case, every rumor spreading algorithm will be a factor of $\Omega(n/\log n)$ slower than PUSH-PULL in the classical telephone model. Below we formalize a fine-grained version of this result, parameterized with maximum and minimum degree of the graph. The proof for this theorem (found in the full version [7]) leverages Theorem 1 and a useful property from [9].

Theorem 2. *Fix some integers δ, Δ, such that $1 \leq \delta \leq \Delta$. There exists a graph G with minimum degree δ and maximum degree Δ, such that every rumor spreading algorithm requires $\Omega(\Delta/(\delta \cdot \phi))$ rounds in the mobile telephone model. In addition, for every graph with minimum degree δ and maximum degree Δ, the optimal rumor spreading algorithm terminates in $O(\Delta/(\delta \cdot \phi) \cdot \log n)$ rounds in the mobile telephone model.*

6   PUSH-PULL with $b = 0$

We now study the performance of PUSH-PULL in the mobile telephone model with $b = 0$ and $\tau = \infty$. We investigate its performance with respect to the optimal rumor spreading performance bounds from Sect. 5. In more detail, we consider the following natural variation of PUSH-PULL, adapted to our model:

> In even rounds, nodes that know the rumor choose a neighbor at random and attempt to establish a connection to PUSH the message. In odd rounds, nodes that do not know the rumor choose a neighbor at random and attempt to establish a connection to PULL the message.

We study this PUSH-PULL variant with respect to both graph conductance and vertex expansion. We begin by considering the performance of this algorithm with respect to graph conductance. Theorem 2 tells us that for any minimum and maximum degree δ and Δ, respectively, the optimal rumor spreading algorithm completes in $O(\Delta/(\delta \cdot \phi) \cdot \log n)$ rounds, and there are graphs where $\Omega(\Delta/\delta)$ rounds are necessary. Interestingly, as noted in Sect. 2, Daum et al. [4] proved that the above algorithm terminates in $O(\mathcal{T} \cdot \frac{\Delta}{\delta} \cdot \log n)$ rounds, where $\mathcal{T}$ is the optimal performance of PUSH-PULL in the classical telephone model. Because $\mathcal{T} \in O((1/\phi)\log n)$ in the classical setting, the above algorithm should terminate in $O(\frac{\Delta}{\delta \cdot \phi} \cdot \log^2 n)$ rounds in our model—nearly matching the bound from Theorem 2. Put another way, rumor spreading potentially performs poorly with respect to graph conductance, but PUSH-PULL with $b = 0$ nearly matches this poor performance.

Arguably, the more important optimal time complexity bound to match is the $O((1/\alpha)\log n)$ bound established in Theorem 1, as it is similar to the performance of PUSH-PULL in the telephone model. In the full version of this paper [7], however, we prove the following (motivating our subsequent investigation of the $b = 1$ case):

Lemma 4. *There is a graph G with constant vertex expansion, in which the above algorithm would need at least $\Omega(\sqrt{n})$ rounds to spread the rumor, with high probability.*

7 PUSH-PULL with $b = 1$

In the previous section, we established that PUSH-PULL in the mobile telephone model and $b = 0$ fails to match the optimal vertex expansion bound by a factor in $\Omega(\sqrt{n})$ in the worst case. Motivated by this shortcoming, we turn our attention to the setting where $b = 1$. In particular, we consider the following natural variant of PUSH-PULL adapted to our model with $b = 1$. We call this algorithm *productive PUSH* (or, PPUSH) as nodes leverage the 1-bit tag to advertise their informed status and therefore keep connections productive.[4]

> At the beginning of each round, each node uses a single bit to advertise whether or not it is *informed* (knows the rumor). Each informed node that has at least one uninformed neighbor, chooses an uninformed neighbor with uniform randomness and tries to form a connection to send it the rumor.

We now analyze PPUSH in a connected network G with vertex expansion α and stability factor $\tau \geq 1$. Our goal is to prove the following theorem:

---

[4] We drop the PULL behavior form PUSH-PULL in this algorithm description as it does not help the analysis. Focusing just on the PUSH behavior simplifies the algorithm even further.

Theorem 3. *Fix a dynamic network G of size n with vertex expansion α and stability factor at least τ, $1 \leq \tau \leq \log \Delta$. The PPUSH algorithm solves rumor spreading in G in $(1/\alpha)\Delta^{1/\tau}\tau \log^3 n$ rounds, with high probability in n.*

To prove this theorem, the core technical part is in studying the success of PPUSH over a stable period of τ rounds, which we summarize below. This analysis bounds the number of new nodes that receive the message in the stable period with respect to the size of the maximum matching defined over the informed and uninformed partitions at the beginning of the stable period. In the full version of this paper [7], we then connect this analysis back to the vertex expansion of the graph (leveraging our earlier analysis from Sect. 5 connecting α to edge independence numbers), and carry it through over multiple stable periods until we can show rumor spreading completes. The combination of these two steps provides the above theorem.

Matching Analysis. The main theorem for this analysis lower bounds the number of rumors that spread across a bipartite subgraph of the network over r stable rounds. Missing proofs below can be found in the full version [7].

Theorem 4. *Fix a bipartite graph G with bipartitions L and R, such $|R| \geq |L| = m$ and G has a matching of size m. Assume G is a subgraph of some (potentially) larger network G', and all uninformed neighbors in G' of nodes in L are also in R. Fix an integer r, $1 \leq r \leq \log \Delta$, where Δ is the maximum degree of G. Consider an r round execution of PPUSH in G' in which the nodes in L start with the rumor and the nodes in R do not. With constant probability: at least $\Omega(\frac{m\Delta^{-1/r}}{r \log n})$ nodes in R learn the rumor.*

We start with some helpful notation. For any $L' \subseteq L$ and $R' \subseteq R$, let $G(L', R')$ be the subgraph of G induced by the nodes L' and R'. Similarly, let $N_{L',R'}$ and $deg_{L',R'}$ be the neighbor and degree functions, respectively, defined over $G(L', R')$.

We begin with the special case $r = 1$. We then move to our main analysis which handles all $r \geq 2$. (Notice, our result below $r = 1$ provides an approximation of $O(\sqrt{\Delta \log \Delta})$ which is tighter than the Δ approximation for this case claimed by Theorem 4. We could refine the theorem claim to more tightly capture performance for small r, but we leave it in the looser more general form for the sake of concision in the result statement.)

Lemma 5. *For $r = 1$, PPUSH produces a matching of size $\Omega(m/\sqrt{\Delta \log \Delta})$, with constant probability.*

We start now the proof of the $r \geq 2$ case by making a claim that says if for a given large subset of L that has a relatively small degree sum, a couple rounds of the algorithm run on this subset will either generate a large enough matching, or leave behind a subset with an even smaller degree sum.

Lemma 6. *Fix any $i \in [r]$, $L' \subseteq L$, and $R' \subseteq R$, such that: $|R'| \geq |L'| \geq m/16$; $\sum_{u \in L'} deg_{L',R'}(u) \leq m\Delta^{1-\frac{i-1}{r}}$; all uninformed neighbors of L' in G' are in R';*

and $G(L', R')$ has a matching of size $|L'|$. With high probability in n, one of the following two events will occur if we execute PPUSH with the nodes in L' knowing the rumor and the nodes in R' not knowing the rumor:

1. within two rounds, at least $\Omega(\frac{m\Delta^{-1/r}}{r\log n})$ nodes in R' learn the rumor; or
2. after one round, we can identify subsets $L'' \subseteq L'$, $R'' \subseteq R'$, with R'' containing only nodes that do not know the rumor, such that $|R''| \geq |L''| \geq (1 - 1/r)^2 \cdot |L'|$; $\sum_{u \in L''} \deg_{L'', R''}(u) \leq m\Delta^{1-\frac{i}{r}}$; R'' contains all uninformed neighbors of L'' nodes in G'; and $G(L'', R'')$ has a matching of size $|L''|$.

We now leverage Lemma 6 to prove Theorem 4. The following argument establishes a base case that satisfies the lemma preconditions of Lemma 6 and then repeatedly applies it r times. Either: (1) a matching of sufficient size is generated along the way (i.e., case 1 of the lemma statement applies); or (2) we begin round r with a set L' with size in $\Omega(m)$ that has an average degree in $\Theta(\Delta^{1/r})$—in which case it is easy to show that in the final round we get a matching of size $\Omega(\frac{m\Delta^{-1/r}}{r\log n})$.

Proof (of Theorem 4). Fix a bipartite graph G with bipartitions L and R with a matching of size $|L| = m$, and a value r, as specified by the theorem statement preconditions. If $r = 1$, the claim follows directly from Lemma 5. Assume in the following, therefore, that $r \geq 2$.

We claim that we can apply Lemma 6 to $L' = L$, $R' = R$, and $i = 1$. To see why, notice that this definition of L' satisfies the preconditions $L' \subseteq L$, $R' \subseteq R$, and $|R'| \geq |L'| \geq m/16$. It also satisfies the condition requiring all of the uninformed neighbors of L' to be in R'. Finally, because we fixed $i = 1$, it holds that: $\sum_{u \in L'} \deg_{L', R'}(u) \leq m\Delta^{1-\frac{i-1}{r}} = m\Delta$, as there are m nodes in L' each with a maximum degree of Δ.

Consider this first application of Lemma 6. It tells us that, w.h.p., either we finish after one or two rounds, or after a single round we identify a smaller bipartitate graph $G(L'', R'')$, where L'' and R'' satisfy all the properties needed to apply the Lemma to $L' = L''$, $R' = R''$, and $i = 2$. We can keep applying this lemma inductively, each time increasing the value of i, until either: (1) we get through $i = r - 1$; (2) an earlier application of the lemma generates a sufficiently large matching to satisfy the theorem; or (3) at some point before either option 1 or 2, the lemma fails to hold. Since the third possibility happens with probability polynomially small in n at each application, we can use a union bound and conclude that with high probability, it does not happen in any of the iterations. Ignoring this negligible probability, we focus on the other two possibilities.

Before that, let us discuss a small nuance in applying the lemma r times. We need to ensure that the specified L' sets are always of size at least $m/16$, as required to keep applying the lemma. Notice, however, that we start with an L' set of size m, and the lemma guarantees it decreases by a factor of at most $(1 - 1/r)^2$. Therefore, after $i < r \leq \log \Delta$ applications, $|L''| \geq (1 - 1/r)^{2i} \cdot m > (1/4)^{2i/r} \cdot m > (1/4)^2 \cdot m = m/16$.

Going back to the two possibilities, if option 2 holds, we are done. On the other hand, if option 1 holds, we have one final step in our argument. In this case, we end up with having identified a bipartite subgraph $G(L'', R'')$ with a maximum matching of size at least $|L''| \geq m/16$. We also know $\sum_{u \in L''} deg_{L'', R''}(u) \leq m\Delta^{1 - \frac{i}{r}} = m\Delta^{1/r}$ as $i = r - 1$. In this case, it holds trivially that at most $m/32$ nodes u of L'' have $deg_{L'', R''}(u) \geq 32\Delta^{1/r}$. Hence, at least $m/32$ nodes u have degree at most $32\Delta^{1/r}$. Now, each of these proposes to its own match in R'' with probability at least $\Delta^{-1/r}/32$. Thus, we expect $\Theta(m\Delta^{-1/r})$ nodes of R'' to receive proposals directly from their matches. Note that these events are independent. Moreover, we have $m\Delta^{-1/r} = \Omega(\log n)$ as otherwise the claim of the theorem would be trivial. Therefore, w.h.p., $\Theta(m\Delta^{-1/r})$ nodes of R'' receive proposals from their pairs. Hence, at least $\Theta(m\Delta^{-1/r})$ nodes of R'' get informed, thus completing the proof.

References

1. Baumann, H., Fraigniaud, P., Harutyunyan, H.A., De Verclos, R.: The worst case behavior of randomized gossip protocols. Theoret. Comput. Sci. **560**, 108–120 (2014)
2. Chierichetti, F., Lattanzi, S., Panconesi, A.: Rumour spreading and graph conductance. In: Proceedings of the ACM-SIAM Symposium on Discrete Algorithms (SODA) (2010)
3. Clarkson, T., Gorse, D., Taylor, J., Ng, C.: Epidemic algorithms for replicated database management. IEEE Trans. Comput. **1**, 52–61 (1992)
4. Daum, S., Kuhn, F., Maus, Y.: Rumor spreading with bounded in-degree. arXiv preprint arXiv:1506.00828 (2015)
5. Fountoulakis, N., Panagiotou, K.: Rumor spreading on random regular graphs and expanders. In: Serna, M., Shaltiel, R., Jansen, K., Rolim, J. (eds.) APPROX 2010. LNCS, vol. 6302, pp. 560–573. Springer, Heidelberg (2010)
6. Frieze, A.M., Grimmett, G.R.: The shortest-path problem for graphs with random arc-lengths. Discrete Appl. Math. **10**(1), 57–77 (1985)
7. Ghaffari, M., Newport, C.: How to discreetly spread a rumor in a crowd. http://people.cs.georgetown.edu/~cnewport/pubs/gn-disc2016.pdf. Also available on arXiv
8. Giakkoupis, G.: Tight bounds for rumor spreading in graphs of a given conductance. In: Proceedings of the Symposium on Theoretical Aspects of Computer Science (STACS) (2011)
9. Giakkoupis, G.: Tight bounds for rumor spreading with vertex expansion. In: Proceedings of the ACM-SIAM Symposium on Discrete Algorithms (SODA) (2014)
10. Giakkoupis, G., Sauerwald, T.: Rumor spreading and vertex expansion. In: Proceedings of the ACM-SIAM symposium on Discrete Algorithms (SODA), pp. 1623–1641. SIAM (2012)
11. Karp, R., Schindelhauer, C., Shenker, S., Vocking, B.: Randomized rumor spreading. In: Proceedings of the Annual Symposium on Foundations of Computer Science (FOCS), pp. 565–574 (2000)

Depth of a Random Binary Search Tree with Concurrent Insertions

James Aspnes[1(✉)] and Eric Ruppert[2(✉)]

[1] Yale University, New Haven, USA
james.aspnes@gmail.com
[2] York University, Toronto, Canada
ruppert@cse.yorku.ca

Abstract. Shuffle a deck of n cards numbered 1 through n. Deal out the first c cards into a hand. A player then repeatedly chooses one of the cards from the hand, inserts it into a binary search tree, and then adds the next card from deck to the hand (if the deck is empty). When the player finally runs out of cards, how deep can the search tree be?

This problem is motivated by concurrent insertions by c processes of random keys into a binary search tree, where the order of insertions is controlled by an adversary that can delay individual processes. We show that an adversary that uses any strategy based on comparing keys cannot obtain an expected average depth greater than $O(c + \log n)$. However, the adversary can obtain an expected tree height of $\Omega(c \log(n/c))$, using a simple strategy of always playing the largest available card.

1 Introduction

In the worst case, the height of a binary search tree (BST) can be linear in the number of keys that it stores. However, if the tree is constructed by inserting the keys one by one in a random order, then the average node depth, and even the height of the tree, will be logarithmic [9]. Here, we consider how much worse these measures become if insertions are performed concurrently by multiple processes. Consider the tree shown in Fig. 1. Suppose three processes wish to insert keys 12, 13 and 16 simultaneously. The processes will compete to insert their keys into the slot at the right child of the node containing key 11. The shape of the resulting tree depends upon which process succeeds first, and this can be determined by a number of system-dependent factors. For example, the scheduling of steps by different processes is affected by cache misses, timesharing and other events that are difficult to predict or analyze. This scheduling will, in turn, determine which process acquires a lock first (in a lock-based BST implementation) or performs a CAS first (in a CAS-based non-blocking BST implementation), and hence which insertion takes effect first. Similarly, in a transactional memory system, the order of insertions may depend on many details of the implementation of transactional memory that are outside the direct control of the BST insertion algorithm. Since the insertion algorithm has no control over these factors, if we wish to provide a worst-case analysis of the BST being constructed, we can imagine

© Springer-Verlag Berlin Heidelberg 2016
C. Gavoille and D. Ilcinkas (Eds.): DISC 2016, LNCS 9888, pp. 371–384, 2016.
DOI: 10.1007/978-3-662-53426-7_27

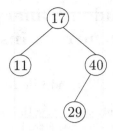

Fig. 1. An example binary search tree.

an adversary choosing which of the concurrent insertions occurs first. This will make our analysis sufficiently general to cover any kind of synchronization used to coordinate the insertions by different processes.

Thus, we consider the following experiment, in which c processes simultaneously insert n random keys into an initially empty BST. Fix an ordered universe U and a probability distribution on that universe. The c processes first choose c keys from U independently at random using this distribution. The c processes attempt to insert these c keys concurrently. The adversary chooses any one of the c values to become the root of the BST (by scheduling the corresponding process p so that it succeeds in installing that value at the root). Process p completes its insertion and draws the next key, again independently at random from the fixed probability distribution, and attempts to insert it. Once again, the adversary can choose any one of the c pending insertions to take effect next, and this procedure is repeated until all n keys have been inserted. We assume that the BST does not permit duplicate keys.

The adversarial scheduler is intended to model difficult-to-predict factors like cache misses or processes being interrupted by higher priority processes. These factors may depend on the memory addresses accessed by the processes, which may in turn depend on the relative order of the random keys chosen by the processes. Beyond this ordering information, the precise values of the keys chosen are unlikely to have any effect on the scheduling of processes. Thus, we assume the adversary is *comparison-based*: it decides which key to insert next based only on the relative order among the c keys of pending operations and the keys that have already been inserted.

As discussed in Mahmoud's monograph [9], if all keys are chosen independently at random from the same distribution, the resulting ranks of the keys form a random permutation of $\{1, \ldots, n\}$, where each permutation is equally likely. Since we consider only comparison-based adversaries, we can envision the concurrent construction of our random BST as follows. We start with an empty BST. We shuffle a deck of n cards labelled with keys 1 to n. The first c cards make up the adversary's initial hand. At each step, the adversary chooses one card to play from its hand, inserts that card's key into the BST and, if the deck is not yet empty, replaces the card by drawing the top card from the deck and adding it to the hand. We are interested in two measures of the resulting random

BST. The depth of a node is the number of edges along the path from the root to that node. The **average depth** is the sum of all the node depths divided by n. The **height** is the maximum of all node depths. Our goal is to establish bounds on the expected values of these measures, where the expected value is taken over all random permutations.

We show that the expected average depth is $O(c + \log n)$. This bound is tight within a constant factor: if the adversary always chooses the largest key among the pending insertions, the expected average depth will be $\Omega(c + \log n)$. Unlike the case of sequential insertions, we show that the expected height can be significantly larger than the average depth: we prove that the adversary that always chooses the largest key causes the expected height to be $\Omega(c \log(n/c))$.

2   Related Work

The height and average depth of randomly constructed BST has been extensively studied and is a classic problem in average-case complexity. Even the earliest papers [1,15] on BSTs included a discussion of the expected average depth of nodes in a tree built from random keys, showing that it is $O(\log n)$. Robson [13] showed that the expected height of a BST built by inserting a random permutation of $\{1, \ldots, n\}$ is at most $(4.311...) \log n + o(\log n)$. The constant factor was shown to be exact by Devroye [5]. Reed [12] proved an even tighter result, showing that the expected height is $(4.311...) \log n - (1.953...) \log \log n + O(1)$. The variance of the height is also known to be $O(1)$ [6,12]. More detailed information is known about the exact distribution of node depths in random trees. Mahmoud's monograph [9] provides an overview of many results of this area. The analysis of random trees constructed using deletions as well as insertions has had very limited success. There have been some empirical studies of this scenario, however (see [4]).

In our paper, we start with a random permutation and allow an adversary to reorder the permutation in a constrained way. A complementary scenario was considered by Manthey and Reischuk [10]: they instead begin with a permutation chosen by the adversary and then randomly perturb it (in a limited way) and analyze the expected height of the resulting BST.

Since BSTs play a central role in computer science, concurrent implementations of them are of great practical importance. If only insertions are supported, it is fairly trivial to implement a BST. For example, a non-blocking implementation can be designed using the compare-and-swap primitive as follows. To insert a key k, first search for the key k. We assume that duplicate keys are not permitted in the BST, so if the key k is found during this search, the insertion terminates without altering the tree. Otherwise, the search reaches a nil child pointer. The process then attempts to install a leaf containing k in place of that nil pointer. If CAS is available, a single CAS can effect this change. Alternatively, for a lock-based implementation, the process can acquire a lock for the child pointer, check that it is still nil, replace the nil pointer, and release the lock. If either of these ways of updating the tree fail (because another process has already replaced the nil pointer with a different non-nil value), then the insertion can simply continue searching down the tree from its current location and try again to insert the new key k. The standard algorithm to search for keys in a BST will work even if insertions are being done concurrently.

In the case of the CAS-based implementation described above, it is easy to see that the number of steps performed by an insertion is proportional to the depth of the node it eventually adds to the tree, since it does a constant amount of work at each step along the path to that node. Thus, the total number of steps to construct a random tree of n nodes is proportional to the sum of the node depths, which has expected value $O(n(c + \log n))$, according to our result. (The total number of CAS steps is $O(nc)$: each of the n successful CAS steps can cause at most one failed CAS step at each other process, for a total of $O(nc)$.)

Coordinating updates to the tree becomes considerably more difficult if deletions can also occur. Ensuring the BST is *balanced*, so that the height of the tree is logarithmic, adds significant additional complications to concurrent implementations of BSTs. Lock-based balanced BSTs have long been studied. As early as 1978, Guibas and Sedgewick [8] sketched a lock-based implementation when they introduced their balanced red-black trees. For a more up-to-date example, see Bronson et al.'s lock-based implementation of an AVL tree [2]. Ellen et al. [7] gave a non-blocking implementation of an unbalanced BST from CAS instructions. There have been several subsequent non-blocking BST implementations, including one that extends the scheme of [7] to yield a balanced BST [3], ensuring that the height is $O(c + \log n)$ whenever there are n keys in the tree and c pending operations on it. However, concurrent balanced trees are considerably more complex than unbalanced ones, and the tree rotation operations that are required to maintain balance incur a significant overhead. In applications where keys will be inserted in random order, our work suggests that this overhead and additional complexity can be avoided by using unbalanced trees without sacrificing good search times in the resulting BST.

3   Problem Statement

We are given a **deck** of n cards with unique keys from some ordered universe U, which are shuffled according to a uniform random permutation π. We start with an empty BST. At each step, a player (representing the adversary) chooses to insert into a BST one card from a **hand** consisting of the first c cards in the permutation that have not yet been inserted, or, if fewer than c cards remain, all remaining cards.

In making this decision, the player can only observe the cards in the hand and the tree; it cannot predict the order of the remaining cards in the deck. Cards already inserted in the tree or present in the hand at some step are called **dealt**; the remaining cards are called **undealt**.

A **play** consists of taking one card from the hand and inserting it into the tree. The game continues for n plays. We formalize the notion of a comparison-based adversary as follows. When deciding which card to play, the player can only observe the relative order of the dealt cards. In particular, if two permutations π

and π' produce the same relative order of their first t cards, then the play after t cards have been dealt will be from the same position in both π and π'. Note that the dealt cards at this time will always be the first t cards in the permutation π.

We have two measures of performance for an adversary strategy:

1. The **expected height** is the expected maximum depth of any node in the binary search tree after all n plays, where the expectation is taken over all choices of the permutation π.
2. The **expected average depth** of all nodes in the tree under the same conditions.

4   An Upper Bound on Expected Average Depth

In this section, we prove the following upper bound on the expected average depth of a random BST.

Theorem 1. *For every comparison-based adversary, the expected average depth of a random BST is $O(c + \log n)$.*

Proof. To simplify the argument, we assume that the player is deterministic. This means that when conditioning on various events we do not need to take into account any random choices made by the player. However, the argument applies equally well to a randomized player, as such a player can be described as a random mixture of deterministic players, and hence the expected average depth for a randomized player will be a weighted average of the expected average depths for various deterministic players.

Number the cards from 1 to n in the order they are dealt. Let A_{ij} be the indicator variable for the event that, in the final tree, card i is a proper ancestor of card j. Then the depth of j is exactly $\sum_i A_{ij}$, and the total depth of the tree is $\sum_j \sum_i A_{ij}$. Interchanging the summations gives $\sum_i \sum_j A_{ij}$, which shows that the total depth is equal to the sum of the number of proper descendants of each node. In the argument below, we will bound this sum instead, booking the expected number of proper descendants of a card i, conditioned on the information available to the player, as soon as it is inserted into the tree.

Let R be the order relation on the shuffled cards, so that $i <_R j$ means that the i-th card in the deck is less than the j-th card in the deck. Recall that we assume all $n!$ permutations of the deck are equally likely.

Define time t, for $c \le t \le n$, as the first time at which $t \ge c$ cards have been dealt, of which c are held in the player's hand and $t - c$ have already been inserted in the tree. We will define a supermartingale process that bounds the expected return to the player up to time n, and use a separate argument to handle the insertion of the last c cards. (See the appendix for background on supermartingales.)

Let R_t be the subrelation of R that includes only cards 1 through t. Since the player is comparison-based, R_t includes all information available to the player at time t. No new information is revealed to the player after time n, because the

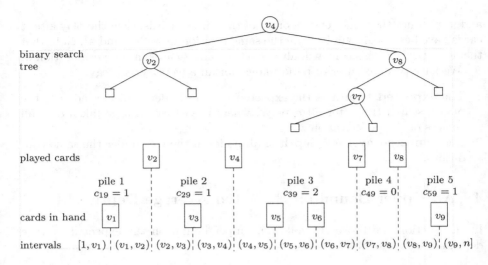

Fig. 2. An example when $t = 9$ and $c = 5$. The values on the cards are $v_1 < v_2 < \cdots < v_9$. 4 cards have been inserted into the tree and 5 cards are in the player's hand. The small squares in the tree represent nil pointers.

last of the n cards is dealt at time n. For any undealt card $j > t$, we have that all $(t + 1)!$ permutations of $\{1, \ldots, t, j\}$ are equally likely, and conditioning on R_t, we get that all $t + 1$ possible positions of j relative to cards $1, \ldots, t$ are equally likely. So the probability that j appears in each of these positions is $\frac{1}{t+1}$, and summing over all $n - t$ undealt cards gives an expected number of $\frac{n-t}{t+1}$ undealt cards in each of these positions.

We now look at the expected return to the player, in terms of the number of proper descendants, of playing a particular card at time $t < n$. Because the tree contains $t - c$ nodes, it has $t - c + 1$ null leaf pointers at which we might insert a new card. Let c_{kt}, the multiplicity of leaf k, be defined as the number of cards in the hand that would be inserted at k. We will refer to the set of these c_{kt} cards as the k-th pile at time t. See Fig. 2 for an example.

Suppose now that we insert one of these c_{kt} cards i_t at leaf k. Each of the remaining $c_{kt} - 1$ cards will eventually become a descendant of i_t. When $t \le n$, so will an average of $(c_{kt} + 1)\frac{n-t}{t+1}$ undealt cards. So for $t \le n$, we have

$$
\mathrm{E}\left[\sum_j A_{i_t j} \,\middle|\, R_t\right] = c_{kt} - 1 + (c_{kt} + 1)\frac{n - t}{t + 1}
$$

$$
= (c_{kt} + 1)\left(1 + \frac{n - t}{t + 1}\right) - 2
$$

$$
= (c_{kt} + 1)\frac{n + 1}{t + 1} - 2. \tag{1}
$$

One way to interpret (1) is that $(c_{kt} + 1)\frac{n+1}{t+1}$ is the expected number of leaf pointers in the final subtree rooted at i_t. Subtracting one gets the number of nodes in this subtree, and subtracting one again removes the subtree's root i_t to get the number of proper descendants.

The values of c_{kt} may evolve over time in a complex way as new cards are dealt and as the player chooses which cards to play based on the current state. We will track the effect of these choices using a shape function proportional to $\sum_k c_{kt}^2$ that will reflect the player's future ability to accrue expected descendants by playing cards from large piles.

Let c'_{kt} be the number of cards that can be inserted under the k-th leaf after i_t is inserted but before any new card is dealt. Playing a card splits c_{kt} into two new piles of size $c'_{k_1 t}$ and $c'_{k_2 t}$, where $c'_{k_1 t} + c'_{k_2 t} = c_{kt} - 1$; the remaining piles are unaffected, so that each $c_{\ell t}$ for a pile that does not contain i_t becomes $c'_{\ell' t}$ for some distinct ℓ'. After playing a card, replacing that card in the hand by dealing a new card adds one to each $c'_{\ell t}$ with probability $\frac{c'_{\ell t}+1}{t+1}$, since the new card is equally likely to fall into any of the $t + 1$ intervals shown at the bottom of Fig. 2.

Splitting c_{kt} into $c'_{k_1 t}$ and $c'_{k_2 t}$ reduces the sum of the squares by at least $2c_{kt} - 1$, since $(c'_{k_1 t})^2 + (c'_{k_2 t})^2 - c_{kt}^2 = (c'_{k_1 t})^2 + (c'_{k_2 t})^2 - (c'_{k_1 t} + c'_{k_2 t} + 1)^2 = -2c'_{k_1 t}c'_{k_2 t} - 2(c'_{k_1 t} + c'_{k_2 t} + 1) + 1 \le -(2c_{kt} - 1)$. Dealing a new card to pile ℓ increases the sum by $2c'_{\ell t} + 1$. So for $t < n$,

$$
\mathrm{E}\left[\sum_\ell c_{\ell,t+1}^2 - \sum_\ell c_{\ell t}^2 \;\middle|\; R_t\right]
$$

$$
\le -(2c_{kt} - 1) + \sum_\ell (2c'_{\ell t} + 1)\frac{c'_{\ell t} + 1}{t + 1}
$$

$$
= 1 - 2c_{kt} + \frac{2}{t+1}\left(\sum_\ell (c'_{\ell t})^2 + \sum_\ell c'_{\ell t}\right) + \sum_\ell \frac{c'_{\ell t} + 1}{t+1}
$$

$$
\le 1 - 2c_{kt} + \frac{2}{t+1}\left(\left(\sum_\ell c'_{\ell t}\right)^2 + \sum_\ell c'_{\ell t}\right) + \sum_\ell \frac{c'_{\ell t} + 1}{t+1}
$$

$$
= 1 - 2c_{kt} + \frac{2}{t+1}\left((c-1)^2 + (c-1)\right) + 1
$$

$$
= 2 - 2c_{kt} + \frac{2c(c-1)}{t+1}. \tag{2}
$$

We will now define a supermartingale process $X_c, X_{c+1} \ldots, X_n$ to bound the expected increase in $\sum_i \sum_j A_{ij}$ up to time n. In this context, the supermartingale property means that $X_t \ge \mathrm{E}[X_{t+1} \mid R_t]$ for all t, from which it can be shown by induction that $X_c \ge \mathrm{E}[X_n \mid R_c]$. We will structure this process so that X_c is a fixed bound and X_n always exceeds $\sum_i \sum_j A_{ij}$.

Let χ_{it} be the indicator variable for the event that the i-th card dealt from the deck is in the tree at time t. This decision is made based on values observable in R_{t-1}.

Define

$$X_t = U_t + V_t + W_t,$$

where

$$U_t = \sum_{i=1}^{n} \chi_{it} \mathrm{E}\left[\sum_{j=1}^{n} A_{ij} \,\middle|\, R_t\right]$$

is the expected total descendants of all nodes already inserted,

$$V_t = \frac{n+1}{2(t+1)} \sum_{\ell=1}^{t-c+1} c_{\ell t}^2$$

is a scaled version of the shape factor discussed above, that will offset changes to U_t that depend on which card is played at time t, and

$$W_t = \sum_{s=t}^{n-1} \left(2\frac{n+1}{s+1} - 2 + (n+1)\frac{c(c-1)}{(s+1)^2}\right).$$

pays for the total expected changes to U_t and V_t that do not depend on which card is played at time t.

Let us now demonstrate that $X_c, \ldots, X_n$ is in fact a supermartingale with respect to $R_c, \ldots, R_n$. We will start by considering U_{t+1}. Since $\chi_{i,t+1}$ is completely determined by R_t, we have

$$\mathrm{E}\left[U_{t+1} \mid R_t\right] = \sum_{i=1}^{n} \mathrm{E}\left[\chi_{i,t+1}\mathrm{E}\left[\sum_{j=1}^{n} A_{ij} \,\middle|\, R_{t+1}\right] \,\middle|\, R_t\right]$$

$$= \sum_{i=1}^{n} \chi_{i,t+1}\mathrm{E}\left[\mathrm{E}\left[\sum_{j=1}^{n} A_{ij} \,\middle|\, R_{t+1}\right] \,\middle|\, R_t\right]$$

$$= \sum_{i=1}^{n} \chi_{i,t+1}\mathrm{E}\left[\sum_{j=1}^{n} A_{ij} \,\middle|\, R_t\right]$$

$$= U_t + \mathrm{E}\left[\sum_{j=1}^{n} A_{i_t j} \,\middle|\, R_t\right]$$

$$= U_t + (c_{kt}+1)\frac{n+1}{t+1} - 2, \tag{3}$$

where k is the number of the pile that contains i_t. In the second-to-last step, we use the fact that only χ_{i_t} changes between t and $t+1$. The last step applies (1).

Now we turn to V_t. For $t < n$, use (2) to get

$$
\begin{aligned}
\mathrm{E}\left[V_{t+1} \mid R_t\right] &= \frac{n+1}{2(t+2)} \mathrm{E}\left[\sum_{\ell=1}^{t-c+2} c_{\ell,t+1}^2 \;\middle|\; R_t\right] \\
&< \frac{n+1}{2(t+1)} \mathrm{E}\left[\sum_{\ell=1}^{t-c+2} c_{\ell,t+1}^2 \;\middle|\; R_t\right] \\
&\leq \frac{n+1}{2(t+1)} \left(\sum_{\ell=1}^{t-c+1} c_{\ell t}^2 + 2 - 2c_{kt} + \frac{2c(c-1)}{t+1}\right) \\
&= V_t + \frac{n+1}{t+1} - c_{kt}\frac{n+1}{t+1} + (n+1)\frac{c(c-1)}{(t+1)^2}.
\end{aligned} \tag{4}
$$

When we add U_{t+1} and V_{t+1} together, the $c_{kt}\frac{n+1}{t+1}$ terms on the right-hand sides of (3) and (4) cancel out, so we are left with

$$
\mathrm{E}\left[U_{t+1} + V_{t+1} \mid R_t\right] < U_t + V_t + 2\frac{n+1}{t+1} - 2 + (n+1)\frac{c(c-1)}{(t+1)^2}. \tag{5}
$$

Since the extra terms on the right-hand side of (5) are precisely the value of $W_t - W_{t+1}$, we have $\mathrm{E}\left[X_{t+1} \mid R_t\right] = \mathrm{E}\left[U_{t+1} + V_{t+1} + W_{t+1} \mid R_t\right] < U_t + V_t + W_t = X_t$, and the supermartingale property holds. It follows that $\mathrm{E}\left[X_n\right] = \mathrm{E}\left[U_n + V_n + W_n\right] \leq U_c + V_c + W_c = X_c$.

Let us look now at U_n, V_n, and W_n. We have

$$
\begin{aligned}
U_n &= \sum_{i=1}^{n} \chi_{in} \mathrm{E}\left[\sum_{j=1}^{n} A_{ij} \;\middle|\; R_n\right] \\
&= \sum_{i=1}^{n} \chi_{in} \sum_{j=1}^{n} A_{ij}.
\end{aligned}
$$

This misses all pairs ij where i is among the c cards left in the hand at time n. However, at this point the remaining play of the game is purely deterministic, and it is straightforward to see that the player's optimal strategy is to play the cards under each leaf in increasing order, adding $\sum_{k=1}^{n-c+1} \binom{c_{kn}}{2} \leq \sum_{k=1}^{n-c+1} \frac{1}{2}c_{kn}^2 = V_n$ to the total. So we have $U_n + V_n \geq \sum_{ij} A_{ij}$. But $W_n = 0$, so this means $X_n \geq \sum_{ij} A_{ij}$.

Now let us return to the start of the process. At time c, we have $\chi_{ic} = 0$ for all i, so $U_c = 0$. We have only one $c_{\ell c}$, which equals c, so $V_c = \frac{(n+1)c^2}{2(c+1)} = O(cn)$.

Using $H(n)$ to denote the nth harmonic number,

$$W_c = \sum_{s=c}^{n-1} \left(2\frac{n+1}{s+1} - 2 + (n+1)\frac{c(c-1)}{(s+1)^2} \right)$$

$$< 2(n+1)\left(H(n) - H(c) \right) + (n+1) \cdot c(c-1) \cdot \int_{x=c}^{\infty} \frac{1}{x^2}dx$$

$$= O(n\log(n/c)) + (n+1) \cdot c(c-1) \cdot \frac{1}{c}$$

$$= O(cn + n\log n).$$

It follows that $\mathrm{E}\left[\sum_{ij} A_{ij} \right] \leq \mathrm{E}\left[X_n \right] \leq X_c = O(cn + n\log n)$. Dividing by n to convert the total to an average then gives the claimed bound. $\qquad\square$

4.1   A Matching Lower Bound

A simple strategy for the comparison-based adversary gets expected $\Omega(c + \log n)$ average depth, matching the bound in Theorem 1.

Theorem 2. *There is a comparison-based adversary that yields an expected average depth of $\Omega(c + \log n)$.*

Proof. Consider the comparison-based adversary that always inserts the largest card in its hand. Let m be the upper median in the initial hand of c cards (i.e., the $\lceil \frac{c+1}{2} \rceil$th smallest card in the hand). With probability at least $1/2$, there are at least $\lfloor n/2 \rfloor$ cards in the deck that are smaller than m. When this occurs, m is placed at depth at least $\lceil c/2 \rceil - 1$ and at least $\lfloor n/2 \rfloor$ keys are placed in the left subtree of m. Even if that subtree is perfectly balanced, the leaf nodes of that subtree alone have a total path length of at least $(n/4)(\lceil c/2 \rceil + \lfloor \log \lfloor n/2 \rfloor \rfloor - 1) = \Omega(n(c + \log n))$. So, with probability $1/2$, the average depth of all nodes will be at least $\Omega(c + \log n)$, and hence the expected average depth will also be $\Omega(c + \log n)$. $\qquad\square$

5   A Lower Bound on Expected Height

In this section, we show a lower bound on the expected height of a BST obtained by the particular adversary strategy that always plays the largest available card.

We first introduce some notation from the calculus of finite differences that will be useful in the proof. The **forward difference operator** Δf is defined by

$$\Delta f(k) = f(k+1) - f(k).$$

This operator satisfies the summation by parts formula,

$$\sum_{k=m}^{n} a(k)\Delta b(k)$$

$$= \sum_{k=m}^{n} a(k)b(k+1) - \sum_{k=m-1}^{n-1} a(k+1)b(k+1)$$

$$= a(n+1)b(n+1) - a(m)b(m) - \sum_{k=m}^{n} b(k+1)\Delta a(k). \qquad (6)$$

The **falling factorial** $(x)_c$ is defined by

$$(x)_c = x(x-1)(x-2)\dots(x-c+1).$$

Then, we have

$$
\begin{aligned}
\Delta(k-1)_c &= (k)_c - (k-1)_c \\
&= (k)(k-1)_{c-1} - (k-c)(k-1)_{c-1} \\
&= c(k-1)_{c-1}. \qquad (7)
\end{aligned}
$$

Theorem 3. *There is a comparison-based adversary strategy that yields a BST with expected height $\Omega(c\log(n/c))$.*

Proof. We consider the leftmost path in the BST, assuming the adversary always plays the largest available card. Let L_i be the value on the i-th card that appears in the leftmost path (starting from the root of the BST), and let X_i be the total number of cards whose values are strictly less than L_i (i.e., $X_i = L_i - 1$). Let $X_0 = n$. When the leftmost path has length i, then no card less than L_i has yet been played, and as long as the hand contains any card greater than L_i, playing this card does not increase the length of the leftmost path. It follows that the leftmost path increases only when the hand consists entirely of cards less than L_i, and that L_{i+1} is the largest of the $\min(c, X_i)$ cards present in the hand at this time.

This can be used to show that $H(X_i)$ does not drop too quickly on average, giving a lower bound on the expected length of the leftmost path. Here, $H(n)$ denotes the nth harmonic number, $H(n) = \sum_{i=1}^{n} \frac{1}{i}$.

We now consider the effect of playing a card less than L_i. Suppose the value of the random variable X_i is x. For any $k \le x$, the probability that c cards chosen uniformly without replacement from the x smallest cards are all at most k is exactly $(k)_c/(x)_c$, and the probability that the largest of these c cards is exactly k is $(k)_c/(x)_c - (k-1)_c/(x)_c = \Delta(k-1)_c/(x)_c$. Now let us compute, for $x \ge c$,

$$\Pr\left[X_{i+1} = k - 1 \mid X_i = x\right] = \Delta(k-1)_c/(x)_c, \text{for } c \le k \le x,$$

and

$$E[H(X_{i+1}) \mid X_i = x]$$

$$= \sum_{k=c}^{x} H(k-1)\Delta(k-1)_c/(x)_c$$

$$= \frac{1}{(x)_c}\left(H(x)(x)_c - H(c-1)(c-1)_c - \sum_{k=c}^{x}(k)_c\Delta H(k-1)\right) \quad \text{by (6)}$$

$$= H(x) - \frac{1}{(x)_c}\cdot\sum_{k=c}^{x}\frac{(k)_c}{k}$$

$$= H(x) - \frac{1}{(x)_c}\cdot\sum_{k=c}^{x}(k-1)_{c-1}$$

$$= H(x) - \frac{1}{(x)_c}\cdot\sum_{k=c}^{x}\frac{\Delta(k-1)_c}{c} \quad \text{by (7)}$$

$$= H(x) - \frac{1}{c\cdot(x)_c}((x)_c - (c-1)_c)$$

$$= H(x) - \frac{1}{c}.$$

Let $Y_i = H(X_i) + i/c$. Then

$$E[Y_{i+1} \mid X_0,\ldots,X_i] = E[H(X_{i+1}) \mid X_0,\ldots,X_i] + \frac{i+1}{c}$$

$$= H(X_i) - \frac{1}{c} + \frac{i+1}{c}$$

$$= H(X_i) + \frac{i}{c}$$

$$= Y_i$$

The remainder of the proof uses martingales, which are described in the appendix. The sequence $\{Y_i\}$ is a martingale with respect to $\{X_i\}$. Let τ be the first index at which $X_\tau \leq c - 1$. Then τ is not only a lower bound on the depth of the tree, but is also a stopping time with respect to $\{X_i\}$. It follows from Doob's Optional Stopping Theorem that $E[Y_\tau] = E[Y_0] = H(n)$. So, we have $H(n) = E[Y_\tau] = E[H(X_\tau) + \tau/c] = E[H(X_\tau)] + E[\tau]/c$. Solving for $E[\tau]$ gives $E[\tau] = c(H(n) - E[H(X_\tau)]) \geq c(H(n) - H(c-1)) = c\sum_{k=c}^{n}\frac{1}{k} = \Omega(c\log(n/c))$. □

6   Conclusion

We considered a node-oriented (or internal) BST, where keys are stored both in internal nodes and leaves. Some concurrent implementations of BSTs are based on leaf-oriented (or external) BSTs, where the keys are stored only in the leaves, and internal nodes are used only to direct searches to the appropriate leaf. Our height lower bound extends to leaf-oriented trees. It would be interesting to see whether our average depth upper bound does too.

Although the comparison-based adversaries discussed here are intended to model schedulers accurately (and pessimistically), it might be interesting to see whether even stronger malicious adversaries could force the height or average depth of random trees to grow higher by using the actual values of the keys. For example, if keys are drawn uniformly at random from the interval $[0, 1]$, and the initial hand consisted of $c = 3$ cards labelled with $0.03, 0.45$ and 0.54, the adversary would be better off choosing 0.03 as the root to ensure a more lopsided tree, whereas if the initial hand contained 0.46, 0.55 and 0.97 the adversary should choose 0.97 as the root.

Acknowledgements. Funding for the second author was provided by the Natural Sciences and Engineering Research Council of Canada.

A   Background on Martingales

Here, for the sake of completeness, we present background information about martingales that is used in our paper, following the presentation of Mitzenmacher and Upfal's textbook [11].

We say that a sequence $Y_0, Y_1, \ldots$ of random variables is a **martingale** with respect to another sequence $X_0, X_1, \ldots$ of random variables if for all $n \geq 0$

- Y_n is a function of $X_0, X_1, \ldots, X_n$,
- $E[|Y_n|] < \infty$, and
- $E[Y_{n+1} \mid X_0, X_1, \ldots, X_n] = Y_n$.

The last property is called the **martingale property**. When X_n contains all the information in the X_i for $i < n$, we can write it more succinctly as $E[Y_{n+1} \mid X_n] = Y_n$.

A random variable τ that takes values from $\mathbb{N}$ is a **stopping time** with respect to $X_0, X_1, \ldots$ if, for all $n \geq 0$, the event $\tau = n$ depends only on $X_0, X_1, \ldots, X_n$.

See [14, Sect. 10.10] for a proof of Doob's Optional Stopping Theorem, of which the following is a special case.

Theorem 4. *If $Y_0, Y_1, \ldots$ is a martingale and τ is a stopping time, both with respect to $X_0, X_1, \ldots$, and τ is bounded, then $E[Y_\tau] = E[Y_0]$.*

For some applications, it makes sense to replace the martingale property with an inequality. A **supermartingale** is a process defined as above except that $Y_n \geq E[Y_{n+1} \mid X_0, \ldots, X_n]$; where a martingale stays the same on average, a supermartingale is non-increasing on average. A straightforward induction shows that supermartingales satisfy $Y_k \geq E[Y_n \mid X_0, \ldots, X_k]$ whenever $k \leq n$.

References

1. Booth, A.D., Colin, A.J.T.: On the efficiency of a new method of dictionary construction. Inf. Control **3**(4), 327–334 (1960)
2. Bronson, N.G., Casper, J., Chafi, H., Olukotun, K.: A practical concurrent binary search tree. In: Proceedings of the 15th ACM Symposium on Principles and Practice of Parallel Programming, pp. 257–268 (2010)
3. Brown, T., Ellen, F., Ruppert, E.: A general technique for non-blocking trees. In: Proceedings of the 19th ACM Symposium on Principles and Practice of Parallel Programming, pp. 329–342 (2014)
4. Culberson, J., Munro, J.I.: Explaining the behaviour of binary search trees under prolonged updates: a model and simulations. Comput. J. **32**(1), 68–75 (1989)
5. Devroye, L.: A note on the height of binary search trees. J. ACM **33**(3), 489–498 (1986)
6. Drmota, M.: An analytic approach to the height of binary search trees II. J. ACM **50**(3), 333–374 (2003)
7. Ellen, F., Fatourou, P., Ruppert, E., van Breugel, F.: Non-blocking binary search trees. In: Proceedings of the 29th ACM Symposium on Principles of Distributed Computing, pp. 131–140 (2010)
8. Guibas, L.J., Sedgewick, R.: A dichromatic framework for balanced trees. In: Proceedings of the 19th IEEE Symposium on Foundations of Computer Science, pp. 8–21 (1978)
9. Mahmoud, H.M.: Evolution of Random Search Trees. Wiley, New York (1992)
10. Manthey, B., Reischuk, R.: Smoothed analysis of binary search trees. Theoret. Comput. Sci. **378**(3), 292–315 (2007)
11. Mitzenmacher, M., Upfal, E.: Probability and Computing: Randomized Algorithms and Probabilistic Analysis, Chap. 12. Cambridge University Press, Cambridge (2005)
12. Reed, B.: The height of a random binary search tree. J. ACM **50**(3), 306–332 (2003)
13. Robson, J.M.: The height of binary search trees. Aust. Comput. J. **11**(4), 151–153 (1979)
14. Williams, D.: Probability with Martingales. Cambridge University Press, Cambridge (1991)
15. Windley, P.F.: Trees, forests and rearranging. Comput. J. **3**(2), 84–88 (1960)

Priority Mutual Exclusion: Specification and Algorithm

Chien-Chung Huang[1] and Prasad Jayanti[2(✉)]

[1] Chalmers University of Technology, Gothenburg, Sweden
villars@gmail.com
[2] Dartmouth College, Hanover, USA
prasad@cs.dartmouth.edu

Abstract. Mutual exclusion is a fundamental problem in distributed computing. In one well known variant of this problem, which we call *priority mutual exclusion*, processes have priorities and the requirement is that, whenever the critical section becomes vacant, the next occupant should be the process that has the highest priority among the waiting processes. Instead of first capturing this vague, but intuitively appealing requirement by a rigorously specified condition, earlier research rushed into proposing algorithms. Consequently, as we explain in the paper, none of the existing algorithms meet the reasonable expectations we would have of an algorithm that claims to respect process priorities. This paper fixes this situation by rigorously specifying the priority mutual exclusion problem and designing an efficient algorithm for it. Our algorithm supports an arbitrary number of processes and, when configured to support m priority levels (m can be any natural number), the algorithm has $O(m)$ RMR complexity on both DSM and CC machines.

1 Introduction

Mutual Exclusion [5] is a fundamental problem in distributed computing. This problem and its variants—such as readers-writers exclusion [3], group mutual exclusion [8], and abortable mutual exclusion [12]—are extensively researched. One such well-known variant, known as *priority* mutual exclusion, is the subject of this paper.

In the *priority mutual exclusion problem*, each process, as it moves from the Remainder section to the Try section, picks a number, called its priority. Informally, the requirement is that processes enter the CS by the priority order: when selecting which process enters the CS next, the algorithm must pick the process whose priority is the highest among the waiting processes. This statement has an intuitive appeal, but its meaning is vague. Unfortunately, instead of first capturing this intuitive requirement of "enter by priority" by a rigorously specified condition, prior works on priority mutual exclusion that we are aware of [4,6,7,10] rushed to propose algorithms.

In this paper, we make two contributions. First, we give a rigorous specification for the priority mutual exclusion problem and explain how existing

© Springer-Verlag Berlin Heidelberg 2016
C. Gavoille and D. Ilcinkas (Eds.): DISC 2016, LNCS 9888, pp. 385–398, 2016.
DOI: 10.1007/978-3-662-53426-7_28

algorithms do not meet this specification; thus, they do not meet some reasonable expectations we would have for an algorithm that claims to respect priority. Our second contribution is a novel algorithm that fills this gap. The algorithm supports a finite number m of priority levels, but can handle an arbitrary and unknown number of processes. It has $O(m)$ RMR complexity on both CC and DSM machines. The algorithm uses the *swap* operation, where $swap(X, v)$ writes the value v in the shared variable X and returns X's previous value.

2   Specification of Priority Mutual Exclusion

We consider a system that consists of asynchronous processes that communicate by applying atomic operations on shared variables. The program of each process is a loop that consists of two sections of code—Try section and Exit section. We say a process is in the Remainder section if its program counter points to the first statement of the Try section; and that it is in the Critical section (CS) if its program counter points to the first statement of the Exit section. The Try section, in turn, consists of two code fragments—a *doorway*, followed by a *waiting room*—with the requirement that the doorway is a bounded "straight line" code [9]. Intuitively, a process "registers" its request for the CS by executing the doorway, and then busywaits in the waiting room until it has the "permission" to enter the CS. Initially, all processes are in their Remainder section. Each time a process p executes the first step of the Try section, it selects a number, which is p's *priority* until it returns to the Remainder section.

A *run* is a (finite or infinite) sequence of steps, where each step is executed by some process at some time. An *attempt* in a run is $(p, [t, t'])$, where p is a process, t is a time when p enters the Try section, and t' is the earliest time after t when p returns to the Remainder section. Notice that a process may have many attempts in a run. If $\alpha = (p, [t, t'])$ and $\beta = (q, [\tau, \tau'])$ are any two attempts in a run, we say:

- α is an attempt by p.
- priority(α) is p's priority during the attempt α.
- α is *active* at time s if $t \leq s \leq t'$.
- α is in the Waiting Room (respectively, Try, CS, or Exit) at time s if p is in the Waiting Room (respectively, Try, CS, or Exit) at s and $t \leq s \leq t'$.
- α *doorway precedes* β if the time when p completes the doorway during the attempt α is before the time when q enters the doorway during the attempt β.

The *Priority Mutual Exclusion Problem* is to design the code for the Try and Exit sections so that five properties—the three stated below and the two defined in Sects. 2.1 and 2.2—hold in all runs.

- *Mutual Exclusion:* At most one process is in the CS at any time.
- *Bounded Exit:* There is an integer b such that every process completes the Exit section in at most b of its steps.

- *Livelock Freedom:* On the assumption that no process permanently stops taking steps in the Try and Exit sections and no process stays in the CS forever, if a process is in the Try section at a point in time, then some process is in the CS at a later point in time.

The remaining two properties capture priorities. Since these properties are new, we have motivated and carefully defined them in the next two subsections.

2.1 Priority Entry

Intuitively, the purpose of the bounded doorway is to make it possible for a process to "register" its priority and its interest in the CS, without being hindered by other processes. Accordingly, if a high priority process p completes the doorway before a lower priority process q even enters the doorway, it makes sense to require that q does not enter the CS before p.

What else must we ensure? Consider a scenario where, while p is in the CS and q is in the waiting room, a process r of higher priority than q enters the Try section, completes the doorway, and enters the waiting room. Later, when p leaves the CS, we would want r, and not q, to enter the CS, even though q has been waiting much longer than r.

To capture the above expectations, we define a *"dominates"* binary relation, denoted $\succ$, on the set of attempts in a run as follows:

Definition 1. For any two attempts α and α' in a run, we say α *dominates* α', written $\alpha \succ \alpha'$, if

priority(α) > priority(α') and α doorway precedes α', or
priority(α) > priority(α') and there is a time when some process is in the CS, α is in the waiting room, and α' is in the Try section.

The next property states what it really means for processes to enter the CS by priority order.

- *Priority Entry:* If α and α' are any two attempts in a run such that $\alpha \succ \alpha'$, then α' does not enter the CS before α.

2.2 Wait-Free Progress for Dominator

The Priority Entry property stated above only ensures that a low priority process does not race ahead of a higher priority process into the CS, but it makes no guarantee that the higher priority process is not obstructed by a lower priority process. This observation motivates the need to formulate a property that guarantees that, under suitable conditions, a high priority process' progress to the CS is not hindered by a lower priority process.

To understand what this property should be fleshed out, consider a scenario where a process q is in the CS, a process p is in the waiting room, and a set S of additional processes are in the Try section. Assume that p has a higher priority than every process in the set S. Then, p dominates every process in S. Suppose now that q leaves the CS, completes the Exit section, and goes back to the remainder section. Assuming that no new processes will enter the Try section with a priority higher than p's, process p finds itself in a favorable situation where no process is in the CS or the Exit section, and p dominates every other process in the Try section forever. Under these circumstances, it makes sense to require that p be able to enter the CS in a finite number of its own steps, regardless of whether other processes are slow, fast, or have crashed. Thus, we are led to the following property: If no process is in the CS or the Exit section and a process p in the waiting room dominates forever every other process in the Try section, then p enters the CS in a finite number of its own steps. More precisely:

– *Wait-free Progress for Dominator:* If an attempt α by a process p is in the waiting room at time τ, no process is in the CS or the Exit section at τ, and, for all $\tau' \geq \tau$, α dominates every attempt that is active at τ', then p enters the CS during the attempt α in a finite number of its steps, regardless of whether other processes take any steps or crash.

3   Stronger Version of Priority Mutual Exclusion

So far we have been silent on the order in which processes of the same priority may enter the CS, and on whether a process can obstruct another process of the same priority. In particular, the properties stated above allow a process p to be stuck in the waiting room while another process q of equal priority repeatedly enters and leaves the CS. We could prevent such a scenario by requiring that processes of equal priority enter the CS in the FCFS order: if p and q have the same priority and p doorway-precedes q, then q does not enter the CS before p.

Similarly, if p and q have the same priority and p doorway-precedes q, we might wish to strengthen the "Wait-free Progress for Dominator" property by requiring that q does not obstruct p's entry into the CS.

To capture these ideas, it is convenient to weaken the earlier defined "dominates" relation slightly by replacing ">" with "$\geq$" in the first condition, as follows:

Definition 2. For any two attempts α and α' in a run, we say α *weakly dominates* α', written $\alpha \succ_w \alpha'$, if

priority$(\alpha) \geq$ priority(α') and α doorway precedes α', or
priority$(\alpha) >$ priority(α') and there is a time when some process is in the CS, α is in the waiting room, and α' is in the Try section.

Notice that, for any two attempts α and α', $\alpha \succ \alpha'$ implies $\alpha \succ_w \alpha'$. Now, we can capture both Priority Entry and FCFS (among processes of equal priority) together as follows:

– *Priority Entry + FCFS*: If α and α' are any two attempts in a run such that $\alpha \succ_w \alpha'$, then α' does not enter the CS before α.

And we can strengthen the "Wait-free Progress for Dominator" property by replacing "$\succ$" with the weaker "$\succ_w$" in its definition:

– *Strong Wait-free Progress for Dominator*: If an attempt α by a process p is in the waiting room at time τ, no process is in the CS or the Exit section at τ, and, for all $\tau' \geq \tau$, α weakly dominates every attempt that is active at τ', then p enters the CS during the attempt α in a finite number of its steps, regardless of whether other processes take any steps or crash.

Finally, we define the *Strong Priority Mutual Exclusion Problem* as designing the code for the Try and Exit sections so that the following five properties hold in all runs: Mutual Exclusion, Livelock Freedom, Bounded Exit, Priority Entry + FCFS, and Strong Wait-free Progress for Dominator.

4   Discussion of Previous Research

The idea of dividing the Try section into a bounded doorway and waiting room is due to Lamport [9], who introduced this structure to capture FCFS—a fairness condition for Mutual Exclusion. Our specification of the Priority Mutual Exclusion Problem is inspired by Bhatt and Jayanti's formulations of the Readers-Writers Exclusion Problem [1]. To the best of our knowledge, there are four papers that proposed algorithms of bounded RMR complexity for the priority mutual exclusion problem [4,6,7,10], but no prior work has attempted a rigorous specification of the problem. Below, we briefly describe why the algorithms in [4,6,7,10] do not meet our specification.

4.1   Algorithms of Markatos [10] and Craig [4]

Markatos' and Craig's algorithms, which are adaptations of Mellor-Crummey and Scott's queue-based mutual exclusion algorithm [11], do not satisfy Priority Entry because they admit the following scenario:

– While a process p is in the CS, three processes q, r, and s enter the Try section and queue themselves up in that order (q, followed by r, followed by s). Assume that s has a higher priority than both q and r.
– q and s complete their doorways, but r stops in the doorway before setting the link at q to point to r.
– p leaves the CS and makes the "best effort" to traverse the queue of waiting processes to locate the highest priority process. It sees q, but will not be able to see the next element r in the queue (since r has not yet installed a link at q to point to r). Because p can't see r, it can't see s either. Thus, q is the only waiting process that p is aware of. So, p lets q into the CS.

In the above scenario, $s \succ q$, yet q enters the CS before s, thereby violating Priority Entry.

4.2   A Second Algorithm of Markatos [10]

Another algorithm in Markatos' paper adapts Burns' algorithm [2] for standard mutual exclusion. In Markatos' algorithm, when a process p leaves the CS, it scans all n processes to find out which ones are waiting and lets into the CS the highest priority process among them. To implement this strategy, p reads $want[1], want[2], \ldots, want[n]$ in that order, where $want[i]$ is a shared flag that process i sets to request the CS. This algorithm violates Priority Entry because it admits the following scenario:

- Process p is in the CS while all others are in the remainder section. Then, p leaves the CS and reads *false* in $want[1]$ (because process 1 is in the remainder section).
- Process 1 enters the Try section with a high priority, completes the doorway, and proceeds to busywait in the waiting room. (During the doorway, process 1 sets $want[1]$, but p does not notice it because it has already gone past 1.)
- Process 2 enters the Try section with a low priority, completes the doorway (setting $want[2]$ along the way), and proceeds to busywait in the waiting room.
- p reads *true* in $want[2]$ and *false* in $want[3], want[4], \ldots, want[n]$. Believing that process 2 is the only waiting process, p lets process 2 into the CS.

In the above scenario, process 1 dominates process 2 because it has a higher priority and doorway-precedes process 2. Therefore, process 2 entering the CS before process 1 is a violation of Priority Entry.

4.3   Johnson and Harathi's Algorithm [7]

Johnson and Harathi's algorithm maintains a list of waiting processes, ordered by their priority. For example, if the list is p, q, r, it means that three processes are waiting, p has the highest priority, q has the second highest priority, and r has the least priority. When a process enters the Try section, it traverses this list and attempts to insert itself at the appropriate position (so as to preserve the priority order of the list). When a process leaves the CS, if the list is not empty, it removes the first process in the list and lets it into the CS. The algorithm uses CAS to manipulate the queue.

Consider a scenario involving four processes a, b, c, x, where a, b, c have the same priority and x has a higher priority. Suppose that a is in the CS; the list has b, c; and x is in the Try section, trying to insert itself at the front of the list. Suppose that a then leaves the CS and acts on the list (to remove the front element) concurrently with x, which also acts on the list to insert itself at the front. Suppose that a succeeds and x fails (because a's CAS succeeds and x's CAS fails). Then, the situation is that b is in the CS, a is back in the remainder section, and x has still not inserted itself in the list. Suppose that a then comes back and inserts itself in the list (to make the list c, a). As b leaves the CS, as before suppose that b and x act on the list concurrently, b's CAS succeeds and x's CAS once again fails. We can repeat the above actions forever to ensure that

x will never be able to insert itself into the list, even though x never ceases to take steps.

The above scenario is damning: even though x has higher priority than all others and takes steps repeatedly forever, it is stuck in the Try section without being able to even get into the wait-queue! In particular, the algorithm violates Priority Entry.

4.4   Jayanti's Algorithm [6]

Jayanti's algorithm satisfies Priority Entry, but violates "Wait-free Progress for Dominator" by admitting the following scenario. While a process p is in the CS, a high priority process q inserts its name into the wait-queue, which is maintained as a priority queue (using LL/SC). Then, p leaves the CS, depositing a token in a central location (to indicate that the CS is vacant) and proceeding to inspect the priority queue. A low priority process r then enters the Try section, inserts its name in the priority queue, grabs the token from the central location, and goes back to the priority queue to hand the token to the highest priority waiting process. However, before r finds out that q is the highest priority waiting process, process p completes the Exit section and goes back to the remainder section, which is possible with that algorithm. At this point, there is no process in the CS or the Exit section, and q dominates r. Yet, q cannot enter the CS until r hands it the token, violating "Wait-free Progress for Dominator."

5   The Auxiliary *Lock* object

Our priority mutual exclusion algorithm, described in the next section, is designed using auxiliary objects that we call *lock* objects. In this section, we specify this object and state how it can be efficiently implemented.

5.1   Specification of a Lock Object

A *lock object* L is an abstraction that helps solve FCFS mutual exclusion, and is specified in Fig. 1. Its state is represented by (i) L.waitqueue, the sequence of processes waiting for the lock, and (ii) L.open, which is *true* if and only if the lock is available. A process p requests the lock by executing L.request$_p$(), which appends p to the wait queue. When the lock is not open, p can open it by executing L.release$_p$(). After p requests the lock, it can execute L.isGranted$_p$() to attempt to own the lock. If the lock is open and p is at the front of the wait queue, the attempt succeeds—i.e., the lock is granted to p, p is removed from the queue, and the lock is no longer open. Finally, p can find out if one or more processes are waiting for the lock by executing L.areProcsWaiting(). We named this object a lock object because it is trivial to solve FCFS mutual exclusion using this object, as follows:

State

    L.waitqueue: Sequence of processes, initially empty

    L.open: Boolean, initially *true* if we want the lock to be open initially,
           and *false* otherwise

Operations

    Precondition: $p \notin L$.waitqueue

    L.request$_p()$

        append p to L.waitqueue

    Precondition: L.open is false

    L.release$_p()$

        L.open $=$ *true*

    Precondition: $p \in L$.waitqueue

    L.isGranted$_p()$

        if $(L$.open $==$ *true*$) \wedge (p$ is at the front of L.waitqueue$)$

            remove p from L.waitqueue

            L.open $=$ *false*

            return *true*

        else return *false*

    L.areProcsWaiting$_p()$

        return $(L$.waitqueue $==$ *empty*$)$

Fig. 1. Specification of a lock object L

        L.request$_p()$

        repeat till L.isGranted$_p()$ returns *true*

        CRITICAL SECTION

        L.release$_p()$

5.2   Implementing the Lock Object

Mellor-Crummey and Scott [11] and Craig [4] designed constant RMR algorithms for FCFS mutual exclusion using shared variables that support the *swap* operation. With a straightforward adaptation of their algorithm, we get an implementation of the lock object, which we omit due to space constraints. The result that we achieve is summarized as follows:

Theorem 1. There is an algorithm that correctly implements a lock object L (using read, write, and swap operations) under the assumption that L.open $=$ *false* in every interval during which a process p executes L.areProcsWaiting$_p()$. On both DSM and CC machines, executing any of L.request$_p()$, L.release$_p()$, or L.areProcsWaiting$_p()$, or repeatedly executing L.isGranted$_p()$ until it returns *true* incurs only $O(1)$ RMRs.

6 The Algorithm

In this section, we present a novel priority mutual exclusion algorithm that supports priorities from a set $\{1, 2, \ldots, m\}$, can handle an arbitrary and unknown number of processes, and has $O(m)$ RMR complexity on both DSM and CC machines.

The algorithm employs m lock objects LOCK$[1 \cdots m]$. When a process p enters the Try section with a priority $\pi \in \{1, 2, \ldots, m\}$, it inserts itself in the wait-queue of LOCK$[\pi]$, the lock associated with priority π. When p leaves the CS, it checks if processes are waiting in any of the wait-queues. If there are, it releases the highest priority lock whose wait-queue is nonempty. On the other hand, if no processes are waiting, p leaves a token in a "depository" DEP so that a process q that enters the Try section in the future can grab the token and enter the CS. These ideas lead to our first attempt towards an algorithm, which we present in Fig. 2. Two lines (2 and 7) are currently left blank, which we will fill later. The code is described informally as follows.

Process p picks a priority π (Line 0) and inserts itself in the wait-queue of LOCK$[\pi]$, the lock associated with its priority (Line 1). Since it is possible that the depository contains the token, p attempts to grab the token from the depository (Line 3). If the depository contains the token, p grabs it and simultaneously erases the token from the depository by swapping the integer π (its priority). If p gets the token, it opens LOCK$[\pi]$ (Line 4) so that the process at the front of its wait-queue is granted the lock, enabling that process to proceed to the CS (note that p knows that LOCK$[\pi]$'s wait-queue is nonempty because p itself is in that wait-queue). The process p then busywaits until it is granted the lock and then enters the CS (Line 5). When p leaves the CS, it goes through all locks, from 1 to m, to identify the highest priority nonempty wait-queue, if there is any (Lines 8 to 10). If $k \neq 0$ when the for-loop on Line 9 terminates, it means that some processes are waiting at LOCK$[k]$ and p found the wait-queues associated with locks $k+1, k+2, \ldots, n$ to be empty. In this case, p skips Line 11 and releases LOCK$[k]$ (Line 12), which enables the earliest process waiting on that lock to enter the CS. On the other hand, if $k = 0$ when the for-loop on Line 9 terminates, it means that p found all wait-queues to be empty. In this case, p puts a token in the depository DEP (Line 11) so that a process q that enters the Try section in the future can grab the token and proceed to the CS. The *swap* operation at Line 11 enables p to both deposit the token in DEP and simultaneously read into k what was in DEP. If $k = \bot$, p infers that since the time that p had cleared the depository at Line 6 no process executed Line 3; in this case, p skips Line 12 and exits to the remainder section, aware that the token it left behind in DEP will be picked up by a process that enters the Try section in the future. On the other hand, if the swap operation at Line 11 swaps into k a positive integer, p infers that since the time it had cleared DEP at Line 6, some process q of priority k executed the swap operation at Line 3. The value that this swap operation returned to q could not have been "token" since p had not deposited the token in DEP by that time. So, q must have skipped Line 4 and be busywaiting at Line 5 for grant of access to LOCK$[k]$. If p takes no action and

Shared variables

DEP $\in \{token, \perp, 1, 2, \ldots, m\}$, initialized to *token*; supports *swap* operation

LOCK$[1 \ldots m]$: array of m lock objects; initially all are closed,

         i.e., $\forall i$, LOCK$[i]$.open $= false$

```
0.    select a priority π ∈ {1, 2, ..., m}
1.    LOCK[π].request_p()
2.
3.      if swap(DEP, π) == token
4.          LOCK[π].release_p()
5.    repeat till LOCK[π].isGranted_p() returns true
      Critical Section
6.    DEP = ⊥
7.
8.    k = 0
9.    for i = 1 to m
10.       if LOCK[i].areProcsWaiting_p() then k = i
11.   if k = 0 then k = swap(DEP, token)
12.   if k ∈ {1, 2, ..., m} then LOCK[k].release_p()
```

Fig. 2. First attempt towards a priority mutual exclusion algorithm: code shown is for process p

---

moves on to the remainder section, q will busywait forever at Line 5, leading to livelock. To prevent this situation, p releases LOCK$[k]$ (Line 12), which enables the process r at the front of that lock's wait-queue (which is possibly, but not necessarily, q) to enter the CS. There is however a nasty race condition here: the depository DEP currently contains the token, which means that a process s that might now enter the Try section with a new priority π executes Lines 0 through 3, grabs the token at Line 3, releases its lock at Line 4, so finds the lock granted at Line 5, and enters the CS that already contains r, violating mutual exclusion! We prevent this scenario by placing a "gate" to regulate access to the depository. Specifically, our final algorithm, presented in Fig. 3, is obtained by making the following three small additions to the code described so far:

- A new shared variable GATE, which can take on two values—*open* or *closed*. Initially, the gate is open, i.e., GATE $= open$.
- Line 2, which ensures that a process p attempts to grab the token at Line 3 only if it finds the gate open. The swap operation at Line 2 lets p close the gate and simultaneously learn if the gate was open just before the operation.
- Line 7, where an exiting process opens the gate.

With these changes, the algorithm prevents violation of mutual exclusion because, as we now explain, an exiting process either wakes up a waiting process or leaves the token behind for later pick up, but never does both. Consider a process p as it leaves the CS. When p's for-loop at Lines 9 and 10 terminates, either $k = 0$

Shared variables

GATE $\in \{open, closed\}$, initialized to *open*; supports *swap* operation

DEP $\in \{token, \bot, 1, 2, \ldots, m\}$, initialized to *token*; supports *swap* operation

LOCK$[1 \ldots m]$: array of m lock objects; initially all are closed, i.e.,
      $\forall i$, LOCK$[i]$.open $= false$

```
0.    select a priority π ∈ {1, 2, . . . , m}
1.    LOCK[π].request_p()
2.    if swap(GATE, closed) == open
3.        if swap(DEP, π) == token
4.            LOCK[π].release_p()
5.    repeat till LOCK[π].isGranted_p() returns true
      Critical Section
6.    DEP = ⊥
7.    GATE = open
8.    k = 0
9.    for i = 1 to m
10.       if LOCK[i].areProcsWaiting_p() then k = i
11.   if k = 0 then k = swap(DEP, token)
12.   if k ∈ {1, 2, . . . , m} then LOCK[k].release_p()
```

Fig. 3. Priority mutual exclusion algorithm: code shown is for process p. Supports limited priorities from $\{1, 2, \ldots, m\}$, but an arbitrary and unknown number of processes.

or $k \in \{1, 2, \ldots, m\}$. If $k > 0$, p skips Line 11 and executes Line 12; thus, p opens a lock but does not leave the token in the depository, thereby giving no scope for any violation of mutual exclusion. For the remaining case, suppose that $k = 0$, which implies that p found every wait-queue to be empty when it executed the for-loop on Lines 9 and 10. It follows that all wait-queues were empty at the point when p had executed Line 6. Therefore, during the interval I spanning from when p had executed Line 6 to when p executes Line 11, at most one process could have gone past the gate at Line 2 and onto Line 3 (because the first process to execute Line 2 closes the gate). If no process executed Line 3 during the interval I, when p executes Line 11 to put the token in the depository, the swap operation returns $\bot$ (because p had put $\bot$ in DEP at Line 6), so p skips Line 12 and goes back to the remainder section without waking anyone from a wait-queue (so there is no scope for violating mutual exclusion). On the other hand, if exactly one process q of priority π executes Line 3 during the interval I, q would read $\bot$ from DEP at Line 3 (because p had put $\bot$ in DEP at Line 6) and busywait at Line 5. And when p executes Line 11 to put the token in the depository, the swap operation returns $\pi \in \{1, 2, \ldots, m\}$ (that q put into DEP). In this case, p executes Line 12 to open LOCK$[\pi]$, while still leaving the token in the depository. However, there is no danger of some other process picking up this token because the gate is closed at this point, so no process will be able to get to Line 3 to grab the token! Hence, mutual exclusion won't be violated. This is just the intuition, and the next section provides a rigorous proof of all properties.

6.1   Proof of Mutual Exclusion and Livelock Freedom

We present a rigorous proof of correctness, which we found to be as challenging as the algorithm. The crux lies in identifying the invariant, presented in Fig. 4. The proof that the algorithm satisfies the invariant is by induction, which is omitted due to space constraints.

Lemma 1 (Mutual Exclusion). *The algorithm satisfies Mutual Exclusion.*

Proof. Immediate from Part (4) of the invariant.   ∎

Lemma 2 (Bounded Exit). *The algorithm satisfies Bounded Exit.*

Proof. Obvious since the exit section involves no waiting and consists of at most $m + 4$ steps.   ∎

Lemma 3 (Livelock Freedom). *The algorithm satisfies Livelock Freedom.*

Proof. Let C be any configuration in which no process is in the CS or the exit section (i.e., $\forall p : PC_p \notin \{7, 8, 9, 10, 11, 12\}$) and at least one process is in the Try section (i.e., $PC_p \in \{2, 3, 4, 5\}$ for some p). To prove the lemma, we argue below that some process is guaranteed to eventually enter the CS. We begin by noting that Part (7a) of the invariant is false in C. Then, it follows from (7) that exactly one of (7b) or (7c) is true.

Case 1: Assume that (7c) is true and (7b) is false. Then, there are three subcases: (i) DEP = token and GATE = *open*, or (ii) DEP = token and $PC_p = 3$ for some p, or (iii) $PC_p = 4$ for some p.

In Subcase (i), it follows from Part (6) of the invariant that all processes in the Try section are at Lines 2. Whichever process executes Line 2 first, it finds that GATE = *open* and moves to Line 3, thereby bringing the configuration to Subcase (ii).

In Subcase (ii), it follows from Part (5) of the invariant that GATE = *closed* and no process other than p is at Lines 3 or 4. Thus, we have the gate closed, p at Line 3, all other processes at Lines 0, 1, 2, or 5, and none of the locks in an open state (since (7b) is false in the case under consideration). So, no process can go past Line 5 or enter Line 3 until p executes a step. When p executes Line 3, it finds the token in DEP and moves to Line 4, thereby bringing the configuration to Subcase (iii).

In Subcase (iii), p is at Line 4 and, by Part (1) of the invariant, the wait-queue of LOCK$[\pi_p]$ is nonempty. When p executes Line 4, it opens this lock, thereby bringing the configuration to Case (2), which we deal with below.

Case 2: Assume that (7b) is true, i.e., some lock ℓ is open. Then, by Part (2), the wait-queue associated with this lock is nonempty. Let q be the process at the front of this queue. By (1), q is at one of Lines 2, 3, 4, or 5. When q moves to Line 5 and executes the first iteration of the repeat-until loop at Line 5, q finds the lock granted to it (because lock ℓ is open), so moves to Line 6 (i.e., enters the CS).

We conclude from the above that livelock is not possible.   ∎

1.
$$\forall p \, \forall \ell : (p \in \text{LOCK}[\ell].\text{wait-queue} \Leftrightarrow (PC_p \in \{2, 3, 4, 5\} \wedge \pi_p = \ell))$$

2.
$$\forall \ell : (\text{LOCK}[\ell].\text{open} \Rightarrow \text{LOCK}[\ell].\text{wait-queue} \neq \epsilon)$$

3.
$$\forall \ell \, \forall \ell' \neq \ell : (\text{LOCK}[\ell].\text{open} \Rightarrow \neg \text{LOCK}[\ell'].\text{open})$$

4.
$$\forall p \, \forall q \neq p : ((PC_p \in \{6, 7, 8, 9, 10, 11, 12\} \Rightarrow PC_q \notin \{6, 7, 8, 9, 10, 11, 12\}))$$

5.
$$\forall p : ((PC_p = 4 \vee (PC_p = 3 \wedge \text{DEP} = token)) \Rightarrow (\text{GATE} = closed \wedge \forall q \neq p : PC_q \notin \{3, 4\}))$$

6.
$$(\text{DEP} = token \wedge \text{GATE} = open) \Rightarrow \forall p : PC_p \in \{0, 1, 2\}$$

7.
$$((a) \wedge \neg(b) \wedge \neg(c)) \vee (\neg(a) \wedge (b) \wedge \neg(c)) \vee (\neg(a) \wedge \neg(b) \wedge (c)), \text{where}$$

(a) $\exists p : PC_p \in \{6, 7, 8, 9, 10, 11, 12\}$
(b) $\exists \ell : \text{LOCK}[\ell].\text{open}$
(c) $(\exists p : PC_p = 4) \vee ((\text{DEP} = token) \wedge (\text{GATE} = open \vee \exists p : PC_p = 3))$

8.
$$\forall p : ((PC_p \in \{7, 8, 9, 10, 11\} \wedge \text{DEP} \neq \bot) \Rightarrow$$
$$(\text{DEP} \in \{1, 2, \ldots, m\} \wedge \text{LOCK}[\text{DEP}].\text{wait-queue} \neq \epsilon))$$

9.
$$\forall p : ((PC_p \in \{10, 11\} \wedge k_p > 0) \Rightarrow ((1 \leq k_p < i_p) \wedge \text{LOCK}[k_p].\text{wait-queue} \neq \epsilon))$$

10.
$$\forall p : ((PC_p \in \{10, 11\} \wedge k_p = 0 \wedge \forall j \in \{i_p, i_{p+1}, \ldots, m\} :$$
$$\text{LOCK}[j].\text{wait-queue} = \epsilon) \Rightarrow ((a) \vee (b) \vee (c)))$$

(a) $(\text{GATE} = open) \wedge (\text{DEP} = \bot) \wedge (\forall q \neq p : PC_q \in \{0, 1, 2\})$
(b) $(\text{GATE} = closed) \wedge (\text{DEP} = \bot) \wedge (\exists q : PC_q = 3 \wedge (\forall r \neq q : PC_r \notin \{3, 4\}))$
(c) $(\text{GATE} = closed) \wedge (\text{DEP} \in \{1, 2, \ldots, i_p - 1\}) \wedge$
    $(\forall q : PC_q \notin \{3, 4\}) \wedge \text{LOCK}[\text{DEP}].\text{wait-queue} \neq \epsilon$

11.
$$\forall p : (PC_p = 12 \Rightarrow \text{LOCK}[k_p].\text{wait-queue} \neq \epsilon)$$

Fig. 4. Invariant satisfied by the algorithm

Due to space limitation, we omit the proof of the Priority Entry + FCFS and Strong Wait-free Progress for Dominator properties, and proceed to state the main result of this work.

Theorem 2. *The algorithm in* Fig. 3 *correctly solves the Strong Priority Mutual Exclusion Problem for an arbitrary and unknown number of processes, when priorities are drawn from* $\{1, 2, \ldots, m\}$. *The algorithm has* $O(m)$ *RMR complexity on both DSM and CC machines.*

References

1. Bhatt, V., Jayanti, P.: Constant RMR solutions to reader writer synchronization. In: PODC 2010: Proceedings of the Twenty-Ninth Annual Symposium on Principles of Distributed Computing, pp. 468–477 (2010)
2. Burns, J.E.: Mutual exclusion with linear waiting using binary shared variables. SIGACT News **10**(2), 42–47 (1978)
3. Courtois, P.J., Heymans, F., Parnas, D.L.: Concurrent control with "readers" and "writers". Commun. ACM **14**(10), 667–668 (1971)
4. Craig, T.: Queuing spin lock algorithms to support timing predictability. In: Proceedings of the 14th IEEE Real-time Systems Symposium, pp. 148–156. IEEE (1993)
5. Dijkstra, E.W.: Solution of a problem in concurrent programming control. Commun. ACM **8**(9), 569 (1965)
6. Jayanti, P.: Adaptive and efficient abortable mutual exclusion. In: PODC 2003: Proceedings of the Twenty-Second Annual Symposium on Principles of Distributed Computing, pp. 295–304. ACM, New York (2003)
7. Johnson, T., Harathi, K.: A prioritized multiprocessor spin lock. IEEE Trans. Parallel Distrib. Syst. **8**, 926–933 (1997)
8. Joung, Y.J.: Asynchronous group mutual exclusion (extended abstract). In: PODC 1998: Proceedings of the Seventeenth Annual ACM Symposium on Principles of Distributed Computing, pp. 51–60. ACM, New York (1998)
9. Lamport, L.: A new solution of Dijkstra's concurrent programming problem. Commun. ACM **17**(8), 453–455 (1974)
10. Markatos, E.: Multiprocessor synchronization primitives with priorities. In: Proceedings of the 1991 IFAC Workshop on Real-Time Programming, pp. 1–7 (1991)
11. Mellor-Crummey, J.M., Scott, M.L.: Algorithms for scalable synchronization on shared-memory multiprocessors. ACM Trans. Comput. Syst. **9**(1), 21–65 (1991)
12. Scott, M., Scherer III., W.: Scalable queue-based spin locks with timeout. In: Proceedings of the Eight Symposium on Principles and Practice of Parallel Programming, June 2001

Information Spreading in Dynamic Networks Under Oblivious Adversaries

John Augustine[1], Chen Avin[2], Mehraneh Liaee[3], Gopal Pandurangan[4], and Rajmohan Rajaraman[3(✉)]

[1] IIT Madras, Chennai 600036, India
augustine@iitm.ac.in
[2] Ben-Gurion University of the Negev, 84105 Beersheba, Israel
avin@cse.bgu.ac.il
[3] Northeastern University, Boston 02115, USA
{mehraneh,rraj}@ccs.neu.edu
[4] University of Houston, Houston, TX 77204, USA
gopalpandurangan@gmail.com

Abstract. We study the problem of *gossip* in dynamic networks controlled by an adversary that can modify the network arbitrarily from one round to another, provided that the network is always connected. In the gossip problem, there are n tokens arbitrarily distributed among the n network nodes, and the goal is to disseminate all the n tokens to every node. Our focus is on *token-forwarding* algorithms, which do not manipulate tokens in any way other than storing, copying, and forwarding them. An important open question is whether gossip can be realized by a distributed protocol that can do significantly better than an easily achievable bound of $O(n^2)$ rounds.

In this paper, we study oblivious adversaries, i.e., those that are *oblivious to the random choices* made by the protocol. We consider RAND-DIFF, a natural distributed algorithm in which neighbors exchange a token chosen uniformly at random from the difference of their token sets. We present an $\tilde{\Omega}(n^{3/2})$ lower bound for RAND-DIFF under an oblivious adversary. We also present an $\tilde{\Omega}(n^{4/3})$ lower bound under a stronger notion of oblivious adversary for a class of randomized distributed algorithms—*symmetric knowledge-based algorithms*— in which nodes make token transmission decisions based entirely on the sets of tokens they possess over time. On the positive side, we present a centralized algorithm that completes gossip in $\tilde{O}(n^{3/2})$ rounds with high probability, under any oblivious adversary. We also show an $\tilde{O}(n^{5/3})$ upper bound for RAND-DIFF in a restricted class of oblivious adversaries, which we call *paths-respecting*, that may be of independent interest.

J.A. was supported by IIT Madras New Faculty Seed Grant, IIT Madras Exploratory Research Project, and Indo-German Max Planck Center for Computer Science (IMPECS). G.P. was partially supported by NSF grants CCF-1527867 and CCF-1540512. M.L. and R.R were partially supported by grants NSF CCF-1422715, NSF CCF-1535929, and ONR N00014-12-1-1001.

© Springer-Verlag Berlin Heidelberg 2016
C. Gavoille and D. Ilcinkas (Eds.): DISC 2016, LNCS 9888, pp. 399–413, 2016.
DOI: 10.1007/978-3-662-53426-7_29

1   Introduction

In a dynamic network, nodes (processors/end hosts) and communication links can appear and disappear over time. The networks of the current era are inherently dynamic. Modern communication networks (e.g., Internet, peer-to-peer, ad-hoc networks and sensor networks) and information networks (e.g., the Web, peer-to-peer networks and on-line social networks), and emerging technologies such as drone swarms are dynamic networked systems that are larger and more complex than ever before. Indeed, many such networks are subject to continuous structural changes over time due to sleep modes, channel fluctuations, mobility, device failures, nodes joining or leaving the system, and many other factors [1,9,14,18,25,29,31]. Therefore the formal study of algorithms for dynamic networks have gained much popularity in recent years and many of the classical problems and algorithms for static networks were extended to dynamic networks. During the past decade, new dynamic network models have been introduced to capture specific applications [9,10,16,18,25,30], and the last few years have witnessed a burst of research activity on broadcasting, flooding, random-walk based, and gossip-style protocols in dynamic networks [3–8,11–13,15,19–22,26,27,33,34].

Our paper continues this effort and studies a fundamental problem of information spreading, called *k-gossip*, on dynamic networks. In k-gossip (also referred to as *k-token dissemination*), k distinct pieces of information (tokens) are initially present in some nodes, and the problem is to disseminate all the tokens to all the nodes, under the constraint that one token can be sent on an edge per round of synchronous communication. This problem is a fundamental primitive for distributed computing; indeed, solving n-gossip, where each node starts with exactly one token, allows any function of the initial states of the nodes to be computed, assuming the nodes know n [26]. This problem was analyzed for static networks by Topkis [35], and was first studied on dynamic networks for general k in [26], and previously for the special case of one token and a random walk in [6].

In this paper, we consider *token-forwarding* algorithms, which do not manipulate tokens in any way other than storing, copying, and forwarding them. Token-forwarding algorithms are simple and easy to implement, typically incur low overhead, and have been widely studied (e.g., see [28,32]). In any n-node *static* network, a simple token-forwarding algorithm that pipelines tokens up a rooted spanning tree, and then broadcasts them down the tree completes k-gossip in $O(n + k)$ rounds [32,35]; this is tight since $\Omega(n + k)$ is a trivial lower bound due to bandwidth constraints. A central question motivating our study is whether a linear or near-linear bound is achievable for k-gossip on dynamic networks. It is important to note that algorithms that *manipulate* tokens, e.g., network coding based algorithms, have been shown to be efficient in dynamic settings [21], but are harder to implement and incur a large overhead in message sizes.

Several models have been proposed for dynamic networks in the literature ranging from stochastic models [6,13] to weak and strong adaptive adversaries [26]. In this paper we consider one of the most basic models known as the *oblivious adversary* [6] or the *evolving graph* model [16,17,24,33]. In this model, the adversary is unaware of any random decisions of the algorithm/protocol and must fix the sequence of graphs before the algorithm starts. The oblivious adversary can choose an arbitrary set of communication links among the (fixed set) of nodes for each round, with the only constraint being that the resulting communication graph is connected in each round. Formally, *oblivious adversary* fixes an infinite sequence of connected graphs $\mathcal{G} = G_1, G_2, \ldots$ on the same vertex set V; in round t, the algorithm operates on graph G_t. The adversary knows the algorithm, but is unaware of the outcome of its random coin tosses.

The oblivious adversary model captures worst-case dynamic changes that may occur independent of the algorithm's (random) actions. On the other hand, an *adaptive* adversary can choose the communication links in every round — depending on the actions of the algorithm — and is much stronger. Indeed, strong lower bounds are known for these adversaries [15,23]: in particular, for the *strongly adaptive adversary*[1], there exists a $\tilde{\Theta}(nk)$ lower bound[2] for k-gossip, essentially matching the trivial upper bound of $O(nk)$.

The main focus of this paper is on closing the gap for the complexity of k-gossip under an oblivious adversary between the straightforward upper bound of $O(nk)$ and the trivial lower bound of $\Omega(n+k)$. In particular, can we achieve an upper bound of the form $\tilde{\Theta}(n+k)$? In fact, it is not even clear whether there even exists a *centralized* algorithm that can do significantly better than the naive bound of $O(nk)$.

The starting point of our study is RAND-DIFF, a simple local randomized algorithm for k-gossip. In each round of RAND-DIFF, along every existing edge (u, v) at that round, u sends a token selected uniformly at random from the difference between the set of tokens held by u and that held by node v, if such a token exists. Note that in RAND-DIFF, a node is aware of the tokens that its neighbours have and therefore RAND-DIFF guarantees progress, i.e., exchange of a missing token along *every* edge where such a progress is possible. Moverover, by using randomization it tries to keep the entropy of token distribution as high as possible in the presence of an adversary. RAND-DIFF is optimal for static networks, while for dynamic networks under an oblivious adversary, it completes k-gossip in $\tilde{O}(n+k)$ rounds for certain initial token distributions which take any token-forwarding algorithm $\tilde{\Omega}(nk)$ rounds under adaptive adversaries [15][3]

1.1   Our Contributions

We present lower and upper bounds for information spreading under the oblivious adversary model.

---

[1] In each round of the strongly adaptive adversary model, each node first chooses a token to *broadcast* to all its neighbors, and then the adversary chooses a connected network for that round with the knowledge of the tokens chosen by each node.

[2] The notation $\tilde{\Omega}$ hides polylogarithmic factors in the denominator and $\tilde{O}$ hides polylogarithmic factors in the numerator.

[3] Actually, [15] shows the $O(n\text{polylog}(n))$ bound applies even for a weaker protocol called SYM-DIFF, where the token exchanged between two neighbouring nodes is a random token from the *symmetric difference* of the token sets of the two nodes.

Lower Bound for RAND-DIFF. We show that RAND-DIFF requires $\tilde{\Omega}(n^{\frac{3}{2}})$ rounds to complete n-gossip under an oblivious adversary with high probability[4] (Sect. 2). Our proof shows that even an oblivious adversary can block RAND-DIFF using a sophisticated strategy that prevents some tokens from reaching certain areas of the network. Although the adversary is unaware of the algorithm's random choices, the adversary can exploit the randomization of the algorithm to act against its own detriment.

Lower bound for symmetric knowledge-based algorithms. We use the technical machinery developed for the RAND-DIFF lower bound to attack a broad class of randomized k-gossip algorithms called *symmetric knowledge-based (SKB) algorithms*, which are a subclass of the knowledge-based class introduced in [26] (Sect. 2.3). In any round, the token sent by a node in a knowledge-based algorithm is based entirely on the set of tokens it possesses over time; an SKB algorithm has the additional constraint that if two tokens first arrived at the node at the same time, then their transmission probabilities are identical. SKB algorithms are quite general in the sense that each node can use any probabilistic function that may depend on the node's identity and the current round number to decide which token to send in a round. Indeed, this offers an attractive algorithmic feature that does not exist in RAND-DIFF: exploitation of information on the history of token arrivals. We show that this may not help achieve a near-linear bound: any SKB algorithm for n-gossip requires $\tilde{\Omega}(n^{\frac{4}{3}})$ rounds whp, under a stronger kind of oblivious adversary, which is also allowed to add tokens from the universe of n tokens to any node in any round.

We do not know whether either of the above lower bounds is tight. Our bounds do raise some intriguing questions: Can n-gossip be even solved in $O(n^{2-\epsilon})$ rounds (for some constant $\epsilon > 0$) rounds by any algorithm? Are there restricted versions of the oblivious adversary that are more amenable to distributed algorithms? We present two upper bound results that partially answer these questions.

Upper bound for RAND-DIFF **under restricted oblivious adversaries.** We introduce a new model for dynamic networks which restricts the oblivious adversary in the extent and location of dynamics it can introduce (Sect. 3). In the *paths-respecting* model, we assume that in each round, the dynamic network is a subgraph of an an underlying *infrastructure graph* $\mathcal{N}$; furthermore, for every pair (s, d) of nodes in $\mathcal{N}$, there exists a set N_{sd} of simple vertex-disjoint paths from s to d in $\mathcal{N}$ such that in any round the adversary can remove at most $N_{sd} - 1$ edges from these paths. The paths-respecting model is quite general and of independent interest in modeling and analyzing protocols for dynamic

---

[4] Throughout, by "with high probability" or *whp*, we mean with probability at least $1 - 1/n^c$, where the constant c can be made sufficiently large by adjusting other parameters in the analysis.

networks.[5] A basic special case of the paths-respecting model is one where $\mathcal{N}$ is a λ-vertex-connected graph and the adversary fails at most $\lambda - 1$ edges in each round. Even for this special case, it is not obvious how to design fast distributed algorithm for n-gossip. In Sect. 3, we also present examples in this model where the adversary can remove a constant fraction of the edges of an infrastructure graph. We show that RAND-DIFF completes n-gossip in $\tilde{O}(n^{5/3})$ rounds under the *paths-respecting model* (Sect. 3). From a technical standpoint, this result is the most difficult one in this paper; it relies on a novel delay sequence argument, which may offer a framework for other related routing and information dissemination algorithms in dynamic networks.

A $\min\{nk, \tilde{O}((n + k)\sqrt{n})\}$ **centralized algorithm for** k**-gossip.** Finally, we present a centralized algorithm (cf. Sect. 4) that completes k-gossip in $\min\{nk, \tilde{O}((n+k)\sqrt{n})\}$ rounds (and hence n-gossip in $\tilde{O}(n^{\frac{3}{2}})$ rounds) whp, under an oblivious adversary. This answers the main open question affirmatively, albeit in the *centralized* setting. This result provides the first *sub-quadratic* token dissemination schedule in a dynamic network controlled by an oblivious adversary. One of the key ingredients of our algorithm is a load balancing routine that is of independent interest: n tokens are at a node, and the goal is to distribute these tokens among the n nodes, without making any copies of the tokens. This load balancing routine is implemented in a centralized manner; its complexity in the distributed setting under an oblivious adversary, however, is open. We believe that our centralized algorithm is a step towards designing a possible subquadratic-round fully distributed algorithm under an oblivious adversary.

Due to space constraints, we have to omit many proofs; we refer the reader to the full paper for all missing proofs [2].

2 An $\tilde{\Omega}(n^{1.5})$ Lower Bound for RAND-DIFF

In this section, we show that there exists an oblivious adversary under which RAND-DIFF takes $\tilde{\Omega}(n^{3/2})$ rounds to complete n-gossip whp. We will establish this result in two stages. In the first stage, we will introduce a more powerful class of adversaries, which we refer to as *invasive* adversaries. Like an oblivious adversary, an invasive adversary can arbitrarily change the graph connecting the nodes in each round, subject to the constraint that the network is connected. In addition, an invasive adversary can add, to each node, an arbitrary set of tokens from the existing universe of tokens. Similar to an oblivious adversary, an invasive adversary needs to specify, for each round, the network connecting the nodes as well as the tokens to add to each node, in advance of the execution of the gossip algorithm.

In Sect. 2.1, we will first show that there exists an invasive adversary under which RAND-DIFF takes $\tilde{\Omega}(n^{3/2})$ rounds to complete n-gossip whp. In Sect. 2.2,

---

[5] Indeed, an infrastructure-based model captures many real-world scenarios involving an underlying communication network with dynamics restricted to the network edges. This is unlike the case of a general oblivious adversary where the graph can change arbitrarily from round to round.

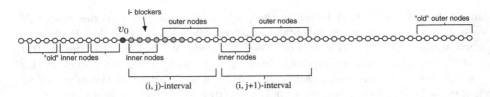

Fig. 1. The dynamic line network for the lower bound for RAND-DIFF

we will simulate the token addition process using RAND-DIFF and extend the lower bound claim to oblivious adversaries.

2.1 Lower Bound Under an Invasive Adversary

Our invasive adversary proceeds in $\sqrt{n}/(2\log n)$ *phases*, each phase consisting of $\Omega(n)$ rounds, divided into *segments* of $\sqrt{n}$ rounds each. Throughout the process, the network is always a line, you can refer to Fig. 1 throughout the description on the network. We build this line network by attaching two line networks – which we refer to as *left* and *right* lines – each of which has the same designated source node v_0 at one of its ends. The size of the left line keeps growing with time, while the size of the right line shrinks with time. After the end of each segment, we move $\log n$ nodes closest to v_0 in the right line to the left line, so the size of the left line at the start of segment j of phase i is exactly $((i-1)\frac{\sqrt{n}}{3}+j-1)\log n$.

At the start of each phase, we label the nodes in the right line (other than the source v_0) as v_1 through v_p (where p is the number of nodes in the right line at that time). For any j, we refer to set $\{v_l : 2(j-1)\sqrt{n} \le l < 2j\sqrt{n}\}$ as the (i,j)-interval. We refer to the first $\log n$ nodes of the (i,j)-interval as the (i,j)-inner nodes, and the remaining $2\sqrt{n}-\log n$ nodes as the (i,j)-outer nodes.

Initially, v_0 has all of the n tokens and every other node has no token. We arbitrarily partition the *tokens* into $\sqrt{n}$ groups of $\sqrt{n}$ tokens each. We use B_i to denote the ith group, and refer to any token in B_i, $1 \le i \le \sqrt{n}/(2\log n)$ as an *i-blocker* since the adversary will use the tokens in B_i in phase i to impede the progress of tokens not in $\cup_{j \le i}B_j$. Let $M(u)$ denote the set of tokens in node u at any time.

At a high level, our adversary operates as follows. Throughout segment j of phase i, the adversary keeps the line unchanged. At the start of segment j, the adversary adds randomly chosen subsets of tokens from B_i to the $\sqrt{n}$ nodes of (i,j)-interval which are the $\sqrt{n}$ consecutive nodes adjacent to v_0 from the right. We argue that this action ensures that in subsequent $\varepsilon\sqrt{n}$ rounds, no token outside the set $\cup_{i' \le i}B_{i'}$ makes it to an (i,j)-outer node. Since in each phase the adversary uses the same set of $\sqrt{n}$ tokens, namely B_i, as "blockers", it can continue this for $\Omega(\sqrt{n}/\log n)$ phases, and ensure that whp, no token in, say $B_{\sqrt{n}}$, has reached the right line in $\Omega(n^{3/2}/\log n)$ rounds. We now formally describe how our adversary operates.

Phase i, $1 \le i \le \sqrt{n}/(2\log n)$:

- **Segment j, $1 \le j \le \sqrt{n}/3$:** The network is a line, that has two parts. The first part is the left line with v_0 at one end, connected to all the (i',j')-inner nodes, where either A: $i' < i$ or B: $i' = i$ and $j' < j$. The second part is a line with v_0 at one end connected to (i, j')-intervals in sequence, $j' \geq j$, followed by (i, j')-outer nodes, $j' < j$.

- **Pre-Segment Insertion:** For each token τ in B_i and each node v among the first $\sqrt{n}$ nodes of (i, j)-interval nodes: adversary inserts τ in v independently with probability $1/2$.
- **Run:** Execute RAND-DIFF for $\varepsilon\sqrt{n}$ rounds of segment j.
- **Post-Segment Shifting:** The adversary moves the (i, j)-inner nodes to the left line, and the (i, j)-outer nodes to the right end of the line and connect the $(i, j + 1)$-interval to v_0.
- **Post-Phase Insertion:** For every node in the right line, the adversary inserts any token missing from B_i.

Lemma 1. *In every round of phase i and segment j, for any of two adjacent nodes u and v on the (i, j)-inner nodes, the probability that $|M(u) - M(v)|$ is less than $\sqrt{n}/16$ is at most $e^{-\Omega(\sqrt{n})}$.*

Proof. Let X be the random variable denoting the number of tokens node u has but node v does not have, at the start of segment j. Clearly, X equals $\sum_{\tau \in B_i} I_\tau$, where I_τ is the indicator variable for token τ; I_τ is 1 if u has token τ and v does not have τ; otherwise it is 0. Using linearity of expectation, we obtain $E[X] = \sum_{\tau \in B_i} E[I_\tau]$. Since the adversary adds each token to each node with probability of $1/2$ independently, we have $E[I_\tau] = 1/4$ and $E[X] = \sqrt{n}/4$. Using a standard Chernoff bound argument, we obtain that the probability that $X \leq \sqrt{n}/8$ is $e^{-\Omega(\sqrt{n})}$. During the remainder of segment j, since each node has two neighbors on the line, node v may receive at most $2\varepsilon\sqrt{n}$ new tokens. Thus, $|M(u) - M(v)|$ is at least $\sqrt{n}/8 - 2\varepsilon\sqrt{n}$ whp (for $\varepsilon \leq 1/32$, this difference is at least $\sqrt{n}/16$).

Lemma 2. *In segment j of phase i, the probability that any token in $\cup_{i'>i} B_{i'}$ reaches an (i, j)-outer node is at most $1/n^9$.*

Proof. Let α be an arbitrary token in the set $\cup_{i'>i} B_{i'}$. By Lemma 1, the probability that at an arbitrary round token α is sent from one node to its adjacent node on (i, j)-interval is at most $16/\sqrt{n}$. The probability that token α goes further than $\log n$ steps during segment j (which is $\varepsilon\sqrt{n}$ rounds) is at most $\binom{\varepsilon\sqrt{n}}{\log n}\left(\frac{16}{\sqrt{n}}\right)^{\log n}$, which is $O(1/n^{10})$. Now using union bound, we obtain that the probability that any token in $\cup_{i'>i} B_{i'}$ reaches any i-outer node is at most $n/n^{10} = 1/n^9$.

Lemma 3. *At the end of phase i, the set of tokens in any node $\neq v_0$ in the right line is $\cup_{i' \leq i} B_{i'}$ whp.*

Proof. The proof is by induction on i. For convenience, we set the induction base case to be $i = 0$ and assume B_0 is the empty set. So the base case, at the start of the algorithm, is trivial since initally every node other than v_0 has no tokens. For the induction step, we consider phase $i > 0$. Let R_i denote the set of nodes in the right line at the end of phase i. We first observe that $R_i \subseteq R_{i-1}$. By the induction hypothesis, it follows that the token set at every node in R_i at the end of phase $i-1$ is precisely $\cup_{i'<i} B_{i'}$. Furthermore, the adversary guarantees that every node in R_i has all tokens from B_i at the end of phase i.

It remains to prove that no token from $\cup_{i'>i} B_{i'}$ arrives at any node in R_i during phase i. Our proof is by contradiction. Let v be the first node in R_i to receive a token τ from $\cup_{i'>i} B_{i'}$ in phase i. Since v is first such node, it received τ from v_0 or from an (i,j)-inner node since R_i is the union of the sets of all (i,j)-outer nodes. Now, v can be connected to such an (i,j)-inner node only during segment j. By Lemma 2, however, no (i,j)-outer node receives a token from $\cup_{i'>i} B_{i'}$ whp.

Theorem 1. *Under the invasive adversary defined above, whp,* RAND-DIFF *requires* $\Omega(n^{3/2}/\log n)$ *rounds to complete n-gossip.*

Proof. Each phase consists of $\sqrt{n}/3$ segments, with each segment having $\epsilon\sqrt{n}$ rounds. So the total number of rounds after $\sqrt{n}/(2\log n)$ phases is $\Omega(n^{3/2}/\log n)$. We obtain that after $\sqrt{n}/(2\log n)$ phases, the size of the left line is at most $n/2$, implying that the right line has $\Omega(n)$ nodes. By Lemma 3, whp, every node in the right line is missing at least one token, completing the proof of the theorem.

2.2   Lower Bound Under an Oblivious Adversary

In this section, we extend the lower bound established in Sect. 2.1 to oblivious adversaries. Thus, the adversary can no longer insert tokens into the network nodes; the pre-segment insertion and post-phase insertion steps of the adversary of Sect. 2.1 are no longer permitted. We simulate these two steps using RAND-DIFF and a judicious use of (oblivious) network dynamics.

Theorem 2. RAND-DIFF *requires* $\Omega(n^{3/2}/\log n)$ *rounds whp under an oblivious adversary.*

2.3   Lower Bound for Symmetric Knowledge-Based Algorithms

In this section, we present a lower bound for a broad class of randomized algorithms for gossip, called *symmetric knowledge-based (SKB)* algorithms. We first introduce some notation. For round t, we define $a_t : U \times V \to T$, where U is the universe of all tokens and V is the set of all nodes: if τ is at u at the start of round t, then $a_t(\tau, u)$ is the time that τ first arrived at u; otherwise $a_t(\tau, u)$ is $\perp$.

Definition 1. *An SKB algorithm is specified by a collection of functions* $P_{t,u} :$ $U \to [0,1]$, *where* $P_{t,u}(\tau)$ *is the probability with which* u *sends* τ *to each of its neighbors in round* t, *satisfying the following properties:*

- **Token transmission:** *for any* t, *if* $a_t(\tau, u) = \perp$, *then* $P_{t,u} = 0$, *the different token sending events for a node in round* t *are mutually exclusive, and* $\sum_{\tau \in U} P_{t,u}(\tau) \le 1$.

- **Symmetry:** *for any* τ_1, τ_2 *such that* $a_t(\tau_1, u) = a_t(\tau_2, u)$, $P_{t,u}(\tau_1) = P_{t,u}(\tau_2)$.

We note that the $P_{t,u}$ may differ arbitrarily from node to node and round to round. The symmetry property and the resulting dependence on the arrival times of tokens are the only constraint on the algorithm.

We now show that there exists an invasive adversary under which SKB takes $\Omega(\frac{n^{4/3}}{\log n})$ rounds to complete n-gossip whp. In order to block the progress of an arbitrary token, the adversary inserts a subset of m tokens, for a suitable choice of m, at the same time as that token reaches a node. We refer to this subset of tokens as a **Blocker Set**. A random selection of the blocker sets, a judicious repetition of this process, together with appropriate network dynamics, yields the desired lower bound.

Theorem 3. *Under an invasive adversary,* SKB *requires* $\Omega(\frac{n^{4/3}}{\log n})$ *rounds whp.*

3   Analysis of RAND-DIFF Under a Paths-Respecting Adversary

In this section, first we introduce a new model, the *paths-respecting* adversary, under which we show that RAND-DIFF completes n-gossip in $\tilde{O}(n^{5/3})$ rounds whp.

3.1   The Paths-Respecting Model

In the paths-respecting model we assume that there is an underlying infrastructure network $\mathcal{N}$ such that at the start of every round t, the network N_t laid out by the adversary is a subgraph of $\mathcal{N}$; we refer to any edge in $\mathcal{N} - N_t$ as an *inactive* or *failed edge* in round t. Before presenting the model, we note that the assumption of an infrastructure network is essentially without loss of generality. For instance, it captures 1-interval connectivity, a central dynamic network model of Kuhn et al [26]: we can let $\mathcal{N}$ be the complete graph and require that N_t be a connected subgraph of $\mathcal{N}$ for each t.

Definition 2. *The* **paths-respecting** *model places some constraints on* $\mathcal{N}$ *and the set of edges that the adversary can render inactive in any given round. In particular, we assume that for every pair* (s, d) *of nodes in* $\mathcal{N}$, *there exists a set* N_{sd} *of simple vertex-disjoint paths from* s *to* d *such that the total number of inactive edges of paths in* N_{sd} *in any round is at most* $|N_{sd}| - 1$.

Before analyzing the paths-respecting model, we present two examples. First, a natural special case of this model is one where $\mathcal{N}$ is a λ-vertex-connected graph and the adversary fails at most $\lambda - 1$ edges in each round. If $\lambda = 2$, then a simple example is that of a ring network in which an arbitrary edge fails in each round. In this example, the adversary is significantly restricted in the number of total edges it can fail in a given round; yet, it is not obvious how a distributed token-forwarding algorithm can exploit this fact since for any pair of vertices, no specific path between the two may be active for more than n rounds over an interval of λn rounds. A radically different example of the paths-respecting model in which the adversary can fail *a constant fraction* of edges in each round is the following: $\mathcal{N}$ consists of a set of r *center* vertices and a set of $n - r$ *terminals*, with an edge between each center and each other vertex. Any two vertices have at least $r - 1$ vertex-disjoint paths between them. An adversary can remove edges between $\lfloor(r - 2)/2\rfloor$ of the centers and all the terminals – and hence, nearly half of the edges of the network – while satisfying the constraint that at most $r - 2$ edges are removed in any collection of $r - 1$ vertex-disjoint paths passing through the centers.

Our main result here is the analysis of RAND-DIFF in the paths-respecting model.

Theorem 4. *Under any n-node paths-respecting dynamic network, RAND-DIFF completes n-gossip in $O(n^{5/3} \log^3 n)$ rounds whp.*

Our proof of Theorem 4 proceeds in a series of arguments, beginning with a restricted version of the paths-respecting model, and successively relaxing the restriction until we have the result for the paths-respecting model. Fix a token τ, and source s that has τ at the start of round 0. Let d be an arbitrary node in the network. In our analysis, we focus our attention on the set N_{sd} of vertex-disjoint paths between s and d such that the total number of inactive edges of N_{sd} in any round is at most $|N_{sd}| - 1$. In Sect. 3.2, we analyze RAND-DIFF under the assumption that the lengths of all paths in N_{sd} are within a factor of two of one another, and the adversary fails at most one edge in any path. In Sect. 3.3, we drop the restrictions that at most one edge is inactive in any path and path lengths are near-uniform, and complete the proof of Theorem 4.

3.2   Near-Uniform Length Paths and at Most One Inactive Edge per Path

Lemma 4. *Suppose there exists an integer $l > 0$ such that the length of each path in N_{sd} is in $[l, 2l)$. Further suppose that in addition to the conditions of the paths-respecting model, for every path in N_{sd}, the adversary can fail at most one edge in the path in any round. Then, the token τ is at d in $O(n^{5/3} \log n)$ rounds whp.*

The proof of Lemma 4 is a *delay sequence argument* that proceeds backwards in time. Delay sequence arguments have been extensively used in the analysis of routing algorithms [28]. A major technical challenge we face in our analysis, distinct from previous use of delay sequence arguments, is network dynamics. The number of possible dynamic networks, even subject to the paths-respecting model, is huge and our analysis cannot afford to account for them independent of the actions of the algorithm.

3.3   Removing Restriction on Path Lengths and Inactive Edges per Path

We first extend the claim of the preceding section to the case where the adversary can fail an arbitrary number of edges in any path of N_{sd}, subject to the constraint imposed by the paths-respecting model that the number of inactive edges in N_{sd} is at most $|N_{sd}| - 1$. We continue to make the assumption of near-uniform path lengths. In a round, call a path *active* if none of its edges is failed, *1-inactive* if exactly one of its edges is inactive, and *dead* if more than one of its edges are inactive. Since the adversary can fail at most $|N_{sd}| - 1$ edges among $|N_{sd}|$ disjoint paths, it follows that the number of active paths is at least one more than the number of dead paths. This is the only constraint we place on the adversary that we analyze in this section: the number of active paths is at least one more than the number of dead paths.

Lemma 5. *Suppose there exists an integer $l > 0$ such that the length of each path in N_{sd} is in $[l, 2l)$. Further assume that the number of dead paths is in $[a, 2a)$ for some a, in each round. Then, under* RAND-DIFF, τ *is at d in $O(n^{5/3} \log n)$ rounds whp.*

Now, we extend Lemma 5 by removing the constraint on the number of dead paths.

Lemma 6. *Suppose there exists an integer $l > 0$ such that the length of each path in N_{sd} is in $[l, 2l)$. Then, in the paths-respecting model, using* RAND-DIFF, *the token τ is at d in $O(n^{5/3} \log^2 n)$ rounds whp.*

We now complete the proof of Theorem 4 by removing the assumption of near-uniform path lengths in the paths of N_{sd}. This is a standard argument in which we incur another multiplicative factor of $\log n$ in our bound.

4 Centralized k-gossip in $\min\{nk, \tilde{O}((n + k)\sqrt{n})\}$ rounds

In this section we present a centralized algorithm that completes k-gossip in $\tilde{O}((n + k)\sqrt{n})$ rounds against any oblivious adversary. Since k-gossip can be completed in nk rounds by separately broadcasting each token over n rounds, this yields a bound of $\min\{nk, \tilde{O}((n+k)\sqrt{n})\}$ on centralized k-gossip using token forwarding.

In the full paper, we give a simple argument that a $\tilde{O}(n^{3/2})$-round algorithm for n-gossip implies a $\tilde{O}((n + k)\sqrt{n})$-round algorithm for k-gossip. We present our centralized algorithm for n-gossip in two parts. We first solve a special case of n-gossip – n-broadcast – in which all the tokens are located in one node. We then extend the claim to arbitrary initial distributions of the n tokens. We start by introducing two useful subroutines: *random load balancing* and *greedy token exchange*.

4.1 Random Load Balancing and Greedy Token Exchange

In the random load balancing subroutine, we have a set F of nodes, each of which contains the same set T of at least n *items* (each item is a copy of some token), and a set R of nodes such that $F \cup R$ is the set of all n nodes. The goal is to distribute the items among nodes in R such that the following properties hold at the end of the subroutine: (B1) each item in T is in exactly one node in R; (B2) every node has either $\lfloor |T|/|R| \rfloor$ or $\lceil |T|/|R| \rceil$ items; (B3) the set X of items placed at any subset $S \subseteq R$ of nodes is drawn uniformly at random from the collection of all subsets of T of size $|X|$.

LoadBalance(F, T, R): Assign a rank to each item in T using a random permutation. In round i, $i \in [|T|]$:

1. Identify a node $v \in R$ that has been distributed fewer than $\lfloor |T|/|R| \rfloor$ items yet, and is closest to a node in F, say v_0, among all such nodes in R.
2. Let P denote a shortest path from v_0 to v. Let ℓ be the number of edges in P, and let (v_{j-1}, v_j), $0 \le j < \ell$, denote the jth edge in P; so $v_\ell = v$. Then, v_0 sends item of rank i to v_1; in parallel, for every edge (v_{j-1}, v_j), $1 \le j < \ell$, v_{j-1} sends an arbitrary item it received earlier in this subroutine to v_j.

Lemma 7. *The subroutine* **LoadBalance**(F, T, R) *completes in* $|T|$ *rounds and satisfies the properties (B1), (B2), and (B3).*

The greedy token exchange is a one round subroutine in which the goal is to maximize the number of new tokens received at each node in that round.

GreedyExchange: Fix a round. For each node v, let $S(v)$ be the set of tokens that node v has at the start of the round. Let N_v denote the set of neighbors of v. Let U_v be the set $\cup_{u \in N_v} S(u) \setminus S(v)$. For each node v, we perform the following operations. Construct a bipartite graph H_v, in which one side is the set N_v, and the other side is the set U_v. For each $u \in N_v$ and $\tau \in U_v$, there is a link between u and τ if token $\tau \in S(u)$. Compute a maximum bipartite matching M_v in H_v. If (τ, u) is in M_v, then u sends token τ to v.

Lemma 8. *In each round, the subroutine* **GreedyExchange** *maximizes, for each node v, number of new tokens that can be added to the node in that round.*

4.2 n-broadcast

We now present a $\tilde{\Theta}(n^{3/2})$-round algorithm for n-broadcast, where all tokens are located initially in a single node. The algorithm consists of $O(\log n)$ *stages*. Let U denote the set of all n tokens. We now describe each stage. Call a node *full* if it has all of the n tokens at the start of the stage, and *non-full* otherwise. Let R denote the set of non-full nodes at the start of the stage, and let $r = |R|$. The stage consists of $\Theta(\sqrt{n} \log n)$ identical phases. Each phase consists of a sequence of steps divided into two segments: distribution and exchange.

Distribution segment: Distribute the n tokens among the non-full nodes R in the network, as evenly as possible, in n rounds by running **LoadBalance**(F, R, U).

Exchange segment: Starting with the distribution of tokens as specified in the preceding distribution segment; i.e., each full node has all tokens, and each non-full node has exactly the tokens distributed in the above segment, run n rounds of **GreedyExchange** maximizing the total number of new tokens received by the nodes in each round.

Theorem 5. *The n-broadcast problem completes in $O(n^{3/2}\log^2 n)$ rounds whp.*

4.3   n-gossip

Our centralized algorithm for arbitrary n-gossip instances is as follows.

Consolidation stage: (a) For each token i, in sequence: for $\sqrt{n}$ rounds, every node holding token i broadcasts token i (i.e., flooding of token i); (b) Identify a set S of $\tilde{O}(\sqrt{n})$ nodes such that every token is in some node in S; arbitrarily assign each token to a node in S that has the token.

Distribution stage: Each node in S makes $\sqrt{n}$ copies of each of its allocated tokens, for a total of $n^{3/2}$ tokens in all, including copies. If any node in S has a token multiset of fewer than n tokens, then it adds dummy tokens to the multiset to make it of size n. Let T_u denote the multiset of tokens at u. For each node u in S, we ensure that each node receives a distinct random token from the multiset of u: **LoadBalance**$(\{u\}, V, T_u)$.

Exchange stage: Maximize the number of token exchanges in each round by repeatedly calling **GreedyExchange**, until some node, say s, has at least $n - c\sqrt{n}\log n$ tokens, for a constant c that is chosen sufficiently large. If n-gossip is not yet completed, then: (a) Run n-broadcast with source s to complete the dissemination of the $n - c\sqrt{n}\log n$ tokens at s; (b) Run at most $c\sqrt{n}\log n$ separate broadcasts, spanning n rounds, disseminating the remaining at most $c\sqrt{n}\log n$ tokens to all nodes.

Theorem 6. *Our centralized algorithm completes in $O(n^{3/2}\log^2 n)$ rounds, whp.*

5   Concluding Remarks

Our work leaves several intriguing open problems and directions for future research: Is there a hybrid of RAND-DIFF and a knowledge-based algorithm that can achieve sub-quadratic complexity? What is the best bound for n-gossip achieved by centralized token-forwarding? Explore paths-respecting and related models further to gain a better understanding of network dynamics from a practical standpoint.

References

1. Augustine, J., Pandurangan, G., Robinson, P., Upfal, E.: Towards robust and efficient computation in dynamic peer-to-peer networks. In: SODA, pp. 551–569 (2012)
2. Augustine, J., Avin, C., Liaee, M., Pandurangan, G., Rajaraman, R.: Information spreading in dynamic networks under oblivious adversaries (2016). arXiv:1603.06109

3. Augustine, J., Molla, A.R., Morsy, E., Pandurangan, G., Robinson, P., Upfal, E.: Storage and search in dynamic peer-to-peer networks. In: SPAA, pp. 53–62 (2013)
4. Augustine, J., Pandurangan, G., Robinson, P.: Fast byzantine agreement in dynamic networks. In: PODC, pp. 74–83 (2013)
5. Augustine, J., Pandurangan, G., Robinson, P., Roche, S., Upfal, E.: Enabling robust and efficient distributed computation in dynamic peer-to-peer networks. In: FOCS, pp. 350–369 (2015)
6. Avin, C., Koucký, M., Lotker, Z.: How to explore a fast-changing world (cover time of a simple random walk on evolving graphs). In: Aceto, L., Damgård, I., Goldberg, L.A., Halldórsson, M.M., Ingólfsdóttir, A., Walukiewicz, I. (eds.) ICALP 2008, Part I. LNCS, vol. 5125, pp. 121–132. Springer, Heidelberg (2008)
7. Baumann, H., Crescenzi, P., Fraigniaud, P.: Parsimonious flooding in dynamic graphs. In: PODC, pp. 260–269 (2009)
8. Baumann, H., Crescenzi, P., Fraigniaud, P.: Parsimonious flooding in dynamic graphs. Distrib. Comput. 24(1), 31–44 (2011)
9. Bollobás, B., Riordan, O.: The diameter of a scale-free random graph. Combinatorica 24(1), 5–34 (2004)
10. Broder, A., Kumar, R., Maghoul, F., Raghavan, P., Rajagopalan, S., Stata, R., Tomkins, A., Wiener, J.: Graph structure in the web. Comput. Netw. 33(1–6), 309–320 (2000)
11. Casteigts, A., Flocchini, P., Quattrociocchi, W., Santoro, N.: Time-varying graphs and dynamic networks. Int. J. Parallel Emergent Distrib. Syst. 27(5), 387–408 (2012)
12. Clementi, A.E.F., Monti, A., Pasquale, F., Silvestri, R.: Broadcasting in dynamic radio networks. J. Comput. Syst. Sci. 75(4), 213–230 (2009)
13. Clementi, A.E.F., Macci, C., Monti, A., Pasquale, F., Silvestri, R.: Flooding time in edge-markovian dynamic graphs. In: PODC, pp. 213–222 (2008)
14. Cooper, C., Frieze, A.: Crawling on simple models of web graphs. Internet Math. 1, 57–90 (2003)
15. Dutta, C., Pandurangan, G., Rajaraman, R., Sun, Z., Viola, E.: On the complexity of information spreading in dynamic networks. In: SODA, pp. 717–736 (2013)
16. Ferreira, A.: Building a reference combinatorial model for manets. IEEE Netw. 18(5), 24–29 (2004)
17. Ferreira, A., Goldman, A., Monteiro, J.: On the evaluation of shortest journeys in dynamic networks. In: NCA, pp. 3–10 (2007)
18. Flaxman, A., Frieze, A.M., Upfal, E.: Efficient communication in an ad-hoc network. J. Algorithms 52(1), 1–7 (2004)
19. Georgiou, C., Gilbert, S., Guerraoui, R., Kowalski, D.R.: On the complexity of asynchronous gossip. In: PODC, pp. 135–144 (2008)
20. Gurevich, M., Keidar, I.: Correctness of gossip-based membership under message loss. In: PODC, pp. 151–160 (2009)
21. Haeupler, B.: Analyzing network coding gossip made easy. In: STOC, pp. 293–302 (2011)
22. Haeupler, B., Karger, D.: Faster information dissemination in dynamic networks via network coding. In: PODC, pp. 381–390 (2011)
23. Haeupler, B., Kuhn, F.: Lower bounds on information dissemination in dynamic networks. In: Aguilera, M.K. (ed.) DISC 2012. LNCS, vol. 7611, pp. 166–180. Springer, Heidelberg (2012)
24. Jarry, A., Lotker, Z.: Connectivity in evolving graph with geometric properties. In: DIALM-POMC, pp. 24–30 (2004)

25. Kempe, D., Kleinberg, J., Kumar, A.: Connectivity and inference problems for temporal networks. JCSS **64**(4), 820–842 (2002)
26. Kuhn, F., Lynch, N., Oshman, R.: Distributed computation in dynamic networks. In: STOC, pp. 513–522 (2010)
27. Kuhn, F., Oshman, R., Moses, Y.: Coordinated consensus in dynamic networks. In: PODC, pp. 1–10 (2011)
28. Leighton, F.T.: Introduction to Parallel Algorithms and Architectures: Arrays, Trees, and Hypercubes. Morgan-Kaufmann (1991)
29. Liben-Nowell, D., Novak, J., Kumar, R., Raghavan, P., Tomkins, A.: Geographic routing in social networks. PNAS **102**(33), 11623–11628 (2005)
30. O'Dell, R., Wattenhofer, R.: Information dissemination in highly dynamic graphs. In: DIALM-POMC, pp. 104–110 (2005)
31. Pandurangan, G.: Distributed algorithmic foundations of dynamic networks. In: Halldórsson, M.M. (ed.) SIROCCO 2014. LNCS, vol. 8576, pp. 18–22. Springer, Heidelberg (2014)
32. Peleg, D.: Distributed Computing: A Locality-Sensitive Approach. SIAM (2000)
33. Das Sarma, A., Molla, A.R., Pandurangan, G.: Fast distributed computation in dynamic networks via random walks. In: Aguilera, M.K. (ed.) DISC 2012. LNCS, vol. 7611, pp. 136–150. Springer, Heidelberg (2012)
34. Sarwate, A.D., Dimakis, A.G.: The impact of mobility on gossip algorithms. In: INFOCOM, pp. 2088–2096 (2009)
35. Topkis, D.M.: Concurrent broadcast for information dissemination. IEEE Trans. Soft. Eng. **11**, 1107–1112 (1985)

Non-Bayesian Learning in the Presence of Byzantine Agents

Lili Su[✉] and Nitin H. Vaidya

Department of Electrical and Computer Engineering,
University of Illinois at Urbana-Champaign, Champaign, USA
{lilisu3,nhv}@illinois.edu

Abstract. This paper addresses the problem of non-Bayesian learning over multi-agent networks, where agents repeatedly collect partially informative observations about an *unknown* state of the world, and try to collaboratively learn the true state. We focus on the impact of the Byzantine agents on the performance of consensus-based non-Bayesian learning. Our goal is to design an algorithm for the *non-faulty* agents to collaboratively learn the true state through local communication.

We propose an update rule wherein each agent updates its local beliefs as (up to normalization) the product of (1) the likelihood of the *cumulative* private signals and (2) the weighted geometric average of the beliefs of its incoming neighbors and itself (using Byzantine consensus). Under mild assumptions on the underlying network structure and the global identifiability of the network, we show that all the non-faulty agents asymptotically agree on the true state almost surely.

Keywords: Distributed learning · Byzantine agreement · Fault-tolerance · Adversary attacks · Security

1 Introduction

Learning is closely related to decentralized hypothesis testing, which has received a significant amount of attention [3,6,8,24,28]. The traditional decentralized detection framework consists of a collection of spatially distributed sensors and a fusion center [24,28]. The sensors independently collect *noisy* observations of the environment state, and send only *summary* of the private observations to the fusion center, where a final decision is made.

Distributed hypothesis testing in the *absence* of fusion center is considered in [1,2,6,10]. In particular, Gale and Kariv [6] studied the problem in the context of social learning, where a fully Bayesian belief update rule is studied.

To avoid the complexity of Bayesian learning, a non-Bayesian learning framework that combines local Bayesian learning with consensus was proposed by

This research is supported in part by National Science Foundation awards NSF 1329681 and 1421918. Any opinions, findings, and conclusions or recommendations expressed here are those of the authors and do not necessarily reflect the views of the funding agencies or the U.S. government.

C. Gavoille and D. Ilcinkas (Eds.): DISC 2016, LNCS 9888, pp. 414–427, 2016.
DOI: 10.1007/978-3-662-53426-7_30

Jadbabaie et al. [8], and has attracted much attention [9,11,14,15,18–20]. Jadbabaie et al. [8] considered the general setting where external signals are observed during each iteration of the algorithm execution. Specifically, the belief of each agent is repeatedly updated as the arithmetic mean of its local Bayesian update and the beliefs of its neighbors, combining iterative consensus algorithm with local Bayesian update. It is shown [8] that, under this learning rule, each agent learns the true state almost surely. The publication of [8] has inspired significant efforts in designing and analyzing non-Bayesian learning rules with a particular focus on refining the fusion strategies and analyzing the (asymptotic and/or finite time) convergence rates of the refined algorithms [9,11,14,15,18–21]. Among the various proposed fusion rules, in this paper we are particularly interested in the log-linear form of the update rule, in which, essentially, each agent updates its belief as the geometric average of the local Bayesian update and its neighbors' beliefs [9,11,14,15,18–21]. The log-linear form (geometric averaging) update rule is shown to converge exponentially fast [9,19]. Taking an axiomatic approach, the geometric averaging fusion is proved to be optimal [14]. An optimization-based interpretation of this rule is presented in [19], using dual averaging method with properly chosen proximal functions. Finite-time convergence rates are investigated independently in [11,15,20]. Both [15,21] consider time-varying networks, with slightly different network models. Specifically, [15] assumes that the union of every consecutive B networks is strongly connected, while [21] considers random networks. In this paper, we consider static networks for ease of exposition – our results can be easily generalized to time-varying networks.

The prior work implicitly assumes that the networked agents are reliable in the sense that they correctly follow the specified distributed algorithm. However, in some practical multi-agent networks, this assumption may not hold. For example, in social networks, it is possible that some agents are adversarial, and try to prevent the true state from being learned by the good agents. In this paper, we focus on the fault-tolerant version of the non-Bayesian framework proposed in [8]. In particular, we assume that an unknown subset of agents may suffer Byzantine faults – agents suffering Byzantine faults can behave arbitrarily. The Byzantine fault-tolerance problem was introduced by Pease et al. [16] and has attracted intensive attention from researchers [4,5,13,25,27]. For the Byzantine fault-tolerant non-Bayesian learning problem, the goal is to design an algorithm that enables all the non-faulty agents learn the underlying true state.

Contributions: The existing algorithms [9,11,15,18,20,21] are not robust to Byzantine agents, since the malicious messages sent by the Byzantine agents are indiscriminatingly utilized in the local belief updates. On the other hand, incorporating Byzantine consensus is non-trivial, since the *effective* communication networks are *dependent* on the choice of received messages (i.e., local beliefs) that need to be trimmed away, which is in turn *dependent* on all the random local observations obtained so far. This dependency makes it non-trivial to adapt analysis of previous algorithms to our setting.

To circumvent the technical difficulties, we consider a different update rule wherein each agent updates its local beliefs as (up to normalization) the product of (1) the likelihood of the *cumulative* private signals and (2) the weighted geometric average of the beliefs of its incoming neighbors and itself (using Byzantine consensus). In contrast to the existing algorithms [11, 15], where only the *current* private signal is used in the update, our proposed algorithm relies on the *cumulative* private signals. As it can be seen later, the likelihoods of the *cumulative* signals are easy to compute – only a constant number multiplication operations is needed per iteration. Under mild assumptions on the underlying network structure and the global identifiability of the network, we show that all the non-faulty agents asymptotically agree on the true state almost surely.

Weaker assumptions on the network structure and global identifiability are characterized in our recent work [23] where different learning rules are considered.

2   Problem Formulation

Network Model: Our network model is similar to the model used in [22, 27]. We consider a synchronous system. A collection of n agents (also referred as *nodes*) are connected by a *directed* network $G(\mathcal{V}, \mathcal{E})$, where $\mathcal{V} = \{1, \ldots, n\}$ and $\mathcal{E}$ is the collection of *directed* edges. For each $i \in \mathcal{V}$, let $\mathcal{I}_i$ denote the set of incoming neighbors of agent i. In any execution, up to f agents suffer Byzantine faults. For a given execution, let $\mathcal{F}$ denote the set of Byzantine agents, and $\mathcal{N}$ denote the set of non-faulty agents. We assume that each non-faulty agent knows f, but does not know the *actual* number of faulty agents $|\mathcal{F}|$. Possible misbehavior of faulty agents includes sending incorrect and mismatching (or inconsistent) messages. The Byzantine agents are also assumed to have complete knowledge of system, including the network topology, underlying running algorithm, the states or even the entire history. The faulty agents may collaborate with each other adaptively [12]. Note that $|\mathcal{F}| \leq f$ and $|\mathcal{N}| \geq n - f$ since at most f agents may fail. (As noted earlier, although we assume a static network topology, our results can be easily generalized to time-varying networks.)

Observation Model: Our observation model is identical to that used in [8, 11, 21]. Let $\Theta = \{\theta_1, \ldots, \theta_m\}$ be a set of m environmental states, which we call *hypotheses*. In the t-th iteration, each agent *independently* obtains a private signal about the environmental state θ^*, which is initially unknown to each networked agent. However, the private signals may not be sufficient for the agents to learn the true state θ^* individually. Thus, collaboration is needed for θ^* to be learned.

Each agent i knows the structure of its private signals, which is represented by a set of parameterized marginal distributions $\mathcal{D}^i = \{\ell_i(w_i|\theta)| \theta \in \Theta, w_i \in \mathcal{S}_i\}$, where $\ell_i(\cdot|\theta)$ is the distribution of private signal when θ is the true state, and $\mathcal{S}_i$ is the finite private signal space. For each $\theta \in \Theta$, and each $i \in \mathcal{V}$, the support of $\ell_i(\cdot|\theta)$ is the whole signal space, i.e., $\ell_i(w_i|\theta) > 0$, $\forall w_i \in \mathcal{S}_i$ and $\forall \theta \in \Theta$. Precisely, let s_t^i be the private signal observed by agent i in iteration t, and let $\mathbf{s}_t = \{s_t^1, \ldots, s_t^n\}$ be the signal profile at time t (i.e., signals observed by the agents in iteration t). Given an environmental state θ, the signal profile $\mathbf{s}_t$ is generated according to the joint distribution $\ell_1(s_t^1|\theta) \times \cdots \times \ell_n(s_t^n|\theta)$. In addition, let $s^i_{1,t}$ be the cumulative private signals obtained by agent i up to iteration t, and $\mathbf{s}_{1,t} = \{s^1_{1,t}, \ldots, s^n_{1,t}\}$ be the signal profile history up to time t.

In this paper, we present a sufficient condition on the collaborative identifiability (Sect. 4.1) for the non-faulty agents to learn the true state θ^*.

Local Beliefs: Each agent i maintains a belief vector $\mu^i \in \mathbb{R}^m$, which is a distribution over the set Θ, with $\mu^i(\theta)$ being the probability with which the agent i *believes* that θ is the true environmental state. Since no signals are observed before the execution of an algorithm, the belief μ^i is often initially set to be uniform over the set Θ, i.e., $\left(\mu^i_0(\theta_1), \ldots, \mu^i_0(\theta_m)\right)^T = \left(\frac{1}{m}, \ldots, \frac{1}{m}\right)^T$.[1] In this work, we also adopt the above convention. (For our results to hold, it suffices to have $\mu^i_0(\theta) > 0, \forall \theta \in \Theta, i \in \mathcal{V}$.)

Correctness: Recall that θ^* is the true environmental state. We say the networked agents collaboratively learn θ^* if for every non-faulty agent $i \in \mathcal{N}$

$$\lim_{t \to \infty} \mu^i_t(\theta^*) = 1 \text{ almost surely.} \tag{1}$$

3   Byzantine Consensus

Byzantine consensus has attracted intensive attention [4,5,13,25–27]. While the past work mostly focuses on scalar inputs, the more general vector (or multidimensional) inputs have been studied recently [13,25,26]. Complete communication networks are considered in [13,26], where tight conditions on the number of agents are identified. Incomplete communication networks are studied in [25]. Closer to the non-Bayesian learning problem is the class of *iterative approximate Byzantine consensus algorithms*, where each agent is only allowed to exchange information about its state with its neighbors. In particular, our learning algorithm builds upon the *Byz-Iter* algorithm proposed in [25] for iterative Byzantine consensus with vector inputs in incomplete networks. [25] provides a matrix representation of the non-faulty agents' states evolution, which is useful in our analysis as well. To make this paper self-contained, in this section, we briefly review the algorithm *Byz-Iter* and its matrix representation.

3.1   Algorithm *Byz-Iter* [25]

Algorithm *Byz-Iter* is based on Tverberg's Theorem [17].

Theorem 1. *[17] Let f be a nonnegative integer. Let Y be a multiset containing vectors from $\mathbb{R}^m$ such that $|Y| \geq (m+1)f + 1$. There exists a partition $Y_1, Y_2, \cdots, Y_{f+1}$ of Y such that Y_i is nonempty for $1 \leq i \leq f+1$, and the intersection of the convex hulls of Y_i's are nonempty, i.e., $\cap^{f+1}_{i=1} \mathsf{Conv}(Y_i) \neq \varnothing$, where $\mathsf{Conv}(Y_i)$ is the convex hull of Y_i for $i = 1, \cdots, f+1$.*

---

[1] In this paper, every vector considered is a column vector.

The proper partition in Theorem 1, and the points in $\cap_{i=1}^{f+1}\mathsf{Conv}(Y_i)$, are referred as *Tverberg partition of Y* and *Tverberg points of Y*, respectively.

For convenience of presenting our algorithm in Sect. 4, we present *Byz-Iter* (described in Algorithm 2) below using *One-Iter* (described in Algorithm 1) as a primitive. The parameter $\mathbf{x}^i$ passed to *One-Iter* at agent i, and $\mathbf{y}^i$ returned by *One-Iter* are both m-dimensional vectors. Let $\mathbf{v}^i$ be the state of agent i that will be iteratively updated, with $\mathbf{v}_t^i$ being the state at the end of iteration t and $\mathbf{v}_0^i$ being the input of agent i. In each iteration $t \geq 1$, a non-faulty agent performs the steps in *One-Iter*. In particular, in the message receiving step, if a message is not received from some neighbor, that neighbor must be faulty, as the system is synchronous. In this case, the missing message values are set to some default value. Faulty agents may deviate from the algorithm specification arbitrarily. In *Byz-Iter*, the value returned by *One-Iter* at agent i is assigned to $\mathbf{v}_t^i$.

Algorithm 1. Algorithm *One-Iter*   with input $\mathbf{x}^i$ at agent i

---

1 $Z^i \leftarrow \emptyset$;
2 Transmit $\mathbf{x}^i$ on all outgoing links;
3 Receive messages on all incoming links. These message values form a multiset R^i of size $|\mathcal{I}_i|$;
4 **for** *every* $C \subseteq R^i \cup \{\mathbf{x}^i\}$ *such that* $|C| = (m+1)f+1$ **do**
5 | add to Z^i a *Tverberg point* of multiset C
6 **end**
7 Compute $\mathbf{y}^i$ as follows: $\mathbf{y}^i \leftarrow \frac{1}{1+|Z^i|}\left(\mathbf{x}^i + \sum_{\mathbf{z} \in Z^i} \mathbf{z}\right)$;
8 Return $\mathbf{y}^i$;

Algorithm 2. Algorithm *Byz-Iter* [25]: t-th iteration at agent i

---

1 $\mathbf{v}_t^i \leftarrow$ *One-Iter*$(\mathbf{v}_{t-1}^i)$;

3.2   Correctness of Algorithm *Byz-Iter*

We briefly summarize the aspects of correctness proof of Algorithm 2 from [25] that are necessary for our subsequent discussion. By using the Tverberg points in the update of $\mathbf{v}_t^i$ above, effectively, the extreme message values (that may potentially be sent by faulty agents) are trimmed away. Informally speaking, trimming certain messages can be viewed as ignoring (or removing) incoming links that carry the outliers. [25] shows that the effective communication network thus obtained can be characterized by a "reduced graph" of $G(\mathcal{V}, \mathcal{E})$, defined below. It is important to note that the non-faulty agents **do not** know the identity of the faulty agents.

Definition 1. *A reduced graph $\mathcal{H}(\mathcal{N}, \mathcal{E}_\mathcal{F})$ of $G(\mathcal{V}, \mathcal{E})$ is obtained by (i) removing all faulty nodes $\mathcal{F}$, and all the links incident on the faulty nodes $\mathcal{F}$; and (ii) for each non-faulty node (nodes in $\mathcal{N}$), removing up to mf additional incoming links.*

Definition 2. *A source component in any given reduced graph is a strongly connected component (of that reduced graph), which does not have any incoming links from outside that component.*

It turns out that the effective communication network is potentially time-varying (partly) due to the time-varying behavior of faulty nodes. Assumption 1 below states a condition that is sufficient for Algorithm 1 [25] to work.

Assumption 1. *Every reduced graph of $G(\mathcal{V}, \mathcal{E})$ has a unique source component.*

Let $\mathcal{C}$ be the set of all the reduced graph of $G(\mathcal{V}, \mathcal{E})$. Define $\chi \triangleq |\mathcal{C}| < \infty$. Let $\mathcal{H} \in \mathcal{C}$ be a reduced graph of $G(\mathcal{V}, \mathcal{E})$ with source component $\mathcal{S}_\mathcal{H}$. Define

$$\gamma \triangleq \min_{\mathcal{H} \in \mathcal{C}} |\mathcal{S}_\mathcal{H}| \geq 1, \tag{2}$$

i.e., γ is the minimum source component size among all the reduced graphs.

Theorem 2. *[25] If Assumption 1 holds, using Algorithm 1, all the non-faulty agents reach consensus asymptotically, i.e., $\lim_{t\to\infty} |\mathbf{v}_t^i - \mathbf{v}_t^j| = 0, \forall i, j \in \mathcal{N}$.*

The proof of Theorem 2 relies on a matrix representation of the state evolution.

3.3   Matrix Representation [25]

Let $|\mathcal{F}| = \phi$ (thus, $0 \leq \phi \leq f$). Without loss of generality, assume that agents 1 through $n - \phi$ are non-faulty, and agents $n - \phi + 1$ to n are Byzantine.

Lemma 1. *[25] Suppose that Assumption 1 holds. The state updates performed by the non-faulty agents in the t–th iteration ($t \geq 1$) can be expressed as*

$$\mathbf{v}_t^i = \sum_{j=1}^{n-\phi} \mathbf{A}_{ij}[t] \mathbf{v}_{t-1}^j, \tag{3}$$

where $\mathbf{A}[t] \in \mathbb{R}^{(n-\phi) \times (n-\phi)}$ is a row stochastic matrix for which there exists a reduced graph $\mathcal{H}[t]$ with adjacency matrix $\mathbf{H}[t]$ such that $\mathbf{A}[t] \geq \beta \mathbf{H}[t]$, where $0 < \beta \leq 1$ is a constant that depends only on $G(\mathcal{V}, \mathcal{E})$.

Let $\mathbf{\Phi}(t, r) \triangleq \mathbf{A}[t] \cdots \mathbf{A}[r]$ for $1 \leq r \leq t + 1$. By convention, $\mathbf{\Phi}(t, t) = \mathbf{A}[t]$ and $\mathbf{\Phi}(t, t + 1) = \mathbf{I}$. Using prior work on coefficients of ergodicity [7], under Assumption 1, it was shown [25,29] that

$$\lim_{t \geq r,\ t\to\infty} \mathbf{\Phi}(t, r) = \mathbf{1}\pi(r), \tag{4}$$

where $\pi(r) \in \mathbb{R}^{n-\phi}$ is a row stochastic vector. Recall that χ is the total number of reduced graphs of $G(\mathcal{V}, \mathcal{E})$, and β is defined in Lemma 1, and $\phi \triangleq |\mathcal{F}|$. Also define $\nu \triangleq \chi(n - \phi)$. The convergence rate in (4) is exponential.

Theorem 3. *[25]* $|\Phi_{ij}(t, r) - \pi_j(r)| \leq (1 - \beta^\nu)^{\lceil \frac{t-r+1}{\nu} \rceil}$ *for all* $t \geq r \geq 1$.

The next lemma is a consequence of the results in [25].

Lemma 2. *[25] For any* $r \geq 1$, *there exists a reduced graph* $\mathcal{H}[r]$ *with source component* $\mathcal{S}_r$ *such that* $\pi_i(r) \geq \beta^{\chi(n-\phi)}$ *for each* $i \in \mathcal{S}_r$. *In addition,* $|\mathcal{S}_r| \geq \gamma$.

With the above background on Byzantine vector consensus, we are now ready to present our algorithm and its analysis.

4   Byzantine Fault-Tolerant Non-Bayesian Learning

We will use a modified version of the geometric averaging update rule that has been investigated in previous work [11,15,18,20] to take into account of Byzantine faults. In particular, in each iteration, the likelihood of the *cumulative* observations $s_{1,t}^i$ (instead of the likelihood of the *current* observation s_t^i only) to is used to update the local beliefs.

For $t \geq 1$, the steps to be performed by agent i in the t–th iteration are listed below, where in step 4, N_t^i is the normalization factor such that $\sum_{p=1}^m \mu_t^i(\theta_p) = 1$. Note that faulty agents can deviate from the algorithm specification. The algorithm below uses *One-Iter* presented in the previous section as a primitive. Recall that $s_{1,t}^i$ is the cumulative local observations up to iteration t. Since the observations are i.i.d., it holds that $\ell_i(s_{1,t}^i|\theta) = \prod_{r=1}^t \ell_i(s_r^i|\theta)$. So $\ell_i(s_{1,t}^i|\theta)$ can be computed iteratively in Algorithm 3. The main difference of Algorithm 3 with respect to the algorithms in [11,15,18,20] is that (i) our algorithm uses a Byzantine consensus iteration as a primitive (in line 1), and (ii) $\ell_i(s_{1,t}^i|\theta)$ used in line 5 is the likelihood for observations from iteration 1 to t (the previous algorithms instead use $\ell_i(s_t^i|\theta)$ here). Observe that the consensus step is being performed on log of the beliefs, with the result being stored as η_t^i (in line 1) and used in line 4 to compute the new beliefs.

Algorithm 3. Byzantine Tolerant Non-Bayesian Learning: Iteration $t \geq 1$ at agent i

---

1 $\eta_t^i \leftarrow$ *One-Iter*$(\log \mu_{t-1}^i)$;
2 Observe s_t^i;
3 **for** $\theta \in \Theta$ **do**
4 $\quad$ $\ell_i(s_{1,t}^i|\theta) \leftarrow \ell_i(s_t^i|\theta)\, \ell_i(s_{1,t-1}^i|\theta)$;
5 $\quad$ $\mu_t^i(\theta) \leftarrow \frac{1}{N_t^i}\left(\ell_i(s_{1,t}^i|\theta) \exp\left(\eta_t^i(\theta)\right)\right)$;
6 **end**

Recalling the matrix representation of the *Byz-Iter* algorithm as per Lemma 1, we can write the following equivalent representation of line 1 of Algorithm 3.

$$
\eta_t^i(\theta) = \sum_{j=1}^{n-\phi} \mathbf{A}_{ij}[t] \log \mu_{t-1}^j(\theta) = \log \prod_{j=1}^{n-\phi} \mu_{t-1}^j(\theta)^{\mathbf{A}_{ij}[t]}, \quad \forall \theta \in \Theta. \tag{5}
$$

where $\mathbf{A}[t]$ is a row stochastic matrix whose properties are specified in Lemma 1. Note that $\mu_t^i(\theta)$ is **random** for each $i \in \mathcal{N}$ and $t \geq 1$, as it is updated according to local random observations. Since the consensus is performed over $\log \mu_t^i \in \mathbb{R}^m$, the update matrix $\mathbf{A}[t]$ is also **random**. In particular, for each $t \geq 1$, matrix $\mathbf{A}[t]$ is dependent on *all the cumulative observations over the network* up to iteration t. This dependency makes it non-trivial to adapt analysis from previous algorithms to our setting. In addition, adopting the local cumulative observation likelihood makes the analysis with Byzantine faults easier.

4.1   Identifiability

In the absence of agent failures [8], for the networked agents to detect the true hypothesis θ^*, it is enough to assume that $G(\mathcal{V}, \mathcal{E})$ is strongly connected, and that θ^* is globally identifiable. That is, for any $\theta \neq \theta^*$, there exists a node $j \in \mathcal{V}$ such that the Kullback-Leiber divergence between the true marginal $\ell_j(\cdot|\theta^*)$ and the marginal $\ell_j(\cdot|\theta)$, denoted by $D\left(\ell_j(\cdot|\theta^*)||\ell_j(\cdot|\theta)\right)$, is nonzero; equivalently,

$$
\sum_{j \in \mathcal{V}} D\left(\ell_j(\cdot|\theta^*)||\ell_j(\cdot|\theta)\right) \neq 0, \tag{6}
$$

where $D\left(\ell_j(\cdot|\theta^*)||\ell_j(\cdot|\theta)\right)$ is defined as

$$
D\left(\ell_j(\cdot|\theta^*)||\ell_j(\cdot|\theta)\right) \triangleq \sum_{w_j \in \mathcal{S}_j} \ell_j(w_j|\theta^*) \log \frac{\ell_j(w_j|\theta^*)}{\ell_j(w_j|\theta)}. \tag{7}
$$

Since θ^* may change from execution to execution, (6) is required to hold for any choice of θ^*. Intuitively speaking, if any pair of states θ_1 and θ_2 can be distinguished by at least one agent in the network, then sufficient exchange of local beliefs over strongly connected network will enable every agent distinguish θ_1 and θ_2. However, in the presence of Byzantine agents, the effective communication network may not be strongly connected. Thus, stronger global identifiability is required. The following assumption builds upon Assumption 1.

Assumption 2. *Suppose that Assumption 1 holds. For any $\theta \neq \theta^*$, and for any reduced graph $\mathcal{H}$ of $G(\mathcal{V}, \mathcal{E})$ with $\mathcal{S}_{\mathcal{H}}$ denoting the unique source component,*

$$
\sum_{j \in \mathcal{S}_{\mathcal{H}}} D\left(\ell_j(\cdot|\theta^*) \| \ell_j(\cdot|\theta)\right) \neq 0. \tag{8}
$$

In contrast to (6), where the summation is taken over all the agents in the network, in (8), the summation is taken over agents in the source component only. Intuitively, the condition imposed by Assumption 2 is that all the agents in the source component can detect the true state θ^* collaboratively. If iterative consensus is achieved, the accurate belief can be propagated from the source component to every other non-faulty agent in the network.

4.2   Convergence Results

Our proof parallels the structure of a proof in [15], but with some key differences to take into account our update rule for the belief vector.

For any $\theta_1, \theta_2 \in \Theta$, and any $i \in \mathcal{V}$, define $\psi_t^i(\theta_1, \theta_2)$ and $\mathcal{L}_t(\theta_1, \theta_2)$ as follows

$$\psi_t^i(\theta_1, \theta_2) \triangleq \log \frac{\mu_t^i(\theta_1)}{\mu_t^i(\theta_2)}, \quad \mathcal{L}_t^i(\theta_1, \theta_2) \triangleq \log \frac{\ell_i(s_t^i|\theta_1)}{\ell_i(s_t^i|\theta_2)}. \tag{9}$$

To show Algorithm 3 solves (1), we show that $\psi_t^i(\theta, \theta^*) \xrightarrow{\text{a.s.}} -\infty$, which implies that $\mu_t^i(\theta) \xrightarrow{\text{a.s.}} 0$ for all $\theta \neq \theta^*$ and for all $i \in \mathcal{N}$, i.e., all non-faulty agents asymptotically concentrate their beliefs on the true hypothesis θ^*. We do this by investigating the dynamics of beliefs which is represented in a matrix form.

For each $\theta \neq \theta^*$, and each $i \in \mathcal{N} = \{1, \cdots, n - \phi\}$, we have

$$\psi_t^i(\theta, \theta^*) = \log \frac{\mu_t^i(\theta)}{\mu_t^i(\theta^*)} \stackrel{(a)}{=} \log \left(\prod_{j=1}^{n-\phi} \left(\frac{\mu_{t-1}^j(\theta)}{\mu_{t-1}^j(\theta^*)} \right)^{\mathbf{A}_{ij}[t]} \times \frac{\ell_i(s_{1,t}^i|\theta)}{\ell_i(s_{1,t}^i|\theta^*)} \right)$$

$$= \sum_{j=1}^{n-\phi} \mathbf{A}_{ij}[t] \log \frac{\mu_{t-1}^j(\theta)}{\mu_{t-1}^j(\theta^*)} + \log \frac{\ell_i(s_{1,t}^i|\theta)}{\ell_i(s_{1,t}^i|\theta^*)}$$

$$= \sum_{j=1}^{n-\phi} \mathbf{A}_{ij}[t] \psi_{t-1}^j(\theta, \theta^*) + \sum_{r=1}^{t} \mathcal{L}_r^i(\theta, \theta^*), \tag{10}$$

where equality (a) follows from (5) and the update of μ^i in Algorithm 3, and the last equality follows from (9) and the fact that the local observations are *i.i.d.*.

Let $\psi_t(\theta, \theta^*) \in \mathbb{R}^{n-\phi}$ be the vector that stacks $\psi_t^i(\theta, \theta^*)$, with the i-th entry being $\psi_t^i(\theta, \theta^*)$ for all $i \in \mathcal{N}$. The evolution of $\psi(\theta, \theta^*)$ can be written as

$$\psi_t(\theta, \theta^*) = \mathbf{A}[t]\psi_{t-1}(\theta, \theta^*) + \sum_{r=1}^{t} \mathcal{L}_r(\theta, \theta^*) \tag{11}$$

$$= \mathbf{\Phi}(t, 1)\psi_0(\theta, \theta^*) + \sum_{r=1}^{t} \mathbf{\Phi}(t, r+1) \sum_{k=1}^{r} \mathcal{L}_k(\theta, \theta^*). \tag{12}$$

For each $\theta \in \Theta$ and $i \in \mathcal{V}$, define $H_i(\theta, \theta^*) \in \mathbb{R}^{n-\phi}$ as

$$H_i(\theta, \theta^*) \triangleq \sum_{w_i \in \mathcal{S}_i} \ell_i(w_i|\theta^*) \log \frac{\ell_i(w_i \mid \theta)}{\ell_i(w_i \mid \theta^*)} = -D(\ell_i(\cdot|\theta^*) \parallel \ell_i(\cdot|\theta)) \quad \text{by} \quad (7)$$

$$\leq 0. \tag{13}$$

Let $\mathcal{H} \in \mathcal{C}$ be a reduced graph with source component $\mathcal{S}_\mathcal{H}$. Define C_0 and C_1 as

$$-C_0 \triangleq \min_{i \in \mathcal{V}} \min_{\theta_1, \theta_2 \in \Theta; \theta_1 \neq \theta_2} \min_{w_i \in \mathcal{S}_i} \left(\log \frac{\ell_i(w_i|\theta_1)}{\ell_i(w_i|\theta_2)} \right), \tag{14}$$

$$C_1 \triangleq \min_{\mathcal{H} \in \mathcal{C}} \min_{\theta, \theta^* \in \Theta; \theta \neq \theta^*} \sum_{i \in \mathcal{S}_\mathcal{H}} D(\ell_i(\cdot|\theta^*) \parallel \ell_i(\cdot|\theta)). \tag{15}$$

The constant C_0 serves as an universal upper bound on $\left| \log \frac{\ell_i(w_i|\theta_1)}{\ell_i(w_i|\theta_2)} \right|$ for all choices of θ_1 and θ_2, and for all signals. Intuitively, the constant C_1 is the minimal detection capability of the source component under Assumption 2.

Due to $|\Theta| = m < \infty$ and $|\mathcal{S}_i| < \infty$ for each $i \in \mathcal{N}$, we know that $C_0 < \infty$. Besides, it is easy to see that $-C_0 \leq 0$ (thus, $C_0 \geq 0$). In addition, under Assumption 2, we have $C_1 > 0$.

Now we present a key lemma for our main theorem.

Lemma 3. *Under Assumption 2, for any $\theta \neq \theta^*$, it holds that*

$$\frac{1}{t^2} \sum_{r=1}^{t} \left(\sum_{j=1}^{n-\phi} \Phi_{ij}(t, r+1) \sum_{k=1}^{r} \mathcal{L}_k^j(\theta, \theta^*) - r \sum_{j=1}^{n-\phi} \pi_j(r+1) H_j(\theta, \theta^*) \right) \xrightarrow{\text{a.s.}} 0.$$

The proof of Lemma 3 is different from the analogous lemma in [15], and will be sketched at the end of this section. The complete proof can be found in our extended version [23].

Theorem 4. *When Assumption 2 holds, each non-faulty agent $(i \in \mathcal{N})$ concentrates its belief on the true hypothesis θ^* almost surely, i.e., $\mu_t^i(\theta) \xrightarrow{\text{a.s.}} 0, \forall \theta \neq \theta^*$.*

Proof. Consider any $\theta \neq \theta^*$. Recall from (12) that

$$\psi_t(\theta, \theta^*) = \Phi(t, 1)\psi_0(\theta, \theta^*) + \sum_{r=1}^{t} \Phi(t, r+1) \sum_{k=1}^{r} \mathcal{L}_k(\theta, \theta^*)$$

$$= \sum_{r=1}^{t} \Phi(t, r+1) \sum_{k=1}^{r} \mathcal{L}_k(\theta, \theta^*).$$

The last equality holds as μ_0^i is uniform, and $\psi_0^i(\theta, \theta^*) = 0$ for each $i \in \mathcal{N}$. Since the supports of $\ell_i(\cdot|\theta)$ and $\ell_i(\cdot|\theta^*)$ are the whole signal space $\mathcal{S}_i$ for each agent $i \in \mathcal{N}$, it holds that $\left| \frac{\ell_i(w_i|\theta)}{\ell_i(w_i|\theta^*)} \right| < \infty$ for each $w_i \in \mathcal{S}_i$, and

$$0 \geq H_i(\theta, \theta^*) \geq \min_{w_i \in \mathcal{S}_i} \left(\log \frac{\ell_i(w_i|\theta)}{\ell_i(w_i|\theta^*)} \right) \geq -C_0 > -\infty. \tag{16}$$

By (16), we know that $|\sum_{j=1}^{n-\phi} \pi_j(r+1)H_j(\theta,\theta^*)| \leq C_0 < \infty$. Due to the finiteness of $\sum_{j=1}^{n-\phi} \pi_j(r+1)H_j(\theta,\theta^*)$, we get

$$\psi_t(\theta,\theta^*) = \sum_{r=1}^{t}\left(\Phi(t,r+1)\sum_{k=1}^{r}\mathcal{L}_k(\theta,\theta^*) - r\mathbf{1}\sum_{j=1}^{n-\phi}\pi_j(r+1)H_j(\theta,\theta^*)\right)$$
$$+ \sum_{r=1}^{t} r\mathbf{1}\sum_{j=1}^{n-\phi}\pi_j(r+1)H_j(\theta,\theta^*). \tag{17}$$

For each $i \in \mathcal{N}$, we have

$$\psi_t^i(\theta,\theta^*) = \sum_{r=1}^{t}\left(\sum_{j=1}^{n-\phi}\Phi_{ij}(t,r+1)\sum_{k=1}^{r}\mathcal{L}_k^j(\theta,\theta^*) - r\sum_{j=1}^{n-\phi}\pi_j(r+1)H_j(\theta,\theta^*)\right)$$
$$+ \sum_{r=1}^{t} r\sum_{j=1}^{n-\phi}\pi_j(r+1)H_j(\theta,\theta^*). \tag{18}$$

To show $\lim_{t\to\infty}\mu_t^i(\theta) \xrightarrow{\text{a.s.}} 0$ for $\theta \neq \theta^*$, it is enough to show $\psi_t^i(\theta,\theta^*) \xrightarrow{\text{a.s.}} -\infty$. Our proof has similar structure as that in [15]. From Lemma 3, we get

$$\frac{1}{t^2}\sum_{r=1}^{t}\left(\sum_{j=1}^{n-\phi}\Phi_{ij}(t,r+1)\sum_{k=1}^{r}\mathcal{L}_k^j(\theta,\theta^*) - r\sum_{j=1}^{n-\phi}\pi_j(r+1)H_j(\theta,\theta^*)\right) \xrightarrow{\text{a.s.}} 0. \tag{19}$$

Next we bound the second term of the right hand side of (18).

$$\sum_{r=1}^{t} r\sum_{j=1}^{n-\phi}\pi_j(r+1)H_j(\theta,\theta^*) \leq \sum_{r=1}^{t} r\sum_{j\in\mathcal{S}_r}\pi_j(r+1)H_j(\theta,\theta^*) \qquad \text{by (13)}$$
$$\leq \sum_{r=1}^{t} r\beta^{\chi(n-\phi)}\sum_{j\in\mathcal{S}_r}H_j(\theta,\theta^*) \qquad \text{by Lemma 2}$$
$$\leq -\sum_{r=1}^{t} r\beta^{\chi(n-\phi)}C_1 \qquad \text{by (15) and (13)}$$
$$\leq -\frac{t^2}{2}\beta^{\chi(n-\phi)}C_1. \tag{20}$$

Thus, by (18), (19) and (20), almost surely, $\lim_{t\to\infty}\frac{1}{t^2}\psi_t^i(\theta,\theta^*) \leq -\frac{1}{2}\beta^{\chi(n-\phi)}C_1$. Therefore, $\psi_t^i(\theta,\theta^*) \xrightarrow{\text{a.s.}} -\infty$ and $\mu_t^i(\theta) \xrightarrow{\text{a.s.}} 0$ for $i \in \mathcal{N}$ and $\theta \neq \theta^*$. □

From the proof of Theorem 4, we know that with probability 1, each non-faulty agent learns the true state θ^* exponentially fast in t.

We now sketch the proof of Lemma 3.

Proof (Proof Sketch of Lemma 3). Since $|\mathcal{L}_r^i(\theta, \theta^*)| \leq C_0 < \infty$ for all $i \in \mathcal{N}$ and $r \geq 1$, adding to and subtracting $\frac{1}{t^2} \sum_{r=1}^{t} \sum_{j=1}^{n-\phi} \pi_j(r+1) \sum_{k=1}^{r} \mathcal{L}_k^j(\theta, \theta^*)$ from the target term – the first term on the right hand side of (18), we get

$$\frac{1}{t^2} \sum_{r=1}^{t} \left(\sum_{j=1}^{n-\phi} \Phi_{ij}(t, r+1) \sum_{k=1}^{r} \mathcal{L}_k^j(\theta, \theta^*) - r \sum_{j=1}^{n-\phi} \pi_j(r+1) H_j(\theta, \theta^*) \right)$$

$$= \frac{1}{t^2} \sum_{r=1}^{t} \sum_{j=1}^{n-\phi} (\Phi_{ij}(t, r+1) - \pi_j(r+1)) \sum_{k=1}^{r} \mathcal{L}_k^j(\theta, \theta^*)$$

$$+ \frac{1}{t^2} \sum_{r=1}^{t} \sum_{j=1}^{n-\phi} \pi_j(r+1) \left(\sum_{k=1}^{r} \mathcal{L}_k^j(\theta, \theta^*) - r H_j(\theta, \theta^*) \right). \tag{21}$$

By Theorem 3, $\Phi_{ij}(t, r+1)$ (although random) will converge to $\pi_j(r+1)$ exponentially fast. Additionally, it holds from (14) that $\sum_{k=1}^{r} \mathcal{L}_k^j(\theta, \theta^*) \leq r C_0$. Then, we are able to show that for every sample path,

$$\frac{1}{t^2} \sum_{r=1}^{t} \sum_{j=1}^{n-\phi} (\Phi_{ij}(t, r+1) - \pi_j(r+1)) \sum_{k=1}^{r} \mathcal{L}_k^j(\theta, \theta^*) \to 0.$$

Thus, to prove Lemma 3, it remains to show that

$$\frac{1}{t^2} \sum_{r=1}^{t} \sum_{j=1}^{n-\phi} \pi_j(r+1) \left(\sum_{k=1}^{r} \mathcal{L}_k^j(\theta, \theta^*) - r H_j(\theta, \theta^*) \right) \xrightarrow{\text{a.s.}} 0,$$

i.e., we need to show that almost surely for any $\epsilon > 0$, there exists sufficiently large $t(\epsilon)$ such that $\forall t \geq t(\epsilon)$ the following holds

$$\frac{1}{t^2} \left| \sum_{r=1}^{t} \sum_{j=1}^{n-\phi} \pi_j(r+1) \left(\sum_{k=1}^{r} \mathcal{L}_k^j(\theta, \theta^*) - r H_j(\theta, \theta^*) \right) \right| \leq \epsilon. \tag{22}$$

We prove this by dividing r into two ranges $r \in \{1, \cdots, \sqrt{t}\}$ and $r \in \{\sqrt{t} + 1, \cdots, t\}$. We can show that there exists $t_1(\epsilon)$ such that

$$\frac{1}{t^2} \left| \sum_{r=1}^{\sqrt{t}} \sum_{j=1}^{n-\phi} \left(\sum_{k=1}^{r} \mathcal{L}_k^j(\theta, \theta^*) - r H_j(\theta, \theta^*) \right) \right| \leq \frac{\epsilon}{2} \quad \text{for all } t \geq t_1(\epsilon).$$

Now consider $\frac{1}{t} \sum_{r=\sqrt{t}+1}^{t} \sum_{j=1}^{n-\phi} \pi_j(r+1) \frac{r}{t} \left(\frac{1}{r} \sum_{k=1}^{r} \mathcal{L}_k^j(\theta, \theta^*) - H_j(\theta, \theta^*) \right)$.

Since $\mathcal{L}_k^j(\theta, \theta^*)$'s are i.i.d., from strong LLN, we know that

$$\frac{1}{r} \sum_{k=1}^{r} \mathcal{L}_k^j(\theta, \theta^*) - H_j(\theta, \theta^*) \xrightarrow{\text{a.s.}} 0, \quad \text{as } r \to \infty.$$

That is, with probability 1, a sample path converges. Now, focus on each convergent sample path. For sufficiently large $r(\epsilon)$, it holds that for any $r \geq r(\epsilon)$,

$$\left| \frac{1}{r} \sum_{k=1}^{r} \mathcal{L}_k^j(\theta, \theta^*) - H_j(\theta, \theta^*) \right| \leq \frac{\epsilon}{2}. \tag{23}$$

Recall that $r \geq \sqrt{t}$. Thus, we know that exists sufficiently large $t_2(\epsilon)$ such that $\forall t \geq t_2(\epsilon)$, $r \geq \sqrt{t}$ is large enough and (23) holds.

Therefore, (22) holds almost surely, proving the lemma.   □

5   Conclusion

This paper addresses the problem of consensus-based non-Bayesian learning over multi-agent networks when an unknown subset of agents may be adversarial (Byzantine). We propose an update rule where each agent updates its local beliefs as (up to normalization) the product of (1) the likelihood of the cumulative private signals and (2) the weighted geometric average of the beliefs of its incoming neighbors and itself (using Byzantine consensus algorithm *Byz-Iter*). In contrast, only the newly obtained private signals are used in updating local beliefs in previous algorithms [11,15,18]. We show that all the agents will identify a common optimal θ almost surely. Weaker assumptions on the network structure and global identifiability are characterized in our recent paper [23] where an alternative family of learning rules are considered.

References

1. Bajovic, D., Jakovetic, D., Moura, J.M., Xavier, J., Sinopoli, B.: Large deviations performance of consensus+ innovations distributed detection with non-gaussian observations. IEEE Trans. Signal Process. **60**(11), 5987–6002 (2012)
2. Cattivelli, F.S., Sayed, A.H.: Distributed detection over adaptive networks using diffusion adaptation. IEEE Trans. Signal Process. **59**(5), 1917–1932 (2011)
3. Chamberland, J.-F., Veeravalli, V.V.: Decentralized detection in sensor networks. IEEE Trans. Signal Process. **51**(2), 407–416 (2003)
4. Dolev, D., Lynch, N.A., Pinter, S.S., Stark, E.W., Weihl, W.E.: Reaching approximate agreement in the presence of faults. J. ACM **33**(3), 499–516 (1986)
5. Fekete, A.D.: Asymptotically optimal algorithms for approximate agreement. Distrib. Comput. **4**(1), 9–29 (1990)
6. Gale, D., Kariv, S.: Bayesian learning in social networks. Games Econ. Behav. **45**(2), 329–346 (2003)
7. Hajnal, J., Bartlett, M.: Weak ergodicity in non-homogeneous markov chains. In: Mathematical Proceedings of the Cambridge Philosophical Society, vol. 54, pp. 233–246. Cambridge University Press (1958)
8. Jadbabaie, A., Molavi, P., Sandroni, A., Tahbaz-Salehi, A.: Non-bayesian social learning. Games Econ. Behav. **76**(1), 210–225 (2012)
9. Jadbabaie, A., Molavi, P., Tahbaz-Salehi, A.: Information heterogeneity and the speed of learning in social networks. Columbia Business School Research Paper, (13–28) (2013)

10. Jakovetic, D., Moura, J.M., Xavier, J.: Distributed detection over noisy networks: large deviations analysis. IEEE Trans. Signal Process. **60**(8), 4306–4320 (2012)
11. Lalitha, A., Sarwate, A., Javidi, T.: Social learning and distributed hypothesis testing. In: IEEE International Symposium on Information Theory, pp. 551–555. IEEE (2014)
12. Lynch, N.A.: Distributed Algorithms. Morgan Kaufmann, San Francisco (1996)
13. Mendes, H., Herlihy, M.: Multidimensional approximate agreement in Byzantine asynchronous systems. In: Proceedings of the Forty-fifth Annual ACM Symposium on Theory of Computing, STOC 2013, pp. 391–400. ACM, New York (2013)
14. Molavi, P., Tahbaz-Salehi, A., Jadbabaie, A.: Foundations of non-bayesian social learning. Columbia Business School Research Paper (2015)
15. Nedic, A., Olshevsky, A., Uribe, C.A.: Nonasymptotic convergence rates for cooperative learning over time-varying directed graphs. ArXiv e-prints 1410.1977 (2014)
16. Pease, M., Shostak, R., Lamport, L.: Reaching agreement in the presence of faults. J. ACM **27**(2), 228–234 (1980)
17. Perles, M.A., Sigron, M.: A generalization of tverberg's theorem. ArXiv e-prints 0710.4668 (2007)
18. Rad, K.R., Tahbaz-Salehi, A.: Distributed parameter estimation in networks. In: 49th IEEE Conference on Decision and Control (CDC), pp. 5050–5055. IEEE (2010)
19. Shahrampour, S., Jadbabaie, A.: Exponentially fast parameter estimation in networks using distributed dual averaging. In: 52nd IEEE Conference on Decision and Control, pp. 6196–6201. IEEE (2013)
20. Shahrampour, S., Rakhlin, A., Jadbabaie, A.: Distributed detection: finite-time analysis and impact of network topology (2014)
21. Shahrampour, S., Rakhlin, A., Jadbabaie, A.: Finite-time analysis of the distributed detection problem. In: 2015 53rd Annual Allerton Conference on Communication, Control, and Computing (Allerton), pp. 598–603. IEEE (2015)
22. Su, L., Vaidya, N.: Reaching approximate Byzantine consensus with multi-hop communication. In: Pelc, A., Schwarzmann, A.A. (eds.) SSS 2015. LNCS, vol. 9212, pp. 21–35. Springer, Heidelberg (2015)
23. Su, L., Vaidya, N.H.: Defending non-Bayesian learning against adversarial attacks. ArXiv e-prints, June 2016
24. Tsitsiklis, J.N.: Decentralized detection by a large number of sensors. Math. Control Signals Syst. **1**(2), 167–182 (1988)
25. Vaidya, N.H.: Iterative Byzantine vector consensus in incomplete graphs. In: Chatterjee, M., Cao, J., Kothapalli, K., Rajsbaum, S. (eds.) ICDCN 2014. LNCS, vol. 8314, pp. 14–28. Springer, Heidelberg (2014)
26. Vaidya, N.H., Garg, V.K.: Byzantine vector consensus in complete graphs. In: Proceedings of the ACM Symposium on Principles of Distributed Computing, PODC 2013, pp. 65–73. ACM, New York (2013)
27. Vaidya, N.H., Tseng, L., Liang, G.: Iterative approximate Byzantine consensus in arbitrary directed graphs. In: Proceedings of the ACM Symposium on Principles of Distributed Computing, pp. 365–374. ACM (2012)
28. Varshney, P.K.: Distributed bayesian detection: Parallel fusion network. In: Distributed Detection and Data Fusion, pp. 36–118. Springer, New York (1997)
29. Wolfowitz, J.: Products of indecomposable, aperiodic, stochastic matrices. Proc. Am. Math. Soc. **14**(5), 733–737 (1963)

Asynchronous Computability Theorems
for t-Resilient Systems

Vikram Saraph[1]([⊠]), Maurice Herlihy[1], and Eli Gafni[2]

[1] Department of Computer Science, Brown University, Providence, USA
{vsaraph,mph}@cs.brown.edu
[2] Department of Computer Science, UCLA, Los Angeles, USA
eli@cs.ucla.edu

Abstract. A task is a distributed coordination problem where processes start with private inputs, communicate with one another, and then halt with private outputs. A protocol that solves a task is t-resilient if it tolerates halting failures by t or fewer processes. The t-resilient asynchronous computability theorem stated here characterizes the tasks that have t-resilient protocols in a shared-memory model. This result generalizes the prior (wait-free) *asynchronous computability theorem* of Herlihy and Shavit to a broader class of failure models, and requires introducing several novel concepts.

1 Introduction

A *distributed system* is a collection of $n + 1$ sequential automatons, called *processes*, that cooperate to solve a problem, called a *task*. Here, processes communicate by reading and writing a shared memory. Processes are *asynchronous*: there is no bound on their relative execution speeds, and up to $t \leq n$ processes can *fail* by crashing (taking no more steps). A *protocol* is a program that solves a task, where each process must halt with a correct output after a finite number of steps. A protocol is *t-resilient* if it tolerates crash failures by t or fewer processes. When $t = n$, we say the protocol is *wait-free*.

As discussed in more detail in Sect. 9, the question of which tasks have t-resilient protocols has a long history. Fischer *et al.* [6] showed that the fundamental *consensus* problem has no 1-resilient protocol in message-passing systems. Later, the *Asynchronous Computability Theorem* (ACT) of Herlihy and Shavit [14] characterized which tasks have wait-free protocols in shared-memory and message-passing models. More recently, Gafni *et al.* [9] gave a general formulation applicable, in principle, to a variety of computational models.

This paper presents the *t-resilient* ACT, characterizing which tasks have t-resilient protocols in shared memory models. As we will see, this generalization is not straightforward: it requires introducing several novel constructs and insights.

Before we can explain the contribution of this paper, we need to introduce some terminology in the next section.

© Springer-Verlag Berlin Heidelberg 2016
C. Gavoille and D. Ilcinkas (Eds.): DISC 2016, LNCS 9888, pp. 428–441, 2016.
DOI: 10.1007/978-3-662-53426-7_31

2   Elements of Combinatorial Topology

Our mathematical model employs concepts from combinatorial topology, a kind of generalization of graph theory to higher dimensions. A complete formal statement of the model appears in Herlihy *et al.* [12]. Here, we give a concise summary to make this document as self-contained as possible.

A *simplicial complex* (or just *complex*) $\mathcal{K}$ consists of a finite set V along with a collection of subsets of V closed under containment. An element of V is called a *vertex*, and each set in $\mathcal{K}$ is called a *simplex*. A simplex σ has *dimension* $\dim(\sigma) = |\sigma| - 1$. A subset of a simplex is called a *face*. We use "k-simplex" as shorthand for "k-dimensional simplex" and similarly for "k-face". The dimension $\dim(\mathcal{K})$ of a complex is the maximal dimension of its simplexes. A simplex of maximal dimension in $\mathcal{K}$ is called a *facet* of $\mathcal{K}$. A complex is *pure* if all its facets have the same dimension. The set of simplexes of $\mathcal{K}$ having dimension at most m is called the *m-skeleton* of $\mathcal{K}$, denoted $\mathrm{skel}^m(\mathcal{K})$. Simplicial complexes are a natural way to generalize graphs to higher dimensions.

For complexes $\mathcal{K}$ and $\mathcal{L}$, a *vertex map* $\phi : \mathcal{K} \to \mathcal{L}$ carries vertices of $\mathcal{K}$ to vertices of $\mathcal{L}$. If in addition ϕ carries simplexes of $\mathcal{K}$ to simplexes of $\mathcal{L}$ then it is called a *simplicial map*. A *carrier map* $\Phi : \mathcal{K} \to 2^{\mathcal{K}}$ takes each simplex $\sigma \in \mathcal{K}$ to a subcomplex $\Phi(\sigma) \subseteq \mathcal{L}$ such that for $\sigma, \tau \in \mathcal{K}$, $\Phi(\sigma \cap \tau) \subseteq \Phi(\sigma) \cap \Phi(\tau)$. A simplicial map $\phi : \mathcal{K} \to \mathcal{L}$ is *carried by* a carrier map $\Phi : \mathcal{K} \to 2^{\mathcal{L}}$ if for every simplex $\sigma \in \mathcal{K}$, $\phi(\sigma) \subseteq \Phi(\sigma)$. Let Δ^n be a simplex whose vertices are labeled with $(n+1)$ distinct process names. If Φ is a carrier map, and σ a simplex of $\Phi(\Delta^n)$, then the *carrier* of σ in Δ^n is the smallest face τ of Δ^n such that $\sigma \in \Phi(\tau)$.

Although complexes are defined in a purely combinatorial way, they can also be realized as topological spaces. Following Munkres [19], a *geometric n-simplex* is the convex hull of a set of $n + 1$ affinely-independent points in a Euclidean space of appropriate dimension. A *geometric complex* is a collection of geometric simplexes closed under containment such that every pair of distinct simplexes has disjoint interiors. The point-set occupied by a simplex σ or complex $\mathcal{K}$ is denoted $|\sigma|$ or $|\mathcal{K}|$, and is called its *polyhedron*.

A *subdivision* of a simplex σ is a complex $\mathrm{Sub}(\sigma)$ such that $|\mathrm{Sub}(\sigma)| = |\sigma|$. Figure 1 illustrates several useful subdivisions: the *barycentric* subdivision Bary $\mathcal{K}$

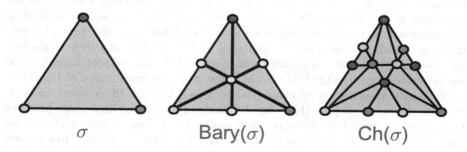

$$\sigma \qquad \mathsf{Bary}(\sigma) \qquad \mathsf{Ch}(\sigma)$$

Fig. 1. Barycentric and standard chromatic subdivisions

and the *standard chromatic subdivision* Ch($\mathcal{K}$). A subdivision is a special case of a carrier map. A simplicial map ϕ from one subdivision of Δ^n to another is *carrier-preserving* if for every simplex σ in the first subdivision, σ and $\phi(\sigma)$ have the same carriers.

Formally, a task is defined by a triple $(\mathcal{I}, \mathcal{O}, \Gamma)$, where $\mathcal{I}$ and $\mathcal{O}$ are the task's *input* and *output* complexes, and $\Gamma : \mathcal{I} \to 2^{\mathcal{O}}$ is a carrier map. An initial configuration where each process P_i is assigned input value v_i is represented as an n-simplex $\sigma = (s_0, \ldots, s_n) \in \mathcal{I}$, where each vertex s_i is labeled with P_i and v_i. Similarly, a legal final configuration where each process P_i halts with output value w_i is represented as n-simplex $\tau = (t_0, \ldots, t_n) \in \mathcal{O}$, where each vertex t_i is labeled with P_i and w_i. For each $\sigma \in \mathcal{I}$, $\Gamma(\sigma) \subseteq \mathcal{O}$ is the set of legal final configurations when the processes that appear in σ participate in the task.

When labeling vertices with process names, we sometimes refer to *coloring* those vertices. A *properly-colored* simplex is one whose vertices are labeled with distinct process names, and a *chromatic* complex is one whose simplexes are properly colored. A simplicial map ϕ between chromatic complexes is *color-preserving* if for all vertices $v \in \mathcal{I}$, v and $\phi(v)$ are labeled with the same color.

3 Contributions

Informally, the wait-free ACT states that a task $(\mathcal{I}, \mathcal{O}, \Gamma)$ has a wait-free protocol if and only if there is a subdivision Sub($\mathcal{I}$) of $\mathcal{I}$ and a simplicial map $\phi : \text{Sub}(\mathcal{I}) \to \mathcal{O}$ that approximates (technically, is carried by) the task's carrier map $\Gamma : \mathcal{I} \to 2^{\mathcal{O}}$. The t-resilient ACT stated here replaces that subdivision with a specific carrier map, denoted Ch_t^N and defined later, asserting that task $(\mathcal{I}, \mathcal{O}, \Gamma)$ has a t-resilient protocol if and only if there is a simplicial map $\phi : \text{Ch}_t^N(\mathcal{I}) \to \mathcal{O}$ carried by Γ. We also give a continuous version of this theorem.

One contribution of this paper is to propose a novel way to generalize the well-known wait-free *immediate snapshot* (IS) protocol of Borowsky and Gafni [1]. Operationally, an *immediate snapshot* takes place in two contiguous steps. In the first step, a process writes its view to a word in memory, possibly concurrently with other processes. In the very next step, it takes a snapshot of that memory, possibly concurrently with other processes. The name comes from the requirement that the snapshot step take place *immediately after* the write step. Combinatorially, the IS protocol is associated with the standard chromatic subdivision. Recall that simplex Δ^n has vertices labeled with the $(n + 1)$ distinct process names. Each process starts on the vertex of Δ^n labeled with its name, and the processes converge to their matching vertices on some simplex of Ch(Δ^n).

It is not immediately obvious how to generalize the IS protocol to be t-resilient. Here, we propose the *delayed snapshot* protocol, a three-phase protocol that runs one round of wait-free IS, followed by a phase where each process waits for $n + 1 - t$ processes to catch up, and then some processes run a second round of wait-free IS. For the t-resilient ACT, this protocol (and its associated complex) play a role analogous to that of IS in the wait-free ACT, suggesting that t-resilient delayed snapshot is the "natural" generalization of the wait-free immediate snapshot.

A second contribution of this paper is the following topological observation. As geometric objects, the input complex $\mathcal{I}$ and its subdivision $\mathrm{Sub}(\mathcal{I})$ have the same polyhedrons: $|\mathcal{I}| = |\mathrm{Sub}(\mathcal{I})|$, often summarized by saying that subdivision leaves "topology" unchanged. In the t-resilient ACT theorem, by contrast, the subdivision is replaced by the carrier map Ch_t^N, where $|\mathrm{Ch}_t^N(\mathcal{I})| \subseteq |\mathcal{I}|$. Applying Ch_t^N to $\mathcal{I}$ changes the topology by tearing "holes" in the polyhedron $|\mathcal{I}|$. Informally, creating "holes" in the input complex increases computational power, by increasing flexibility to wrap around obstructions when constructing a simplicial map to approximate Γ. In this way, the theorem draws a connection between computational power (the ability to solve more tasks) and topological structure (more "holes" means that more tasks have protocols).

A third contribution is new insight into the power of waiting. In a wait-free protocol, no process can wait for others to take a step, because those others may have undetectably crashed. In a t-resilient protocol, by contrast, it is safe to wait for all but t processes to take steps. We provide a proof that any task that has a t-resilient protocol has a protocol with only a single waiting step: all steps before and after can be executed wait-free. It was known [12, Chapter 5] that a single waiting step was sufficient for "colorless" tasks where outputs are independent of process names, but as far as we know, this property had not been proved for tasks in general.

4   Delayed Snapshot Protocol

Let $\mathcal{C}$ be a simplicial complex with subcomplex $\mathcal{A} \subseteq \mathcal{C}$. Define the *deletion* of $\mathcal{A}$ in $\mathcal{C}$, written $\mathrm{dl}(\mathcal{A}, \mathcal{C})$, to be the subcomplex of $\mathcal{C}$ consisting of all simplexes that do not intersect $\mathcal{A}$.

Informally, the delayed snapshot complex $\mathrm{Ch}_t(\Delta^n)$ is the subcomplex of the two-round immediate snapshot complex $\mathrm{Ch}^2(\Delta^n)$ obtained by removing any simplexes that meet a low-dimensional skeleton of Δ^n.

Definition 1. *The complex* $\mathrm{dl}(\mathrm{Ch}^2(\mathrm{skel}^{n-t-1}(\Delta^n)), \mathrm{Ch}^2(\Delta^n))$, *which is denoted* $\mathrm{Ch}_t(\Delta^n)$, *is the* delayed snapshot complex. *It is the subcomplex of* $\mathrm{Ch}^2(\Delta^n)$ *obtained by removing all simplexes of* $\mathrm{Ch}^2(\Delta^n)$ *that intersect* $\mathrm{skel}^{n-t-1}(\Delta^n)$.

Figure 2 shows $\mathrm{Ch}_1(\Delta^2)$.

The *iterated immediate snapshot* protocol consists of a sequence of immediate snapshot protocols, each executed with a distinct array, where the output of one round's immediate snapshot is the input to the next. The corresponding complex is the subdivision constructed by repeatedly composing the standard chromatic subdivision.

In the *delayed snapshot task* $(\Delta^n, \mathrm{Ch}_t(\Delta^n), \mathrm{Ch}_t)$, each process starts on the vertex of Δ^n labeled with its name, halts on a vertex of $\mathrm{Ch}_t(\Delta^n)$ labeled with its name, and all processes converge on a single simplex of $\mathrm{Ch}_t(\Delta^n)$. Protocol 1 shows a delayed snapshot protocol. Processes share two $(n+1)$-element arrays,

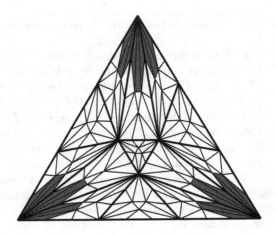

Fig. 2. $Ch_1(\Delta^2)$ as a subcomplex of $Ch^2(\Delta^2)$. The grayed-out simplexes are discarded from $Ch^2(\Delta^2)$ to obtain $Ch_1(\Delta^2)$.

mem0 and mem1, and a shared variable, done. Each process calls the wait-free immediate snapshot protocol to store its name in mem0 and take a snapshot of that array (Lines 6–8). Here, the **immediate** block's first line assigns to that process's element in mem0 and the second line immediately assigns an atomic snapshot of mem0 to a local variable, snap0. If the process does not see at least $n+1-t$ processes in snap0, it waits until done is set to true. Otherwise, it stores snap0 in mem1, takes an immediate snapshot of mem1, sets done to true, and then returns (Lines 12–16).

Theorem 1. *Protocol 1 is a t-resilient delayed snapshot protocol.*

Proof. Since the protocol consists of two successive immediate snapshots on clean memory, the processes converge to a simplex of $Ch^2(\Delta^n)$. To see why each non-faulty process executing the protocol eventually returns, consider the set of all non-faulty processes. Because we consider only t-resilient executions, there must be at least $n+1-t$ such processes. Let P be the last non-faulty process to complete the first, wait-free immediate snapshot (Lines 6–8). Since P is last, P must observe the effects of at least $n+1-t$ processes, including itself. Therefore P does not wait at Line 10 and proceeds to execute the second immediate snapshot wait-free. Before returning, P signals other waiting processes by setting done to *true*. The remaining processes then stop waiting and join the second immediate snapshot.

Finally, we check that each process chooses a vertex in $Ch_t(\Delta^n)$. Define process P as above. Before writing to done, P must have written its view to mem1. Thus any process blocked at Line 10 will see P's view. But this view includes at least $n+1-t$ processes, so any subsequent process taking a snapshot of mem1 will see at least $n+1-t$ processes as well. But the vertices of $Ch_t(\Delta^n)$ correspond exactly to the local views in which processes see at least $n+1-t$ processes, so each process will choose a vertex in $Ch_t(\Delta^n)$.

```
1   shared mem0[n+1];
2   shared mem1[n+1];
3   shared done;
4   done := false;
5   protocol DelayedSnapshot(id):
6       immediate
7           mem0[id] := id;
8           snap0 := snapshot(mem0);
9       if |snap0| ≤ n − t then
10          while not done
11              skip
12      immediate
13          mem1[id] := snap0;
14          snap1 := snapshot(mem1);
15      done := true;
16      return snap1;
```

Algorithm 1. Delayed snapshot protocol

5   Protocol Complex Properties

Let $\mathrm{Ch}_t^N(\mathcal{I})$ denote the N-fold composition of $\mathrm{Ch}_t(\mathcal{I})$, for some $N > 0$. Operationally, the complex corresponds to a protocol composed from N instances of delayed snapshot. We call this complex the *protocol complex* for this protocol. In this section, we discuss useful combinatorial properties of the delayed snapshot protocol complex, which are eventually used to prove the main theorems.

Roughly speaking, a pure n-dimensional simplicial complex is *shellable* if it can be constructed by "gluing" facets together along their $(n − 1)$-faces.

Definition 2. *Let C be a pure complex of dimension n, and let $\psi_0, \ldots, \psi_s$ be an enumeration of its facets. Then $\{\psi_i\}$ is called a shelling order if for all j, the complex $\bigcup_{i=0}^{j} \psi_i \cap \psi_{j+1}$ is pure of dimension $n − 1$. A complex with a shelling order is said to be shellable.*

In the proofs to follow, we use the notation $\ell : \mathbb{N} \rightarrow C$ to denote a shelling order $\psi_0, \ldots, \psi_s$ on a simplicial complex C, where ℓ is a partial function such that $\ell(i) = \psi_i$.

Theorem 2. $\mathrm{Ch}(\Delta^n)$ *is shellable.*

Proof. Following Kozlov [18], a one-round immediate snapshot execution by processes $P_0, \ldots, P_n$ is described by an *ordered partition* $S_0, \ldots, S_m$, where the S_i are disjoint sets of processes. Operationally, the processes in S_0 all write and scan concurrently, followed by the processes in S_1, and so on.

Let $S_0, \ldots, S_m$ be the ordered partition whose simplex is σ. Define $\mathrm{Flip}_i(\sigma)$:

$$\mathrm{Flip}_i(\sigma) = \begin{cases} \{P_i\} \cup S_1, \ldots, S_m & \text{if } S_0 = \{P_i\} \\ \{P_i\}, S_0 \setminus \{P_i\}, S_1, \ldots, S_m & \text{if } |S_0| > 1 \text{ and } P_i \in S_0 \end{cases}$$

Flipping an execution changes exactly one process's view, so σ and $\mathrm{Flip}_i(\sigma)$ share an $(n-1)$ face.

Let $\Delta^n = (v_0, \ldots, v_n)$. Define the *extended star* of v_i to be the union of $\mathrm{St}(v_i, \mathrm{Ch}(\Delta^n))$ with $\mathrm{Flip}_i(\sigma)$ for each facet σ of $\mathrm{St}(v_i, \mathrm{Ch}(\Delta^n))$. $\mathrm{Lk}(v_i, \mathrm{Ch}(\Delta^n))$ is isomorphic to $\mathrm{Ch}(\Delta^{n-1})$, which is shellable by the induction hypothesis. The link's shelling order induces a shelling order on $\mathrm{St}(v_i, \mathrm{Ch}(\Delta^n))$. The shelling order for the extended star is constructed by appending, in any order, the flipped simplexes to the star's shelling order. The shelling order for $\mathrm{Ch}(\Delta^n)$ is constructed by concatenating the shelling orders for the extended stars, and eliminating duplicates.

Every facet of $\mathrm{Ch}(\Delta^n)$ is included in this order because every execution $S_0, \ldots, S_m$ is either a facet of some $\mathrm{St}(v_i, \mathrm{Ch}(\Delta^n))$ (if S_0 is a singleton) or one flip away from some star.

For $\sigma \in \mathrm{Ch}(\Delta^n)$, define $\mathrm{Ch}_\sigma(\sigma) = \mathrm{Ch}^2(\sigma) \cap \mathrm{Ch}_t(\sigma)$, the restriction of Ch_t to σ. $\mathrm{Ch}_\sigma(\sigma)$ is $\mathrm{Ch}(\sigma)$ without the simplexes that intersect certain vertices.

Theorem 3. $\mathrm{Ch}_\sigma(\sigma)$ *is shellable.*

Proof. Let the missing vertices be $\{v_i : i \in I\}$, for some index set I. The shelling order is the concatenation of the shelling orders for the extended stars of all the vertices *not* in I.

Theorem 4. $\mathrm{Ch}_t(\Delta^n)$ *is shellable.*

Proof. We inductively construct a shelling order on $\mathrm{Ch}_t(\Delta^n)$ by concatenating the shelling orders for each $\mathrm{Ch}_\sigma(\sigma)$. Let ℓ be the shelling order on $\mathrm{Ch}(\Delta^n)$ constructed in Theorem 2. Enumerate the facets $\sigma \in \mathrm{Ch}(\Delta^n)$ as $\sigma_i = \ell(i)$. Inductively assume $\mathrm{Ch}_{\sigma_i}(\sigma_i)$ is attached, and let $\mathcal{C}_i$ denote the complex constructed so far, with shelling order ℓ_i. Let α be any ordering on the vertices of σ_{i+1} such that every vertex v already contained in $\mathcal{C}_i$ precedes every vertex w not contained in $\mathcal{C}_i$. Let $\ell_{\alpha, \sigma_{i+1}}$ be the shelling order constructed earlier for $\mathrm{Ch}_{\sigma_{i+1}}(\sigma_{i+1})$, with vertices ordered by α. Append $\ell_{\alpha, \sigma_{i+1}}$ to ℓ_i to obtain a shelling order ℓ_{i+1} on $\mathcal{C}_{i+1} = \mathcal{C}_i \cup \mathrm{Ch}_{\sigma_i}(\sigma_i)$.

Definition 3. *Let S^k denote the k-dimensional sphere. A complex $\mathcal{K}$ is k-connected if, for all $0 \le m \le k$, any continuous map $f : S^m \to |\mathcal{K}|$ can be extended to a continuous $F : D^{m+1} \to |\mathcal{K}|$, where the sphere S^m is the boundary of the disk D^{m+1}.*

One way to think about this property is that any map f of the k-sphere that cannot be "filled in" represents a k-dimensional "hole" in the complex. Indeed, S^k itself is m-connected for $m < k$, but not k-connected.

Let $\mathcal{K}$ be a complex, and σ a simplex in $\mathcal{K}$. The *link* of σ in $\mathcal{K}$, written $\mathrm{Lk}(\sigma, \mathcal{K})$, is the smallest subcomplex of $\mathcal{K}$ consisting of simplexes τ disjoint from σ such that $\sigma \cup \tau$ is a simplex. One can think of the link of σ as a small subcomplex that encompasses σ but does not contain it.

Definition 4. *A pure n-dimensional complex $\mathcal{K}$ is* link-connected *if for all $\sigma \in \mathcal{K}$, $\mathrm{Lk}(\sigma, \mathcal{K})$ is $(n - \dim(\sigma) - 2)$-connected.*

Informally, link-connectivity ensures that a complex cannot be "pinched" too thinly. To prove link-connectivity of $\mathrm{Ch}_t^N(\Delta^n)$, we prove the stronger claim that $\mathrm{Ch}_t^N(\Delta^n)$ is a *combinatorial manifold* (or simply *manifold*). A manifold is a pure simplicial complex in which the link of each vertex is either a topological disk or a sphere.

Definition 5. *Let $\mathcal{K}$ be a pure n-dimensional complex. A simplex $\sigma \in \mathcal{K}$ is called* regular *if $\mathrm{Lk}(v, \mathcal{K})$ is an $(n - \dim(\sigma) - 1)$-sphere when σ is not contained in the boundary of $\mathcal{K}$, and $\mathrm{Lk}(v, \mathcal{K})$ is an $(n - \dim(\sigma) - 1)$-disk otherwise. The complex $\mathcal{K}$ is a* combinatorial manifold *if all its vertices are regular.*

Lemma 1. *Combinatorial manifolds are link-connected.*

Proof. It is known that every simplex in a combinatorial manifold $\mathcal{K}$ is regular [10]. In particular, each link in $\mathcal{K}$ is sufficiently connected, so $\mathcal{K}$ is link-connected.

We can glue together $\mathrm{Ch}_t^N(\Delta^n)$ from copies of $\mathrm{Ch}_t^{N-1}(\Delta^n)$ according to the shelling order on $\mathrm{Ch}_t(\Delta^n)$. At each step, we ensure that every attached vertex remains regular.

Theorem 5. $\mathrm{Ch}_t^N(\Delta^n)$ *is link-connected.*

To demonstrate the $(t - 1)$-connectivity of $\mathrm{Ch}_t^N(\Delta^n)$, we use the *Nerve Lemma*, a classical result from combinatorial topology.

Definition 6. *Let $\mathcal{K}$ be a simplicial complex and let $\{\mathcal{K}_i\}_{i \in I}$ be a collection of subcomplexes covering $\mathcal{K}$, which is to say that $\bigcup_{i \in I} \mathcal{K}_i = \mathcal{K}$. Then the* nerve complex *$\mathcal{N}(\{\mathcal{K}_i\}_{i \in I})$ is a simplicial complex whose vertices are the $\mathcal{K}_i$ and whose simplexes are collections $\{\mathcal{K}_j\}_{j \in J}$ such that $\bigcap_{j \in J} \mathcal{K}_j$ is nonempty.*

The nerve complex of a simplicial cover encodes how the components of the cover intersect with one another. The complex obtained in this way sometimes shares connectivity properties with the original complex, as described by the Nerve Lemma below. Kozlov [16] contains an excellent statement and proof of the Nerve Lemma.

Lemma 2 (Nerve Lemma). *Let $\{K_i\}_{i \in I}$ be a simplicial cover of $\mathcal{K}$, and let k be some fixed integer. For any nonempty $J \subseteq I$, define $\mathcal{K}_J = \bigcap_{j \in J} \mathcal{K}_j$, and suppose that $\mathcal{K}_J$ is $(k - |J| + 1)$-connected or empty for all such J. Then $\mathcal{K}$ is k-connected if and only if $\mathcal{N}(\{\mathcal{K}_i\}_{i \in I})$ is k-connected.*

The next corollary is a direct consequence of the Nerve Lemma, and will also prove useful in showing topological connectivity of the t-resilient protocol complex. A statement of this corollary is found in Herlihy *et al.* [12].

Corollary 1. *If $\mathcal{K}$ and $\mathcal{L}$ are k-connected complexes such that $\mathcal{K} \cap \mathcal{L}$ is $(k - 1)$-connected, then $\mathcal{K} \cup \mathcal{L}$ is also k-connected.*

Similar to the approach for link-connectivity, we can piece together $\mathrm{Ch}_t^N(\Delta^n)$ from copies of $\mathrm{Ch}_t^{N-1}(\Delta^n)$ and iteratively apply the above corollary to obtain the following.

Theorem 6. $\mathrm{Ch}_t^N(\Delta^n)$ *is* $(t-1)$-*connected.*

6   Single-Round Waiting

We now construct a map from the one-round protocol complex to any N-round protocol complex. Operationally, this means that any task solvable t-resiliently can be solved using only one delayed snapshot round, followed by some number of wait-free immediate snapshot rounds, implying that only one waiting statement is necessary in any protocol.

If $Y \subseteq X$ are topological spaces, then a *retraction* [11] from X to Y is a continuous map $f : X \rightarrow Y$ such that f restricted to X is the identity.

Define the complex

$$\mathrm{Bary}_t(\Delta^n) = \{\sigma \in \mathrm{Bary}(\Delta^n) : \forall v \in \sigma, \dim(\mathrm{Car}(v, \mathrm{Bary})) \geq n - t\}.$$

That is, $\mathrm{Bary}_t(\Delta^n)$ is the induced subcomplex of $\mathrm{Bary}(\Delta^n)$ defined by vertices whose carriers have dimension at least $n - t$.

Lemma 3. $\mathrm{Bary}_t^\circ(\mathcal{I}) = |\mathrm{Bary}_t(\mathcal{I})| - |\mathrm{skel}^{n-t}(\mathcal{I})|$ *retracts to* $|\mathrm{Bary}_{t-1}(\mathcal{I})|$.

We can iteratively apply Lemma 3 to obtain the following theorem.

Theorem 7. *There is a map* $f : |\mathrm{Ch}_t(\mathcal{I})| \rightarrow |\mathrm{Bary}_t(\mathcal{I})|$ *that is continuous and carrier-preserving.*

We use topological connectivity of $\mathrm{Ch}_t^N(\mathcal{I})$ to map $\mathrm{Bary}_t(\mathcal{I})$ into the former.

Theorem 8. *There is a map* $f : |\mathrm{Bary}_t(\mathcal{I})| \rightarrow |\mathrm{Ch}_t^N(\mathcal{I})|$ *that is continuous and carrier-preserving.*

We make use of the following theorem, based on an algorithm of Borowsky and Gafni [2].

Theorem 9. *Let* $\mathcal{I}$ *and* $\mathcal{O}$ *be chromatic complexes,* $\Gamma : \mathcal{I} \rightarrow 2^{\mathcal{O}}$ *a carrier map such that* $\Gamma(\sigma)$ *is link-connected for each* $\sigma \in \mathcal{I}$, *and* $f : |\mathcal{I}| \rightarrow |\mathcal{O}|$ *a continuous map carried by* Γ. *Then there exists a chromatic, carrier-preserving simplicial map* $\phi : \mathrm{Ch}^N(\mathcal{I}) \rightarrow \mathcal{O}$, *for some sufficiently large* N, *also carried by* Γ.

As a technical aside, Theorem 9 is a color-preserving analog of the classical *simplicial approximation theorem* [19], which states that any continuous map from complex's polyhedron to another's can be approximated by a simplicial map from a sufficiently subdivided complex to the other. Here, the link-connectivity condition on $\mathrm{Ch}_t^N(\Delta^n)$ is necessary to ensure that the map ϕ can be made color-preserving.

Theorem 10 (Wait Reduction). *For any $N > 0$ there is a chromatic, carrier-preserving, simplicial map $\phi : \mathrm{Ch}^M(\mathrm{Ch}_t(\mathcal{I})) \rightarrow \mathrm{Ch}_t^N(\mathcal{I})$ for some sufficiently large M.*

Proof. Existence of a continuous, carrier-preserving $f : |\mathrm{Ch}_t(\mathcal{I})| \rightarrow |\mathrm{Ch}_t^N(\mathcal{I})|$ follows from Theorems 7 and 8, and the claim follows from Theorem 9.

It follows that there is a t-resilient read-write protocol that simulates N rounds of delayed snapshots with only a single delayed snapshot, followed by some number of wait-free immediate snapshots.

7 t-ACT Theorems

We state two alternative versions of the t-resilient asynchronous computability theorem: a discrete version, which characterizes solvability in terms of the existence of a chromatic simplicial map, and an equivalent continuous version, which provides the same characterization in terms of the existence of a continuous function.

7.1   Discrete t-ACT

Theorem 11 (Discrete t-ACT). *A task $(\mathcal{I}, \mathcal{O}, \Gamma)$ has a t-resilient read-write protocol if and only if there exists a color-preserving, carrier-preserving, simplicial map $\phi : \mathrm{Ch}_t^N(\mathcal{I}) \rightarrow \mathcal{O}$ for some natural number N.*

Proof. Given such a map, consider the following protocol. Each process with input vertex v runs N rounds delayed snapshot rounds, choosing a vertex w in $\mathrm{Ch}_t^N(\mathcal{I})$. Now decide $x = \phi(w)$. This protocol satisfies the task specification because ϕ is carried by Γ.

In the other direction, we sketch an argument that any t-resilient protocol can be put into normal form as an equivalent sequence of t-resilient delayed snapshots, each operating on its own region of memory.

It is known that any wait-free read-write protocol can be expressed in normal form as a *layered immediate snapshot* protocol [12, Chapter 14]: the execution occurs as a sequence of (asynchronous) layers (rounds). Each layer has its own $(n + 1)$-element array, where process P_i writes its current state to the ith array element, takes an immediate snapshot of that array, and the value returned by that snapshot becomes P_i's new state. After the last such layer, P_i applies a decision map to its final state to choose an output value.

In a t-resilient model, we can guarantee that each layer's immediate snapshot returns states written by at least $n + 1 - t$ distinct processes by waiting until enough processes have finished the prior layer (as in Line 10 of Algorithm 1). We call such a layer a *barrier* layer.

Given a t-resilient protocol expressed as a sequence of barrier layers, we can add a wait-free layer between each pair of barrier layers without reducing the protocol's computational power (informally, the decision map can just ignore the new snapshots). A sequence of $2L$ layers that alternates wait-free and barrier layers is a sequence of L delayed snapshot layers.

We could choose to replace $\mathrm{Ch}_t^N(\mathcal{I})$ in the discrete t-ACT with the complex $\mathrm{Ch}^M(\mathrm{Ch}_t(\mathcal{I}))$, using the wait reduction theorem. Though we do not do this for the discrete t-ACT, we will do so for continuous t-ACT in the next section.

7.2   Continuous t-ACT

While the discrete t-ACT provides a clean characterization of t-resilient solvability, there is an even more succinct statement replacing simplicial maps with continuous functions. The main difference is that we lose any notion of process names, since there is no clear continuous analog of *chromatic* simplicial maps. To address this, we give an alternative to the discrete t-ACT, subject to a link-connectivity condition on the output complex.

Theorem 12 (Continuous t-ACT). *Let $T = (\mathcal{I}, \mathcal{O}, \Gamma)$ be an $(n+1)$-process task such that $\Gamma(\sigma)$ is link-connected for all $\sigma \in \mathcal{I}$. Then there is a t-resilient read-write protocol for T if and only if there is a continuous, carrier-preserving $f : |\mathrm{Ch}_t(\mathcal{I})| \to |\mathcal{O}|$.*

Proof. First suppose we have a t-resilient protocol for task T. The discrete t-ACT ensures there is a chromatic, carrier-preserving, simplicial map $\phi : \mathrm{Ch}_t^N(\mathcal{I}) \to \mathcal{O}$. We apply Theorem 10 to turn ϕ into a chromatic, carrier-preserving, simplicial map $\phi' : \mathrm{Ch}^M(\mathrm{Ch}_t(\mathcal{I})) \to \mathcal{O}$. Then let $f = |\phi'|$, the geometric realization of ϕ'. Recalling that Ch^M does not change the topology of simplicial complexes, we get a continuous, carrier preserving $f : |\mathrm{Ch}_t(\mathcal{I})| \to |\mathcal{O}|$.

In the other direction, given a continuous, carrier-preserving $f : |\mathrm{Ch}_t(\mathcal{I})| \to |\mathcal{O}|$, there is a chromatic, carrier-preserving simplicial map $\phi : \mathrm{Ch}^M(\mathrm{Ch}_t(\mathcal{I})) \to \mathcal{O}$. Operationally, this provides us a t-resilient protocol for solving T, in which each process executes one round of delayed snapshot, followed by M rounds of immediate snapshots, halting on a vertex v in $\mathrm{Ch}^M(\mathrm{Ch}_t(\mathcal{I}))$. The process decides $\phi(v)$, which is correct because ϕ is carrier-preserving.

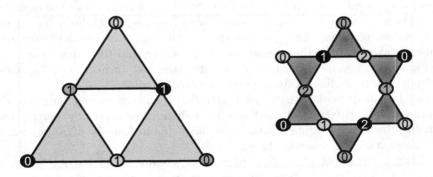

Fig. 3. Test-and-set and Fetch-and-increment tasks

8   Applications

Here are some applications of the t-resilient ACT.

Lemma 4. *If $\mathcal{K}$ and $\mathcal{L}$ are chromatic complexes, $\mathcal{K}$ is link-connected, and $\phi :$ $\mathcal{K} \to \mathcal{L}$ is color-preserving, then the subcomplex $\phi(\mathcal{K}) \subseteq \mathcal{L}$ is also link-connected.*

In the following two tasks, processes have only their names as inputs. In the *test-and-set* task, exactly one participating process decides 0, and the rest decide 1. Figure 3 shows this task's output complex $\mathcal{O}$. If there were a t-resilient test-and-set protocol, there would be a color-preserving simplicial map $\phi : \mathrm{Ch}_t^n(\Delta^n) \to \mathcal{O}$. It is not hard to see that the image of $\mathrm{Ch}_t^n(\Delta^n)$ must be all of $\mathcal{O}$. But $\mathrm{Ch}_t^n(\Delta^n)$ is link-connected, while $\mathcal{O}$ is not, contradicting Lemma 4.

In the *fetch-and-increment* task, if k processes participate, they decide distinct integers between 0 and $k - 1$. Figure 3 shows this task's output complex $\mathcal{O}$. By the same argument, there can be no a color-preserving simplicial map $\phi : \mathrm{Ch}_t^n(\Delta^n) \to \mathcal{O}$ because $\mathcal{O}$ is not link-connected.

In the k-set agreement task, each process has a private input, each process decides some process's input, and no more than k distinct inputs can be decided. We can use the t-resilient ACT to see that there is a t-resilient $(t + 1)$-set agreement protocol. Without loss of generality, assume each process's input is its own name, so the task's input complex is the simplex Δ^n. Simply assign each vertex v in $\mathrm{Ch}_t(\Delta)$ the least process name in v's carrier.

We can also use the t-resilient ACT to see that there is no t-resilient t-set agreement protocol. Omitting details, start by "coloring" each vertex of $\mathrm{Ch}_t(\Delta)$ with its decision value. We can extend this coloring from $\mathrm{Ch}_t(\Delta^n)$ to all of $\mathrm{Ch}^2(\Delta^n)$ simply by assigning each additional vertex a decision value from its carrier. The result is called a *Sperner coloring*, and the classical Sperner's Lemma [12, Chapter 4] states that at least one n-simplex in $\mathrm{Ch}^2(\Delta^n)$ has all $n + 1$ colors. Going back from $\mathrm{Ch}^2(\Delta^n)$ to $\mathrm{Ch}_t(\Delta^n)$ requires discarding at most $n - t$ vertices from any simplex, leaving at least $t + 1$ colors on some simplex of $\mathrm{Ch}_t(\Delta^n)$. This simplex corresponds to an execution where $(t + 1)$ distinct values are chosen, violating the t-set agreement condition. It is straightforward to extend this construction to any $\mathrm{Ch}_t^N(\Delta)$ by considering the N-fold *relative subdivision* [19] of $\mathrm{Ch}_t(\Delta^n)$ in $\mathrm{Ch}^2(\Delta^n)$.

9   Related Work

The original ACT [14,15] applied only to wait-free read-write memory. Some prior approaches used simulation [4] to reduce certain t-resilient "colorless" protocols to wait-free "colorless" protocols. Herlihy and Rajsbaum [13] derived task solvability conditions for *colorless tasks* which, roughly speaking, can be defined independently of process identities. The t-resilient model is a special case of adversarial shared-memory models [5].

We use the *immediate snapshot* (IS) protocol of Borowsky and Gafni [3], later extended by Raynal and Stainer [20] extended to encompass failure detectors. Kozlov [17] was the first to prove that the standard chromatic subdivision produced by immediate snapshot is, in fact, a subdivision. Gafni *et al.* [9] give a general theorem for task solvability for a class of computational models, but they do not give an explicit characterization of the protocol execution complex for *t*-resilient computations In this paper, by contrast, we give an explicit construction for all complexes, as well as an explicit and novel protocol for *t*-resilient delayed snapshot.

Another approach is to reduce the problem of constructing *t*-resilient protocols to that of constructing wait-free protocols. Gafni and Kuznetsov [7,8] make progress in this direction, considering a more general failure model that permits irregular failure patterns, but a weaker notion of protocol correctness, called "weak solvability". They provide a way to transform a task T to another task T' such that if T is weakly solvable in the general model, then T' is weakly wait-free solvable.

10 Remarks

This paper proposes a novel generalization of the ACT to *t*-resilient read-write memory. The generalized theorem is expressed in two equivalent ways: in terms of the existence of a simplicial map between simplicial complexes, and also in terms of the existence of a continuous map between polyhedrons of simplicial complexes. The algorithmic construction introduces a novel *t*-resilient delayed snapshot protocol, generalizing the wait-free immediate snapshot protocol of Borowsky and Gafni.

References

1. Borowsky, E., Gafni, E.: Immediate atomic snapshots and fast renaming, August 1993
2. Borowsky, E.: Capturing the power of resiliency and set consensus in distributed systems. Ph.D. thesis, University of California, Los Angeles (1995)
3. Borowsky, E., Gafni, E.: A simple algorithmically reasoned characterization of wait-free computations. In: Proceedings of the 16th Annual ACM Symposium on Principles of Distributed Computing, pp. 189–198, August 1997
4. Borowsky, E., Gafni, E., Lynch, N.A., Rajsbaum, S.: The BG distributed simulation algorithm. Distrib. Comput. **14**(3), 127–146 (2001)
5. Delporte-Gallet, C., Fauconnier, H., Guerraoui, R., Tielmann, A.: The disagreement power of an adversary. In: Keidar, I. (ed.) DISC 2009. LNCS, vol. 5805, pp. 8–21. Springer, Heidelberg (2009)
6. Fischer, M., Lynch, N.A., Paterson, M.S.: Impossibility of distributed commit with one faulty process. J. ACM **32**(2), 374–382 (1985)
7. Gafni, E., Kuznetsov, P.: On l-resilience, hitting sets, and colorless tasks. In: Proceedings of the 29th ACM SIGACT-SIGOPS Symposium on Principles of Distributed Computing, PODC 2010, pp. 81–82. ACM, New York (2010)
8. Gafni, E., Kuznetsov, P.: Turning adversaries into friends: simplified, made constructive, and extended. In: Lu, C., Masuzawa, T., Mosbah, M. (eds.) OPODIS 2010. LNCS, vol. 6490, pp. 380–394. Springer, Heidelberg (2010)

9. Gafni, E., Kuznetsov, P., Manolescu, C.: A generalized asynchronous computability theorem. In: ACM Symposium on Principles of Distributed Computing, PODC 2014, Paris, France, pp. 222–231, 15–18 July 2014

10. Glaser, L.C.: Geometrical Combinatorial Topology, vol. 1. Van Nostrand Reinhold, New York (1970)

11. Hatcher, A.: Algebraic Topology. Cambridge University Press, Cambridge (2002)

12. Herlihy, M., Kozlov, D., Rajsbaum, S.: Distributed Computing Through Combinatorial Topology. Elsevier, Boston (2013)

13. Herlihy, M., Rajsbaum, S.: The topology of distributed adversaries. Distrib. Comput. **26**(3), 173–192 (2013)

14. Herlihy, M., Shavit, N.: The topological structure of asynchronous computability. J. ACM **46**(6), 858–923 (1999)

15. Herlihy, M.P., Shavit, N.: The asynchronous computability theorem for t-resilient tasks. In: Symposium on Theory of Computing (STOC), pp. 111–120. ACM, May 1993

16. Kozlov, D.: Combinatorial Algebraic Topology. Springer, Heidelberg (2008)

17. Kozlov, D.N.: Chromatic subdivision of a simplicial complex. Homology, Homotopy Appl. **1**(14), 1–13 (2012)

18. Kozlov, D.N.: Combinatorial topology of the standard chromatic subdivision and weak symmetry breaking for 6 processes. CoRR, abs/1506.03944 (2015)

19. Munkres, J.R.: Elements of Algebraic Topology. Addison Wesley, Reading (1984)

20. Raynal, M., Stainer, J.: Increasing the power of the iterated immediate snapshot model with failure detectors. In: Even, G., Halldórsson, M.M. (eds.) SIROCCO 2012. LNCS, vol. 7355, pp. 231–242. Springer, Heidelberg (2012)

Upper Bounds for Boundless Tagging with Bounded Objects

Zahra Aghazadeh$^{(\boxtimes)}$ and Philipp Woelfel

Department of Computer Science, University of Calgary, Calgary, Canada
{zaghazad,woelfel}@ucalgary.ca

Abstract. A fundamental technique used in the design of shared memory algorithms is *tagging*, where registers or other shared objects get augmented with additional values, called tags. In this paper, we provide a framework for tagging, and prove upper bounds for the complexity of this problem. We define new types that allow processes to generate tags infinitely often, store them to or retrieve them from other objects, use them safely, and release them when they are not needed any more. We present asymptotically optimally time efficient implementations of those types from objects of bounded size. In particular, our tags need only objects of logarithmic size, and operations on them can be performed in constant step complexity. In addition to the straightforward applications that use tags directly, our implementations can also be used for memory reclamation in a number of algorithms, such as those based on single compare-and-swap universal or read-copy-update.

1 Introduction

A standard technique in shared memory algorithms is *tagging*, where registers or other shared objects get augmented with additional values, called tags. Such tags can serve multiple purposes: One is to allow processes to distinguish multiple writes of the same value. This can, for example, be used to avoid the ABA problem. (The ABA problem occurs when two subsequent reads of the same register return the same value, even though at some point between those reads the value was different.)

In many algorithms, processes proceed in rounds. When a process writes to shared objects, it can augment its written data values with a tag, that consists of the process's current round number and possibly its process ID. Other processes can then use the tags read from shared objects to distinguish whether the corresponding data values were written by a process in the same or in different rounds. Each time a process starts a new round, it needs to find a new unique tag that it can use throughout its round as an identifier of that round. In some applications (e.g., [21,26]), it is important that tags are ordered (e.g., later rounds should

---

This research was undertaken, in part, thanks to funding from the Canada Research Chairs program and from the Discovery Grants program of the Natural Sciences and Engineering Research Council of Canada (NSERC).

© Springer-Verlag Berlin Heidelberg 2016
C. Gavoille and D. Ilcinkas (Eds.): DISC 2016, LNCS 9888, pp. 442–457, 2016.
DOI: 10.1007/978-3-662-53426-7_32

have higher tags than earlier ones); in others, the only requirement is that tags are unique. (e.g., [3, 7, 13]).

A standard technique for tagging is as follows: To generate a new tag a process p increments a local variable c, and then uses (p, c) as the tag. But in many algorithms this leads to an unbounded number of tags, and thus shared base objects need to be able to store values of unbounded size. The problem of bounding tags is a special case of the bounded timestamp problem. But timestamps provide more functionality than sometimes needed: In addition to uniqueness, they also satisfy a temporal order relation. This functionality is costly: In all known algorithms (e.g. [10–12, 15, 19]), operations to maintain timestamps for n processes have step complexity at least $\Omega(n)$. Moreover, any timestamp system requires 2^n timestamps [18], and thus they must be stored in objects of size at least n bits. This limits the number of processes that can participate in algorithms relying on timestamp systems, especially if the tags (or timestamps) need to be stored in the same object together with the data they are augmenting.

We investigate the natural question, whether tagging is easier, if no order relation is required. There is evidence that this is the case: Several applications that use tagging rely on ad-hoc techniques to recycle tags with only constant step complexity overhead. Examples are implementations of LL/SC objects [6, 20] or FIFO queues [25] from CAS objects and registers, transformations that augment objects with concurrent Write() or reset() operations [2, 3], and a construction of ABA-detecting registers [4]. But a systematic study of the complexity of tagging was missing. We fill this gap.

We define new types that maintain a finite pool of tags. A process can efficiently find a free tag from that pool and communicate it to other processes by storing it in a shared object. Other processes can obtain references to tags by reading them from shared objects, and later release those reference via a dedicated method. The main safety property provided by our abstraction is that whenever a process obtains a new tag from the pool, then immediately before that the tag was free, i.e., no process had a reference to it. New tags can be taken from the pool infinitely many times, as long as the algorithm that uses this abstraction guarantees that the number of tags to which processes have references to, is bounded (by some parameter τ).

Often, tags need to augment other data that is written to objects. Our abstraction provides methods through which data/tag pairs can be stored into and retrieved from objects. We present two variants of our types; they mainly differ in what operations can be used to store or retrieve data/tag pairs. In the first type, called *taggable registers*, these operations are reads and writes; the second type, called *taggable LL/SC*, supports load-linked/store-conditional (LL/SC) operations. We present implementations from atomic base objects, which correspond to the operations that can be used to communicate data/tag pairs: Our taggable registers are implemented from registers only, and taggable LL/SC objects from LL/SC objects and registers. Each of those implementations is wait-free, all operations have constant step complexity, shared base objects have bounded size (typically it is logarithmic in the number of processes), and the number of base objects used is bounded (typically polynomially in the number of processes).

Considering tags as memory addresses, our taggable objects can be directly used for memory reclamation in a number of algorithms, and allow certain operations to be wait-free, where other memory reclamation techniques guarantee only lock-freedom. Popular techniques for memory reclamation are Michael's Hazard Pointers (HP) [23], and Herlihy et al.'s Pass-the-Buck (PB) [16]. Naively applying those techniques to data structures based on compare-and-swap universal [5,9,24] or read-copy-update [22], usually requires that even non-modifying operations are at most lock-free, even though without memory reclamation, those operations could be wait-free. Using our taggable objects for memory reclamation, wait-freedom of such read-only operations can be preserved, and in fact, only a constant step complexity overhead is added. Other algorithms that use ad-hoc memory reclamation have trivial wait-free solutions using our taggable objects [2,3,14].

The core reason why other memory reclamation techniques do not achieve wait-freedom even for certain non-modifying operations, is that retrieving the reference of a memory block and protecting it are separated into two distinct operations. Suppose a process wants to access a memory block (e.g., the top element of a stack) after having read its address from a shared object (e.g., a pointer to the top of the stack). Then the process must first make an attempt to protect that node from being released (e.g., by setting a hazard pointer), and then check whether it succeeded doing so by testing if the node is still part of the data structure (e.g., it is still pointed to by the stack pointer). If that test fails, the memory block may have already been released, and thus cannot be safely accessed anymore. Then the process's attempt to make progress failed. This is different with our taggable object implementations: Retrieving a tag from a taggable register or taggable LL/SC object automatically protects the tag from being released, and is achieved through a wait-free operation with constant step complexity.

For this purpose, our abstraction works best, if only a fixed node needs to be protected, such as the root of a tree, or the top element of a stack. In the case of general linked data structures, where any node may have to be protected (e.g. a linked list), our taggable objects do not achieve better progress conditions than other memory reclamation techniques. (See also Sect. 2.2.)

Memory reclamation techniques such as HP or PB often rely on the operating system to provide methods for allocation and deallocation of memory blocks. The time and space complexity of those allocation methods, or their progress guarantees, are not part of the analysis. Some schemes, such as DEBRA [8], also manage pools of memory blocks, and provide (de-)allocation methods. However, these schemes usually use lock-free linked list, and therefore are not wait-free. Our taggable object implementation manages its own pool of tags, and does not rely on any external methods for memory allocation. Consequently, unlike memory reclamation solutions such as HP or PB, progress is not dependent on the progress of the system's memory allocation layer.

A disadvantage of our implementations may be that a sufficiently large pool of shared objects needs to be preallocated. It is not hard to accommodate our implementations so that the pool of tags is dynamically resized, if the system provides methods for memory allocation and deallocation; but this is beyond the scope of this paper. Moreover, one could conceive a system, where essentially all available memory addresses are tags; our results show that in such a system memory allocation and reclamation is possible with only constant time overhead. Even though the space of our implementations is polynomial (in several parameters, including the number of processes), it may be too high for practical use. But the main goal of this research is not to provide a finished practical system. Instead we aim to devise a new abstraction and demonstrate its usefulness for a variety of applications (see Sect. 2.1 for selected examples). We show that the abstraction has a time efficient, polynomial space implementation, and can yield wait-freedom, where other techniques cannot.

2   Taggable Objects

Throughout, n denotes the number of processes in the system. The types we introduce are called taggable register array (TRA) and taggable LL/SC array (TLSA). Each is instantiated by two parameters, m and τ, and maintains an array $R[0 \ldots m-1]$ of size m. The parameter τ is, roughly, a bound on the number of tags that can be simultaneously referenced by processes; a formal definition will be provided below. To specify the values of the parameters m and τ, we will sometimes write (m, τ)-TRA and (m, τ)-TLSA. The tags come from the domain $T = \{0, \ldots, \Delta(m, n, \tau) - 1\}$, where Δ is a some function. (In our implementations, Δ is a polynomial, albeit with large constant degrees; see Sect. 2.3.) The components of the array R behave essentially as registers (for TRA) and as LL/SC objects (for TLSA), respectively, but they provide additional functionality.

In the following, we provide a *sequential* specification of the types TLSA and TRA. Our implementation described in Sect. 3 is linearizable. Both types support the operations GetFree() and Release(). Operation GetFree() returns a free tag g from pool T, and as a result g is *in use*. Method Release(g) takes as parameter a tag g that is in use, and as a result g ceases to be in use. (But even when a tag has been released, it may not be free because other processes may still need access to it, as explained below.)

Once a tag is put in use through a GetFree() method, processes can augment data values with them, and communicate the resulting data/tag pairs via the shared objects of array R. In case of type TRA, this is done with the operations Write() and Read(). Specifically, Write()$i, (x, g)$ writes the pair (x, g) consisting of a tag g and a data value x to $R[i]$, and Read()i returns the pair stored in $R[i]$. Similarly, in case of type TLSA, tags can be stored in and retrieved from R using operations LL() and SC() that behave like the corresponding operations on LL/SC objects: Operation LL(i) returns the current pair stored in $R[i]$, and SC($i, (x, g)$) attempts to write the pair (x, g) to $R[i]$, and returns a Boolean value indicating whether the write succeeded or not (if it does not succeed, $R[i]$ remains unchanged). Operation $\mathsf{SC}(i, (x, g))$ by p succeeds if and only if p previously executed $\mathsf{LL}(i)$, and since then no other successful $\mathsf{SC}(i, \cdot)$ operation was performed.

As a result of an $\mathsf{LL}()$ or a $\mathsf{Read}()$ that returns a pair (x, g), a process has tag g *protected*, and can from then on safely use that tag. (The meaning of safe is explained later.) Once a process needs no access to g anymore, it can call $\mathsf{Unprotect}(g)$. Since multiple $\mathsf{LL}()$ or $\mathsf{Read}()$ operations may return the same tag, a tag may be protected multiple times. If p executed k $\mathsf{LL}()$ or $\mathsf{Read}()$ operations that returned tag g, and ℓ $\mathsf{Unprotect}(g)$ operations, then p protects g exactly $k - \ell$ times. A process must not call $\mathsf{Unprotect}(g)$ unless it protects g at least once, so $k - \ell$ cannot become negative. We say a process *protects* a tag to indicate that the process protects it at least once.

The goal of these methods is that access to tags is always safe, in the sense that no process is poised to use a tag g, when a $\mathsf{GetFree}()$ method returns g. To make this precise, we distinguish between *free* and *occupied* tags. A tag g is *occupied*, if

– it is in use (i.e., a $\mathsf{GetFree}()$ returned g and was not followed by a $\mathsf{Release}(g)$);
– some process *protects it* (i.e., p executed more $\mathsf{LL}()$ or $\mathsf{Read}()$ calls that returned g, than it executed $\mathsf{Unprotect}(g)$ calls); or
– a pair $(\cdot, g)$ is stored in some element of array R.

A tag g is called *free*, if it is not occupied. The safety property guaranteed by types TLSA and TRA is that whenever a $\mathsf{GetFree}()$ method returns a tag, that tag is free.

Safety can, of course, only be ensured if processes access tags properly. In particular, when a process calls $\mathsf{SC}(\cdot, (\cdot, g)))$, it must protect tag g, when it calls $\mathsf{Release}(g)$, g must be in use, and when it calls $\mathsf{SC}(\cdot, (\cdot, g)))$, g must be occupied. Moreover, in order to not run out of free tags, the algorithm using our taggable objects must ensure that there are never more than τ tags in use or protected. Processes can achieve that by releasing and unprotecting sufficiently many tags. For example, in the applications presented below, we choose $\tau = n$ and $\tau = 2n$, because at any point each process protects only one and two tags, respectively, and the algorithm ensures that the total number of protected and in use tags is bounded by n and $2n$, respectively.

Note that $\mathsf{Release}(g)$ is the counterpart of $\mathsf{GetFree}()$, and $\mathsf{Unprotect}(g)$ the counterpart of $\mathsf{Read}()$ or $\mathsf{LL}()$. But if a process begins to protect a tag g as a result of a $\mathsf{Read}()$ or $\mathsf{LL}()$ method, it needs to call $\mathsf{Unprotect}(g)$ itself, while any process can call $\mathsf{Release}(g)$ for an in-use tag g, no matter which process received t from a $\mathsf{GetFree}()$ call. This property will allow us later to design an extension of this type that can replace other memory reclamation techniques, such as HP or PB, for list based data structures.

To illustrate the usefulness of our abstraction, we describe some simple applications.

2.1 Example Applications

Round-Based Algorithms. In a recent mutual exclusion algorithm [13], processes make multiple attempts to enter the critical section. In each such attempt, a process p increments a round number, c, and when it writes to some objects, it writes pairs of the form (x, c). The only purpose of writing round numbers is that if some other process reads different pairs, say (x, c) and (x', c') written by p, then it can decide by comparing c and c', whether those pairs were written by p in the same or in different rounds. The temporal order relation between rounds is irrelevant. Since there is no bound on the number of attempts a process makes, correctness can only be ensured by unbounded registers to store the round numbers; therefore, the authors describe an ad-hoc way of recycling round numbers in that particular algorithm. With our abstraction, this becomes trivial: We can use an (m, τ)-TRA object, where m is the number of registers that need to store round numbers in the algorithm, and $\tau = O(n)$. At the beginning of a round, a process calls GetFree(), and uses the returned tag, g, as its round number. During the round, it uses the methods Write() and Read() provided by the TRA object whenever it wants to write or read a value from a register that may store a round number (tag). At an appropriate point after reading a tag, it unprotects the tag with Unprotect(), and at the end of the round it releases its own round number by calling Release(g).

Pointer Swinging. Many shared memory algorithms are based on the following template: There is a pointer, X, that points to a block of objects that store the current state of the data structure. A process may modify the data structure as follows: First it allocates a new block B of objects. Then it reads the current state, computes the new state and writes the new state to B. Finally, the process tries to change X so that it points to B.

A simple universal construction, called *single compare-and-swap universal (SCU)* [5] is based on this technique. Many lock-free data structures [9,24], and McKenny and Slingwine's *read-copy-update (RCU)* mechanism employed by the Linux kernel use similar pointer swinging techniques [22]. Other examples are the implementation of a CAS object from name consensus and registers [14], and a construction to augment a wide class of objects with wait-free reset or write operations [2,3].

Under the assumption that memory is unbounded, the algorithms mentioned above are trivial. But implementations in bounded space are very difficult, and it is not surprising that a significant amount of the technical work in [2,3,14] is devoted to ad-hoc memory reclamation.

Our taggable array types provide an abstraction that allows an elegant solution to the memory reclamation problem encountered in those algorithms: For X we use either a $(1, 2n)$-TRA or a $(1, 2n)$-TLSA object. Each tag $g \in \{0, \dots, \Delta(1, n, 2n) - 1\}$ is associated with a block $B[g]$ of registers, and X simply stores a tag that is an index of the current block. To "allocate" a new block, a process can simply call GetFree() to obtain an index g' of an unused block. After successfully updating X to g', the process can call Release(g') to indicate that it is not using block $B[g']$ anymore. The semantics of the taggable object then guarantess that no GetFree() returns an index to an occupied block, i.e., one that a process may be about to change.

```
// C is a (1,2n)-TLSA; Since C has only one component, we omit the array
   index 0 from C.LL() and C.SC() statements.
// B is an array of size Δ(1,n,2n).
```

update(x)
1   $g' := C.\text{GetFree}()$
2   **repeat**
3      $g := C.\text{LL}()$
4      $b := B[g]$
5   Determine new state from b and x; write to $B[g']$
6      $C.\text{Unprotect}(g)$
7   **until** $C.\text{SC}(g')$
8   $C.\text{Release}(g')$
9   **return** b

read()
10   $g := C.\text{LL}()$
11   $b := B[g]$
12   $C.\text{Unprotect}(g)$
13   **return** b

Fig. 1. SCU with Bounded Memory and Wait-Free Read.

To illustrate this, we present in Fig. 1 pseudocode for a universal construction based on SCU with bounded memory, and a wait-free read method. Operation update(x) updates the object based on parameter x and returns its previous value, and operation Read() returns the object's value. Note that memory reclamation for SCU can also easily be achieved with techniques such as HP or PB, but then read-only operations are lock-free instead of wait-free, and memory allocation must be provided by the system.

Another example is that of a stack implementation with a wait-free peek() operation. Michael [23] applied his HP technique to the IBM Free-List algorithm [17]. We can replace Hazard Pointers by using a TLSA object S to store the address of the top element of the stack. As a result, an S.LL() operation does not only return a reference to that top element, it also protects it. This way, it is straight-forward to obtain a wait-free peek() operation.

2.2 Extended Specification

With the specification described above, our taggable objects cannot easily be used for memory reclamation in linked data structures, unlike HP or PB. Consider for example a linked list implementation. A natural way of using our primitives would be to associate a tag with every node that may be used in the list. But in order to protect the next pointer of a node, the node itself would have to be a component of the taggable array $R[0 \dots m-1]$. Therefore, each tag (which corresponds to an address of a node) would have to be in the domain $\{0, \dots, m-1\}$. But for our implementation, the size of the tag domain, $\Delta(m, n, \tau)$, is always larger than m.

It is easy to extend our types, so that our objects can be used in a similar way as HP and PB for linked data structures. To do that, we allow that tags that are in use can be communicated to other processes not only through the taggable array R, but also through other objects in the system. However, it is then not possible to read and protect a tag in one operation; instead, similar as in HP and PB, a process can attempt to protect a tag, but must afterwards ensure that the tag has not yet been released by some other process (typically by checking that it is still part of the data structure).

To facilitate this, we add a method Protect(g) to the TRA or TLSA specification, which takes as argument a tag g and returns nothing. A process can call Protect(g) for a tag g at any point. The Protect(g) call by process p increases the number of times p has tag g protected, provided that at the point of the Protect(g)call the tag is occupied (recall that this a sequential specification). Otherwise, p must call Unprotect(g) immediately, before executing any other operation on the TRA or TLSA object. These primitives can be used in much the same way as, e.g., Hazard Pointers: After a process p obtained the address g of a node (which corresponds to a tag) in a linked data structure (e.g., it read it from the next pointer of a linked list), p tries to protect that node by calling Protect(g). Then p checks if the node is still in the data structure. If not, p must immediately call Unprotect(g). Otherwise, the node is protected from being reclaimed, so it can be safely accessed until p calls Unprotect(g).

2.3   Main Result

We present implementations of taggable register and taggable LL/SC arrays with constant step complexity, using only a bounded number of bounded size base objects.

Theorem 1. *Let $M(m, n, \tau)$ be a sufficiently large polynomial. There are linearizable implementations*

- *of type (m, τ)-TRA, from $M = M(m, n, \tau)$ registers of size $O(\log M)$ bits, such that each operation has constant step complexity; and*
- *of type (m, τ)-TLSA from $M = M(m, n, \tau)$ registers and LL/SC objects of size $O(\log M)$ bits, such that each operation has constant step complexity.*

In both implementations, the tag domain is $\{0, \ldots, \Delta(m, n, \tau) - 1\}$, where Δ is a polynomial function.

We obtain the following upper bounds: $M(m, n, \tau) = O(mn^5 + n^3 \tau)$ and $\Delta(m, n, \tau) = O(m^2 n^6 + n^2 \tau^2 + mn^4 \tau)$. We believe that it is possible to reduce these values, but doing so would make the algorithms more complicated. Note that an LL/SC object can be implemented from a single compare-and-swap (CAS) object and from $O(n)$ registers, in such a way that each LL() and each SC() operation has constant step complexity [6,20].

In the following, we describe the implementation of the TLSA object. Full correctness proofs and our implementation of TRA will be made available in the full version.

3   TLSA Implementation

In this section, we present our TLSA Implementation from registers and LL/SC objects, as depicted in Fig. 2. To simplify the algorithm, we use *ABA-detecting registers* [4]. An ABA-detecting register provides the operation DWrite(x), which writes value x to the object, and operation DRead(), which returns the current value of the object and a Boolean flag. The flag is **true**, if and only if the process executed an earlier DRead() operation, and a DWrite() was performed after that. An ABA-detecting register with constant step complexity can be implemented from $O(n)$ registers [4].

3.1   Managing Tags

Let $T = \{0, \ldots, \Delta(n, m, \tau) - 1\}$ be the domain of tags. Tags are organized in $\beta \cdot n$ *blocks* $b_0, \ldots, b_{\beta n-1}$, where $\beta = mn(2n + 5) + \tau + 2n + 1$, and each block contains $\delta = 2n\beta + n$ tags. Each block is *owned* by exactly one of the n processes, and each process owns β blocks. Block b_i contains tags $i \cdot \delta, \ldots, i \cdot (\delta + 1) - 1$ and is owned by process $\lfloor i/\beta \rfloor$.

The algorithm ensures that when a process returns the first free tag of some block b_i in a GetFree() method, then not only that tag is free, but in fact all tags in that block are. During its next δ GetFree() method calls the process returns only tags from block b_i, and with every such method call it executes a constant amount of work to identify a new block that contains only free tags.

To protect tags in a specific block from being freed, a process p uses two ABA-detecting register arrays, Emp_p and Use_p, each of size βn. In a GetFree() method that returns tag $g \in b_i$, process p increments the value of $Use_p[i]$, and in a Release(g) method it decrements it. Therefore, the algorithm maintains (roughly) the invariant that $\sum_{p=0}^{n-1} Use_p[i]$ is the total number of tags in block b_i that are in use. The value of $Emp_p[i]$ gets incremented and decremented by process p via methods Protect() and Unprotect(), respectively. We say a tag g is *employed* k times by process p, if that process called Unprotect(g) ℓ times for some value $\ell \geq 0$, and Protect(g) $k + \ell$ times. Note that Protect() and Unprotect are not only used as external methods, but as sub-routines for other methods. For example, a process calls Protect(g) during a LL() method, in order to protect tag g from being freed, while the process is trying to decide if that LL() can return g.

Our algorithm maintains the invariant that if $E(i) := \sum_{p=0}^{n-1}(Emp_p[i] + Use_p[i]) = 0$, then all tags in block b_i are free. Hence, in a GetFree() method, in order to find a block b_i that contains only free tags, a process p needs to find an index i such that it owns b_i and $E(i) = 0$. Process p can check if $E(i) = 0$ using $O(n)$ steps as follows: It reads the ABA-detecting registers $Emp_0[i], Use_0[i], \ldots, Emp_{n-1}[i], Use_{n-1}[i]$, and computes the sum of their values. If the sum is 0, it reads these ABA-detecting registers again, and uses the flags returned by DRead() operations to ensure that none of the register values has changed; essentially this is a double collect as in the standard snapshot implementation [1]. If no register changed, then there was a point at which $E(i) = 0$,

```
// Tag domain T = {0,...,nβδ−1}
shared:
    LL/SC R[m]
    ∀p ∈ [n]: int Emp_p[nβ]
    ∀p ∈ [n]: int Use_p[nβ] = 0
    ∀i ∈ [m]: LL/SC H_i[n]
```

$$// \; \beta = mn(2n+5) + \tau + 2n + 1$$
$$// \; \delta = 2n\beta + n$$

```
local to process p, and with global scope:
    bool flag_p[m] = 0
    int emp_p[nβ]
    int ρ = 0, j = 0
    int tag_p = pβ − 1
    ∀i ∈ [m]: int q_i = 0
    Queue rsrvQ_p[m]  (each initially contains
                       2n+4 elements of value ⊥)
```

Method SC_p(i, (x, g))

14 **if** $flag_p[i] = 1$ **then return false**
15 Protect(g)
16 $(x', g', p') := H_i[q_i].\mathsf{LL}()$
17 **if** $R[i].\mathsf{SC}(x, g) = $ **false then**
18 | Unprotect(g)
19 | **return false**
20 updateQ(i, g)
21 **if** $(x', g', p') = (\bot, \bot, \bot)$ **then**
22 | $H_i[q_i].\mathsf{SC}(x, g, p)$
23 **else if** $p' = p$ **then**
24 | Protect(g')
25 | updateQ(i, g')
26 (q_i++) mod n
27 **return true**

Method LL_p(i)

28 $flag_p[i] = 0$
29 **repeat**
30 | $H_i[p].\mathsf{LL}()$
31 **until** $H_i[p].\mathsf{SC}(\bot, \bot, \bot)$
32 $retv := (x, g) := R[i].\mathsf{LL}()$
33 Protect(g)
34 $(x', g', p') := H_i[p].\mathsf{LL}()$
35 **if** $(x', g', p') \ne (\bot, \bot, \bot)$ **then**
36 | $retv := (x', g')$
37 | Unprotect(g)
38 | Protect(g')
39 | $(x'', g'') := R[i].\mathsf{LL}()$
40 | **if** $(x'', g'') \ne (x', g')$ **then**
41 | | $flag_p[i] := 1$
42 **return** $retv$

Method Release_p(g)

43 $u := Use_p[\lfloor g/\delta \rfloor].\mathsf{DRead}()$
44 $Use_p[\lfloor g/\delta \rfloor].\mathsf{DWrite}(u - 1)$

Method GetFree_p()

45 tag_p++
46 $(x, f) := Emp_{\rho \bmod n}[p\beta + j].\mathsf{DRead}()$
47 $(x', f') := Use_{\rho \bmod n}[p\beta + j].\mathsf{DRead}()$
48 **if** $\rho < n$ **then** $sum := sum + x + x'$
49 **if** $n \le \rho < 2n$ **then** $sum := sum + f + f'$
50 $(\rho++)$ mod $3n$
51 **if** $\rho = 2n \wedge sum \ne 0$ **then**
52 | $sum := 0; \rho := 0$
53 | $(j++)$ mod β
54 **else if** $2n \le \rho < 3n$ **then**
55 | $Use_{\rho \bmod n}[p\beta + j].\mathsf{DWrite}(0)$
56 **else if** $\rho = 0$ **then**
57 | $tag_p := (p\beta + j) \times \delta$
58 | $(j++)$ mod β
59 $u := Use_p[\lfloor tag_p/\delta \rfloor].\mathsf{DRead}()$
60 $Use_p[\lfloor tag_p/\delta \rfloor].\mathsf{DWrite}(u + 1)$
61 **return** tag_p

Method Protect_p(g)

62 $emp_p[\lfloor g/\delta \rfloor]++$
63 $Emp_p[\lfloor g/\delta \rfloor].\mathsf{DWrite}(emp_p[\lfloor g/\delta \rfloor])$

Method Unprotect_p(g)

64 $emp_p[\lfloor g/\delta \rfloor]--$
65 $Emp_p[\lfloor g/\delta \rfloor].\mathsf{DWrite}(emp_p[\lfloor g/\delta \rfloor])$

Method updateQ_p(i, g)

66 $rsrvQ_p[i].\mathsf{enq}(g)$
67 $g' := rsrvQ_p[i].\mathsf{deq}()$
68 **if** $g' \ne \bot$ **then** Unprotect(g')

Fig. 2. Implementation of an (m, τ)-TLSA

and thus at that point all tags in b_i were free. The algorithm ensures that if a tag g is free, then no process calls Protect(g). Hence, once the value of $E(i)$ is 0, it does not change until a GetFree() method returns a tag from b_i. Therefore, if p detects that $E(i)$ had value 0 at some point t, then all tags in b_i are still free unless p returned a tag from b_i in a GetFree() method after t.

Note that up to here, each process p only needs to increment or decrement "its own" registers $Emp_p[i]$ or $Use_p[i]$. Therefore, we need no concurrent counter implementations.

A problem is that even when $E(i) = 0$, each individual register $Use_q[i]$ can be positive or negative, even though $\sum_{q=0}^{n-1} Use_q[i] \geq 0$. (Process q may have decremented the value of $Use_q[i]$ when releasing a tag from b_i, while a different process p originally obtained that tag from a GetFree() operation during which it incremented $Use_p[i]$.) In order to avoid that the values of those registers grow very large over time, p can reset all registers $Use_q[i]$, $q \in \{0, \ldots, n-1\}$, to 0, during n DWrite() operations. The fact that $E(i) = 0$ guarantees that no other process concurrently accesses any of those registers, while they are being reset. To summarize, for each block b_i, in $O(n)$ steps, process p can check if $E(i) = 0$, and if yes, reset all registers $Use_q[i]$, $q \in \{0, \ldots, n-1\}$.

Our implementation guarantees that among the β blocks owned by process p, there is always at least one block b_i with $E(i) = 0$. Hence, to find such a block, process p can test each of its β blocks with the procedure described above. As a result it takes $O(n\beta)$ steps to find a free block and reset the corresponding employment counters. We distribute this work over $O(n\beta)$ of p's GetFree() operations, during each of which a constant number of the required steps get executed. A sufficiently large block size of $\delta = 2n\beta + n$ guarantees that p finds a new block with $E(i) = 0$ before it runs out of tags in its current block.

In the following, we describe the implementation in detail. Methods Protect() and Unprotect() simply increment or decrement a single writer component of array Emp_p. In method Release(g), process p decrements $Use_p[i]$, where b_i is the block containing tag g, using a DRead() followed by a DWrite(). Recall that no other process writes to $Use_p[i]$, while p executes Release(g).

The GetFree() Operation. We use a local variable tag_p (with global scope) to keep track of the last tag p obtained from a GetFree() operation. In line 45, process p increments that variable, so that its value is now the next free tag in the block that p is currently using. The rest of the method is devoted to performing a constant number of steps of the work required for finding a new free block, i.e., a block b_i for which $E(i) = 0$. Variable j keeps track of the block that p is currently checking whether it is free. More precisely, the block being checked has index $i = p\beta + j$. Variable $\rho \mod n$ indicates the process whose variables $Emp_{\rho \mod n}[i]$ and $Use_{\rho \mod n}[i]$ are being summed up. Over time, each of those variables needs to be read twice to perform a double collect on all these registers, and, if b_i is identified as a free block, then the variables $Use_0[i], \ldots, Use_{n-1}[i]$ need to be reset. Therefore, ρ takes values in $\{0, \ldots, 3n-1\}$.

In lines 46–47, p uses DRead() to read $Emp_{\rho \mod n}[p\beta + j]$ and $Use_{\rho \mod n}[p\beta + j]$. If $\rho < n$, then this is the first time p reads those variables during the current "double collect", so it sums up the returned values in line 48. If $n \leq \rho < 2n$, then this is the second time that p is reading those variable during the current double collect, so it adds the flags returned from the DRead operations to the sum in line 49 (recall that each flag is 0 if the corresponding value has not changed since the previous read, and otherwise it is 1). After that p increments ρ modulo $3n$ in line 50.

If $\rho = 2n$ after the increment, then p has completed its double collect. If $sum \neq 0$, then $E(i) > 0$ (where $i = p\beta + j$), and so the process prepares for moving on to a new block to check in its subsequent GetFree() calls. To that end, p increments j mod β, and resets ρ and sum in lines 52–53. Otherwise, $sum = 0$, and the process identified a free block b_i. In this case, during this and the next $n - 1$ GetFree() calls, $2n \leq \rho < 3n$; in line 55 of those calls, p resets $Use_0[i], \ldots, Use_{n-1}[i]$. If $\rho = 0$, then p has made $3n$ GetFree() calls that dealt with block b_i, where $i = p\beta + j$, and thus it identified b_i as free and reset all Use variables of that block. Hence, the GetFree() method can return the first tag, $(p\beta + j) \cdot \delta$, from block b_i. Therefore, p sets tag_p to that value in line 57. In line 58 process p then increments j modulo β so that it begins the search for another free block in its next GetFree() call. In either case, in lines 59–60 process p increments the value of $Use_p[\lfloor tag_p / \delta \rfloor]$ to indicate that the tag it returns is now in use; the GetFree() operation linearizes with the write to $Use_p[\lfloor tag_p / \delta \rfloor]$.

3.2   Load and Store

For the ease of description, we assume in the following that $m = 1$ (i.e., array R contains only one element), and we ignore the data values that are augmented by tags when storing or loading them from $R[0]$. We write LL() instead of LL(0), SC(g) instead of SC($0, (\cdot, g)$), and R instead of $R[0]$.

To execute an LL() operation on the TLSA object, a process q must perform two tasks: It has to identify a tag g that is stored in R at some point during the LL() operation (that point will be the linearization point), and it has to employ g, i.e., call Protect(g) (which increments $Emp_q[i]$, where b_i is the block containing g). The difficulty is that q must do all this while $E(i) > 0$, because otherwise the process q that owns block b_i may in the meantime begin using tags from that block for its GetFree() operations. In particular, if such a GetFree() returns g, the safety condition of TLSA would be violated.

We deal with this in the following way: Each time a process p executes an SC(g) operation on the TLSA object, it chooses a different process q (in a round robin fashion), and tries to provide tag g as a hint that q can use in an LL() operation in case the tag it found on R is not "safe" to use. The hint will be stored in the component $H[q]$ of a shared *hint array* $H[0..n-1]$ of LL/SC objects (each component of H stores either $(\bot, \bot)$ or a pair consisting of a tag and a process ID). Process p also uses a local *reserved queue*, $rsrvQ_p$, which always stores $2n+4$ such pairs or $\bot$ elements. (For $m > 1$, there will be m hint arrays H_i and queues $rsrvQ_p[i]$, $0 \leq i < m$, one for each component of R. Moreover, in the pseudocode, instead of pairs, these objects store triples, each containing a data value in addition to a tag and process ID.) Queue $rsrvQ_p$ is used to keep track of the last $n + 2$ hints that have been provided by p to other processes, as well as the last $n + 2$ tags that have been successfully stored in R. A tag g is inserted into the queue by calling helper method updateQ(g). The algorithm maintains the invariant that all tags in $rsrvQ_p$ are employed, so updateQ(g) is only called after a tag g has been employed. In addition to enqueuing g into p's reserved queue, the method also dequeues an element from that queue, and unemploys it. I.e., this method ensures that the reserved queue always has the same length. Method updateQ() will be called at least once and at most twice during each successful SC() call, and not at all during an unsuccessful one. Therefore, once a tag has been employed by process p and added to p's reserved queue $rsrvQ_p$, it will remain employed throughout p's next $n + 1$ successful SC() calls.

The SC() Operation. At the beginning of an SC(g) operation by p on the TLSA object, process p first checks its local variable $flag_p$, and if that is set, it returns **false** immediately (line 14). The reason for that will be explained later, when we describe method LL(). Next, p employs g by calling Protect(g) in line 15. Then, in line 16, process p loads $H[q]$, where q is the process to which p may provide a hint in this SC() operation. (Recall that q changes in a round robin fashion with each of p's SC() calls, see line 26.) Then an attempt is made to store g into R using an R.SC(g) operation (line 17). The point when this happen will be the linearization point of p's SC() operation on the TLSA object. If that attempt to store g in R fails, then p unemploys g again by calling Unprotect(g) and returns **false** to indicate that its SC() on the TLSA object failed (lines 18–19). Otherwise, updateQ(g) is called in line 20, and thus g remains employed throughout p's next $n + 1$ successful SC() operations. Then p makes an attempt to provide g as a hint to process q, if $H[q]$ does not already contain a hint. To do that, the value g gets stored into $H[q]$ if and only if $H[q] = (\bot, \bot)$ when p loaded it earlier, and $H[q]$ has not changed since then (lines 21–22). If $H[q]$ already contains a hint g' previously provided by p, then p calls Protect(g') followed by updateQ(g') to ensure that the hint remains employed for another $n + 1$ successful SC() operations by p (23–25). Finally, p increments q modulo n and returns **true** (lines 26–27).

The LL() Operation. Now consider process p's LL() operation on the TLSA object. First, p resets $flag_p$ in line 28; we postpone an explanation to the end of this section. In lines 29–31, process p resets $H[p]$ by repeating $H[p]$.LL() and $H[p]$.SC($\bot, \bot$) operations, until an $H[p]$.SC($\bot, \bot$) succeeds. (Any other process will only change the value of $H[p]$ when its value is $(\bot, \bot)$, so p needs at most two attempts to reset $H[p]$.) Then p executes an LL() operation on R to obtain a tentative tag g, and employs that tag by calling Protect(g) (lines 32–33). After that p reads $H[p]$ in line 34. If $H[p] = (\bot, \bot)$, then no process provided a hint to p since p reset $H[p]$ at the beginning of its ongoing LL() operation. In particular, this is true for the process q that stored tag g in R prior to p's R.LL(). This implies that q has executed at most $n - 1$ complete and successful SC() methods since then, because in n consecutive successful SC() methods q attempts to provide a hint to every process. Since tag g remains employed throughout $n + 1$ successful SC() methods by q, following the one in which q stored it into R, tag

g is still employed by q when p reads $(\perp, \perp)$ from $H[p]$; specifically, it has been continuously employed starting from the point when p read g from R until p employed it itself prior to reading $H[p]$. As a result, p can safely use tag g and return it from its LL() method in line 42. In this case, the linearization point of the LL() method is when q loads g from R in line 32.

Now suppose that $H[p]$ contains a pair $(g', p') \neq (\perp, \perp)$ when p loads it in line 34. Then it is ensured that, during a successful SC(g'), process p' must have executed an $H[p]$.LL() and a subsequent $H[p]$.SC(g', p') operation since p reset $H[p]$ in line 31 of its LL() operation on the TLSA object. During that SC(g'), p' successfully stored g' into R (line 17), and this must have happened after p reset $H[p]$ in line 31, and before it read (g', p') from it in line 34. Thus, p's LL() operation can return tag g', and its linearization point will be immediately after g' got stored into R by p' (which happened at the linearization point of the SC(g') by p'). Moreover, the SC() method ensures that g' remains employed as long as the pair (g', p') remains in $H[p]$, and only p can reset that LL/SC object itself. Hence, p can now simply call Protect(g') in line 38 and be sure that g' has continuously been employed since the linearization point of its LL() operation on the TLSA object. Since p's LL() will not return tag g, it also calls Unprotect(g) in line 37.

But here is the catch: the linearization point of p's LL() operation may lie before p executed R.LL(). Inbetween that linearization point and p's R.LL() operation in line 32, a successful SC() operation of some other process, r, may have linearized. If following its LL() of the TLSA object, p executes SC() on that object, then that SC() may succeed because, the R.SC() operation in line 17 succeeds (because p has a "valid link" to R). But the semantics of the TLSA object dictates that this SC() must fail, because of r executed a successful SC() between the linearization point of p's LL() and p's following SC(). To deal with this case, process p loads R one more time after it has decided to use hint g' (line 39). If the value of R is not equal to g', then p sets the local flag $flag_p$ (lines 40–41), which will force its next SC() operation to fail immediately (line 14). (Note that the fact that R does not contain g' implies that a successful SC() must have linearized since the linearization point of p's ongoing LL().) If the value of R is equal to g', then p does not set the flag, but now the linearization point of its LL() is the point of p's last load of R (line 39), when the value is g'.

4   Conclusion

We presented the first study on the complexity of tagging, and showed that tags can be bounded with only constant time overhead. Using our taggable objects for memory reclamation, can in some cases lead to wait-free read-only operations, where other memory reclamation techniques yield only lock-freedom. We see it as an important contribution of this paper to present the right abstraction, and provide building blocks that can be easily reused. We hope that this simplifies future attempts to prove upper bounds on algorithmic problems, as researchers can simply use the primitives presented here, and do not have to find ad-hoc solutions for bounding tags. The space complexity of our implementations may be too high for practical use. We hope that future research can reduce the space overhead and may eventually lead to practical solutions.

Acknowledgements. We thank Lisa Higham for valueable discussions related to our abstraction, and Hagit Attiya for helpful literature pointers.

References

1. Afek, Y., Attiya, H., Dolev, D., Gafni, E., Merritt, M., Shavit, N.: Atomic snapshots of shared memory. J. ACM **40**(4), 873–890 (1993)
2. Aghazadeh, Z., Golab, W., Woelfel, P.: Making objects writable. In: Proceeding of 33rd PODC, pp. 385–395 (2014)
3. Aghazadeh, Z., Woelfel, P.: Space- and time-efficient long-lived test-and-set objects. In: Aguilera, M.K., Querzoni, L., Shapiro, M. (eds.) OPODIS 2014. LNCS, vol. 8878, pp. 404–419. Springer, Heidelberg (2014)
4. Aghazadeh, Z., Woelfel, P.: On the time and space complexity of ABA prevention and detection. In: Proceeding of 34th PODC, pp. 193–202 (2015)
5. Alistarh, D., Censor-Hillel, K., Shavit, N.: Are lock-free concurrent algorithms practically wait-free? In: Proceeding of 46th ACM STOC, pp. 714–723 (2014)
6. Anderson, J.H., Moir, M.: Universal constructions for multi-object operations. In Proceeding of 14th PODC, pp. 184–193 (1995)
7. Attiya, H., Rachman, O.: Atomic snapshots in o(n log n) operations. SIAM J. Comp. **27**(2), 319–340 (1998)
8. Brown, T.A.: Reclaiming memory for lock-free data structures: there has to be a better way. In: Proceeding of 34th PODC, pp. 261–270 (2015)
9. Clements, A.T., Kaashoek, M.F., Zeldovich, N.: Scalable address spaces using RCU balanced trees. In: Proceeding of 17th ASPLOS, pp. 199–210 (2012)
10. Dolev, D., Shavit, N.: Bounded concurrent time-stamping. SIAMJC **26**(2), 418–455 (1997)
11. Dwork, C., Herlihy, M., Waarts, O.: Bounded round numbers. In: Proceeding of 12th PODC, pp. 53–64 (1993)
12. Dwork, C., Waarts, O.: Simple and efficient bounded concurrent timestamping or bounded concurrent timestamp systems are comprehensible! In: Proceeding of 24th ACM STOC, pp. 655–666 (1992)
13. Giakkoupis, G., Woelfel, P.: Randomized mutual exclusion with constant amortized RMR complexity on the DSM. In: Proceeding of 55th FOCS, pp. 504–513 (2014)
14. Golab, W., Hadzilacos, V., Hendler, D., Woelfel, P.: RMR-efficient implementations of comparison primitives using read and write operations. Distr. Comp. **25**(2), 109–162 (2012)
15. Haldar, S., Vitányi, P.M.B.: Bounded concurrent timestamp systems using vector clocks. J. ACM **49**(1), 101–126 (2002)
16. Herlihy, M., Luchangco, V., Martin, P.A., Moir, M.: Nonblocking memory management support for dynamic-sized data structures. ACM Trans. Comp. Syst. **23**(2), 146–196 (2005)
17. IBM. IBM system/370 extended architecture, principles of operation. Technical report, 1983. Publication No. SA22-7085
18. Israeli, A., Li, M.: Bounded time-stamps. In: Proceeding of 28th FOCS, pp. 371–382 (1987)

19. Israeli, A., Pinhasov, M.: A concurrent time-stamp scheme which is linear in time and space. In: Proceeding of 6th WDAG, pp. 95–109 (1992)
20. Jayanti, P., Petrovic, S.: Efficient and practical constructions of LL/SC variables. In: Proceeding of 22nd PODC, pp. 285–294 (2003)
21. Lamport, L.: A new solution of Dijkstra's concurrent programming problem. Commun. ACM **17**(8), 453–455 (1974)
22. McKenney, P.E., Slingwine, J.D.: Read-copy update: using execution history to solveconcurrency problems. In: Proceeding of 10th PDCS, pp. 509–518 (1998)
23. Michael, M.: Hazard pointers: safe memory reclamation for lock-free objects. IEEE Trans. Parallel Distrib. Syst. **15**(6), 491–504 (2004)
24. Michael, M., Scott, M.L.: Simple, fast, and practical non-blocking and blocking concurrent queue algorithms. In: Proceeding of 15th PODC, pp. 267–275 (1996)
25. P. Tsigas and Y. Zhang. A simple, fast and scalable non-blocking concurrent FIFO queue for shared memory multiprocessor systems. In Proc. of 13th SPAA, pp. 134–143, 2001
26. Vitányi, P., Awerbuch, B.: Atomic shared register access by asynchronous hardware (detailed abstract). In: Proceeding of 27th FOCS, pp. 233–243 (1986)

Brief Announcements

Brief Announcement:
Local Distributed Verification

Alkida Balliu[1,2]($\boxtimes$), Gianlorenzo D'Angelo[2], Pierre Fraigniaud[1],
and Dennis Olivetti[1,2]

[1] CNRS and University Paris Diderot, Paris, France
[2] Gran Sasso Science Institute, L'aquila, Italy
alkida.balliu@gssi.infn.it

Abstract. It is known that the hierarchy induced by local decision in networks where the certificates may depend on the actual identities of the nodes collapses at the first level [Korman et al., 2010]. We show that, if the certificates cannot depend on the actual identities of the nodes, then the hierarchy also collapses, but at the second level, while the first and second levels are different.

1 The Framework

Following the guidelines of [3], we define a *configuration* as a pair (G, ℓ) where $G = (V, E)$ is a connected simple graph, and $\ell : V(G) \to \{0, 1\}^*$ is a function assigning a *label* $\ell(u)$ to every node $u \in V$. A *distributed language* $\mathcal{L}$ is a Turing-decidable set of configurations. Note that the membership of a configuration to a distributed language is independent of the identity that may be assigned to the nodes. The class LD is the set of all distributed languages that are locally decidable [3]. That is, LD is the class of all distributed languages $\mathcal{L}$ for which there exists a local algorithm $\mathcal{A}$ (i.e., an algorithm $\mathcal{A}$ running in a constant number of rounds in the LOCAL model [6, 8]) satisfying that, for every configuration (G, ℓ), we have $(G, \ell) \in \mathcal{L} \iff \mathcal{A}$ accepts (G, ℓ), where one says that $\mathcal{A}$ accepts if it accepts at *all* nodes. More formally, given a graph G, let $\mathrm{ID}(G)$ denote the set of all possible identity assignments to the nodes of G (with distinct non-negative integers). Then LD is the class of all distributed languages $\mathcal{L}$ for which there exists a local algorithm $\mathcal{A}$ satisfying the following: for every configuration (G, ℓ),

$$(G, \ell) \in \mathcal{L} \Rightarrow \forall \mathrm{id} \in \mathrm{ID}(G), \forall u \in V(G), \mathcal{A}(G, x, \mathrm{id}, u) = \text{accept}$$
$$(G, \ell) \notin \mathcal{L} \Rightarrow \forall \mathrm{id} \in \mathrm{ID}(G), \exists u \in V(G), \mathcal{A}(G, x, \mathrm{id}, u) = \text{reject}$$

where $\mathcal{A}(G, x, \mathrm{id}, u)$ is the output of Algorithm $\mathcal{A}$ at node u running on the instance (G, ℓ) with identity-assignment id.

A. Balliu, P. Fraigniaud and D. Olivetti—Received additional supports from the ANR project DISPLEXITY.
P. Fraigniaud—Additional supports from the INRIA project GANG.

C. Gavoille and D. Ilcinkas (Eds.): DISC 2016, LNCS 9888, pp. 461–464, 2016.
DOI: 10.1007/978-3-662-53426-7

The class NLD [3] is the non-deterministic version of LD, i.e., the class of all distributed languages $\mathcal{L}$ for which there exists a local algorithm $\mathcal{A}$ *verifying* $\mathcal{L}$, i.e., satisfying that, for every configuration (G, ℓ),

$$(G, \ell) \in \mathcal{L} \Rightarrow \exists c \in \mathcal{C}(G), \forall \text{id} \in \text{ID}(G), \forall u \in V(G), \mathcal{A}(G, x, c, \text{id}, u) = \text{accepts}$$
$$(G, \ell) \notin \mathcal{L} \Rightarrow \forall c \in \mathcal{C}(G), \forall \text{id} \in \text{ID}(G), \exists u \in V(G), \mathcal{A}(G, x, c, \text{id}, u) = \text{rejects}$$

where $\mathcal{C}(G)$ is the class of all functions $c : V(G) \rightarrow \{0, 1\}^*$, assigning a *certificate* $c(u)$ to each node u. Note that the certificates c may depend on both the network and the labeling of the nodes, but should be set independently of the actual identity assignment to the nodes of the network. In the following, for the sake of simplifying the notations, we shall omit specifying the domain sets $\mathcal{C}(G)$ and $\text{ID}(G)$ unless they are not clear from the context.

It follows from the above that NLD is a class of distributed languages that can be locally *verified*, in the sense that, on legal instances, certificates can be assigned to nodes by a *prover* so that a *verifier* $\mathcal{A}$ accepts, and, on illegal instances, the verifier $\mathcal{A}$ rejects (i.e., at least one node rejects) systematically, and cannot be fooled by any fake certificate.

In [2], NLD was proved to be exactly the class of distributed languages that are closed under lift. Hence, NLD does not contain all distributed languages. In contrast, LCP (for locally checkable proofs), defined in [4], is the class of all distributed languages $\mathcal{L}$ for which there exists a local algorithm $\mathcal{A}$ verifying $\mathcal{L}$ in the following sense: for every configuration (G, ℓ),

$$(G, \ell) \in \mathcal{L} \Rightarrow \forall \text{id} \in \text{ID}(G), \exists c \in \mathcal{C}(G), \forall u \in V(G), \mathcal{A}(G, x, c, \text{id}, u) = \text{accepts},$$
$$(G, \ell) \notin \mathcal{L} \Rightarrow \forall \text{id} \in \text{ID}(G), \forall c \in \mathcal{C}(G), \exists u \in V(G), \mathcal{A}(G, x, c, \text{id}, u) = \text{rejects}.$$

Note that, in LCP, the certificates can depend on the identity assignment to the nodes. It is known that LCP contains all distributed languages, since every distributed language has a proof-labeling scheme [5].

2 Our Contributions

Following up the approach recently applied to *distributed graph automata* in [7], we observe that the class LD and NLD are in fact the basic levels of a "local hierarchy" defined as follows. Let $\Sigma_0 = \Pi_0 = $ LD, and, for $k \geq 1$, let Σ_k be the class of all distributed languages $\mathcal{L}$ for which there exists a local algorithm $\mathcal{A}$ satisfying that, for every configuration (G, ℓ),

$$(G, \ell) \in \mathcal{L} \iff \exists c_1, \forall c_2, \ldots, Q c_k, \mathcal{A} \text{ accepts } (G, \ell) \text{ with certificates } c_1, c_2, \ldots, c_k$$

where the quantifiers alternate, and Q is the universal quantifier if k is even, and the existential one if k is odd. The class Π_k is defined similarly, by starting with a universal quantifier, instead of an existential one. The certificates $c_1, c_2, \ldots, c_k$ should not depend on the identity assignment to the nodes. Hence, NLD $= \Sigma_1$, and, for instance, Π_2 is the class of all distributed languages $\mathcal{L}$ for which there exists a Π_2-algorithm, that is, a local algorithm $\mathcal{A}$ satisfying the following: for every configuration (G, ℓ),

$$(G, \ell) \in \mathcal{L} \Rightarrow \forall c_1, \exists c_2, \forall \mathrm{id}, \forall u \in V(G), \mathcal{A}(G, x, c_1, c_2, \mathrm{id}, u) = \text{accept};$$
$$(G, \ell) \notin \mathcal{L} \Rightarrow \exists c_1, \forall c_2, \forall \mathrm{id}, \exists u \in V(G), \mathcal{A}(G, x, c_1, c_2, \mathrm{id}, u) = \text{reject}.$$

Our main results are the following.

Theorem 1. $\mathsf{LD} \subset \Pi_1 \subset \mathsf{NLD} = \Sigma_2 \subset \Pi_2 = \mathsf{All}$, *where all inclusions are strict.*

That is, $\Pi_1 \supset \Pi_0$, while $\Sigma_2 = \Sigma_1$, and the whole local hierarchy collapses to the second level, at Π_2. We complete our description of the local hierarchy by a collection of separation and completeness results regarding the different classes and co-classes in the hierarchy. In particular, we revisit the completeness results in [3], and show that the notion of reduction introduced in this latter paper is too strong, and may allow a language outside NLD to be reduced to a language in NLD. We introduce a more restricted form of local reduction, called *label-preserving*, which does not have this undesirable property, and we establish the following.

Theorem 2. NLD *and* Π_2 *have complete distributed languages for local label-preserving reductions.*

Finally, Fig. 1 summarizes all our separation results.

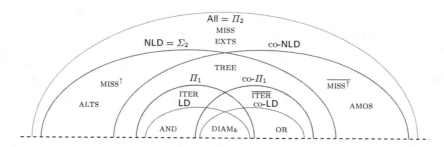

Fig. 1. Relations between the different decision classes of the local hierarchy.

A extended version of this brief announcement can be found in [1].

References

1. Balliu, A., D'Angelo, G., Fraigniaud, P., Olivetti, D.: Local Distributed Verification. Technical report arXiv:1605.03892 (2016)
2. Fraigniaud, P., Halldórsson, M.M., Korman, A.: On the impact of identifiers on local decision. In: Aguilera, M.K., Querzoni, L., Shapiro, M. (eds.) OPODIS 2014. LNCS, vol. 8878, pp. 224–238. Springer, Heidelberg (2012). doi:10.1007/978-3-642-35476-2_16

3. Fraigniaud, P., Korman, A., Peleg, D.: Towards a complexity theory for local distributed computing. J. ACM **60**(5), 35 (2013)
4. Göös, M., Suomela, J.: Locally checkable proofs. In: PODC, pp. 159–168 (2011)
5. Korman, A., Kutten, S., Peleg, D.: Proof labeling schemes. Distrib. Comput. **22**(4), 215–233 (2010)
6. Peleg, D., Computing, D.: A locality-sensitive approach. SIAM (2000)
7. Reiter, F.: Distributed graph automata. In: LICS, pp. 192–201 (2015)
8. Suomela, J.: Survey of local algorithms. ACM Comput. Surv. **45**(2), 24 (2013)

Brief Announcement: A Step Optimal Implementation of Large Single-Writer Registers

Tian Ze Chen$^{(\boxtimes)}$ and Yuanhao Wei$^{(\boxtimes)}$

Department of Computer Science, University of Toronto, Toronto, Canada
{tianze.chen,yuanhao.wei}@mail.utoronto.ca

A register is a fundamental object that supports READ and WRITE operations. Implementing large ℓ-bit registers from small k-bit registers in a wait-free manner is a classic problem in distributed computing. We consider this problem for single-writer atomic registers shared by n readers. This problem arises naturally in practice when ℓ-bits need to be written atomically on a system that provides only k-bit registers.

The *space complexity* of an implementation is the number of shared k-bit registers that it uses and the *step complexity* is the number of shared register operations. Note that $\Omega(\ell/k)$ steps are required for READ operations [3]. Also, any implementation requires $\Omega(\ell/k)$ space, since 2^ℓ different values might need to be represented.

Peterson [4] presented an ℓ-bit single-writer register implementation using $\Theta(n\ell/k)$ space in 1983. Peterson's implementation uses $\Theta(\ell/k)$ steps for READ, $\Theta(n\ell/k)$ steps for WRITE, and works for all $k \geq 1$.

In 1991, Vidyasankar [5] showed that atomic ℓ-bit registers can be implemented from two regular ℓ-bit registers and one atomic binary register. WRITE performs 2 regular writes and 2 atomic writes. READ performs at most 2 regular reads and 1 atomic read.

Later, Chaudhuri and Welch [3] presented an implementation of regular ℓ-bit registers from regular binary registers with step complexity $\Theta(\ell)$ for both READ and WRITE, using $\Theta(2^\ell)$ space.

Chaudhuri, Kosa and Welch [2] presented an atomic ℓ-bit register implementation from atomic binary registers in which each WRITE operation performs only one step. However, the step complexity of READ and the space complexity are both $\Theta(4^\ell)$.

Recently, Aghazadeh, Golab and Woelfel [1] implemented an ℓ-bit *multi-writer* register shared by n processes from k-bit *multi-writer* registers with step complexity $\Theta(\ell/k)$ for both READ and WRITE. Their implementation uses $\Theta(n^2\ell/k)$ registers and requires that $k \in \Omega(\log n)$.

Observations. Using Chaudhuri and Welch's implementation for the regular ℓ-bit registers in Vidyasankar's algorithm gives an implementation of an atomic ℓ-bit register from regular binary registers and one atomic binary register with $\Theta(\ell)$ step complexity and $\Theta(2^\ell)$ space complexity. We call this the CWV implementation.

© Springer-Verlag Berlin Heidelberg 2016
C. Gavoille and D. Ilcinkas (Eds.): DISC 2016, LNCS 9888, pp. 465–467, 2016.
DOI: 10.1007/978-3-662-53426-7

Aghazadeh et al.'s implementation can be modified to implement an ℓ-bit *single-writer* register from k-bit *single-writer* registers with $\Theta(\ell/k)$ step complexity and $\Theta(n\ell/k)$ space complexity, provided that $k \in \Omega(\log n)$.

Main Contributions. In this paper, we present an implementation of atomic ℓ-bit single-writer registers from atomic k-bit single-writer registers with $\Theta(\ell/k)$ step complexity that works for all $k \geq 1$. Our implementation uses $O(n\ell/k)$ registers, which is the same as Peterson's implementation and the single-writer variant of Aghazadeh et al.'s implementation.

We prove the following result, which shows that our implementation is step optimal.

Theorem 1. *Any regular ℓ-bit single-writer register implementation from atomic k-bit single-writer registers with $O(\ell/k)$ step complexity for READ requires $\Omega(\ell/k)$ step complexity for WRITE.*

Our register implementation is the composition of a *tree based* implementation and a *buffer based* implementation. Although our tree based implementation can be replaced by the CWV implementation, we will present it briefly because it is interesting.

We begin by describing Chaudhuri and Welch's regular register implementation. They use a complete binary tree where each leaf represents a different register value and each internal node stores a *switch*, a shared binary register that selects between its two children. Their regular register read operation, REGREAD, traverses down the tree, following the switches, until it reaches a leaf and returns the value of that leaf. Their regular register write operation, REGWRITE, starts at the leaf with the value it wishes to write and traverses up the tree, changing each switch on the path to point to that leaf. Note that leaves are not represented in shared memory.

To make their implementation atomic, we first use atomic registers, rather than regular registers, for the switches at height 1. If α is the value of the leaf that is currently reachable from the root by following switches and β is the value of the leaf that is its sibling, then a REGWRITE of β would be atomic, since it changes only the switch at their parent. Consider a tree with $\binom{2^\ell}{2}$ height 1 nodes such that every pair of values are siblings in the tree. To atomically write the value β to a register containing the value α, the writer first changes the switches to point to a leaf with value α whose sibling has value β. Then the writer changes their parent's switch to point to the leaf with value β. WRITE operations are linearized when this switch changes. READ performs the same steps as REGREAD.

Using a 2^k-ary tree, we can generalise this implementation to use k-bit registers rather than binary registers. The resulting step complexity is $\Theta(\ell/k)$ and the space complexity is $\Theta(4^{\ell/k})$. The same generalization can be applied to the CWV algorithm.

Our tree based implementation can be modified to implement an ℓ-bit counter that supports a single incrementer and any number of readers. Since the value can only be incremented, we only need each pair of consecutive values (modulo 2^{ℓ}) to be siblings in the tree. Hence the space complexity can be reduced to $\Theta(2^{\ell/k})$ and the step complexity remains the same. Our counter is a factor of two faster than the CWV implementation and has the same asymptotic space complexity.

Our buffer based implementation uses this counter as well as known techniques, such as announcement arrays, round robin helping, and handshake objects, to implement an atomic ℓ-bit register with $\Theta(\ell/k + (\log n)/k)$ step complexity and $\Theta(n\ell/k + n(\log n)/k)$ space complexity.

A *buffer* is an array of $\lceil \ell/k \rceil$ k-bit registers used to represent an ℓ-bit value. As in Peterson's implementation, our buffer-based implementation uses an array of buffers G, and a pointer V to the currently active buffer in G. However, in our implementation, G contains $4n$ buffers, instead of 2, and V is implemented using a $\lceil \log_2 4n \rceil$-bit single-incrementer counter. Like Aghazadeh, Golab and Woelfel's implementation, our implementation uses round robin helping, except that it uses handshaking and completion bits to coordinate the helping.

At a high level, a reader announces the index of the element in G that it wants to read in a single-reader single-writer array. The writer helps the reader by writing that element, as well as the most recent value it wrote to two single-reader buffers. Each of these arrays is accompanied by a completion bit. The completion bit is set when the write to the array is finished to indicate that it is safe to read from the array.

When $\ell \leq (\log_2 n)/2$, both our tree based implementation and the CWV implementation have $\Theta(\ell/k)$ step complexity and $O(n/4^k)$ space complexity. When $\ell > (\log_2 n)/2$, our buffer based implementation has $\Theta(\ell/k)$ step complexity and uses $\Theta(n\ell/k)$ registers. Combining the algorithms based on the value of ℓ yields the following theorem.

Theorem 2. *There is an implementation of an atomic ℓ-bit single-writer register from atomic k-bit single-writer registers with $\Theta(\ell/k)$ step complexity and $O(n\ell/k)$ space complexity.*

References

1. Aghazadeh, Z., Golab, W., Woelfel, P.: Making objects writable. In: Proceedings of the 2014 ACM symposium on Principles of Distributed Computing, pp. 385–395. ACM (2014)
2. Chaudhuri, S., Kosa, M.J., Welch, J.L.: One-write algorithms for multivalued regular and atomic registers. Acta Inf. **37**(3), 161–192 (2000)
3. Chaudhuri, S., Welch, J.L.: Bounds on the costs of multivalued register implementations. SIAM J. Comput. **23**(2), 335–354 (1994)
4. Peterson, G.L.: Concurrent reading while writing. ACM Trans. Program. Lang. Syst. **5**(1), 46–55 (1983)
5. Vidyasankar, K.: A very simple construction of 1-writer multireader multivalued atomic variable. Inf. Process. Lett. **37**(6), 323–326 (1991)

Brief Announcement: Deterministic MST Sparsification in the Congested Clique

Janne H. Korhonen[✉]

School of Computer Science, Reykjavík University, Reykjavik, Iceland
janne.h.korhonen@gmail.com

Abstract. We give a simple deterministic constant-round algorithm in the congested clique model for reducing the number of edges in a graph to $n^{1+\varepsilon}$ while preserving the minimum spanning forest, where $\varepsilon > 0$ is any constant. This implies that in the congested clique model, it is sufficient to improve MST and other connectivity algorithms on graphs with slightly superlinear number of edges to obtain a general improvement. As a byproduct, we also obtain an alternative proof showing that MST can be computed deterministically in $O(\log \log n)$ rounds.

1 Introduction

MST in the Congested Clique. The *congested clique* [5] is a specialisation of the standard CONGEST model of distributed computing; in the congested clique, each of the n nodes of the network can send a different message of $O(\log n)$ bits to each other node each synchronous communication round. The congested clique model has attracted considerable interest recently, as the fully connected communication topology allows for much faster algorithms than the general CONGEST model.

Minimum spanning tree is perhaps the most studied problem in the congested clique model, and a good example of the power of the model. The Lotker et al. [5] paper introducing the congested clique model gave an $O(\log \log n)$-round deterministic MST algorithm. Subsequently, even faster randomised algorithms have been discovered: the $O(\log \log \log n)$-round algorithm by Hegeman et al. [2], and the recent $O(\log^* n)$-round algorithm by Ghaffari and Parter [1].

MST Sparsification. Both of the above fast randomised MST algorithms are based on fast randomised *graph connectivity* algorithms. To solve MST, they use a reduction of Hegeman et al. [2] from MST to graph connectivity; this works by (1) reducing general MST into two instances of MST on graphs with $O(n^{3/2})$ edges using a randomised sampling technique of Karger et al. [3], and (2) reducing MST on sparse graphs to multiple independent instances of graph connectivity.

In this work, we take a closer look at the sparsification step of the Hegeman et al. [2] reduction. Specifically, we show that it is possible to obtain much stronger sparsification for connectivity problems in constant rounds without using randomness:

© Springer-Verlag Berlin Heidelberg 2016
C. Gavoille and D. Ilcinkas (Eds.): DISC 2016, LNCS 9888, pp. 468–470, 2016.
DOI: 10.1007/978-3-662-53426-7

Theorem 1. *Given a weighted graph $G = (V, E)$ and an integer k, we can compute in $O(k)$ rounds an edge subset $E' \subseteq E$ with $|E'| = O(n^{1+1/2^k})$ such that E' contains one minimum spanning forest of G.*

In particular, Theorem 1 implies that graphs with slightly superlinear number of edges are the hardest case for connectivity problems in the congested clique, as graphs with linear number of edges can be learned by all nodes in constant rounds using the routing protocol of Lenzen [4]. Alas, our sparsification technique alone fails to improve upon the state-of-the-art even for deterministic MST algorithms, though applying Theorem 1 with $k = \log \log n$ does give an alternative deterministic $O(\log \log n)$ algorithm for MST in the congested clique.

2   Deterministic MST Sparsification

Let $\mathcal{S} = \{S_1, S_2, \ldots, S_\ell\}$ be a partition of V. For integers i, j with $1 \leq i \leq j \leq \ell$, we define

$$E_{ij}^{\mathcal{S}} = \{\{u, v\} \in E : u \in S_i \text{ and } v \in S_j\},$$

and denote by $G_{ij}^{\mathcal{S}}$ the subgraph of G with vertex set $S_i \cup S_j$ and edge set $E_{ij}^{\mathcal{S}}$.

Definition 1. *For $0 < \varepsilon \leq 1$, graph $G = (V, E)$ and partition $\mathcal{S} = \{S_1, S_2, \ldots, S_\ell\}$ of V, we say that $(G, \mathcal{S})$ is ε-sparse if $\ell = n^\varepsilon$, each $S \in \mathcal{S}$ has size at most $n^{1-\varepsilon}$ and for each i, j with $1 \leq i \leq j \leq \ell$, we have $|E_{ij}^{\mathcal{S}}| \leq 2n^{1-\varepsilon}$.*

If $(G, \mathcal{S})$ is ε-sparse, then G can have at most $2n^{1+\varepsilon}$ edges. Moreover, we will now show that we can *amplify* this notion of sparseness from ε to $\varepsilon/2$ in constant rounds. Observing that for any graph $G = (V, E)$ and $\mathcal{S} = \{\{v\} : v \in V\}$, we have that $(G, \mathcal{S})$ is 1-sparse, we can start from arbitrary graph and apply this sparsification k times to obtain sparsity $1/2^k$, yielding Theorem 1.

For convenience, let us assume that the all edge weights in the input graph in distinct, which also implies that the minimum spanning forest is unique. If this is not the case, we can break ties arbitrarily to obtain total ordering of weights. Recall that each node in V receives its incident edges in G as input.

Lemma 1. *Given a graph $G = (V, E)$ with distinct edge weights and unique MSF $F \subseteq E$, and a globally known partition $\mathcal{S}$ such that $(G, \mathcal{S})$ is ε-sparse, we can compute a subgraph $G' = (V, E')$ of G and a globally known partition $\mathcal{T}$ such that $(G', \mathcal{T})$ is $\varepsilon/2$-sparse and $F \subseteq E'$ in constant number of rounds.*

Proof. To obtain the partition $\mathcal{T} = \{T_1, T_2, \ldots, T_{n^{\varepsilon/2}}\}$, we construct each set T_i by taking the union of $n^{\varepsilon/2}$ sets S_j. Clearly sets T_i constructed this way have size $n^{1-\varepsilon/2}$, and this partition can be constructed by the nodes locally. Since $(G, \mathcal{S})$ is ε-sparse, we now have that

$$|E_{ij}^{\mathcal{T}}| = \sum_{x:\, S_x \subseteq T_i} \sum_{y:\, S_y \subseteq T_j} |E_{xy}^{\mathcal{S}}| \leq (n^{\varepsilon/2})^2 2n^{1-\varepsilon} = 2n.$$

We assign arbitrarily each pair (i, j) with $1 \leq i \leq j \leq n^{\varepsilon/2}$ as a *label* for distinct node $v \in V$. The number of such pairs (i, j) is at most $(n^{\varepsilon/2})^2 = n^{\varepsilon} \leq n$, so this is always possible, though some nodes may be left without labels. The algorithm now proceeds as follows:

1. Distribute information about the edges so that node with label (i, j) knows the full edge set $E_{ij}^{\mathcal{T}}$. Since $\left|E_{ij}^{\mathcal{T}}\right| \leq 2n$, this can be done in constant rounds using the routing protocol of Lenzen [4].
2. Each node with label (i, j) locally computes a minimum spanning forest $F_{ij}^{\mathcal{T}}$ for the subgraph $G_{ij}^{\mathcal{T}}$ using information obtained in previous step. Since $|T_i \cup T_j| \leq 2n^{1-\varepsilon/2}$, we also have $\left|F_{ij}^{\mathcal{T}}\right| \leq 2n^{1-\varepsilon/2}$.
3. Redistribute information about the sets $F_{ij}^{\mathcal{T}}$ so that each node knows which of its incident edges are in one of the sets $F_{ij}^{\mathcal{T}}$. Again, this takes constant rounds.

Taking $E' = \bigcup_{(i,j)} F_{ij}^{\mathcal{T}}$, we have that $(G', \mathcal{T})$ is $\varepsilon/2$-sparse. To see that E' also contains all edges of F, recall the fact that an edge $e \in E$ is in MSF F if and only if it is the minimum-weight edge crossing some cut (V_1, V_2), assuming distinct edge weights (see, e.g. Karger et al. [3]). If edge $e \in E_{ij}^{\mathcal{T}}$ is in F, then it is minimum-weight edge crossing a cut (V_1, V_2) in G, and thus also minimum-weight edge crossing the corresponding cut in $G_{ij}^{\mathcal{T}}$, implying $e \in F_{ij}^{\mathcal{T}}$. □

Acknowledgements. We thank Magnús M. Halldórsson, Juho Hirvonen, Tuomo Lempiäinen, Christopher Purcell, Joel Rybicki and Jukka Suomela for discussions, and Mohsen Ghaffari for sharing a preprint of [1]. This work was supported by grant 152679-051 from the Icelandic Research Fund.

References

1. Ghaffari, M., Parter, M.: MST in log-star rounds of congested clique. In: Proceedings of the 35th ACM Symposium on Principles of Distributed Computing (PODC 2016) (2016)
2. Hegeman, J.W., Pandurangan, G., Pemmaraju, S.V., Sardeshmukh, V.B., Scquizzato, M.: Toward optimal bounds in the congested clique: graph connectivity and MST. In: Proceedings of the 34th ACM Symposium on Principles of Distributed Computing (PODC 2015), pp. 91–100 (2015)
3. Karger, D.R., Klein, P.N., Tarjan, R.E.: A randomized linear-time algorithm to find minimum spanning trees. J. ACM **42**(2), 321–328 (1995)
4. Lenzen, C.: Optimal deterministic routing and sorting on the congested clique. In: Proceedings of the 32nd ACM Symposium on Principles of Distributed Computing (PODC 2013), pp. 42–50 (2013)
5. Lotker, Z., Patt-Shamir, B., Pavlov, E., Peleg, D.: Minimum-weight spanning tree construction in $O(\log \log n)$ communication rounds. SIAM J. Comput. **35**(1), 120–131 (2005)

Brief Announcement: Symmetricity in 3D-space — Characterizing Formable Patterns by Synchronous Mobile Robots

Yukiko Yamauchi[✉], Taichi Uehara, and Masafumi Yamashita

Graduate School of ISEE, Kyushu University, Fukuoka, Japan
yamauchi@inf.kyushu-u.ac.jp

Mobile Robot System. We consider distributed coordination of autonomous mobile robots moving in the three-dimensional space (3D-space). Each robot is an anonymous point and executes a common algorithm. It has neither any access to the global coordinate system nor any explicit communication medium. Its unit action is a *Look-Compute-Move cycle*, where it observes the positions of other robots (Look phase), computes the next position and the route to reach there by a common algorithm (Compute phase), and moves to the computed next position (Move phase). In a Look phase, each robot observes the positions of other robots in its *local coordinate system*, i.e., x-y-z Cartesian coordinate system. The origin of the local coordinate system is the current position of the robot, and the directions of the axes and the unit distance are arbitrary. We assume that all coordinate systems are right-handed. Hence each local coordinate system is obtained by a translation, a rotation, a uniform scaling, or a combination of them on the global coordinate system. In a Compute phase, if the input to the common algorithm is the observation obtained in the preceding Look phase, the algorithm is called *oblivious*, otherwise *non-oblivious*. In a Move phase, if all robots reach their next positions, the movement is called *rigid*. *Non-rigid* movement allows the robots to stop en route; each robot moves at least an unknown minimum moving distance δ, but after that it may stop at any point on the route. There are three types of synchrony among the robots: We consider discrete time $t = 0, 1, 2, \cdots$. In the *fully-synchronous (FSYNC) model*, at each time instant, the robots execute a Look-Compute-Move cycle synchronously with each of the Look phase, Compute phase, and the Move phase completely synchronized. In the *semi-synchronous (SSYNC) model*, a non-empty subset of the robots execute a Look-Compute-Move cycle at each time instant, with each of the three phases completely synchronized. In the *asynchronous (ASYNC) model*, we do not put any assumption on the execution of the Look-Compute-Move cycles except that the length of each cycle is finite.

Pattern Formation Problem. The pattern formation problem requires the robots to form a given target pattern from an initial configuration.

Y. Yamauchi — This work was supported by a Grant-in-Aid for Scientific Research on Innovative Areas "Molecular Robotics" (No. 24104003 and 15H00821) of MEXT, Japan, and JSPS KAKENHI Grant Numbers JP15H02666, JP15K11987, JP15K15938.

© Springer-Verlag Berlin Heidelberg 2016
C. Gavoille and D. Ilcinkas (Eds.): DISC 2016, LNCS 9888, pp. 471–473, 2016.
DOI: 10.1007/978-3-662-53426-7

Let $R = \{r_1, r_2, \ldots, r_n\}$ be the set of anonymous robots. We use r_i just for description. We denote the position of robot r_i (in the global coordinate system Z_0) at time t by $p_i(t)$. The *configuration* of the robots at time t is a set of points $P(t) = \{p_1(t), p_2(t), \ldots, p_n(t)\}$. We assume that any initial configuration $P(0)$ contains no multiplicity. An *execution* of an algorithm ψ from an initial configuration $P(0)$ is a sequence of configurations $P(0), P(1), P(2), \cdots$. Note that there exist many executions depending on the local coordinate systems of the robots in $P(0)$, asynchrony, and non-rigid movement. A target pattern F is a set of positions of n points observed in Z_0. The pattern formation problem allows uniform scaling, translation, rotation, and their combinations on F. We say an algorithm ψ forms F from an initial configuration $P(0)$ if for any execution $P(0), P(1), P(2), \cdots$, there exists $t \geq 0$ such that for any $t' \geq t$, $P(t') = P(t)$ and $P(t) \simeq F$. When there exists an algorithm that forms F from P, we say F is formable from P. Our goal is to characterize the formable patterns and reveal the formation power of the robots.

In the two-dimensional space (2D-space), the set of formable patterns are characterized by using the notion of *symmetricity*. For a given set of points P, consider a decomposition of P into regular m-gons centered at the center $c(P)$ of the smallest enclosing circle of P. The symmetricity $\rho(P)$ of P is the maximum of such m, except that $\rho(P) = 1$ when $c(P) \in P$. It has been shown that irrespective of obliviousness and asynchrony, the robots can form a target pattern F from an initial configuration P if and only if $\rho(P)|\rho(F)$ [1–3]. The impossibility is shown by the worst case, where both the positions of the robots and their local coordinate systems are symmetric. Because the observations of the robots forming a regular $\rho(P)$-gon are the same, their next positions form a regular $\rho(P)$-gon again. Then the robots can never break their symmetricity $\rho(P)$. This result immediately holds for the oblivious FSYNC robots with rigid movement, and this fact determines the limit of the formation power of the non-oblivious ASYNC (thus SSYNC) robots with non-rigid movement since these models allow initial empty memory content, the FSYNC schedule, and rigid movement. Regarding the formable patterns, existing papers show oblivious pattern formation algorithms for each of the FSYNC, SSYNC, and ASYNC models with non-rigid movement [1–3].

On the other hand, the definition of symmetricity is based on the following simple symmetry breaking algorithm: When $c(P) \in P$ in an initial configuration P, the robot on $c(P)$ can translate P to an asymmetric configuration by just leaving its current position.

Our Results. Symmetricity in 2D-space is essentially the order of the *cyclic group* that acts on a given set of points. We extend the notion of symmetricity in 2D-space to 3D-space by using the rotation groups. In 3D-space, there are five kinds of rotation groups, the *cyclic groups*, the *dihedral groups*, the *tetrahedral group*, the *octahedral group*, and the *icosahedral group*. Each of the rotation groups is recognized as the set of rotation operations on a regular pyramid, a regular prism, a regular tetrahedron, a regular octahedron, and a regular icosahedron, respectively. Specifically, each rotation group is defined as a set of rotation axes and their arrangement. When a rotation axis admits rotations by $2\pi/k, 4\pi/k, \cdots$, and 2π, we call the axis k-*fold rotation axis*. Let $\mathbb{S} = \{C_k, D_\ell, T, O, I \mid k = 1, 2, \cdots, \ell = 2, 3, \cdots\}$, where C_k ($k = 1, 2, \cdots$) is a cyclic group with a single k-fold rotation axes, and D_ℓ ($\ell = 2, 3, \cdots$) is a dihedral group with a single ℓ-fold rotation axis (principal axis) and ℓ 2-fold rotation axes perpendicular to the principal axes. C_1 consists of only the identity element. Then we define the *rotation group* and the *symmetricity* of a set of points in 3D-space.

Definition 1. *Let P be a set of n points in 3D-space. The rotation group $\gamma(P)$ of P is the rotation group in $\mathbb{S}$ that acts on P and none of its proper supergroup in $\mathbb{S}$ acts on P.*

Clearly $\gamma(P)$ is uniquely determined for any set of points P. If a rotation axis of $\gamma(P)$ contains some point of P, we say the rotation axis is *occupied*.

For two groups $G, H \in \mathbb{S}$, an *embedding* of G to H is an embedding of each rotation axis of G to one of the rotation axes of H so that any k-fold axis of G overlaps a k'-fold axis of H satisfying $k|k'$ with keeping the arrangement of the rotation axes of G.

Definition 2. *Let P be a set of n points in 3D-space. The symmetricity $\varrho(P)$ of P is the set of rotation groups $G \in \mathbb{S}$ that acts on P (thus $G \preceq \gamma(P)$) and there exists an embedding of G to unoccupied rotation axes of $\gamma(P)$. If all rotation axes of $\gamma(P)$ are occupied, $\varrho(P)$ consists of C_1.*

Then we show the following theorem that characterizes the set of formable patterns for FSYNC robots in 3D-space.

Theorem 1. *Regardless of obliviousness, FSYNC robots can form a target pattern F from an initial configuration P if and only if $\varrho(P) \subseteq \varrho(F)$.*

The necessity is clear from the existence of a symmetric initial configuration with symmetric local coordinate systems for each $G \in \varrho(P)$. For the solvable instances, we designed an oblivious pattern formation algorithm that consists of a symmetry breaking phase, an embedding phase, and a perfect matching phase. The symmetry breaking phase is essentially the same as the symmetry breaking in 2D-space; the robots on rotation axes leave their current positions. We can show that the rotation group of any resulting configuration is in the symmetricity of an initial configuration. Because of the condition of Theorem 1, the robots can agree on a perfect matching between the current configuration and an embedded target pattern, and complete the pattern formation.

References

1. Fujinaga, N., Yamauchi, Y., Ono, H., Kijima, S., Yamashita, M.: Pattern formation by oblivious asynchronous mobile robots. SIAM J. Comput. **44**(3), 740–785 (2015)
2. Suzuki, I., Yamashita, M.: Distributed anonymous mobile robots: formation of geometric patterns. SIAM J. Comput. **28**(4), 1347–1363 (1999)
3. Yamashita, M., Suzuki, I.: Characterizing geometric patterns formable by oblivious anonymous mobile robots. Theor. Comput. Sci. **411**, 2433–2453 (2010)

Brief Announcement: Mending the Big-Data Missing Information

Hadassa Daltrophe[✉], Shlomi Dolev, and Zvi Lotker

Ben-Gurion University of the Negev, 84105 Beer-sheva, Israel
{hd,dolev}@cs.bgu.ac.il, zvilo@cse.bgu.ac.il

Introduction, Model and Motivation. One of the main challenges that arise while handling big-data is not only the large volume, but also the high-dimensions of the data. Moreover, part of the information at the different dimensions may be missing. Assuming that the true (unknown) data is d-dimensional points, we suggest representing the given data point (which contains lack information at different dimensions) as a k-affine subspace embedded in the Euclidean d dimensional space $\mathbb{R}^d$. A data object that is incomplete in one or more features corresponds to an affine subspace (called flat, for short) in $\mathbb{R}^d$, whose dimension, k, is the number of missing features.

This representation yields algebraic objects, which help us to better understand the data, as well as study its properties. A central property of the data is clustering. Clustering refers to the process of partitioning a set of objects into subsets, consisting of similar objects. Finding a good clustering is a challenging problem. Due to its wide range of applications, the clustering problem has been investigated for decades, and continues to be actively studied not only in theoretical computer science, but in other disciplines, such as statistics, data mining and machine learning. A motivation for cluster analysis of high-dimensional data, as well as an overview on some applications where high-dimensional data occurs, is given in [3].

Our underlying assumption is that the original data-points, the real entities, can be divided into different groups according to their distance in $\mathbb{R}^d$. Formally, the data set satisfy the following assumptions: *(i)* There are m clusters. *(ii)* Each cluster is modeled as a ball in $\mathbb{R}^d$. *(iii)* All k-flats which belong in the same cluster are intersected with the ball of the cluster. *(iv)* Each k-flat that belong to a cluster is selected uniformly among all k-flats that intersect the ball's cluster. A data set that satisfies these assumptions will be called *separable data*.

The distance between a flat and a point (the center of the ball) is well-defined, hence, the classic clustering problems, such as k-means or k-centers (see [2] Chap. 8), can be defined on a set of flats. The clustering problem when the data is k-flats is to find the center of the balls that minimizes the sum of the distance between the k-flats and the center of their groups, which is the nearest center among all centers. However, Lee & Schulman [4] argues that the running time of an approximation algorithm, with any approximation ratio, cannot be polynomial in even one of m (the number of clusters) and k (the dimension of the flats), unless $P = NP$. We overcome this obstacle by approaching the problem differently. Using a probabilistic assumption based on the distribution of the data, we achieve a poly-logarithmic algorithm, which we use to identify the

© Springer-Verlag Berlin Heidelberg 2016
C. Gavoille and D. Ilcinkas (Eds.): DISC 2016, LNCS 9888, pp. 474–476, 2016.
DOI: 10.1007/978-3-662-53426-7

flats' groups. Moreover, the presented probability arguments can help us in better understanding the geometric distribution of high dimensional data objects, which is of major interest and importance in the scope of big-data research.

Our Contributions. We face the challenge of mending the missing information at different dimensions by representing the objects as affine subspaces. In particular, we work within the framework of flats in $\mathbb{R}^d$, where the missing features correspond to the (intrinsic) dimension of the flat. This representation is accurate and flexible, in the sense that it saves all the features of the origin data; it also allows for algebraic calculation over the objects.

We study the pairwise distance between the flats, and based on our probabilistic and geometrical results, we developed a polylogarithmic algorithm that achieves clustering of the flats with high probability.

The main result of the study is summarized in the following theorem, while the precise definition and the detailed proof are presented in the full paper [1].

Theorem 1. *Given the separable data set* $\mathbf{P}$ *of* n *affine subspaces of dimension* k *in* $\mathbb{R}^d$, *for any* $\epsilon > 0$ *and for sufficiently large* d *(depending on* ϵ*), with probability* $1 - \epsilon$, *we can cluster* $\mathbf{P}$ *using their pair-wise distance projection in* $poly(n, k, d)$ *time.*

Remarks:

- In addition to proving good performance for high dimensions as required in the scope of big-data, we also show that the algorithm works well for low dimensions. We addressed this issue through empirical studies.
- Using sampling, we achieve a *poly-logarithmic* running time. Namely, instead of running the algorithms with the whole n flats set, we apply the algorithm with a sample of $\log n$ flats that were picked uniformly at random. The reason we can use sampling is due to our assumption about the distribution of the data.

Algorithm. Given the set $\mathbf{P}$ of n k-flats in $\mathbb{R}^d$, our goal is to cluster the flats according to the unknown set of balls, namely, to separate $\mathbf{P}$ into m groups such that every group $P_i \in \mathbf{P}$ contains n/m flats that intersect the same unit ball $\mathbb{B}_{c_i}^d$. We suggest the following procedure for the clustering process. The first step is to find the distance and the midpoint between every pair of flats in $\mathbf{P}$. Next, we filter the irrelevant midpoints using their corresponding distances such that midpoints with a distance greater than two are dropped and those with a distance ≤ 2 are grouped together. We justify this step by the observation that when two flats P_i and P_j arise from the same cluster then the probability that the distance between them is less than 2 is $P\left(dist(P_i, P_j) \leq 2\right) = 1$. Moreover, when P_i and P_j arise from different clusters we show that for any $\epsilon > 0$, $\lim_{d \to \infty} \Pr\left(dist(P_i, P_j) \geq 2\left(\Delta - \epsilon\right)\right) = 1$. In the final step of the algorithm we check which group contains $O(n/m)$ flats and output those groups. We argue that these simple steps provide the expected clustering procedure with high probability.

Our suggested algorithm is executed in a distributed fashion. Given a set of processors, such that each one of them has an access to the whole set of flats, every processor randomly picks a pair of flats and calculate their midpoints. If the distance between the pair is less than two, the processor saves the midpoint in shared memory. The processors continue this procedure until enough midpoints were collected as defined by the given threshold.

Conclusion. The analysis of incomplete data is one of the major challenges in the scope of big-data. Typically, data objects are represented by points in $\mathbb{R}^d$, we suggest that the incomplete data is corresponding to affine subspaces. With this motivation we study the problem of clustering k-flats, where two objects are similar when the Euclidean distance between them is small. The study presented a simple clustering algorithm for k-flats in $\mathbb{R}^d$, as well as studied the probability of pair-wise intersection of these objects.

The key idea of our algorithm is to formulate the pairs of flats as midpoints, which preserves distance features. This way, the geometric location of midpoints that arise from the same cluster, identify the center of the cluster with high probability. When the dimension d is big enough, the corresponding distance of flats that arise from different clusters approach the mean distance of the cluster's center. Using this, we can eliminate the irrelevant midpoints with high probability.

In addition, using experimental results, we support our claim that the algorithm works well in low dimensions as well. Finally, we achieve a polylogarithmic running time using a distributed algorithm that involves sampling.

References

1. Daltrophe, H., Dolev, S., Lotker, Z.: Mending the big-data missing information. CoRR, abs/1405.2512 (2016)
2. Hopcroft, J., Kannan, R.: Foundations of data science1 (2014)
3. Kriegel, H.P., Kröger, P., Zimek, A.: Clustering high-dimensional data: a survey on subspace clustering, pattern-based clustering, and correlation clustering. ACM Trans. Knowl. Discov. Data **3**(1), 1:1–1:58 (2009)
4. Lee, E., Schulman, L.J.: Clustering affine subspaces: hardness and algorithms. In: Proceedings of the Twenty-Fourth Annual ACM-SIAM Symposium on Discrete Algorithms, pp. 810–827. SIAM (2013)

Brief Announcement: Set-Consensus Collections are Decidable

Carole Delporte-Gallet[1]($\boxtimes$), Hugues Fauconnier[1], Eli Gafni[2], and Petr Kuznetsov[3]

[1] IRIF, Université Paris Diderot, Paris, France
cd@liafa.univ-paris-diderot.fr
[2] UCLA, Los Angeles, CA, USA
[3] Télécom ParisTech, Paris, France

Abstract. A natural way to measure the power of a distributed computing model is to characterize the set of tasks that can be solved in it. In general, however, the question of whether a given task can be solved in a given model of computation is undecidable, even if we only consider the wait-free shared-memory model. In this paper, we address this question for a restricted class of models and tasks. We show that the question of whether a collection C of (j, ℓ)-*set consensus* tasks, for various ℓ (the number of processes that can invoke the task) and j (the number of distinct outputs the task returns), can be used by n processes to solve wait-free k-set consensus is decidable. Moreover, we provide a simple $O(n^2)$ decision algorithm, based on a dynamic programming solution to the Knapsack problem. We then present an adaptive wait-free set-consensus algorithm that, for each set of participants, achieves the best level of agreement that is possible to achieve using C. Overall, this gives us a complete characterization of a model equipped with a collection of set-consensus tasks through its *set-consensus power*. Therefore, the question of determining the relative power of models defined by set-consensus collections is decidable and, moreover, has an efficient solution.

1 Motivation

A plethora of models of computation were proposed for distributed environments. The models vary in timing assumptions they make, types of failures they assume, and communication primitives they employ. It is hard to say *a priori* whether one model provides more power to programmer than the other. A natural way to measure this power is to characterize the set of distributed tasks that a model allows for solving. In general, however, the question of whether a given task can be solved in the popular *wait-free* model, i.e., tolerating asynchrony and failures of an arbitrary subset of processes, is undecidable [7].

In this paper, we address this question for a restricted class of models and tasks. We consider models in which n completely asynchronous processes communicate through shared-memory but in addition can access *set-consensus* tasks. A (j, ℓ)-set-consensus task solves set-consensus among ℓ processes, i.e., the task

C. Gavoille and D. Ilcinkas (Eds.): DISC 2016, LNCS 9888, pp. 477–479, 2016.
DOI: 10.1007/978-3-662-53426-7

can be accessed by up to ℓ processes with *propose* operations that take natural values as inputs and return natural values as outputs, so that the set of outputs is a subset of inputs of size at most j. Set consensus is a generalization of consensus, and as well as consensus [8] exhibits the property of *universaliyy*: ℓ processes can use (j, ℓ)-set consensus and read-write registers to implement j state machines, ensuring that at least one of them makes progress [6]. In this paper, we explore what level of agreement, and thus "degree of universality", can be achieved using combinations of a collection of set-consensus tasks.

The special case when only one type of set consensus can be used in the implementation was resolved in [3, 4]: (j, ℓ)-set consensus can be used to implement (k, n)-set consensus if and only if $k \geq j \lfloor n/\ell \rfloor$. Indeed, by splitting n processes into groups of size ℓ we trivially solve $j \lfloor n/\ell \rfloor$-set consensus.

Characterizing a general model in which processes communicate via an arbitrary collection C of possibly different set-consensus tasks is less trivial. For example, let C be $\{(1, 2), (2, 5)\}$, i.e., every 2 processes in our system can solve consensus and every 5 can solve 2-set consensus. What is the best level of agreement we can achieve using C in a system of 9 processes? One can easily see that 4-set consensus can be solved: the first two pairs of processes solve consensus and the remaining 5 invoke 2-set consensus, which would give at most 4 different outputs. One can also let the groups of the first 5 and the remaining 4 each solve 2-set consensus. (In general, any two set-consensus tasks (j_1, ℓ_1) and (j_2, ℓ_2) can be used to solve $(j_1 + j_2, \ell_1 + \ell_2)$.) But could we do $(3, 9)$-set consensus with C?

2   Results

We propose a simple way to characterize the power of a set-consensus collection. By convention, let (j_0, ℓ_0) be $(1, 1)$, and note that $(1, 1)$-set consensus is trivially solvable.

Theorem 1. *We show that a collection* $C = \{(j_0, \ell_0), (j_1, \ell_1), \ldots, (j_m, \ell_m)\}$ *solves* (k, n)-*set consensus if and only if there exist* $x_0, x_1, \ldots, x_m \in \mathbb{N}$, *such that* $\sum_i \ell_i x_i \geq n$ *and* $\sum_i j_i x_i \leq k$.

Thus, determining the power of C is equivalent to solving a variation of the Knapsack optimization problem, where each j_i serves as the "weight" of an element in C, i.e., how much disagreement it may incur, and each ℓ_i serves as its "value", i.e., how many processes it is able to synchronize. We describe a simple $O(n^2)$ algorithm for computing the power of C in solving set consensus among n processes using the dynamic programming approach [1].

The sufficiency of the condition is immediate. The necessity of the condition is much less trivial to derive. It required a carefully crafted simulation algorithm, showing that if a collection not satisfying the condition solves (k, n)-set consensus, then $k + 1$ processes can solve k-set consensus, contradicting the classical wait-free set-consensus impossibility result [2, 9, 10].

Coming back to the collection $C = \{(1, 2), (2, 5)\}$, our characterization implies that 4-set consensus is the best level of set consensus that can be achieved by 9 processes with C. Observe, however, that if only 2 processes participate, then they can use C to solve consensus, i.e., to achieve the "perfect" agreement.

A natural question is whether we could *adapt* to the participation level and ensure the best possible level of agreement in any case?

Theorem 2. *Let C be s set-consensus collection, n be an integer. There exist an optimally adaptive algorithm for C*

Intuitively, for the currently observed participation, our algorithm employs the best algorithm and, in case the participating set grows, seamlessly relaxes the agreement guarantees by switching to a possibly less precise algorithm assuming the larger set of participants.

Our results thus imply that the question of whether one model defined by a set-consensus collection implements another model defined by a set-consensus collection is *decidable* and, moreover, it has an efficient solution.

3   Conclusion

We conjecture that the ability of any "reasonable" shared-memory system to solve set consensus, captured by its j-set-consensus numbers, characterizes precisely its computing power, e.g., with respect to solving tasks or implementing deterministic objects.

A preliminary version of the full paper is in [5].

References

1. Andonov, R., Poirriez, V., Rajopadhye, S.V.: Unbounded knapsack problem: dynamic programming revisited. Eur. J. Oper. Res. **123**(2), 394–407 (2000)
2. Borowsky, E., Gafni, E.: Generalized FLP impossibility result for t-resilient asynchronous computations. In: STOC, pp. 91–100. ACM Press, May 1993
3. Borowsky, E., Gafni, E.: The implication of the borowsky-gafni simulation on the set-consensus hierarchy. Technical report, UCLA, 1993. http://fmdb.cs.ucla.edu/Treports/930021.pdf
4. Chaudhuri, S., Reiners, P.: Understanding the set consensus partial order using the Borowsky-Gafni simulation. In: Babaoğlu, Ö., Marzullo, K. (eds.) WDAG 1996. LNCS, vol. 1151, pp. 362–379. Springer, Heidelberg (1996). doi:10.1007/3-540-61769-8_23
5. Delporte-Gallet, C., Fauconnier, H., Gafni, E., Kuznetsov, P.: Set-consensus collections are decidable. Technical report, ArXiv (2016)
6. Gafni, E., Guerraoui, R.: Generalized universality. In: Katoen, J.-P., König, B. (eds.) CONCUR 2011. LNCS, vol. 6901, pp. 17–27. Springer, Heidelberg (2011). doi:10.1007/978-3-642-23217-6_2
7. Gafni, E., Koutsoupias, E.: Three-processor tasks are undecidable. SIAM J. Comput. **28**(3), 970–983 (1999)
8. Herlihy, M.: Wait-free synchronization. ACM Trans. Prog. Lang. Syst. **13**(1), 123–149 (1991)
9. Herlihy, M., Shavit, N.: The topological structure of asynchronous computability. J. ACM **46**(2), 858–923 (1999)
10. Saks, M., Zaharoglou, F.: Wait-free k-set agreement is impossible: the topology of public knowledge. SIAM J. Comput. **29**, 1449–1483 (2000)

Brief Announcement: A Log*-Time Local MDS Approximation Scheme for Bounded Genus Graphs

Saeed Akhoondian Amiri[1(✉)] and Stefan Schmid[2]

[1] TU Berlin, Berlin, Germany
saeed.amiri@tu-berlin.de
[2] Aalborg University, Aalborg, Denmark

Abstract. This paper shows that the results by Czygrinow et al. (DISC 2008) and Amiri et al. (PODC 2016) can be combined to obtain a $O(\log^* n)$-time local and deterministic approximation scheme for Minimum Dominating Sets on bounded genus graphs.

1 Local MDS Approximation Scheme

It is well-known that fundamental graph problems such as the Minimum Dominating Set (MDS) problem cannot be solved efficiently by distributed algorithms on general graphs. However, over the last years, researchers have found several very fast distributed algorithms for sparse families of networks, such as constant-degree graphs and planar graphs.

This paper presents a deterministic $O(\log^* n)$-time MDS $(1+\epsilon)$-factor approximation algorithm for a more general graph family: graphs of constant genus. The algorithm relies on: (1) a slight modification of the clusting algorithm for planar graphs presented by Czygrinow et al. [2], and (2) the recent constant approximation result by Amiri et al. [1] for MDS on graphs of bounded genus. Due to space constraints, we refer the reader to the prior work for more background.

We suppose familiarity with basic graph theory and graphs on surfaces [4]. We consider simple finite undirected graphs unless stated explicitly otherwise. We denote the set of all integers by $\mathbb{N}$. For a graph $G = (V, E)$, we write $E(G)$ resp. $V(G)$ to denote the edge set resp. vertex set of graph G. For a *weighted* graph G, we define an edge weight function as $w : E(G) \rightarrow \mathbb{N}$. For a sub-graph $S \subseteq G$, we write $W(S)$ for $\Sigma_{e \in E(S)} w(e)$, and call it the total edge weight of S. We contract an edge $\{u, v\}$ by identifying its two ends, creating a new vertex uv, but keeping all edges (except for parallel edges and loops). Additionally, if the graph is weighted and $\{u, x\}, \{v, x\} \in E(G)$, we set the edge weight of $\{uv, x\}$ to $w(uv, x) := w(u, x) + w(v, x)$. Let $S \subseteq G$ be a set of vertices, then $G[S]$ is an

---

Research supported by the European Research Council (ERC) under the European Union's Horizon 2020 research and innovation programme (ERC consolidator grant DISTRUCT, agreement No 648527).

© Springer-Verlag Berlin Heidelberg 2016
C. Gavoille and D. Ilcinkas (Eds.): DISC 2016, LNCS 9888, pp. 480–483, 2016.
DOI: 10.1007/978-3-662-53426-7

induced subgraph of G on vertices of S. The *degeneracy* of a graph G is the least number d for which every induced subgraph of G has vertex degree at most d.

We need the following lemma for the sake of completeness.

Lemma 1. *Let $\mathcal{G}$ be a class of graphs of genus at most g. Then the degeneracy of every graph $G \in \mathcal{G}$ is in $O(\sqrt{g})$.*

Proof. We prove the lemma for graphs with orientable genus g; an analogous argument works for graphs of non-orientable genus g. Let $G \in \mathcal{G}$ with genus at most g, and suppose the degeneracy of G is c. We prove that $c \in O(\sqrt{g})$. Let us denote by v, e the number of vertices and edges of G, respectively. By the Euler formula, we have: $e \leq 3 \cdot v + 6g - 6$ [1]. On the other hand, by definition of the degeneracy, every vertex in G has degree at least c, so $\frac{c \cdot v}{2} \leq 3v + 6g - 6 \Rightarrow c \leq \frac{12g - 12}{v} + 6$ (1). To find the maximum value of c for a fixed genus, we must minimise v. A complete graph on v vertices has genus at most $v^2/12$ [4], therefore by plugging it into (1), we obtain that $c \leq \sqrt{12g} + 6$.

Definition 1 (Pseudo-Forest [2]). *A pseudo-forest is a directed graph in which every vertex has an out-degree at most 1.*

For a directed graph G, if we ignore the edge directions, we write $\bar{G}$.

Different variations of the first part of the following lemma have already been proved in the literature. However, to be able to provide exact numbers and for completeness, we include a proof here. Let G be a graph and let $\mathcal{F}$ be a family of forests such that for all $F \in \mathcal{F}$, we have $F \subseteq G$. We say that $\mathcal{F}$ is a *forest cover* of G, if for every edge $e \in E(G)$, there is a forest $F \in \mathcal{F}$ such that $e \in E(F)$.

Lemma 2. *There is a constant c_1 such that for an edge weighted graph G of genus g, we can find, in two communication rounds, a pseudo-forest F such that $\bar{F}$ is a spanning sub-graph of G and $W(\bar{F}) \geq \frac{W(G)}{c_1 \cdot \sqrt{g}}$.*

Proof. By Lemma 1, the degeneracy of a graph G of genus g is in $O(\sqrt{g})$. The degeneracy is within factor two of the arboricity [3], and the arboricity equals the size of at least a forest cover $\mathcal{F}$ of G. Therefore, there is a constant c_1' such that $|\mathcal{F}| \leq c_1' \cdot \sqrt{g}$. Hence, there is a forest $F_1 \in \mathcal{F}$ such that $W(F_1) \geq W(G)/(c_1' \cdot \sqrt{g})$. Similarly to the proof of Fact 1 in [2], for a vertex v, we choose an edge $\{v, u\}$ of largest weight, and direct it from v to u. If we happen to choose an edge $\{v, u\}$ for both vertices u and v, we direct it from v to u, using the larger identifier as a tie breaker. This algorithm creates a pseudo-forest F. $\bar{F}$ is a spanning sub-graph of G and it has a total edge weight of at least half of $W(F_1)$, so $W(\bar{F}) \geq W(G)/(2 \cdot c_1' \cdot \sqrt{g})$. We set $c_1 = 2 \cdot c_1'$. Note that we found F in two rounds. $\square$

Lemma 3. *There is a local algorithm which takes an $0 < \epsilon < 1$ and an edge-weighted graph G of genus at most g as input, runs in $O(\log^* n + 1/\epsilon \cdot \sqrt{g})$*

communication rounds and returns a set of clusters $C_1, \ldots, C_l$ partitioning G, such that, each cluster has a constant diameter. Moreover, if we contract each C_i to a single vertex to obtain a graph H, then $W(H) \leq \epsilon \cdot W(G)$.

Proof. Let $t := 4 \cdot c_1 \cdot \sqrt{g}$. By applying the HEAVYSTARS algorithm from [2] on the pseudo forest provided in the proof of Lemma 2, we obtain stars of weight $\frac{|E(G)|}{t}$. We also run the algorithm CLUSTERING provided in [2], but we set the number of iterations in the algorithm to $\log(\frac{1}{\epsilon})/\log(\frac{t}{t-1})$; the rest of the algorithm is left unchanged. A similar line of proof for the original algorithm, proves the claim of the lemma. Just note that $\log(\frac{x}{x-1}) \geq 1/x$ for $x > 1$. □

Theorem 1. *Given a $0 < \delta < 1$ and a graph G of genus at most g, the Minimum Dominating Set can be approximated in $O(\log^* |G| + g^2 \sqrt{g})$ time within a factor of $1 + \delta$.*

Proof. Suppose OPT is the optimal dominating set of G. By [1], we can find a dominating set D of G such that for some constant c, we have $|D| \leq c \cdot g \cdot |OPT|$. This can be done in a constant number of communication rounds. For a vertex $v \in G$, we denote the neighbours of v in G by $N[v]$ i.e., $N[v] = v \cup \{u \in V(G) \mid \{u, v\} \in E(G)\}$. Suppose $|D| = t$.

Let us order the vertices of D arbitrarily, and suppose $d_1, \ldots, d_t$ is such an ordering. Create a partition $(V_1, \ldots, V_t)$ of $V(G)$ such that $V_i = \{v \in N[d_i] \mid v \in (G - D - \bigcup_{j<i} V_j)\} \cup \{d_i\}$. We next contract each V_i to a single vertex v_i to obtain a graph H. We assign an edge weight to H, i.e., for all $e \in E(H)$, we set $w(e) := 1$. It is clear that $W(H) = |E(H)|$. H has genus at most g and it has at most $3|D| + 6g - 6$ edges (see Lemma 4 of [1]). Set $\epsilon = \delta/((6 + 12g) \cdot c \cdot g)$. When we apply the algorithm in Lemma 3, it finds clusters $C_1, \ldots, C_l$ such that the total edge weights between clusters amount to at most $\epsilon \cdot |E(H)|$. Note that as $\epsilon \in \Omega(1/g^2)$, the algorithm uses $O(\log^* |G| + 1/\epsilon \cdot \sqrt{g}) = O(\log^* |G| + g^2 \sqrt{g})$ communication rounds.

For a cluster C_j, suppose $V(C_j) = \{v_{j_1}, \ldots, v_{j_k}\}$, and let U_j be an induced subgraph of G on vertices of a subgraph $X = \bigcup_{i=1,\ldots,k} V_{j_i}$, i.e. $U_j := G[X]$. We find the optimum dominating set S_i in each U_j. Moreover, we know that each C_i had a constant diameter therefore, each U_j will have a constant diameter. Hence, finding an optimum dominating set within each U_i can be done in a constant number of communication rounds. Now take a dominating set $S = \bigcup S_i$. First of all, it is clear that S is a dominating set of G. To prove the upper bound, let D^* be a set of vertices of D which have a neighbour in other clusters, i.e., $D^* = \{w \in D \mid \text{if } w \in U_i \text{ then } \exists j \neq i \text{ and } \exists x \in U_j \text{ such that } \{w, x\} \in E(G)\}$. By the CLUSTERING algorithm and the above counting, we have $|D^*| \leq 2\epsilon |E(H)| \leq 2\epsilon(3|D| + 6g - 6) \leq 2\epsilon \cdot c \cdot g \cdot (3|D| + 6g) \leq \delta|OPT|$. On the other hand, we know that $|S| \leq |OPT \cup D^*| \leq (1 + \delta)|OPT|$. □

References

1. Amiri, S.A., Schmid, S., Siebertz, S.: A local constant factor mds approximation for bounded genus graphs. In: Proceedings of the ACM PODC (2016)

2. Czygrinow, Andrzej, Hańćkowiak, Michal, Wawrzyniak, Wojciech: Fast distributed approximations in planar graphs. In: Moses, Yoram (ed.) DISC 2015. LNCS, vol. 9363, pp. 78–92. Springer, Heidelberg (2008). doi:10.1007/978-3-540-87779-0_6
3. Dean, A.M., Hutchinson, J.P., Scheinerman, E.R.: On the thickness and arboricity of a graph. J. Comb. Theor. Ser. B **52**(1), 147–151 (1991)
4. Mohar, B., Thomassen, C.: Graphs on Surfaces. Johns Hopkins University Press (2001)

Brief Announcement: On the Space Complexity of Conflict Detector Objects

Claire Capdevielle$^{(\boxtimes)}$, Colette Johnen, and Alessia Milani

Universite Bordeaux, LaBRI, UMR 5800, 33400 Talence, France
ccapdevi@labri.fr

A conflict detector is a one-shot shared-memory object introduced by Aspnes and Ellen in [1]. It supports a single operation, $check(v)$, with input v from a set of values and returns a boolean response. It has the following two properties: (i) in any execution that contains a $check(v)$ operation and a $check(v')$ operation with $v \neq v'$, at least one of these two operations returns $true$ (to indicate a conflict); (ii) in any execution in which all check operations have the same input value, they all return $false$. The conflict detector was introduced to prove tight bounds on the individual step complexity of wait-free adopt-commit objects implemented using multi-writer registers. Adopt-commit objects can be used to implement round-based protocols for set-agreement and consensus [3]. Aspnes and Ellen show that we can implement an adopt-commit object using a conflict detector plus a constant number of registers and vice versa. They also show that the individual step complexity of adopt-commit objects and conflict detectors differ by a small additive constant.

In this paper we study the *space* and *solo-write complexity* of conflict detectors (and then of adopt-commit objects), answering a question left open in [1]. The solo-write complexity is the maximal number of writes performed in a solo execution of a single *check* operation, taken over all possible input values. The space complexity is the number of registers an algorithm uses.

Our Results. We prove a $\Theta(\min(\sqrt{n}, \log m / \log \log m))$ bound on the space and solo-write complexity of a wait-free conflict-detector implemented using multi-writer registers for n anonymous processes and where m is the size of the input values set. Processes are anonymous meaning that they have no identifiers and thus they execute the same program. In particular, on the negative side, the following lower bound holds.

Theorem 1. *Any n-process anonymous wait-free conflict detector algorithm must have space complexity $\Omega(\min(\sqrt{n}, \log m / \log \log m))$ and solo-write complexity $\Omega(\min(\sqrt{n}, \log m / \log \log m))$. Moreover, if the algorithm is input-oblivious (the sequence of registers written in a solo execution does not depend on the input value), then the bounds become $\Omega(\sqrt{n})$.*

Theorem 1 easily derives from the bounds we present in a previous work [2]. In particular, we proved the same bounds on the space complexity and the

Partially supported by the ANR project DISPLEXITY (ANR-11-BS02-014). This study has been carried out in the frame of the Investments for the future Programme IdEx (ANR-10-IDEX-03-02).

C. Gavoille and D. Ilcinkas (Eds.): DISC 2016, LNCS 9888, pp. 484–486, 2016.
DOI: 10.1007/978-3-662-53426-7

solo individual write complexity to implement a consensus object considering algorithms that in absence of contention only operate on registers. To implement the corresponding asymptotically optimal consensus algorithm (presented in [2]) we proposed a new abstraction, called *value-splitter*, which is similar to a conflict detector. A value-splitter supports a single operation, $split(v)$ taking a parameter v in a domain of values V and returning a boolean response, and ensures that, for all $v, v' \in V$, and in every execution: (i) if $split(v)$ and $split(v')$ return *true*, then $v = v'$; (ii) If a $split(v)$ operation completes before any other $split$ operation is invoked, then it returns *true*. A conflict detector trivially implements a value splitter. Then, Theorem 1 derives from the fact that the space and the solo write complexity of the consensus algorithm presented in [2] is constant if we do not count the space and solo write complexity of the value-splitter implementation.

On the positive side we present an algorithm that implements a wait-free anonymous conflict detector using $O(\sqrt{n})$ atomic registers (Algorithm 1). Our algorithm improves the *input-oblivious* conflict detector presented in [1] which uses a linear number of registers. Also together with the *non input-oblivious m-values* conflict detector presented in [1] (whose space and solo write complexity is in $O(\log m / \log \log m)$) contributes to prove that the lower bound is tight. Despite the $\Omega(n)$ bound on the space complexity of obstruction-free consensus recently proved in [4], our result is still interesting since it dismantles the difficulty to implement consensus proving the cost to detect the existence of different input values. Also, the tight bounds on the solo-write complexity improve the results in [1] proving that many of these steps are writes.

Theorem 2. *Algorithm 1 implements a wait-free input-oblivious conflict detector for n anonymous processes with solo-write and space complexities in $O(\sqrt{n})$.*

Shared variables:
Array of registers $R[0 \ldots b - 1]$ with $b^2 - 4 > 4n$ and $b \geq 4$. Initially $\perp$

Procedure: $check(v)$

1   $i \leftarrow 0$;
2   $next\_writing \leftarrow 0$;
3   **while** $next\_writing < b$ **do**
4      $i \leftarrow 0$;
5      $res \leftarrow Read(R[i])$;
6   **while** $i < b \wedge res \neq \perp$ **do**
7   **if** $res \neq v$ **then return** *true*;
8         $i + +$;
9   **if** $i \neq b$ **then** $res \leftarrow Read(R[i])$;
10   **end**
11   **if** $i < b \wedge i = next\_writing$ **then**
12        $Write(R[i], v)$;
13        $next\_writing \leftarrow i + 1$;
14   **else** $next\_writing \leftarrow i$;
15 **end**
16 **return** *false*;

Algorithm 1: Input-oblivious conflict-detector

In the following we describe the main ideas of the Algorithm 1. A process p stores in a local variable *next_writing* the index of the register it is expected to write next. Then, the write is applied only if both the following conditions are satisfied: after reading all the registers p does not detect a value different from its input value and the value of *next_writing* corresponds to the index of the first register whose read by p returned the initial value $\perp$. If p reads its own input value from a register it has not yet written, there is another process q executing a *check* operation with the same input value v and q is more advanced in the computation than p. In this case p has to increment its variable *next_writing* in order to move to write to the next register q is expected to write (line 14). Since a process writes registers in increasing order, this jump by p facilitates the detection of conflicting values. In fact, future steps by p will not cover values different from v that some other process may write in registers previously written by q.

References

1. Aspnes, J., Ellen, F.: Tight bounds for adopt-commit objects. Theory Comput. Syst. **55**(3), 451–474 (2014)
2. Capdevielle, C., Johnen, C., Kuznetsov, P., Milani, A.: On the uncontended complexity of anonymous agreement. In: OPODIS (2015, to appear)
3. Gafni, E.: Round-by-round fault detectors: unifying synchrony and asynchrony. In: PODC, 1998, 143–152 (1998)
4. Zhu, L.: A tight space bound for consensus. In: STOC 2016, pp. 345–350 (2016)

Brief Announcement: Public Vs. Private Randomness in Simultaneous Multi-party Communication Complexity

Orr Fischer, Rotem Oshman, and Uri Zwick[✉]

Blavatnik School of Computer Science, Tel-Aviv University, Tel Aviv, Israel
zwick@tau.ac.il

1 Introduction

In his seminal 1979 paper introducing the notion of two-party communication complexity, Yao [3] mentions "one situation that deserves special attention": two players receive private inputs and send randomized messages to a third player who then produces the output. Yao asked what is the communication complexity of the Equality function EQ_n in this model: the two players receive vectors $x, y \in \{0,1\}^n$ and the goal is to determine whether $x = y$. Only private randomness is allowed. (With public randomness, EQ_n can be solved in $O(1)$ bits).

Seventeen years later, Yao's question was answered: Newman and Sezegy [2] showed that EQ_n requires $\Theta(\sqrt{n})$ bits to solve simultaneously using private randomness. Moreover, Babai and Kimmel [1] showed that for *any* function f, if the deterministic simultaneous complexity of f is $D(f)$, then the private-coin simultaneous communication complexity of f is $\Omega(\sqrt{D(f)})$, so in this sense private randomness is of only limited use for simultaneous protocols.

In this note we study multi-player simultaneous communication complexity. We consider the *number-in-hand* model, where each player receives a private input. We show that the effect of private randomness in the multiple player case is essentially *the same* as it is for two players. We first extend the $\Omega(\sqrt{D(f)})$ lower bound of [1] to the multi-player setting, and show that for any k-player function f, the private-coin simultaneous communication complexity of f is $\Omega(\sqrt{D(f)})$. We then show, perhaps surprisingly, that the extended lower bound is still tight in some cases.

Consider the function $\mathrm{ALLEQ}_{k,n}$, which generalizes EQ_n to k players: each player i receives a vector $x_i \in \{0,1\}^n$, and the goal is to determine whether all players received the same input. It is easy to see that the deterministic communication complexity of $\mathrm{ALLEQ}_{k,n}$ is $\Omega(nk)$ (not just for simultaneous protocols), and each player must send n bits to the referee in the worst case. We thus obtain a lower bound of $\Omega(\sqrt{nk})$ for the private-coin simultaneous complexity of $\mathrm{ALLEQ}_{k,n}$. We show that this lower bound is almost tight by giving a simple simultaneous private-coin protocol for $\mathrm{ALLEQ}_{k,n}$ where each players sends only $O(\sqrt{n/k} + \log(\min\{n,k\}))$ bits to the referee, for a total of $O(\sqrt{nk} + k\log\min\{k,n\})$ bits. This matches the lower bound of $\Omega(\sqrt{nk})$ when $k = O(n/\log^2 n)$. We also show that $\mathrm{ALLEQ}_{k,n}$ requires $\Omega(k\log n)$ bits, so in fact our upper bound for $\mathrm{ALLEQ}_{k,n}$ is tight.

© Springer-Verlag Berlin Heidelberg 2016
C. Gavoille and D. Ilcinkas (Eds.): DISC 2016, LNCS 9888, pp. 487–489, 2016.
DOI: 10.1007/978-3-662-53426-7

2   Lower Bound

Let $R_\epsilon(f)$ denote the private-coin randomized simultaneous communication complexity of f, i.e., the total number of bits sent in the worst-case by any simultaneous protocol for f with error probability at most ϵ.

For a k-player function f, let $\dim_i(f)$ be the number of *distinct* inputs that the i-th player has. (Two inputs x_i, x_i' are *indistinct* if for every joint input x_{-i} of all the other players, $f(x_i, x_{-i}) = f(x_i', x_{-i})$.) Generalizing an observation of [1], it is easy to see that to compute f, the i-th player must send at least $\log \dim_i(f)$ bits in the worst case, and thus $D(f) = \sum_{i=1}^{k} \lceil \log \dim_i(f) \rceil$.

Babai and Kimmel [1] prove that for any 2-player private-coin protocol Π with constant error $\epsilon < 1/2$ we have $\text{CC}_1(\Pi) \cdot \text{CC}_2(\Pi) \geq \Omega(\log \dim_1(f) + \log \dim_2(f))$, where CC_i is the number of bits sent by player i. Using this property we show by a reduction from 2-party to k-party that for any k-*player* private-coin protocol Π that computes some function f with constant error $\epsilon < 1/2$, and for each $i \in [k]$, $\text{CC}_i(\Pi) \cdot \left(\sum_{j \neq i} \text{CC}_j(\Pi) \right) = \Omega(\log \dim_i(f))$. Summing up we have:

Theorem 1. *For any k-player function f and $\epsilon > 0$, $R_\epsilon(f) = \Omega(\sqrt{D(f)})$.*

Similarly, for any k-player function f and constant error probability $\epsilon < 1/2$ we have $R_\epsilon^\infty(f) = \Omega(\sqrt{D^\infty(f)/k})$, where $D^\infty, R_\epsilon^\infty$ denote the *maximum* number of bits sent by a single player. (This does not follow immediately from Theorem 1 because we compare maximum to maximum.)

3   Tight Upper Bound for AllEq

To show that our lower bound is tight, we give a protocol for $\text{ALLEQ}_{k,n}$ where each player sends $O(\sqrt{n/k} + \log(\min(n,k)))$ bits, for a total of $O(\sqrt{nk} + k \log(\min(n,k))) = O(\sqrt{D(\text{ALLEQ}_{k,n})})$ bits. We show in the full paper that $R_\epsilon(\text{ALLEQ}) = \Omega(k \log n)$, so the protocol is optimal.

Intuitively, the "hard" cases for $\text{ALLEQ}_{k,n}$ are those where any two inputs that differ only on a small number of coordinates. To overcome this difficulty, each player encodes its input using a predetermined *error correcting code* which blows up the size by only a constant factor and ensures that the relative Hamming distance of the encodings of any two differing inputs is at least some constant $\delta \in (0,1)$. Each player then partitions its encoded input into roughly k blocks.

If $x_i \neq x_j$, the encoded inputs differ in a *constant fraction* of the blocks; if players i, j choose the same *random* block, there is constant probability that they would differ in this block. We face two problems: first, we do not have shared randomness, so players cannot choose the same random block; and second, the size of each block is roughly $O(n/k)$ bits, so how can we check if the players agree on the block or not?

To overcome the first difficulty, we observe that if $\text{ALLEQ}(x_1, \ldots, x_n) = 0$, then some player i received a *minority* input x_i: at most $k/2$ other players have the same input. The probability that one of the $k/2$ disagreeing players sends the same block player i sent is at least:

$$1 - \left(1 - \frac{1}{\#\text{blocks}}\right)^{k/2} \geq 1 - \left(1 - \frac{1}{k}\right)^{k/2} \geq 1 - \left(e^{-1/k}\right)^{k/2} = 1 - e^{-1/2}.$$

Given that player j with $x_j \neq x_i$ sent the same block as player i, with constant probability the block sent is one they disagree on. In this case the referee should be able to detect the difference. But, we cannot afford to have each player send an entire block, and therefore use a "succinct representation" for blocks, which still catches a difference with good probability. The representation we use is simply the 2-player EQ protocol from [1], applied to a block instead of the entire input. Each player sends roughly $O(\sqrt{n/k})$ bits representing its selected block, as well as the index of that block ($O(\log k)$ bits). If two players that disagree on a block both send it, which occurs with constant probability, the referee detects the difference with constant probability. Thus the overall error probability is constant. As the protocol of [1] has one-sided error, so does our protocol.

References

1. Babai, L., Kimmel, P.G.: Randomized simultaneous messages: solution of a problem of Yao in communication complexity. In: Proceedings of CCC 1997, pp. 239–246 (1997)
2. Newman, I., Szegedy, M.: Public vs. private coin flips in one round communication games. In: Proceedings of 28th STOC, pp. 561–570 (1996)
3. Yao, A.C-C.: Some complexity questions related to distributive computing (preliminary report). In: Proceedings of 11th STOC, pp. 209–213 (1979)

Brief Announcement: Beeping a Maximal Independent Set Fast

Stephan Holzer$^{(\boxtimes)}$ and Nancy Lynch

Massachusetts Institute of Technology (MIT), Cambridge, USA
holzer@mit.edu, lynch@csail.mit.edu

Abstract. We adapt a recent algorithm by Ghaffari for computing a Maximal Independent Set in the LOCAL, so that it works in the significantly weaker BEEP network model. For networks with maximum degree Δ, our algorithm terminates locally within time $O((\log \Delta + \log(1/\varepsilon)) \cdot \log(1/\varepsilon))$, with probability at least $1 - \varepsilon$. Moreover, the algorithm terminates globally within time $O(\log^2 \Delta) + 2^{O(\sqrt{\log \log n})}$ with high probability in n, the number of nodes in the network. The key idea of the modification is to replace explicit messages about transmission probabilities with estimates based on the number of received messages.

1 Introduction

Computing a Maximal Independent Set (MIS) is a widely studied problem in distributed computing theory. One of the weakest models of communication in which this problem has been studied is the BEEP model, e.g., [13]. For that model, we obtain:

Theorem 1 (Global termination complexity). *Our algorithm computes an MIS within $O(\log^2 \Delta) + 2^{O(\sqrt{\log \log n})}$ rounds w.h.p., where n is the number of nodes in the network and $\Delta \leq n$ is the maximum degree of any node.*

This improves over the state-of-the-art algorithm [3] for a large range of values of the parameter Δ. We obtain this bound by translating Ghaffari's algorithm [2] for the LOCAL model into the BEEP model. We adapt the proof of Theorem 1.2 of [2], which infers a global bound from a local bound stated in Theorem 1.1 of [2]. In particular we state a local bound in Theorem 2 and use Theorem 2 to replace Theorem 1.1 of [2] in the proof of Theorem 1.2 of [2]. We argue that this replacement works also for the BEEP model.

Theorem 2 (Local termination complexity). *In our algorithm, for each node v, the probability that v decides whether it is in the MIS within $O((\log \Delta + \log(1/\varepsilon)) \cdot \log(1/\varepsilon))$ rounds is at least $1 - \varepsilon$.*

S. Holzer and N. Lynch—Supported by: AFOSR Contract Number FA9550-13-1-0042, NSF Award 0939370-CCF, NSF Award CCF-1217506, and NSF Award CCF-AF-1461559.

© Springer-Verlag Berlin Heidelberg 2016
C. Gavoille and D. Ilcinkas (Eds.): DISC 2016, LNCS 9888, pp. 490–493, 2016.
DOI: 10.1007/978-3-662-53426-7

Note that this local bound is only a factor of $O(\log(1/\varepsilon))$ larger than the $O(\log \Delta + \log(1/\varepsilon))$ bound for the algorithm in the LOCAL model [2]. The key idea in the proof and algorithm of Theorem 2 is that, instead of maintaining full information about its neighbors' states, a node keeps a single binary estimate for the aggregate state of its entire neighborhood.

2   Models and Definitions

LOCAL and BEEP Models: In both models, the network is abstracted as an undirected graph $G = (V, E)$ where $|V| = n$. All nodes wake up simultaneously. Communication occurs in synchronous rounds. In the LOCAL model (e.g., [2]), each node knows its graph neighbors. Nodes communicate reliably, where in each round nodes can exchange an arbitrary amount of information with their immediate graph neighbors. On the other hand, in the BEEP model (e.g., [1, 3]), nodes do not know their neighbors. Nodes communicate reliably and a node can choose to either beep or listen. If a node v listens in slot[1] t it can only distinguish between silence (no neighbor beeps in slot t) or the presence of one or more beeps (at least one neighbor beeps in in slot t).

Graph-related Definitions: A set of vertices $I \subseteq V$ is an *independent set* of G if no two nodes in I are neighbors in G. An independent set $I \subseteq V$ is a *maximal independent set (MIS)* of G if, for all $v \in V \setminus I$, the set $I \cup \{v\}$ is not independent. An event occurs *with high probability* (w.h.p.), if it occurs with probability at least $1 - n^{-c}$ for some constant $c \geq 1$.

3   Algorithms

The MIS algorithm of [2] runs for R:$=\beta(\log \Delta + \log(2/\varepsilon)) = O(\log \Delta + \log(1/\varepsilon))$ rounds, where $\beta = 1300$. In each round t, each node v has a *desire-level* $p_t(v)$ for joining the MIS, which initially is set to $p_0(v) = 1/2$. Ghaffari [2] calls the total sum of the desire-levels of neighbors of v its *effective-degree* $d_t(v)$, i.e., $d_t(v) = \sum_{u \in N(v)} p_t(u)$. The desire-levels change over time depending on whether or not $d_t(v) \geq 2$. In each round, node v gets *marked* with probability $p_t(v)$. If v is marked, and no neighbor of v is marked, v joins the MIS and gets removed along with its neighbors. Using the power of the LOCAL model, in each round t, nodes exchange exact values of $p_t(u)$ with all their neighbors.

   In implementing this algorithm in the BEEP model, we do not require that a node v learn the exact values of $p_t(u)$ for all neighbors u in order to compute $d_t(v)$. Instead, we allow node v to decide, based on how many beeps v receives within a certain number of rounds, whether $d_t(v)$ is more likely to be larger than 1 or smaller than 3. To make this decision, we define an *interval* to consist of $I := 1000(\ln(1500) + \ln(2/\varepsilon))$ consecutive slots. We use one interval in the BEEP model to emulate each round of the algorithm [2] in the LOCAL model.

---

[1] To disambiguate, we refer to the rounds of the BEEP model as *slots*.

During part of an interval, the algorithm computes the ratio of the number of beeps received $(b_t(v))$ to the total number of slots in which v listened during the interval $(c_t(v))$. Node v decides to update its desire-level:

$$p_{t+1}(v) = \begin{cases} p_t(v)/2, & \text{if } b_t(v)/c_t(v) > \frac{5}{6} \\ \min\{2p_t(v), 1/2\}, & \text{if } b_t(v)/c_t(v) \leq \frac{5}{6} \end{cases}$$

Thus, we replace the condition $d_t(v) \geq 2$ in the algorithm of [2] by the condition $b_t(v)/c_t(v) > \frac{5}{6}$.

4   Local Analysis of our MIS Algorithm

We demonstrate that for each node v, the accuracy of deciding whether v's effective degree is high or low is good enough to translate the algorithm of [2] into the BEEP model, i.e., our algorithm does not require v to learn exact desire-values of its neighbors. We say node v is a *good node* in an interval t, if at the end of the interval the following three conditions are satisfied: (i) $c_t(v) > I/3$, and (ii) if $b_t(v)/c_t(v) > \frac{5}{6}$, then $d_t(v) \geq 1$, and (iii) if $b_t(u)/c_t(v) \leq \frac{5}{6}$, then $d_t(v) \leq 3$.

Lemma 1 *A good node v always (i) draws correct conclusions about whether its effective degree is high or low, and (ii) adjusts its desire-values in the same way as in the algorithm of [2].*

Lemma 1 allows us to modify the analysis of [2] to obtain statements about good nodes. To argue that this applies to large parts of the graphs, we show that most nodes are good:

Lemma 2 *For any interval, the probability that a node v is good is at least $1 - 2e^{-I/1000}$.*

To prove Lemma [2], we use a Chernoff Bound to bound the probability that $b_t(v)/c_t(v)$ reflects whether the effective degree is high or low based on the condition $b_t(v)/c_t(v) > \frac{5}{6}$ rather than $d_t(v) \geq 2$.

We define two kinds of *golden intervals* for a node v, by analogy with the definition of *golden rounds* in [2]: Interval t is a golden interval of type-1, if $b_t(v)/c_t(v) \leq \frac{5}{6}$ and $p_t(v) = 1/2$. Interval t is a golden interval of type-2, if $b_t(v)/c_t(v) > \frac{5}{6}$ and at least $d_t(v)/10$ of $d_t(v)$ is contributed by neighbors u with $d_t(u) \leq 3$. Using Lemmas 1 and 2 we show:

Lemma 3 *In each type-1 (resp., type-2) golden interval, with probability at least $1/1000$, v joins the MIS (resp., one of v's neighbors joins the MIS). If $R/13$ intervals are golden, then the probability that v has not decided whether it is in the MIS during the first R intervals is at most $\varepsilon/2$.*

Lemma 4 *By the end of interval R, with probability at least $1 - 1500e^{-I/1000}$, either v has joined, or has a neighbor in, the (computed) MIS, or at least one of its golden interval counts reached $R/13$.*

We prove Lemma 4 by adapting ideas of [2]. Theorem 2 follows from combining Lemmas 3 and 4.

References

1. Afek, Y., Alon, N., Bar-Joseph, Z., Cornejo, A., Haeupler, B., Kuhn, F.: Beeping a maximal independent set. Distrib. Comput. **26**(4), 195–208 (2013)
2. Ghaari, M.: An improved distributed algorithm for maximal independent set. In: Proceedings of the 2015 ACM-SIAM Symposium on Discrete Algorithms, pp. 270–277 (2016)
3. Scott, A., Jeavons, P., Xu, L.: Feedback from nature: an optimal distributed algorithm for maximal independent set selection. In: Proceedings of the 2013 ACM Symposium on Principles of Distributed Computing, pp. 147–156 (2013)

Author Index

Printed in the United States
By Bookmasters